THE CONCISE ENCYCLOPEDIA OF

ARCHAEOLOGY

THE CONCISE ENCYCLOPEDIA OF

Archaeology

EDITED BY LEONARD COTTRELL

THE CONTRIBUTORS

P. J. ADAMS
J. ALDEN MASON
F. R. ALLCHIN
A. J. ARKELL
D. G. BRIDSON
DOUGLAS H. CARPENTER
ANTHONY CHRISTIE
J. DESMOND CLARK
JOHN CHADWICK
SONIA COLE
J. M. COOK
LEONARD COTTRELL
AHMAD HASAN DANI
GUY DANIEL
P. E. P. DERANYAGALA
A. DIGBY
JOHN D. EVANS
C. J. GADD
D. H. GORDON
GEOFFREY GRIGSON
G. LANKESTER HARDING
THOR HEYERDAHL
P. HULIN
G. W. B. HUNTINGFORD
R. W. HUTCHINSON
VERA S. KATRAK
J. EDWARD KIDDER JR
JAMES KIRKMAN
G. E. LAW
L. S. B. LEAKEY
C. B. M. Mc BURNEY
ALEXANDRA MACFARLANE
B. D. MALAN
RAYMOND A. MAUNY
J. V. S. MEGAW
T. C. MITCHELL
MARGARET ALICE MURRAY
KENNETH OAKLEY
J. J. ORCHARD
ROBIN PLACE
A. HINGSTON QUIGGIN
REAY ROBERTSON-MACKAY
A. F. SHORE
H. S. SMITH
ROGER SUMMERS
LORD WILLIAM TAYLOUR
D. J. WISEMAN
H. M. WORMINGTON

HAWTHORN BOOKS INC. NEW YORK
Publishers

 All inquiries should be addressed to Hawthorn Books Inc., 70 Fifth Avenue, New York City 10011. This book was designed and produced by George Rainbird Ltd, London. *The Concise Encyclopedia of Archaeology* is published simultaneously in Canada. Library of Congress Catalogue No. 60-10337. Suggested Decimal Classification: 571.03.

FIRST EDITION 1960

SECOND PRINTING 1964

PRINTED IN THE NETHERLANDS

CONTENTS

Classified List *page* 7

Editor's Note 15

"What is Archaeology?" by the Editor 17

Chart of the cultural traditions of Early Man 30

The Concise Encyclopedia 33

For Further Reading 501

Notes on Contributors 510

THE COLOR PLATES

I	Africa: prehistoric rock painting from Tassili	49
II	Ajanta: ceiling detail	68
III	Aztecs: funerary urn	85
IV	Babylon: relief of a dragon	104
V	Easter Island: Statues	154
VI	Etruscans: sarcophagus from Cerveteri	171
VII	Kansu: Sung dynasty vase	237
VIII	Lascaux: painting of bison	256
IX	Luxor: the temple	273
X	Mexico: wall painting from Teotihuacán	292
XI	Mycenae: tholos tomb	342
XII	Persepolis: carving	359
XIII	Petra: rock cut temple	377
XIV	Sanchi: the Great Stupa	396
XV	Stonehenge: stone circle	446
XVI	Tutankhamun's tomb: exterior	463

The picture on the jacket and endpapers is of the step pyramid of Zoser at Saqqara.

Photo: Fiona Wilkie

CLASSIFIED LIST

This has been compiled to help those wishing to study a particular area or topic in more detail.

AFRICA

MAP page 471

Africa, East
Africa, Eastern Coast Ruins
Plates 1–4, pages 51–54
Africa, North
Africa, Prehistoric Art in
Colour plate I, page 49; plate 5, page 55
Africa, Stone Age Man in
Africa, Stone Age Man in South
Africa, West
Plates 6–7, pages 56–57
Ain Hanech
Atlanthropus
Australopithecus
Boskop Skull
Bushmen
Capsian
Ethiopia
Hamitic People
Magosian
Meroe
Plate 89, page 283
Negroes, Origin of the
Nubia *Plate 102, page 330*
Olduvai Gorge
Olorgesailie
Oranian
Rhodesia Man
Sangoan
Singa Skull
Stellenbosch
Sudan
Plates 129–130, pages 429–430
Tassili Frescos
Colour plate I, page 49
Zimbabwe
Plates 149–150, pages 469–470

AMERICA

MAP page 472

America, Early Man in
Plate 12, page 62
Amer-Indians
Plate 13, page 63
Aztecs
Colour plate III, page 85; plates 19, 21–22, pages 89, 91–92
Chichen Itzá
Plate 40, page 144
Eskimos
Plate 46, page 150
Incas
Plate 64, page 204
Machu Picchu
Maya
Plates 82–84, pages 276–278
Mexico
Colour plate X, page 292; plates 91–92, 94, pages 285–286, 288
Peruvians
Plate 112, page 340

ARCHAEOLOGISTS AND HISTORIANS

Anning, Mary
Belzoni, Giovanni Battista
Boucher de Perthes, Jacques
Breasted, James
Plate 30, page 100
Breuil, Henri
Browne, Thomas
Buckland, William
Buffon, Georges
Carter, Howard
Champollion, Jean-François
Cunningham, Alexander
Cuvier, Georges
Darwin, Charles
Evans, Arthur
Plate 47, page 151
Foote, Robert
Frere, John
Garstang, John
Grotefend, George
Hutton, James
Koldewey, Robert
Layard, Austen
Plate 72, page 246
Lepsius, Karl
Lyell, Charles
Manetho

Mariette, Auguste
Marshall, John
Maspero, Gaston
Miller, Hugh
Pendlebury, John
Petrie, William Flinders
Plate 111, page 339
Pitt-Rivers, Augustus
Rawlinson, Henry
Plate 118, page 384
Reisner, George
Schliemann, Heinrich
Plate 123, page 389
Smith, George
Stein, Aurel
Usher, James
Ventris, Michael
Wallace, Alfred
Woolley, Leonard
Plate 147, page 467

EARLY MAN AND GEOLOGICAL PERIODS

MAP page 474

Abbevillian
Acheulian
Africa, Prehistoric Art in
Colour plate I, page 49; plate 5, page 55
Africa, Stone Age Man in
Africa, Stone Age Man in South
Ain Hanech
America, Early Man in
Plate 12, page 62
Altamira
Plate 8, page 58
Antler Pick
Anyathian
Argon Potassium Dating
Arrow-heads
Arrow-straightener
Artifact
Atlanthropus
Aurignacian
Plates 18, 20, pages 88, 90
Australopithecus
Azilian
Bac-son
Basketry
Beaker People
Plate 24, page 94
Boreal
Borer
Borneo
Boskop Skull
Bow
Brachiate
Bronze Age
Burin
Bushmen
Caenozoic
Capsian
Carbon Fourteen Dating
Causeway Camp
Cave Men
Celebes
Celt
Ceylon, Stone Age Man in
Chalcolithic
Châtelperronian
Cheddar Man
Plate 35, page 139
Chellean
Chert
Chopper
Chou-kou-tien
Clactonian
Cleaver
Coelacanth
Coprolite
Core
Creswellian
Cro-magnon
Dea Mater
Dinosaur
Dog
Domestication of Animals
Dordogne
Earth, Age of the
Earth Goddess
Ecology
Emmer Wheat
Eocene Epoch
Eolith
Flake
Flexed Burial
Flint
Flint Mine
Fluorine Dating
Fluviatile
Fossil
Fossil Apes
Fossil Man
Fossils, Living
Geological Periods
Gibraltar Skull
Gigantopithecus
Glacial
Plate 50, page 190
Gravettian
Plate 52, page 192
Grimaldi
Haematite
Halafian
Hand-axe
Plate 55, page 195
Harpoon
Heidelberg Jaw
Hoa-binh
Hominid
Horizon
Hoxne
India, Prehistoric
Iron Age
Plate 62, page 202
Japan, Prehistoric
Java Man
Lamma Island
Laos
Lascaux
Colour plate VIII, page 256
Levalloisian
Lung Shan
Macrolith
Magdalenian
Plate 77, page 251
Maglemosian
Magosian

Mammoth
Meganthropus
Mesolithic
Mesozoic
Microlith
Midden
Miocene Epoch
Mojokerto
Mousterian
Plate 98, page 326
Natufian
Neanderthal Man
Neolithic
Obsidian
Olduvai Gorge
Oligocene Epoch
Olorgesailie
Oranian
Oreopithecus
Palaeobotany
Palaeolithic
Palaeolithic, Further Asian
Palaeontology
Palaeozoic Era
Palstave
Paviland Cave
Perigordian
Piltdown Skull
Plate 115, page 381
Pithecanthropus
Pliocene Epoch
Plough
Pluvial
Pollen Analysis
Pongid
Pottery
Predmostian
Prehistoric Art
Plates 116–117, pages 382–383
Prehistory
Primates, Prehuman Evolution of
Quaternary Period
Plate 113, page 379
Quartz
Quern
Rhodesia Man
Sangoan
Scraper
Sedimentary Rocks
Simian Shelf
Sinanthropus
Plate 127, page 393
Singa Skull
Sledge
Solo
Solutrean
Star Carr
Stellenbosch
Stone Age
Stone Tools
Stratification
Tardenoisian
Tassili Frescos
Colour plate I, page 49
Tertiary Period
Totems
Trepanning
Type-site
Typology
Urn People
Varves
Wheel
Woodhenge
Yang-shao
Zinjanthropus

EGYPT

MAP page 475

Abydos
Akhnaton
Ba
Book of the Dead
Canopic Jars
Canopus Decree
Cartouche
Coptic Language
Deir el Medinah
Demotic
Egypt *Plate 44, page 148*
Faiyum
Giza
Heb-sed
Heliopolis
Hierakonpolis
Hieratic
Hieroglyphs
Plate 57, page 197
Karnak
Plates 65, 67, pages 239, 241
Lotus
Luxor
Colour plate IX, page 273; plate 74, page 248
Mastaba Tomb
Medinet Habu
Plate 85, page 279
Memphis
Plate 88, page 282
Merimde
Moeris, Lake
Mummies *Plate 99, page 327*
Nag Hammadi
Nome
Obelisk
Plate 103, page 331
Oxyrhyncus
Palermo Stone
Papyrus
Philae
Plate 114, page 380
Punt
Pyramids
Rosetta Stone
Plate 119, page 385
Sais
Saqqara
Endpapers; plate 120, page 386
Sarcophagus
Scarabs
Serapeum
Sphinx
Suez Canal
Tanis
Tell el Amarna

Thebes
Plate 141, page 441
Tomb Robbery Papyri
Tutankhamun, Tomb of
Colour plate XVI, page 463; plate 145, page 465
Ushabti
Valley of the Kings

EUROPE

MAP page 476

Abbevillian
Acheulian
Altamira
Plate 8, page 58
Aurignacian
Plates 18, 20, pages 88, 90
Avebury
Broch
Carnac *Plate 29, page 99*
Celtic Fields
Châtelperronian
Cheddar Man
Plate 35, page 139
Chellean
Clactonian
Crannogs
Creswellian
Cro-magnon
Cromlech
Dolmen
Dordogne
Druids
Etruscans
Colour plate VI, page 171; plate 48, page 152
Gibraltar Skull
Gravettian
Plate 52, page 192
Grimaldi
Hallstatt
Plates 53–54, pages 193–194
Heidelberg Jaw
Heuneburg
Hoxne
Köln-Lindenthal
Lake Dwellings
Lascaux
Colour plate VIII, page 256
Leubingen
Plate 73, page 247
Levalloisian
Lynchet
Magdalenian
Plate 77, page 251
Maglemosian
Maiden Castle
Plate 75, page 249
Mediterranean, the Western
Plate 86, page 280
Megalith
Menhir
Minorca, Megalithic Remains in
Plate 96, page 290
Mousterian, *Plate 98, page 326*
Neanderthal Man
Paviland Cave
Perigordian
Piltdown Skull
Plate 115, page 381
Predmostian
Silbury Hill
Skara Brae
Plate 128, page 394
Somme-Bionne
Star Carr
Stonehenge *Colour plate XV, page 446*
Sutton Hoo *Plate 136, page 436*
Tardenoisian
La Tène
Plates 139–140, 142, pages 439–440, 442
Tolund Man
Plate 143, page 443
Vix, the Treasure of
Woodhenge

FAR EAST

MAPS page 473 and page 480

Ainu
Angkor
Anuradhapura
Plates 14–15, pages 64–65
Anyang
Plates 11, 16, pages 61, 66
Anyathian
Asuka
Bac-son
Bali
Borneo
Borobudur
Plate 27–28, pages 97–98
Buddhist Art and Architecture
Plate 31, page 101
Celebes
Ceylon, Stone Age Man in
Chams
Plates 32, 34, pages 102, 138
Chang-sha
Chen-la
Chia-hsiang Hsein
Plates 33, 36–37, pages 137, 140–141
Chou-kou-tien
Chryse
Dagoba
Dong-son
Dvararati
Easter Island
Colour plate V, page 171; plate 43, page 147

Fu-nan
Gigantopithecus
Great Wall of China
Plate 51, page 191
Haniwa
Heian
Hindu Art and Architecture
Hmawza
Hoa-binh
Hsing-lung Hsien
Plate 58, page 198
Hsiang-t'an Shan
Indonesian
Ise
Japan, Prehistoric
Java Man
Kansu
Colour plate VII, page 237; plate 66, page 240
Khmer
Korea
Kra
K'un-Lun
Lacquer
Lamma Island
Laos
Ligor
Lopburi
Lung-men
Plate 76, page 250
Lung Shan
Majapahit
Mison
Mlu Prei
Mojokerto
Nara
Oc-eo
Oracle Bones
Pagan
Plate 105, page 333
Palaeolithic, Further Asian
Palembang
Philippines
Polonnaruwa
P'ong-tuk
Prambanan
Shih Chai Shan
Plate 126, page 392
Siemreap
Plate 125, page 391
Sigiriya
Sinanthropus
Plate 127, page 393
Solo
T'ai
Tra-kieu
Tun-huang
Yang-shao
Yueh
Yün-kang

GENERAL

Acropolis
Aepyornis
Agglutinative
Agriculture
Air Photography
Alphabet
Amphora
Amulet
Archaeology
Antler Pick
Archaic
Argon Potassium Dating
Arrow-heads
Arrow-straightener
Artifact
Aryan
Ashlar Masonry
Atlantis
Barrow
Basketry
Batter
Boats
Boreal
Borer
Bow
Brachiate
Breccia
Bronze Age
Burin
Carbon Fourteen Dating
Cartouche
Causeway Camp
Celt
Celtic Fields
Cenotaph
Chalcolithic
Chamber Tombs
Champlevé
Chert
Chopper
Cinerary Urn
Cire Perdue Process
Cist
Cleaver
Cloisonné
Clothing
Plate 38, page 142
Codex
Coinage
Colossus
Copper
Coprolite
Core
Crannogs
Cromlech
Culture
Culture Sequence
Cuneiform
Cursive Writing
Cyclopean Masonry
Dea Mater
Dinosaurs
Dog
Dolmen
Domestication of Animals
Dromos
Earth, Age of the
Earth Goddess
Ecology
Electron
Emmer Wheat
Eolith
Epigraphy
Faience
Figurine

Flake
Flexed Burial
Flint
Flint Mine
Flood, the
Fluorine Dating
Fluviatile
Glacial
Glacis
Glyph
Haematite
Hand-axe
Plate 55, page 195
Hanging Gardens
Harpoon
Hieratic
Hieroglyphs
Horizon
Hypaethral
Ideograms
Inhumation
Iron Age
Plate 62, page 202
Krater
Lake Dwellings
Lingua Franca
Lustral
Lynchet
Macrolith
Mammoth
Mastaba Tomb
Megalith
Megaron
Menhir
Microlith
Midden
Numismatics
Obsidian
Ophir
Ossuary
Ostrace
Palaeobotany
Palaeontology
Palstave
Papoura
Papyrus
Phonograms
Pictograms
Pisé
Pit Graves
Plough
Pluvial
Pollen Analysis
Pottery
Prehistory
Quartz
Quern
Repoussé
Sarcophagus
Scarabs
Schist
Scraper
Seals
Sedimentary Rocks
Seven Wonders of the World
Shaft Graves
Sledge
Sphinx
Stadium
Steatite
Stela
Stone Circles
Stratification
Stratum
Stupa
Tell
Temenos
Tessera
Tholos Tombs
Torc
Totems
Transhumance
Tree-ring Dating
Trepanning
Tuff
Tumulus
Type-site
Typology
Uncials
Varves
Weep-hole
Wheel

GREECE AND THE EASTERN MEDITERRANEAN

MAP page 477

Achaeans
Acropolis
Athens
Chamber Tombs
Cimmerians
Cyclades
Plate 42, page 146
Cyclopean Masonry
Dorians
Dromos
Gournia
Hagia Triada
Helladic
Hellenic
Herodotus
Homer
Ionians
Plate 60, page 200
Knossos
Plates 68–70, pages 242–244
Lycians
Lydians
Mallia
Mediterranean, the Eastern
Megaron
Minoan Civilization
Plates 93, 95, pages 287, 289
Minoan Scripts
Minotaur
Mycenae
Colour plate XI, page 342; plates 100, 104, pages 328, 332
Olympia
Orchomenos
Phaistos
Phrygians
Pylos
Tholos Tombs
Tiryns
Plate 144, page 444
Troy
Tylissos

INDIA

MAP page 478

Ajanta *Colour plate II, page 68*
Amaravati
Plates 9–10, pages 59–60
Arikamedu
Aryan
Asoka Maurya
Cave Temples
Buddhist Art and Architecture
Plate 31, page 101
Ellora *Plate 45, page 149*
Gandhara
Plate 49, page 189
Harappa
Plate 56, page 196
Hindu Art and Architecture
India
India, Prehistoric
Indus Valley Civilization
Plate 59, page 199
Mathura
Plates 78, 80, pages 252, 254
Mauryan Empire
Plates 79, 81, pages 253, 275
Mohenjo-Daro
Plate 97, page 325
Rigveda
Sanchi
Colour plate XIV, page 396; plate 121, page 387
Sarnath
Plates 122, 124, pages 388, 390
Stupa
Taxila
Plate 137, page 437

THE MIDDLE EAST

MAP page 479

Accadians
Alaca Höyük
Amorites
Assyrians
Plate 17, page 87
Baalbek
Plate 23, page 93
Babylon, *Colour plate IV, page 104*
Behistun Rock
Plate 25, page 95
Boghazköy
Plate 26, page 96
Byblos
Canaanites
Ctesiphon
Plate 41, page 145
Dead Sea Scrolls,
Plate 39, page 143
Ephesus
Fertile Crescent
Flood, the
Gilgamesh Epic, the
Halafian
Hammurabi
Hanging Gardens
Hazor
Hebrews
Hittites
Hurrians
Hyksos
Iran
Plate 61, page 201
Iraq
Jericho
Plate 63, page 203
Jerusalem
Jordan
Kassites
King Solomon's Mines
Lachish
Lagash
Plate 71, page 245
Mari
Megiddo
Plate 87, page 281
Mesopotamian Sculpture
Plate 90, page 284
Nabataeans
Natufian
Nimrud
Nineveh
Plate 101, page 329
Nippur
Palestine
Palmyra
Plate 106, page 334
Parthians
Persepolis
Colour plate XII, page 359; plates 107–109, pages 335–337
Petra
Colour plate XIII, page 377; plate 110, page 338
Phoenicians
Ras Shamra
Royal Road
Satrap
Sea Peoples
Sumerians
Plates 131–132, pages 431–432
Susa
Plates 133–134, pages 433–434
Tell
Tell Atchana
Plates 135, 138, pages 435, 438
Tyre
Ur *Plate 146, page 466*
Urartu
Ur-Nammu
Ziggurat
Ziwiye
Plate 148, page 468

ACKNOWLEDGMENTS

The publishers and the Editor are indebted to the Reverend Guy Daniel for his editorial assistance.

They also wish to thank the following for their advice and help: R.D.Barnett, Keeper of the Department of Western Asiatic Antiquities at the British Museum, London; G.H.S.Bushnell, Curator of the Museum of Archaeology and Ethnology, Cambridge; Anthony Christie, Lecturer in the Art and Archaeology of south-east Asia at the School of Oriental and African Studies, University of London; Sonia Cole; J.M.Cook, Reader in Classical Archaeology at the University of Bristol; R.Crossland, Professor of Greek at the University of Sheffield; Glyn Daniel, Lecturer in Archaeology at the University of Cambridge; I.E.S.Edwards, Keeper of Egyptian Antiquities at the British Museum, London; Kenan Erim, Assistant Professor of Classics at New York University and Archaeologist identified with the Princeton Excavations in the Near East; W.B.Fagg, Deputy Keeper of the Department of Ethnography at the British Museum, London; C. J. Gadd, Professor of Ancient Semitic Languages and Civilizations at the School of Oriental and African Studies, University of London; R.W.Hutchinson, formerly Lecturer in Classical Archaeology at the Universities of Cambridge and Liverpool; the late Casper J.Kraemer, Professor of Classics at New York University; Dr Margaret Murray, formerly Assistant Professor of Egyptology at the University of London; Kenneth Oakley, Senior Principal Scientific Officer in charge of the Anthropology Section at the British Museum (Natural History), London; W. Watson, Assistant Keeper of the Department of Oriental Antiquities at the British Museum, London; D.J.Wiseman, Assistant Keeper of the Department of Western Asiatic Antiquities at the British Museum, London.

We are indebted to the following for their assistance with the plates: The Ashmolean Museum, Oxford; The Bodleian Library, Oxford; The Britain China Friendship Association, London; The Trustees of the British Museum, London; The Trustees of the British Museum (Natural History), London; Service des Antiquités, Cairo; Anthony Christie, Esq.; Michael Cubitt, Esq.; Gerald Cubitt, Esq.; Dr Gisèle Freund; Kenya Information Services; M. Henri Lhote; The Trustees of the National Portrait Gallery, London; The Percival David Foundation of Chinese Art, School of Oriental and African Studies, University of London; Miss Ann Flinders Petrie, Department of Antiquities, Tanganyika Government; UNESCO; Miss Fiona Wilkie.

The maps were drawn by Arthur Banks, Esq. The chart on pages 30–31 is based on a chart in *Man the Toolmaker* by K. P. Oakley, with some slight modifications agreed by the author, and is reproduced by permission of the Trustees of the British Museum (Natural History), London.

EDITOR'S NOTE

Interest in archaeology is keener and more widespread now than at any time in the past; so much so that the dividing-line separating the specialist and the "general reader" is narrowing. Newspaper articles and many popular books keep the reader informed of the latest archaeological techniques and discoveries. The result is that the intelligent amateur wants to know more and more, and is sometimes prepared to wrestle with serious professional works which may occasionally take him out of his depth.

This book has been compiled to help such enthusiasts. If, in the course of his study, a reader comes upon a passing reference to, say, Tolund Man or the Tassili Frescos, he can find out more about them here. If he is interested in the lives and personalities of great archaeologists, he will find biographies of such men as Sir Flinders Petrie, Mariette Pasha, Sir Arthur Evans and the Abbé Breuil, to name a few. If his interest is in particular regions, there are long articles on the archaeology of Egypt, east and west Africa, the eastern and western Mediterranean, and other areas. If he wants to know more about how objects are dated, or how stone tools are identified and classified he will find the appropriate articles. A great many archaeological discoveries are described, such as the Tomb of Tutankhamun, Ur of the Chaldees, Alaca Höyük, Jericho, and Knossos. There are articles on places and peoples, cities and civilizations, tombs and techniques, ancient languages and their decipherment. Each article is written by an acknowledged authority on the subject, and the field covered is world-wide, from China to Mexico, from northern Europe to southern Africa.

However, in a book of some 220,000 words, it was clearly impossible to include a reference to every fact of archaeological importance in the world, even if each entry was reduced to a few lines. Personal selection is inevitably involved, and for this the Editor must take responsibility. His choice was guided by the following considerations: the interest of the general reader as well as the specialist; the necessity of including items from many parts of the world, not merely from Europe, the Middle East, and the Americas; and the need to strike a balance between sites and discoveries of world-wide importance and interest, and out-of-the-way terms which the reader might encounter, and of which he required explanations. An example of the first is "Knossos", and of the second "brachiate".

Although the second consideration, "general reader-interest", played a large part in selecting the items, accuracy and intelligibility were equally important. Within these limits this book is a work of reference but it also caters unashamedly for the "dipper-in". Open any page, and the odds are that you are likely to find something curious, interesting or exciting. And if, having become interested in one entry, the reader wishes to pursue the subject further, there is a system of cross-references which enables him to do so. Moreover, although the entries are arranged in alphabetical order, readers who wish to study a particular period, culture or geographical area, will find, on page 7, items conveniently grouped under a number of separate headings.

One important omission will be noticed. There are few references to the archaeology of "classical" Greece and Rome, or to that of medieval Europe. There are, however, contributions on antiquities in the Far East and in America even though some of them are as recent as the sixteenth century A.D. The reason for this apparent inconsistency is that a great many books on classical archaeology already exist, as do works on medieval Europe. Less information is readily available on archaeological sites in such countries as China, Ceylon, Indonesia, India, and South America, even though these may fall within Europe's "historical" period. The main criteria in selecting a subject have been *(a)* is this subject important and interesting, and *(b)* is it one with which the general reader, as distinct from the specialist, is likely to be unfamiliar?

Yet, even allowing for all these provisions, the Editor has to admit that many worth-while subjects which he would like to have included have had to be left out. When a final choice had to be made it became, ultimately, a personal one, though guided by the Editor's advisers, each of whom is a specialist in his particular field, whether it is India, Egypt, the Aegean, western Europe, the Middle East, the Far East, or pre-Columbian America. Each of these eminent authorities was equally anxious that his or her subject should be adequately represented, and the task of arbitrating between them was not always easy. The Editor wishes to express his grateful thanks to these scholars, and to all the many contributors who have made this book possible. He hopes that they, as well as the reader, will consider that the result justifies their joint efforts.

L. C.

NOTE: **Bold type** within any article denotes that there is a separate entry on the place, person or thing which should be consulted for further reference.

WHAT IS ARCHAEOLOGY?

by

LEONARD COTTRELL

"The scientific study of antiquities" says one dictionary – a very inadequate definition. We shall get nearer to the truth if we examine the Greek foundation of the word: *archaios*–ancient; *arché*, beginning; *logos*, discourse. A discourse based on an examination of man's beginnings; is that the answer? Only a partial one, for archaeology is often also concerned with endings; there are few things the archaeologist likes better than a site which has been subjected, in ancient times, to sudden and catastrophic destruction (Pompeii, for instance). From the death of a city, a culture, or a civilization, we can learn a great deal about its life. There is also the equally important question of development. Archaeological research can reveal to us change, progress or deterioration; it is a continuing story which begins with the first appearance of man on earth, and will only end with the final extinction of the species.

Essentially, then, archaeology is the story of man, as revealed by the things he has left behind, whether these are tools, weapons, household articles, furniture, ornaments, buildings, tombs, human or animal remains. Written records on stone, clay, or papyrus are obviously important too, but they appear relatively late in human history, within the last 5,000 years, and then only in certain limited areas. Most archaeological knowledge is derived from the interpretation of things, and not only things in themselves. We may identify an object and understand its purpose and function; but equally important is the situation in which it is found, its association with other objects, or with identifiable soil or rock strata, and its similarity or dissimilarity to objects found on other sites.

Again the study of stratigraphy helps us to establish comparative dates from the levels at which things are found; that of typology enables us to follow the development of a people or "culture" from stylistic changes in the things they made and used. Other specialists can help the archaeologist in his work; the anatomist and the palaeontologist tell him about the physical appearance of ancient peoples by examining their bones. The palaeobotanist, by microscopic examination of seeds, pollen, and other surviving vegetable remains, helps to build up a picture of the flora existing in ancient times, and the climatologist the type of weather. In recent years the nuclear physicist has provided an invaluable technique for dating objects made of organic matter, by measuring the amount of radioactivity present in it.

An old-style antiquarian such as Sir Thomas Browne, who wrote so movingly about "funerary urnes lately discovered in a field in Norfolk" would be bewildered by the technical language of the modern archaeologist. It is a far cry from Browne's "to be pyramidally extant is a fallacy in duration" to the following title of an article in an Egyptological journal "A special use of the *sdm.f* and *sdm.n.f* Forms"...

The Editor admits that his sympathies are with Sir Thomas Browne. While respecting and admiring the technical expertise of the modern archaeologist, and recognizing the need for the amateur to understand these techniques (hence this book) it seems to him important that one should not lose sight of the wood for the trees, the "wood" being the wonderful, moving story of man's progress from the animal to the human state; his successive experiments, successes and failures in the art of living. Just as the explorer extends our knowledge of the earth which is our home, so the archaeologist should enlarge our comprehension of ourselves. Instead of being confined to a brief, blinkered vision of our own segment of time, our eyes should be opened to the whole vast panorama of human development.

Curiosity about the past is no recent thing. The ancient Egyptians kept records; so did the Babylonians. In classical times Herodotus travelled thousands of miles, eagerly searching for the history of the many peoples with whom he came in contact. Pausanias went to Mycenae some sixteen centuries before Schliemann. Diodorus the Sicilian, Strabo and Pliny were all curious about the past. Even the study of geology is very ancient. Nineteenth-century scientists such as Huxley and Darwin examined fossils of animals, and postulated that the world was far, far older than man, and that over a period of millions of years there had been changes in the earth's crust; so that what had once been under sea was now on a mountain-top. More than 2,500 years before Huxley, a Greek philosopher named Xenophanes found fossilized remains of sea shells in the mountains of Sicily, and the imprint of seaweed and fishes in a quarry near Syracuse, and correctly interpreted them.

Scientific curiosity, such as the Greeks exhibited, grew dim in the Middle Ages, imprisoned within a religious orthodoxy which frowned on rational inquiry. But there were still "antiquarians". With the Renaissance the liberated spirit of man again began searching and probing into the past. There was a cult of Antiquity. Greek and Roman art was rediscovered. Statues were dug up to enrich private museums and collections. In the seventeenth and eighteenth centuries we see the beginnings of scientific archaeology; such men as Sir Thomas Browne examined and reflected on the significance of ancient objects, and here and there a few bold spirits even dared to question the Church's dogma that man's history extended no further back than about 4000 B.C. But at this time their voices were scarcely heard.

Even in the seventeenth century travellers to Egypt and the Middle East surveyed the Pyramids. Professor Greaves, in the time of Charles I, wrote an excellent treatise on them, and other travellers brought back tales of Babylon and Nineveh. The works of classical historians, Herodotus, Pliny and the rest, were re-examined. But scientific inquiry was still inhibited by the necessity of keeping within a literal interpretation of biblical chronology. Archaeology was still in chains.

Towards the end of the eighteenth century it began to break free. By the beginning of the nineteenth, with the decipherment of the Rosetta Stone and the re-discovery of the ancient Egyptian language, modern archaeology may be said to have begun. But for a long time it remained little more than an occupation for romantic treasure-seekers and antiquity hunters. This was the period when Egypt and Mesopotamia were plundered ruthlessly for works of antiquity which were assembled in European museums and private collections, undated, and at the time, undatable – objects only of curiosity.

At this period begin the great names; Mariette, Maspero, Petrie, Brugsch in Egypt, Layard and Botta in Mesopotamia, Pitt-Rivers in Britain, others in Europe and America. In India and the Far East also curiosity was beginning to stir. In Ceylon Major Forbes explored the ruined cities of Anuradhapura and Polunnaruwa, and compiled a list of Sinhalese kings, the first of whom reigned more than 500 years before Christ. In Europe men began to probe much further back in time; in the limestone hills of the Dordogne, in the Dorset chalk, in the caves of Altamira in Spain, men looked on the work, the tools, the remains of ancestors who had lived at a time so remote than even the pharaohs seemed, by comparison, of yesterday. Darwin had published *The Origin of Species*. Huxley made his historic speech at Oxford. Archbishop Usher's tidy little chronology "dislimned like mist" and men looked back, not to an act of Creation in 4004 B.C. but to a yawning abyss of time which seemed bottomless. Some refused even to look. And geologists proved that, compared with the age of the earth, the emergence and development of Homo sapiens was as a day compared with a thousand years.

Against this background the archaeologists of the nineteenth and twentieth centuries have attempted to chart the comparatively brief progress of man from savagery to civilization. Archaeology ceased to be a treasure-hunt and a collector's hobby. With Pitt-Rivers and Petrie scientific excavation began, in which the aim was not merely to find objects but to establish a reliable system of comparative dating, even of buildings and artifacts which were made long before the invention of written records. Gradually, patiently, the history of man's successive attempts at civilization has been pieced together; the "tells" of Mesopotamia – layer after layer of successive occupation – began to give up their secrets; from fragmented pottery, from tools and weapons, wall foundations, funerary furniture, archaeologists were able to trace the movement of peoples, their wars and conquests, religious beliefs, social customs; and when the ancient writings were deciphered, even something of their thoughts.

In Greece, long believed to be the birthplace of western civilization, Schliemann, Evans and others discovered that there had existed, in prehistoric Europe, a rich and literate civilization a thousand years before the age of Pericles. Homer, who had been regarded as a recorder of myths and folk-tales, was proved to have been describing a civilization which once existed, though it had vanished in his time. "We know now", said Sir Arthur Evans, "that the old legends were true".

And not only the Homeric legends. In India the discovery of great cities at Harappa and Mohenjo-Daro, datable to more than 2000 B.C., and the evidence of their sack and pillage, indicated that the ancient Hindu myths concerning Indra (in the *Rigveda*) may well commemorate the original invasion of the Indus Valley by Aryan conquerors.

Near Peking in China, were discovered the remains of one of man's earliest ancestors, Sinanthropus. In the same country, at Anyang, archaeologists found evidences of a highly developed "riverine" culture, with a writing-system, roughly contemporaneous with the Middle Kingdom in ancient Egypt (about 2000 B.C.). At Folsom, in North America, remains were found of Palaeolithic men, hunters and tool-makers, dating back to at least 10,000 B.C. and probably much earlier. And in Africa, hitherto almost virgin territory for the prehistorian, proto-human remains were found of such vast antiquity as to suggest that Darwin's shrewd guess – that Africa may have been the birthplace of the human race – may well have been true.

Looked at in this way archaeology is exciting. An airman's view of the prehistoric landscape shows a clear and intelligible sequence of development, a progressive extension of knowledge.

It is like reading the last chapter of a well-written detective-story in which the deductions from all the clues scattered throughout the book are analysed and then assembled into a coherent pattern. But in fact the story is made up from the work of a very large number of individual scholars, each working within the limits of his own particular field. If the airman comes down from the higher altitudes, and lands, he may well find one devoted man spending a lifetime examining and interpreting archaeological "finds" in one small area. That man is only vaguely aware of what is going on beyond the mountains which circumscribe his view. Indeed he may be indifferent to discoveries made outside his own territory. But if he does his job properly, recording, photographing and describing, it does not matter if he dies and is forgotten. Another scholar, perhaps of a different nationality, living at a later time and in another part of the world, can read the former scholar's work, and perhaps find the missing piece in the jigsaw puzzle which he himself is trying to solve. This is why an international standard of techniques and working methods is so important. Three hundred years ago Sir Thomas Browne wrote magnificently about his "funerary urnes", but we do not know what they looked like, what objects were found in association with them, at what level they were found, how they compared with other "urnes" discovered in other parts of Britain or Europe. If Browne had been writing today, a future archaeologist living in 2260 A.D. would know as much about them as Browne himself – and probably more.

One can think of many examples of this vital correlation between the discoveries of scholars living and dead. In 1876 Schliemann found, at Mycenae, a bull's head in silver with a rosette, between its horns. Years after the death of Schliemann, another archaeologist found, at Vapheio in Greece, a cup ornamented with reliefs showing the capture of a bull. Still later, in the early years of the twentieth century, Sir Arthur Evans, excavating at Knossos, in Crete, came upon painted frescos depicting young men and girls leaping over the horns of a charging bull, scenes which reminded him of the Greek legends concerning Theseus and the Minotaur – a bull-monster. Today we can be reasonably certain that there existed, in Minoan Crete, a religious cult in which the bull – symbol of fertility – figured prominently. We also know that the invaders of Greece in the second millennium B.C. came into contact with this earlier Cretan civilization and adopted some of its customs and beliefs.

In the nineteenth century Egyptologists noticed, in a certain tomb in the Theban Necropolis, painted scenes representing a procession of alien people presenting gifts to the Pharaoh Tuthmosis III. These people wore a dress which was quite unfamiliar and non-Egyptian. They carried offerings in the form of ornaments, vessels, and weapons which were noticeably non-Egyptian, and among them was a model of a bull's head. In the Egyptian hieroglyphic writing these people were described as "the Keftiu", but nobody knew who "the Keftiu" were. Many years later Sir Arthur Evans discovered, at Knossos in Crete, frescos of men dressed exactly like those represented in the Theban tomb. The mysterious "Keftiu" were the inhabitants of Minoan Crete in 1500 B.C.

Here is a more dramatic example. In 1922 Howard Carter discovered the fabulous tomb of Tutankhamun, an Egyptian pharaoh whose sepulchre had miraculously survived more then 3,000 years, with nearly all its funerary furniture intact. The girl-wife of the king was named Ankhesenamun, and it was known that some months after the death of the young pharaoh (who died at about the age of 17) the queen married a powerful Egyptian courtier named Ay. He was probably about sixty years of age. In ancient Egypt succession to the throne passed through the female line; a man could not become pharaoh unless he married the daughter of the preceding pharaoh, which is why Ay was so anxious to marry Ankhesenamun. Human nature has changed very little in 3,000 years, so that one imagines that a seventeen-year-old girl would not be anxious to marry a man over thrice her age.

Some years after the discovery of Tutankhamun's tomb a German archaeologist was working in the ruins of the city now called Boghazköy, in Asia Minor, more than seven hundred miles distant from the capital of Egypt. He found a large number of baked-clay writing-tablets which had formed part of the archives of the Hittite kings who formerly inhabited Boghazköy. Among these archives was a number of letters addressed by a Hittite king named Shubbiluliuma to an unknown Egyptian princess. Her letters have not survived, but it was clear from Shubbiluliuma's replies that the Egyptian princess was desperately anxious to find a husband. She had invited Shubbiluliuma to send one of his unmarried sons to Egypt, so that the princess, whose husband had recently died, could marry him. "So" she wrote "he may become king of Egypt".

Herr Edel, a noted German scholar, has succeeded in identifying the unknown Egyptian princess with Ankhesenamun. According to Egyptian funerary ritual, the deceased king's body had to remain for a hundred days in a bath of natron prior to mummification. Those hundred days gave Ankhesenamun her chance. Determined not to marry Ay she had written in desperation to the Hittite king. "You have many sons. Send me one of them, that he may marry me and become king of Egypt." In the end Shubbiluliuma did send one of his sons, but he never reached Thebes. Probably he was murdered by one of Ay's agents. Ay married Ankhesenamun and became king of Egypt, and the unhappy widow of Tutankhamun disappears from the scene.

This is a romantic, passionate, human story, but it is not an imaginative creation. It is factually true, and the archaeological records prove it. For one brief moment the veil is lifted, and we come into contact with human beings like ourselves. Unhappily such incidents are rare, and for most of the time one must piece together the human story from the utilitarian objects which human beings have left behind.

"Romance" is almost a dirty word among some archaeologists. One can readily understand why, and sympathize. For far too long, in novels, films and plays, the archaeologist has been represented, not as a patient seeker after truth, but either as a vulgar treasure-seeker lusting for hidden gold, or a pathetic, slightly comic creature doddering about among bones and scraps of pottery – a refugee from life. Both stereotypes are demonstrably false.

The saddest aspect of this travesty is that the reality is often so much more "romantic" than the fictitious creation of the scriptwriter. One must admit that the adventure experienced by the modern archaeologist is usually intellectual. One thinks of Michael Ventris, poring over the navigator's table in an R.A.F. bomber returning from a raid on Berlin, puzzling over the mysterious "Linear B" script which Sir Arthur Evans discovered at Knossos. When he was a seventeen-year-old schoolboy at Stowe, Ventris had heard the 80-year-old scholar, discoverer of the Minoan civilization, lecture on this unknown writing system which for forty years he had tried to interpret. Seventeen years later, when still only thirty-four, Ventris had translated it – a feat greater than that of Champollion, who deciphered the Egyptian hieroglyphs. Champollion had a "bilingual clue". Ventris had not.

One thinks of Henry Rawlinson, hanging perilously from the Behistun Rock in Persia, laboriously transcribing the cuneiform writing which he was eventually to translate, thus revealing to the modern world the literature of ancient Babylonia. There is the young Flinders Petrie, sent out to Egypt in the 'eighties by his cranky father to investigate the quasi-religious "Great Pyramid" theories of Piazzi Smyth, and discovering something much more impressive. "The mean thickness of the eastern joint of the northern casing stones is a fiftieth of an inch"... he wrote"... therefore the mean variations of the cutting of the stone from a straight line is but ... *one hundredth part of an inch*... these joints, with area of seventy-five square feet each, were not only worked as finely as this, but cemented throughout. Though the stones were brought as close as one five-hundredth of an inch, in fact into contact, the mean opening of the joint was one fiftieth of an inch, yet the builders managed to fill the joint with cement, despite the great area of it, and the weight of the stone, some sixteen tons..." Five thousand years ago, the Great Pyramid had been built with almost as much precision as a modern machine-tool.

There was also physical adventure, often of the most alarming kind. Smith, discoverer of the Temple of Diana at Ephesus, being shot through the chest by a fanatic, yet surviving; Layard galloping across the Armenian mountains in his hurry to be the first to excavate Nimrud, and arriving at the British Residence at Baghdad, ragged and penniless; Hiram Bingham, the American explorer, scrambling, breathless, up the final slopes of the gorge of the Urubamba in Peru, hearing the roar of waters far below, and seeing, for the first time, the sacred city of the Incas, Macchu Picchu, which even the Spanish *conquistadores* never discovered. There was Petrie, camping in the desert near the pyramid at Hawara, with a gun at his side, and finding, in a rocky crevice, the half-eaten corpse of a tomb-robber; and Howard Carter, discoverer of the tomb of Tutankhamun, esconced with his armed guard high in the Theban cliffs, engaging in a brisk gun-battle with Arab plunderers who had come to rob the tomb of Queen Hatshepsut. There was Hilprecht, another American archaeologist, watching the smoke rising from his burning tents as Beduins looted his camp at Nippur. If Hollywood is looking for "true-life" stories about archaeologists, involving physical adventure and violence, it need not employ fiction-writers.

But few archaeological adventures are of this robust physical kind. Much of the archaeologist's work would appear dull to the layman; the painstaking digging, month after month, of a site which yields no objects of artistic or intrinsic value; the routine measurement, photographing and drawing of strata; the classification, in the workshop and laboratory, of hundreds of tiny fragments of pottery; the ultimate publication of the finds, so that other scholars shall have ready access to the information. Such work is going on all the time, in the universities and museums of the world; the general public never hears of it, unless a "dig" happens to reveal something which appeals to the imagination of the layman. Yet it is probably true to say that the greater part of our knowledge of the remote past is derived from his patient, relatively unrewarding work.

In any case, the romance and excitement of archaeological research is not confined to the discovery of rare or beautiful objects. Archaeology is a search for knowledge, not primarily for things. A few tiny scraps of Roman pottery, below the grass of some British hill-fort, may be enough to prove that the fort was built in pre-Roman times. A minute scrap of bitumen from mummy-wrappings, found inside an otherwise empty sarcophagus, proves that it once contained a body, and that fact may be of vital importance to the history of a dynasty. One insignificant little Egyptian statuette of known date, discovered in association with certain Minoan objects under the Palace of Knossos, enabled the excavators to date not only those objects, but similar artifacts found on other sites, perhaps hundreds of miles away. The mere imprint, on dried earth, of a wooden harp from which every trace of wood had decayed, enabled Sir Leonard Woolley to reconstruct, down to the last detail, an instrument played by the court musicians of Sumeria 3,000 years ago.

The work of many archaeologists is confined within a certain period beginning with the Neolithic (New Stone) Age, of which the earliest manifestations are found in central Asia probably round about 10,000 B.C. From that time onwards we can study the lives of men who had ceased to depend entirely on hunting, but were able to live for considerable periods in one spot, and thus develop the arts of agriculture, stock-rearing, spinning, weaving, and the making of pottery vessels for storing food. This marked a revolution in human behaviour, and laid the foundations of modern civilization. However, compared with the entire history of man, this period of some 12,000 years represents only *one twenty-fifth* part of the whole (some prehistorians would put the proportion at *one fortieth*). That is why, in this book, we have included items dealing with much earlier periods, right back to the Palaeolithic (Old Stone) Age and the pre-Palaeolithic ages even though some might argue that such remote epochs are the province of the prehistorian rather than the archaeologist.

The fascination of Neolithic and post-Neolithic archaeology is that it deals with human beings who, in many ways, were very like ourselves. The fascination of prehistory is of the opposite kind; in the earliest beginnings we are faced with creatures which are not apes, and yet still not men. And even later, in Palaeolithic times, when we find stone tools obviously shaped by a human will, we are dealing with people so remote from ourselves that we can only enter in their minds through imagination. Sometimes the artist – the composer Stravinsky, for instance, in "The Rite of Spring" – may bring us nearer to the spirit and atmosphere of prehistoric times than the scientist. To many laymen the main obstacle to an appreciation of prehistoric archaeology is the paucity of the objects found. We have all looked bewilderedly at the rows upon rows of carefully classified implements, hand-axes, knives, borers, scrapers, etc., labelled Aurignacian, or Mousterian, or Gravettian, and retired baffled, or perhaps bored.

Yet the subject can be absorbing and stimulating, provided one recognizes that these "cultures" so painstakingly catalogued are only the prehistorian's "tools of trade", convenient labels and nothing more. Always, ultimately, the study is not of things but of human beings. The careful classifications show us where and how certain primitive human beings lived; the mode of life can be guessed at by the tools they used: hand-axes for use both as weapons and tools; knives for cutting up the animal-skins, awls for piercing them; bone needles for sewing them together. Then there are those mysterious "cave-shelters" such as one finds in the now-fertile valleys of the Dordogne and the Vézère, in France. Here, when the glaciers of the last Ice Age penetrated far south into Europe, primitive man looked out from the cave mouth, watching for the return of the wild animals upon which he depended for very life. There you will see the remains of his fires, used both for cooking and for keeping the more ferocious beasts at bay. There you will see, at Le Moustier for instance, the figures he carved on the rocks within the cave. And in the gravels prehistorians discovered the primitive stone tools which he made and used, equipment devised by his superior brain to compensate for his own pitiful frailty compared with the strength of the wild beasts.

Benjamin Franklin's definition of man as a "tool-making animal" still holds good. Some animals, e.g. gorillas, have been known to use tools, such as a piece of wood or bone and, even to maintain, though not to create, fire. But only man can *make* tools. About thirty million years ago, in the period which the geologists called Miocene, there lived in east Africa a certain species of monkey-like creatures. About a hundred of them were found on Rusinga Island, in Kenya, and one of them, labelled Proconsul, had certain un-ape-like characteristics which, it has been suggested, may indicate that it belonged to the primal strain from which both man and apes are descended.

During the early Pliocene period other types of ape developed which were adapted to living in trees, as certain types of ape do today. But there were other apes who preferred to live in the open country. So, in time, they developed their pelvic girdles and hind legs in such a way as to enable them to move easily on their hind legs only. It is believed that this upright posture enabled the human race to evolve. Once he had learned to walk upright, man, or sub-man, had the free use of his fore-limbs and hands. He could pick up and examine objects. His fore-paws (or "hands") became more highly developed, whereas his feet did not. Nevertheless, even today, in Japan, there are artists capable of making fine drawings with a brush held between the first and second toes; and the same capacity has been observed among Europeans whose hands have become useless through paralysis.

These sub-men also developed fine eyes, which could see both near and distant objects clearly. Above all they developed their brains. Whereas other animals specialized (in the genetical sense) mainly in bone and muscle, only man's ancestors specialized in their brains. In time, the human brain ceased merely to control and direct the physical actions of the body, as in the lower animals. It developed *self-consciousness*, and the capacity for conceptual thought. "Consciousness" says a well known prehistorian "is the mistletoe on the oak tree... Man is the only animal which can stand outside the window and see itself talking". Three hundred years ago an Italian doctor named Galliani had observed that "man is the only animal which takes an interest in things which don't concern it."

This is no place to describe the evolution of man, from man-ape to primeval, from primeval to primitive, from primitive to modern. But at least it can be said that, at widely-separated places on the earth's surface, remains have been found of creatures which had more in common with ourselves than our ape-like ancestors. The oldest known example is Australopithecus, which means "southern ape" and was found in Africa. He probably lived about a million years ago. In the same continent was discovered the more developed species, Paranthropus and Telanthropus. In Java was found Pithecanthropus erectus, who walked like a man. In China there was Sinanthropus who could make quartz tools and who used fire. In Britain there was Swanscombe Man who was also a tool-maker.

We do not yet know from which species our own ancestor, Homo sapiens, is derived. Mr Desmond Clark states that "anatomists are generally agreed that the genus Pithecanthropus is probably ancestral to the genus Homo, and may in turn have evolved from a form very similar to that of Australopithecus. This does not imply, however, that the Far Eastern population of this genus was itself the ancestral group, as the actual transition from the one to the other may have occurred in some other part of the world" (*The Prehistory of Southern Africa* by J.D.Clark, 1959). On the other hand some authorities, such as the author of the article on Primates, suggest that such species as Australopithecus and Pithecanthropus were "side-tracks" from the main evolutionary road, and that we derived through a more direct, but as yet undiscovered route, from the ancestors of the Proconsul apes.

But it does appear that Homo sapiens may have originated in Africa, and then, with the melting of the glaciers at the end of the Ice Age, migrated to Europe, where he found, already living there, a more primitive but distantly related species of men which we call Homo neanderthalis. Because he had had the opportunity for development in warmer latitudes, Homo sapiens was superior to Neanderthal Man and eventually replaced him. He was a skilful hunter, and produced the magnificent cave art which one finds at such places as Les Trois Frères, Lascaux and Altamira. Why he painted these vivid pictures of animals in the dim recesses of caves – places which could not have been his home – has never been fully explained, though there are theories. Most prehistorians agree that the paintings had some religio-magical significance. It may well be that we see here a manifestation of the religious impulse in Man. At Les Trois Frères, in France, one can see a picture, painted on the cave-wall, of a "medicine man" wearing the horns of a reindeer. It has been suggested that at times when the animals, on whom man depended for his food supply, had not returned, the tribe retired to the depths of the cave and there took part in a religious ceremony during which the medicine-man induced in the worshippers a trance-like state which made them highly suggestible. Then he may have ritually "killed" the painted animals with his spear (some cave-paintings show bison, reindeer etc. transfixed by spears) and sent the tribe away convinced that soon the animals would return, and that there would be good hunting; the starving women and children would be fed. It is a fascinating and, as yet, unproven theory, but prehistory is a discipline which allows room for the exercise of imagination.

By contrast Neolithic and post-Neolithic times are as of yesterday. Between 12,000 and 20,000 years ago, probably in central Asia, climatic changes may have turned what had been steppe country, in which man and animals wandered freely, into desert. But there were always the oases, here there was a constant supply of water, vegetation and fertile soil. Gradually both men and animals may have been pushed back to these waterholes. Some animals, lingering near the fringes of the camps in search of food, may have become so tame that it became possible to domesticate them. Besides hunting animals, man also tamed and bred them for food and clothing. Certain beasts such as the ox and the sheep became, in the words of the late V.Gordon Childe, "living larders and walking wardrobes". Round about the same period the reasoning, reflecting brain of man may have noticed that certain wild seeds, accidentally spilled on fertile soil, sprouted in due season. So agriculture was born. It was no longer necessary to wander perpetually, as one's ancestors had done for threescore millennia, hunting for food. One could stay in one spot and both rear and grow food.

All this took place quite recently, within 20,000 years at the most. All man's experiments in civilization, i.e. corporate living – Sumerian, Egyptian, Indus Valley, Minoan, Chinese, Mexican, Peruvian began when he had learned to grow food and domesticate animals; from man the hunter to man the farmer. Only when human beings were able to live in settled communities, in one place, for considerable lengths of time, did civilization become possible.

Between 5000 and 3000 B.C., man found, in at least two places, conditions which permitted him to settle, not in isolated communities, oases such as that of Jericho, but along broad river valleys in which the soil was annually re-fertilized by flooding. One was the Nile Valley; the other was the valley of the Tigris-Euphrates in Mesopotamia. The Nile had the additional advantage of being hemmed in on each side by inhospitable deserts – a deterrent to enemies, whereas the civilization of Sumer, in Mesopotamia, lacked this protection. Probably for this reason civilization was slower to develop in Sumer than it was in Egypt, in which rose, round about 3000 B.C., the first large, self-contained monolithic state owing allegiance to a single ruler. In Sumer cohesion was more difficult, and for a long period – before the arrival of Hammurabi of Babylon – men lived in independent city-states often at war with each other or with enemies from beyond.

But in both cases the pattern of development was the same. The possibility of a settled existence led to the building of permanent homes, at first of mud-brick. Stone tools gave place to those made of metal, at first of copper, then of bronze, and finally of iron. The annual re-fertilization of the land from mud carried downstream by the river made agriculture relatively easy. Also there was an abundance of wild game near the river banks, so that one did not have to wander far in search of animals. Hunting, which had formerly been a condition of existence, became a sport. Without too much exaggeration one might compare the Egyptian tomb-paintings depicting the hunting of wildfowl with photographs of the British Prime Minister shooting grouse.

And something else happened, much more important. For the first time in the history of the human race, man was able to produce a surplus of wealth above his own immediate requirements, which could be used to store against famine, and to support a new non-producing class of specialists; the literate class which could store and transmit knowledge; administrators, priests, engineers, architects and specialized craftsmen in stone, wood, and metal. Also "conspicuous consumption" makes its first appearance in the form of the splendid furniture, jewellery and ornaments used by the aristocracy.

With metal tools and organized labour, man could build magnificently in wood and stone. 5,000 years ago the Egyptians raised the Great Pyramid, a solid block of masonry 750 feet along each base-line, and over 450 high, constructed of twelve-ton stone blocks fitted together with mathematical precision, and orientated with such accuracy that compass errors can be checked against it. Moreover until a mere 150 years ago it was the highest building in the world. Similar feats were achieved in Mesopotamia, where the Sumerians erected huge towers called ziggurats, artificial mountains looming above the plain. In the Indus Valley of

India, at Mohenjo-Daro and Harappa, the inhabitants of the fertile valley achieved similar features of engineering and architecture. Somewhat later, round about 2000 B.C. the Chinese had developed another riverine civilization, together with a writing-system, remains of which have been discovered at Anyang.

On the American continent, into which man penetrated relatively late, such major developments had to wait for a further 2,500 years. And the same seems to apply to eastern Asia, apart from China. As for Africa, it seems that the wastes of the Sahara effectively prevented Egyptian knowledge penetrating farther south than the Sudan. South of the Zambesi men were still living in the Stone Age. In Europe knowledge of agriculture, animal husbandry, and the craft of making metal tools and weapons spread slowly from east to west. In the island of Crete immigrants from Asia and north Africa, who arrived there before 3000 B.C. gradually developed a civilization as sophisticated and complex as that of Egypt. It was imitated by the Myceneans. But throughout the rest of Europe there were only isolated tribes, living precariously in forest clearings and along river valleys, who copied in stone the rare and precious metal weapons brought by trade from the more advanced Mediterranean regions.

Yet even before 1500 B.C. Mediterranean peoples had sailed through the Straits of Gibraltar and settled along the coast of Spain and in Britain, taking with them their knowledge of agriculture, stock-rearing, metallurgy, and architecture. Their great megalithic tombs and stone circles may be indirectly derived from the tholos tombs of Mycenean Greece, or even from Egypt. Quite recently archaeologists detected, carved on the stones of Stonehenge, a British sun-temple, the clear outline of a Mycenean dagger.

It is significant that nearly all the great monuments which have survived from the ancient world are religious; temples or tombs. One thinks of the Egyptian pyramids, which were the tombs of kings; the Egyptian temples such as that of Karnak, so huge that a hundred men could stand on the capital of one of the gigantic columns; one recalls the Sumerian and Babylonian ziggurats – of which the biblical Tower of Babel is a memory – the alignments at Carnac, in Brittany, and the circles of Stonehenge and Woodhenge in England. In India and Ceylon there are the Buddhist stupas or towers. In Mexico and Peru there are the pyramidal sun-temples of the Aztecs, the Mayas, and the Incas. All are religious monuments. In most cases the temporary homes of men have disappeared almost entirely, but their temples have survived.

Inevitably, one is reminded of the mysterious and sinister caves in France, Spain, and elsewhere, where our primitive ancestors, hunters and cave-dwellers, listened to the voice of their medicine-men, as modern primitives in Australia and Africa do today.

There is a reason for this. In that remote period it would be natural that the most intelligent and perceptive of the tribe would gain intellectual ascendancy. Poet, artist, philosopher, priest – all were one. Those with the most highly-developed brains and imaginations became the élite. In our own day the man-in-the-street recognizes that the hydrogen bomb exists. He has seen it on the newsreel. He has read about it in his newspaper. But he does not know how it works, whereas the scientist does. Primitive man saw lightning, heard thunder, saw floods devastate his land. He watched, without understanding them, the slow, inevitable progress of the seasons. But it was the priest or medicine-man who told him when the river would rise, when the rain would fall, when to plant and when to reap.

But the priest had to explain these things, both to himself and to his followers. It is not suggested that the intellectual class deliberately misled its followers. But the only way to explain what we call "natural forces" was to humanize them. Thunder, rain, lightning, flood, the sea, the land, the mountains, the plain, birth, love, death, sickness, disease, could be comprehended only in human terms. In the words of Professor Frankfort: "The fundamental difference between the attitudes of modern and ancient man as regards the surrounding world is this; for modern, scientific man the phenomenal world is primarily an 'It'. For ancient – and also for primitive man it is 'Thou'... Primitive man has only one mode of thought, one mode of expression, one part of speech – *the personal*. This does not mean that primitive man, in order to explain natural phenomena, imparts human characteristics to an inanimate world... The world appears to primitive man neither inanimate or empty but abundant with life; and life has individuality, in man or beast or plant, and in every phenomenon which confronts man – the thunderclap – the sudden shower – the eerie unknown clearing in the wood – the stone which hurts him when he stumbles while on a hunting trip. Any phenomenon may at any time face him, not as an 'It' but a 'Thou'." (*The Intellectual Adventure of Ancient Man* by H. Frankfort, Chicago U.P., copyright by the University of Chicago, 1946).

So the medicine-man, the interpreter of what we call "nature" becomes the priest; and in primitive society not only the priest but the scientist, the engineer, the mathematician, the astronomer. This, surely, is vital to the study of archaeology. If we think of the Egyptian, Babylonian, Aztec priests as we think of Christian bishops in the twentieth century we shall miss the point.

Confronted with an ancient temple we may be tempted to think "Yes, these people made tools and weapons, lived in comfortable houses, made bread and wine, fell in love, married and had children, and died, just as we do. And they also built churches." If we take this superficial view we shall never understand the world of our ancestors. To them the temple was like a power-house, a source of energy. Within it, and the men who served it, lay all life, all power, all understanding. It is for this reason that our ancestors expended far more time, care, and love in building the homes of their gods, and in preparing the tombs of their dead, than we do.

In some civilizations, e.g. that of ancient Egypt, the priestly caste secured such a hold over the people that Egyptian society remained relatively static for nearly 3000 years. Examine a carved relief of 2700 B.C. and compare it with another of 300 B.C. and, apart from stylistic development, you will see little change. Tradition, though it stabilizes society, can also inhibit and restrain development.

In other societies, e.g. that of Greece, this was not so. Unlike the Egyptians or the Babylonians, the Persians, the Mayas and the Aztecs, the Greeks thought freely. They examined existing doctrines, criticizing, accepting or rejecting them, and this, presumably, is why we feel more at home with the Greeks than with the people of the earlier civilizations. Yet other peoples, for instance those of India and the Far East, and the aboriginal inhabitants of America, may have apprehended reality through more spiritual channels. Without delving into metaphysics, which are outside the scope of this book, one fact seems fairly clear: man evolved from the animal to the human state through that "mistletoe-growth" of consciousness from which developed that "spiritual" element which the ancient Egyptians called the *ka* and which we call "the soul". Despite the cynical comment of the famous surgeon who, when dissecting a human body, said that he had "failed to find any trace of the soul", a great many of us are convinced of its existence. Whatever it is, this is the mainspring of our moral convictions, the motivating force behind those acts of altruism and self-sacrifice of which the lower animals have no experience. But one fact at least appears certain. Archaeology, by revealing the panorama of human development, shows us that man became man by the exercise of consciousness. When he ceases to wonder and reflect he will perish. The spirit of the man who first saw fire and considered how he could create and control it is still with us; the nuclear physicist can release the source of the sun's energy, but he is not afraid of it. The man who first thought how to make a primitive stone tool which could amplify the power of his arm, now devises electronic devices for operating machinery which dispenses altogether with human effort. The man who determined to climb and conquer the mountains which hemmed in his tribe has his modern equivalent in the scientist who wants to conquer outer space.

Archaeology, then, is not just a means of escaping from the present, an exploration of the dead forgotten past. Rightly understood, it is a means of enlarging our understanding of ourselves. By looking back along the road we have travelled we gain a better appreciation of the hazards ahead.

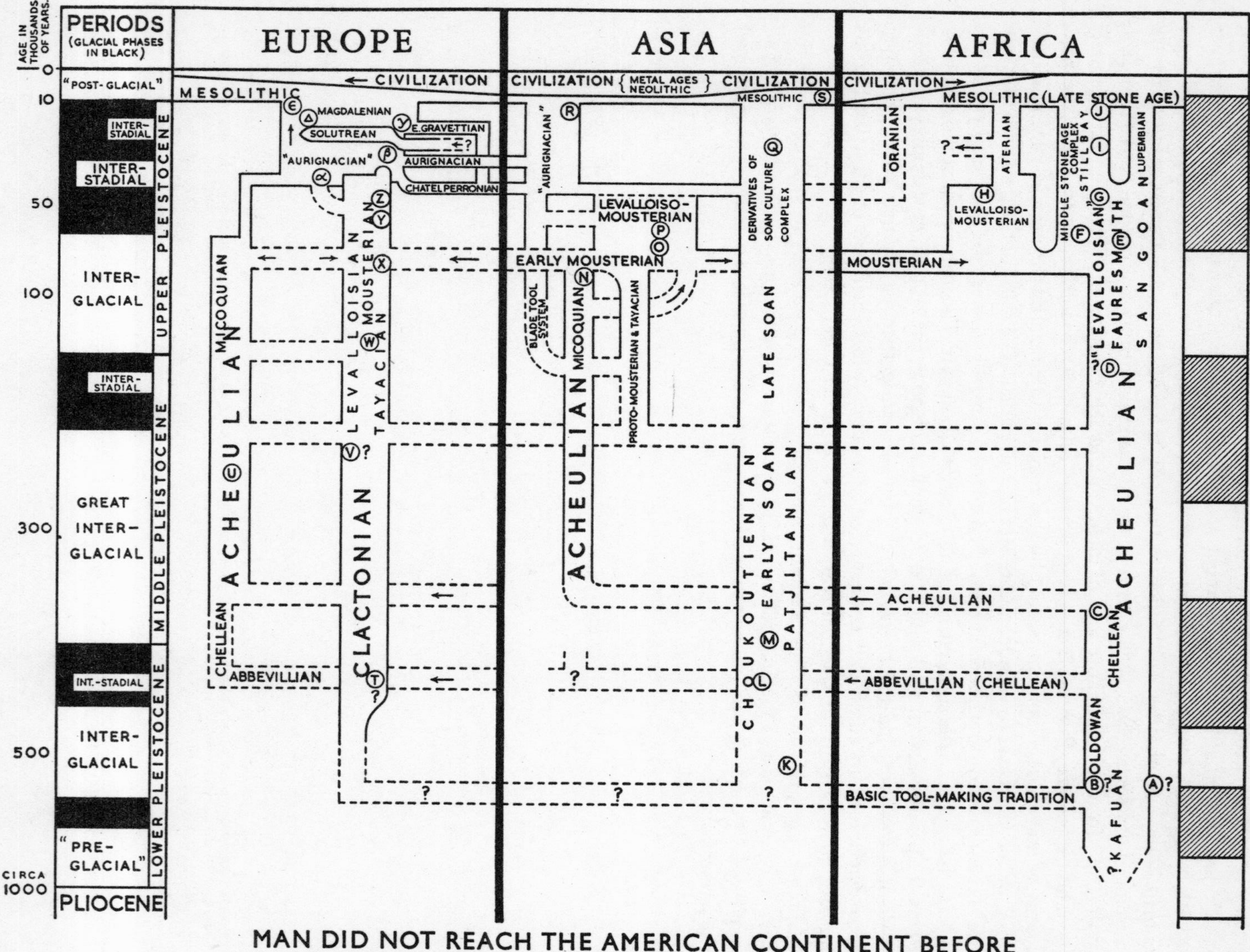

MAN DID NOT REACH THE AMERICAN CONTINENT BEFORE THE CLOSING STAGES OF THE ICE AGE C. 15,000 B.C.

Distribution and Suggested Relationships of

THE CULTURAL TRADITIONS OF EARLY MAN

The glacial periods shown on the chart are generally regarded as corresponding with the advances of ice in the Alps which have been named: Günz, Mindel I–II, Riss I–II, Würm I–III. The pluvial periods recognized in Africa (shaded in column) are now named: Kageran, Kamasian, Kanjeran ("Upper Kamasian") and Gamblian.

An encircled letter plotted in relation to the name of a culture shows that fossils remains of a bearer of the tradition have been found in deposits of the age and location indicated. Thus **U** in the European Acheulian indicates the skull found in deposits dating from the end of the second interglacial, at Swanscombe, Kent.

The following is a key to the localities of fossil hominids: **A** Makapan Limeworks (S. Africa); **B** Kanam (Kenya); **C** Ternifine (Algeria); **D** Kanjera (Kenya); **E** Saldanha (S. Africa); **F** Florisbad (S. Africa); **G** Broken Hill (N. Rhodesia) and Eyasi (Tanganyika); **H** Huau Fteah (Cyrenaica); **I** Singa (Sudan), Boskop and Matjes River (S. Africa); **J** Fish Hoek (S. Africa); **K** Sangiran (Java); **L** Chou-kou-tien (near Peking); **M** Trinil (Java); **N** Galilee; **O** Tabun, Mt Carmel; **P** Skhul Cave, Mt Carmel; **Q** Ngandong, Solo River (Java); **R** Hotu Cave (Iran); **S** Wadjak (Java); **T** Heidelberg (Germany); **U** Swanscombe (Kent); **V** Steinheim (Germany); **W** Fontéchevade (France); **X** Ehringsdorf (Germany); **Y** Gibraltar; **Z** La Chapelle-aux-Saints (France); α Châtelperron and Combe Capelle (France); β Cro-magnon (France); γ Predmost (Czechoslovakia); δ Chancelade (France); ε Cheddar and Aveline's Hole (Somerset), Whaley (Derbyshire).

The remains from **A** belong to Australopithecus; those from **K, L, M,** and possibly **C** and **T** to the Pithecanthropus group of men; those from **Y** and **Z** to the Neanderthal group; those from **E, G, H, N, O, P, V,** and **X** are neanderthaloids showing various degrees of affinity to Homo sapiens; remains from **D, F, I, J, R,** α-ε are referable to Homo sapiens.

A

Abbevillian. This culture of the Lower **Palaeolithic** takes its name from Abbeville in northern France. It was once known as the Chellean, after finds made at Chelles, but was changed in deference to the more typical **stone tools** found at Abbeville.

These hunters reached France in a warm interglacial period at the beginning of the Pleistocene, over half a million years ago. Their characteristic tool was the **hand-axe,** a pear-shaped lump of flint with a heavy butt and pointed end. As time went on, this was refined by more highly-developed techniques of flint-working, in **Acheulian** levels. Experiments by archaeologists have demonstrated that the Abbevillians shaped their hand-axes by battering a block of flint against a stone anvil. This resulted in the removal of large flakes, leaving a core of the desired shape with deep flake-scars. The blows were struck from alternate sides all round the edge, the flint being turned over after each blow. A wavy edge resulted, very different from the straight edge, or delicate S-twist, of the Acheulians. The butt of the Abbevillian hand-axe was often left unworked, preserving the cortex or outer surface of the flint.

The hand-axe served as an all-purpose tool. The butt could have been used for crushing, the sharp edges for skinning animals and cutting, and the point for digging. It was an exceedingly long-lived design, continuing for thousands of years, becoming only more finely worked.

Although Abbevillian hand-axes were first identified in France, recent discoveries indicate that the culture had its origin in Africa. At **Olduvai Gorge,** four distinct levels containing Abbevillian hand-axes were found, lying above the layer containing Leakey's Oldowan pebble-tools, the oldest yet known.

Abydos. One of the most ancient cities of Upper Egypt, Abydos lies some 320 miles south of Cairo. Founded by pre-Menite kings, the city and its temples were rebuilt continuously from the first to the thirtieth dynasties, for it was the chief centre of the cult of Osiris. On one site ruins were excavated to a depth of eighteen feet, revealing ten temples built successively on one spot, between the first and twenty-sixth dynasties (3200 B.C.–500 B.C.). One mile south of this series of temples is the Great Temple of Abydos built by Seti I in the nineteenth dynasty, much of which still remains standing. On the walls is the "Table of Abydos" on which is carved a list of kings, a panegyric on Ramses II and various mythological subjects. There are also seven chapels for the worship of kings and the principal gods. Nearby is a smaller temple of Ramses II, also containing fine wall-carvings.

One mile away, in the desert, are tombs of early kings, some covering more than 3,000 square yards. In the town there is a cemetery for private people with many rich tombs dating from the first dynasty to Roman times. Large numbers of inscribed **stelae,** funerary slabs, have been found there.

Many interesting objects were found in the ruins and tombs, including fine ivory carvings, glazed figures and tiles, a vase of Menes glazed green and inlaid with purple **hieroglyphics,** and a fine ivory statuette of Cheops.

Abyssinia, *see* Ethiopia.

Accadians. A Semitic people dwelling in northern Babylonia, the Accadians took their name from the important city of Accad (non-Semitic Agade) which became the principal city of the Babylonian Semitic Empire. Accad was situated on the left bank of the Euphrates. It became the seat of the powerful Sargon I (about 2800 B.C. or later) who had control over the whole of Babylonia, subjugating also Elam and Mesopotamia and invading Syria and Palestine four times. The word Accad was often used loosely in **cuneiform** inscriptions to signify the whole of Babylonia. The Accadian language superseded Sumerian, especially as a vehicle of commercial correspondence. As such it was widely used throughout the Middle East.

Achaeans. The general term used by Homer for the Greeks is not the classical *Hellenes,* but *Akhaioi* or Achaeans. The original form of the name was *Akhaiwoi,* whence came the Latin *Achivi.* The Greeks derived the name from a mythical ancestor *Akhaios,* son of Xuthus and brother of Ion, the ancestor of the **Ionians.** In the classical period Achaea was the name both of a part of Thessaly and of the district on the north coast of the Peloponnese fronting onto the Corinthian Gulf. In the third and second centuries B.C. the cities in the latter area formed the Achaean league; and when the Romans finally overran Greece, they adopted Achaea as the name of their province.

Modern writers mostly use Achaeans as a name for the Greek population of the **Mycenaean** period (about 1650–1100 B.C.), though there is no evidence in contemporary documents (*see* **Minoan Scripts**) for the name used by these people themselves. **Hittite** documents, however, refer to a kingdom of *Ahhijawa*, which is generally thought to be Greek, though its location is uncertain. The Egyptian mention of *iqjws* (possibly *Aqiyawasa*) among the **Sea Peoples** is often believed to be a further reference to the Achaeans, but there are good reasons for questioning this identification. Linguistically, Achaean is sometimes used to mean the common ancestor of the Arcadian and Cypriot dialects, and the Mycenaean dialect of the Linear B inscriptions.

Achaemenians *or* **Achaemenids,** *see* Iran.

Acheulian. This is sometimes known as Abbeville-Acheulian, since the **Abbevillian** culture can be seen as merely the first phase of the main Acheulian culture. The type-site from which this, one of the earliest **Palaeolithic** cultures, takes its name is at St Acheul in northern France.

Palaeolithic man, who flourished in the Pleistocene or European Ice Age period (*see* **Quaternary Period**) and fashioned **stone tools** by chipping (not grinding and polishing), falls into a number of groups, each definable by the type of stone implement it left. The men of the Abbeville-Acheulian culture left tools known as **hand-axes.** These hand-axes were of two broad types: those with a point and a round butt for holding, and "ovates" which were trimmed to a thin edge round their whole circumference. The earliest (Abbevillian) hand-axes are crudely made, but later examples show some improvement with variations in shape to suit different purposes.

The Acheulian culture begins in Europe and traces have been found in Britain and nearly all parts of Africa, in the Near East and southern India. Little is known of the habitat of Acheulian man but the great majority of his tools have been found near rivers and lakes or embedded in river gravels, and this suggests that his way of life was closely associated with inland water.

Acropolis. The citadel-on-a-hill, especially that of **Athens,** but extended to other Greek or Greek-colonized cities as well.

Aegean Civilization, *see* Minoan Civilization *and* Mycenae.

Aepyornis. A bird of Madagascar exterminated by man in historic times. Its eggs were the largest known to science, holding about two gallons, and it is possible that they gave rise to the stories in *The Arabian Nights* of the roc, that enormous bird which could carry off people – as it did Sinbad. The aepyornis, however, like the ostrich, was unable to fly.

Africa, East. East Africa, in the political sense, comprises Kenya Colony and Protectorate, Tanganyika Territory, and Uganda Protectorate; geographically, it includes also Somalia, the Horn of Africa. It is a land of contrasts owing to the great variations in altitude, and hence in climate. The land below 3,000 feet is mostly barren desert or thorny bush and was avoided in prehistoric times, as it is today. The highlands, above 5,000 feet, are now the most densely populated part of the country; but, during the early part of the Stone Age, hunters lived for the most part on the open plains between 3,000 and 5,000 feet, camping beside the shores of Lake Victoria and the Rift Valley lakes.

In east Africa, as nowhere else in the world, man's ancestry can be traced back for about 25,000,000 years. The earliest skull of an ape, named Proconsul (*see* **Primates, Prehuman Evolution of**), was found on Rusinga Island in Lake Victoria and it is believed that both man and the modern great apes may be descended from such a form. There is a long gap in the fossil record between these **Miocene** apes and the curious Australopithecines (*see* **Australopithecus**), which lived in the cape Province and elsewhere in South Africa about half a million years ago, towards the end of the Lower Pleistocene.

The first crude pebble-tools date from this period, though it is not known whether they were made by true men or perhaps by the Australopithecines.

A human jaw from Kanam, on the shores of the Kavirondo Gulf of Lake Victoria, was apparently associated with pebble-tools and Lower Pleistocene fauna. It seems to have a vertical chin, a feature which is unique for this early period; but a tumour may have exaggerated the depth of the bone. The only other contemporary human remains from east Africa are a jaw fragment from Laetolil, and two milk teeth from **Olduvai Gorge,** both in northern Tanganyika; possibly these may represent the Australopithecines.

The Olduvai teeth are more than twice as big as a modern child's; this may mean that the individual was gigantic, or it may simply mean that he had a very powerful jaw. Certainly many of the animals hunted by early man were enormous; there were sheep as large as buffaloes and pigs the size of a rhinoceros. At Olduvai there is evidence that men drove these animals into a swamp and butchered them nearby with stone tools. Pebble-tools form a rough cutting edge. Gradually they evolved into the first **hand-axes** of the Chelles-Acheul culture, which become more advanced in successive beds. Many thousands of hand-axes, cleavers and stone balls have been found in this magnificent gorge, as well as numerous remains of fossil mammals. The animal bones were split open to extract the marrow and skulls were smashed to get at the brains. (*See also* **Zinjanthropus**.)

Several other **Acheulian** sites are known in east Africa, including **Olorgesailie** in the Kenya Rift Valley, Nsongezi in Uganda and Isimila Karongo in Tanganyika. At all these sites **stone tools** have been found in incredible profusion. Such camps must have been occupied over long periods, since they were situated near drinking places where game would congregate. Rainfall was more regular and more evenly distributed over most of Africa during four major pluvial periods in the Pleistocene; lakes existed then at Olduvai and Olorgesailie, both of which are in extremely arid country today.

The makers of the hand-axe culture in east Africa are represented only by fragments of four skulls from Kanjera, near Kanam. In one case the forehead region has been preserved; it is quite smooth, as in modern man, with no projecting brow-ridges. This feature makes the Kanjera skulls quite unlike any other fossils of comparable age, but the dating is not absolutely certain.

A skull from Eyasi in northern Tanganyika is roughly contemporary with **Rhodesia Man** and **Neanderthal Man** and, like these types, it has very pronounced brow-ridges, a flat vault to the cranium and thick walls. It was accompanied by an early Upper Pleistocene fauna and rather crude stone tools made on flakes; by that time, the hand-axe culture had died out.

During the dry period which followed the third pluvial, people moved up to higher altitudes; the **Fauresmith** culture is found beside permanent streams in the highlands of Kenya and Ethiopia. Two main cultures existed during the Middle Stone Age at the time of the fourth pluvial period. The **Sangoan** is found in forested country, which has over forty inches mean annual rainfall at the present time; it is characteristic of many parts of central Africa and extends into Uganda and western Kenya. The Stillbay extends over the drier country of eastern Africa, from the Horn to the Cape; typical implements are small points, flaked over both surfaces, which were presumably hafted as spears or daggers.

The Kenya Capsian, which is similar to the **Capsian** of Tunisia, has only been found in the Rift Valley of Kenya and northern Tanganyika and is believed to have been contemporary with the Stillbay, though it is far more advanced. Microlithic tools of obsidian include backed-blades, burins or gravers, end-scrapers and crescents or lunates which must have been barbs for harpoons, spears, or possibly arrows. The earliest pottery is also associated with this culture, as well as beads made from ostrich egg-shell and bone awls for sewing leather. The long, narrow skulls of the Kenya Capsians are of Mediterranean type and show no traces of negroid characteristics.

The Kenya Capsians were followed in the Rift Valley by the Elmenteitans, who are represented by two racial types. One was tall, with long, narrow skulls and long faces, like the Kenya Capsians; the other was short, with round skulls and broad faces. These two types continued in this part of east Africa until the **Iron Age**, when Negroids first appeared.

The Stillbay people were succeeded by the Magosians and then the Wiltons. Some of the Wilton people lived out in the open, others in rock shelters, and others again beside the shores of lakes. Many skeletons of these lake-side dwellers were found near Kanam, associated with huge shell mounds. They were heavily built people, with large skulls and small faces reminiscent of the **Bushmen.** Contemporary with the Wiltons were the Nachikufans, who lived in the woodland regions of north Rhodesia and Tanganyika. They were probably responsible for the earliest rock paintings of Tanganyika, which are mainly centred on Kondoa.

Nearly two hundred rock painting sites have been studied in this area and several hundred more are known to exist.

In Somalia, two distinctive cultures arose between the Magosian and the Wilton. The Doian, which is confined to southern Somalia, is named after the sand which covers much of this country and is known to the Somali as *doi*. The Hargeisan is found in the northern part of the plateau and the Gulf of Aden rift; in some ways it is rather similar to the Kenya Capsian, though it was considerably later.

In most parts of east Africa there are few signs of a **Neolithic** way of life, but instead the people seem to have continued as hunters and food-gatherers until the Iron Age. In the Rift Valley of Kenya and northern Tanganyika, however, there were settled communities and presumably some kind of food production from about 3000 B.C. onwards. These people were the makers of the so-called Stone Bowl culture, of which there were four variants.

The earliest settlement was at Hyrax Hill, near Nakuru, where all female burials were accompanied by shallow stone platters. Rather later, the characteristic stone bowls were deeper and shaped like pudding basins. Skulls of these people are much longer and narrower than those of any of the present inhabitants of Africa. The third variant of the Stone Bowl culture is associated with a peculiar method of burial which suggests *sati*. At a site near Nakuru, one skeleton had been buried carefully in the contracted position and covered with red ochre. Parts of eight dismembered skeletons had been thrown amongst a pile of rocks against the face of a cliff; presumably they were either slaves or wives killed at the same time.

The fourth variant of the Stone Bowl culture, from the Njoro river cave, has been dated to about 1200 B.C. by **radio-carbon**. These people cremated their dead and the process of slow combustion turned many perishable objects into charcoal and so preserved them. These objects include skin clothing, string bags, plaited cords, and a carved wooden vessel decorated with a honeycomb pattern. Both male and female skeletons were accompanied by stone bowls, pestles and mortars. Many hundreds of beads were also found, some in groups forming complete necklaces, as well as pendants and bone awls.

The date when the knowledge of iron-working reached east Africa is not known; probably this art spread from the kingdom of **Meroe** on the Nile, but it may have been several hundreds of years after Meroe's decline in the fourth century A.D. before the secrets of iron working were known south of the Sahara. This was largely due to that impenetrable barrier of papyrus, the *sudd*, which blocked the Nile route and caused the isolation and stagnation of countries beyond the Sudan.

Stone-walled enclosures and hut circles in Nandi, western Kenya, show that the population during the Iron Age must have been about ten times as great as it is today in this region. In parts of northern Tanganyika there are traces of cultivation terraces and irrigation ditches, and in other areas wells and cairns, dating from a period before the arrival of the present inhabitants. Probably some of these structures may be attributed to **Hamitic** people from the Horn, who ruled much of western Uganda before the sixteenth century A.D. Traditionally known as the Bachwezi, they are said to have been light-skinned and very tall. They are believed to have been responsible for extensive earthworks, the largest of which is at Bigo, on the south bank of the Katonga river. The outer ring of trenches is nearly three miles long and the ditches are twelve feet deep. Probably Bigo was a huge cattle kraal, into which the animals could be driven when danger threatened.

The largest settlement of this period was at Ntusi, eight miles from Bigo. The middens are full of animal bones and potsherds, some of which are decorated with red paint. Links between the Iron Age people and recent inhabitants exist at Masaka Hill and Mubende Hill. Masaka Hill is alleged to have been the residence of Bachwezi chiefs, who surrendered a ceremonial drum to the Babito succeeding them. Mubende Hill is supposed to have been the home of a priestess of the spirit of small pox, to whom pilgrims came to present offerings. The site today is marked by a giant "witch tree", some 350 years old. Near it have been found iron objects, potsherds decorated with paint like those of Ntusi, and several large globular vessels. Large pots were sometimes used as burial urns, as at Nkongora in Toro, where an urn was found containing an adult and an infant skeleton.

One of the few early Iron Age settlements which has been excavated is at Hyrax Hill, near Nakuru. Various iron objects were found, as well as cowrie shells and Arab water-pipe bowls, showing that trade with the coast had started. The site must be later than the seventh century A.D., but how much later is not known.

The dates of Iron Age sites in east Africa are at present purely conjectural and must remain so until systematic excavations are carried out and objects are dated either by radio-carbon or by correlation with sites at the coast, where imported pottery, coins and beads often give an indication of their age.

Africa, Eastern Coast Ruins. Along the east coast of Africa, from Mogadishu to Mozambique, on the islands of Pemba, Zanzibar, Mafia, the Comoros and at the north end of Madagascar, are found ruins of mosques, tombs and houses. These are the remains of colonial Arab settlements which seem to have been most prosperous in the fifteenth century A.D.

The earliest written information on this coast are two inscriptions, one in the mosque of Kizimkazi dated H. 500 (A.D. 1107), the other on the tower of the Great Mosque at Mogadishu dated H. 636 (A.D. 1238). Excavations have been carried out in Kenya by J. S. Kirkman for the Trustees of the Royal National Parks at Gedi, Kilepwa, Ungwana, Mnarani and Takwa, in Pemba at Ras Mkumbuu and in Tanganyika at Kilwa: also in Tanganyika by N. Chittick at Kisimani Mafia, and in Madagascar by M. Poirier at Nossi Manja. None of these excavations has shown any evidence of occupation earlier than the thirteenth or, less likely, the twelfth century A.D. The archaeological evidence therefore does not yet support the literary or traditional records, which would take back the history of these settlements to periods ranging from the seventh to the ninth centuries. However, relatively little work has been done on this two thousand odd miles of coast, and undue emphasis cannot be laid on the *ex absentia* argument.

The map (p. 471) shows the position of the principal monuments of this colonial Arab culture, which was marked from its inception by non-Arab features resulting from the mixed racial components – Arab, Persian, Bantu, Galla, Indian – of the people by whom it was developed.

The walls of these buildings were made of random rubble set in red earth or coral lime mortar, with a plastered face. Doorways generally had pointed arches of cut coral, without keystones or voussoirs but often with two stones set vertically above the apex on the outside face. These are perhaps derived from India. Roofs were flat or, rarely, a series of small square cupolas or barrel vaults. Floors were of lime concrete with drainage pits closed by a circular stone with a small aperture. In the walls were niches for lamps or bowls, sometimes in the shallow pilasters of the door-frames or in rows along the walls.

The most important buildings were the mosques – plain rectangular structures, usually covered by a flat lime concrete roof carried on square or rectangular piers. The standard plan included one or two anterooms and a veranda with a cistern fed from a well by a conduit, usually at the east, sometimes at the south end. The *mihrab* or *qibla*, showing the direction of Mecca, consisted of a recess with a pointed or trefoliate arch, frequently embellished with porcelain bowls and surrounded by a herringbone border of cut coral. The *mimbar* or pulpit was a short flight of three steps, standing about four feet high.

More interesting than the mosques are the remarkable pillar tombs – solid pillars, polygonal, circular or square, varying in height between fifteen and thirty feet and in girth between two and five feet. They are believed to be related to the phallic pillars erected by the Galla which are found in **Ethiopia** and Somalia, and are evidence of the essentially mixed colonial culture of the coast. They are stated to be the prerogative of *sharif* or holy men, and are today regarded askance by most orthodox Muslims as a Shia deviation. None of the tombs which have been investigated is earlier than the fourteenth century.

The other monuments were domestic buildings and town walls. The standard house of the sites which have been investigated was of bungalow type with a sunken court in front and a triple series of rooms. These consisted of a long room with a lavatory at the end and either a second long room with two small rooms and a store at the back, or two suites of two rooms each with a store in one room. At the side were often two additional rooms, one a kitchen, the other perhaps a room where the ladies of the house could meet their friends. The largest residential building excavated has been the Palace at Gedi, which has a plan like the letter H and is surrounded by open courts. A larger building, probably of the same type, is on the island of Songo Mnara near Kilwa.

The town walls were of no great strength or height, being nine feet high and eighteen inches thick, and the gates mere enclosures in the walls where strangers could be examined before dispersing among the buildings. The areas of these towns varied between five (Takwa) and forty-five acres (Gedi and Ungwana).

The culture was Muslim but cosmopolitan and included iron and probably beads from India, glass and glazed earthenware from the Near East, and porcelain from China. Local products comprised a fairly wide range of local earthenware – jars, cooking pots, eating bowls, lamps and toilet vessels, and shell beads. The economic basis was the export of ivory, rhinoceros horn, gold, leopard skins, and tortoise-shell to the Far East. Copper coins provided the medium of small exchange at Kilwa, Mafia, Zanzibar and probably Mogadishu: in other places cowries were used.

Apart from the medieval ruins, there are similar colonial Arab monuments dating from the sixteenth to the nineteenth centuries, and two fine ones at sixteenth century Portuguese castles – Fort Jesus, Mombasa and San Sebastiao, Mozambique. *See* plates 1–4, pages 51–54.

Africa, North. From the point of view of human geography north Africa might be likened to an immense peninsula. The fertile uplands of the Atlas Massif, extending from Tunis to Morocco, are defined almost as effectively by the Sahara to the south as they are by the sea to the north and west; to the east they are linked along 600 miles of coast by a narrow isthmus-like strip of slightly attenuated desert to the much smaller fertile area of the Cyrenaican Gebel. This in turn is joined by a similar "isthmus" to the Nile Delta, and farther to the east again to the fertile hills of Judaea. During long periods of desiccation in the **Pleistocene** the Nile Valley would have provided almost the only link for men and most other mammals between northern and central Africa. At other times a rainfall much greater than at present maintained waterholes, and even semi-permanent streams, across wide areas of the western Sahara. To the east, however, the present Great Sand Sea of Libya seems to have remained more or less desert virtually throughout the Pleistocene.

The first prehistoric antiquities to be observed in northern Africa were probably a remarkable series of large rock engravings, noted just over a century ago by the explorer Heinrich Barth at Tel Isaghan in the Fezzan, 500 miles south of Tripoli. Following the tradition of his day Barth attributed them to Greek or Egyptian sources; they are now known to be the easternmost of a chain of similar sites of undoubted native origin that extend westward to the Atlantic seaboard along the desert foot-hills of the Atlas and the Tripolitanian plateau.

Scattered outliers of related type can be found as far south as the Hoggar Mountains in the central Sahara; the same influence can be detected here and there along the Hoggar-Tibesti Ridge in vaguely comparable finds, and some authorities would even see a connection with decorated sites in Nubia and the Upper Egyptian desert.

Aesthetically and archaeologically the most significant are the Tel Isaghan group, comprising some thirty or more sites in southern Tripolitania, a few characteristic examples in central Tunisia, a large and important cluster of finds in southern Algeria centring on the southern slope of the Ksour Range, and finally a slightly less well defined group far to the west in southern Morocco and the Rio de Oro. Most typically the sites consist of large, even life-sized, engravings on rock surfaces near modern or extinct waterholes and intermittent water-courses. The subjects are mainly animals such as the giraffe, elephant, hippopotamus, rhinoceros, and even crocodile, all betokening a much more abundant rainfall than the present. Other compositions show desert and steppe species such as the antelope and gazelle, and finally herds of cattle some of which seem to be domesticated. The latter are often of rougher execution and some are certainly later in date.

In the southern Atlas there is a curious recurrent design of a sheep (apparently the same as the modern *ovis longipes*) wearing a disc-like device on its head with lateral appendages – the whole reminiscent of the well-known Middle Kingdom Egyptian Amun-Ra symbol of a ram wearing the sun disk flanked by two rearing cobras. Since the Algerian engravings are often in as good a naturalistic style as some of the earlier group it seems reasonable to attribute at least the closing stages of the tradition in question to the second millennium B.C. A further argument to the same effect is provided by a group of reasonably well executed human figures from the Fezzan – apparently in the same technique as the animal engravings – which can be interpreted with confidence as derived from the ithyphallic dwarf god *Bes* also typical of the Egyptian Middle Kingdom.

On the other hand the pluvial period to which many of the engravings should correspond, to judge by their subjects, especially those in now totally waterless desert regions, is believed to have been at its peak in the sixth millennium B.C. Although a higher rainfall than the present is still indicated in the fifth millennium in both Lower and Upper Egypt (evidence is cited in association with the Badarian culture and with the Neolithic "A" stage of the **Faiyum**, the latter certainly of late fifth millennium date), and would presumably have been felt throughout the northern Sahara, it would seem to have been long past its maximum as late as the second millennium. Moreover the bulk of the best naturalistic scenes are clearly the work of hunters rather than pastoralists, to judge by the acute anatomical observation which is characteristic of such peoples. The human figures, which accompany them in some instances, are of archers taking part in a hunt, often wearing animal masks. Some of the human figures, belonging perhaps to the latest phases of the style, show interesting features of dress. The hair is worn in a curious side ringlet or looped pigtail, a penis sheath protects the male organ and an animal tail is seen depending from the back of a kilt-like garment. Tattooed designs appear on wrist and forearm. All these are features of the ancient Libyan tribes as recorded on Egyptian monuments and decorations from the fourth millennium B.C. and some still survived as late as classical times. Compare this dress with that of **Minoan** Crete.

Overlaying the early series there are often found rock-cut designs and paintings of widely different styles and dates generally much cruder in manner. Among these are some representing charioteers (certainly no earlier than late second millennium date), camels (fourth century B.C. to recent), and horsemen (first millennium B.C. to recent).

The early series thus reveals the presence of hunting and pastoral peoples all along the northern borders of the desert from Morocco to Egypt, sharing a number of highly characteristic culture traits at least from the fourth millennium B.C. This impression of widespread cultural uniformity in northern Africa from relatively early times is reinforced by a study of the languages of the area. Thus the indigenous speech from the borders of Egypt to the Atlantic coast up to the Arab invasion in the eighth century was everywhere of **Hamitic** or Berber derivation. To this day non-Semitic Berber dialects survive as far east as Siwa and even Gara in the western Egyptian desert, and are spoken by a high proportion of the population throughout the Atlas Massif.

Again, the physical type of the Berber speakers can be readily distinguished from the much lighter built and more aquiline features of the descendants of the Arab invaders. Although both language and physical type naturally overlap, the difference is readily perceived as one passes westwards from Cyrenaica to regions bordering on the Maghreb such as northern Tripolitania. As to the antiquity of the Berber languages, this is sufficiently proved by fragments, mainly personal and tribal names, nicknames of animals, etc., preserved on Egyptian monuments from the second millennium B.C. onwards.

The name "Libyan" which has been loosely applied by scholars to nearly all the ancient native peoples of northern Africa, should strictly be used only of those of the eastern half of the coast from Tunis to Egypt. There can be no real doubt that the word originates in the name *Rbw* applied by the Middle Kingdom Egyptians to the tribes inhabiting the Cyrenaican Gebel; no distinction is made in Egyptian script between *l* and *r*, while the *w* would certainly become the Greek *u* and hence give rise to the Greek *Libues* of which "Libya" is the Latin form.

The ancient Egyptian monuments further provide us with not a few details of the life and customs of the Libyans at that time. They appear to have been organized in a number of loosely related nomadic tribes ruled by hereditary chieftains, though they were capable on occasion of combining in force, as when they attacked Egypt during the reign of Merneptah in the thirteenth century B.C., at least 100,000 strong. From the same sources we learn something of their material culture. Owing to the poverty of north Africa in metal ores their weapons and implements were normally of wood and stone right down to classical times. The mainstay of their economy seems to have been cattle and sheep-herding, no doubt supplemented on occasion by hunting. No direct evidence of agriculture or trade on any scale is known before Greek times in Cyrenaica, or before the foundation of Carthage in the Maghreb.

Apart from the glimpses of life and history afforded by Greek and Egyptian sources, and the desert art sites mentioned above, our knowledge of cultural development and intercourse in northern

Africa from the earliest times derives almost entirely from a study of **stone tools.** This study, it should be noted, is today far removed from the rigidly typological analyses of an earlier generation of prehistorians. The recognition and isolation of tool forms and techniques of manufacture is followed by research into their associations, their geographical distribution, and such ecological evidence as can be deduced from food debris, climatic indications, and so on. Last but not least, greatly improved geological dating can now be supplemented by absolute dating in years with the **radiocarbon** technique.

By these methods we are gradually learning to recognise the characteristic traces of various hunting communities, their geographical range, their movements from one area to another, and even something of their mutual degree of intercourse or isolation from contemporary groups in neighbouring territories.

Although the earlier stages of human development and migration in northern Africa as elsewhere cannot be dated with any certainty in absolute time units since radio-carbon has as yet a range of not more than 50,000 years, we know, by correlation with the ice ages of the northern hemisphere, that the earliest traces go back to a period in the order of three-quarters of a million years.

At the very beginning of the Pleistocene indeed, at a period estimated at about one million years before the present (on the strength of radium, not radiocarbon analyses) the first modern types of mammals make their appearance in north Africa. They include the first somewhat primitive representatives of horse, cattle, rhinoceros, elephant, etc., together making up the so-called Villafranchian assemblage. At its first appearance the Villafranchian fauna seems to have had free access across the Sahara and, via land bridges across the Mediterranean, to have spread as far north as central Europe. Towards the end of the Villafranchian episode the extremely important site of **Ain Hanech** in northern Algeria yields some of the earliest certain traces of human occupation known anywhere in the world.

It is interesting to note that the extremely primitive tool forms of Ain Hanech – roughly trimmed pebbles – find their nearest analogies in the famous stratified sites of **Olduvai Gorge** in east Africa. There they can be seen to give rise by slow transition and improvement to the much more specialized and standardized tools known to prehistorians as "**hand-axes**"; these again in the great succession of layers at Olduvai cover a period in the order of not less than 50,000 years (during which intense climatic desiccation must have closed the Sahara to human migration), and gradually give rise to further and more specialized tool forms still, among which is the ingeniously produced "cleaver".

It would appear that, soon after this cultural event in central Africa, the climate once again improved and men and animals were able to pass freely across the Sahara from south to north and there is evidence of a second human migration from that source to the Atlas Massif. Spectacular finds of human fossils recently made at Ternifine in Algeria show that the human strain involved was of a peculiarly primitive kind, comparable to the very earliest human fossils from south-east Asia and central Europe. In all three areas they are associated with an assemblage of fossil animals transitional between the Villafranchian and the more evolved forms of the Middle and Upper Pleistocene. In Morocco further highly significant finds provide geological evidence to show that the migration in question took place during the temperate Gunz-Mindel period which separates the first and antepenultimate **glacials** of more northerly latitudes.

In eastern north Africa the sequence of events does not seem to have been exactly the same. The Nile would at all times have provided a viable corridor of intercourse with central Africa, and it is not therefore surprising that the first hand-axe users seem to have penetrated to the north at a more primitive stage of cultural developments. Subsequently, during a return of adverse climatic conditions which interrupted the flow of hand-axe makers to the Atlas, the Nile seems to have been used by later and more advanced men originating in central Africa as a way of passing northward to the Delta whence they fanned out westward to Cyrenaica, and eastward to Palestine.

The most important of such later events was probably the spread of an evolved **flake** industry of Middle **Palaeolithic** character, the **Levalloiso-Mousterian**, practised by a strikingly similar human strain of Neanderthaloid characteristics contemporaneously in the Cyrenaican Gebel and the hills of Judaea, during the early Upper Pleistocene. This period seems to correspond with the beginning of the last or Würm glaciation in Europe. At the same time the evidence from the Atlas suggests that the ancient human stock introduced with the first hand-axes had remained there largely undisturbed and isolated from the evolutionary trends of both the great population south of the Sahara and the areas at the outlet of the Nile corridor.

The role of northern Africa during a still later period of migration, that of the spread of Homo sapiens of modern type at the expense of the extinct Neanderthaloid or Palaeanthropic strains, has been much discussed in the past. The origin of this new human type, the bearer of the Upper Palaeolithic culture, and author of the famous cave paintings and other works of art in western Europe, has frequently been sought in western or west-central Asia. According to this view their spread westward into Europe and along the south Mediterranean shore would have begun about the middle of the Würm phase of Europe. Radio-carbon dates, though few in number, as far as they go certainly support the idea and suggest that the movement started about or shortly before 30,000 B.C. At one time it was supposed that north Africa might have provided one of the corridors of access to south-west Europe. This idea is now abandoned since the earliest remains of Upper Palaeolithic character in the Atlas, known as the **Capsian** culture, have been shown to correspond most nearly in type to a post-glacial stage of cultural evolution in Europe, and on radio-carbon evidence can hardly be earlier than 10,000 B.C. The final phase only of the Capsian has been directly dated, namely to 7000 B.C., but for various reasons the duration of the tradition is most unlikely to have exceeded 2,000–3,000 years.

East of the Sirtican Desert, in the Cyrenaican Gebel, however, a large stratified site, the Haua Fteah, has recently yielded an industry strikingly like the earliest Upper Palaeolithic of western Asia, and carbon-dated to approximately 29,000 B.C. It would appear that this Cyrenaican industry represented an isolated outpost of the original spread, which would have been held up by the natural barrier of the Sirtican Desert during the arid conditions known to have prevailed at the time. Judging by the associated physical type the Capsian culture might well have been brought to Tunisia by a long delayed migration from Cyrenaica. On the other hand a sharply contrasted coastal culture, the **Oranian,** which apparently overlaps the Capsian in time, may well have come in the reverse direction and ultimately originated in south-west Europe. In its extreme extension it appears to have occupied the entire north African coastline, and in Egypt at least to have penetrated some distance inland.

In the Atlas Massif both Oranian and Capsian seem gradually to have given place to an industry containing pottery, ground stone, pressure-flaked arrow-heads and, in a few cases, unmistakable evidence of domestic sheep and cattle. It is this type of industry in the western half of northern Africa that is the hallmark of the so-called **Neolithic** or Capsian tradition, and is regularly associated with the art sites described above. It would seem that the western peoples who came under Middle Kingdom influence in the second millennium and were later in contact with Carthaginians, Romans, and finally the invading Arabs of the eighth century A.D. (the ancestors in fact of the modern Berber-speaking peoples) were themselves the distant survivors of a very ancient stock of "Mediterranean" and non-African origin, who reached the area at least as early as the tenth millennium B.C. But, whether they arrived then or even earlier, there can be little doubt that their ultimate homeland lay to the north and east of Africa.

In Cyrenaica the process of penetration can probably be followed in greater detail. In the Haua Fteah a distinctly west Asiatic type of flint industry suddenly displaced the Oranian at about 6000 B.C. or soon after; by 4800 it had grafted on to its material culture traits such as burnished self-coloured pottery, ground stone adzes, and possibly material culture such traits as burnished self-coloured pottery, ground stone adzes, and possibly domestic sheep or goats, all most easily derived from the Levantine coast viá Lower Egypt. In the latter area at least the Asiatic origin of both the earliest domesticated grains and animals is no longer in serious doubt. From the sixth millennium B.C. onwards then, apart from Egypt itself, the days of north Africa as an originator of major cultural advances were over. The inhabitants become little more than middlemen in the transmission of borrowed culture traits, southward to central Africa, and northward to south-western Europe.

Africa, Prehistoric Art in. The beginning of artistic expression goes back in Africa probably to the later part of the Early **Stone Age** but it is not until Late Stone Age times – at the end of and immediately following the termination of the Pleistocene period – that an artistic tradition represented in paintings and engravings on the walls of caves and rock shelters is found. The main regions where this art is met with are north-west Africa and the Sahara, the Horn of Africa, northern Tanganyika, Rhodesia, south and south-west Africa. There is no direct evidence that any of these art groups are related to each other, but it is probable that culture contact at various times may have been largely responsible for spreading the techniques of rock drawing from north to south.

In French North Africa the art is usually in the form of engravings and is associated with the **Capsian** culture the later stages of which have been dated by **carbon fourteen** methods to between 6500 and 6000 B.C. Here and in the Sahara there are depicted animals either now extinct, such as the giant buffalo and wild ox, or whose habitat is far removed from that where the engravings are found, for example, the hippo and elephant. In the central and eastern parts of the Sahara are found naturalistic paintings of pastoral and domestic scenes with many cattle, done by a nomadic, stock-owning, **Neolithic** people prior to the last desiccation of the Sahara.

There is little direct evidence for dating the south and east African rock art but it is likely, in view of the way the rock weathers, that all of this art should be measured in centuries and not in millennia. Some of the finest naturalistic paintings of wild animals and hunting scenes are found in southern Rhodesia and the Union of South Africa. A number of different and developing artistic styles can be distinguished with regional specialization which reach their ultimate expression in the beautiful polychrome paintings of the Drakensberg in South Africa and the Brandberg in South West Africa. On the central plateau in the Transvaal and Orange Free State, ridges and kopjes of dolerite were favoured places for engraving drawings of the animals the hunters could watch grazing in the valley below their look-out. These engravings were either directly incised into the rock with a freedom of line that has hardly been surpassed or else they were pecked or punched on to the rock by means of a stone punch.

The paintings were all done with natural mineral colours – reds, yellows, browns, purples or black from **haematite** or limonite, or white from kaolin. The paint was probably mixed with fat – **Bushmen** used the marrow fat of the eland – and was applied in a variety of ways. Brushes were made by using a feather or fine hairs bound to a stick. Sometimes a bone or wooden stylus was used for fine lines. The fine shading of some of the polychrome work suggests that the mouth may have been used as a spray-gun, while some of the cruder work was certainly done with the finger.

In South Africa there is good evidence to associate the Bushmen with the later cave paintings and it is likely that none of those that survive today dates to before the beginning of the Christian era, though the artistic tradition stretches back much further.

These engravings and paintings may in part have been a form of sympathetic magic to aid the band or an individual in the hunt or to protect them from harm or misfortune. Many on the other hand were undoubtedly painted for pleasure and as records of events – fights and hunting scenes, magico-religious ceremonies, and ordinary domestic pursuits for example. Many of these prehistoric artists were possessed of very high artistic merit and besides preserving for us a unique record of the lives of these people and other racial groups with which they came into contact, their work is often quite outstanding and must be ranked among the great artistic traditions of the world. (*See also* **Prehistoric Art.**) *See* colour plate 1, plate 5, page 55.

Africa, Stone Age Man in. Since earliest times the pattern of human culture has been dictated by the topography and the changing climate, rainfall and vegetation. The open central plateau region of southern Africa has yielded the earliest evidence of man anywhere in the world. From the fillings of old caves in limestone country have come many remains of Australopithecines (the "southern apes" – *see* **Australopithecus**), early **hominids** most probably in the direct line of human descent. They are of Lower Pleistocene Age and have been found at Taungs in the northern Cape and at Sterkfontein and Makapan in the Transvaal in association with a fossil fauna of Omo-Kanam age. In appearance Australopithecus had certain ape-like features, notably the large protruding jaw and face, but in brain size he falls between ape and man and his body was essentially human in form. He undoubtedly used tools though prehistorians are divided as to whether he also possessed the ability to make them, or whether the primitive stone chopping-tools made on pebbles and found associated with him at Sterkfontein in 1957, were made by some more advanced hominid. Pebble tools are also found in several early high-level fluviatile deposits belonging to the dry period separating the Lower and Middle Pleistocene and it seems likely that the creature who made them will be found to have been of Australopithecine stock, perhaps of the more advanced, but allied form, Telanthropus.

Two long periods when the climate was wetter than today (Kamasian and Kanjeran **pluvials**) followed during the Middle Pleistocene. The human culture of those times is known as the Abbeville-Acheulian and together with the pre-Abbeville-Acheulian pebble cultures make up the Earlier **Stone Age** lasting for some 400,000 years. Numerous Abbeville-Acheulian sites are known from river gravels in south and central Africa and the characteristic **stone tools** are pear-shaped and pointed **hand-axes** and axe-shaped cleavers with numbers of unspecialized flake tools. Tools were often made from large flakes struck from hard-grained rocks. The most complete succession is found in the valley of the Vaal where there occurs an evolutionary progression of culture from crude to highly developed forms showing the beginnings of the Middle Stone Age prepared **core** technique.

The physical type responsible for this culture in southern Africa is as yet unknown. Finds from east and north Africa, however, suggest that it approximated to the Pithecanthropoid form though with a more Homo sapiens brain case. Many extinct animals are associated. Man still preferred to live in open country and probably relied for his meat upon scavenging or community hunting. Forest/savannah was largely unoccupied until the desiccation marking the decline of the Kanjeran pluvial. No knowledge of fire making seems to have penetrated to southern Africa until the very end of the Early Stone Age. Charcoals and a hearth, with wooden digging-sticks and other worked wood, have been found in waterlogged deposits at the Kalambo Falls at the south end of Lake Tanganyika, while other hearths occur in the Cave of Hearths at Makapan.

Transitional cultures succeeded the Acheulian and are grouped in what is called the First Intermediate period. The Fauresmith, adapted to open grassland and high country, is found mainly in the south-west. The **Sangoan** belongs to the woodland and forest regions of the north and east and includes many wood-working tools. The human type has been termed proto-Australoid, or Rhodesiois, and is related to the **Neanderthal** race of Europe. The Saldanha fossil man from north of Cape Town is associated with a late Fauresmith industry and a fossil of mixed extinct and modern species. Sangoan man was probably of the same stock which seems to have continued into early Middle Stone Age times in central Africa, where it is represented by Rhodesia Man from Broken Hill, a massive-browed, robust individual with sloping forehead, low vaulted cranium and protruding face. Florisbad man from the Orange Free State is another near contemporary human fossil of less "rugged" appearance.

The Middle Stone Age, belonging to the Upper Pleistocene, is contained in deposits of the Gamblian pluvial. It probably began about 75,000 years ago and lasted until 12,000 to 10,000 years ago. Tools are now often hafted and the cultures are based on the prepared core and faceted **flake.** Regional specialization now occurs – equatorial forest (Lupemban), savannah (Rhodesian Stillbay, Pietersburg) and grass and scrubland (Mazelspoort, Stillbay, Mossel Bay etc.) cultures having evolved. Fossil human remains are all of modern type with degrees of hybridization between a large-brained Boskopoid, a small-brained Bushmanoid and a long-headed, long-faced Caucasoid form.

About 12,000 to 10,000 years ago "neanthropic" elements became evident in the sub-continent and the Magosian cultures of those times are grouped in the Second Intermediate period. They are transitional between the Middle and Later Stone Ages and their **microlithic** "blade and **burin**" elements may be derived from the Kenya Capsian of east Africa.

By about 6000 B.C. the microlithic revolution was complete and the Later Stone Age began. Two main culture complexes are now found – the fully microlithic Wilton, and the Smithfield which, perhaps on account of the raw material used, has largely preserved its **macrolithic** proportions. The Wilton appears to have been established at an early date north of the Limpopo and later to have spread down both sides of the continent to mingle with the Smithfield along the south coast. Special forest (Tshitolian) and woodland (**Nachikufan**) cultures are found in the north. The Smithfield, characterized by scrapers of various kinds, is found mainly in the central plateau south of the Limpopo and is associated with fine naturalistic rock engravings. The Wilton is associated more with the rock paintings which are among the art treasures of the world today. South of the Zambesi the makers of these cultures were chiefly of **Bushman** and "Hottentot" (Bush-**Boskopoid**) physical stock, hybridized with other racial elements.

In some parts the Stone Age continued until very recent times and can be connected with the Bushmen and, less certainly, with the Hottentots.

Africa, Stone Age Man in South. In the middle of the nineteenth century, while **Boucher de Perthes** was demanding scientific recognition of his discoveries of stone artifacts in the gravels of the Somme, Thomas Holden Bowker, a farmer in the Albany district of the Cape of Good Hope, was already making similar discoveries in his own area. Early attempts at cultural and chronological classification of the finds failed in the absence of an appreciation of stratigraphic evidence and because of a tendency to follow too closely the classifications and terminology proposed for finds in Europe.

It was not until 1923 that the basis for a more scientific understanding of the Stone Age began to emerge through the efforts of Professor A. J. H. Goodwin. His ideas received general acceptance at a conference held in Pretoria in 1926 where a classification and terminology specifically adapted to South Africa was adopted. Two major divisions of the **Palaeolithic** were recognized; an Earlier Stone Age comprising the **hand-axe** complex, and a Later Stone Age which included all subsequent cultures.

It was soon realized that the so-called Later Stone Age was too comprehensive and in 1928 Goodwin advocated that a Middle Stone Age group of cultures be recognized, chronologically and typologically intermediate between the Earlier and Later Stone Ages, and comprising the important industries which were based upon the prepared striking platform or "**Levalloisian**" technique. Adequate stratigraphic data were adduced in support of these major divisions. At the same time a system of cultural terms based on South African site-names was introduced, thus giving full recognition to the differences between South African and western European conditions and the impossibility of reliable correlations between the two areas. The only departure from this has been the abandoning of the term "Stellenbosch" for "South African Chelles-Acheul".

At the Third Pan-African Congress on Prehistory at Livingstone in 1955 it was resolved to introduce two additional major chronological and cultural periods, the First Intermediate Period embracing industries of Fauresmith and Sangoan type between the Earlier and Middle Stone Ages, and the Second Intermediate Period embracing industries of Magosian type between the Middle and Later Stone Ages.

In the Earlier Stone Age human origin has been claimed for flakes and broken pebbles from the upper calcified crust of the Basal Older Gravels of the Vaal River and from deposits contemporary with Australopithecine remains at the Limeworks Caves in the Makapan's Valley in the central Transvaal and these "artifacts" have been regarded as comparable with the Upper Kafuan of Uganda. Subsequently the validity of the Kafuan culture both in Uganda and South Africa has been seriously challenged and it is generally agreed that much stronger evidence for their validity is required.

The South African Chelles-Acheul culture-complex was originally termed the "Stellenbosch culture" after a site near that town. In the type area, i.e. the southern mountain region of the Cape Province, deposits including Chelles-Acheul remains are thin and no stratigraphy within them has so far been noted. On purely typological grounds rather ill-defined Early, Middle and Later phases are recognized. There is, however, little doubt that the material formerly regarded as comprising the "Stellenbosch culture" of the south-western Cape Province embraces long developments through several stages and includes in its latest phase material which further research will enable us to assign to the First Intermediate period.

The most characteristic **stone tools** of this culture are hand-axes and cleavers of a variety of forms showing progressive improvements in techniques, large flake tools, and polyhedral choppers and hammer-stones. Characteristic of the southern region are tools made from waterworn boulders of quartzite on which considerable areas of the natural outer surface are retained.

Extensive studies of gravels of the Vaal River from Vereeniging to Douglas have led to important results for the interior Highveld of the Union. A group of Basal Older Gravels occur at heights from three hundred to fifty feet above the river. Where they are undisturbed they contain only artifacts of "Kafuan" and "Olduwan" form whose validity is open to question.

A second group of gravels, the Younger Gravels, rest on terraces at forty feet and twenty feet and on the present river-bed. In and on these Younger Gravels five well-differentiated stages of the Chelles-Acheul culture have been recognized, and these are supported by typological and technological evidence. On the eroded surface of the calcified layers of wind-borne sands which lie above the gravel artifacts of the Fauresmith culture are found, and these occur also in the time-equivalent Youngest Gravels which are found at the base of soil profiles in tributary streams of the Vaal River. The Younger Gravels are separated by silts and clays from later grit-bands containing Middle Stone Age remains, which in turn are separated by further silts and humus from Later Stone Age artifacts which occur on and near the present surface.

Chelles-Acheul Stage I typically comprises fairly crude hand-axes on **cores**, showing bold and steep flake-scars produced by a stone-on-stone technique, while evidence of a block-on-block technique is by no means uncommon. Cleavers are rare but present, and equally crude. Choppers and polyhedral hammer-stones on cores are common and a few flake scrapers are found.

Stage II is represented by a similar range of artifacts, generally somewhat larger and showing some technical advance. In Stage III an entirely new primary technique appears by which heavy elongate cores were prepared for the production of heavy side-struck **flakes** which were then secondarily trimmed by a wood-on-stone technique to make very refined hand-axes and cleavers of a variety of forms. Stage IV is characterized by a development of the primary technique by which heavy round, high-backed cores were made to yield end-struck flakes of trapezoidal cross-section. Stage V of the South African Chelles-Acheul lacks these techniques and shows some reversion to the use of cores to make extremely refined hand-axes of many forms. Cleavers now become less abundant, but small scrapers on flakes and rock fragments appear.

Two cultures flourished during the First Intermediate Period; the Fauresmith and Sangoan.

The Fauresmith is fully developed over most of the Union of South Africa and indeed over those parts of southern Africa which lie within the savannah and grassland belts.

By contrast, the Sangoan occurs as the counterpart of the Fauresmith in forest and riverine contexts. While the Fauresmith is probably a local cultural expression, the Sangoan is intrusive from the Belgian Congo and northern Rhodesia.

The Fauresmith culture is represented most abundantly in the western Orange Free State, the northern Cape Province and the Transvaal and shows considerable regional variation. In the extreme south it has only recently been identified, notably at the important fossil-bearing site near Hopefield which has yielded an interesting human skull which differs only in slight detail from the Broken Hill specimen of Rhodesian Man. Typical of the Fauresmith culture are hand-axes, many of which are reduced in size to four inches and less in length. Large flake scrapers of irregular form are common. An important feature of this culture is the presence of cores and flakes with faceted striking platforms. The Fauresmith is seen as a transitional culture between the Earlier and Middle Stone Ages in South Africa.

The **Sangoan** culture occurs mainly in the coastal area of Natal, apparently having penetrated southward down the eastern seaboard via southern Rhodesia and Portuguese East Africa, though some evidence of Sangoan influence has been seen in the central Transvaal. In addition, the northern part of South West Africa seems to have received Sangoan influences from Angola. The recognition of the Sangoan in South Africa is a recent development and much remains to be learned of its nature and distribution in this area.

During the Middle Stone Age period a number of cultures and local variants flourished in fairly restricted areas. By these times the hand-axes and cleavers which characterized the Earlier Stone Age had disappeared completely, to be replaced by smaller and lighter flake and blade tools made almost exclusively by prepared striking platform techniques.

Stone tools of the South African Middle Stone Age include a wide range of scrapers, lance-heads, points, backed blades, scrapers, **burins**, etc. such as in Europe typify Middle and Upper Palaeolithic industries. Secondary trimming by pressure-flaking now makes its appearance. In the southern and eastern littoral the Stillbay culture predominates. The Mossel Bay culture is an equivalent variant showing less elaborate secondary trimming possibly as a result of the choice of fine-grained quartzitic sandstone. In the central Orange Free State the Vlakkraal industry provides a comparable developmental stage and is preceded by a cruder expression. In the central Transvaal the Pietersburg culture shows various stages of development culminating in well-made unifaced triangular points, while a variant in the eastern Transvaal is characterized by elaborate bifaced pressure-trimmed points comparable with those of the Stillbay in the south. The Glen Grey culture of the eastern Cape Province extends to east Griqualand on the borders of Basutoland and Natal where it exhibits a two-stage development. The Alexandersfontein variant is found in the northern Cape and western Orange Free State but has not been fully described, while a number of other Middle Stone Age industries in other parts of South Africa await fuller study.

Stratigraphic evidence for the chronological relationships between the various regional expressions of Middle Stone Age cultures is lacking.

The Second Intermediate period embraces those cultures of **Magosian** type which represent a transition from the prepared striking platform technique of the Middle Stone Age to the microlithic cultures of the Later Stone Age. The South African Magosian was first described under the name "Modderpoort culture" which was soon abandoned in favour of the term South African Magosian. This culture is found in abundance in the hill country of the eastern Orange Free State and Basutoland and has also been reported in Natal, the northern Cape, the northern Transvaal and the northern part of South West Africa. A coastal variant in the southern mountain region is known as the "Howieson's Poort variation". In these industries artifacts based on a prepared striking platform technique are much refined and reduced in size, while microlithic blades and, occasionally, crescents, backed blades and small end-scrapers appear. While these industries clearly provide technological and typological links between the Middle Stone Age and the Wilton culture of the Later Stone Age, there is evidence of a noticeable time-space between the Magosian and the Later Stone Age microlithic cultures.

The cultures of the later Stone Age, the last major subdivision of the Stone Age in South Africa, are the Smithfield complex, the Wilton, and the industries found in shell middens of the "Strandlopers" along the coasts. The later phases are certainly the work of **Bushmen** of historic times who occupied considerable areas of the country when the first European settlers arrived and whose remnants still inhabit the Kalahari area. By Later Stone Age times the prepared striking platform technique had been abandoned, giving place to simple blade techniques.

The Smithfield industries are centred on the basins of the Vaal and Upper Orange rivers. The Smithfield A and B phases are almost entirely restricted to this area and to indurated shale as a raw material, but a variant known as Smithfield N is common in Natal and the western borders of that province. The Smithfield C and Wilton cultures are microlithic. At Umgazana on the Pondoland coast a late Smithfield variant appears to be the result of a group of Smithfield A people who penetrated to the coast where they exchanged hunting for a beach-combing subsistence in which fish and shellfish constituted major elements of the food supply.

Abundant along the coasts of South Africa are extensive shell mounds probably of varying date, but all falling within the Later Stone Age. They are associated with the "Strandlopers", that is, groups of people who in the interior of the country enjoyed the Smithfield C or Wilton cultures but on the coast subsisted almost entirely on shellfish and such fish as they could trap in enclosures of stones crudely thrown together in intertidal waters, the remains of which are still commonly seen. These middens contain very few well-made artifacts but large numbers of waterworn beach pebbles fractured in use.

Common to all later Stone Age industries are bored stones (perforated spheres) and the reamers used for perforating them, grindstones, mullers and pounders, and beads of ostrich eggshell.

It is clear that the Stone Age inhabitants of South Africa did not develop beyond a hunting and food-gathering stage of subsistence. There is sporadic evidence of the introduction of grinding techniques for tool-making during the Later Stone Age and a few polished axes of Neolithic type have been found, but nothing whatever to suggest even the most rudimentary attempts at food production by domestication of plants or animals.

The gravels, sands, silts and clays of the Vaal River basin have been interpreted as evidence for alternating wet and dry climatic phases during the **Quaternary period** in South Africa, and evidence from the Little Caledon River deposits has been adduced in support of this. In the Vaal and Little Caledon valleys direct correlations of cultural and climatic phases have been claimed. There can be little doubt that South Africa did undergo significant climatic fluctuations during the Stone Age, but recent authorities have challenged the validity of the detailed climatic sequence and cultural correlations. The evidence for what at one time seemed a satisfactory climatic succession not only in South Africa but in southern Africa as a whole has been shown to be entirely open to question.

No country rivals South Africa for its richness in rock art, either in quantity or variety. This art is expressed in two forms, paintings in overhanging rock shelters in the mountain areas, and petroglyphs (rock-carvings) on exposed rock surfaces of the Karoo and Highveld.

Both forms of art expression were practised over many centuries, but there is no acceptable evidence of any art before the Later Stone Age. There is ample reason to attribute much of the art to the Bushmen who practised the Wilton and Smithfield industries, while claims for the presence of other artist peoples are entirely speculative, though a considerable proportion of the paintings in the southern region has been credited to the Hottentots. Superpositions of art styles, treatments and techniques occur frequently in painted sites, but sequences observed in one site are often contradicted in another, and attempts to arrive at generally valid series or sequences over extensive areas are open to question. Certainly, a number of different regions must be recognized within which artistic expressions are similar and contrast with those of other regions. Thus rock paintings of the Transvaal are for the most part simple monochromes with occasional bichromes, the shelters of the southern mountain region contain hand imprints, rows of finger-dots and rather crude representations rare or absent elsewhere, and the rocks of the Drakensberg range contain complicated compositions and elaborate shaded polychrome figures in which the art of rock painting reaches its maximum artistic development.

The petroglyphs of the Highveld are executed by two major techniques: incised lines or "true engravings", and "rock peckings" in which figures are delineated by removing the patina by repeated and closely-spaced blows with a sharp stone. As must be expected, these techniques imposed far stricter limitations on the artists than did the use of paint, but nevertheless were exploited in a number of ways. So we get simple outlines, simple silhouettes, partly filled-in figures and, in the best engravings, excellent representation of such anatomical details as the eye or ear or folds of the skin and even occasionally some attempt at representing the moulding of an animal's body. Composition is almost entirely absent and even the portrayal of relationships between more than one figure is rare. Although line engraving reached great heights in a restricted area near Johannesburg and was perhaps surpassed in quality only by some magnificent pecked engravings in the western Transvaal, the art of the petroglyphs elsewhere is on the whole simple and not of a high artistic order. Superpositions in petroglyphs are far less common than in paintings and have been studied in detail only at Vosburg where a long sequence of styles bears witness to the fact that this art, like rock painting, was practised over a considerable period.

Africa, West. The territory described here includes French West Africa and the adjacent countries of Gambia, Portuguese Guinea, Sierra Leone, Liberia, Ghana and Nigeria.

Throughout prehistory and history, there have been two major divisions in west Africa: the Sahara with a fringe of savannah to the south of it on the one hand, and the forest and wooded savannah country on the other. These divisions are due to climate; the almost waterless country in the north is the land of nomads (Moors, Tuaregs, Tedas, and Fulani on the southern border), while the southern regions have sufficient rainfall to allow agriculturalists to grow their crops. These are, in fact, two entirely different worlds.

In the savannah country, large empires could thrive and support a dense population of war-like tribes, constantly having to defend themselves against predatory Berbers from the Sahara. North of the tsetse fly area, horses could be kept, giving the tribes the redoubtable advantage of cavalry over their Saharan and forest neighbours.

This, of course, applies to historic times. What about the prehistoric and protohistoric period?

Palaeolithic surface sites have been found in many places in the Sahara, sometimes hundreds of miles away from the nearest wells, proving that the desert was not so arid at that time. At some of these sites, such as El Beyyed and Toufourine, **hand-axes** have been found by the hundreds. In the south, on the other hand, where vegetation covers everything, **stone tools** of the Early Stone Age are very rare. They are brought to light only when exposed by large-scale mining, quarrying or other works (Bauchi plateau tin mines and the diamond mines of French Guinea) are examples.

It has not yet been possible to establish a satisfactory climatic and chronological sequence in the west, as has been done in east Africa. But the Sahara seems to be linked with the north African Palaeolithic province and the south with the **Sangoan** equatorial forest complex.

We have better information for **Neolithic** times. Once more, probably after a period of severe desiccation, the Sahara ceased to be a desert. Mighty rivers flowed across it and large swamps, like Lake Chad or Bahr el Ghazal today, allowed people to thrive in many different places. Innumerable sites have yielded rich and varied material: arrow- and spear-heads, scrapers, harpoons, arm-rings, beads and so on. Also dating from this period are numerous rock-engravings and paintings, particularly in the Saharan Mountains, at **Tassili** des Ajjers, Hoogar, Adrar des Ilforas, Air and Tibesti. These pictures show large herds of cattle and flocks of sheep and goats grazing in a green Sahara, while there are also hunting scenes. Elephants, rhinoceroses, hippopotamuses and giraffes, depicted at these sites, are found today only far to the south.

Very few human skeletal remains have been found and all come from the extreme south of the Sahara. The best-known type is that of the Negroid Asselar man.

Towards the very end of Neolithic times in the Sahara, during the last millennium B.C., horse-drawn carts, such as those described by **Herodotus** in the country of the Garamantes, crossed the desert. There were two main routes: in the west, between southern Morocco and the bend of the Niger round Timbuktu via Zemour and Adrar in Mauritania; and in the east, between Fezzan and the bend of the Niger round Gao, by Tassili des Ajjers, Hoggar and Adrar des Iforas. Both routes are marked by rock-paintings and engravings showing carts; they are to be found only along these ways and nowhere else among the hundreds of sites known in the desert.

Did voyagers come to west Africa by sea in ancient times? This has been a theme of bitter controversy among historians. Some affirm that Nechao's Phoenicians about 600 B.C., Sataspes the Persian about 470 B.C., Hanno the Carthaginian and Euthymenes of Marseilles in the fifth century B.C., and Polybius the Greek about 146 B.C., all explored the west African coasts; others, however, deny these voyages, totally or partially.

Controversies rage chiefly around Hanno's periplus, the majority of scholars until recently having been in favour of a voyage of exploration to Sierra Leone if not to Gabon. But modern criticism points out the practical impossibility for the square-sailed and rudderless boats of antiquity, even for galleys, to come back from Senegal to Cape Juby against the very strong winds and the current, which are contrary to the return voyage throughout the year. A recent work of G. Germain proves that the author of the periplus borrowed from Herodotus and others, and concludes that it is a literary exercise rather than a reliable document. The only certain fact is that the ancients knew the coasts of Morocco as far as Cape Juby, as well as the Canary Islands.

What about the interior? Ptolemaeus' map of about A.D. 141 shows that the Romans, who at that time were going to China, India and Zanzibar and had explored the valley of the Nile up to the Bahr el Ghazal swamps, did not know the interior of north-west Africa. Tuat and Fezzan oases were the southernmost points surely identified on the map. A few Roman coins, mostly of late Imperial times, have been found in the Sahara between Fezzan and Iforas. The fortress of Abalessa, legendary burial place of Tin Hinan, the ancestral queen of the Tuaregs, has been excavated west of the Hoggar Mountains. Roman lamps, bits of glass, beads and the imprint of a Constantine coin were brought to light.

The most important events of this period were the introduction of the camel to the Sahara during Roman times and of iron to Negro Africa. Occasionally, camels came from Arabia to Egypt even before the Christian era: they are mentioned by several authors. But they do not seem to have reached north Africa before the first century B.C. and it was not until the third century that they could be found in numbers in Tripolitania. This animal was to change completely the life of the Saharans. The predatory Libyans, ancestors of the Tuaregs, were now able to make quick raids on the Roman provinces and retire to the desert where nobody could follow them. They could do the same in the southern Sahara against neighbouring negro tribes. The beginning of Libyan expansion in the north and south, therefore, was due to the coming of the camel.

History began in west Africa only in the seventh to eighth centuries with the first Arab raids (Kawar, A.D. 666; western Mauritania, A.D. 734). Already by

Photo: Mission Henri Lhote

PLATE I. PREHISTORIC ART IN AFRICA: rock painting from Tassili in the Sahara, about 6000 B.C.

Photo: Kenya Information Services

PLATE 1. AFRICA, EASTERN COAST RUINS: tomb on Lamu Island.

A

B

Photos: Kenya Information Services

PLATE 2. AFRICA, EASTERN COAST RUINS: (A) celadon and Ming bowls found at Gedi. (B) Part of the ruins of the great mosque at Gedi.

Photo: Kenya Information Services

PLATE 3. AFRICA, EASTERN COAST RUINS: pillar tomb outside the ruined palace of Gedi.

PLATE 4. AFRICA, EASTERN COAST RUINS: aerial view of the ruined city of Gedi.

Photo: Kenya Information Services

Photo: H. N. Chittick (Tanganyika Antiquities Department)

PLATE 5. PREHISTORIC ART IN AFRICA: painting of giraffes in red from the Singida district, central Tanganyika.

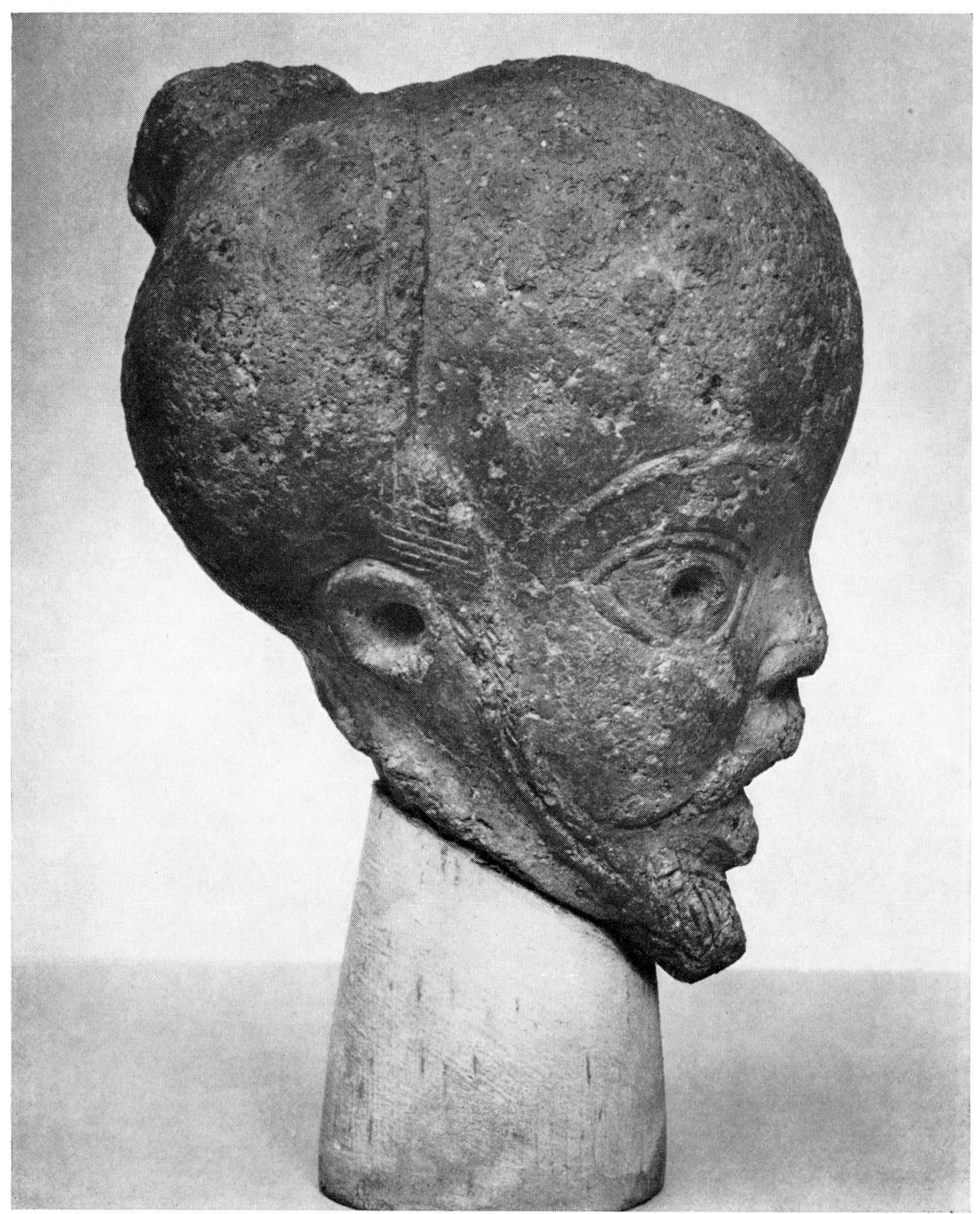

Photo: British Museum

PLATE 6. WEST AFRICA: terracotta head of the Nok culture, probably between 400 and 200 B.C., excavated at Wamba, northern Nigeria. Height 5½ inches. *(Copyright Bernard Fagg, Jos, N. Nigeria)*

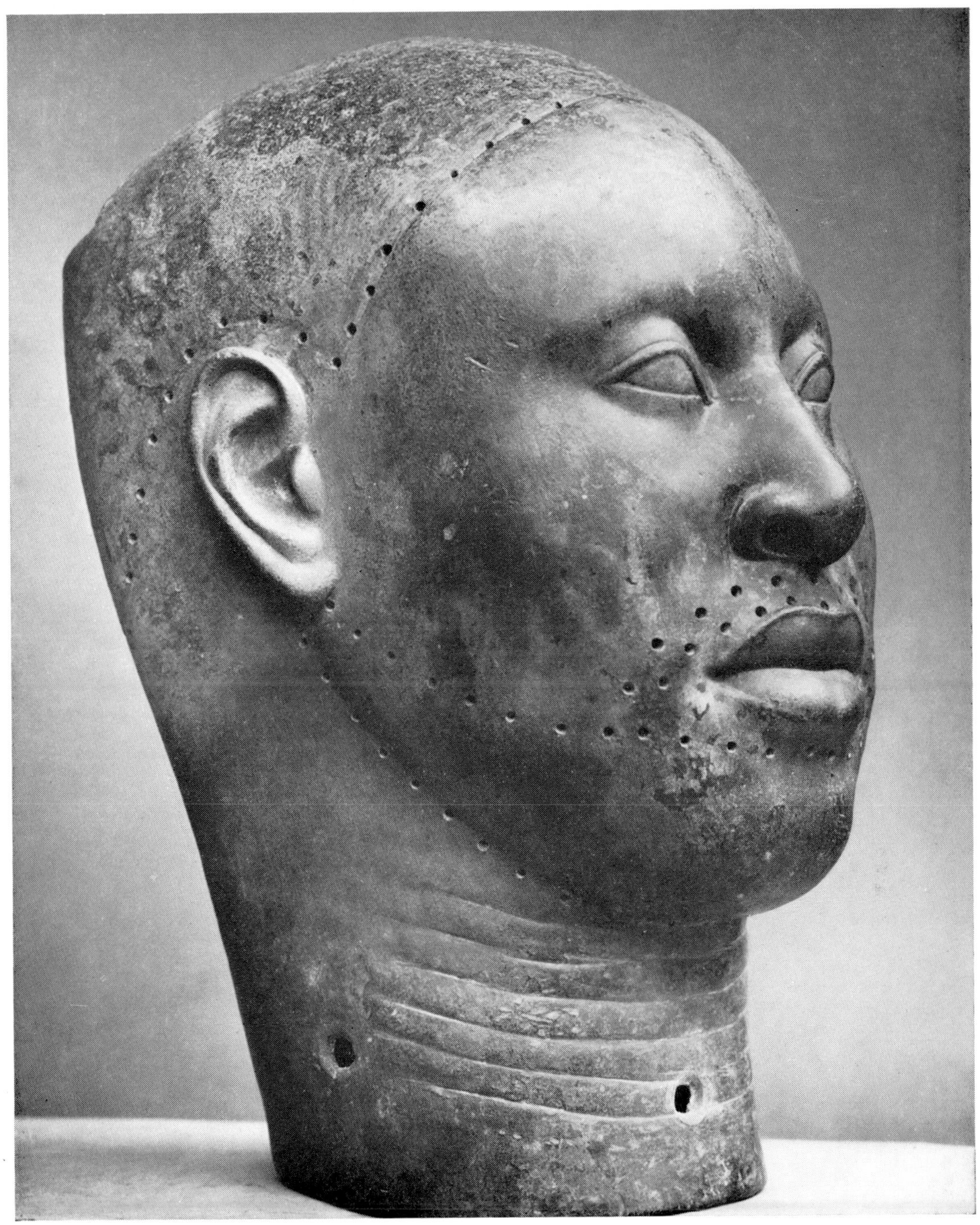

Photo: British Museum

PLATE 7. WEST AFRICA: bronze head from Ife, probably about fourteenth century A.D., excavated in 1938. Height 12 inches. *(British Museum, London)*

Photo: Exclusive News Agency

PLATE 8. ALTAMIRA: cave painting of a deer, Magdalenian period.

Photo: British Museum

PLATE 9. AMARAVATI: slab supporting a lion. (*British Museum, London*)

Photo: British Museum

PLATE 10. AMARAVATI: caryatid of a dwarf. *(British Museum, London)*

Photo: from "Archaeology in China" by William Watson, Max Parrish and Co. Ltd., London

PLATE II. ANYANG: chariot burial from Ta-Ssu-k'ung, near Anyang, Shang dynasty.
(By courtesy of the Britain-China Friendship Association)

Photo: Denver Museum of Natural History

PLATE 12. EARLY MAN IN AMERICA: Folsom point and associated fossil bison ribs embedded in matrix. Type-site Folsom New Mexico. *(Denver Museum of Natural History, Denver)*

Photo: Peabody Museum of Archaeology and Ethnology

PLATE 13. AMER-INDIANS: the house under the rock in Arizona known as Be-ta-ta-kin, Pueblo Indian culture. *(Peabody Museum of Archaeology and Ethnology, Harvard University)*

Photo: Hunting Aerosurveys Ltd

PLATE 14. ANURADHAPURA: aerial view of the Ruwanweli Stupa founded in about 150 B.C. and subsequently restored and enlarged.

Photo: P. E. P. Deraniyagala

PLATE 15. ANURADHAPURA: semicircular stone threshold slab.

Photo: John R. Freeman and Co.

PLATE 16. ANYANG: pottery goblet, Shang dynasty. *(British Museum, London)*

Photo: *Unesco*

PLATE II. AJANTA: ceiling detail from cave I, sixth to seventh century A.D.

the middle of the eighth century, a trade route had been established between southern Morocco and Ghana – this name appears as early as A.D. 800 in Al-Fazarie – by the Umayyads, who dug wells in the middle of the desert.

The Arabs were attracted there by the desire to proselytize and also by the gold of **Nubia** in the Sudan. It should be remembered that today's rich goldfields were not known then and that western Sudan was throughout the Middle Ages the most important source of gold in the world: Boure, Galam, Lobi, Bito were then considered to be El Dorados. In these countries gold was bartered, sometimes by way of silent trade (*see* **Coinage**), against the salt of the Sahara, which came chiefly from Teghaza, and against copper and manufactured goods from the Middle East, north Africa and Europe.

Powerful empires existed in the Sudanese belt during the whole of the Middle Ages. The first was Ghana, the capital of which, Kumbi Saleh, was still referred to by local chroniclers centuries after it was destroyed in A.D. 1240. It was remembered in Mauritanian tradition so well that Bonnel de Mézières could locate it in 1914 and carry out extensive excavations (others were made between 1949 and 1951). Kumbi is a large ruined town, approaching one square mile in area, with huge cemeteries of Moslem collective graves on both sides of the city. The houses are built in stone with elaborate architecture similar to that of old Mauritanian cities: Walata, Tichitt, Wadan, Chinguetti. All the material found during the excavations is medieval (Arabic inscriptions, early enamelled pottery, iron tools and weapons). The town must be the city of Ghana inhabited by Arab merchants of which El-Bekri speaks in about A.D. 1067. The king's capital, mentioned by the same author, has still to be found.

Marble tombstones inscribed with Kouric Arabic characters, dating from A.D. 1100 to 1120, have been dug out of a royal cemetery near Gao. They were carved in Almeria, in Spain.

The Mali Empire succeeded that of Ghana in A.D. 1240 and reached its peak in 1325 when the Sultan Mansa Moussa made his pilgrimage to Mecca, taking with him a fortune in gold and spending it in Cairo and the holy towns of Arabia. His capital has not been surely identified: the most probable site is Niani, on the River Sankarani.

The last of these huge Sudanese states was the Songai Empire, with first Kukia and then Gao as the capital. It lasted until 1591, when it was destroyed by the Moroccans of Djuder. No archaeological remains represent that period other than the tomb of Askia El Hadj Mohammed and mosques in Timbuktu.

Archaeological research is now carried out in several countries in west Africa. In Nigeria, the Bauchi Plateau tin-fields have yielded the fine terracottas of the Nok culture, dated from the beginning of the Christian era onwards. Here, too, wonderful fourteenth-century brass heads and statues were found in the old capital of Ife. In French West Africa, excavations have been carried out at Kumbi Saleh, Gao, Es-Suk in the Iforas, Teghaza salt-mine, mounds in Lower Senegal, and stone circles in Senegal. *See* plates 6–7, pages 56-57.

Agade, *see* Accadians.

Age of the Earth, *see* Earth, Age of the.

Agglutinative. As applied to architecture, a system (or lack of it) by which rooms are added to a building as they are needed, no attempt being made to plan the building as a whole; it is also called "cellular architecture".

Agriculture. Man was a hunter and a foodgatherer in both the **Palaeolithic** and the **Mesolithic** periods. **Neolithic** man was the first to invent agriculture – the deliberate sowing of selected seeds and the careful weeding of the cultivated plot with the intention of producing a crop for food. This was a tremendous step forward in the history of man, the first great move in that Neolithic revolution which led man away from savagery and on to, first, barbarism, and ultimately civilization.

The first that we know to have done this were the people of the **Natufian** culture on the slopes of Mount Carmel in Palestine. They hunted with Mesolithic-type **stone tools,** but they also set **flints** in bone tools and used these as sickles; the gloss which is still to be seen on the flints was imparted to them by the silica in the stems of the unknown grasses which the Natufians reaped.

Similar sickles were used by the people of **Siyalk** I in Iran, and round about the same time the people of the **Faiyum** in Egypt were using wooden-handeld sickles, again with flint teeth. Cereal grains have been discovered on the latter site.

They are already developed forms and a long way from the original wild grasses; the barley is of a kind still grown in primitive parts of north Africa.

The plants which were cultivated by Neolithic man varied according to those which were available in the areas concerned; they include barley, maize, millet, sweet potatoes, wheat and yams. The two most important plants were undoubtedly wheat and barley, and it is on these two that the civilizations of the **Fertile Crescent** were based.

The invention of agriculture was the cause of an extraordinary increase in population. The tiny Palaeolithic settlements round the lake in the Faiyum were succeeded by a string of comparatively populous Neolithic hamlets which soon developed into villages of peasant farmers, and it was not long before these were to be found strung out along the length of the lower Nile; they grew rapidly in size and importance until civilization burst into flower by about 3000 B.C.

This pattern is repeated elsewhere. In Europe, for instance, the Neolithic skeletons which have been unearthed are more than a thousand times as numerous as the Palaeolithic ones, and this is so even though the Neolithic age in Europe lasted less than two thousand years whereas the Palaeolithic age there was certainly more than two hundred thousand years long.

At first the type of agriculture was what is known as "shifting cultivation". The ground would be worked until its fertility was used up and it lost heart; the villagers would then move on to another tract – a process which can be traced happening at the Neolithic site at **Köln-Lindenthal** in Germany.

As the population grew, unoccupied land became scarcer and this manoeuvre more difficult, and it was then that the discovery of the importance of manuring the land came to the rescue. The discovery was probably made empirically; people would notice that the land on which the cattle were kept grew better crops and dimly realize why; but the net result was that the villagers were able to restore the lost fertility to the ground and so make it possible for them to continue living in the same place year after year.

The earliest agricultural digging tool was a kind of hoe; this was used for many hundreds of years until man invented the **plough**.

Ain Hanech. This prehistoric site lies in the ancient lacustrine depression existing in the neighbourhood of Saint-Arnauld, near Sétif, in the Algerian department of Constantine in north Africa. During the Villafranchian period, this depression became filled with gravel and clay, in which many mammals were bogged down. Fauna have been discovered here of archaic-appearing Proboscidea (the elephant family) and also three-toed Equidae (the horse family) of a typical Villafranchian type. Many unchipped pebbles have also been found and about fifty polyhedral stone balls were discovered in 1947. These balls are made of dolomite, which is a rock occurring in outcrops near the edges of this former lake bed. They are about the size of an orange and their surfaces display traces of chipping. They are comparable with the spheroids found in Uganda, Tanganyika, south Africa and India. In fact, they belong to an archaic pebble-culture of Villafranchian date. In 1952 further excavations revealed more of these polyhedral pebbles, on which the surface chipping was much more clearly defined. Artifacts were also found resembling a primitive form of **Chellean** hand-axe. In this year about one hundred implements were discovered in about 1083 cubic yards of deposit. But the most important find was a number of **hand-axes** discovered by workmen after a storm. These are coarse and clumsy. The points are not well-defined and project from a portion that is generally trihedral in section. The edges are twisted. Their importance lies in the fact that they display very archaic features, and show that man was present in north Africa at the beginning of the **Quaternary period.**

Ainu. Now confined to the northernmost parts of Japan and to Sakhalin and Yezo, the Ainu seem once to have covered a considerably larger area. The fact that blood-group evidence points to connections with the Kha of the Annamite Chain, while certain physical features seem to connect them with the archaic White stock of Australia, gives some indication of their importance in the history of the further parts of Eurasia and the Pacific. They are a remarkably hirsute people, a fact which distinguishes them sharply from the predominantly mongoloid peoples among whom they live, though there is much evidence for mongoloid admixture, particularly noticeable in the female. There is some reason to associate them with the northern Japanese **Neolithic**, while their famous bear cult seems to link them closely with northern Eurasiatic religious systems. They were long a threat to the expanding Japanese power, though in the Heian period Ainu were recruited for the imperial bodyguard. In a series of bitter campaigns culminating in the early ninth century A.D. they were gradually driven back to the north of Hokkaido. It seems likely that their defence was aided by Japanese settlers who wished to maintain an area outside imperial control as a private trading zone. The full extent of their contribution to Japanese culture has still to be determined, as has their position in the wider sphere of Asian and Pacific prehistory.

Air Photography. Once the subsoil has been disturbed it can never be replaced exactly as it was before. Centuries later, plants will still flourish on the disturbed patch in a different fashion from the undisturbed part, and the subsoil, if carefully excavated, will be seen to have a different look and texture.

Archaeologists have been familiar with this fact for a long time and have always looked carefully for traces of disturbance in the subsoil, knowing that these were signs of past occupation, but it was not until after the first world war that they came to realize that such traces could be identified in photographs taken from the air. British Royal Air Force officers drew the attention of O. G. S. Crawford, then archaeological officer to the British Ordnance Survey, to photographs which showed the existence of hitherto unsuspected indications of man's occupations of ancient sites. Amongst other early discoveries made in this way was that of an avenue at **Stonehenge** which had previously been completely unknown; **Woodhenge** owes its discovery to air photography.

Two main methods of air photography are used by archaeologists in exploring ancient sites: vertical photographs and oblique photographs.

When, for instance, a ditch is dug across a chalk down, the resulting disturbance will show up on a vertical air photograph of growing crops hundreds of years after the ditch has been filled in. Because the soil is moister where the ditch was dug the corn will grow more strongly there, and will consequently show up as a darker band on a photograph, though indistinguishable from ground level. Alternatively, if there are the remains of a pavement or the foundations of a house below the surface, the corn will grow less strongly and therefore appear as a lighter patch on an air photograph.

Oblique photographs taken when the sun is at the right angle will show, for instance, the existence of strips such as those which divide **Celtic fields** by the shadows which these cast; sometimes they are visible from the ground when the sun is low and casting a long shadow, but often they are only identifiable as the result of air photographs; and with the help of such photographs it is possible to plot and map even the known ones very much more quickly than can be done on the ground.

Ajanta. The Buddhist caves at Ajanta, situated in the Aurangabad district of Bombay on the northern escarpments of the Deccan lava plateau of India, were excavated in the cliffs of a wild and lonely ravine of great scenic beauty, and formed no doubt a monastic centre near enough to the great trade routes of western India to derive patronage from passing merchants and caravan leaders as well as from royal patrons. There are twenty-nine principal caves. Architecturally they conform to the other great sites of the region: the earlier caves, which are usually assigned to the second and first centuries B.C., comparing with those of Karle, Kanheri and Nasik; and the latter with those of **Ellora.** But the special glory of Ajanta lies in the great wealth of paintings which adorns its walls. These are often termed frescos, but the technique is slightly different from that of the true fresco. The surface was prepared with a cow-dung plaster and finished with a white gypsum on which the painting was later executed. It is generally held that the earliest examples in caves nine and ten date from the first century B.C., but it has also been convincingly argued that none is earlier than the opening of the second century A.D. However, the great majority of the paintings in the other caves were executed under the patronage of the Vakataka rulers in the sixth and seventh centuries A.D. Although painted for a religious purpose the murals convey also a secular message and, as with the reliefs at **Sanchi** (*see* colour plate XIV, plates 31, 121, pages 101, 387), are a mine of information for the whole life of the times. *See* colour plate II.

Akh, *see* Ba.

Akhnaton. This was the name, meaning "it is well with the [sun-] disk", adopted by the heretic pharaoh Amenhotep IV (1380–1362 B.C.) who renounced the old Egyptian gods and established a monotheistic cult with Aten, the sun's disk, as the sole object of worship – probably the first monotheistic religion in history. Since **Thebes** was associated with the old religion, Akhnaton transferred his capital from there to Akhetaton ("horizon of the sun's disk", modern **Tell el Amarna**). He inspired a distinctive style of naturalistic sculpture which had a profound effect on Egyptian art, and composed hymns to Aten which are masterpieces. But his preoccupation with his new religion meant that he neglected the administration of his country and Egypt's Asiatic empire; complaints in the Amarna Letters form evidence of this. His solar cult did not survive his reign. His wife was the beautiful Nefertiti. He was succeeded by his half-brother Tutankaten who, after the country's rejection of the new religion, changed his name to **Tutankhamun.**

Alaca Höyük. This is a *höyük* or **tell** near the small town of Alaca situated in a central position on the Anatolian Plateau in Turkey about one hundred miles to the east of Ankara and at the junction of three ancient routes, those to the Black Sea, the Aegean, and Mesopotamia. A key site for the archaeology of the plateau, it was continuously occupied from about 4000 B.C. onwards, although its most important phase is pre-Hittite.

Discovered by W.G. Hamilton in 1835, it was subsequently visited and rather ineffectively excavated at fairly frequent intervals up to 1927. From 1935–49 extensive excavations were carried out by the Turkish Historical Association under the direction of Dr Hamit Zubeyr Kosay; they proved to be one of the most spectacular excavations in Turkish archaeology.

The layers and the phases have been numbered from the top downwards and hence Phase IV is the earliest. This phase, the Late **Chalcolithic**, begins about 3000 B.C. and is contemporary with the first settlement at Troy; the culture is also known from Alishar and Gölücek. It is known at Alaca only from deep soundings in a limited area which revealed brick-built houses with stone foundations, a domestic economy based on the Anatolian **Neolithic**, **a flexed burial**, a few simple objects of copper, button seals, pottery which has finely incised squares and triangles, true handles, fruit stands, and some white-on-black painted ware. It shows little, if any, influence from the Mediterranean.

Phase III is, however, the one for which the site is really famous, comprising the "Royal Tombs" of Early **Bronze Age** II date. This used to be called the Copper Age in Turkey and before Dr Kosay's excavations it was only known from the rather modest agricultural community at Alishar. But here were the aristocracy of the same culture, thirteen tombs filled with rare and costly objects, crowded together into an area of only some thirty yards by thirty. They remained unique until 1957 when excavations at Horoztepe in north Anatolia revealed two very similar graves, which only serve to confirm the splendour of the Anatolian Early Bronze Age.

That male and female were sometimes buried together seems to show that the cemetery represented a secular group, and rich female graves demonstrate the high social position of women in that society. The objects themselves give a glimpse of the funeral procession, the corpse richly decked out in gold pins and belt-buckles, with diadems, bracelets and anklets all of gold; carried along with it, various vessels bowls, jugs, stemmed chalices (very often of gold and silver and richly decorated with repoussé designs) and even a wooden chest inlaid with gold and silver bands. Weapons buried with the men included spherical mace-heads, battle-axes and one dagger with a blade of an extremely valuable metal, iron. Strange metal "standard-heads" with an open-work lattice or animal models were held aloft, often with an attachment which jangled. Unique from Horoztepe was a rectangular sistrum of similar design which could have been used as a rattle to excite devotees. Little is known about the religion except that it must have been based on a mother-goddess fertility cult, and that the emphasis on the stag and lion in figurines indicate the mentality of a mountain people. Copper female figurines are common and a single *Kourotrophos* figurine (mother suckling a child) comes from Horoztepe.

The tombs themselves were shallow rectangular pits four metres by eight in size. The contracted body was usually placed in one corner facing south and with a pile of religious objects in front of it. A flat wooden roof was covered over with earth and the outline of the grave marked with stones. The final ceremony included a sacrifice of animals and a ritual feast.

It is not possible to give an exact date for these tombs, although they fall within the period 2600–2300 B.C. and are contemporary with **Troy** II. Stratigraphical evidence shows that the royal cemetery was in use for several generations, the final burials being contemporary with those at Horoztepe. This culture is uniform all over the Anatolian Plateau, and has some good parallels in the Early Helladic Bronze Age and from Troy II where some of the items from the Alaca tombs (mainly spiral and hammer-headed pins) also turned up. The bossed gold plaques are found later in bone in the Castelluccio culture of Sicily. Despite these connections this culture seems to be native to Anatolia for there are no strong Mesopotamian influences, nor does it seem to have contributed very much to the Aegean.

Much of the wealth of the nobility of Alaca must have been based on trade, and they seem to have imported their fine metal work from northern Anatolia where there must have been advanced metal workshops with techniques of repoussé, sheet-working, soldering, and wire drawing. The style is, again, a native Anatolian one.

Phase II covers both the Middle and Late Bronze Age and also the period of the **Hittite** Empire. To this phase belong the most spectacular architectural works, including the town wall built on a huge made-up platform, the main barbican gate with twin towers (the famous Sphinx Gate), with reliefs of a bull and a priest-king at the base of the towers. A short distance inside this gate stood the main temple with an open loggia façade, surrounded by its own walled enclosure and double gate.

Finally, Phase I consists of Phrygian, Roman, Byzantine, Seljuk and Ottoman occupation. *See* plate 26, page 96.

Alalakh, *see* Tell Atchana.

Alishar, *see* Alaca Höyük.

Alphabet, The. Writing first took the form of **pictograms,** in which a picture represented an object. The next steps were for the picture to represent, first an idea – an **ideogram,** and then an actual spoken sound – a **phonogram.** The latter can be syllabic, when each sign represents a syllable, usually simply a consonant followed by a vowel; or it can be alphabetic, when the sign represents one sound, whether it be a consonant or a vowel.

The most familiar example of the pictographic form of writing is the Egyptian **hieroglyphics**, though by the time this first becomes known to us it is already composed of both pictograms and ideograms. Less familiar is the older **cuneiform** writing which was developed in Mesopotamia; the earliest examples we have date from the fourth millennium B.C. and are already partly ideographic. How much further back in time we should need to go to discover the beginning of writing is a mystery to which we shall probably never know the answer.

Both hieroglyphic and cuneiform writing developed to the syllabic stage, where the signs represent syllables, and the Egyptians took hieroglyphics still further and used the signs to represent single consonants. But the conservatism of the Egyptian priests was such that, though their writing had reached the stage where it could have been developed into an alphabetic form, they never took the final step. Nor did the Sumerians advance in cuneiform beyond the syllabic stage. Neither, far to the east, did the Chinese; indeed, their writing has never progressed to a purely phonetic stage and has remained ideographic to the present day so that the Chinese scholar has to learn thousands of characters.

The first purely alphabetic writing appeared amongst the **Phoenicians** sometime before 1500 B.C.; it is the ancestor of all the western alphabets.

The Phoenicians were merchants and sea-traders, and it is probably to this fact that their invention of the alphabet is due. In both Egypt and Mesopotamia it was to the interest of the priests and the professional clerks to keep their system of writing difficult and hard to learn; thereby they enjoyed a privileged position and an importance in the eyes of their fellows. The Phoenicians, however, had an incentive. They needed an easy and quick form of writing; it was essential for the rapid discharge of business; and sheer necessity drove them to the point where inspiration led them to produce the first alphabet. From discoveries made at **Ras Shamra** and **Byblos** it appears that, for good measure, they actually produced two alphabets. One, which did not survive, had thirty characters; the other had twenty-two characters, all consonants; the vowels were not written, an omission for which various explanations have been attempted, but none successfully.

The Phoenicians carried their alphabet to Greece somewhere between 1000 and 700 B.C. The Greeks discarded certain consonants and added new ones; other consonants, for which there was no equivalent in the Greek language, they used for vowels. A further refinement introduced by the Greeks was to change the method of writing; previously it had been from right to left across the page, and the Greeks altered this to from left to right.

From Greece the reformed alphabet travelled to Rome and so to the western European world. Eastward the alphabet was taken by traders to Mesopotamia, existing there side by side with cuneiform, and on to Iran. It reached India and had a significant influence on the creation there, by 300 B.C., of an **Aryan** alphabet.

Altamira, in the Santander province of northern Spain, is the most famous and in many ways the most remarkable painted cavern of the Old **Stone Age;** the paintings, grouped in one sector of the cave, were discovered in 1879, though they were not widely accepted as genuine until 1902.

The name Altamira means "high view", and the cave opens in a ridge in rolling limestone country between the sea and the Picos de Europa, mountains which continue the barrier of the Pyrenees westward. On a good day the mountains are visible from the cave. Through the Old Stone Age, and especially in its closing phases, the climate round Altamira was less severe than across the plains and plateaux of France. Game abounded, fish were plentiful in the rivers and the Bay of Biscay, and conditions favoured a final elaboration of **Palaeolithic** culture.

In 1868 a shift of soil and rock first revealed the entrance. In 1878 a landowner and amateur archaeologist of the neighbourhood, Don Marcelino de Sautuola, visited the Paris Exhibition, among the features of which were the new archaeological discoveries of France. He was impressed by the evidence on view of the early hunting cultures, particularly by the engraved tools and weapons from the rock shelters of the **Dordogne**, which more than suggested a new dimension in the history of man. Back in his native province Don Marcelino began to explore local caverns (of which there is an abundance) with a new keenness.

He had examined the Altamira Cave in a cursory way in 1875, before his visit to Paris, and had noticed drawings in black outline which did not impress him at the time as prehistoric or significant. Now he returned and dug into the filling of the threshold.

Accounts of the discovery of the paintings have the variety of legend. It seems certain, however, that Don Marcelino, while he was excavating – or delving, had a small daughter with him, that she strayed under a roof of limestone, and, thinking she saw bulls painted on the knobs of rock above her head, came running back to her father crying "*Toros! Toros!*" ("Bulls! Bulls!" – animals of which a Spanish child would be well aware). Her father described the paintings in a pamphlet he called *Brief Notes on Some Prehistoric Objects of the Province of Santander* (1880), stating his belief that the painted images must be coeval with the **artifacts** he dug up in the mouth of the cave.

The bull-like creatures were in fact bison, painted in several colours (predominantly in red ochre, with black manganese shading). Bison had been a principal game animal in the damp, partly wooded coastal corridor below the mountains. A few other animals were also delineated in the cave, including a red deer hind and a splendidly naturalistic wild boar, two more species of the damp woodland.

Altamira became a brief wonder – and enigma. But opinion was not primed yet with a wide sufficiency of evidence, and most archaeologists believed a well-known French palaeontologist who reported that the paintings were neither Palaeolithic nor even prehistoric. They were variously ascribed to art students and Roman legionaries; and Don Marcelino de Sautuola was even suspected of a hand in forging the paintings and then of trying to pass them off on to the learned world. Sceptical French archaeologists (possibly a little anxious to reserve *la gloire* of Palaeolithic discoveries for France and the Dordogne) suspected a trick of Spanish clericalism in the whole matter; and Don Marcelino died before later discoveries confirmed the correctness of his own conclusions.

Until the last years of the century the Altamira paintings were more or less forgotten. Then in 1895 animal drawings of a date unquestionably Palaeolithic were found when the French cave of La Mouthe, outside Les Eyzies, was opened and excavated. Discoveries piled up in quick procession. In Marsoulas Cave fine coloured images of bison were recognized in 1897. The celebrated (but now, alas, very faded and faint) paintings of reindeer, rhinoceroses, mammoth and bison in the Font-de-Gaume cave became known in 1901.

Full of these discoveries the archaeologists, Emile Carthailac of an older school and Henri **Breuil** of the younger school, visited forgotten Altamira in 1901, at once realizing the age and quality of the paintings which spread across the low ceiling of the cave.

Altamira was frequented as a shrine of animal

increase over a long period; but the best of the paintings, grouped in the one shallow sector of the cave system, are **Magdalenian**, belonging to the latest, most assured, and elaborate (though not most vital) phase of the art of the Old Stone Age hunters. Bison cows and bulls are painted over preliminary "drawing" – i.e. over preliminary engraved indications – on boss-like projections of limestone.

The figured animals are large, up to six feet long, and although the cave has been open to visitors for more than half a century, the damp Cantabrian climate has preserved the pigment very well, so that the roof glows with the blood colour of these powerful creatures in the shine of lamps spaced across the floor.

The connoisseur of archaeological sites will be pleased by the tact with which the Spaniards introduce Altamira. A neat road up hill, a neat car park by eucalyptus trees, a neat museum, a neat dark hole into the hillside. The pleasant surroundings are rural or pastoral rather than dramatic. In extent the cave is not impressive. The floor is apt to be wet and muddy, the roof (since the whole cave was shaken and threatened by quarrying nearby) is shored with huge rectangles of concrete. The effect is one of visiting primeval works of art and hunting magic in the sub-basement of an office block. But if there are cave sites more savage and extraordinary both in Spain and France, as well as Palaeolithic drawings and paintings which are more vital, Altamira continues to enjoy its own historical supremacy. It helped to revolutionize our ideas of human development, and of the cave shrines so far discovered **Lascaux** (*see* colour plate VIII) is Altamira's only rival for opulence of image and colour. (*See also* **Prehistoric Art.**) *See* plate 8, page 58.

Al Ubaid, *see* Sumerians.

Amaravati. The site generally designated Amaravati lies on the south bank of the River Krishna (Kistna) in the Guntur district of India, a short distance from the site of the ancient city of Dhanyakataka, once the capital of the Satavahana Empire. When it first came to the attention of antiquarians in 1796 it was still cased in much of its original brickwork and sculptured stone slabs. In 1816 a careful survey was made. Today, as the result of continued depredations, the mound has almost vanished, but it is clear that in its original form it constituted a large Buddhist **stupa** richly adorned with sculptured stonework, which must have been in the second century A.D. by far the finest monument in the Buddhist world. There is evidence of three main phases of construction: early, showing strong influence from **Sanchi** and the north-west Deccan; mature, in which the art reached its high water mark; and late, during which the standard of the work was maintained at a high level. The early phase may be dated to the first century A.D., the mature to the second and early third centuries, and the late to the third and perhaps early fourth. The characteristic style represented by this work, and by that of other sites in the area, particularly the nearby Nagarjunikonda (now to be submerged in a great irrigation project to which it is giving its name), spread far beyond the Andhra country, and appears to have been among the first sculptural styles to have reached Ceylon. In its later phases its influence, particularly in certain distinctive forms of Buddha image, has been traced in several parts of south-east Asia. *See* plates 9-10, pages 59-60.

Amarna, *see* Tell el Amarna.

Amenhotep IV, *see* Akhnaton.

America, Early Man in. The fact that all human skeletons found in the New World are those of Homo sapiens, coupled with the absence of higher primates, has convinced anthropologists that man did not originate in the western hemisphere and that the ancestors of the American Indian must have come from the Old World. The Mongoloid physical characteristics of the Indians indicate an Asiatic source. A glance at a world map will show that, until well developed watercraft were available, men could have followed only one route, moving from Asia to America by way of the Bering Strait. Here the two continents are separated by only fifty-six miles, and at certain times in the past they were connected by a land bridge.

Until 1926 it was generally believed that man had been present in the New World for only a few thousand years before the beginning of the Christian era. In that year, however, artifacts were found near Folsom, New Mexico, in clear association with the articulated bones of extinct bison believed to be some 10,000 years old. Since that first discovery much additional evidence of the antiquity of man in the western hemisphere has been found.

American archaeologists are agreed that America has been inhabited for more than 10,000 years and that man was present during the terminal Pleistocene (Ice Age) period. Many accept dates in excess of 20,000 years ago which fall within the time of the last major **glaciation**, the Wisconsin. A small minority is convinced that man entered America at a much earlier date, in pre-Wisconsin times, but most archaeologists do not believe that adequate evidence has been presented.

The term "Palaeo-Indian" is often used to refer to the earliest inhabitants of America. The Palaeo-Indian period is the first in the developmental sequence. In the United States there is increasing evidence that, during this period, people who lived on the eastern side of the Rocky Mountains and those who lived on the western side had somewhat different ways of life and produced different types of tools. In some areas, particularly in the south-west, both types of life were represented. Those who lived in Alaska and northern Canada followed still another pattern. These three traditions are sometimes designated the Palaeo-eastern, the Palaeo-western, and the Palaeo-northern.

The Palaeo-eastern tradition emphasized the hunting of big game animals, including species which are now extinct. Most **stone tools,** which included many types of cutting and scraping implements, were made from flakes. The most characteristic artifacts were projectile points, generally more or less lanceolate in outline and usually finely flaked by pressure. They are believed to pre-date the introduction of the bow and are thought to have been used with dart throwers or spears.

The most famous type, although not the oldest, of these projectile points is the Folsom, named after the site that first provided proof of the antiquity of man in North America. These are lanceolate points with concave bases usually marked by ear-like projections. Their average length is about two inches. The most characteristic feature is the fluting produced by the removal of a longitudinal flake from either face. The flutes usually extend over most of the length of the point. The makers of Folsom points were primarily hunters of bison of species now extinct. **Radiocarbon** dates and geological studies indicate an age of some 10,000 years. Folsom points have been found only in the Great Plains.

Among the older types are similar points, often called Clovis points, which are much more widely distributed. They have been found in every state east of the Rocky Mountains, in the south-west, and in a few localities in the Great Basin and in California. These are fluted lanceolate points with parallel or slightly convex sides and concave bases, usually some three inches or more in length, although sometimes smaller. The fluting, which usually extends about half-way from base to tip, was normally produced by the removal of multiple flakes.

It has not yet been possible to date most fluted points in the eastern United States, either geologically or by the radio-carbon method, but since the fluted point horizon appears to pre-date the **Archaic** horizon, which began some 8,000–10,000 years ago in some areas, they must be ancient. At the type station, near Clovis, New Mexico, they were found in a **stratigraphic** position underlying Folsom points. At this site and at three others, Clovis points have been found in association with the bones of mammoth. It is thought that Clovis points were the prototypes from which the more specialized Folsoms developed in the Plains. In some areas, however, the more generalized type may have persisted into Folsom times.

Among points found stratigraphically below Folsoms are the Sandia points first found in a cave of the same name in New Mexico. They are lanceolate points, two or three inches long, characterized by an inset on one side which produces a single shoulder. Some found in another site are fluted. The practice of fluting points appears to be a New World development, for fluted points have not been reported from Asia. In Sandia Cave bones of mammoth, mastodon, bison, horse, and camel were found in the same horizon with the distinctive points. Geological evidence suggests that this horizon dates back to a time before the last major advance of the Wisconsin ice. Most Sandia points have come from the southern Plains, but a few have been found in Canada.

From Folsom times onward the Palaeo-Indians of the plains were bison hunters. During the time from about 9,000 to 7,000 years ago they produced lanceolate points, many of which were characterized by extraordinarily fine parallel flaking. Two of the best known types were Plainviews, points that resembled Clovis points but were unfluted, and Scottsbluff points which had parallel flaking and broad stems. The latter have been found in several sites in association with other artifacts which produce a complex to which the name Cody has been given. The most diagnostic of the associated implements are Eden points, which are narrower relative to their length than are the Scottsbluffs, and distinctive knives with transverse blades, shouldered on one side.

Farther east various complexes were developing which are attributed to the next stage in the sequence of development, the Archaic. The Archaic people were gatherers as well as hunters and fishermen, and some depended to a great extent on shell fish. There was some use of polished as well as chipped implements and certain groups used some copper. Most projectile points were fairly large and notched or stemmed.

Most of the people of the Palaeo-western tradition who lived on the western side of the Rocky Mountains, particularly those in the Great Basin and in portions of the south-west, placed a greater emphasis on food gathering than on hunting. In general, projectile points were less important and they were often stemmed or notched. Choppers, keeled scrapers, commonly made from cores and flaked by percussion, and grinding stones were characteristic tools. The term "Desert Cultures" is sometimes applied to manifestations of this tradition.

At Tule Springs in southern Nevada flakes and a few crude tools have been found in a deposit which contains bones of extinct Pleistocene animals. Charcoal, thought to be of human origin, is more than 23,800 years old according to the radiocarbon test. Another Nevada site, known as Gypsum Cave, contained **artifacts** and the remains of extinct ground sloths. Gypsum Cave projectile points are lozenge or diamond shaped with small tapering stems. Radiocarbon dates for samples from this site range from 8,527 to 10,455 years ago. In Danger Cave, a deep stratified site in Utah, thousands of artifacts were found. They included corner and side-notched points and many grinding stones. Samples from the lower zone produced radiocarbon dates of more than 11,000 years ago. Grinding stones were the most characteristic artifacts of the Cochise culture of south-eastern Arizona and south-western New Mexico. Artifacts of the earliest stage were found in a deposit which yielded bones of mammoth, extinct horse, and bison.

Radiocarbon dates from Washington and Oregon suggest that the north-west was occupied by at least 10,000 years ago. There was greater emphasis on hunting and, in some areas, on fishing. Some of the early inhabitants used **burins** for working elk antler. In the desert areas of southern California various artifacts have been found on fossil beaches and terraces of large former lakes. Some archaeologists believe that the occupation, which must have occurred at a time of great moisture, dates back to the last great pluvial of the Pleistocene, but others believe that the lakes were produced by a more recent pluvial, and the issue is still in doubt. The best known of these assemblages are those found near Lake Mohave and in the Pinto Basin.

The Palaeo-northern tradition of Alaska and northern Canada is characterized by specially prepared cores, the prismatic flakes struck from them, small tools made from these flakes, and burins. The best known of the northern complexes is the Denbigh represented at the Iyatayet site, which lies on the west side of Cape Denbigh in Norton Sound. The artifacts of this complex were separated from more recent Eskimo artifacts by a layer of sterile laminated clay. They include cores, blades, and burins, reminiscent of Old World forms of Upper Palaeolithic and Mesolithic age, and some lanceolate points similar to New World types. Geological evidence suggested a date of about 8,500 years ago. Radiocarbon dates varied from about 3,500 to about 5,000 years ago, but the samples appear to have been contaminated by grass roots. The age of these finds is still in question.

South of the United States there is also evidence for the antiquity of man. In Tamaulipas, Mexico, a series of cave sites has yielded evidence of early occupation. One of the early complexes, the Lerma, has been dated at more than 9,000 years ago by the radiocarbon method. Lerma points are doubly pointed laurel leaf types. In the Valley of Mexico three sites have been discovered where artifacts have been found in unmistakable association with the bones of mammoths in a formation attributed to the terminal Pleistocene.

Points resembling the Lerma type have been found at El Jobo, Venezuela. These were surface finds and cannot be dated, but radiocarbon dates from a site in central Argentina indicate that such implements were being made there some 8,000 years ago. One of the best known of early South American sites is Palli Aiki, a cave with stratified deposits, which lies on the north shore of the Strait of Magellan in Patagonia. Large points, usually stemmed with concave bases, and various stone and bone tools were found associated with the charred bones of extinct sloth, horse, and guanaco at the lowest level. A radiocarbon date of 8,639 ± 450 years ago was obtained from a sample from this horizon.

Very little is known of the physical appearance of the first Americans. Most of the discoveries of human skeletal remains attributed to the Palaeo-Indian period have been discredited. The most generally accepted discovery was made near Midland, Texas, where a partial human skeleton with a long headed skull was found in a deposit that may be some 12,000 years old. Two other skeletons, Minnesota Man, found near Pelican Rapids, Minnesota, and Tepexpan Man, found in the Valley of Mexico, are regarded as ancient by some archaeologists but not by others. The former lay under clays laid down in sedimentary layers in a glacial lake shortly after the last major advance of the continental ice sheets. The latter was found near the localities where there is incontrovertible evidence of the contemporaneity of men and mammoth, and it was in the same formation. Unfortunately, however, in both instances, the manner in which these skeletons were excavated makes it impossible to be certain that they were not intrusive into the deposits in which they were found. Recent investigations indicate that there is no evidence for any great age for the so-called "Lagoa Santa Race" in Brazil. *See* plate 12, page 62.

Amer-Indians. This is a general name for the early native inhabitants of the American Continent. The civilization reached its highest point in Central America and Peru and it was entirely distinct from the culture of the Old World. For instance, the wheel, the plough, the use of money and iron were all unknown.

There seems to have been little contact between the very early occupants of these vast spaces, but it seems clear that the Continent was populated by successive waves of immigrants coming from the Old World across the Bering Strait.

In North America the earliest traces are of a stone-flaking people using the Folsom point for their weapons, a thin blade with a broad flake-scar along each side. Farther south, the south-western states of the USA with New Mexico form an area in which the Basket-makers lived but their earliest remains can hardly be dated earlier than the Christian era. They made interlaced baskets, wore animal skins and fibre sandals. Some of their pottery has been discovered and at the end of their period they used the bow and arrow instead of a spear.

By about A.D. 700 the Basket-maker culture was succeeded by the Pueblo and whole sites have been identified by the method of studying tree-rings. Their dwellings became rather more advanced, with several rooms and an underground chamber for ceremonial purposes. Slipped pottery of this period is common and cotton cloth came into use.

The next period, Pueblo II, is marked by the appearance of houses built entirely above ground, and by the use of rather more elaborate pottery.

From A.D. 1100 to 1300 was the Pueblo III era, in which the outlying districts were left in favour of a central concentration, large communal houses of stone were built and pottery designs enriched and greatly varied. After this time we come to the age of recorded history, and the last notable antiquities of North America are the remains of the Mound-builders, found largely in the Mississippi Basin. Their work in copper was highly skilled, and they left behind many elaborately carved stone pipes to show that they knew all about tobacco.

Mexico and Central America developed different cultures, including that of the **Aztecs** whose capital dates from about A.D. 1325. They came from farther north and were a highly warlike and barbarous crew of nomads, amongst whom human sacrifice was practised on a vast scale. Their skill in working gold, silver and other metals was considerable, and they were accomplished potters. Their architecture is notable for huge columns and the famous plumed serpents, and they left signs of marked development in agriculture.

The **Maya** civilization was spread over what is now Honduras, Guatemala and part of Mexico. Some of their cities date from the fourteenth century A.D., and their culture lasted until the coming of the Spaniards in 1511. Their origin is uncertain, but they were given to building monoliths dated by their own calendar which supply some rather uncertain evidence as to their history.

Mayan architecture is characterized by pyramids crowned with temples and elaborate dwellings for priests. Their carving of wood, freestone and jade was highly skilled but they rarely used metals. Their pottery included cylindrical beakers, tripods and bowls in excellent colours, and they were adept at picture writing and fresco work.

Farther south, in El Salvador, Nicaragua and Costa Rica the order of cultures is very difficult to trace, but in western Panama there have been rich finds of gold and pottery, especially in graves.

In **Peru**, many advanced cultures seem to have developed with remarkable rapidity and much of the pottery is particularly rich in colours, as many as eight appearing on the same vessel. The final civilization was that of the **Incas**, with their famous saucers with bird-head handles.

All through South America the archaeological story continues in much the same way. In Ecuador, for instance, Inca remains are found throughout the highlands, but the countries developed their own arts, such as the large painted effigy jars found in Ecuador, and some very early stone chairs.

Colombia is notable for fine examples of gold work, for large burial urns and for a wealth of flat gold and copper figurines, stone statues and broad-winged pendants.

As one proceeds farther to the south, the country becomes more inaccessible, or certainly must have been so in very early times. It is therefore no longer possible to find the remains of cultures so markedly distinctive as those of the Aztec, the Maya, and the Inca. In all the South American countries, finds have been made of early pottery, jewellery, metal-work and so forth. And buildings have been unearthed which give a clue to the development of architecture, to burial customs and to many other aspects of local life. But to treat them all in detail would require a whole series of large volumes, and the literature already dealing with them is immeasurably extensive and highly specialized.

It is in Central America and Peru that the archaeologist has found remains of the greatest interest. Some of the discoveries in North America go back to an early date, but the cultures of the greatest importance are those of the Aztec, the Maya and the Inca. *See* plate 13, page 63.

Amorites. These were a group of Semitic nomads who moved into the **Fertile Crescent** of Mesopotamia, Syria and Palestine and dominated it from about 2200 to 1700 B.C. Excavations between 1935 and 1938 at the Amorite capital **Mari** on the Middle Euphrates (modern Tell el Hariri, Syria) brought to light more than twenty thousand tablets, attesting to their high organization, artistic ability and building skill. The immense palace of their king covered over fifteen acres. They were finally overwhelmed from the north by the Hittites and Indo-European invaders. The term "Amorites" was used by the Babylonians to denote the inhabitants of Palestine and Syria; the Egyptians limited it to the hill-men in central Palestine and northern Syria. In the Bible the name was used for some of the pre-Israelite inhabitants of Palestine and Jordan.

Amphora. A large storage vessel with two handles (plural – amphorae or amphoras). *See* plate 70, page 244.

Amulet. An amulet is an article which is believed by its owner to have the power to ward off evil. Originally amulets were natural objects with what were considered to be magical properties, such as a precious or a semi-precious stone, or a misshapen piece of wood or rock in which the eye could trace the likeness of some deity or animal. From this it was a short step to deliberately carving or shaping the object into the direct likeness of something believed to possess the power to keep evil away or to bring the owner good luck. After the invention of writing, amulets sometimes took the form of charms inscribed on paper and carried in a locket.

Angkor. The word Angkor derives from the Sanskrit *nagara* – city, which occurs widely as a loan-word in south-eastern Asia. While its primary meaning is retained to mean either city or state, by extension it is applied to temples which by virtue of their more durable materials tend to survive long after the surrounding buildings in wood and bamboo have disappeared. Compare Malay: *negeri, negri;* Thai: *nakhom;* Javanese: *negoro;* Cambodian: *angkor.* (*See also* **Siemreap.**)

Animals, Domestication of, *see* Domestication of Animals.

Anning, Mary (1799–1847). Lyme Regis, on the south coast of England, is particularly rich in fossils. Mary Anning's father was a carpenter who collected, and sold to tourists, the fossilized remains of ammonites and belemnites, shellfish of the **Mesozoic** era. He died in 1810 and his daughter continued his work, beginning a career which was to bring her the title of the world's "most eminent female fossilist". In 1812, at the age of twelve, she uncovered an ichthyosaur (extinct marine animal with a huge head and tapering body), which is now in the British Museum. She seemed to have an uncanny instinct for the right place to search and, besides numerous other finds, discovered the first plesiosaur (extinct marine reptile) in 1824 and the first pterodactyl (extinct winged reptile) in 1826. She was befriended by, and corresponded on equal terms with, many eminent geologists of her day, among them Dr **Buckland** and Baron **Cuvier**.

Antler Pick. Neolithic Man used picks made from deer antlers in **flint mines**. Such picks were still being used in the **Bronze Age**.

Anuradhapura. This site in Ceylon was occupied from perhaps 200 B.C. until about A.D. 780 when it was abandoned as a result of Tamil raids. The surviving remains are almost wholly connected with Buddhism which appears to have been introduced into Ceylon in the Asokan epoch. The cultural connections with south India are clearly traceable, though sometimes areas farther north seem to have influenced the island. In its turn Ceylon seems to have played an important part in the transmission of Indian culture eastwards, particularly in the early period. The **stupas** or dagobas of Anuradhapura are of a number of types, but all consist of three basic components: a base, a dome and a superstructure. The present buildings on the site were much enlarged and remodelled in antiquity, but the *Mahavamsa*, the Great Chronicle, gives an account of them which adds to our archaeological information. Many of the stupas attained a great size; Ruwanweli has a diameter of 254 feet and the finial is 180 feet above ground level. The relic chamber is in the brick-built dome. Altar projections, *wahalkada*, at the cardinal points are a feature of many dagobas. Some are surrounded by concentric rows of stone pillars (e.g., Thuparama). The *viharas* (halls) are rectangular in plan, with brick walls, and ranges of stone interior pillars to support the roof. The entrance is in the long face, which is approached by a staircase, fronted by a moonstone. This feature, which precedes most of the entrances to Anuradhapuran buildings, is a semicircular stone threshold slab decorated in zones with carvings of beasts, geese and lotus. The Lohapasada, of which only the foundations remain – 1600 granite pillars on a 250-feet-square base – was, according to the *Mahavamsa*, a nine-storied building of wood, with a copper-sheathed roof, decorated with jewels and ivory. After a fire in the fourth century A.D., it was rebuilt in five stories.

The sculpture of this period has a certain grand simplicity, probably deriving in part from the nature of the stone used, which does not allow any great portrayal of details. There is a tendency to large-scale work, with somewhat archaic and rigid poses. Some of the seated figures seem to relate to Kushana styles, rather than to those of **Amaravati** and Nagarjunikonda which is the source for the standing figures. No paintings from the earliest periods have survived, but those from **Sigiriya** are remarkable. These too have affinities with Amaravati, and these links with south India persist into Pallava times, as can be seen from the carvings on boulders of a low cliff surrounding a tank at the Isurumuniya Vihara. This work is very close in style and technique to that of Mamallapuram. *See* plates 14-15, pages 64-65.

Anyang was in Honan Province, China. The archaeological investigation of this site established the definite existence of the Shang dynasty (about 1450–1050 B.C.), hitherto only known from documentary sources of disputed reliability. The culture has been described, by Eberhard, as that of a peasant civilization with towns. Of these Anyang was one. It was surrounded by a mud wall (*compare* **Lung Shan**) with the ruler's palace in the middle, surrounded by the rectangular houses of the palace dependants, notably artisans. Bronze was worked in the town and shows two distinct cultural patterns. The weapons are of a northern Eurasiatic type while the bronze vessels, of great technical skill and beauty, have affinities with southern styles. Bronze was, however, always dear – it is probable that the great ceramic industry of China has developed largely because of the inadequacy of metal supplies – and it was supplemented by a number of earthenware vessels, some of which lack only the characteristic glaze to be classed as true porcelains, the paste being a brilliant white. There is also a simple grey ware, undecorated, in contrast to the white which often shows stamped patterns of the type found on some of the bronzes. Silk was in use, another southern trait in the Shang culture, and a number of vegetable fibres including hemp, but there is no evidence for the use of wool. Writing, in rudimentary characters, was in use: about 2,000 characters, against perhaps 50,000 for the whole period of Chinese history. Much of the writing was in the form of oracular consultations (*see* **Oracle Bones**).

Agriculture was carried on without the plough, though a spade held by one worker and towed by a rope by a second was in use, as well as a hoe. Irrigation was in use. Crops included rice, wheat and millet; cattle, water-buffaloes, sheep, pigs and dogs were domesticated; horses were rare. Horses became more common in Middle Shang times, apparently under influence from nomadic peoples from the north-west. The wheeled vehicle – a form of war chariot – appears at this time and with it the emergence of a controlling nobility which led, in turn, to the development of a feudal society. The possession of the war chariot also enabled the Shang dynasty to extend its territorial sway. This probably led to its downfall, for its military techniques were in advance of the available administrative and communication systems, and rebellions grew more frequent. One of these led to the collapse of the dynasty at the hands of the most powerful of its feudatories, the state of Chou (about 1050 B.C.). There is clear evidence of human sacrifice at Shang sites, and burials, particularly of the nobility, were accompanied by large-scale offerings. The burials were associated with chariots – a feature which has western affinities. From the skeletal evidence, it is obvious that the ethnic make-up was like that of present-day northern China, but some of the cultural pattern of the Chinese was still missing. The religion was still primarily concerned with agrarian fertility, the family system still pronouncedly matriarchal. Ancestor-worship of the classic kind was still to appear. The fusion of Shang and Chou was to establish a full Chinese cultural pattern. *See* plates 11, 16, pages 61, 66.

Anyathian. This term, which comes from the Burmese *anyatha* – a native of Upper Burma, is applied to the Palaeolithic industries of Burma, particularly of the Irrawaddy Valley. The tools, which are of silicified **tuffs** and fossil wood, date from the beginning of the Middle Pleistocene onwards; there is evidence to suggest a considerable persistence of Palaeolithic types into the Holocene (*see* **Quaternary Period**). The industry consists of various types of choppers and chopping-tools, **core** tools, with a few simple **flakes**. (Their primitive appearance is, in fact, a probable result of the nature of the raw material, flint being unknown in Burma.) The choppers are mostly made on cores, flaked usually on one side only, to produce a round, oval or straight cutting-edge. Only occasionally are they made on flakes. The chopping-tools are always on cores, usually on pebbles. The edge is sinuous, and produced by alternate flaking. A tabular form of this is made on a core with a straight, slightly rounded or even pointed edge and is characterized by its square or rectangular section, in contrast with the round or oval forms of the other types. This is often classified as a hand-adze. The scrapers are generally only to be distinguished by size from the other groups. They are formed on both cores and on flakes. As is the case with other **Further Asian Palaeolithic** industries, the Anyathian is characterized by a marked preference for adze rather than axe forms.

Apes, Fossil, *see* Fossil Apes.

Archaean. The oldest era of the earth's history, beginning some 520,000,000 years ago. It saw the beginnings of life in the form of seaweeds and of invertebrate animals. It is sometimes divided into the Azoic, or life-less, era, and the Proterozoic era when life first began to stir. It was succeeded by the **Palaeozoic** era.

Archaeology. Anything that a man makes is in some small way a reflection of himself and of the outlook of the culture in which he lives. It will probably also, for man is very conservative and dislikes change, be a copy, if with subtle differences, of what his predecessors have made in the same line.

Archaeologists have made use of these two facts in their exploration of the past, and of the **cultures** that existed before history began. They dig up with extreme care the relics that are to be found on ancient sites and, by examining all that they find with meticulous thoroughness, are able to piece together an immense amount of information about the people who used to occupy the site, their ways, their habits, the details of their daily lives.

The job is a skilled one because so much has perished and has to be identified by subtle signs, invisible to the untrained eye. A wooden post may decay and disappear, but leave a hole running through the earth which can be filled with plaster of paris and so enable the shape of the post to be recovered. A piece of matting can decay entirely, and yet its imprint in the soil, if carefully exposed, can be sufficiently recovered for a photograph to be taken of it. Very damp conditions can, somewhat paradoxically, be very good for preservation; the article on **Tolund Man** (*see* plate 143, page 443) tells of the remarkable discovery that was made in 1950 in a peat bog in Denmark.

For dating his finds the archaeologist relies on the principle of stratification – that the oldest part of a site is always to be found at the lowest level, with later ages leaving their deposits in order of time from the bottom upwards. By digging from the top downwards the archaeologist can trace the different types of object or building from the latest and most advanced specimens back to the earlier and more primitive ones – a procedure known as typology, the study of the way types changes. Types, especially of pottery, can be compared with similar finds from sites elsewhere, and so a picture built up of trading and communications.

Sometimes the archaeologist makes spectacular finds, such as at **Vix, Sutton Hoo** (*see* plate 136, page 436), **Tutankhamun's Tomb** (*see* plate 145, page 465), but more often his finds are flakes of flint, sherds of pottery, broken bones, which he treasures as much as gold because they enable him to build up the history of man from its earliest beginnings, more than half a million years ago.

Archaic. A term which is used sometimes of prehistory in general, sometimes of the early stages of civilization.

Argon Potassium Dating. Potassium is an element that occurs commonly in minerals. One kind of potassium atom, potassium^{40}, is radioactive and decays very slowly to argon. Argon is a gas and is retained between the grains of the mineral. The age of a mineral containing potassium can be estimated by finding how much of the original potassium^{40} has changed to argon. This is done by measuring the ratio of argon to potassium^{40} in the mineral. If the grain size is large a correction must be made for argon which escapes. The method is useful on a geological time scale for measuring ages of rocks greater than 10,000,000 years.

Arikamedu. Since 1775 occasional finds of Roman coins have testified to the ancient trade with southern India which was known from Greek, Latin and Tamil sources, but the archaeology of the area has been little studied and the **culture sequence** remained largely unknown until 1937. In that year remains including Roman pottery were discovered at Arikamedu, a site two miles from the city of Pondicherry (then a French possession) on the south-east coast of India. Between 1944 and 1949 three seasons of excavation were carried out by French workers, including J. M. Casal, and one by the Indian Archaeological Department under the direction of Sir Mortimer Wheeler. As a result it can be said that a small Iron Age settlement existed there which at a certain date was augmented by a trading station importing Roman goods including Arretine ware, amphorae, glass, etc.

The importance of the site was recognized by Wheeler; it lay in the fact that the Roman products, particularly the Arretine ware, gave a means of cross-dating to the local culture sequence. He further showed that this sequence was comparable to that found at Brahmagiri and Chandravalli several hundred miles away on the Deccan Plateau, although the Roman export objects were not found there. From the excavation at Arikamedu, then, and from the subsequent work carried out in south India, a foundation has been laid for our knowledge of the culture sequence of late prehistoric and early historic times.

In the Deccan Plateau there is evidence of **Neolithic** culture which is described elsewhere (*see* **India, Prehistoric**). This culture may be divided into a lower and upper phase. There are indications, which still await proof, that during the upper phase the culture spread to the south-east coast.

Throughout the peninsula the next culture may be described as **Iron Age**. It is mainly known from a profusion of stone-cist and stone-circle graves which invariably produce pottery of typical red-and-black ware and characteristic forms. Along with these go a variety of iron implements, also characterized by certain distinct forms. This Iron Age culture is sometimes called, from the type of grave, **megalithic**. The duration of the period in south India is not yet certain, but it may be inferred that it was already flourishing when **Asoka Maurya** carved his rock edicts in the Deccan. The terminal date, at Arikamedu at least, can be fixed with some certainty. Here the red-and-black ware of the graves is found in the settlement area directly underlying the characteristic pottery which accompanies the Roman imports. The date of the imports is the last quarter of the first century B.C. and the first half of the first century A.D.

The next period, which we may call Early Historic, is one in which not only Roman imports arrive but also there is much evidence of culture contacts with north India. Certain pottery types arrive which closely reflect those of the Ganges Valley and the north-west. This is almost certainly the time when north Indian culture became an important feature in the south.

Arrow-heads. Bows and arrows seem to have been invented towards the end of the Upper **Palaeolithic**. Arrow-heads were made of **flint**, flakes being struck from the **core** for this purpose. Such arrowheads continued in use into the **Bronze Age**, then disappeared with the introduction of iron.

Arrow-straightener. A device invented by **Neolithic** man for bending straight the shafts of arrows. Normally made of bone or antler it had a hole through which the shaft was passed, and against which it was strained straight after being heated near a flame.

Artifact. An object produced by the skill of man who shapes or fashions it for his use. It is still disputed whether **eoliths** are artifacts or the result of natural breakages.

Art, Prehistoric, *see* Prehistoric Art.

Aryan is a linguistic term derived from the Sanskrit *Arya*, a name which the Rigvedic (*see* **Rigveda**) conquerors of India used to distinguish themselves from the local non-Aryan populace. Iranian is its variant. The Indo-Iranian forms a language group and also bears some affinity with the Teutonic, Italic, Romance, Celtic, Greek, Slavonic, Baltic, Albanian, and Armenian groups of languages. The discovery of this relationship in the eighteenth century led to the recognition of a family of Indo-European languages. This is a purely linguistic group.

Another step was to speak of a common ancestry of these languages, and it was not difficult to pass from a common tongue to the speakers themselves. Scholars talked of an Indo-European or, more conveniently, an Aryan race, and thus provided fuel for the protagonists of extreme racialism. The philologists have reconstructed a stock of words common to these languages and have built up a picture of the culture which is attributed to the original Indo-Europeans. This culture, as they point out, was **Neolithic** (or, more correctly, **Chalcolithic** as the use of metal was known) with domesticated animals, the horse being the favourite. From the fauna it has been argued that the climate of the original habitat was continental, such as appears in the Eurasiatic continent north of the mountain axis and east of the Alps. From the use of the foreign words, *ayos* and *roundhos*, for metal it is further suggested that the Indo-Europeans lived not far from the **Bronze Age** civilization of western Asia. The habitat is usually placed in one or another region within the wide area lying between the Semitic concentration on the south and the Fino-Ugrian on the north. But archaeology has not yet been able to identify any particular culture as Aryan, much less trace its spread in the countries where the allied languages are spoken today. The main difficulty is due to the fact that both culture and language are mixed products and that various factors influence their formation. The allied cultures and languages need not have a common ancestry, nor can they be attributed to any particular race. The little archaeological detail that is known about the "Aryans" clearly bears out this point.

About 1900 or 1800 B.C. the cuneiform Hittite, an Indo-European language, appears in central Asia Minor, but every feature of the material **Hittite** culture – the **cuneiform** script, religion, literature and material remains – is derived from the previous occupants of the area, the Hattians, who also gave them their name. About the beginning of the sixteenth century B.C. the **Kassite** dynasty was established in Babylon and the kingdom of Mitanni was founded in northern Mesopotamia. The names of Indo-Aryan gods form parts of the names of the Kassite rulers, though their language was not Indo-European. The same is true of the kings of Mitanni, who also worshipped Indo-Aryan gods, though their language was the non-Indo-European speech called the Hurrian. In these cases both the culture and the words are acquired from others. Again it is not possible to associate the Indo-Aryans who invaded north-west India in the second half of the second millennium B.C. with any certain material culture, though various traits have been pointed out. Yet the very fact that some languages bear closer affinity to one another than the others suggests a broad relationship, underlying which may be several factors.

The Indo-European is one such broad group which unites the far-flung elements in a common whole.

Ashlar Masonry. Square-hewn stones used as facing to a wall built of rubble or sometimes of brick.

Asoka Maurya (about 269 – 232 B.C.). Beyond doubt one of the greatest rulers of ancient India, Asoka was the grandson of Chandragupta, the founder of the **Mauryan** dynasty who contributed to the defeat of Alexander the Great in India (326–323 B.C.) and built up a mighty kingdom with its capital at Pataliputra (modern Patna). Some eight years after his accession, following his bloody conquest of the neighbouring state of Kalinga, Asoka was converted to the way of Righteousness (*Dharma*) and became a Buddhist. This change affected his whole life and policy, and henceforth he proclaimed his belief in non-violence and in the conquest of Righteousness, making these the key-notes of his government. He sent out Buddhist missions to many countries including the kings of Syria, Egypt and Macedon, and to other neighbouring states which perhaps already recognized his suzerainty. Tradition has it that his own son headed the mission to Ceylon. Asoka also caused a series of rock edicts to be cut throughout his own domains, and these constitute the first historical documents available in Indian history. Throughout India they are carved in the *Brahmi* script (the ancestor of all later Indian scripts), but in the North-West Frontier of Pakistan several are in the *Kharosthi* script adapted from Aramaic. Finally in eastern Afghanistan there are two inscriptions, the one in Aramaic and the other, recently discovered near Kandahar, in Aramaic and Greek. The pillars of Asoka are described in the article on the **Mauryan Empire**.

Assyrians. The name of this people is a Latinized form of that (Ashur) which they bore in common with their land and their national god. Ashur was also the name of their principal city, the ruins of which stand on the River Tigris in Mesopotamia between its confluences with the Upper and Lower Zab tributaries. But in the years of their greatest ascendancy it was the angle of country between the Tigris and the Upper Zab which contained their seats of power, **Nineveh**, Kalhu, and Arbail, and formed the kernel of their homeland.

About the middle of the third millennium B.C. the inhabitants of Ashur had a material culture hardly differing from the **Sumerians** in the south, and subsequently, in the periods of **Accad** (about 2300 B.C.) and the third dynasty of **Ur** (about 2000 B.C.), the land of Ashur was still subject to these alien if related rulers. The eighteenth century B.C. saw the first period of Assyrian ascendancy, under Shamshi-Adad I, but their leader was an immigrant and there was nothing specifically Assyrian about his rule. Not until the middle of the fourteenth century, when the centre of affairs had moved into the west, did the Assyrians appear in their full identity as one of the contenders, with Mitanni, **Egypt**, the **Hittites**, and the **Babylonians**, for supremacy in the world of western Asia. Their fortunes underwent several vicissitudes, but from the reign of Tiglath-Pileser III (745–727 B.C.) dated the final expansion of Assyria into an empire embracing not only all the lands from the Zagros mountains to the Levant, but even, for a time, Egypt itself. It is in this final character, of warriors and oppressors, that the Assyrians are known to the modern world, chiefly through the narratives and allusions of the Old Testament, where they have an odious reputation which their own records, disclosed only in the last century, do little to redeem. This vast but short-lived empire came to a catastrophic end in 612 B.C. with the fall and destruction of Nineveh, after which the Assyrians disappeared as a nation for ever.

In a measure hardly equalled elsewhere the "king of Assyria" concentrated the forces and genius of his people, and is now seen as the "oriental despot" to perfection. Both literature and art put him in the forefront of interest; he was the agent on earth of the national god Ashur, and as leader in war, as planner and executive in peace, both service of the gods and welfare of the people were alike his supreme responsibility. In these functions individual kings are variously portrayed by their records, often copious, and they attain thus some degree of personal character. As these records are mainly of war the king too often appears as a ruthless conqueror, boasting without restraint of his wrath, his heroism, his victories, and the abominable cruelties which he wreaked upon his victims. Behind such self-portraits, as of the merciless Ashur-nasir-pal II (883–859 B.C.), disappear the figures of more enlightened and constructive monarchs such as Sennacherib (704–681 B.C.) who was

Photo: *Gisèle Freund*

PLATE III. AZTECS: funerary urn.

Photo: British Museum

PLATE 17. ASSYRIANS: Ashur-nasir-pal and a winged eagle-headed god before the sacred tree, relief from Nimrud. *(British Museum, London)*

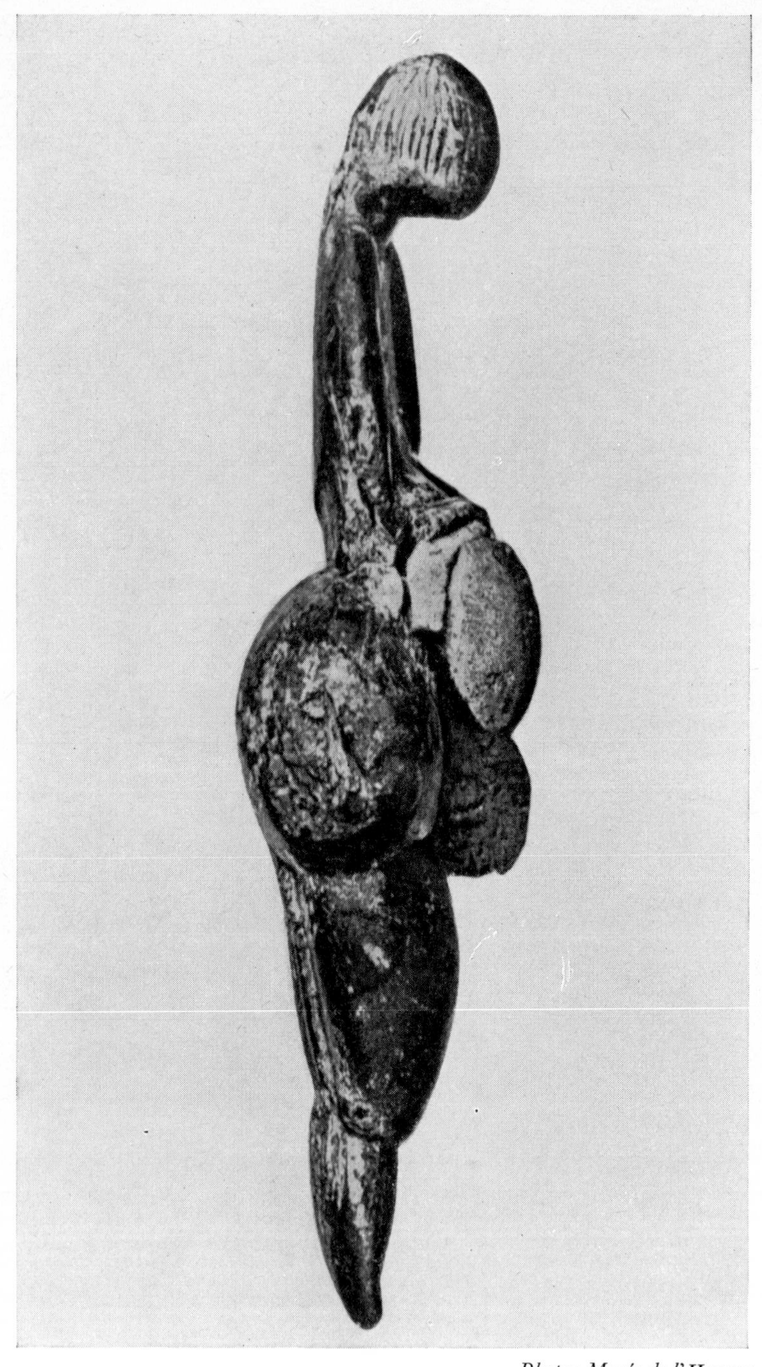

Photo: Musée de l'Homme

PLATE 18. AURIGNACIAN: Venus of Lespugne from the Haute Garonne, France. *(Musée de l'Homme, Paris)*

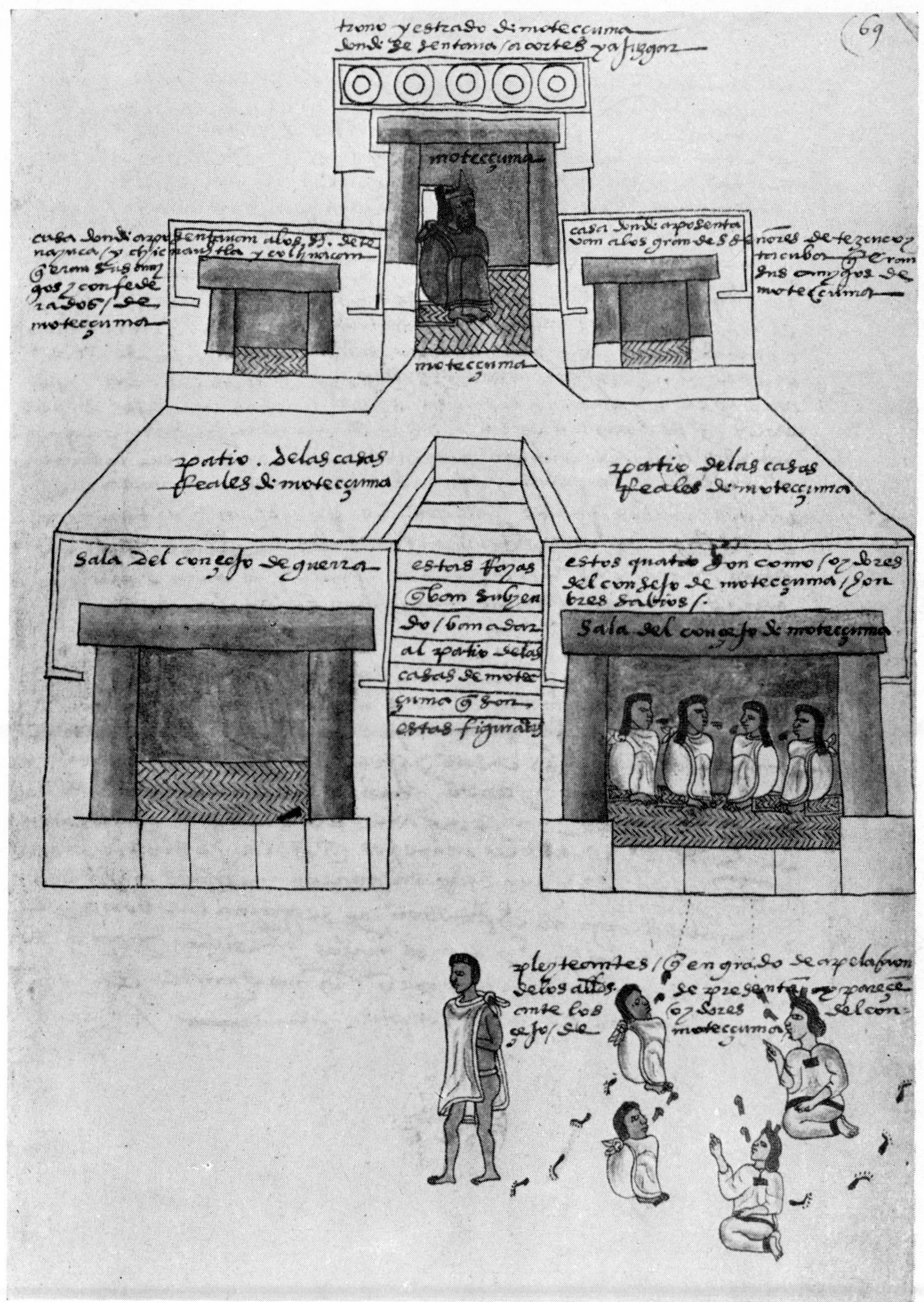

Photo: University Press, Oxford

PLATE 19. AZTECS: page from the Codex Mendoza showing Montezuma's Palace. The Codex Mendoza was prepared in about A.D. 1540 by the order of Don Antonio de Mendoza, the first Viceroy of New Spain, for the Emperor Charles V and is an account of the life and customs of Mexico at that time. *(Bodleian Library, Oxford)*

Photo: Naturhistorisches Museum

PLATE 20. AURIGNACIAN: the Venus of Willendorf, one of the best known fertility figures. *(Naturhistorisches Museum, Vienna)*

Photo: British Museum

PLATE 21. AZTECS: turquoise mosaic pectoral ornament in the form of a double headed serpent, believed to be part of the treasure given by the Aztec ruler Montezume to Hernando Cortez and sent by him to the Emperor Charles v. Length 18 inches. *(British Museum, London)*

Photo: British Museum

PLATE 22. AZTECS: Andesite mask representing the god Xipe Totec, fourteenth century A.D.
(British Museum, London)

Photo: A. C. Barrington Brown

Plate 23. Baalbek: the Temple of Jupiter.

Photo: British Museum

PLATE 24. BEAKER PEOPLE: beaker found with a skeleton at Denton, Lincolnshire. *(British Museum, London)*

Photo: Exclusive News Agency

PLATE 25. BEHISTUN ROCK: detail of relief, showing Ahura Mazda, winged god of the Persians, grasping the ring which conferred kingship.

Photo: Exclusive News Agency

PLATE 26. ALACA HÖYÜK: stone symbol at foot of one of the Hittite sphinxes.

Photo: Anthony Christie

PLATE 27. BOROBUDUR: Buddha figure on upper terrace. The figure was originally enclosed in a stupa of the type seen in the background.

Photo: Exclusive News Agency

PLATE 28. BOROBUDUR: gallery carving – upper register: the bath of the Buddha; lower register: a Jataka story. The large vessel with outriggers is typical of south-eastern shipping in the early centuries of the Christian era.

PLATE 29. CARNAC: the alignments.

Photo: Oriental Institute, University of Chicago

PLATE 30. James Henry BREASTED (1865–1935), photograph.

Photo: India Office Library, Commonwealth Relations Office

PLATE 31. BUDDHIST ART AND ARCHITECTURE: under the Bo-tree the Bodhisattva attains Enlightenment and becomes the Buddha (the scene depicts the Bodhi shrine at Bodh Gaya), detail of east gateway, Sanchi.

A

B

Photo: Anthony Christie

PLATE 32. CHAMS: (A) dancing girl, probably a heavenly being. (B) *Dvarapala*, or temple doorkeeper; the ferocious expression is designed to repel the forces of evil. Tenth to eleventh century A.D.

Photo: Detroit Institute of Arts

PLATE IV. BABYLON: relief of a dragon from the Ishtar Gate at Babylon. (*Detroit Institute of Arts, Detroit*)

much more than the "wolf on the fold" abhorred by biblical and modern tradition. At home he was a town-planner and an engineer of great public works and water-supplies, himself a notable inventor with a keen interest in devising new technical processes and introducing to his country foreign resources such as the cotton shrub, thereby bestowing upon his people a novel clothing material.

Military expeditions were generally led by the king himself, whose prowess is belauded by the inscriptions, while his figure appears dominant in the carved pictures which adorned the walls of his palace. The army excelled most in the capture, by ramps and battering-rams, of walled cities, from which captives and rich spoils were carried off, and hostile rulers haled out to submission and often to death; rebels whose defiance had been most flagrant were sometimes doomed to fiendish tortures, such as being impaled or skinned alive. Insistence upon such scenes and descriptions has given the Assyrians a character of barbarity to the disregard of their attainments in the ways of civilization.

The Assyrians had early in their history an assembled body of laws, and their business was ruled by written agreements, the observance of which, and the disputes arising therefrom, were adjudicated on by regular courts and enforced by characteristically severe penalties. These private "contracts" and business letters were but one branch of the literary activity in which the Assyrians took such pride. They chose with care and perfected by a long education a large class of scribes whose writings, preserved in the difficult **cuneiform** script upon clay tablets, have preserved knowledge of their ancient world in such detail as we hardly possess even for the classical periods of Greece and Rome. Literature was fostered and even personally cultivated by kings, who had early begun the practice of collecting clay "books" (as they also collected zoological and botanical specimens), and the still extensive remains of the library of Ashur-banipal (668–626 B.C.) in the British Museum exhibit the remarkable literary wealth of the Assyrians, not only in religious compositions, but in myths and epics, historical writing, grammatical texts, scientific classification, and even technology. *See* plate 17, page 87.

Asuka is a Japanese cultural period (A.D. 538–645). In this period Yamato State was established and Buddhism was introduced. Relations between Yamato and the three kingdoms of **Korea** formed a link with the northern Wei dynasty of China (A.D. 386–535) and it was from the art of the Wei that the first Japanese Buddhist art derived its inspiration and, by means of Chinese artists, established centres which were to produce work of high artistic excellence. The temporary proscription of Buddhism in China in A.D. 574 was no doubt partly responsible for this efflorescence which led, by A.D. 640, to the construction of at least forty-six temples. Most of these, being in wood, have perished, but much of the Horyuji monastery (A.D. 607, probably rebuilt in the same style in A.D. 708), has survived. The Kondo Golden Hall, the Pagoda, a roofed gallery and gate demonstrate the style and technical skills of this period, the whole being harmoniously spaced and grouped. The sculpture, like the buildings, shows clear evidence of Chinese and Korean influence, and also gives some indication of changes due to the use of bronze and wood where the original models were in stone. A Buddhist triad in the Kondo shows a somewhat stiff archaic manner, but that there was another tradition is clear from a number of images of Kwannon which, while obviously of Chinese inspiration, show a much greater technical mastery and command of material. In painting the progress is not so great and the surviving examples are of "applied" rather than of "pure" art. Metal-work shows considerable advance over that of earlier periods.

Athens is situated on the Attic plain four miles from its harbour, Piraeus. From comparatively small beginnings as a **Mycenaean** centre it became a dominant city of Greece, a strong colonial power, and, especially under Pericles, a great intellectual and artistic centre. It already had a Greek-speaking **Ionian** population in the second millennium B.C. After the collapse of the Mycenaean Empire, civilization in Athens was forced to begin afresh.

Nothing is known of the kings of Athens. From the seventh century B.C. it was ruled by a council of Areopagites made up of aristocratic property owners. Archons or chief magistrates were also drawn from this class. The Archon Solon introduced liberalizing and ultimately anti-aristocratic measures and established a new law-code which remained effective for several centuries. During the latter part of the sixth century B.C. Athens was ruled by tyrants, the second of whom, Hippias, lost support because of his submissiveness to the Persian Darius. In 507 B.C. Cleisthenes founded a democracy in which every Athenian free-man could play his part in the government and in which offices were widely distributed. This enterprise, though ultimately a failure, was the step that was to result in Periclean Athens.

Athens answered the menace of Persian invasion by its victories at Marathon in Attica in 490 B.C., at sea at Salamis in 480 B.C. and the following year at Plataea. In 478–477 B.C. it was asked to organize Greek resources outside the Peninsula for a campaign against Persia. This prospered and Athens was simultaneously founding an empire, but a rupture with Sparta followed and, unable to fight both Sparta and Persia, Athens made peace with the latter in 449 B.C. Pericles came to power at the beginning of this crisis. His chief constitutional innovation was the establishment of completely democratic law courts with citizen juries. The Periclean era was particularly rich in art and literature. During the fifth century B.C. the great tragedies of Aeschylus, Sophocles and Euripides were written; somewhat later (mid-fifth to late fourth century B.C.) came the comedies of Aristophanes and Menander. The Acropolis was rebuilt under Pericles.

The Peloponnesian War against Sparta ruined Periclean civilization. The years 360–350 B.C. were marked by the revolt of Athens' allies and the rise of Macedon, both bringing about the end of Athens' power.

Under the Roman Empire Athens was patronized by the wealth of the Emperors. During this period it was of importance chiefly as an academic centre. Its schools were finally closed in A.D. 529.

The Athenian Acropolis has few Mycenaean remains and what is left dates mostly from the period when it was one of the most important religious centres, especially for the worship of the city goddess Athena. The Parthenon, Erechtheum and Temple of Athena Nike are all part of the scheme for the Acropolis initiated by Pericles and carried out with Phidias as overseer. The Parthenon, begun in 447–446 B.C., contained Phidias' gold and ivory statue of Athena and was decorated with the 524-foot Parthenon Frieze, illustrating the Panathenaic Festival procession, superb pedimental sculptures and ninety-two metopes of combat scenes. The Erechtheum, finished in 407 B.C., housed different cults, its plan being somewhat diffuse as a result. Among its fine stone carvings were the six maiden caryatids of the South Porch. The Americans have been excavating the Athenian civic centre, the Agora, since 1931. Buildings there included the early Council Chamber (*Bouleuterion*), subsequently enlarged, the circular Tholos for the presidents of the Council, long porticoes (*Stoai*) and a firstcentury B.C. concert hall (*Odeion*).

Atlanthropus. The name given to a skull of a **Fossil Man** found in Algeria and regarded as the African parallel to **Pithecanthropus.**

Atlantis. The legend of Atlantis first appears in Plato who says the story came from an Egyptian priest. Atlantis is described as an island, in the Atlantic west of Gibraltar, which was destroyed before 9000 B.C. because of the wickedness of its inhabitants. Guesses at its position have ranged from the Canaries to America. The name was borrowed by the palaeogeographers for the vast continent which, in Jurassic times (some 140 to 170 million years ago), covered the northern hemisphere from western America to England.

Aurignacian. A highly developed Upper **Palaeolithic** culture which succeeded the **Châtelperronian** in central France. It seems likely that the Aurignacians, a people of modern European physical type, migrated to Europe after developing their distinctive culture elsewhere, probably in Asia. Their **stone tools** show fine workmanship: they produced scrapers and **burins** of distinctive types and a typical figure-of-eight shaped blade with rounded ends. They also used bone, horn and ivory, and made necklaces and other personal ornaments. In addition, they developed the arts of cave-painting and sculpture. *See* plates 18, 20, pages 88, 90.

Australopithecus. The name "Australopithecus" – the "southern ape" – was given by Professor Raymond Dart of Johannesburg to a cranium found in 1924 during quarrying at Taungs in Cape Province. Since then a number of other bones have been found in similar circumstances. These have established the presence in South Africa of a group of "near-men" or "man-apes", named, after the first one discovered, the Australopithecinae.

The original Australopithecus cranium was of a young creature. Beside the face and lower jaw there was an almost complete cast of the inside of the skull. The teeth were preserved at an interesting stage, for the first permanent molars could be seen as well as the complete set of milk teeth.

In many ways the cranium resembles a young chimpanzee, although the brain is proportionately bigger than an ape's. The teeth are human in many respects. The dental arch is curved, like that of man, the canine teeth do not project above the other teeth, and the premolars have a human bicuspid shape. The wear on the teeth made by chewing suggests a strange conclusion. Apes, with their projecting canine teeth, move the lower jaw backwards and forwards in chewing. Australopithecus, on the other hand, must have moved its jaws from side to side like a human, for the crowns of the teeth are worn down to an almost flat surface.

This skull, and the other remains of Australopithecinae, have been found in the limestone fillings of caves, which accumulated without clear stratification. It appears from the animal fossils that were found with them, however, that the skulls can be dated to the early part of the Pleistocene, about half a million years ago. (*See also* **Primates, Prehuman Evolution of**.)

Avebury, a small village in Wiltshire, England, about six miles from Marlborough, is famous as one of the most important and interesting sites of archaeological research in England.

In particular, there is a huge **stone circle**, which may be the largest yet known in the world. The modern village of Avebury stands inside this circle which encloses an area of over twenty-eight acres and measures some 1,200 feet in diameter. The circle is made up of about a hundred standing stones and has three entrances, though there were originally four at approximately north, south, east and west. It is surrounded by a huge ditch over forty feet wide at the top but with variations of depth from thirty feet upwards.

Inside the large circle are two very much smaller ones, measuring some 300 feet in diameter and again formed of standing stones. Of these two circles, the northern one had three standing stones at its centre, the southern, one stone.

Originally, as at Stonehenge, the great circle was approached by an avenue consisting of standing stones about fifty feet apart, now known as the West Kennet Avenue. This runs for over a mile to a site where, until 1724, there were two further concentric circles of stone.

To the south-west of the great circle there is another avenue, known as the Beckhampton, of which not so much now remains, but its course is still quite clear. A good deal of destruction took place after the first proper records of the whole site had been made in the eighteenth century.

The whole complex of stone found at Avebury is of the local sarsen and there is no "foreign" stone such as is found at **Stonehenge**. The individual blocks of stone vary in height between five and twenty feet above the ground and from three to twelve feet in breadth. The stones were sunk in rather small sockets, wedged with wood. During the Middle Ages many of the stones were displaced and afterwards buried by soil.

The question of dating the Avebury circles has given rise to a good deal of speculation. A Late **Neolithic** date has been suggested. Ritual deposits or burials near the stones include examples of early **Bronze Age** beaker pottery but the avenue was found to cross an earlier, Late Neolithic site.

Between 1908 and 1938 much excavation was done. The great bank and ditch round the outer perimeter were found to be of the early Bronze Age and there were indications that from the earliest times demolitions and alterations of plan and layout had been made. So it is fair to say that the entire Avebury complex can be classified as being within the early Bronze Age, though not built within any one short period of time.

On the neighbouring downs there are many barrows to be found, including a huge mound on Silbury Hill, and at Overton Hill, to which leads West Kennet Avenue, there are the two smaller circles of stone already referred to, which may in fact precede everything else at this site in date.

Avebury as a whole is remarkable for its huge size and for the complexity of the layout. It is one of a number of British Bronze Age monuments which can come under the general classification of open temples, but there is no indication that it was orientated in any specific direction.

Axe, *see* Hand-axe.

Azilian. The **Mesolithic** Azilian culture is named after the great Mas d'Azil cave forty miles from Toulouse, on the French side of the Pyrenees. The deposits lay above **Magdalenian** layers, demonstrating that the Azilians must have lived after the end of the Pleistocene, about 8000 B.C. They were food-gatherers, not farmers, but had domesticated the dog. As with other Mesolithic cultures, the flint implements are tiny **microliths**, like the "thumb-nail" scrapers used for dressing skins. There was no heavy **stone tool** equipment, but bone and antler were extensively used. Mammoth had become extinct, so that ivory was no longer available, nor was reindeer antler, for these beasts had moved northwards following the retreating ice-sheet. But the red deer was now able to live in southern France, and its antlers were widely used for the harpoons that are typical of the Azilian culture. Most are barbed on both sides, and have a perforation at the base. They were designed to be attached to a shaft by a cord, so that if vegetation brushed out the shaft from the quarry, the harpoon head would remain in the body, and ultimately kill. They were used against land animals, not for fishing as the name suggests.

Curious objects found on Azilian sites are smooth river pebbles, mostly quartzite, painted with red ochre. The designs include stripes, spots, and zigzags, and some might be degenerate representations of the human figure. Some have been found deliberately broken. Their function is unknown, but they may have corresponded to the sacred "churinga" of some Australian aborigines.

Two skull-nests found at Ofnet in Bavaria provide evidence of head-hunting by Azilians. There were six skulls in one, and twenty-seven in the other, all arranged to face west, and covered with red ochre. Neck vertebrae attached to some skulls show marks of cuts.

Azilian sites have been found in caves in the south of France, central Europe, Belgium, and north Britain.

Aztecs. The word Aztec, more properly applied to the culture flourishing in Mexico at the time of the Spanish conquest, is popularly applied to the Tenochcas, the tribe inhabiting Mexico City which they called Tenochtitlán.

Our sources are a number of pictographic records made by the Aztecs themselves and by the Mixtecs, historico-legendary accounts written by Mexicans after the conquest, the descriptions of the Conquistadores, and the work of archaeologists such as Batres, Gamio, Martinez del Rio, and Palacios to mention only a few.

The Tenochcas were a Nahua-speaking tribe, who came into the Valley of Mexico along with other nomads, known as Chichimecs, after the eclipse of the Toltecs. These wanderers must have overcome many of the centres of Toltec culture and settled down, adopting much of the civilization of their predecessors. This hybrid culture derived its elements not only from the Toltecs, but also from the Mixtecs farther south.

The Tenochcas claimed to have started their wanderings from a cave in A.D. 1168. For a time they settled in Chapultepec. But frequent quarrels with their neighbours, culminating in a raid on Tenayuca, led to a combined punitive expedition against them and the enslavement of the majority by the Culhuas. A remnant fled to an island in the Lake of Mexico. This was where they saw an omen, long foretold, of an eagle on a cactus eating a snake, and accordingly founded their city there. Whether this occurred when the remnant fled from the Culhuas is uncertain, but a small band of outlaws, who adopted the eagle and serpent as their name-**glyph** grew into the dominant power in Mexico. They evolved a method of reclaiming land by piling mud from the lake into basketry structures, which were subsequently consolidated and anchored by vegetation and tree roots – the *chinampas* described by the Spaniards.

Gradually they extended their sway, absorbing the neighbouring island of Tlatelolco among other places until at the time of the conquest they dominated most of the country as far as the Gulf Coast. They were unable to make any real headway in Michoacan and their conquests in the south were being resisted by the Mixtecs and Zapotecs in Oaxaca when the Spaniards came.

A sketchy account of their history can be seen in the Mendoza Codex, a post-conquest pictographic document now in the Bodleian Library at Oxford. In this each successive ruler is shown as a seated figure wearing a blue diadem, and with his name-glyph beside him. The years of his reign are shown by the signs for their opening days; and his conquests by a burning temple and the name-glyph of the city concerned. The same names occur many times because the Aztecs did not absorb or colonize their conquests, being content to exact a tribute. At intervals, of course, cities would rebel. Other sections of the Codex deal with the tribute exacted and with the education of the young. The **pictograms** are sometimes **ideograms** like the burning temple; others are syllabic like many of the name-glyphs, and others again are purely illustrative. The calendar was based on a sacred period of 260 days combined with a solar year of 365 days. The first day of the sacred period coincided with the beginning of the solar year once in fifty-two years. They believed that in the past great disasters had occurred on such occasions. The world had been destroyed on four occasions: first by Tezcatlipoca when jaguars ate up mankind; secondly when the wind god Quetzalcoatl, the Feathered Serpent, sent a hurricane; thirdly when Tlaloc the rain god sent a fiery rain and fourthly when Chalchihuitlicue sent floods. One day it would be destroyed again by earthquakes.

All Central American religion was a personification of the forces of nature. All religious endeavour was aimed at controlling or propitiating the gods embodying these forces. In addition to their own tribal deity Huitzilopochtli (Humming-bird Wizard) the Aztecs adopted many of the Toltec gods. Xipe Totec, the flayed skins of whose victims were worn by his priests, possibly to represent rejuvenation, and Tlaloc, both fully established in the Classic period at Teotihuacán, took their places with the Toltec Quetzalcoatl beside newcomers like Tonatiuh and Tezcatilpoca. Chalchihuitlicue, a water goddess, and the ferocious earth goddess Coatlicue, the mother of the gods, who wore a skirt of writhing snakes, and many others found places in the Aztec pantheon.

Special propitiation took place at the beginning of a fifty-two year period. All fires were put out and the ruler anxiously awaited the dawn, firestick in hand, ready to kindle the New Fire as soon as he saw the sun. The old Temples were rebuilt and there was general relief. This practice has been of inestimable value to archaeologists, since the age of an Aztec temple can be determined by the number of times it has been rebuilt. Tenayuca, for example, built in Chichimec times, has no less than eight layers.

Warfare too served the gods. Its main object was to provide prisoners for sacrifice, thus serving simultaneously the needs of public policy in the fields of both foreign policy and religion. Boys started their military training at fifteen, went to war at twenty and were not allowed to cut their hair short until they had taken a prisoner. Repeated failure to take a prisoner led to expulsion from the army and disgrace. The highest awards they could obtain were the right to wear a jaguar skin or an eagle skin.

But war was only one side of Aztec life. Traders brought in the produce of distant parts of Mexico and a stream of tribute flowed in from the conquered cities; jade and sea-shells for their jewellery, feathers for their ceremonial clothing, cacao beans, raw cotton for their spinners, blankets, and beautifully embroidered cloths. A market was held in Tlatelolco, with most careful rules for its proper conduct. Their artisans were skilled in working jade and other hard stones, in casting gold for their jewellery, in the manufacture of feather mosaics and in the making of the beautiful mosaic masks of turquoise.

The city itself, built on an island, was approached by four causeways, wide enough for ten men to walk abreast. In the middle was the ceremonial centre dominated by a great pyramid crowned by the twin temples of Tlaloc and Tezcatlipoca. Nearby was the circular temple of Quetzalcoatl. In the same area were the Tzompantli, where skulls of their victims were preserved, the ball court for a sacred game played with a solid rubber ball, and many other temples. The city, mostly reclaimed from the lake, was intersected by a multitude of canals, laid out in rectangles like the street of a modern American city.

Cortez and his followers owed their successful conquest to a number of causes. The almost ritual view of war was a severe handicap, when the Aztecs were confronted with the practical and ruthless Spaniards. A number of signs and portents indicative of disaster were also a great handicap. Perhaps the most important factor was the loose nature of the Aztec hegemony over their neighbours. The many tributary, but independent, states, always liable to rebel, seized on the arrival of the Spaniards as a heaven-sent opportunity.

When Cortez first arrived at Tenochtitlán, he was received peacefully by Montezuma, whom he seized as a hostage. After a time the Aztecs rose against the Spaniards. Montezuma was killed, and the Spaniards, beset on all sides, and unable to manoeuvre in the narrow streets and canals withdrew across the causeway.

Montezuma was succeeded by his brother Cuitlahuac, who died a few months later, and by Cuauhtemoc. Cortez returned, and with many Indian allies, notably the Texcocans who deserted their Aztec friends, laid siege to Tenochtitlán. After a heroic defence Tenochtitlán was taken, but only after the Spaniards had, as they advanced, pulled down the houses and temples to fill in the canals and to give themselves room to manoeuvre. Consequently Tenochtitlán, unlike most Mexican cities of the

Aztec period has little to offer to the archaeologist, and we are driven to reconstructions based on the Codices and on analogies from other sites for a picture of the city in Aztec times. *See* colour plate III, plates 19, 21–22, pages 89, 91–92.

B

Ba is one of three related but distinct terms used by the ancient Egyptians which correspond to notions conveyed by the English word "soul". The other two are *akh* and *ka*. No Egyptian text tells us clearly the distinction between these three aspects of the individual personality which originally had belonged to the gods and kings alone.

The word *ba* was written in the **hieroglyphic** script with the jebiru-bird; from the time of the New Kingdom the *ba* is regularly depicted as a human-headed bird which hovers over the mummy or drinks from pools of cool water. It is best thought of as an external manifestation (which was not necessarily in the form of a bird) of the soul, surviving after death with the power of entering and leaving the body.

Akh describes the blessed state of the dead man who becomes an "excellent spirit". Unlike the *ba*, the *akh* had no separate entity before death. The word is written by means of the crested ibis, with or without phonetic complements, and derives from a stem meaning "to be beneficial, advantageous". It survives in **Coptic** with the meaning of "ghost" or "demon".

The *ka*, represented by two extended arms, is chiefly associated in the texts with the mortuary cult. The funerary offerings are described as being made to the *ka* of a person. The *ka* may be considered as a person's double, individuality of "self", conceived of as having a separate existence.

It is unlikely that the Egyptians themselves had clear or consistent views concerning the differences between these three terms and too logical or rigid definition of these terms, as if they concealed a systematic and well-formulated doctrine, is likely to mislead.

Baalbek. The magnificent temple ruins at this site in the Lebanon belong to the period of its colonization by Rome as Heliopolis and were erected between the first and third centuries A.D. No traces remain of a previous Phoenician settlement, presumed from the "Baal" (Phoenician sun god) element in the name, or of the Hellenistic town following it. The Roman city was centred round the worship of Helios the sun god, who achieved considerable vogue under the Empire, and Jupiter, worshipped there together with Venus, took on characteristics of a sun god: he was represented locally as a beardless god in long scaly drapery, a whip in his right hand, lightning and ears of corn in his left.

The most important buildings of the great complex of the Acropolis at Baalbek are the Temple of Jupiter Heliopolitanus and the Temple of Venus. The former, built on a huge platform, is approached by way of a great rectangular court (now also containing a fourth-century church that partially obscures the façade of the temple itself as well as the altar situated in the court), a second, hexagonal court, and a propylaeum. Only six of the original fifty-four great columns of the peristyle of the temple survive. In the west supporting wall of the platform are three massive megaliths, possibly the largest blocks used in actual construction; they are sixty-three feet long and thirteen in height and width. The Temple of Venus is better preserved and may be considered as one of the finest products of Roman architecture. During the thirteenth century the Arabs converted the group of temples into a fortress and the site was not cleared until early in the present century. *See* plate 23, page 93.

Babylon, a name famous as few others in history, legend, and literature, is today a vast expanse of confused mounds and hollows extending for some three miles along the east bank of the river Euphrates about seventy miles south of Baghdad in Iraq. Nearby is the modern town of Hillah, partly constructed from the ancient bricks of Babylon. There are now within the ruins about five principal mounds, the most northern of which still bears the name of Babil; these cover the main buildings of the former city. Its name, both in Sumerian (Kedingira) and in Semitic (Babili) means "Gate of (the) god".

Babylon was for so many centuries the capital of the land called Sumer and Accad (the southern part of modern Iraq) that it has given a name to the whole ancient culture which grew up there. But in the earliest historical ages it was unknown, and it remained so except for a few passing references until the foundation there of a first dynasty of

Babylon by west Semitic immigrants in the nineteenth century B.C. These kings had at first to struggle with two rival cities, but the supremacy of Babylon was established in the eighteenth century B.C. by **Hammurabi**, the celebrated law-giver, and was never again contested in its own land, although the city was frequently at strife, especially with the **Assyrians** to the north, and was several times captured and ravaged.

The last age of Babylon was her greatest, and it is this which has left so mighty a memory. Vast works of construction, defensive, religious, and civil, were carried out by the kings of the New Babylonian or Chaldaean dynasty, especially Nebuchadnezzar II (604–561 B.C.) whose almost superhuman creations, soon attributed in legend to more or less fabulous queens, Semiramis and Nitocris, turned Babylon into one of the Seven Wonders of the World and himself into the dramatic figure of magnificence and humiliation immortalized in the Book of Daniel. From the last of his successors the wondrous city was captured (539 B.C.) by the Persians under Cyrus without fighting. It was again partly destroyed by Xerxes in 482 B.C., and was to have been restored by Alexander, but he died there in 323. After this, although the cult and the astronomical schools of Babylon still existed, its population gradually disappeared, especially when a new capital was founded (300 B.C.) at Seleucia on the Tigris.

What has been unearthed of Babylon by modern excavators is almost exclusively the city as it was fashioned by Nebuchadnezzar. The River Euphrates flowed through its midst, and the Greek historian **Herodotus** gives a vivid account of the great walls which, as well as encircling the whole area (whose vastness he much exaggerates), were continued along both river banks, between which there was one bridge only, with piers of burnt brick and a footway of timber which could be withdrawn; the remains of this have been discovered. On the top of the walls were turrets and between them was space enough for a four-horsed chariot to pass. Gates in these walls were numerous, and all, with their housings, were of heavy bronze. Herodotus says there were a hundred, but a much smaller number has been found, most of them bearing the names of gods. Best preserved and most famous is the Ishtar Gate, which stands at the entrance to the principal street, the Processional Way. It is built of bricks so modelled that they make up figures in bas-relief of bulls and dragons. Their surfaces were overlaid with thick coloured enamels, and in front of the gate both sides of the approach had their walls decorated with the same kind of coloured reliefs showing lions and decorative patterns.

Of all the great city's wonderful buildings, most famous in antiquity were the "Tower of Babel" and the "**Hanging Gardens**". The tower (*Etemenanki* – "House of the Foundation of Heaven and Earth") stood in a spacious courtyard on the north side of the street leading to the Euphrates bridge. Since hardly anything of it now remains we depend upon descriptions given by **cuneiform** tablets and by Herodotus, which do not always agree. But it was certainly a huge mass of brickwork rising upwards in decreasing cubes, a stepped pyramid which the Babylonians called a **ziggurat**. Access from the ground began with a triple staircase, as excavation has proved, though Herodotus affirms that the ascent was made by a spiral ramp. At the top was a temple of bricks enamelled bright blue (to imitate the heavens), and within was a splendid couch and a golden table or chair; this was occupied by a priestess with whom the god Marduk was believed to keep company as his wife, the rite of "sacred marriage" upon which the prosperity of the land was thought to depend. On the other side of the street lay the great temple of Marduk called Esagila ("House which Uplifts the Head") with its multitude of sanctuaries and courts. Herodotus relates that its principal divine inhabitant was a seated figure of "Zeus" (i.e. Bel-Marduk) with a throne and pedestal and a table beside him, all of gold and weighing together 800 talents (a talent being about sixty pounds). Outside the fane there stood great altars for sacrifices of different kinds. One of these was also made of gold and near it was another standing figure of the god, twelve cubits high (a cubit was about twenty inches) and of solid gold.
Such was its sanctity that Darius never dared to touch it, but nothing could restrain the cupidity of Xerxes, who slew the high-priest and seized the statue. *See* colour plate IV.

Bac-son in north Viet-Nam is the **type-site** for a Neolithic culture of south-east Asia. (*See* **Hoabinh.**)

Balearic Islands, *see* Mediterranean, the Western *and* Minorca, Megalithic Remains in.

Bali. This small island to the east of Java never came under the influence of Islam and has preserved a culture of Indian, largely Hindu, and native Indonesian type which retains many features that have disappeared from or been overlaid in its larger neighbour. It has retained a caste system, though only about seven per cent of the population are of brahmin (priestly caste), ksatriya (military caste), or vaisya (merchant and agriculturist caste) grade, the rest being sudra (lowest caste). Little is known of the early stages of Balinese cultural history, but small model **stupas** of an esoteric Buddhist sect may date from the ninth century A.D. The Tirta Mupal, a tank round a holy spring, dates from A.D. 962. In A.D. 991 Erlangga, one of the great kings of east Java, was born in Bali. His younger brother ruled as his viceroy in the island and his tomb, with that of his wives, is in a series of rock-cut graves at Tampak-Siring, surrounded by rock shelters which served to house the monks who were attached to the service of the royal graves. In A.D. 1343 the Balinese royal house was overthrown by the Javanese kingdom of **Majapahit** and the centre of power shifted to Pejeng, later to Klungklung. The regent of this last was still regarded as the most senior of the Balinese chiefs, even under Dutch rule. To the Pejeng period belong most of the surviving antiquities of the island. Great skill in stone carving is allied to a love of intricate decoration and a certain avoidance of uncut areas. It might be compared with European baroque.

Barrow. The name now given to a prehistoric burial mound; the old name, tumulus, is still to be found on British Ordnance Survey maps. Barrows were long in **Neolithic** times, and were often family vaults for the chieftains; in the **Bronze Age** they were round and usually contained only one grave. Inhumation was customary in earlier times, cremation in later.

Basketmakers, *see* Amer-Indians.

Basketry. When **Palaeolithic** man began to collect and store food in the shape of berries, nuts, and so on, one of his early inventions must have been some kind of basket, made by weaving grasses, reeds, canes or willow twigs in and out of each other. They could be plastered on the outside with mud or lined inside with skins; in later times they would be daubed with pitch or resin to make them waterproof. Sometimes the basket was decorated by selected fibres being stained or dyed, possibly with magical symbols as a charm against evil influences. The **Aztecs** used basketry mud-containers as a method of land reclamation.

Basketry Structures, *see* Aztecs.

Batter. A method of building in which the walls slope inwards and are thus narrower at the top than at the bottom. Both the Babylonians and the Egyptians worked out formulae for accurately calculating the batter of the sides of a pyramid.

Beaker People. These are named after their characteristic ware: bell-shaped beakers and open bowls decorated with toothed stamps with geometric patterns, normally in horizontal zones. The wide distribution of this ware forms the main evidence for their migrations at the opening of the second millennium B.C. The strongest traces of occupation by the Beaker People have been found in Iberia, Czechoslovakia, south Germany and the British Isles. They came originally from Spain, possibly from near Carmona in the province of Seville, and spread by an Atlantic route to Brittany and Ireland and through the western Mediterranean to southern France, northern Italy, Sardinia and Sicily. Overland they reached central Europe through the Brenner Pass, and the middle Rhineland by the Rhône Valley, and Belfort Gap. Here they came into contact with the battle-axe folk – a people also producing beaker-shaped pots, though with certain characteristics of their own. This region formed a mingling zone for the two peoples and it was from here that the greater number of the Beaker People who spread to England came, though Wessex was colonized from Brittany.

The Beaker People buried their dead in single graves – both flat, and with round barrows above them – and, in western Europe, in **megalithic** tombs. The grave-goods accompanying the burials are our chief source of information about their culture: they include flint arrow-heads, stone arrow-shaft smoothers, flat daggers of metal or flint, metal awls and conical buttons of amber, bone and jet with a v-shaped arrangement of threading holes. The rapid movements of the Beaker People resulted in the spread of bronze metallurgy in central and western Europe. *See* plate 24, page 94.

Beehive Tombs, *see* Tholos Tombs.

Behistun Rock. This is so called after the name of the nearest village, sometimes known also as Bisitun, which is situated at the foot of a precipitous peak some 1,700 feet high in the mountain range of Zagros, in **Iran.** It stands on the right bank of the River Gamasi-ab. The original form of the name was Bagistana, meaning the place of the gods, or of God, and it is mentioned by two classical authors, Diodorus Siculus and Stephen of Byzantium; the ancient road from Ecbatana to Babylon passed by the foot of the scarp. In 516 B.C. Darius I, king of Persia, chose the spot as a suitably impressive place in which to set up a monument to himself; he caused part of the scarp to be smoothed down, and the sculptures and inscriptions for which the rock is so famous to be carved on the smoothed face. The inscriptions, which provided the key to the decipherment of **cuneiform,** are carved nearly 300 feet above the level of the spring which bubbles out at the foot of the mountain; they are extremely difficult to reach, and involve a climb up an almost precipitous rock face. They are in three different forms of cuneiform, the Babylonian, the Persian and the Susian; on the lowest part of the inscribed surface are three columns of Susian and five of Persian, each column being about eleven feet high. Above these is a sloping overhang on which is the Babylonian text, and a carved relief of Darius followed by two officials, with his foot on the prostrate form of his enemy Gaumata. In front of him are nine rebel chiefs with their hands bound behind their backs and ropes around their necks, and above them is a figure of the god Ahura Mazda.

The Persian part of this trilingual inscription was first copied and translated by Sir Henry **Rawlinson** in 1835 and the following years, and from his success with this text the Susian and Babylonian texts were subsequently interpreted, and the secret of cuneiform was broken. The inscriptions reveal how Darius defeated and killed the usurper Gaumata who had seized the throne in the absence of any direct heir after the death of Cambyses, though Darius was of the royal family. The organization of the Persian territories into satrapies or provinces is also described.

Babylonian cuneiform is an extremely complex script, with a great number of different signs none of which is really alphabetic, whereas Persian cuneiform, though derived directly from the Babylonian, is considerably simplified, alphabetic, and has only forty-three signs. There is a rather obscure passage in the Behistun text which seems to suggest that it was Darius who converted Babylonian cuneiform to Persian use, but a very brief inscription of Cyrus in Persian is almost certainly earlier. Main events referred to in the inscription are dated by the day of the month, but no year is mentioned at all; the only clue is that on four separate occasions it is stated that events related in the first column all occurred in the same year. From this it has been deduced that the text is an account of the first year of Darius' reign, and covers the period from autumn 522–spring 520 B.C. *See* plate 25, page 95.

Belzoni, Giovanni Battista (1778–1823), became famous as a collector of antiquities during the early part of the nineteenth century. He worked mainly for Henry Salt, who was the British consul in Egypt, and sent back to England many pieces of sculpture including the colossal head of Ramses II now in the British Museum.

Belzoni was born at Padua in Italy, possibly in 1778. Poor, and of a restless temperament, he travelled about Italy and Europe in search of employment. When he arrived in England he became the "strong man" in theatrical performances, for he was of immense stature and strength. Belzoni, however, wanted to exhibit his other talents, particularly his mechanical skill and knowledge of hydraulics. His chance came when he learned that Mohammed Ali, the ruler of Egypt, might be willing to employ him on irrigation schemes. At first he was hospitably received by the Pasha, but his labour-saving ideas were not popular and the Pasha did not honour his contract with him. Left without money or employment, Belzoni cast about for something else to do, and when the British Consul suggested that he should collect antiquities for him and organize their removal to Cairo, Belzoni readily agreed. This commission involved Belzoni in many disputes with local rulers and with the central government, as well as with rival Italian and French collectors. He and his wife travelled widely in Egypt and Nubia during their four years' stay. One of the high-lights of his search in the **Valley of the Kings** was the discovery of the tomb and sarcophagus of Seti I. The sarcophagus is now in the Soane Museum, London. Belzoni collected papyri from the tombs as well as sculptures and anything else which his great strength and ingenuity could move. His somewhat ruthless methods have been severely criticized, but he was merely following the practice of his times when excavators sometimes used battering-rams, and detailed records of excavations were not kept.

In the spring of 1820, Belzoni held an exhibition of his discoveries in the Egyptian Hall in Piccadilly; eulogistic notices in the press made him the darling of London society. He published an account of his travels in his *Narrative of the operations and recent discoveries within the Pyramids, Temples, Tombs and Excavations in Egypt and Nubia* (1820).

Belzoni was anxious to explore more of Africa, and set out early in 1823 for Timbuktu. He was not able to travel by way of the Atlas mountains and the Sahara, as was his intention, and so took ship for the Bight of Benin, the White Man's Grave, which claimed him as its victim on 3 December, 1823.

Boats. Wood being such a perishable material none of the earliest boats has survived; it is considered that they were some form of canoe. Opinions among the experts vary as to which came first – the dug-out canoe formed from a hollowed-out and roughly shaped tree-trunk, or the bark canoe – though there is a preponderance of opinion in favour of the latter. Another form of early boat was the canoe or coracle (a round boat) that was made of skins stretched tight over a wooden framework.

The discovery of the boat in its earliest and most primitive form, that of a tree-trunk pushed out to float on the surface, must date back to **Palaeolithic** times. The earliest surviving boats date from the **Mesolithic** period. People of the **Maglemosian** culture travelled from Europe to Britain by the land-bridge which connected the two before the English Channel was formed (an event which may have taken place round about 7000 B.C.), but their route took them across rivers where they must certainly have used some kind of water-transport. They also worked their way through the fens which existed where the North Sea now is by means of dug-out canoes. One of these has been found at Perth in Scotland; it dates from 10,000 years ago and is the oldest known boat found in western Europe. It was propelled by broad-bladed wooden paddles.

A narrow-bladed paddle of comparable date which was unearthed at **Star Carr** in Yorkshire, England, is the earliest navigational appliance known. Palaeolithic man kept to rivers and lakes, but Mesolithic man had sufficient confidence in the sea-going powers of his boats to venture on such a crossing as that between northern Ireland and south-western Scotland.

By **Neolithic** times boats were larger and stronger. Canoes have been unearthed at Oban in Scotland and elsewhere which are some forty to fifty feet long. People living in **crannogs** must have used canoes for communications though none of these has survived, perhaps because they were skin-boats. The Polynesians, who were still in the Neolithic stage of development when the white man landed, were then building with **stone tools** boats which were as much as one hundred feet long and could hold up to a hundred people; in such boats they made journeys of anything up to a thousand miles or more, making use of ocean currents to help them on their way. They had evolved methods of charting these currents and recording them in the form of a grid with an interlacing lattice-type pattern of thin wooden strips.

The Polynesians used sails. These were known in Egypt well before 3000 B.C., for vases of a period a little earlier than 3000 B.C. show ships with sails. The sails were square and would be used for running before the wind; any other kind of manoeuvre with them would be practically impossible. Ships sailing from the Nile delta to **Byblos** in Syria would, if the wind were fair, cover the distance in four days; the return journey usually had to be by means of oars, being made against the prevailing wind, and might take as much as ten days.

These Egyptian ships were at first some seventy to one hundred feet in length; later they might be as much as 170 feet, and in the time of the Middle Kingdom, ships are known that are a little over two hundred feet long, sixty-eight feet wide, and could carry one hundred men.

Bodhisattvas, *see* Buddhist Art and Architecture *and* Heian.

Boghazköy is a Turkish village in Anatolia near which the massive ruins of the spectacular fortified **Hittite** city, Hattusas, are to be found. Hattusas is spread out on either side of a gorge and rises up onto a flat-topped hill on which are the ruins of the ancient citadel, called by the Turks Büyükkale. It looks out on a wide cultivated valley to the north. The Hittite king Hattusil I made it his capital in the middle of the sixteenth century B.C. but, with the growth of the Hittite Empire, the original city proved too small and possibly in the fourteenth century, under the ruler Shubbiluliuma, a crescent of new fortifications was thrust out to the south, increasing the area of the enclosed city to over 300 acres. The ruins of these fortifications still give the impression of immense strength; the walls were built of heavy blocks carefully fitted together, the space between the double shell of wall being filled in with rubble. They were raised on ramparts of earth and projecting towers were spaced out along them. Of the five gates in the south wall three are named "Warrior", "Lion" and "Sphinx Gate" from the reliefs decorating them. One of the most massive series of remains in the city is that of the largest temple, which is centred on a rectangular courtyard and surrounded by a complex of storehouses and repositories. There are also the ruins of four smaller temples on the same general plan. The other fairly easily identifiable buildings are the two ranges of storehouses within the citadel; one of these housed the ten thousand tablets discovered earlier this century which form part of a royal archive and have proved of the greatest value in the study of Hittite history.

Book of the Dead. This is the title now commonly given to an ancient Egyptian religious book written on rolls of papyrus inscribed with a heterogeneous collection of magical spells, for which the Egyptian name was *The Book of Coming Forth at Daytime*. Three "books" have been found in the tombs of the wealthier people from the time of the eighteenth dynasty onwards; they were designed to facilitate the passage of the dead man to the world beyond and to ensure his ease and comfort there. They were placed either directly within the coffin or in a special wooden container which formed the pedestal for a status of Osiris. It is customary to divide the spells into a number of "chapters" but few of the *Books of the Dead* contain the complete collection of spells and there is considerable variation in the number and arrangement of spells from book to book. They were written in vertical columns of archaic cursive **hieroglyphs** separated by lines reading from right to left (the normal Egyptian practice), sometimes for obscure reasons in retrograde from left to right; examples have also survived from the Late New Kingdom written in **hieratic** in horizontal lines. They were frequently illustrated with drawings in black outline, and the outline then filled with colours, to which the name vignette is given. The more elaborate *Books of the Dead* are some of the finest examples of ancient book production: the *Papyrus of Ani*, for instançe, now in the British Museum, measures seventy-eight feet in length and one foot three inches in height. Repeated copying has led to many corruptions in the text and sometimes the books show carelessness in the arrangement of the vignettes to the text. In some cases the rolls have apparently been mass-produced, a space being left in the text to receive the purchaser's name, titles and affiliation. These are added in a different hand, often squeezed into an inadequate space: examples are known where these spaces have been left blank.

Though the collection of spells on papyrus is not attested before the eighteenth dynasty, they clearly derive from a similar collection principally found inserted in coffins of the Middle Kingdom, and called *Coffin Texts*. These in turn derive ultimately from the collection of spells discovered on the walls of the chambers inside certain pyramids of the fifth and sixth dynasties. Together the *Pyramid Text*, the *Coffin Text* and the *Book of the Dead* represent our most extensive body of Egyptian religious literature.

The version current at **Thebes** in the eighteenth and nineteenth dynasties contains something like 190 different spells. It includes hymns to the Sun God Ra, and to Osiris, speeches of various gods to the deceased, and magical spells like that commonly inserted on **ushabti** figures, and heart **scarabs.** Other spells contain the formulae to be recited in order to protect the deceased from such dangers and discomforts as dying a second time or eating his own excrement. The importance of good offerings for the future well-being of the deceased is emphasized by the fact that it was the spell to enable the dead man to enter and leave the burial place and to have access to the offering table, that gave its name to the book as a whole.

The most interesting of the spells is that containing the so-called negative confession and psychostasis (chapter 125), with its suggestion of a belief in an ethical standard of human behaviour and divine sanctions. This chapter as we have it now is a conflation of two similar spells. The deceased declares to Osiris that he has not committed certain evil actions ranging from denials of crimes of universal experience like theft, murder and adultery to what might be termed peculiarly Egyptian malformalities like the moving of boundary stones and interference with the irrigation controls. The list concludes with the thrice repeated declaration of the deceased that he is "pure".

The negative confession is repeated in slightly different and longer forms after the deceased has gained admittance to the Great Hall of Double Truth by reciting the magical names of the parts of the doors to the hall. Within, on either side in two equal rows, sit forty-two assessors and the deceased addresses each by name, declaring his innocence of a particular crime. There follows the judgement before Osiris, King of the Underworld, seated on his throne, with Isis and Nephthys behind him, and an assembled company of gods of Heliopolite origin. Before Osiris is the balance in charge of the jackal-headed Anubis; behind Anubis is the ibis-headed Thoth, the scribe of the gods, writing the verdict on a papyrus roll. Present too is the dreaded monster Amenlit, the devourer of the dead, part crocodile, part lion, part hippopotamus, awaiting the heart of the deceased, should it not exactly balance on the scales the feather of Truth. Chapter 125 contains some of the largest and the best of the vignettes: all illustrations naturally show the happy ideal, and the deceased is declared "true of voice". Though it should be remembered that in this as in other spells the inclusion itself would be sufficient security that the verdict would be favourable to the deceased, no matter what in fact his life on earth had been, nevertheless it seems unduly cynical to dismiss it as of no importance as an indication of an ethical content in the Osiris religion.

No clear picture emerges from the *Book of the Dead* of the precise state that one "true of voice" might expect to enjoy. One favourite belief was admission into the Kingdom of Osiris, where the country was flat and intersected by canals, a simulacrum of Egypt itself. Here the deceased would have his plot in the "Field of Reeds", sometimes referred to as the Elysian Fields of the Egyptians where he would plough, sow, reap and enjoy abundance in the company of his family. The picture is that of an ideal Egypt, the deceased serving Osiris as in life he had served the living Pharaoh. Such a belief is however at variance with the provision of ushabti figures and the emphasis elsewhere in the *Book of the Dead* upon the need of offerings from the living. Nothing illustrates better the unsystematic nature of the collection of spells and the habit of the Egyptians of incorporating new religious ideas without discarding older beliefs.

Boreal. In a geological context, this word refers to a dry, continental climate with warm summers and cold winters.

Borer. One of the simpler **flint** tools and therefore more common in the Lower **Palaeolithic.** A borer was a flint chipped on one side only, and put to a great variety of uses.

Borneo. Very little is known of the archaeology of Borneo, the second largest island in the world. Recent work has revealed an extensive system of caves in Niah, Sarawak, with cultures which seem to extend from the **Palaeolithic** to historical times. The finds are claimed to range from **stone tools** which may be comparable with those of the Upper Sohan industry (north-west India) to a number of **Neolithic** cultures with five different types of burial, and a considerable variety of ceramic forms, none of which are the result of using the potter's wheel. Paintings have also been found on the cave walls. From later periods of Bornean history, finds are scattered and difficult to date. A group of inscriptions from Kutei have been assigned to the fifth century A.D. but this is almost certainly a century or more too early. A Buddha image from Kota Bangun is in a so-called Gupta style, and there are a number of buddhist and brahmanic figurines from the Rata Estuary which are probably of the tenth to twelfth centuries A.D. Another group from Sambas belongs to the **Majapahit** period. Large amounts of Chinese export ceramics found at various points on the coasts of the island point to trade with China, and the association of these with iron slag shows clearly that iron was one of the principal exports. The situation of the island in the eastern maritime trade system makes it clear that field work there is likely to throw much light on cultural relations throughout a large area of Further Asia.

Borobudur. The earliest surviving buildings from the period when Java came under Indian influences are probably those of the Dieng group, in the crater of an extinct volcano where some forty buildings still survived in the time of Raffles. Of these eight still remain. They probably date from the early eighth century A.D., as do those of Gedong Sangga. The cult of mountains is apparently fundamental to

Indonesian religious systems, and it was a dynasty which claimed to be Lords of the Mountains who were probably responsible for Java's best known monument, Chandi Borobudur which was erected round about A.D. 800. In consists of six superimposed square terraces, with double projections on each side, surmounted by three circular platforms and a final **stupa**, fifty-two feet in diameter. The side of the lowest terrace is 480 feet. The outer walls of the terraces carry five rows of Buddha figures, ninety-two to a side, arranged in accordance with cosmological principles. The circular platforms carry small lattice-work stupas enclosing further Buddha figures, seventy-two in number, the same Buddha appearing on the top row of the terrace system. In all there are 504 Buddhas. The interior walls of the terraces, to which access is gained by staircases set at the midpoint of each side, form a series of closed galleries which are decorated with low-relief carvings based on Buddhist texts. Further carvings of the same type are found on the basement which was subsequently concealed by a great stone extension whose purpose still remains a subject for debate. In all there are approximately three miles of narrative sculpture. None of these can be seen from the outside, save for those, now concealed, on the basement, and it seems clear that the idea was to construct a closed microcosm. The exterior is ornately decorated in non-narrative style. On reaching the platforms, the worshipper had passed through galleries which became increasingly more austere, and whose illustrations referred to increasingly more esoteric texts, to find himself on an open series of circles without carving. This seems to be the final stage of progression towards a detachment from worldly things, on an ascent to ultimate truth symbolized by the final stupa.

The craftmanship of the carving is high and although the texts illustrated are of Indian origin, the mise-en-scène is Javanese so that the great building is a valuable repertory of the objects of Javanese everyday life and the flora and fauna of its period. It seems likely that shortly after its construction the centre of power shifted, and that Hinduism became a more important force than Buddhism (*see* **Prambanan**). It is interesting to speculate upon the economic implications of the stupa's construction and its possible effect upon the dynasty's later history.

Chandi Mendut, near Borobudur contains a remarkable fine seated Buddha, fourteen feet high, flanked by two Bodhisattvas of the same scale. The carvings on the exterior are of equally high quality and suggest that there was no dearth of skilled artisans in the Kedu area. *See* plates 27–28, pages 97–98.

Boskop Skull. This was found in South Africa in 1913, near Boskop in the Petchefstroom district of the Transvaal. It is far from complete, for the facial bones are missing. It comprises the skull-cap, part of the right temporal bone, and the left half of the lower jaw. Casts of these bones may be seen at the British Museum (Natural History) in London. Enough of the skull remains to show that it is Homo sapiens but with a much larger brain than the present-day average of 1350 c.c. The cranial capacity must have been about 1800 c.c. The brow-ridges are not prominent, and the outline of the skull seen from above is pentagonal, an unusual feature among living men. This, and various other features, show a greater similarity to the modern **Bushmen** of the Kalahari desert than to any other race, although these people are pygmies, with small brains.

Stone implements of the **Levalloisian** tradition were found with the Boskop skull, and these show that it belongs to the South African Middle Stone Age. This corresponds to the Upper **Palaeolithic** of Europe.

This period is of special interest to anthropologists for the study of the origins of the different living races of mankind. A number of skulls has been found in different parts of the world that suggests links between modern races and Palaeolithic stocks. The Boskop Skull is interesting for the light it is thought to throw on the, at present, uncertain origin of the Bushmen. Together with the slightly smaller **Singa Skull**, it suggests that the Bushmen may belong ultimately to a primitive human stock resembling the Australian aborigines. Further finds may provide more evidence of beings at stages of development between the Bushmen and the tall, large-brained "Boskop people".

Boucher de Perthes, Jacques (1788–1868). Jacques Boucher de Crèvecoeur de Perthes was born at Rethel in France, and from an early age showed a strong interest in archaeology and geology. In 1837 he discovered Palaeolithic **hand-axes** (which he called "the first diluvial axes") at Menchecourt and Moulin-Quignon near Abbeville. His first work *De la Création: essai sur l'origine et la progression des êtres* appeared in 1838–41. A further work was published in 1847. Believing at first that the hand-axes were made by men existing at the time of the deluge ("Diluvial Man") he later came to realize that even if the gravels were caused by a single deluge the men who made the tools must have existed beforehand ("Antediluvial Man") and were contemporary with extinct animals.

Boucher de Perthes was not the first to discover that Man's antiquity could be measured in terms of geological time; indeed this had already been done almost half a century earlier, although these finds had remained virtually ignored. He was, however, the first to develop this idea and to bring it to the notice of the scientific world in general.

The French academic world received this publication very badly and, although similar discoveries were made in 1854 at St Acheul, it was not until a group of British scientists made a joint visit five years later that the position began to improve, for de Perthes' conclusions were immediately attacked by the French Academy of Sciences. He bore these reverses with great courage and it was mainly due to him that man's origin was recognized as being infinitely more ancient than the mere 4000 B.C. then imagined. Through him and his successors the whole field of **Palaeolithic** archaeology and human palaeontology has been opened up.

Bow. The bow has been described as the first engine invented by man, for, in bending the bow, the muscles' energy is collected and stored so as to be expended in the instant of discharging the arrow. It is uncertain when the invention was first made but it may have been in **Magdalenian** times toward the end of the Upper **Palaeolithic.**

Brachiate. To swing by the arms from branch to branch, used especially in connection with monkeys' and apes' progress through trees.

Breasted, James Henry (1865–1935), was Professor of Egyptology and Director of the Oriental Institute at Chicago from 1919 until his death in 1935.

He was born at Rockford, Illinois. At twenty-one he was employed in a drug-store but soon decided that he should enter the Church. He quickly proved to be exceptionally adept at learning languages. After two years' study he reached the grave decision that he could not be a minister. He explained his feelings to his mother in this way: he read out his own translation of a passage from the Bible and then the Authorised Version: "Do you see that it is full of mistakes which convey a meaning quite different from the original? I've found scores of such mistakes. I could never be satisfied to preach on the basis of texts I know to be full of mistranslations. It's my nature to seek the sources of everything I study".

His tutor and friend, William Rainey Harper, advised him to go to Berlin in order to study Egyptology under the great German scholar, Adolf Erman. When he had completed his thesis for a doctorate (1894) he was invited to join the team who were working on a dictionary of the Egyptian language. This meant going to Egypt. Breasted combined his first field trip with his honeymoon. It was during this visit that he decided his first task would be to make a record of every inscription which bore any reference to Egypt's history. He envisaged something like Mommsen's *Corpus of Latin Inscriptions.* The results of this journey were published in the five volumes of *Ancient Records of Egypt* in 1906–7.

When he returned to Chicago in 1895 he was given a lectureship with a very meagre salary which he supplemented by travelling all over America giving public lectures. It was ten years before he was again in Egypt in December 1905. His work consisted of copying inscribed monuments in the Nile valley and in Sinai.

In the following year funds were again forthcoming from the Oriental Exploration Fund, largely supported by J.D. Rockefeller, Snr. This time the area covered was along the Upper Nile and into the Sudan. It was an exciting journey and conditions were none too easy.

Financial worries still troubled him and plans which he had entertained for a great Oriental Research Institute were making no perceptible progress. Then came the first world war. In May 1919 J.D. Rockefeller, Jnr, agreed to finance field research in Egypt for a period of five years. Breasted set out for Europe and the East again. He toured the Fertile Crescent (as he himself named the territory bordering on the Arabian desert) and made many purchases of antiquities for the Chicago University Museum. He became even more impressed with the need for immediate salvage work upon inscriptions and antiquities both in Egypt's Museum and in the Valley as a whole. He persuaded Rockefeller to provide the funds for a museum in Cairo, but difficulties arose and the money finally went to the Palestine authorities for a museum in Jerusalem. At last his plans for recording all the historical monuments in Egypt were beginning to become realities. An Epigraphical Survey was sent to work at **Medinet Habu,** and an Architectural Survey began work at **Luxor.** Breasted started work on the publication of the **Mastaba** of Mereruka at **Saqqara.** The work of the Oriental Research Institute now covered a large part of the Middle East with expeditions at **Megiddo, Persepolis,** in Iraq and in Anatolia. In 1926 the Prehistoric Survey of Egypt began work under his guidance.

One of his most valuable books was *A Handbook of Egyptian Religion* which was enlarged and published as *The Dawn of Conscience* (1933). *See* plate 30, page 100.

Breccia. Rock composed of sharply angular stones cemented together.

Breuil, Henri (1877–). L'Abbé Henri Breuil was born in 1877 at Mortain (Manchel), France. He published his first paper when he was twenty-two. After taking a science degree at twenty-seven he proceeded to teach ethnography in Switzerland for five years until in 1910 he was appointed Professor of Prehistoric Ethnography and Director of Research at the Institute of Human Palaeontology in Paris.

Perhaps his study of **Palaeolithic** art will be best remembered. At the beginning of the century he had to fight against general disbelief in the antiquity of Palaeolithic cave paintings. He was mainly responsible for a great series of works published by the Institute of Human Palaeontology, giving a definitive account of the main examples of **cave art** in western Europe. Starting as a young enthusiast in conjunction with Capitan and Pegrony in 1901 he made a study of Combarelles and Font-de-Gaume. Then followed a series of outstanding caves culminating in **Lascaux** (*see* colour plate VIII) in 1940.

Another major contribution to the study of the Palaeolithic was his great influence in the gradual change-over from what was basically a geological to an anthropological approach. He was foremost, earlier in this century, in the gradual amplification of de Mortillet's simple scheme. This actually led to the breaking down of the old "epoch" system, where one "epoch" followed another as in geological strata. Breuil was the first to prove, at the Grotte de Valle in northern Spain in 1909, that two epochs were contemporary (the **Azilian** and the **Tardenoisian**). A paper read by him at an international conference in Geneva in 1912 went a long way towards the break-up of the old **Chellean-Acheulian-Mousterian** system by showing that the sub-divisions were very complex. He had the Chellean changed to the **Abbevillian** and was responsible for having the Aurignacian (originally in Lartet's scheme) finally reinstated in 1912. Breuil had a profound influence on the further subdivision of the Upper Palaeolithic, breaking down the **Aurignacian** and the **Solutrean** each into three phases and the **Magdalenian** into six. It was his study tour of the central and east European material published as *Voyage Paléolithique en Europe Centrale*, that caused him to change to the idea of contemporary groups, a study of **Levalloisian** flakes in 1926 finally completing the process of change towards the modern **"culture"** concept. Six years later he began to distinguish three cultural groups (**Clactonian,** Levalloisian, Tayo-Mousterian) even among the Lower Palaeolithic flake industries. With Obermaier he had the basic idea of a dual civilization in the Lower Palaeolithic, although this has been subsequently very greatly modified.

Frequently very advanced for his times, in 1910 he would not accept **eoliths** as humanly made, and did not accept the pre-Crag tools of East Anglia until some ten years later.

As an international expert on the Palaeolithic, his influence outside France was naturally profound, especially in north and in South Africa (*Cahiers d'Art* 1931).

In 1941 he gave the Huxley Memorial Lecture on "The Discovery of the Antiquity of Man".

Brittany, *see* **Carnac.**

Broch was originally the name in the north of Scotland, and is now the standard archaeological term, for describing certain structures in that area. They are circular in shape and were protective dwellings, made of dry-built stonework, not apparently found elsewhere, belonging to the **Iron Age** and dating from some time between 100 B.C. and A.D. 100 or a little later.

These brochs are usually about twenty-eight feet in diameter of inside measurement and the thickness of the wall at its base is about thirteen feet. Some 500 of them have been discovered, generally on or near land that could be cultivated, and they spread over Orkney, Shetland, the Hebrides, Skye and the northernmost counties of Scotland. Some few have been found further south, and in one near the English border some Roman pottery was discovered of the late first century. More pottery an remains of the same time have been turned up in other brochs, so that it is possible to assign a date to them relative to the Roman occupation.

The typical broch had a roof supported between and inner ring of uprights and the main wall and was like the "wheel-house" found in Uist, Orkney and Shetland, in which internal walls radiated from a central space to hold up a roof above a ring of cells.

Judging from the remains to be found in brochs, which include pottery, bronze ornaments and iron implements, it seems possible that they came from south-west Britain, no doubt by sea, and certain tools for making textiles show a relationship between the two areas. The height of the broch roof seems to have been about eight feet, and the wall went up further into a gallery approached by stairs built within the space made available by the double construction. Farther to the north, the brochs increase in height and in the larger kinds the gallery is always found, very often with out-buildings of considerable strength.

Here and there the broch rose even higher, culminating in quite a tall tower which gave the defences an element of remarkable strength such as can hardly be seen elsewhere in the Europe of such early times.

There is a famous and elaborate broch at Mousa, in Shetland, where the walls incline inwards, windows are entirely lacking and corbelled cells open onto the floor. The wall gallery here has been extended to six storeys, one above another, with a flight of stairs running up to one storey after another. This is an exceptionally elaborate specimen, but there are other brochs nearly as high and there may well have been many more of them.

Bronze Age. The Bronze Age succeeded the **Neolithic** Age, the date at which it did so varying in different parts of the world according to the stage of civilization reached. In Asia Minor, Greece, India, and Mesopotamia it dates from before the third millennium B.C.; in Britain it began round about 1900 B.C.

Bronze is an alloy of **copper** and tin, and the Age is the period when bronze tools and weapons were widely used, though by no means universally; in particular, **stone tools** often continued in use long after the introduction of bronze weapons.

The Bronze Age marked a wide development in trade and the beginning of specialization. Smiths and miners no longer took part in food production but concentrated on production, gaining their living by barter. The reduction of a metal from its ores and the casting of required objects is a skilled process and would lead to the formation of guilds in which the secrets of the craft would be jealously guarded. The Neolithic society had been self-sufficient. The Bronze Age society was not. To obtain the desired goods the household had to produce a surplus for barter with the smith, and the community as a whole had to produce an exportable surplus in exchange for the raw materials from the distant mines. This it was able to do because of two further inventions of the Bronze Age: the ox-drawn **plough**, which enormously increased the amount of land one family could cultivate in a year and the **wheel**, which revolutionized transport.

Browne, Thomas (1605–82). "Tell me how Browne's Urne", a modern poet has asked, "Makes all the past like coloured fireworks burn". No writer more deserves inclusion in a survey of the past than this English doctor who gravely and grandly meditated on human transience. No writer has more inspired archaeologists.

Sir Thomas Browne practised medicine at Norwich in England. In 1658, an urn-field or cemetery of the Late **Bronze Age** came to light in a sandy field at Walsingham, not far away. Browne was thereupon inspired to compose – there is no other word: he writes like a composer at the organ – his famous *Hydriotaphia: Urne Buriall; or, A discourse of the Sepulchral Urnes lately found in Norfolk.*

Five short chapters contain some of the grandest sentences and phrases in the English language:

"He that lay in a golden Urne, eminently above the Earth, was not like to find the quiet of these bones."

"To be knav'd out of our graves, to have our sculs made drinking-bowls, and our bones turned into Pipes, to delight and sport our Enemies, are Tragicall abominations escaped in burning Burials."

"A Dialogue between two Infants in the womb concerning the state of this world, might handsomely illustrate our ignorance of the next."

"Time which antiquates Antiquities, and hath an art to make dust of all things, hath yet spared these minor monuments."

"But the iniquity of oblivion blindly scattereth her poppy."

"Diuturnity is a dream and folly of expectation."

"Man is a Noble Animal, splendid in ashes, and pompous in the grave."

"The Aegyptian Mummies, which *Cambyses* or time hath spared, avarice now consumeth. Mummie is become Merchandize, *Mizraim* cures wounds, and *Pharaoh* is sold for balsoms."

"There is nothing strictly immortall but immortality."

Countless archaeological books have come into the world with a quotation from *Urne Buriall*, their authors as moved as Browne had been by the mystery and the transience of things. Browne had the enquiring and poetical mind, in which archaeology has its roots. The past might seem a great darkness, but that darkness, that inscrutability, must be scrutinized: "'Tis time to observe Occurrences", he said at the beginning of *Urne Buriall*, "and let nothing remarkable escape us: The Supinity of elder dayes hath left so much in silence, or time hath so martyred the Records, that the most industrious heads do find no easie work to erect a new *Britannia*."

The past, in Browne's sense, is still mysterious. Knowing nothing of Bronze Age, Iron Age, and Ages of Stone, he looked at his urns from Walsingham, his "aged cinders" and "long-fired particles" and concluded that it might be possible to guess "what song the Syrens sang", or to work out when "the persons of these Ossuaries entered the famous Nations of the dead". But we could discover nothing of their human individuality, and could give only the thinnest answer to the question, "Who were they?"

"Who were the proprietaries of these bones, or what bodies these ashes made up, were a question above Antiquarism."

True even now. Yet Browne would be delighted with the progress of archaeology and the way it is revealing more and more of man in his infancy and his forgotten glory.

Sir Thomas Browne's life in Norwich was the uneventful one of a general practitioner, a scholar, and a writer.

A long while after death he became an antiquity himself. His coffin in one of the Norwich churches was opened in 1840 and his skull was removed. That skull in which he hatched his magnificent sentences is now an exhibit in the Museum of Norwich Hospital.

Buckland, William (1784–1856). Dr Buckland was an English geologist who discovered the Red Lady of Paviland in **Paviland Cave.** He was an clergyman and therefore considered himself bound by Archbishop **Usher's** chronology. His lectures on geology were the cause of Charles **Lyell** becoming interested in the subject, with revolutionary results.

Buddhist Art and Architecture. It appears that the earliest Buddhist art was inhibited from portraying the Buddha. There thus developed a system of representing him in symbolic form, a practice which persisted even after the original inhibition had disappeared. A tree, the Bodhi-tree *(Ficus religiosa)* represented the enlightenment, a wheel *(dharma-cakra)* represented the teaching and, especially when associated with deer, the first sermon in the deer-park at Benares. A stupa symbolized the attainment of nirvana. This last, a hemispherical structure on a base, and crowned with a superstructure, often in the form of an umbrella, seems to be a sophistication of a primitive burial mound. The practice of erecting pillars at places of particular importance in the faith, or at places which were to be incorporated into the sacred geography of Buddhism as this spread through India, also seems to have been early. The stupas, with which pillars were often associated, were surrounded by ornate railings, *vedika*, by the second century B.C., and complex gateways which, to judge from their arrangement, served to keep out evil spirits, were quickly added. These, known as *torana*, probably lie behind the Japanese *torii*. The carvings at such early sites as Bharhut and **Sanchi** (*see* colour plate XIV, plates 31, 121, pages 000,000) portray other buildings, including palaces and monasteries in wood. The next stage was the development of rock-cut temples of increasing sophistication, which still retain features suitable to wooden architecture. These include both shrines *(caitya)* and monasteries or shelters for retreating monks *(vihara)*. With the development of the free-standing building, three main types are to be found. These are the temple, to house an image or images, the stupa (tope, dagoba, etc.), a solid building which may contain a sacred relic of some kind, and the *vihara* with various buildings required as libraries, preaching halls, etc. The many-staged pagoda, a feature of Chinese and Japanese Buddhist architecture, seems to have originated in northern India, and does not appear to have been used in south-east Asia, except in Viet-Nam under Chinese influence.

By the first century A.D. the use of the Buddha image seems to have been accepted, perhaps under western influence. The development of a complex system of hand positions and poses *(mudra, asana)* enabled these images to fulfil a narrative function, especially when associated with symbols from the earlier period.

The emergence of more complicated forms of Buddhism extended greatly the scope of Buddhist iconography and the repertoire of the Buddhist artist, who was thus enable, by the use of pose, hand gestures and attributes, to portray recognizably a vast pantheon of Buddhas, Bodhisattvas (pure earthly beings who have attained great virtue through numerous rebirths) and spirits, both good and evil, together with such Hindu deities as had been incorporated into the Buddhist system. Narrative carvings and paintings served to record previous lives of the Buddha (*jataka*), episodes in his life as Gautama Buddha, and much of his doctrine as well as later, more esoteric, dogma. Buildings such as **Borobudur** contain some miles of this type of carving. *See also* **Hindu Art and Architecture.** *See* plate 31, page 101.

Buffon, Georges Louis Leclerc (1707–88) was a French naturalist who produced numerous theories in advance of his time. He believed the origin of the earth to have been due to the near approach of another star to the sun, or of an actual collision between the two; and he produced a time-scale for the **age of the earth** vastly longer than anything imagined in his own time, though infinitesimal compared with modern theories. His theory was further developed by Baron **Cuvier.**

Burin. A prehistoric **flint** engraving tool, or chisel. (*See* **Stone Tools.**)

Bushmen. These are closely related, physically and linguistically, to the Hottentots, and the two racial groups are sometimes known as the Khoisan peoples.

The fossil record shows that they have a long ancestry and may be regarded as the oldest indigenous stock of southern Africa. Today the Bushmen number approximately 55,000 and are distributed mainly in the drier parts of Bechuanaland, South West Africa and Angola. Fossil and sub-fossil skeletal remains show, however, that at one time people of Bush race extended throughout southern and eastern Africa into the Sudan, having gradually evolved from a Middle Stone Age, Boskopoid, ancestor. (*See* **Boskop Skull.**)

Linguistically the Bushmen are divided into three main groups – northern, central and southern. The last group is now virtually extinct and among the other two peaceful associations with Bantu and European have resulted in intermarriage and in many of the groups becoming settled and forsaking their original way of life as nomadic hunters and food gatherers.

The Bushman is so distinctive in appearance that he is readily distinguished from other African peoples except the Hottentot. Usually short of stature he is slenderly built with small hands and feet. His head is small, preserving certain infantile (paedomorphic) features. His skin is yellow or yellowish-brown and he has a rather Mongolian-like eye and hair on his head which forms tightly curled spirals or "peppercorns".

Their social organization and material culture are very simple. They live in small hunting bands of from thirty to one hundred members and are directed by the older and more experienced men. Their chief hunting weapon is the bow and poisoned arrow with which they are very proficient. While the men hunt and collect honey the women and girls gather wild fruits and other edible vegetable foods. For clothing they wear skins and they build only simple windbreaks for shelter. Formerly, before being driven into the Kalahari, they occupied country where caves and rock shelters afforded natural protection from the weather and it is here that the most remarkable of their cultural achievements – their naturalistic art – is found. Many of the paintings in these caves are of high artistic merit and depict hunting and domestic scenes which preserve a very complete record of the life and habits of the Bushmen of later **Stone Age** times before the encroachment of the Bantu people and the European into his hunting preserves. Their coming caused him in recent times to become extinct in many of those parts where traces of his former presence are very numerous. (*See* **Africa, Prehistoric Art in.**)

Byblos. The town of Jebeil, situated about twenty miles north of Beirut along the Lebanese coast, looks down from a cliff-top on to the Mediterranean. It marks the ancient site of the once flourishing port and trading centre known to the Graeco-Roman world as Byblos and to the Assyrians and Babylonians in earlier times as Gubla. The town's most valuable export was pine and cedarwood felled inland on the slopes of the Lebanon. This timber found a ready market in Egypt. Apart from their commercial ability the men of Byblos were famous as ship-builders and stone-cutters.

From 1921 to 1924 M. Pierre Montet conducted four seasons of excavation at Byblos under the auspices of the French Académie des Inscriptions et Belles Lettres. After a short interval work was resumed in 1926 by M. Maurice Dunand for the Lebanese Republic and is still in progress. Dunand has traced the earliest occupation of the site to a primitive village community of **Neolithic** farmers who manufactured dull-toned reddish-brown pottery with incised decoration. After an indefinite interval a group of **Chalcolithic** farmers and stock-breeders arrived to found a new village about 3500 B.C. Their hutments were rectangular or circular in plan and were possibly interspersed with cobbled pathways. They made use of silver for personal ornaments, but only a very few copper knives were found in their burials.

By the beginning of the third millennium B.C. Byblos was an expanding township and was probably already trading with Egypt. Wheel-thrown kiln-fired flasks of a type produced at Byblos have been discovered in the royal tombs of the first dynasty, doubtless originally containing some imported liquid. About 2800 B.C. Byblos suffered a temporary set-back when a fire, thought by Dunand to have been accidental, swept through the town. Reconstruction on a grander scale soon began, limestone replacing sandstone even in domestic architecture. To this phase belongs the earliest recognized temple, which may be ascribable to Ba'alat Gebal, the patron goddess of Byblos. Later temples to her were found belonging to phases contemporary with the Old and Middle Kingdoms in Egypt. The former contained fragments of votive alabaster vases bearing the names of Egyptian kings from Khasekhemui (second dynasty) to Pepi II (sixth dynasty). During the period of the twelfth dynasty trade flourished between Egypt and Byblos enabling the latter's **Amorite** princes to construct for themselves magnificent subterranean tombs in which they were buried with rich funeral furniture including objects and ornaments of gold, ivory, ebony and semi-precious stones.

Our archaeological picture of the Byblos of New Kingdom times is meagre, owing firstly to the destruction of the town by the **Sea Peoples** in their march on Egypt in 1194 B.C., and secondly to the considerable disturbance of what remained by the foundations of Hellenistic, Roman and modern buildings.

Under the Romans Byblos assumed vast proportions. Among the public buildings excavated by Dunand particular mention may be made of the amphitheatre with its adjoining baths and an imposing temple to an unidentified male deity.

C

Caenozoic Era. The era of the earth's history which includes the **Tertiary** and **Quaternary Periods.** It was preceded by the **Mesozoic, Palaeozoic** and **Archaean Eras.**

Canaanites. The word Canaanites today usually refers to the Semitic speaking peoples of mixed race who inhabited the area centring on Phoenicia on the eastern coast of the Mediterranean during the **Bronze Age.** The origin of the name Canaan for this area is not known, but in the Nuzu documents it is used to refer to the purple dye obtained from certain species of shellfish found on the eastern Mediterranean coast, and it may be that the area took its name from its most characteristic product. Until the end of the nineteen-thirties, the main source of information about the Canaanites was the Bible, eked out by a few references in classical sources and in Babylonian and Egyptian documents. This condition has been radically altered by the remarkable discoveries made since 1929 by Claude Schaeffer at **Ras Shamra**, the site of ancient Ugarit, on the Syrian coast. The most important discovery at Ras Shamra was a large collection of documents of the fourteenth century B.C., including a certain number of mythological compositions, all written in a special **cuneiform** alphabet on clay tablets, and throwing a flood of light on Canaanite civilization in the Late Bronze Age. The language of these texts is usually classified, together with Hebrew, Phoenician and others, in the north-west Semitic group.

Owing to the continual migrations and invasions suffered by the Syro-Palestine region, it is not yet possible to disentangle the early history of the area but it appears that north-west Semitic languages were being spoken there by the third millennium B.C. It is probable therefore that the Canaanite population consisted of a mixture of the original inhabitants of the area, whose language is unknown, and Semitic-speaking immigrants whose language became dominant. By the second millennium B.C., the distinctively Canaanite civilization was established and, while the area consisted more of a number of city states with varying loyalties than of any lasting unified states, the general standard of culture was uniform. Though the supreme Canaanite god was El, the most prominent was Baal, already familiar from the Bible. There were two fertility goddesses, Anat and Astarte (the Ashtaroth of the Bible), and a fertility aspect of Baal is brought out in one of the myths where he is killed by Mot, the ruler of the dead, and life ceases on the earth until Anat avenges him and restores him to life. There was at this time, as is reflected in the art and literature, a widespread sea trade between the Aegean, Egypt, and Syro-Phoenicia, but the Canaanites suffered a series of severe setbacks in the late second millennium B.C., from invasions of the **Sea Peoples** from the north, and the **Israelites** from the south. A revival took place in the first millennium, based chiefly on sea trading, with its centres at **Tyre** and Sidon, and it was the people of Canaan of this period that the Greeks called **Phoenicians**, though they continued to call themselves Canaanites. Their many trading colonies throughout the Mediterranean became separated politically when the rise of Assyria (*see* **Assyrians**) and the growth of Greek trade began the process which culminated in the absorption of the remaining independent cities into the Persian Empire.

Canoe, *see* Boats.

Canopic Jars. When the ancient Egyptians began to mummify their dead they discovered that the first parts of the body to decay were the viscera. They therefore made a cut on the left side of the lower abdomen and through this opening the viscera were removed. It was, however, essential for the continuation of life after death that all the members should remain together, and so the liver, intestines, kidneys, and stomach were treated with preservatives, wrapped in bandages of linen and placed in jars. The jars first came into use during the **Old Kingdom**. They were kept in a square box made to resemble the coffin, and inscribed with the owner's name and titles, and a magical formula. During the Late New Kingdom and afterwards, stoppers were made in the likeness of the four sons of Horus and a particular organ was assigned to each one. Four goddesses were regarded as the protectresses of these gods; Isis, Neith, Nephthys, and Selkis (*see* **Tutankhamun, Tomb of**). The materials used for Canopic jars during the Old Kingdom included wood, alabaster, pottery and limestone; **faience** was introduced during the New Kingdom and continued in use until Ptolemaic times. With the twenty-first dynasty the viscera were treated with preservative and returned to the body and the art of making Canopic jars declined.

The origin of the name comes from a mistake by scholars who thought that they recognized in the jars the source of the classical belief that the Egyptians worshipped, in the form of a jar with a human head, Canopus, the pilot of Menelaus, who had been buried at Canopus on the Nile.

Canopus Decree. At Canopus, which was the principal port in Egypt for Greek trade before the founding of Alexandria, a great assembly of priests, in 239 B.C. passed an honorific decree conferring, among other things, the title of "Benefactor" on Ptolemy Euergetes. Two copies of the decree are known, inscribed in **demotic, hieroglyphs** and Greek; they were discovered by Karl **Lepsius** in 1866 and were of considerable value in deciphering the first two languages, and in this were only exceeded by the **Rosetta Stone**. (*See* plate 119, page 385.)

Capsian. A **Stone Age** culture peculiar to north Africa, the Capsian dates from the close of the Pleistocene era, succeeding the Aterian culture and continuing throughout the period of the European **Mesolithic** cultures. Distribution was mainly centred round Gafsa in southern Tunisia and Tehessa in south-eastern Algeria. It also flourished in Kenya, where another technique (known as Kenya Capsian) of the post-Gamblian dry phase was found. Traces are occasionally found in caves and rock-shelters, but more normally in open camp-sites, in extensive middens (consisting of thousands of snail-shells for example), and fire-hearths containing ashes.

Artifacts found include various kinds of **stone tools** – **microliths**, backed blades, points, scrapers, **burins**, and simple bone implements.

Carbon Fourteen Dating. All living things contain carbon, and all organic matter (the matter of which plants and animals are composed) is continually exchanging carbon, in the form of carbon dioxide, with the atmosphere, At death this process stops and the carbon compounds decay, break down, and, with the help of bacteria, are reconverted into carbon dioxide.

Most carbon atoms are stable and have an atomic weight of twelve. As a result of the constant bombardment of the atmosphere by cosmic rays from outer space a very small proportion of the carbon atoms is changed into a radioactive form – known as carbon fourteen because these atoms have an atomic weight of fourteen. Being radioactive these atoms are unstable and slowly decay, thereby changing into a stable form of nitrogen with an atomic weight of fourteen.

There is a balance between the creation of new carbon fourteen atoms and their decay into nitrogen fourteen, consequently the number of carbon fourteen atoms in the atmosphere remains constant. Because every living creature is continually exchanging carbon dioxide with the atmosphere, there is the same balance here, with all living organic matter containing the same proportion of radioactive carbon as does the atmosphere. At death, however, the balance begins to change because the supply of carbon fourteen atoms is no longer replenished from the atmosphere. Slowly the process of radioactive decay reduces their number. The half-life, as it is called, of these atoms is 5,000 years, and at the end of that period half of them will have decayed into nitrogen fourteen atoms. The rate is constant and unchanging; nothing can alter it; so that at the end of 5,000 years there will be left half the number of carbon fourteen atoms that are to be found in living organic matter, at the end of 10,000 years one quarter, at the end of 15,000 years one eighth, and so on.

A method of detecting and measuring the amount of carbon fourteen in dead organic matter was developed in the University of Chicago, and the technique is now available to archaeologists who can and do use it for the purpose of constructing a time-scale and of determining the relative age of dead organic matter, such as wooden posts, textiles, and so on, which they find in the course of excavation. The method can only give an approximation in years, and the estimated date will be given as, say, 1848 B.C. ±275 (as in the case of **Stonehenge**), which means that the date lies somewhere between 275 years either side of 1848 B.C., that is, between 2123 B.C. and 1573 B.C.

The method is, unfortunately, expensive and, as it involves the destruction of the material, only used when such material can easily be spared.

Carnac. The south coast of Brittany at the north-western tip of France is the site of one of the richest concentrations of megalithic remains in the whole of western Europe. They probably belong chiefly to the first half of the second millennium B.C. The types of construction employed in these tombs, the objects found in them, and the carvings executed on the walls of some of them all combine to show that their builders were closely connected with the collective-tomb people of the west Mediterranean, particularly those of Spain and Portugal. Their ancestors may, in fact, have originally come to Brittany as immigrants. On the other hand, they also show close connections with various groups of megalithic tombs in western Britain and Ireland, which seem to represent a further extension north-westward of this remarkable "megalithic religion". It has often been suggested that the main cause of this northward expansion of the **megalith**-builders was the search for supplies of tin and copper ores to supply the needs of the **Bronze Age** civilizations of the east Mediterranean. There may be some truth in this, but the whole movement is so complex and extends over such a long period of time that many factors probably played a part. The fact is that despite much patient research the whole process is still involved in considerable obscurity. Nevertheless, the discovery of a blue paste bead of the type distributed by Mycenaean trade in Europe in the fourteenth century B.C. in one of the south Breton tombs gives some support to the idea of an indirect trade in metals with the civilization of **Mycenae** at any rate during the later phases of the megalithic culture.

The Breton remains generally take the form of round and long **barrows**, with stone chambers (but in the case of the latter, sometimes without), stone circles (or **cromlechs**), and alignments of stones. The most remarkable collection of these monuments occurs in the vicinity of the little village of Carnac in the Morbihan. This complex includes megalithic tombs of various kinds, and unchambered barrows, but its dominating feature is the avenues of monoliths known as the Carnac alignments. These are what make it unique of its kind in Europe. They consist of a varying number of parallel rows of upright stones which vary greatly in size and they run without a break for considerable distances.

The main ones fall into three separate groups, known respectively as the Menec, Kermario and Kerlescant alignments. Together they are several miles long and contain several thousand stones. The three groups are arranged so that they form parts of a single line running roughly from south-west to north-east, with intervals of varying length between each set.

The Menec alignments are the most south-westerly. The stones are arranged in eleven rows, which run for a distance of 1,264 yards, the average width being 108 yards. There are 1,099 stones in the alignments themselves, whilst another seventy are arranged to form a cromlech or stone circle at the west end of the lines. The tallest stone in the Menec alignments is thirteen feet high, the smallest a mere twenty-four inches.

The Kermario alignments begin 368 yards, from the north-east end of the Menec ones. They consist of ten lines of stones, 1,213 yards long, and comprising in all 1,029 stones. The lines have a width of about 108 yards on the average. The tallest stone is seven yards high and the smallest just under half a yard. This group may also have had a cromlech at its south-west end, but all trace of this has now disappeared. At a certain point in the Kermario alignments three stones run off at right angles to the south. Perhaps they once formed the beginning of what was once a separate branch of the avenues. Near their eastern end the stones of the alignments pass over a long mound, which, when excavated in 1922, proved to be a burial monument similar in some respects to the British unchambered long barrows. It is roughly rectangular, and from it rises a large upright stone, which is higher than most of those of the alignments, where these pass near it. It has also a different orientation. Near its base it bears four carved zig-zag lines, which may have been intended to represent serpents. Nearby five small polished stone axes were found during the excavations set with their cutting edges uppermost. This part of the Kermario alignments is called the Manio section, and the long mound bears the same name.

A further gap of 433 yards separates the Kermario avenues from those of Kerlescant. The Kerlescant alignments are only 953 yards long, and they consist of 555 stones ranged in thirteen parallel lines. The lines are 150 yards wide. At the point where they pass behind the village of Kerlescant there is a gap in the alignments about 217 yards long. To the west these avenues end in a cromlech of unusual shape. It is roughly square, with rounded corners, and contains thirty-nine stones. On the north side of the cromlech lies a long mound, similar to that covered by the Manio avenues, with a standing stone 13 feet high at its western end. North of the alignments there is another long mound, which this time contains a narrow, corridor-like chamber, which is closed at both ends and divided into two by a septum formed by two slabs near the centre. A circular, porthole-like opening cut in these slabs makes a communication between the two halves of the chamber. In this chamber were found various objects, which included pottery, both plain and of bell-beaker type, flint implements and arrow-heads, pendants, and a polished stone axe.

Remains of a number of other alignments are known in the region around Carnac, some of which end in stone circles. The best preserved is that at Kerzeho, with 1,129 stones.

A number of other barrows containing megalithic burial chambers occur in the vicinity of the Carnac alignments, and they well illustrate the wide variety of these to be found in Brittany. To the south-east of the Menec alignments is the barrow of St Michel, a huge mound about 130 yards long, sixty-five yards broad and twelve yards high, which covers a megalithic tomb-chamber. It is one of the largest in Europe. Farther to the north-east, opposite the Manio end of the Kermario alignments, is a round barrow over thirty-two yards in diameter and about ten feet high. This barrow, known as Kercado, covers a rectangular chamber, in which the usual beads, axes and arrow-heads were found, with plain and bell-beaker pottery, and two remarkable gold plaques. Other tombs include that of Mané Kerioned, which has a V-shaped chamber entered from the narrow end, and Keriaval, which has a long chamber with pairs of symmetrical side chambers branching off it.

The alignments which are the most remarkable feature of the Carnac group of monuments were obviously intended for the performance of sacred rituals, which must have included solemn processions along the avenues to and from the cromlechs. These ceremonies were plainly closely connected with the presence of the great collective tombs, but more than that we cannot say. The alignments are plainly later in date than the long mound over which they pass at Manio. These unchambered long mounds are an early type of monument, which may belong to the later third millennium B.C. The alignments themselves probably belong to the first half of the second millennium B.C. and they could scarcely have been built after 1400 B.C. The later collective tombs with various types of built chamber were probably constructed at different times. Some may be earlier, some contemporary, and others again later than the alignments, even assuming that the latter were all built at the same time, which we cannot prove. *See* plate 29, page 99.

Carter, Howard (1873–1939), famous British Egyptologist, received his training under Sir W. M. Flinders **Petrie** and others. From 1891 to 1899 he conducted excavations on behalf of the Egypt Exploration Fund, after which he joined the Antiquities Service of the Egyptian Government as chief inspector. His greatest discovery was the **Tomb of Tutankhamun** made while working in association with George Herbert, fifth earl of Carnarvon.

Cartouche, derived from a French word meaning an ornamental plaque for inscribing, is the name given to the oval shape which encloses the prenomen and nomen of the Egyptian **pharaohs.** Its significance is obscure. Carefully drawn **hieroglyphs** show that it represents a loop of double thickness of rope the ends of which are knotted, but very early the form was linearly simplified. The same sign is used in the writing of the verb "to enclose" and doubtlessly the cartouche signifies the all-embracing rule of the pharaoh.

Causeway Camp. Enclosures built for defensive purposes in the **Neolithic** times in Europe, causeway camps consisted of two or more concentric rings of banks and ditches round the houses of the settlement. They could be square, round, or oval, and were large enough to provide ample room inside for the cattle. One or more gaps, or causeways, were left as entrances. A famous example in England, enlarged in Celtic times, is **Maiden Castle.**

Cave Art, *see* Prehistoric Art, Altamira *and* Lascaux.

Cave Men. In the early days of archaeology it was believed, as a result of the many discoveries in Europe of the remains of prehistoric man in caves, that **Palaeolithic** man always lived in caves, and the term Cave Man came into popular use as a convenient description of him. It is now known that Palaeolithic man, though he used caves frequently, by no means did so exclusively. In Ireland he lived in **crannogs,** in Switzerland in **lake dwellings,** in Russia in houses built partly below ground, and so on. Even where he lived in caves in the winter, in the summer he often built temporary brushwood huts.

Cave Temples. The rock-cut architecture of India forms a series extending over a millennium and occupying a unique place in the architecture of the Old World. In particular the cave temples of western India and the Deccan provide the finest examples of the style and of the rich sculptures which adorn them.

The earliest specimens of rock-cut architecture in India date from the time of the **Mauryan Empire** and are found in the hills of eastern India adjoining their kingdom of Magadha. Here in the Barabar Hills is a small group of caves dedicated by **Asoka** to the Ajivakas, an unorthodox sect which came into existence at about the same time as Buddhism. One of these caves has the typical façade of a wooden *chaitya* (or assembly) hall cut from the rock around its entrance. It may thus be argued that, while the idea of cave architecture reached India from **Achaemenid** Persia (in much the same way as did the idea of rock-cut inscriptions and the style of stone carving), there was already flourishing in India a distinctive wooden architecture which in characteristically Indian fashion was taken over by the new medium.

The western Indian series is generally agreed to be post-Mauryan, but there is not yet agreement on the age of the earliest specimens. It was formerly thought that some caves might date back to the second century B.C., but this view – founded upon the evidence of palaeography – has been challenged and recently it has been suggested that no caves are prior to the middle of the first century B.C. All the early examples are Buddhist. They generally appear in groups of *chaitya* halls and *viharas* or monasteries for residence. The long *chaitya* halls had an apsidal end in the centre of which was placed a **stupa.** In the earliest examples the wooden prototype was recalled by the pegging of wooden roofing-beams inside the rock vault, but later the beams, too, were carved from the rock. The *viharas* developed from rows of cells into square or oblong caves surrounded by cells cut in the walls, and this pattern, in which a shrine gradually assumed more and more prominence, later became that of the Brahmanical shrine caves. The sites are situated near the west coast ports and along the routes which led thence to the Deccan plateau and the interior. Outstanding examples of the early period (first century B.C. to third century A.D.) are found at Bhaja, **Ajanta** (Caves eight to thirteen), Nasik, Kanheri, Karle and Junnar. Several bear inscriptions of rulers of the Satavahana dynasty, while nearly all have donative inscriptions of monks, merchants or craftsmen. The later period was from the fifth to eighth centuries A.D., and includes much of the finest painting and sculpture at Ajanta (*see* colour plate II) and all of that at **Ellora** (*see* plate 45, page 149). This period saw the first excavations of Brahmanical caves. Of these the earliest is at Udayagiri and dates from the opening of the fifth century. These caves were both Vaishnavite (dedicated to the worship of Vishnu) and Saivite (dedicated to the worship of Siva), and include such masterpieces as the Rameswara and Kailasa caves at Ellora and those at Badami farther south. Also Brahmanical was the cave at Elephanta, which is just south of Bombay, and which excited the interest of many early European travellers. In the final stages of cave art at Ellora several caves were also dedicated to the Jain religion.

Celebes, a large island in the Indonesian archipelago to the east of Borneo, is now called Sulawesi. **Stone tools** from Galumpany indicate connections not only with south China, and indirectly with Japan, but also with certain Polynesian finds, an important link in the history of the peopling of the Pacific. A **Bronze Age** culture is also recorded, but the most important finds so far belong to a **megalithic** culture which has no satisfactory chronology. Urn burials probably belong to this phase also. The finds include large stone vats, with lids which bear stone images of frogs, and stone figures, usually without feet, since they are carved on pillars and the lower part is buried. The sexual organs are emphatically depicted.

Cellular, *see* Agglutinative.

Celt. A prehistoric chisel, axe or adze, usually of stone or bronze, sometimes of iron. (*See also* **palstave.**)

Celtic Civilization, *see* Tène, La.

Celtic Fields. In the late **Bronze Age** people of the **Hallstatt** culture invaded England, introducing the plough and a regular field system. Their fields were squarish and small, often only about a quarter of an acre in size. They formed these Celtic fields, as they are now called, on the chalk downs and the boundaries can still be traced, especially from the air, when the sun is sufficiently low for the remains of the banks to throw a shadow.

Cenotaph. A monument to a person whose body is buried elsewhere.

Cenozoic, *see* Caenozoic.

Ceylon, Stone Age Man in. Ceylon underwent periodic separations and reconnections with the Indian subcontinent during the **Pleistocene.** These have converted the island into a backwater, with relics of fauna and human cultures that throw important light upon those of the mainland. The fact that most of the freshwater fishes of Ceylon are of the same species and sub-species as those of India indicates that the last isolation occurred comparatively recently, while the recurrence in Ceylon of the Shivalik fossil fauna that is unknown in India south of the Godavari River, the presence of an Old **Stone Age** akin to the early Sohan of India and the recent discovery of **Meso-Neolithic** human skeletons together with numerous bone artifacts, an association hitherto more or less unknown from India, all render the Stone Age of Ceylon of unusual interest.

Chakravarti, *see* Mauryan Empire.

Chalcolithic. The term "chalcolithic" (pronounced – "kalko-") is applied to the age which succeeded the **Neolithic** and is largely covered by the **Bronze Age.** Formed from the Greek words for "copper" and "stone", it refers to the period when stone and early metal implements were both in use. Some authorities restrict its use to the time when **copper**

only was being used and the discovery had not yet been made that copper alloyed with tin produced the harder bronze.

Chamber Tombs in Greece were underground cave-like graves cut into the slope of a hillside and approached by a horizontal **dromos** or passage open to the sky and normally at right angles to the hill slope. At **Mycenae** the doorways of the chambers sloped inwards towards the top and had horizontal lintels. The chambers could be oval, round or rectangular. After the dead had been placed in them the doors were blocked and the dromos filled with earth. Those at Mycenae were family graves used over and over again in the course of centuries.

Champlevé. A form of enamelling in which different colours are placed in hollows sunk in the surface of metal.

Champollion, Jean-François (1790–1832), called Le Jeune to distinguish him from his elder brother Jacques Joseph, also an archaeologist, was born at Figeac in France on 22 December, 1790. Influenced by his elder brother, he soon developed a taste for the study of oriental languages and antiquities. He was educated at the Académie de Grenoble and when only sixteen he read there a paper in which he maintained that the **Coptic** language was the ancient language of Egypt. Thereafter he devoted himself to the study of Ancient Egypt. In 1807 he went to Paris where he studied at the School of Oriental languages and at the Collège de France. At the same time he began work on a dictionary and grammar of the Coptic language. In 1814 he published his two volumes entitled *Egypte sous les Pharaons*. In 1819 he returned to Grenoble where he became Professor of History at the Lyceum. He continued his researches into the Coptic language and in 1821 published *Sur L'Ecriture hiératique*. In 1822 he published his *Lettres à M.Dacier sur les hiéroglyphes phonétiques*, and followed it in 1824 with *Sur l'Ecriture démotique* and his celebrated *Précis du Système hiéroglyphique des Anciens Egyptiens, figuratif, idéographique et alphabétique* which caused a sensation for it provided the solution to the problem of translating the Egyptian **hieroglyphics.** In 1824 he was sent to study Egyptian antiquities in the museums of Italy. On his return he was appointed director of the Egyptian Museum at the Louvre. From 1828–30 he conducted a scientific expedition in Egypt with Rosellini, the results of which were published in 1833. In 1831 he received the Chair of Egyptology created specially for him at the Collège de France. His health was already failing and he died in Paris in 1832 with his great *Grammaire Egyptienne* and *Dictionnaire Egyptien* still unfinished. They were published by his brother in 1836 and 1841 respectively, and have been universally acclaimed. Champollion has been acknowledged as the founder of Egyptology, and monuments have been erected in his memory at Figeac, Turin and Florence. (*See also* **Rosetta Stone.**)

Chams. Now reduced to two small groups near Phan Thiet and Phan Rang in south Viet-nam, and the southern end of the Tonle Sap in Cambodia, the Chams once controlled the greater part of the area of Indo-China lying to the east of the Annamite Chain. The Chams speak an Indonesian language and appear to represent the last main body of this group moving southwards from the coastal parts of China to the islands of the Indonesian archipelago. The nucleus of the Cham Empire was formed when a sinized official of a Chinese government in Viet-Nam at the end of the Han dynasty led a revolt and set up a kingdom called Lin-i in A.D. 196. The capital was in the region of **Hue** and was subsequently moved to **Tra-kieu.** There is a distinct probability that the **Dong-son** culture was essentially Cham, and it is clear that the subsequent Indian influences which formed the historical Cham culture interacted with a vigorous native tradition (*See also* **Mi-son.**) *See* plates 32, 34, pages 102, 138.

Chanchan, *see* Peruvians.

Chandi Borobudur, *see* Borobudur.

Ch'ang-sha is situated in Hunan Province, China. A number of tombs of between the third and first centuries B.C. are situated outside the walls of the city which is the chief town of Hunan. The moist nature of the soil has preserved numbers of objects in wood and lacquer. Ch'ang-sha was the capital of the state of Ch'u, a feudal state of sufficient prestige for it to be permitted to retain local kings even after its incorporation into the Han Empire. The material from the site points to a non-Chinese culture with some shamanistic traits. (Shamanism is the primitive religion of the Ural-Altari peoples of Siberia.) The finds include wooden images of monsters with protruding tongues and eyes, and a human head with antlers and a protruding tongue. Wooden figures, presumably of servants, were buried with the dead, and lacquer goods, including toilet cases. The work on these is typical of Han government lacquer factories. One grave yielded the earliest known example of a writing brush.

Châtelperronian. The first of the Upper **Palaeolithic** series of cultures (i.e. those active between the last **glaciation** and the close of the Pleistocene Age about 20,000 years ago) concentrating on blade-production. Blades are long narrow **flakes** with approximately parallel sides. The Châtelperronian culture, which was situated in central France, produced fairly wide ones serving as knives, smaller ones used probably as arrows and javelin points, and scrapers and **burins** for working antler and bone.

Chavin de Huántar, *see* Peruvians.

Cheddar Man. The complete skeleton of Cheddar Man is to be seen in the Cheddar Gorge in England. It is mounted to stand upright in a small museum at the entrance to Gough's Cave.

The cave has been known since 1877. In 1903 the skeleton was found, together with flint implements and an antler *bâton-de-commandement*, a tool now thought to be a **shaft-straightener.** Further excavations in 1927 produced some hundreds more flint tools, another shaft-straightener, bone awls, part of an ivory rod, and perforated shells and teeth that could have been threaded as necklaces. Some other human remains also came to light.

The caves in the sides of the Cheddar Gorge were hollowed out in the soft limestone by water. Several of them were inhabited by bands of hunters towards the end of the **Palaeolithic** period. The population of Britain at this time was Homo sapiens, and tools found with skeletons show that there was close cultural contact with France. The English Channel was not then formed, and once the British ice that corresponded to the Würm **glaciation** had retreated, it was possible for Upper Palaeolithic cultures to develop in Britain.

In Gough's Cave, the flint tools were of the types associated with the **Creswellian** culture, as is shown by the small battered-back blades used as knives. This is a pale reflection of the splendid French **Aurignacian** of the Upper Palaeolithic. **Magdalenian** influence is shown by the presence of the shaft-straighteners.

The bones of Cheddar Man were found near the entrance of the cave, for, with little means of artificial light at his disposal, Palaeolithic Man was forced to live within the range of daylight. The spot where they were dug up is to be seen on the left-hand side in a grotto below the present ground level. *See* plate 35, page 139.

Chellean. This name for a **culture** of the **Palaeolithic** era has now been largely abandoned in favour of **Abbevillian.**

Chelles-Acheul, South African, *see* Africa, Stone Age Man in South.

Chen-la. According to Chinese historical sources, the kingdom of **Fu-nan** was overthrown towards the end of the sixth century A.D. by a feudal vassal known as Chen-la. It has not yet proved possible to identify the Chinese form of the name with any south-east Asian race or place-name, but there is little doubt that the state was a proto-**Khmer** kingdom and marks the historical emergence of the Khmers as a power in south-eastern Asia. The kingdom seems to have been centred about the Lower Mekong, and expanded to include parts of the Mun Valley and much of eastern Thailand. It seems to have acted as a means by which Indian influences were transmitted from the **Chams** to the western side of the Annamite Chain. The art of Chen-la was developed to meet the requirements of an Indianized state. Secular building was in wood: brick was used for religious buildings, but stone was used for some features. The typical building was a single room, rectangular or square in plan, though an octagonal form was also used, notably at Sambhor Prei Kuk. The superstructure was usually in the form of a staged pyramid, but in the rectangular form a gabled upper structure with a ridge crest was also employed. Important sites include those of Phnom Da, Stung Treng, Hanchey, Banteay Prei Nokor and a series of temples to the south of **Siemreap** where the later capitals of Chen-la were established.

The statuary of the Chen-la period is important for the history of Khmer art because it shows a marked transition from strong Indian influences to the emergence of a local style which lies behind later Khmer art.

Cheops, Pyramid of, *see* Pyramids.

Chersonese, *see* Chryse Chersonese.

Chert. A quartz, similar to **flint,** used for tools in **Stone Age** times.

Chia-Hsiang Hsien. This site of the Wu family tombs, (about A.D. 147–68) is situated in Shantung Province, China. These Han dynasty family tombs, together with others of much the same period from Wang-tu Hsien, Hopei, Pei-chai Ts'un, Shantung, and Hsiao-t'ang Shan, throw much light upon Han period culture. By this time the use of a brick-built, underground tomb with a true arch-and-barrel-vault roof was widespread. There are usually a number of main chambers, set north-south with side chambers opening out of them. The interior walls are either painted or covered with low relief carvings of both secular and religious scenes. The finest surviving Han period murals are at Wang-tu Hsien. Here minor officials are depicted, perhaps as attendants on the dead, together with auspicious birds and animals. The figures are outlined in black and coloured in red, blue and yellow. In the relief carvings buildings are shown, sometimes with the outer walls removed to show activities in the interior. The scenes depicted testify to the heterodox character of Han beliefs and society. History, legend, mythology, hunting, feasting are all depicted in an exuberant abundance, and Confucian moral teachings are mixed with scenes of Taoist mysticism. There is no clear break between the earthly world and that of the spirit and of the spirits. The appearance of a painted and carved stone imitation of a lantern roof at Pei-chai Ts'un points to contacts with western Asia in the second century A.D., although the earliest occurrence of an example of this structural feature in China is fifth century. Tombs of this and later periods also contain a variety of models–servants, buildings, boats etc., many of which have survived and provide valuable information about the material culture of China. *See* plates 33, 36–37, pages 137, 140–141.

Chichen Itzá, the greatest city and shrine of the **Maya,** reaching its peak between the eleventh and thirteenth centuries A.D., was in Yucatán, twenty-two miles west of Valladolid. The Itzá were a tribe of Mayan stock formerly inhabiting the city. Many of the monuments of Chichen Itzá belong to the period of the Mexican intrusion and indicate that the invaders were the Toltecs, a tribe from north of Mexico City.

Among its ruined temples are El Castillo, a large temple on a massive base with staircases leading up to it on four sides and feathered-serpent columns of Mexican type, a temple-pyramid with caryatid figures, and the Tiger Temple, decorated with magnificent colour reliefs in Mexican style. The Caracol, an astronomical observatory tower with a snail-shell-like dome, again manifests Mexican influence. Among other remains are the Court of a Thousand Columns, possibly a former market-place, and a well into which human sacrificial victims were thrown.

The city as a centre of Mayan culture came to an end with the Spanish enslavement of Yucatán. *See* plate 40, page 144.

Chimu Kingdom, *see* Peruvians.

Chinampas, *see* Aztecs.

Chopper. A specialized **stone tool,** usually made of **flint.**

Chou-kou-tien is a village near Peking in north China. In a nearby hill are great clefts which, since they were formed in the limestone, have gradually become filled with deposits. They have been described as caves, but excavation has shown that they were in fact wide clefts in which men have sheltered from time to time during the last 500,000 years. Many superimposed strata were found; some contain ashes of ancient fires, stone implements, bones of animals that were utilized as tools, or the remains of meals. Between some occupation layers were sterile deposits, when the cleft had been the home only of hyenas and other wild beasts, and debris had tumbled in from the ground surface from above.

Excavation began at Chou-kou-tien in 1921 after a Swede, Dr Andersson, had noticed pieces of quartz there. As a geologist, he realized that quartz could not occur naturally in that limestone district, and must have been brought there by man. It was hoped that the quartz-users would be discovered, but it was not until 1927 that a human tooth came to light. Later the remains of forty-five individuals (**Sinanthropus**), were found, and it is to these that Chou-kou-tien owes its fame.

A vast number of fossil animal bones has also

been found. There are about twenty kinds of mammals: horse, bear, buffalo, deer, pig, rhinoceros and hyena. Among the extinct animals are the sabre-toothed tiger and giant beaver.

Besides the cleft in which these remains were found, there are a number of others, some older than the one excavated. In the "Upper Cave" was a large number of Homo sapiens bones, with which an Upper **Palaeolithic** type of industry was found. Three skulls are interesting in that they seem to typify three racial types: Mongoloid, Melanesoid, and Eskimoid. (*See* **Fossil Man.**)

Chryse Chersonese (Greek – "Golden Peninsula") is a term used by the classical geographers and usually equated with the Suvarnabhumi of Indian writers. It is generally taken to refer to the **Malay Peninsula** with Burma, but it is probably used both precisely and as a general term like El Dorado for supposedly wealthy lands beyond the known limits of the eastern world.

Cimmerians. The *Kimmerioi* of the Greeks, and the *Gimirraa* of the Assyrians, the Cimmerians have left no inscriptions of their own, and are difficult to connect with any archaeological remains. About the end of the eighth century B.C. they surged over the Caucasus and devastated eastern Anatolia. They finally overran the whole of western Asia Minor to the coast, where **Ephesus** alone among the Greek cities held out against them, in spite of the fact that the Artemesion, the famous shrine of Artemis, which lay outside the city walls, was sacked and burnt.

Cinerary Urn. An urn containing the ashes of a dead person. Such urns have been found in **barrows.**

Cire Perdue Process. A technique for producing bronze figurines or statuettes. A model of the figure was made in wax and coated with clay. The mould was heated so that the wax melted and ran out. (*Cire perdue* is the French for "lost wax".) Molten bronze was then poured into the cavity. When the bronze had cooled the clay was chipped away.

Cist. A prehistoric coffin, usually made of stone or a hollowed-out tree; also a storage place, especially for sacred objects.

Clactonian. The name-site of this Lower **Palaeolithic** culture is an old channel of the Thames at Clacton-on-Sea. The culture apparently begins as early as the **Abbevillian,** and overlaps with the early stages of the **Acheulian.** Its characteristic tools were thick, squat **flakes** of up to six inches across. The culture produced no hand-axes. Three phases of Clactonian implements have been distinguished, culminating in those manifesting the highest skill, which are found principally at High Lodge, Suffolk. Clactonian implements are found in France and England, and there are several deposits in Lower Thames gravels.

Cleaver. A specialized **stone tool,** usually made of **flint.**

Cloisonné. A form of enamelling in which the different colours of the pattern are separated by thin strips of metal.

Clothing. Man in the earliest **Palaeolithic** times will have gone about naked. Clothing probably developed for a variety of reasons–protection from the weather, adornment, the fear of evil magic, and so on. The first form of clothing was very likely a girdle of some kind, used to hold tools and other personal possessions. In course of time this would be extended to form a loincloth or a skirt, and a cloak of some kind would be thrown over the upper part of the body.

Being made of perishable materials all early clothing has disappeared but, if we may judge by contemporary primitive communities, a wide variety of materials would be pressed into service for use as clothing - skins, hair both human and animal, grass, leaves (Genesis 3, 7), bark-cloth, and so on. Skins were undoubtedly the most usual form of costume.

The date at which spinning and weaving were invented lies so far back in prehistory that it is impossible to tell when it took place. It was certainly in **Neolithic** times, for by the **Bronze Age** woven cloth is so commonly used as to make it clear that the invention had taken place many centuries previously.

Various materials were used, differing principally according to their availability which in turn depends upon the area of the earth's surface. In **Egypt** the Neolithic villagers in the **Faiyum** grew flax in order to make linen from it. Cotton, we know, was grown in the **Indus Valley civilization** before 2500 B.C. At about the same time wool and linen were being woven in Mesopotamia, and silk in China.

Of these materials wool falls into a different category from flax, cotton, and silk, since it is almost certainly an artificial product in the sense that it was produced as the result of selective breeding of sheep, for most species of wild sheep have a hairy coat, with only a thin woolly down between the hairs.

With the rise of civilization a wide variety of costume came into existence. The ancient Egyptians wore a loincloth or kilt if they were men, cloaks or dresses if they were women, and the loincloth in some form or other was widely worn. In general clothes were loose and flowing. An exception to this is the clothing worn by the people of the **Minoan civilization.** Here the women wore wide flounced skirts and a blouse or jacket cut low so as to reveal the breasts; the clothes were skilfully shaped to fit the figure, and hence have a surprisingly modern look about them. *See* plate 38, page 142.

Clovis, New Mexico, *see* America, Early Man in.

Cochise Culture, *see* America, Early Man in.

Codex. The earliest books were normally in the form of a long strip of paper, or **papyrus,** wound on two wooden rolls. About the fourth century A.D. this was superseded by the codex (plural – codices), the modern form of book, in which the paper is in sheets sewn together at one side. The oldest known codex dates from about 715 B.C. and was found at **Nimrud.**

Cody, *see* America, Early Man in.

Coelacanth. An instance of a **"living fossil"**.

Coffin Texts, *see* Book of the Dead.

Coinage. Money used as a medium of exchange comes late in the history of mankind and money in the form of coins does not appear until a few centuries B.C. When men lived on food provided by nature in simple self-supporting communities there was probably little communication between the groups. But the provisions of nature are uneven, and from the earliest days there were areas where abundance of game or fish or the fruits of the earth tempted the have-nots to barter with the haves. Such exchanges without the medium of money are common among some of the less developed folk today. Occasionally when relations are unfriendly, this exchange takes the form of "silent trade" (described by **Herodotus** as occurring on the west coast of Africa) when the traders never meet. Goods are left at a certain place. These are collected and goods left in return, without any personal contact. In many native markets goods are still exchanged for goods without any money being used. But for important transactions there has always been a need for some standard by which values could be estimated, not only for the mundane exchange of goods but for the more serious matters of "bride-price" and "blood-money" or wergild (rate at which a man had to be paid for if he were killed in Anglo-Saxon times). For example, values were estimated in cattle in prehistoric Europe, in cowries further east, in shells, knives and hoes in China. Metal tools or weapons were current in Africa, shell strings were used in the Pacific, and wampum in north-east America. Such objects, though awkward or cumbersome, were sufficient for their purpose. Metal currencies were the least cumbersome and the most useful, whether for making into tools, weapons or ornaments, or for exchanging again for other goods. So, as trading developed, metal in varying shapes, of varying values, of varying weights, "portable, durable, divisible and recognizable", came to be preferred by buyers and sellers alike. When the metal was cut up into pieces of even weight, and these were stamped with a mark to show that they were genuine, coinage came into existence.

It is commonly believed that coinage was invented in the eastern Mediterranean about 700 B.C. though the possibility of earlier independent invention in China cannot be ignored. Some authorities date the earliest Chinese round coins about 1000 B.C., others, following Chinese writings and traditions, even 1,000 years earlier. But all are uninscribed and further evidence is needed to place them in their right sequence and approximate centuries.

The assumption that coinage was invented in the eastern Mediterranean rests on firmer foundations. Right across Europe, from Ireland in the west to further India, cattle formed the main standard of value as well as the store of wealth. The "bride-price" of a woman or the "blood-price" of a man was reckoned in cattle. But something more portable, durable, divisible and recognizable was needed for trade, especially in an area where the keen traders of the Greek islands met the merchandise brought by caravan across Asia, and the rich products of Egypt from the south.

It was natural that traders should welcome the use of gold, silver, bronze or iron, which, though representing the value of an ox, could be carried in small bulk in the shape of rods or bars, rings or lumps. Such were the shekels of the Phoenicians and the talents of Greece. But shekels and talents were weights, not coins.

The introduction of stamped coinage has been attributed to Pheidon of Argos, to Midas of Phrygia and to Candaules or Croesus of Lydia, but the origin was probably due to the custom among traders of putting a mark on their lumps of metal to avoid having to weigh them for each transaction. This mark gave assurance of correct weight and value. A city stamp would have more authority than that of a trader and a regal stamp was best of all. Greek cities were quick to take advantage of the new invention, and Athens issued its "owls", Corinth its "foals", and Aegina its "turtles". The first coins to spread over the then-known world were the "philippi" distributed over the Alexandrian Empire, barbarous copies of which formed the coinage of Kent in the first century B.C.

Cöln-Lindenthal, *see* Köln-Lindenthal.

Colossus. A statue of considerably more than life-size (plural – colossi).

Copper. How man learnt to extract metals from their ores is still a matter of guesswork. In the case of copper it may have resulted from the use of malachite (copper carbonate) as a pigment, and pieces being dropped in the fire and reduced in consequence to small pieces of pure copper. The process of producing copper by heating copper ores with charcoal had been discovered in the fourth millennium B.C. in the Middle East, and the discovery that copper could be melted and then cast in any desired shape in a mould followed.

Copper is not to be found everywhere but in certain localities. Cyprus was a particularly famous source in ancient times, so famous, indeed, that it gave its name to the metal. Copper's discovery and use were, therefore, one of the factors which led to trade being organized and to a development from the self-sufficiency of Neolithic times in the direction of civilization.

The next step in the story of copper was the discovery that it was easier to cast copper, and the product was more reliable if it was alloyed, that is, if some other metal was added to it. Experiment probably led to the realization that tin provided the best alloy, and so bronze (ideally eight parts of copper to one of tin) was invented.

The Copper Age had neither the duration of the **Neolithic** period which preceded it, nor the importance of the **Bronze Age** which succeeded it; it is sometimes referred to as the **Chalcolithic** period.

Coprolite is fossilized dung.

Coptic Language. The term "Copt" is a Europeanized form of the Arabic word, itself a corruption of the Greek word *Aigyptos*, applied by the Moslem invaders of Egypt in A.D. 639 to the indigenous, non-Greek speaking population of the country. Their language, to which the term Coptic is given, represents the last and best understood stage of the ancient Egyptian tongue. As a spoken language Coptic died out in the sixteenth century, being superseded by Arabic, the modern tongue of Egypt. It is, however, still in use, in the Bohairic dialect form, as the liturgical language of the ancient Christian Monophysite church, though little understood. Knowledge of the Coptic language never died out among western orientalists; the lexicographical and grammatical aid that it provided was one of the reasons for the rapid progress made in the recovery of the ancient language of Egypt, once the **hieroglyphic** signs on the **Rosetta Stone** had been deciphered.

Core. The central part of a **flint** tool from which the **hand-axe** was shaped. (*See also* **Stone Tools**.)

Crannog is an Irish word used to describe ancient dwellings built, presumably for safety, on artificial islands in lakes. Those in Britain owe their discovery ultimately to the finding of the Swiss Neolithic lake villages (*see* **Lake Dwellings**). The interest aroused by these finds led two Somerset archaeologists, Bulleid and Gray, to investigate low mounds near Glastonbury in England. There they discovered that about 50 B.C. Celts had made an island in what had then been a lake. They had cut down thousands of trees, stripped them of their branches, and laid them on the lake bed. To keep them in place, vertical posts were driven in from above, and a palisade was erected all round the edge of the roughly triangular "island". The floors of the huts consisted of planks laid as floor-boards, and clay was brought in dug-out canoes from pits one and a half miles away, so that fires could be lit with safety in the huts on a central hearth.

The local interest roused by the Glastonbury excavations in their turn led a farmer to discover a second lake village not far away, at Meare. He built some hay ricks on low hummocks, which were the highest ground available. When he dug holes to erect posts for a wire fence round the ricks he found pottery, and took it to Glastonbury to be identified.

Recently, industrial activities have led to the discovery of a number of important crannogs in Ireland. In 1953, in Co. Tyrone, a factory pumped water from a lake. The tops of vertical trunks holding together an artificial island were noticed as the water level fell, and were at first considered to be the remains of an ancient pine forest. An even more important settlement was found at Lough Gara, near Boyle, in 1952. There crannogs of three different periods were found, with about two dozen dug-out canoes which were the only means of communication for crannog-dwellers. A government drainage scheme was responsible for these finds.

Apart from their intrinsic interest, the archaeological importance of crannogs is the preservation by waterlogging of wooden articles which would otherwise have entirely decayed.

Creswellian. At Creswell Crags, a limestone formation on the border of Derbyshire and Nottinghamshire in England with many caves in cliff walls, traces of **Palaeolithic** and **Mesolithic** habitation have been found. In the cave known as "Mother Grundy's Parlour" were **Gravettian**-type **stone tools** including blades often of **microlithic** proportions. Incised figures on bone have also been discovered, the engraving of a horse's head being comparable with **Magdalenian** work. The material found here forms type specimens of what is known as the Creswellian culture, the British offshoot of the Gravettian.

Crete, *see* Minoan Civilization, Knossos, etc.

Cro-magnon. The remains of some **Aurignacian** people – Homo sapiens of a completely modern European type – have been found at Cro-magnon in France. These people, who probably migrated to Europe from Asia, were a tall, finelybuilt race with a high cranium and refined features and were probably the first representatives of the fully evolved Homo sapiens in Europe. (*See also* **Fossil Man.**)

Cromlech. This is an archaeological term which has changed in meaning. Originally it meant a **megalithic** tomb of **Neolithic** times. Later it came to be used for a single standing stone. Now it is more usually reserved for a circle of standing stones of prehistoric date (*see* **Dolmen**).

Ctesiphon. About twelve miles south-east of Baghdad near the road to Hamadan on the east bank of the River Tigris lie some of the most impressive ruins of **Iraq**. The massive vaulted arch and brick façade of the west wing of the crumbling palace are known as the Arch of Ctesiphon, being attributed to Chosroes (Khusrau) the Great (A.D. 531–79). However, many of the architectural remains still standing in that country are today attributed to legendary builders of the past, Sennacherib, Semiramis and Chosroes among them.

In 129 B.C. the site was a camping ground used by the **Parthian** kings from which they surveyed the enemy in the capital Seleucia across the river. By 55 B.C. a palace had been built there and a village developed and eventually, under the **Sassanians,** it became the alternative capital to Seleucia itself.

The surviving building dates from the fourth century A.D. and though it may incorporate some work by Chosroes its origin may best be attributed to the work of Sapor I (A.D. 242–72). The large throne-hall, or Liwan, of Sassanian design still stands today as the widest single-span vault of unreinforced brickwork (twenty-seven yards) in the world. The vaulted roof, twenty-seven yards wide by fifty-four yards long and forty yards high above the pavement, is pierced with small weep-holes as a precaution against damp and the open end of the vast hall may well have been draped with curtains.

Ctesiphon was frequently attacked and fell to Trajan and Lucius Verus but it withstood the army of Queen Zenobia of **Palmyra.** When the Arab invaders under **Khalid ibn Walid** entered in A.D. 637 they are said to have recovered immense booty and found the Liwan, which they adapted as a prayer hall, covered with a vast carpet measuring thirty-three by thirty-three yards.

The original plan of the palace has been traced by a number of German expeditions since 1903. Since the east wing collapsed in 1909 the remaining west façade, with its ten foot-thick mud-brick walls on which traces of wooden tie-beams can be seen, was buttressed by order of Gertrude Bell, the first Director of Antiquities in modern Iraq. *See* plate 41, page 145.

Culture. A stage of development in prehistoric times in which all the **artifacts** have a definite similarity and relationship, so that they can be recognized and identified when they appear elsewhere.

Culture Sequence. The order in which the different stages of cultural development follow each other in an archaeological excavation, the oldest in date being usually at the lowest level.

Cuneiform. The word means "wedge-shaped" and is used of the ancient writing of Sumer, Babylon and Assyria because the letters are built up of wedge-shaped strokes. Cuneiform originated in the fourth millennium B.C. and is the oldest known form of writing; it has survived because it was written on wet clay tablets which were then baked hard (*see* **Behistun Rock, Grotefend, Rawlinson**).

Cunningham, Alexander (1814–93). Major-general in the Indian army, and first Director-general of Archaeology in India, Sir Alexander Cunningham came first to India from England at the age of nineteen with a commission in the Bengal engineers. At the start of his twenty-eight years' military service he came in contact with the scholarly antiquarian, James Prinsep, who fired him with an interest in numismatics and history. His enthusiasm soon developed: in 1837 he visited **Sarnath** (*see* plates 122, 124, pages 388, 390) and did some excavation; in 1848, after a period of duty in Kashmir and Ladakh, he wrote a paper on the temple architecture of that area; and in 1850 he visited **Sanchi** (*see* colour plate XIV, plates 31, 121, pages 101, 387), excavated it, and published a book on the site. The creation of the Archaeological Survey in 1863 was largely the result of his labours, and on retiring from the army he became its first director. During the next twenty-two years he published numerous volumes reporting his discoveries. The reports included the first illustration of typical **Harappan** finds. Other volumes included a corpus of *Inscriptions of Asoka* (1877) (*see* **Mauryan Empire**), *Coins of India* (1891), *Ancient Geography of India* (1871), and studies of the Buddhist remains at Bharhut and Bodh Gaya.

Thus Cunningham set the tradition of broad interests which has since characterized the work of the Archaeological Survey of India, developing alike numismatics, epigraphy, exploration, excavation and conservation. If his excavations were aimed mainly at recovering relics it is because he succeeded in a remarkable way in obtaining the information he required by exploration and other less costly means.

Cursive Writing. Running hand-writing, in which the letters are linked, or run together as they are written; the opposite form is **uncial.**

Cuvier, Georges Leopold (1769–1832). Baron Cuvier was a Frenchman who was inspired by the theories of his fellow-countryman, Georges **Buffon,** and by his own numerous discoveries of fossils, to produce a theory that there had been three separate creations, each of which had been ended by a cataclysm such as the **Flood.** Only so could he explain the presence of fossils in the rocks. He thus paved the way for the theory of enormously big geological eras first set out by Charles **Lyell** in 1830–33.

Cyclades. This group of partly volcanic islands lying between Greece and Crete, was the centre of a flourishing **Bronze Age** culture known as the Cycladic, and divided into the following periods, Early Cycladic (?3000–1900 B.C.), Middle Cycladic (1900–1550 B.C.) and Late Cycladic (1550–1100 B.C.).

No clear evidences have yet been cited for the existence of a Neolithic culture but the **obsidian** abounding on the island of Melos seems to have been exported at a very early date to Crete and the mainland as material for knives and arrow-heads. Pottery and marble figurines of Early Cycladic I type have been found on various sites in Crete and it seems not improbable that the Bronze Age may have started a little later on that island than in the Cyclades, and the bronze pins with birds' heads

Photo: from "Archaeology in China" by William Watson, Max Parrish and Co. Ltd, London

PLATE 33. CHIA-HSIANG HSIEN: mural in red, blue and yellow, outlined with black, of a minor official, possibly an attendant on the deceased, from the "beehive" brick tomb at Wang-tu Hsien, latter Han dynasty. *(By courtesy of the Britain-China Friendship Association)*

Photo: Anthony Christie

PLATE 34. CHAMS: a game of polo, eleventh century A.D.

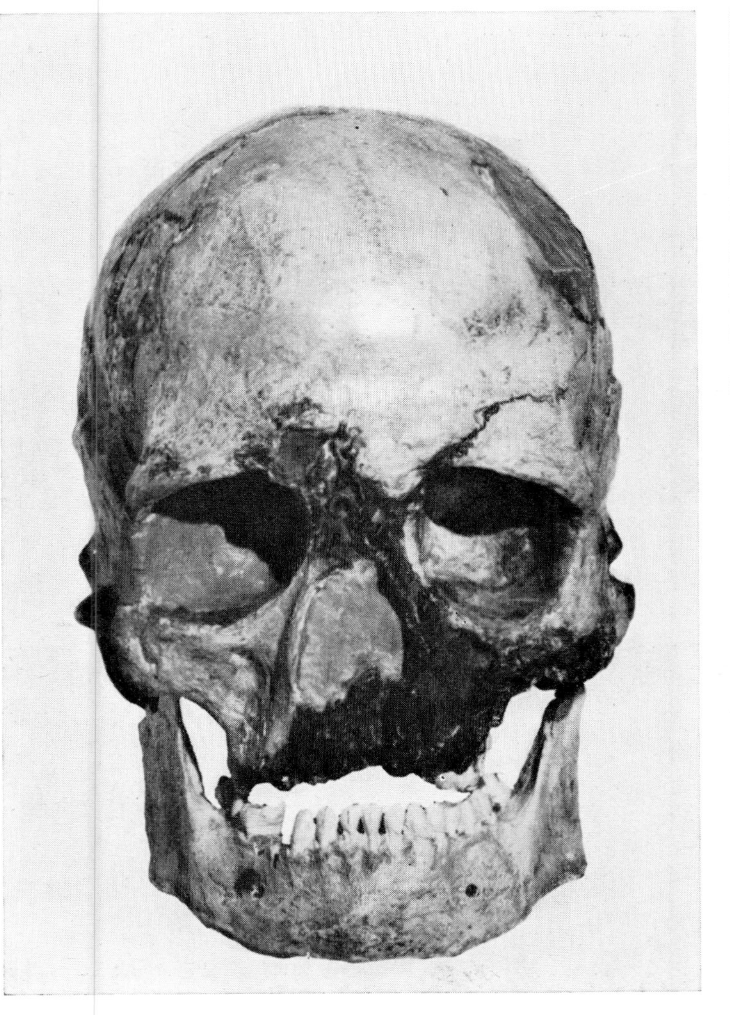

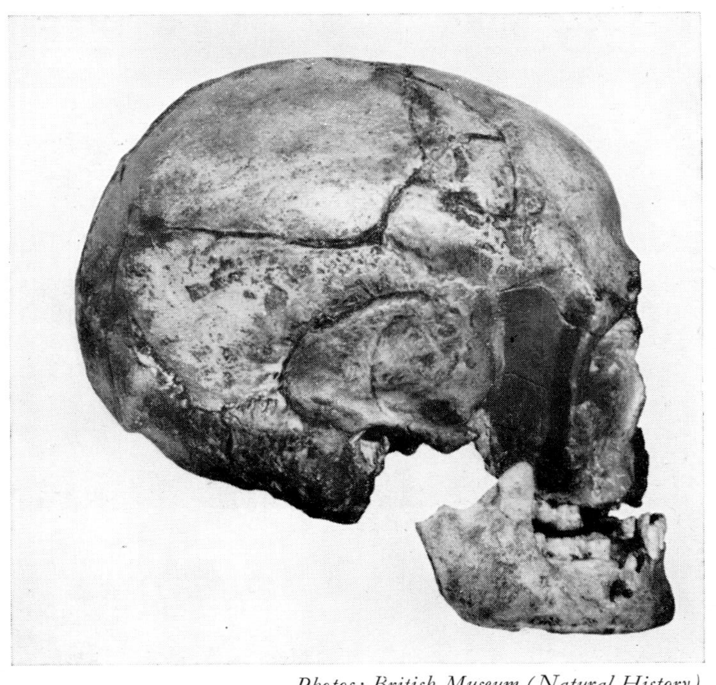

Photos: British Museum (Natural History)

PLATE 35. CHEDDAR MAN: skull of Cheddar Man from Gough's Cave, Cheddar Gorge. *(British Museum (Natural History), London)*

A

Photo: from "Archaeology in China" by William Watson, Max Parrish and Co. Ltd, London

PLATE 36. CHIA-HSIANG HSIEN: (A) part of upper frieze of twenty-four minor officials, possibly attendants on the deceased (B) part of the lower frieze of auspicious birds and beasts. From the "beehive" brick tomb at Wang-tu Hsien, latter part of Han dynasty. *(By courtesy of the Britain-China Friendship Association)*

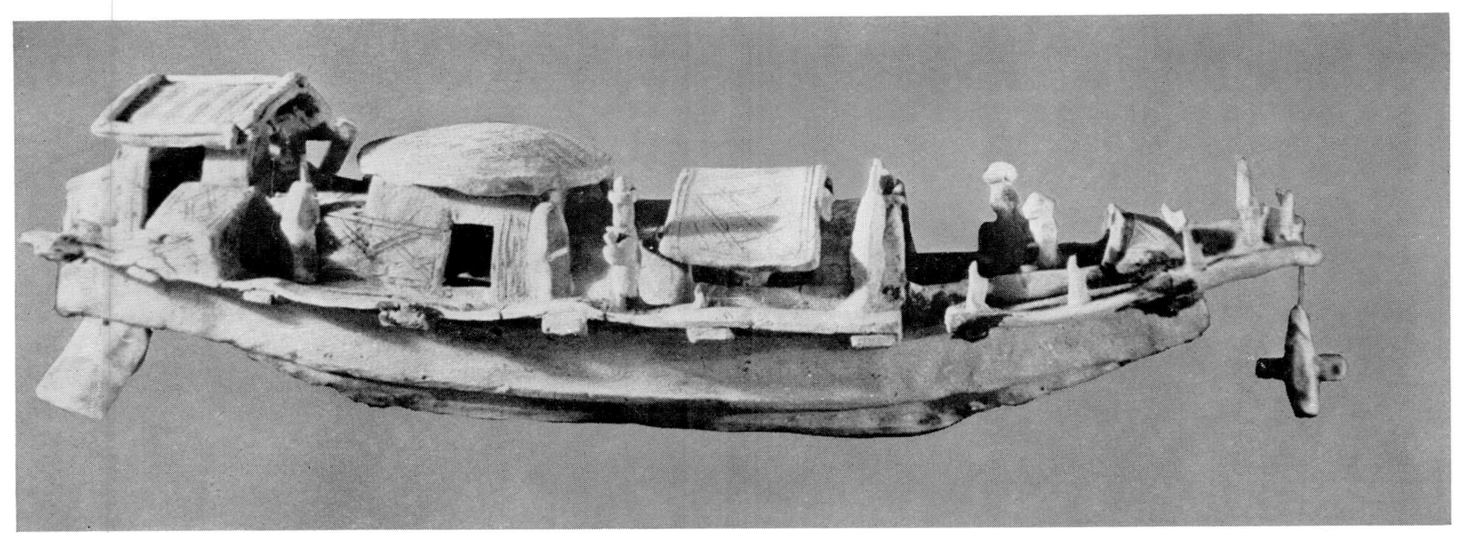

Photo: from "Archaeology in China" by William Watson, Max Parrish and Co. Ltd, London

PLATE 37. CHIA-HSIANG HSIEN: pottery model of a boat from Eastern Suburb, Canton, Kwantung Province, latter part of Han dynasty. *(By courtesy of the Britain-China Friendship Association)*

Photo: National Museum

PLATE 38. CLOTHING: a woman of about 1000 B.C. in an embroidered jersey and hairnet, from an oak coffin, Skrydstrup, Denmark. *(National Museum, Copenhagen)*

Photo: Camera Press

PLATE 39. DEAD SEA SCROLLS: the Second Isaiah Scroll before unrolling. *(By courtesy of The Hebrew University, Jerusalem)*

Plate 40. Chichen Itzá: typical designs used in ornamentation.

Photo: Exclusive News Agency

Photo: Exclusive News Agency

PLATE 41. CTESIPHON: the "Arch of Ctesiphon", a massive vaulted arch popularly attributed to Chosroes the Great. The arch is the widest single-span vault of unreinforced brickwork in the world.

Photo: British Museum

PLATE 42. CYCLADES: mother-goddess figures in marble, early Cycladic period, ? 3000–1900 B.C. *(British Museum, London)*

Photo: Paul Popper

PLATE 43. EASTER ISLAND: rock carving.

Photo: A. F. Kersting

PLATE 44. EGYPT: statue of the god Horus at Edfu.

Photo: Mansell Collection

PLATE 45. ELLORA: Visvakarma cave (number X), upper part, front view, late seventh or early eighth century A.D.

Photo: Canadian National Film Board

PLATE 46. ESKIMOS: woman with braids by an unknown carver from Sugluk.

Photo: National Portrait Gallery

PLATE 47. Arthur John EVANS (1851–1941), portrait by Francis Dodd drawn in 1935. *(National Portrait Gallery, London)*

Photo: British Museum

PLATE 48. ETRUSCANS: sea-horse, probably from the rim of a bowl, 550–500 B.C. *(British Museum, London)*

Photo: Thor Heyerdahl

PLATE V. EASTER ISLAND statues. Only the heads remain above ground today. These statues stand at the foot of the Rano Raraku quarries, where they had been only temporarily raised to have their backs finished before transportation to distant temple platforms.

found on these islands are paralleled by examples from Thermi I, **Troy** I, **Siyalk** IV and **Harappa.**

The most important site is that of Phylakopi excavated by the British School at Athens on Melos where there exist the remains of three successive cities erected above a primitive Early Cycladic I settlement.

The first city of Phylakopi (unlike the settlements on Syra and Siphnos) was without any city wall but had well-constructed rectangular houses of basalt and limestone. The pottery consisted chiefly of the grey incised Early Cycladic type familiar on most of the other islands, but accompanied in the later stages of Phylakopi I by pottery with simple geometric designs in dark brown lustrous paint on a white slip (found also on Syra, Siphnos, etc.).

The second city erected at the beginning of the Middle Cycladic period has left more ambitious remains with well laid out streets and a strong city wall. The influences of the **Minoan civilization** of Crete are illustrated by imports of Kamares wares, by increasing naturalism and the use of polychromy in the local pottery, and by a splendid fresco depicting flying fish probably painted by a Cretan artist. Polychrome jugs of the latest Middle Cycladic style were exported to Crete where examples were found in the Temple Repositories at **Knossos.**

Similar but less important cities existed on Paros and on Thera. Phylakopi II was violently destroyed by fire but was succeeded almost immediately by Phylakopi III, also a walled city.

The Cyclades now fell more under the influence, if not the actual control, of the **Mycenaean** culture of the mainland. A Mycenaean palace complete with a **megaron** hall, secluded quarters for the women and an open courtyard in front was constructed in the centre of the town. The smaller houses followed Cycladic models but the street plans of Phylakopi I, II and III all varied, and did not continue the old pattern. The late Cycladic variety of the native pottery continued to be made but Mycenaean vases were imported in ever increasing numbers.

The settlement on Thera vanished about 1500 B.C. after the volcanic eruption which blew up the whole of the centre of the island.

Mycenaean settlers and culture penetrated to the other islands also, but there appears to have been a general decline not only in the culture but in the actual population of the Cyclades after 1400 B.C.

Dorian-speaking Greeks began to colonize some of the Cyclades such as Thera and Melos in the tenth century B.C. but on the other islands, where the Ionic tongue was spoken, the inhabitants may have been descended from Mycenaean settlers (*see also* **Mediterranean, The Eastern**). *See* plate 42, page 146.

Cyclopean Masonry. Masonry formed of huge uncut blocks of limestone with a filling of smaller stones and rubble; it was much used by the people of **Mycenae** and gained its name because it was believed by the people of **Homer**'s day and after to have been erected by the Cyclops, one-eyed giants of Greek mythology.

Cylinder Seal, *see* Seal.

Cyprus, *see* Mediterranean, the Eastern.

D

Dagoba. Another name for a **stupa.**

Danger Cave, Utah, *see* America, Early Man in.

Darwin, Charles (1809–82), was not the first to put forward a theory of evolution, but he was the first to see his theory become widely accepted and finally established. Born at Shrewsbury in England in 1809 the turning-point in his life came in 1831 when he began a five-year voyage round the world as naturalist on the naval survey ship *Beagle*. In the Galapagos islands he noticed how each island had its own individual species, slightly different from the species both on the other islands and on the mainland. He found it impossible to believe what was then the orthodox view that a different set of animals had been created for each island, and came to the conclusion that there had been a common mainland stock and that the island species had evolved differently as a result of their isolation. Patiently he collected facts which showed that no two individuals, of whatever species, are exactly alike, and that, in the struggle for existence, the one more fitted to adapt itself to life and its changing circumstances would be the one to survive and breed. It was not until 1856 that he felt he had collected enough facts to prove his theory, and in 1859 he finished and published his great book *On the*

Origin of Species by means of Natural Selection. The previous year he had delivered to the Linnean Society in London a paper stating his views, doing so jointly with Alfred Russel **Wallace** who had arrived independently at the same conclusions, though without amassing the information which made Darwin's theory, so formidable, that he and his supporters won a victory for their views.

Dawson, Charles, *see* Piltdown Man.

Dead Sea Scrolls. The ancient Hebrew, Aramaic and Greek manuscripts now known as the Dead Sea Scrolls represent, perhaps, the most sensational archaeological discovery of our age, for these documents, many of which are of books of the Old Testament, are older by at least 1,000 years than the hitherto earliest known Old Testament manuscript. Since the first discovery by a shepherd in 1947, thousands of learned articles and dozens of books have been written about them, although as yet it has only been possible to study and publish less than a third of the total available texts. Since 1947 scarcely a year has passed without some new cave being discovered, and eleven caves are now known from which manuscript material, in large or small quantities, has been recovered. These caves are all in the barren foot-hills on the north-western shores of the Dead Sea in Palestine; some are natural caves in the rock and others are artificially cut in the soft marl.

Cave I produced the only complete scrolls so far found, the great scroll of Isaiah, seven and a half yards long, and some large but incomplete pieces of seven other scrolls; there were also hundreds of tiny fragments of about forty other manuscripts. But the greatest quantity of material came from cave IV, discovered in 1952. In this case there were no complete or even nearly complete scrolls, but about a hundred thousand fragments varying in size from a finger nail to a foolscap sheet, in all states of preservation. The reason for this is that in cave I most manuscripts had been placed in pottery jars, whereas in cave IV they had been simply laid on the ground and so rendered subject to the chemical action of the soil – cave IV is an artificial one in the marl – and to damage by rats, white ant and weevil. Cave XI, found in 1956, has provided some of the best preserved documents, including a scroll which seems to be complete in length but has the lower quarter of it eaten away by damp.

At the beginning, one of the most difficult and important problems was the date of these scrolls: the only available evidence then was the actual form of the letters used, and for these there was practically no comparative material to help. Estimates of their age ranged from the third century B.C. to the eighth A.D., and one scholar even maintained that they were all forgeries. When cave I was excavated in 1949 the objects found in it were not of much assistance for dating purposes, for the pottery was of an unfamiliar type which was thought to belong to the first century B.C. Linen found in the cave gave, when submitted to the **carbon fourteen** test, a central date of A.D. 33, with a margin of error of 200 years on either side. So it was important to try and find something which would give a more accurate date, and only archaeology or the contents of the scrolls could offer such a possibility. The contents have so far failed to provide the necessary information, but archaeology has done so.

Just over half of mile south of cave I was a small ancient ruin known as Khirbet Qumran, and although a surface examination of the pottery seemed to suggest that it was later than the date of the cave, it was the only ancient site in the neighbourhood, and the possibility of a connection could not be ignored. A trial excavation was accordingly started there in 1951, and by a lucky chance there was found, buried in the floor of the first room to be cleared, a jar identical with those from the cave, and beside it on the floor a coin of A.D. 10. So a direct connection between the site and scrolls was established, and a date some sixty years later than that originally proposed by the archaeologists.

In the following year more extended excavations were started; these have been continued each subsequent year, and now the entire history of the site and so of the scrolls, has been firmly established. That this is so is chiefly due to the great number of coins found – more than 500 altogether – which provide an almost continuous sequence for nearly 200 years. A quantity of potsherds and one **ostrace** show that the site was originally a small fort in the **Iron Age**, about the sixth century B.C., which was abandoned a century or so later. It was not reoccupied until the scrolls community established themselves there in the last quarter of the second century B.C.

From this time there is a continuous coin sequence up to the time of Herod the Great; only three coins have been found from his very prosperous reign. But there was clear evidence that the building in its first form had been destroyed by a great earthquake, for there was a crack right through the whole structure from north to south, and the eastern section had sunk some twenty inches lower than the western. It is known from the historian Josephus that in 31 B.C. there was a violent earthquake while Herod was in Jericho with his army, so it seems probable that this is the date of the Qumran destruction and may account for its temporary abandonment, for there are no further coins until 5 B.C., when the place was apparently re-occupied and rebuilt. Occupation now continues up to A.D. 68, which is the latest date attested by any coins found in the actual building. The place was then utterly destroyed by fire, and on the ruins a few rooms were built and inhabited by the Tenth Roman Legion up to about the end of the century, as attested again by coins. It would seem, then, that in the year before the destruction of Jerusalem by Titus, this settlement was destroyed by the Romans and, save for squatters, was never occupied again. But the inhabitants must have had sufficient warning of the approach of the Roman troops to hide their most valued possession – their library – in the caves round about, where it remained undiscovered until a few years ago.

So it is clear from the excavation that none of the scrolls can be later than A.D. 68, and many of them are certainly considerably earlier. This means that the Old Testament manuscripts are older by 1,000 years than the hitherto earliest known ones. The archaeological evidence is conclusive, and has now been generally accepted.

The manuscripts themselves fall into two main classes, books of the Old Testament, and other works of various kinds, the proportion being roughly one-third Old Testament books to two-thirds other works. The most popular books, if quantity can be considered a criterion of popularity, were those of Isaiah, Deuteronomy and Psalms, for there are between ten and fifteen manuscripts of each of these three. Furthermore there are, sometimes in the same book, almost word for word examples of the Massoretic (authorised Hebrew) text; of the Septuagint (early Greek translation) both in its original Hebrew and in Greek; one example of the Samaritan text of Deuteronomy; and often yet another version which differs slightly from all these. Usually this latter version is also superior.

In general, the historical books of the Old Testament seem to favour the Septuagint rather than the Massoretic readings. In six large fragments of Samuel, for example, the Qumran text follows the Septuagint thirteen times when the Greek disagrees with the Massoretic text, as against four cases where the Qumran text agrees with the Massoretic against the Septuagint; three to one in favour of the Greek tradition. But it is too soon yet to draw any firm conclusions on such evidence, for there is still an enormous amount of work in front of the scholars who are piecing together and translating these difficult texts. It does, however, seem clear that the discovery of the Qumran scrolls will not involve any radical changes in the Old Testament text; they will undoubtedly help to explain many hitherto obscure passages and fill in a few gaps, but there will be no question of re-writing the Old Testament.

The other works are of many kinds: Apocryphal books, both known and new, commentaries on Old Testament books, hymns and psalms, liturgies, theological works, and works relating to the sect who lived at Qumran and wrote the scrolls. Among the Apocryphal books there is, for instance, the Book of Tobit in its original Aramaic for the first time; hitherto it has only been known in Greek translation. Some of the new Apocrypha is of great interest, such as *The War between the Children of Light and the Children of Darkness*, and there are others which seem to be peculiar to the sect, such as *The Book of Enoch*, *The Testament of the Twelve Patriarchs*, *The Sayings of Moses*, and so on. The Commentaries are attempts to explain parts of Old Testament books (Habakkuk, Nahum, etc.) in terms of past or present events connected with the sect. This could, of course, provide a good deal of information about their history, except that most allusions are so oblique, and there are so few mentions of identifiable historical figures, that reconstruction of the story must be largely speculation.

From the sectarian manuscripts, of which there are two main works known as *The Manual of Discipline* and *The Zadokite* or *Damascus Document*, it has been deduced that they were the people known as the Essenes, about whom the ancient writers Josephus and Pliny the Elder have hitherto been almost our only sources of information. Pliny's description of their settlement between Jericho and Ain Giddi so closely fits the circumstances of Qumran that there can be no doubt they are one and the same.

We learn from the manuscripts that they considered their founder was one whom they do not name but call the Teacher of Righteousness; he it was, apparently, who led them out into the wilderness to found what can only be described as the earliest monastic establishment. They call themselves the people of the New Testament who have chosen the Way. Love of God and neighbour is the sum of their law. They are the poor in the world, the children of light, the elect of God who shall judge Israel and the nations at the end of days, and so on, and their philosophy approaches very closely that of the early Christians.

The central "sacraments" of the sect were baptism and communion meals; their baptism, like that of John, was on repentance of sins into the community. There is a detailed account of their communion meals of bread and wine, in which the priest first blesses the food which is then shared out among the others in strict order of precedence. Detailed parallels of practice between Essenes and Christians is by no means the whole story; equally important is the common theological world view of the two sects. Both live in the "end of days". Both live in a world in which the powers of righteousness and the powers of evil are engaged in warfare. The Essenes recognize in events of their own days signs of the fulfilment of Old Testament prophecies. According to one manuscript they considered they were called upon "to go into the desert to prepare there the way of the Lord, according as it is written, 'in the desert prepare ye the Way, make straight in the wilderness a highway for our God'". In this there is a clear parallel with John the Baptist, whom many scholars consider was a member of the sect.

At the same time there are many divergencies between the sect and the early Christians, chief of which perhaps is that the Essenes considered salvation was only for those of the sect who were God's elect, whereas Christ preached salvation for all.

No doubt there are many surprises in store for us in this great collection of manuscripts, but it will be many years before translation and publication is complete; when it is, scholars the world over will have in their hands material for the study of the Old Testament and of the origins of the early Christian Church such as has never been seen or dreamt of before. *See* plate 39, page 143.

Dea Mater. Another name for the **Earth Goddess**; the name is Latin for "the goddess mother".

Deir el Medinah. At Deir el Medinah, in the desert near Thebes in Egypt, were housed the workmen who made the tombs of the **Valley of the Kings.** It was founded originally probably by Amenhotep I, though the bricks of the enclosure wall are stamped with the name of Tuthmosis I. It contained about seventy houses, situated on either side of a main street, onto which the houses opened directly. The village flourished throughout the eighteenth dynasty and was probably at its peak under Ramses II; the workmen were buried in tombs near to the village. During the nineteenth and twentieth dynasties the tombs were family affairs, burials taking place through many generations. They were surmounted by small hollow brick pyramids, with limestone capstones. The barrel-vaulted burial chambers were decorated with religious scenes. The rich documentation of the village life from the countless number of **ostraca** found there, relating to the legal, commercial and social activities of the workmen, dries up at the end of the twentieth dynasty, but the chapel belonging to the village was rebuilt in the Ptolemaic period.

Deluge, the, *see* Flood, the.

Demotic. The term "demotic" (Greek *demotikos* – "popular") has been adopted by modern scholars to describe a form of **cursive** script used by the ancient Egyptians from about 700 B.C. down to the third century A.D. (though it is occasionally used with reference to other languages). The script is engraved on the **Rosetta Stone** (*see* plate 119, page 385) below the **hieroglyphs**; its inclusion was necessary to proper promulgation of the decree, since hieroglyphs by this time (196 B.C.) were only understood by the priests.

Demotic, as many of its spellings and forms of individual signs show, is a more cursive derivative of **hieratic**, and was adapted for writing with a pen on papyrus or potsherds ("**ostraca**"), and intended for popular, not monumental use. The vast majority of our demotic texts are legal documents and official and private letters, which are of the greatest importance for Egyptian legal and social history, but a fair number of literary and magico-scientific works survive. In general, elegance has been sacrificed to speed, especially in documents; but the finest hands have rhythm and dignity.

Desert Cultures, *see* America, Early Man in.

Dinkel Wheat, *see* Emmer Wheat.

Dinosaurs. The dinosaurs rioted throughout the **Mesozoic era,** and their fossilized bones have been found in all parts of the world. They ranged in size from about that of a kangaroo to the vast ninety-foot-long Diplodocus, the largest land animal known, which was common in America; their brains were the size of that of a modern kitten. They dominated the earth for about one hundred and twenty million years, a far longer period than any other kind of creature, and became extinct about seventy million years before the appearance of man, whose ancestors during this period were probably the tiny tree-shrews.

Dog. The dog was the first animal to be domesticated by man. This took place in **Mesolithic** times, for its bones have been discovered in European settlements of the **Maglemosian** culture which came to Britain from the east, and in similar settlements of the **Tardenoisian** culture which probably originated in north Africa and spread from there northward across Europe.

Arguments have raged over whether the ancestor of the tamed dog was the wolf, the fox, or the jackal; the most widely accepted theory is the dog is descended from the wolf. Probably packs of wolves haunted settlements for the sake of obtaining surplus meat and bones. Possibly the young were captured and tamed, and a pack of domesticated dogs formed. These were used in the chase and their loyalty kept by a regular supply of food.

The remains of dogs are found on sites throughout **Neolithic** times. Bones dated to 6000 B.C. show that as early as that date there were two types, a species of terrier, and a larger and presumably fiercer kind. By the time that dogs begin to be represented in civilized times it is clear that selective breeding has been in progress for a long time. **Assyrian** sculptures show two main breeds; one a mastiff-like type clearly bred for fighting and guarding purposes, the other a greyhound type equally obviously bred for its speed in hunting. Egyptian paintings and the **mummies** of dogs show that there were several breeds as early as 3000 B.C. – wolfhounds, greyhounds, terriers, possibly even small pet dogs.

Dolmen. This name and **cromlech** originally had the same meaning – a **megalithic** tomb of **Neolithic** times. Now this meaning is reserved for dolmen.

Domestication of Animals. The first animal to be domesticated by man was the **dog.** This took place in **Mesolithic** times. It was not until the **Neolithic** period that any more animals were tamed and domesticated, by which is meant that they were brought under human control and deliberately protected, cared for, and finally bred for specific purposes.

It is thought probable that the termination of the **Ice Age** gave man his opportunity. The northward retreat of the glaciers meant that the rain-bearing clouds from the Atlantic followed a more northerly course. North Africa and Arabia consequently became drier. Deserts began to appear and the animals were forced to cluster round the oases, thus being brought into closer proximity with man. Neolithic man was a cultivator, not a hunter; he would allow the wild grass-eaters to graze on his stubble, protect them from the animals that preyed on them, and soon realized that he had a ready supply of food at hand. Slowly the animals would become tamer, and man would slip almost without realizing it into breeding more suitable domesticated animals by selecting the wilder ones for killing.

Not all attempts at domestication were successful; the Egyptians tried to keep herds of antelopes and gazelle round about 3000 B.C. but failed. Other animals – cattle, goats, pigs, and sheep – proved more tractable and soon became valued not simply as a source of easily obtained meat but as a supply of milk for food and hair or wool for clothing. Selective breeding would again be applied in that the best milkers would be kept and the others used for food. Wool is the result of careful selective breeding for it is almost non-existent on the wild sheep; sheep were being bred for their wool in Mesopotamia before 3000 B.C.

The ass, a native of north-east Africa, was domesticated long before the last mentioned date, presumably as a beast of burden though it is not possible to prove this. It was drawing a plough and pulling a two-wheeled cart or chariot in Mesopotamia round about 3000 B.C. The ox had been used for these purposes for some unknown length of time previously, and the ox-harness was transferred to the ass and, later, the horse. This was unfortunate in that, owing to the position of the horse's windpipe, the ox-harness half-chokes it as it pulls against the band fastening it to the yoke. Not until the invention of the horse-collar in Europe round about A.D. 900 was the horse able to exert its full strength.

The horse seems to have been domesticated after dogs, oxen and asses. Bones appear in levels of the Siyalk II period in **Iran**; they have also been found in a contemporary layer of the Neolithic settlement at Anau in Turkestan, where camel bones have also been unearthed. (An Egyptian model of a camel dates from before 3000 B.C.) It is considered doubtful that horse-riding took place before 1000 B.C., though horses were used for drawing chariots before 2000 B.C.; they were not used in Egypt, however, until the **Hyksos** introduced them in 1650 B.C. Model saddles dating from 2500 B.C. have been found in excavations of the **Indus Valley civilization**, but there is no indication that these were used on horses. Certainly they would not have been used on the ass which was unknown in India at this time, as also was the camel. In the Near East, on the other hand, the ass was the usual riding-animal long before, as well as long after, the horse was first used for this purpose. The Scythians of south Russia bred horses for milking and riding, and possibly, in their raids against the Assyrians and the Europeans halfway through the last millennium B.C., introduced the idea of cavalry to their opponents.

Dong-son, in the Than-Hoa province of Viet-Nam is the name-site of a south-east phase of the Asian **Bronze Age**, sometimes, and probably unwisely, extended to cover the whole area of south-eastern Asia. The culture, which has strong Indonesian traits, perhaps more specifically proto-**Cham,** also shows marked Chinese affinities though it is not necessary to follow some scholars in the view that it is more or less a provincial Chinese culture. Robert Heine-Geldern saw in it strong evidence for **Hallstatt** influence, but this, if present, is so remote as to be almost unrecognizable. Bronze objects, notably drums, had long been known from south-east Asia, but it was not until excavations in 1926–27 that these were found in an archaeological context. A study by Victor Goloubew in 1929 was followed by further excavations, by Olov Janse, in 1936. In addition to a large amount of Chinese material, of Han and later date – the Dong-son graves precede those of the Tang period – a rich corpus of bronze objects, together with small quantities of iron, **stone tools** and **pottery,** was found. The bronze finds include parts of armour, fastenings, knives, digging tools, curious pediform axes and drums, apparently mostly grave miniatures of other larger specimens which had long been known from stray finds. The bronze alloy is characterized by its high lead content which may amount to twenty per cent of the whole. The drums, which were the subject of an earlier study by Franz Heger, are the prototypes for a widespread cult instrument found in south China and widely among the hill peoples of south-eastern Asia; they are decorated with geometrical motifs and scenes which are thought to portray ritual scenes, though their precise interpretation is a matter of controversy. The setting for the scenes provides valuable data about the type of house, and illustrates some aspects of Dong-son culture. The date of the finds is uncertain, but there is nothing to support a date before the second century B.C., and some evidence to suggest its continuance in the early centuries of the Christian era, especially in Indonesia. Its connections with surviving cults in some of the Indonesia islands, and perhaps New Guinea, is probable, but not fully established. The relation between the Dong-son material and that from recent finds from Kunming, Yun-nan, is unclear, but it seems most likely that they are collaterally connected.

Dordogne is a department of south-western France, on the western slopes of the Massif Central, its capital being Périgueux. The region is of very great importance to archaeology and has been the centre of a great deal of most rewarding research.

The Dordogne has, in the first place, thrown much light on the early stages of man himself. In 1868, in a rock-cave near the village of Les Eyzies, remains of the **Cro-magnon** type of Homo sapiens were discovered, very similar in type to others found in French North Africa and known as the Mechta-el-Arbi people.

The men of this Cro-magnon type were very tall, up to nearly six feet in height, while the women were noticeably less so. These men had prominent brow-ridges, with strong jaws and neck muscles. The face was short and broad, but the cranial capacity was often greater than is usual in present-day man, though this is partly explained by their greater bodily measurements. They were quite heavily built. The forearm and shin were long, as compared with the upper arm and thigh. Certain traits of this Cro-magnon man, common in many **Neolithic** peoples, were once explained as indicative of gait or posture, for example of the habit of squatting, but later consideration has suggested that the explanation is better connected with a deficiency of bone as compared with the space required for muscular attachment.

The Cro-magnon type is reputed to be found among the inhabitants of the Dordogne to this very day. At any rate quite a large number of individual men of this type have been discovered all over the area, for instance at Les Eyzies, Cap Blanc, Laussel and elsewhere.

At Montferrand, Périgord, some fifty-six years ago, the Comb Kapelle man was discovered in a rock-shelter right at the bottom of a layer containing **Aurignacian** implements. This man is held to be a specimen of one of the very earliest types of upper **Palaeolithic** Europe.

In 1888 came the discovery of the Chancelade man, near Périgueux in the Dordogne. This man was found on the rock floor of a cave, under deposits containing **Magdalenian** implements. His skull has been compared to that of the Greenland Eskimo, who hunts reindeer in much the same conditions as did the Magdalenians, but his features do not have any of the Mongolian characteristics of the Eskimo.

It is not only in the remains of man himself that the Dordogne has yielded such rich finds. The Magdalenian stage of civilization is named after the cave of La Madeleine in the Dordogne, where signs of a remarkable artistic advance have been discovered, including the much increased use of bone and reindeer antler for the making of spear-heads with levelled, pointed or forked bases, as well as hooked spear-throwers, arrow-straighteners, needles and skin-dressers. Many of these are decorated with engravings or carvings, and it is the Magdalenian period that has become known as the great period of engraving and painting on walls.

To this time belong small plaques of stone beautifully engraved with recognizable animal forms and a few conventionalized small statues of women.

Gradually, in the Magdalenian period, engraving and sculpture were applied to all kinds of objects, usually based on natural animal forms. The naturalistic and decorative arts seem to be more ready to influence one another and often to be combined.

The art of carving, painting and engraving on the walls of caves developed remarkably, and there is a region of the Dordogne, embracing Font-de-Gaume, Combarelles, Bernifal, La Mouthe and the famous **Lascaux** where this development can be seen in many stages.

Cave paintings nearly always take the shape of single animals, such as the horse, reindeer, bison, red deer or ibex. Scenery is very rare, and human figures not at all common. The pictures are seldom life-size but vary from a few inches in width to about a yard. They were probably done with a brush, the colours being derived from red, yellow and brown ochre and black. These materials were ground up and mixed with fat on a slate or stone, and light was provided by small stone lamps burning fat, with perhaps a wick of moss. The engravings were executed with a flint burin, with a strong sharp edge.

Breuil has shown that this art of wall painting falls into two distinct cycles. The first begins with rather vague tracings made by two or more figures in the clay which sometimes covers the walls of caves. Soon after distinct animal shapes become recognizable, and then followed imitators in red or yellow paint.

In the next stage came an effect of modelling or shading, and black paint made its appearance, though only monochrome was attempted, with no combination of colours.

The second cycle is marked by sculptured friezes of animals, and at last comes the stage of the superb polychromes, using red, yellow and black all at once, such as are seen at their finest at **Altamira.**

Without question, the Dordogne is the region where this astonishing development in Neolithic art can best be studied. It was Breuil who first made so exact an examination of it as to divide the period of development into distinct stages. So much has been written about the cave paintings and sculptures of the Dordogne, and so many people from all over the world have been to see them, that they may have eclipsed the other aspects of Dordogne archaeology in the public estimation. But the importance of the traces of Cro-magnon man himself in the region should not be overlooked.

Dorians. Little is known of the process by which the aboriginal inhabitants of Greece and the Aegean (Pelasgians, Leleges, Carians, etc.) were absorbed or expelled by the Greek-speaking Indo-European tribes who invaded this region. In general the Greeks seem to have entered Greece by land from the north. Most scholars hold that the first wave of them (perhaps the **Ionian** race) arrived in central and southern Greece at the end of the Early **Bronze Age.** It is not clear whether the **Shaft Grave** dynasty of **Mycenae** (about 1600 B.C.) represents another wave of Greek-speaking immigrants, or (as Sir Arthur **Evans** believed) a Cretan penetration of southern Greece; but there is little doubt that in the later stages of the Late Bronze Age Greek-speaking people known as **Achaeans** were established in the Mycenaean kingdoms of the Peloponnese, and that Aeolians then occupied Boeotia and Thessaly. The Dorians, together with other north-west Greek tribes, formed the last main wave of Greek immigrants into the southern regions.

Ancient Greek tradition speaks of the Dorian conquest of southern Greece (the "Return of the Heraclidae" from the northern mountain region) as occurring eighty years after the Trojan War. In the Homeric epic there are several direct or implied references to Dorians or Dorian organization in Greece and the islands; but these are rare exceptions, and the Greece that **Homer** depicts is in general that of the Achaean heroes before the coming of the Dorians. It has commonly been supposed that it was the Dorians who overthrew the declining Mycenaean kingdoms at the end of the Late Bronze Age (about 1100 B.C.); and this view is no doubt substantially correct. But the Dorian attacks may have begun earlier than this, and the actual conquest must have been a gradual process lasting perhaps a century or two. Corinth and Megara do not seem to have been occupied by the Dorians before about 900 B.C., and **Athens** was never conquered by them. Many refugees from the shattered Mycenaean kingdoms migrated to the islands and the west coast of Asia Minor; they carried with them some traditions of Mycenaean culture and literature, and their descendants in Ionia played a dominant part in the Greek Renaissance in the eighth to seventh centuries B.C.

In the Early **Iron Age** the Dorians were established in the Peloponnese, whence they spread to Crete, the southern **Cyclades**, Rhodes, Cos and Cnidus. They farmed the more low lying areas. In Sparta they reduced the remnant of the pre-existing population to the condition of serfs ("*helots*"), but did not dispossess the inhabitants of the hill country. Dorians or related people settled also as landowners in the rich plains of Thessaly, where again the older population was made subject (*penestae*).

The centuries following the arrival of the Dorians constitute the Greek Dark Age (about 1100–750 B.C.). The introduction of iron weapons, of a geometrical style of pottery decoration and of cremation of the dead occurred about the same time as the Dorian conquest in the Peloponnese; and scholars at one time supposed that these were all Dorian innovations. But the recent excavations in the Kerameikos (Dipylon) Cemetery at Athens have shown that the Geometric style there developed from the Mycenaean without any interruption, and cremation seems to have been a widespread practice in these troubled times. In fact there seem to be no general archaeological criteria by which the Dorians can be recognized at the beginning of the Early Iron Age, and archaeology gives no very clear indications of their first appearance.

In the Late Mycenaean world a remarkable uniformity of culture seems to have been achieved; and if the Dorians lived for some generations on the fringes of this world before its collapse, it may be supposed that they absorbed some of its culture. In that case the individual characteristics (such as social structure, dialects and local pottery styles) which distinguish the different Greek peoples in early historical times may be regarded as having developed and become increasingly marked in the Dark Age, when the unity of the Mycenaean world was shattered and intercourse between the various regions was at its lowest ebb.

The two leading Dorian states in early times were Argos and Sparta, whose royal houses claimed descent from the "Dorian" hero Heracles. Sparta, where the Dorians formed a ruling caste, was a police state in which military training took the first place. The Dorians distinguished themselves as athletes and were the principal competitors in the games at the Olympic festivals. They were robust and orderly, but unimaginative, taking little interest in the intellectual and commercial movements of early Greece; and they were slow to embrace city life. They produced excellent bronzework, but apart from this they showed little artistic talent. Their choral music was distinctive and admired for its moderation; the Doric dialect, however, was a rough one and in itself ill-suited to literature.

When it was quickened by contact with lighter and more volatile Greek strains the Doric temper was capable of developing qualities of appreciation and initiative. In Corinth, which occupied a commanding situation at the crossing of the land and sea routes, the franchise was not restricted to the Dorian settlers and an important mercantile city came into being. Corinth founded many colonies in the eighth century and afterwards, the most famous being Syracuse (about 734 B.C.), and she played a leading part in trade with Italy and other countries. Corinthian artists and craftsmen were numerous and highly skilled; Corinthian pottery is found in bulk on sites in and outside the Greek world.

The massive Doric order of architecture, especially well-suited to temples set on citadels or crests, reflects the character of the Dorians. Corinth seems to have been the centre where gabled buildings with tiled roofs and painted terracotta facings were first developed, and from about 600 B.C. monumental stone buildings were being constructed in the Doric style. Most of the great buildings of classical Athens also were wholly or largely in the Doric order.

Dromos. A long open passage-way cut in to the hillside as an approach to a **tholos** or **chamber tomb**.

Druids. The Druids were a powerful religious body found among the Celtic peoples of both Gaul and Britain. Their decline was caused by the Roman invasion in these regions or finally by the spread of Christianity in those parts of Britain unoccupied by the Romans.

Most of the information extant about the Druids relates to those in Gaul. The first historical mention of Druids was made by a Greek, Sotion of Alexandria about 200 B.C. when news of them as philosophers had already spread to Greece. The main description, however, is by Julius Caesar who had to deal with them in the process of conquering Gaul in 58 B.C. His information may not always be accurate but at least he had a personal friend (Divitiacus) who was a Druid. From a Roman point of view of course, theirs was an inferior culture and this is probably why Caesar made no attempt to record Druid philosophy.

Their function was not only as priests of their religion, but as teachers of their philosophy and judges of cases both civil and criminal. As priests they were by no means devoid of political power and, owing allegiance to an archdruid, were organized on a national basis and hence above that most powerful factor in Celtic politics, the clan or intertribal dispute. They were therefore probably the only unitive force among the Celts of Gaul and Britain. Roman suppression claimed to have been on account of their cruel practices, is much more likely to have taken this as a convenient excuse for eliminating a dangerous political element in the Roman Empire.

Of the religion itself practically nothing is known except that they believed in the immortality of the soul (as, it is also believed, many prehistoric peoples did) and in its transmigration after death. These beliefs were probably independently arrived at and not necessarily acquired from Greek philosophers. The Druids (and the Gauls) claimed descent from a Supreme Being who was head of the Celtic pantheon, and indeed Druidism seems to be merely one branch of ancient Celtic religion. Human sacrifice has probably been overemphasized as one of the Druids' religious rites. The victims may in any case have been criminals who were used for this purpose when available but not necessarily as a regular rite. Men were burnt alive in wicker cages in the shape of immense figures, and divining carried out by the killing of a human being. These rites have undoubtedly captured the imagination from Roman times onwards. Disobedience was punished by banning from sacrifice, this being apparently a kind of excommunication. A further ritual, described by Pliny, was that of cutting mistletoe. Their knowledge included astronomy, doubtless mixed up with astrology.

With the Roman occupation of Gaul their power was broken and by the late first century A.D. they had sunk to mere magicians. As late, however, as the fourth century there were still Gauls who boasted of their Druid ancestors.

Turning to Britain we find that in A.D. 61 Tacitus mentions Druids in Anglesey; this is the only concrete reference to those in Britain who must have been contemporary with the first century B.C. Gaulish Druids. The absence of any reference to Druids in southern and eastern England in Roman times may have been partly due to Belgic influence, but this is rather doubtful. Druids did, however, exist in Ireland and Scotland, possibly as early as the second century B.C., and they are a stray traditional element in Irish literature.

The Druids are therefore a particular section of **La Tène** religion about which we happen to have written evidence. As their religion seems to have been basically Celtic it is impossible to say whether such Celtic religious sites as Llyn Cerrig Bach, Anglesey, were Druid or not (apart from the evidence of Tacitus). At the moment no Druid monument can be pointed out. Much confusion has been caused in Britain by seventeenth- and eighteenth-century antiquaries attributing Neolithic and Bronze Age **megalithic** monuments such as **Avebury** and **Stonehenge** to the Druids. This was partly caused by a lack of a proper perspective in prehistory. They deduced, correctly, that these monuments were pre-Roman, the Druids were pre-Roman, therefore the monuments were Druid! It is worth repeating that they most certainly are not.

Dvaravati is the name given to a kingdom of the lower Menam, Thailand, which probably at first formed part of the Empire of **Fu-nan.** It gained some degree of independence from the latter, and seems to have been recognized by the Chinese as an independent Buddhist kingdom, at least in the seventh century A.D. Archaeological finds in the area between **Lopburi**, Ratburi and Prachin show a certain homogeneity which points to a common cultural pattern, and there is evidence to suggest that the people were probably **Mons**, a group now found principally in Lower Burma, although its speakers are found far more widely from eastern Siam to northern Burma and Assam. Such sites as S'i Tep, Pra Pathom and **P'ong tuk** probably belong to Dvaravati. A number of images of Vishnu with a mitre-like headdress suggest some cultural link with the eastern part of southern India. There is, in addition, a considerable body of work in stucco which seems to belong to a secular art of a non-Buddhist character. By the middle of the tenth century A.D. the area seems to have formed part of the **Khmer** Empire, but the traditions of Dvaravati persisted and were continued by the **Thai** when they took over control of the Menam Delta from the Khmer and the name was preserved in the names of the capitals Ayuthia and Bangkok: the full title of the former is Krung Devamahanagara Dvaravati Sri Ayudhya Mahatilaka Bhavanaratna Rajadhani Puriramya.

Earth, Age of the. Archbishop **Usher** dated the creation of the earth to 4004 B.C. In 1778 the Frenchman Georges **Buffon** pushed the date further into the past, to more than 60,000 years ago. In 1830 Charles **Lyell** showed that the age could only be measured in millions of years. The generally accepted date at the present time is some 4,500,000,000 years ago. This is based on the time, which is known, that it takes radioactive uranium to decay into lead. By this method the oldest rocks so far known – at Rice Lake, Manitoba – are dated to about 2,100,000,000 years ago.

Earth Goddess. It is thought that prehistoric man may have worshipped an Earth Goddess, for figurines of female form (*see* plates 18, 20, pages 88, 90) pregnant and with exaggerated breasts and buttocks, have been found, for instance, on **Aurignacian** sites as far apart as the Pyrenees and Russia.

Easter Island is a small, hilly and treeless island of volcanic origin, located at twenty-seven degrees south some 2,000 miles off the Pacific coast of Chile, and almost an equal distance from the nearest islands in Polynesia. Its triangular surface area covers only forty-five square miles, with some extinct volcanoes rising to a maximum height of 1,500 feet. Being one of the loneliest islands in the world, Easter Island remained unknown to Europeans until 1722 when it was accidentally hit upon by the Dutch Admiral Jacob Roggeveen on Easter day, hence its name.

Roggeveen found the island to be already inhabited by a primitive native population, which the Dutch visitors described as of an apparently mixed breed; some had darker skins whereas others were "quite white" and looked like Europeans. Near the shore some rows of gigantic grey figures were observed, carrying great red cylinders on top of their heads.

Easter Island was next visited by Gonzales in 1770, by Cook in 1774 and by La Perouse in 1786. From their time Easter Island has been renowned as the centre of one of the greatest archaeological mysteries of the world. The giant figures first seen by Roggeveen were found to be hewn out of single blocks of stone, some measuring thirty feet in height.

They were raised on top of stepped ceremonial platforms of beautifully carved and fitted stone masonry, and Cook had never seen more perfect mason's work even in the best buildings in England. The giants who had not already fallen from their platforms were still carrying cyclopean "hats" or "wigs" of red **tuff** weighing many tons. Cook noticed specifically that many of the stone foundations and fallen statues showed a marked degree of erosion and decay, and he marvelled at the engineering skill of the unknown architects of the dim past who had raised these wonderful monuments on an island now inhabited by mere primitive savages.

In 1862 the island was almost depopulated through a Peruvian slave raid followed by a smallpox epidemic and with the death of the learned men among the natives, most of the important local traditions were lost for posterity. It was now merely archaeology that could give the answers to the mystery of the stone giants.

The first serious attempt to carry out an archaeological survey of the island was made in 1914 by a private British expedition led by Mrs Katherine Routledge. Mrs Routledge and her companions discovered and mapped numerous *ahus*, or ceremonial terraces, prehistoric roads, dwellings, and over 400 stone statues which were found scattered all over the barren island. She also made a thorough survey of the extinct crater of Rano Raraku towards the eastern headland of the island, where she examined numerous unfinished statues still left in the niches of the ancient quarries just as if they had been suddenly abandoned by the ancient sculptors. In 1934 the Belgian archaeologist Henri Lavachery landed on the island together with the French ethnologist Alfred Métraux. Whereas Mrs Routledge had mainly surveyed monuments and architecture, Lavachery extended the scope of the surface archaeology of Easter Island by concentrating his investigations on the numerous interesting petroglyphs (rock carvings) and relief carving abounding on the island. In 1955 a private Norwegian expedition led by Thor Heyerdahl brought four archaeologists to Easter Island, starting the first local excavations in search of possible cultural **stratigraphy** and also of material permitting **carbon fourteen** datings. Major excavations were performed by A. Skjolsvold in the slopes and refuse-mounds of the Rano Raraku statue quarries; by W. Mulloy in the classic *ahu* complex of Vinapu; and by E. N. Ferdon in the ceremonial centre of Orongo; while C. S. Smith led a series of test diggings in various sections of the island. These investigations resulted in the clear-cut stratigraphy of three distinct cultural epochs in the pre-European era of Easter Island. Although many major archaeological problems are still to be solved on the island, the following facts are now established.

Easter Island had already been discovered and settled by **Neolithic** seafarers in the earliest centuries of the Christian era. Carbon fourteen datings revealed that in about A.D. 380 plus or minus a hundred years a huge defence position had been constructed to fortify the eastern headland of Poike. At the meeting place of two lava flows an artificial ditch with rectangular bottom and rampart on the upper side had been cut into the rock, some twelve feet deep, about forty feet wide, and nearly two miles long. These first settlers of Easter Island arrived as experts in **cyclopean** stone masonry. At intervals along the coast and particularly near all bays and landing places, they built huge platforms with the retaining walls facing the sea formed by colossal cut and polished blocks of stone, often polygonal in shape and fitted together so precisely without cement that a knife blade could not be inserted in the joints. Anthropomorphic stone statues of human size or a little bigger were an important culture element during the first epoch, but they were carved from different types of stone and did not resemble in form the large monuments of the second epoch which made the island so famous. Furthermore the first epoch statues were not standing on top of the stone platforms, but were raised on the ground.

There is a marked break between the first and second epochs, and there is evidence to suggest that the island might even have experienced a period of depopulation. Although the exact timing of this first cultural change remains to be fixed, it is apparent that all first epoch structures were either partly or entirely torn down and rebuilt in the second epoch. Carefully shaped and polished stones from the first epoch platforms were mixed with unworked boulders and lava blocks, and even with deliberately broken fragments of second epoch statues, to form the peculiar *ahus* so characteristic of the subsequent Easter Island architecture. The central platform of the *ahu* was extended with lateral wings and the inland wall was filled in to form a ramp or incline down to a ceremonial court on the inland side. The surface of the extended platform was strengthened and large slabs were inserted to serve as foundation stones for the gigantic superimposed stone busts which were characteristic of this period. The large image *ahus* were primarily destined to serve as a sort of pedestal for rows of statues, although secondary vaults and **cists** were often built inside the *ahus* to hold single or group burials. With their backs to the sea, the statues are invariably facing the inland court. Most *ahus* carried four to six statues or less, but Ahu Tongariki carried fifteen statues.

In contrast to the wide variety and realistic form of the first epoch statues, the giant monuments of the second epoch followed a rather homogenous and highly conventionalized pattern. Heads, tall in proportion to the body, are carved on full length torsos ending in a flat and flaring base without legs. The arms are carved vertically down the sides with the hands bent in such a manner that the long fingers meet at the base of the abdomen on each side of a masculine member. Breasts and navel are carved in relief. The head is abruptly truncated above the straight-cut and deep orbits to form a flat base for the superimposed cylindrical top-knot of red tuff. The nose is long and slim with flaring nostrils, the eyes are represented as oval depressions below the protruding eyebrows, the mouth is small with sharp, narrow and protruding lips and the ears are depicted with artificially extended earlobes hanging down the sides of the head. Whereas black basalt or red tuff were often used for carving the heterogenous first epoch statues, the second epoch statues were carved from the yellow-grey tuff of the Rano Raraku crater. The sculptors' tools in the quarries were crudely pointed picks of hard basalt, with pumice-stones for the final polishing.

The front and sides of the statues were carved and smoothly polished to the last detail before the back was detached from the rock of the quarry. The statues were next transported down the slopes of the crater to be temporarily raised in excavated pits in the debris while the backs were finally shaped and polished. At last the statues were put down again to be transported by many natives pulling with ropes to the respective *ahus* for which the individual statues were destined. Through an ingenious method of building a steadily increasing pile of stones underneath the statue, the local natives made the statues rise into the air until they assumed a standing position on top of the *ahu*. Not until standing at their destination on an *ahu* did the statues receive the concavities marking their eyes, and the stone cylinders on top of their heads. The largest statue ever raised on an *ahu* measured thirty-two feet, weighed about fifty tons and carried a ten-ton stone cylinder on top of its head. The largest standing statue at the quarry measured forty feet when excavated and the largest of all which is left unfinished measured sixty-nine feet. The largest of all top-knots measures 600 cubic feet and weighs roughly thirty tons. There are seven miles between the image quarry and the top-knot quarry and from these points the giant stones have been dragged to all parts of the island.

About A.D. 1680 a civil war put an end to the second epoch culture. All work in the quarries ceased abruptly and the victors even commenced to overthrow the statues on the *ahus* the last of which was dragged down about 1840 during a cannibal feast. The only statues standing in our time are those without eyes which were temporarily set in deep pits below the quarries while their backs were finished. According to native tradition, during the civil war twelve generations ago, the ancestors of the present population exterminated a previous island population with light skin and reddish hair who enlarged their earlobes artificially in the manner depicted on their statues. These "long-ears" were massacred in a huge pyre lit in the defence ditch at Poike. Archaeological excavation with carbon fourteen dating strongly supports these native claims.

Whereas the victorious third epoch Polynesians, of whom some 900 survive on the island today, probably arrived in sailing canoes from the Marquesas group, there is archaeological and botanical evidence to the effect that one, or possibly both of the two earlier cultures were of South American origin.

The mysteries of Easter Island also include a number of wooden tablets with **ideographic** inscriptions, found in the hands of the living islanders. The writing system is of unique type, the art of which is lost among the present natives, and in spite of repeated claims to the contrary, no one has so far been able to read the script. Of recent years secret family caves have also been discovered on the island containing decayed remains of tablets and wooden images, and quantities of small lava sculptures of bizarre forms. **Artifacts** found through excavations are limited to different types of stone adzes, **obsidian** points, a variety of stone and bone fish-hooks, bone needles, polished stone bowls, fragments of small sculptures and pendants and earplugs of stone, bone and shell. Paved landing places and petroglyphs and mural paintings of large reed-boats with sails reveal an active maritime culture during the earlier periods, although the arriving Europeans found nothing but frail miniature canoes barely capable of carrying two people in a cramped position. *See* colour plate v, plate 43, page 147.

Ecbatana, *see* Iran.

Ecology is the study of the habits of living organisms, their methods of life and relationship to their surroundings.

Eden points, *see* America, Early Man in.

Egypt lies in the north-east corner of the African continent but culturally it has always belonged to the world of the eastern Mediterranean basin and Near East, situated as it is at one extremity of the Fertile Crescent, that almost continuous belt of fertile regions which form an arc of settled communities running from Egypt through Palestine and Syria across to the riverain lands of the Euphrates and Tigris. Though part of this world Egypt nevertheless retained a certain isolation from it owing to its geographical position and topographical features: for no other country in the Ancient World excelled it, as the Greek historian Diodorus Siculus noted, in the strength of its natural frontiers.

Secure within these frontiers, Egypt very early developed a settled and ordered way of life along the Nile, which alone enabled life to be sustained.

Of the total area contained within the modern frontiers, not much more than a thirtieth can be irrigated. The Nile, flowing from south to north, has created a narrow valley which is enclosed on either side by a cliff face or low escarpment beyond which lie the barren expanses of the high *gebel*.

Crowded within this narrow strip is today one of the densest populations of the world; and though it is impossible to calculate the extent of the population in the ancient period, all possible agricultural land was utilized and the wisdom books of Ancient Egypt contain admonitions not to build homes on it. The villages were constructed of sun dried Nile mud on the edge of the valley or on land not inundated.

Regularly each year about the middle of June the river slowly begins to swell as the steady flow of the Nile is joined by the increasing volume of the Blue Nile and Atbara Rivers, due to the melting snows and tropical monsoon in the Abyssinian highlands. By the middle of July the increase in volume has become rapid and the river begins to overflow its banks.

In November the waters recede, at first gradually and then more rapidly. In January, February and March the fields from which the water has retired, gradually dry up and in April the river reaches its lowest level.

It is impossible to say how early the Egyptians began to control the distribution of the water by an irrigation system. Traditionally Menes, the founder of the first dynasty, is credited with the construction of dykes. Throughout the Pharaonic period the regular method of irrigation was similar to that now known as "basin irrigation" and still practised in parts of Upper Egypt. The flood water was conducted on to the fields by means of canals and the water retained in basins by the construction of dykes. The ideal length of time for the water to remain is from forty to sixty days which allows the matter brought down by the Nile in suspension to settle. The water is then returned to the main stream by means of drainage canals and the alluvial soil is ready for cultivation.

A second method of irrigation whereby the flood water was stored up and fed through canals to the land as it was needed resulted in the possibility of perennial irrigation. This method was probably not used by the ancient Egyptians before the New Kingdom, from which time onwards there is some evidence for summer crops. The method involved the use of a water-raising instrument such as the *shadoof* (a bucket suspended from a wooden arm with a counterpoise weight) for transferring water from the canals to the land.

In ancient times two main cereal crops were grown: barley and **emmer wheat.** Fruit, vegetables and flax were grown in abundance. The textiles of Egypt were famous throughout the ancient Middle East.

It is to a great extent from the geographical features that certain elements in the history of ancient Egypt resulted. The conservatism of Egyptian civilization, many aspects of which altered little over a period of 3,000 years, was perhaps to be expected in a valley isolated from the outside world by desert and sea, so that continuity of habits and customs could remain unbroken. Similarly, Egypt's initial slowness in expanding and acquiring an empire can be seen as partly due to this position. Further, Egypt's wealth and luxury could not have existed without the fertility provided by the Nile.

The dates of the divisions of Egyptian history used in the following account are very approximately as follows: the Prehistoric period – before 3188 B.C.; the Archaic period (first and second dynasties) – 3188 to 2815 B.C.; the Old Kingdom (third to sixth dynasties) – 2815 to 2294 B.C.; the First Intermediate period (seventh to tenth dynasties) – 2294 to 2132 B.C.; the Middle Kingdom (eleventh and twelfth dynasties) – 2132 to 1777 B.C.; the second Intermediate period (thirteenth to seventeenth dynasties) – 1777 to 1573 B.C.; the New Kingdom (eighteenth to twentieth dynasties) – 1573 to 1090 B.C.; the Late New Kingdom (twenty-first to twenty-fifth dynasties) – 1090 to 663 B.C.; the Saite period (twenty-sixth dynasty) – 663 to 525 B.C.; the Late period (twenty-seventh to thirty-first dynasties) – 525 to 332 B.C.

No conclusion is possible about the state of civilization in the Nile Valley in the **Palaeolithic** period. In the **Neolithic** period, during which the Egyptians-to-be probably arrived in the region from west Asia and Africa, it seems likely that the **nome** land divisions came into existence and that these were fairly early on grouped into two kingdoms with capitals in the Delta and Upper Egypt. During the last quarter of the fifth millennium the Delta ruler conquered and colonized the south, founding the capital of the newly united Egypt at **Heliopolis**. The Heliopolitan kingdom later split again and this split lasted until the beginning of the historical period.

In the Neolithic period mixed farming was already practised and cereals grown, in addition to hunting, fishing and food gathering being carried on. The people lived in light, perishable huts; basketry was much used – for instance to fashion underground silos – and weaving and leather-working were carried on. The flint implements of this period – arrow- and lance-heads, knives, clubs and axes – are very fine, but only a comparatively small amount of metal, chiefly copper, was yet in use. Pottery was fashioned without the wheel at this stage, a flat stick being used to shape the inside, the hand, the outside; towards the close of the Neolithic period, however, rotary motion was being used to finish the necks of vases. Characteristic pottery was, early on, a soft, brown, highly burnished ware with white line patterns, the lips of the pots blackened from being placed mouth downwards in the kiln, and later, a pink-brown ware with a red line design and no facing. During this period stone was little used for building but stone vases of great elegance were produced.

The Archaic period, which was followed by the Old Kingdom, opened with the reunification of Egypt which took place, under Menes, the first king of the first dynasty, and the concern of the rulers of the first and second dynasties who followed him seems to have been to establish an absolute monarchy with a claim to divine descent, under which the administration was firmly centralized. The third dynasty ruler Zoser established the capital of Egypt at Memphis and the erection of his step pyramid at **Saqqara** (designed by his architect and vizier Imhotep who, according to tradition, also founded the temple at Edfu, *see* plate 44, page 148) began an era of great building. This was continued by the fourth dynasty rulers Snefru, Cheops and Chephren, the first of whom built pyramids at Meidum and Dashur, the second, the Great Pyramid at Giza, and the third, another pyramid, also at Giza. Snefru carried out victorious expeditions into Nubia but though, during the first Intermediate period (seventh to tenth dynasties), this attempt to dominate the neighbouring regions was continued, with punitive expeditions against the Bedouins and the colonization of Nubia, at home power seeped away from the rulers, the nomarchs became hereditary and greatly strengthened, and anarchy resulted. The Delta was invaded by Bedouins, Lower Egypt underwent a social revolution, the peasants revolting against the rich, and for a period cultivation ceased there with resultant famine. Two separate kingdoms – one in Upper Egypt centred on **Thebes**, and the other in Middle Egypt with its capital at Heracleopolis struggled for power, the conflict finally ending with the victory of Thebes and the re-unification of Egypt under Menthuhotep II of the eleventh dynasty.

The Archaic period and Old Kingdom saw the development of religious thought with a strong belief in an afterlife, and the cult of the sun god Ra, centred on Heliopolis, became powerful in the fifth dynasty. A solar calendar, later adopted and spread, though in a modified form, by Caesar, came into being. Much of the Nile Valley came under cultivation and a system of canals for retaining flood-water was started.

These periods saw great advances in the sphere of art, especially sculpture, as well as in that of building. While the few representations of organic forms surviving from the Prehistoric period are clumsy, those of the Archaic period and Old Kingdom are often full of life and action. From the Archaic period, besides the rude colossi of the God Min from Coptos, dates work showing great keenness of observation – ivory figures of men, women and animals from **Hierakonpolis** and **Abydos**, and glazed pottery figures; some reliefs on slate of this period, too, have great charm. The fourth dynasty saw the growth of a convention of spare grandeur in sculpture and also saw, the development of great vigour in reliefs, with a wealth of variety and detail.

There were developments, too, in the fashioning of tools and artifacts. Copper tools became increasingly used; these were apparently first cast and then hammered with stone hammers.

As early as the fourth dynasty the **cire perdue** process was being used for casting metal figures. Already in the first dynasty gold jewellery showed great skill. Glazed pottery was already being used for beads in the Prehistoric period, but early in the Historic period glazed tiles, figures and toggles also appeared.

During these periods, and especially in the first dynasty, hard stones were still used for vases. Stone was also employed for reliefs, mace-heads and tombstones. Stone working received a great impetus in the fourth dynasty, the skill reaching a peak in the construction of the **pyramids**.

Turned forms of pottery appear in the first dynasty though until the twelfth dynasty the lower part of pots were finished with a knife. Characteristic of the Archaic period are grand jars two to three feet high, while the typical fourth dynasty ware was short, rough pots and bowls.

The Middle Kingdom saw a revival of the power of the pharaoh under Menthuhotep III who also went on further victorious expeditions in Nubia, and the rulers of the twelfth dynasty continued his policy of strength at home and prestige abroad. The cult of Osiris, God of the Dead, became popular although the pharaohs themselves supported the cult of the God Amun propagated by the Theban school of priests. At the end of the twelfth dynasty, however, came another breakdown of central government, and a swift succession of weak kings, the last of whom put up little resistance to the invasion of the **Hyksos** who established their capital at Avaris in the Delta. After a nominal domination of 500 years, during which their rule was effective only in the Delta and Middle Egypt, the Hyksos were driven out by Ahmoses, the founder of the eighteenth dynasty.

In the sphere of art, the Middle Kingdom is marked by a new style of low relief, showing considerable refinement. Stoneworking continued to be of a very high standard, the twelfth-dynasty granite sarcophagus of Senusret III being one of the finest pieces of Egyptian stone cutting known. The twelfth dynasty produced a characteristic hard, thin ware, the pots frequently having spherical bases, while large light brown jars were manufactured for storage.

During the New Kingdom immense advances were made in all the refinements of civilization; it was a period of great artistic activity and of great building. It was, too, an era of conquest abroad, initiated by Tuthmosis III who became overlord of Nubia and of much of the Middle East, from the Euphrates to the Hittite Kingdom. Egypt's vassals in these regions were forced to pay tribute money which brought her new wealth and she became increasingly open to new influences from abroad. During this period the priests of the god Amun worshipped at Thebes increased in power and this was possibly partly responsible for **Akhnaton's** establishment, as a form of resistance, of his monotheistic solar cult away from Thebes at **Tell el Amarna**. This was, however, abandoned after the rule of his immediate successor Smenkere. Though the nineteenth dynasty was still a period of glory for Egypt, the twentieth saw a decline in her strength and in that of the pharaohs, power within Egypt falling increasingly into the hands of the priests of Amun.

In the eighteenth dynasty the great temple at **Karnak** was begun by Tuthmosis I and additions to the magnificence of Karnak continued to be made throughout the nineteenth and twentieth dynasties. In the eighteenth dynasty, too, Queen Hatshepsut's three-terraced funeral temple was built at **Deir el Bahri** and the great temple was constructed at **Luxor**. During the nineteenth dynasty, under Ramses II, the rock-cut temple of Abu Simbel was constructed. The twentieth dynasty, too, saw the construction of further monuments: a temple at **Medinet Habu**, three more temples at Karnak.

The New Kingdom is characterized by an entirely new art style, which reached its most extreme form under Akhnaton. The style emphasized the human rather than the remote divine nature of the rulers it portrayed and sculpture gained a new naturalism, sometimes bordering on caricature as well as grace, vivacity and at times emotionalism. Portraiture flourished under Akhnaton. Painting was a favourite medium and the surviving frescos are full of life and, frequently, comedy. By the reign of the nineteenth dynasty pharaoh Ramses II, however, the new convention had become outworn and lifeless.

Glass in the sense of glassy matter was first used in the eighteenth dynasty. At first, black and white glass, pasty in quality, was used for small vases. Later, glass was mainly used for very delicate mosaics. Beads were made by winding glass threads on copper wire. Blown glass, however, did not appear before the coming of the Greeks and Romans. Under Amenhotep II and Akhnaton new colours for glazes appeared, – purple, violet, red, yellow and white being added to the earlier green and blue.

Typical New Kingdom pottery was, in the eighteenth dynasty, a soft ware with a red rim. Under Tuthmosis III this was decorated with red and black lines, under Amenhotep III with blue paint. In the late eighteenth and nineteenth dynasties a thick hard ware with white specks made its appearance.

The latter part of Egypt's ancient history, from the Late New Kingdom to the coming of Alexander the Great was a time of weakening and disintegration. Already in the twentieth dynasty the pharaoh's power was on the wane, and control was falling more into the hands of the priests of Amun.

This tendency culminated in the priest Herihor becoming pharaoh. Tanite, Theban, Libyan and Ethiopian dynasties succeeded one another with a slight revival of Egyptian strength under the Saite dynasty. This was, however, followed by the Persian conquest and domination (only interrupted by half a century of independence from 404 to 341 B.C.) which lasted until the arrival of Alexander the Great in 332 B.C.

Elam, *see* Susa.

Electron or **Electrum.** An alloy of gold and silver.

Ellora or **Elura.** The rock-cut cave site of Ellora stands on a small tributary of the Godavari River in the north-west Deccan. It is now in the Bombay State and lies some forty miles south-west of **Ajanta** (*see* colour plate II). It was first described by the French traveller Thevenot in the latter half of the seventeenth century, and since that time has excited the admiration of many visitors. The caves are excavated on the scarp of a lava plateau and this gives them a distinctive character different from that of most other **cave temples** of west India which are cut in sheer cliffs. There are some thirty-five caves of which just under half are Buddhist and Hindu and a small number Jain. Just as the later caves at Ajanta are associated with the Vakataka dynasty and those of Badami with the early Chalukyas, so those of Ellora are associated with the Rashtrakutas. The earlier caves have been generally accepted to be among the Buddhist group, situated at the southern end of the line. Of them the caves one to three, the Dherawara, probably belong to the latter half of the sixth century. Somewhat later is the great Mahawara monastery cave (number five) the hall of which measures some fifty-eight feet by one hundred and seventeen feet. Of the Buddhist caves perhaps the most famous is number ten, the Visvakarma (dating from the late seventh to early eighth century). This is a *chaitya* (or assembly) hall some eighty-six feet deep with a **stupa** in its apsidal end adorned with a colossal image of the Buddha in the teaching posture. Next come the caves of about the same date known respectively as Do Thal and Tin Thal (two-storeyed and three-storeyed); they typify the late Buddhist monastery caves carved on more than one floor, with a broad open courtyard in front. The façade of the Tin Thal rises to a height of nearly fifty feet and its simple design must be regarded as one of the masterpieces of cave architecture.

The Brahmanical caves date from the mid-seventh and eighth centuries. We may recognize three main types: first, that of the two - storeyed Dasavatara cave (number fifteen), a large pillared hall deriving from the Buddhist *vihara* (monastery), with its shrine cut in the far wall; second, deriving from the latter is the hall with shrine cut as a separate entity at the back and having a circumambulatory path around it, as in the Ramesvara cave (number twenty-one), and Ravan's cave (number fourteen), the former having startlingly beautiful sculptures; and thirdly, late in the series, the cruci-

Photo: by courtesy of the magazine "Italy's Life", published by the Ente Nazionale Industrie Turistiche, Rome

PLATE VI. ETRUSCANS: sarcophagus from Cerveteri showing a married couple reclining on a bed while dining. (*Museum of the Villa Giulia, Rome*)

form hall with the shrine standing isolated in the centre, as in the lovely Dumar Lena (more correctly Dhumar Lena, number twenty-nine). Finally and in a class by itself, is the great temple of Kailasa (Siva's paradise), cut from the living rock in emulation of the Kailasanatha temple of Rajasinha Pallava at Kanchipuram. It was probably constructed during the reign of the Rashtrakuta ruler Krishna I (about A.D. 756–73). Adorned with a wealth of superb sculpture this shrine must be reckoned as one of the greatest achievements of Indian architecture and civilization. Latest in point of time is a small group of Jain caves, dating probably from the ninth century, of which the Indra Sabha (number thirty-two) is most noteworthy. *See* plate 45, page 149.

Elmenteitan Culture, *see* Africa, East.

Emmer Wheat. Wheat is a domesticated form of wild grass. Emmer wheat is a form of the wild emmer grass and was grown round the eastern Mediterranean and in western Europe; it is superior to the dinkel wheat, developed from the wild dinkel grass, which was cultivated in central Europe and elsewhere and has been identified from prehistoric settlements. The wild ancestor of the modern wheat is unknown; it may have been the result of crossing emmer wheat and some other grass.

Eoanthropus, *see* Piltdown Man.

Eocene Epoch. The name Eocene (Greek *eos*, dawn; *kainos*, recent) has been given to that epoch of earth history, between 70 and 45 million years ago, which marked the beginning of **Tertiary** times and heralded the dawn of modern life. During this interval of approximately 25 million years the ancestral forms of many modern animals first appeared.

It is thought that the continents and oceans attained their present-day distribution during Eocene times. In some regions the sea-bed gradually sank to form "basins of deposition", such as the London and Paris Basins, whilst a narrow and relatively deep ocean called "Tethys" extended across southern Europe, as far as the East Indies. The climate was generally warmer than now, for tropical and temperate conditions appear to have been more widespread.

There was considerable volcanic activity in many parts of the world during Eocene times – in the Arctic, northern Britain, southern India and east Africa. Widespread earth-movements also took place, although never on such a scale as in later Tertiary epochs; a divergence between northern American and west European faunas during later Eocene times indicates a break in the land connection.

The vegetation of the Eocene landscape was almost modern in aspect; ferns and conifers were common, but flowering plants, including deciduous trees, were dominant. Fishes and invertebrate animals of Eocene seas were also similar to present-day forms. Vertebrate animals, especially birds and mammals, bore little resemblance to living types, however, but their spectacularly rapid evolution began during the Eocene period. The most primitive mammals – five-toed creatures with small brains and low-crowned teeth – evolved into more varied types with bodies and brains of increasing size, and teeth and limbs adapted to many different modes of life. All the main groups of placental mammals, including rodents, insectivores, primates, carnivores, hoofed herbivores and whales, flourished in Eocene times. Large flightless birds of an ostrich type had developed, but older stocks of toothed birds gradually died out.

Eolith. The earliest form of stone tool (hence the name – "stone of the dawn") eoliths date back to before the **Palaeolithic** era, over 500,000 years ago. It is doubtful whether they are naturally fractured stones picked up and used by the first near-men, or whether they are **artifacts.**

Ephesus. One of the twelve **Ionian** cities of Asia Minor, Ephesus was situated on the west coast of Lydia, near the mouth of the River Caijster and commanded the great river basins of the Hermus and the Meander. Its strategic position partly accounted for its importance as a centre of commerce. The Greeks established Artemis as the deity of the city, though the Artemis worshipped there bore a strong resemblance to the Asiatic goddess of nature celebrated nearby in pre-Ionian times; she was the virgin mother of all life, especially wild-life, and the embodiment of fertility and the productive power of the earth.

Ephesus fell under the rule of the Persians and even remained subordinate to her in the Ionian revolt of 500 B.C. against Persia. After the ultimate defeat of the Persians, Ephesus paid tribute to Athens for a time. In the fourth century B.C. it once again came under Persian domination. Alexander established democratic government there. The city subsequently came into the hands of the Attalids of Pergamum and was bequeathed to Rome by them. Under Rome its prosperity increased: it became the chief city and principal port in the province of Asia. It was heavily fined by Rome for its support of the Mithridatic revolt. When St Paul founded a Christian church there under Timothy and John it was known to be addicted to the practice of occult arts and the tradition of Artemis persisted. In A.D. 262 the Goths destroyed the city and temple and Ephesus never recovered its power. In A.D. 431 a general council of the Church was held there. In later years the city gradually decreased in size as a result of malaria, and the temple of Artemis, after being used by local builders as a quarry, became silted up and buried with river mud. It was not rediscovered until 1869.

The most significant ruins at Ephesus are a stadium, 687 feet long, and fragments of a great theatre and of an *odeum* or concert-hall. The site of the famous Temple of Artemis is to the north-east of the city; this was occupied by early sanctuaries, then by a gigantic archaic temple built about 600 B.C. This was fired in the fourth century and its successor was perhaps the largest Greek temple ever constructed. It became one of the **Seven Wonders of the World.** Its altar was in part decorated by Praxiteles. The sculptured drums and pedestals of some of its columns are now in the British Museum. The Temple was burnt by the Goths and finally deserted after the Edict of Theodosius closing pagan temples.

Epigraphy. The study of inscriptions on monuments, coins, statues, etc.

Eskimos. These are a people living in the Arctic and sub-Arctic regions extending over 6,000 miles from east Greenland to the Bering Strait and as far as Siberia. They are the only people to inhabit both the Old and New Worlds and centuries ago they stretched even farther, from the mouth of the St Lawrence River on the west to the Siberian coast on the east.

The Eskimos cannot be classified into tribes. They are more properly divided into geographical units, forming three main cultural groups which might be styled as eastern, central and western; they possess a common language differing from group to group only in the use of words rather than variations of grammar.

Eskimo art is of very considerable archaeological interest, since it shows clear signs of direct descent from an ancient form of civilization. Now, as always, its production is dependent upon the very small number and variety of materials upon which the artist can draw, as, for instance, ivory from the tusks of the walrus, the antlers of reindeer and the skins of other animals.

Even with these limitations, remarkable skill has been shown for hundreds of years in the graphic arts, – their engraving on walrus tusks for example – and in sculpture, this latter including – many weird masks of skin or wood, portraying birds and human beings with a very decided character of their own.

Small figures carved in ivory, bone or wood of a great age have been found, probably designed to be children's toys, and these often show a remarkable grasp of form even though the actual treatment may be crude. Human beings are the most common subjects, very often without any attempt to delineate arms or faces, while highly fantastic creatures are also quite common, no doubt representing spirits good and evil.

Paintings are few and far between, but in Alaska drums have been found painted to illustrate stories and local events. On the other hand, examples of work in relief are numerous, such as a wide variety of tools and implements, often decorated with various forms of animals, particularly seals.

Almost all Eskimo art forms are the product of men, and it seems that the women's work has always been limited to the work on skins used in the making of clothing.

As closer touch has been established between the Eskimo and other nations, their traditional skills have lost a great deal of their originality, but carving in wood or ivory still bears traces of the ancient standards. *See* plate 46, page 150.

Ethiopia. The kingdom of Ethiopia, often called Abyssinia, lies in the highlands west of the Red Sea. The basic ethnic stock of the country is **Hamitic**, but from perhaps the seventh century

B.C. it was colonized by Semitic immigrants from southern Arabia who, coming originally as traders, eventually formed a kingdom with its capital at Aksum. These immigrants called themselves Agazyan and Habashat (whence "Abyssinia"), and they dominated the Hamitic peoples through their superior culture. Their city of Aksum, though no longer a capital, is still a sacred city, and the kings were crowned there till 1868.

The Habashat and Agazyan brought with them a language which eventually became known as Ge'ez (pronounced something like *gherz*). It is written in a syllabic alphabet of south Arabian origin in which the vowels are shown by modification of the radical letters, of which there are thirty-two, each with seven forms. From Ge'ez developed the three chief modern languages, Tigrinya, Tigre, and Amharic. Ge'ez ceased to be spoken about the tenth century A.D. though it continued to be the language of the church and of literature. Amharic is now the official language of the country.

The kings of Ethiopia claimed descent from Menelik, son of Solomon and the Queen of Sheba. This is a fiction; but the Solomonian or Israelite dynasty has nevertheless a long ancestry. Aksum was in full vigour at the beginning of the Christian era, and Christianity was introduced in A.D. 333. The new religion gained a firm hold on the Ethiopians, and penetrated deep into their lives. The kingdom of Aksum fell into decline after the sixth century, and from then till the early tenth century A.D. we know little or nothing about it. About 911 the Solomonian dynasty was overthrown by a queen of the Falasha called Yodit (Judith), who in three years "covered Ethiopia with ruins". She was expelled by a new dynasty called Zague, which ruled till 1268, when the throne reverted to the Solomonians.

Archaeologically, Ethiopia is as yet hardly explored. Something is known of the original kingdom of Aksum in the north, including the city of Aksum and sites at Kohayto, Tokonda, Yeha, and on the coast at Zulla. The chief Aksumite architectural features are obelisks, up to sixty feet high, cut from a single block of granite into the representation of a many-storied castle; stepped and recessed walls; thrones on steps with a roof supported by squared stone pillars; and dams. Aksum Cathedral, founded in the fourth century, was destroyed by Granye in 1535, and rebuilt about 1615. It was the most sacred place in Ethiopia.

In central Ethiopia there is a number of churches cut out of solid rock. The largest group of these is at Lalibala, where there are eleven, made in the twelfth century. The method was to isolate a block of rock (reddish volcanic **tuff**) by digging a trench round it; the rock was then cut with adzes into the shape of a church, with all the architectural features of a built-up church, and the roof at ground level.

In southern Ethiopia, in the Harar uplands in the east, there are found cairns up to ten feet high; graves, including a cist-grave of south Indian type; earth-works, one with the middle bank deliberately broken at intervals; and extensive terracing on the hillsides. South and west Harar **dolmens** occur, which were probably never covered with earth or stones, cairns, stone-walled enclosures and town-sites, ruined mosques, and graves. In the country west of the chain of lakes Zeway-Shala-Abaya-Chamo are found large numbers of stones carved with swords in relief, anthropomorphic stones, menhirs and stone circles (Soddo region); phallic menhirs and anthropomorphic stones (Gurage region); plain and phallic menhirs (Sidamo region); and cairns with carved stone peristaliths (Webi Shabelle region).

Etruscans. This people lived in an area north of the River Tiber, between the Apennines in the east, and the coast of Italy to the west. For about a hundred years from 616 B.C. the kings of Rome were Etruscans, and as a nation they were in the forefront of the culture of their day and age, with special skill in the use of metals and minerals. Moreover, their military genius enabled them to spread their sphere of influence to Rome, Lombardy and the Adriatic sea.

As early as 1000 B.C., Etruria was settled by people from the north whose civilization is known as Southern Villanovan. But by early in the seventh century B.C. they had been succeeded by a people of another origin who no longer burned the bodies of their dead but buried them in trench-graves. Their art was highly developed and included decorative ornaments with an eastern touch, shown in vases of quite new shapes and undoubted importations from Greece and Asia Minor.

Their work in bronze is notable and covers all kinds of products from small mirrors to chariots. They excelled in the making of terracottas, jewellery, life-size figures and pottery. Their wall-paintings and their architecture show a high degree of accomplishment but never, perhaps, rivalled those of Greece itself, and a comparison between a Greek marble statue and an Etruscan terracotta shows the difference between their standards of artistry and technical skill. *See* colour plate VI, plate 48, page 152.

Evans, Arthur John (1851–1941). Sir Arthur Evans was, archaeologically speaking, "born in the purple". His father John Evans had married his cousin Harriet Dickinson, daughter of the head of the printing firm of John Dickinson, and was in his spare time a distinguished antiquary, author of the standard books on the **Neolithic** and **Bronze Age** periods of northern Europe.

Arthur Evans was born at Nash Mills in England in 1851 and educated at Harrow and at Brasenose College, Oxford. Even as a boy he went flint-hunting with his father in France but his own interests were turned rather towards ancient coins and he read history at Oxford. In 1871 he visited the Dalmatian coast, to be fascinated by its cultures and its peoples, and roused to sympathy with the Slavs and Albanians of Bosnia and Herzegovina (now Yugoslavia) in their struggle against the oppressive rule of Turkey. In 1873 he visited the Scandinavian countries but in 1875 was back in Bosnia, and in Sarajevo when the revolt of that country broke out. He wrote a book on the sufferings of the Slavs which was quoted by Gladstone of whose party he was an ardent supporter. In 1877 the powers intervened to save Serbia from Turkey; Bosnia, however, was not granted her freedom but was occupied by Austria. Evans was sent out by C.P. Scott as special correspondent for the *Manchester Guardian* in the Balkans and was based on Ragusa; there he renewed an acquaintance with the historian Freeman who was visiting that city, fell in love with his daughter Margaret and married her after his return to England in 1878, when he and Margaret visited **Schliemann's** finds from **Troy** then on exhibition in London. The newly-married couple returned to Ragusa but in 1881 Evans was imprisoned by the Austrians for his pro-Bosnian sympathies, and he and his wife were expelled from the country. He applied for, but failed to obtain, the new chair of Classical Archaeology at Oxford. In 1883 he and his wife visited Greece for the first time, saw Schliemann digging at **Orchomenos** and his treasures from **Mycenae**, and visited his sites in the Argolis, visits which riveted Evans' attention to the Mycenaean culture of the Greek Bronze Age.

In 1884 Evans was appointed Keeper of the Ashmolean Museum, Oxford, which was suffering badly as a result of many years' neglect. Years of hard but successful struggle in the reorganization of the Ashmolean were enlivened by individual researches into different archaeological fields, such as articles on Sicilian coins and the excavation of a late Celtic urnfield (*see* **Urn People**) at Aylesford, and by visits to south Russia, Bulgaria and Greece.

In 1893 Margaret Evans died at Alassio on the way to Greece. The same spring Evans worked in the Athens Museum on the engraved seals there, devoting special attention to some prism seals with hieroglyphic symbols in an unknown script, and was told they had come from Crete. On 15 March, 1894, Evans landed for the first time at Herakleion, which he always refused to call by any name but Candia, bought some antiquities, visited the private collections of I. Mitsotakis and M. Kalokairinos and that of the Syllogos of Herakleion, walked over the site of **Knossos,** and conferred with Dr Joseph Hazzidakis, the Cretan archaeologist, on the possibilities of excavating it. He even purchased about a quarter of the site. Before he could complete his negotiations about the rest of the site the Cretan revolution broke out in 1896. An armistice was proclaimed. Evans in England and Hazzidakis in Crete organized funds for the victims but fighting broke out afresh and Greece declared war on Turkey. After the cessation of hostilities Evans returned to Crete in 1898 accompanied by D.G. Hogarth and J.L. Myres. On 28 March, 1899. Evans accompanied by Duncan MacKenzie and by his architect Theodore Fyfe began the excavation of Knossos and in the first week discovered the fine fresco known as the "cup-bearer", and clay tablets inscribed with symbols of what was later to be known as Linear Script B (*see* **Minoan Scripts**). In 1900 Evans described in *The Times* "The Council Chamber of Minos" and "The Bath Chamber", later to be known as "The Throne Room" and "The Lustral Area". By the following year he had cleared most of the area west of the central court and his father Sir John Evans, now seventy-seven years old, visited the excavations. On his return to England Evans was honoured with degrees by the Universities of Dublin and Edinburgh, and at the Glasgow meeting of the British Association outlined his chronology for the new civilization he had discovered in Crete, dividing the Bronze Age culture into Early, Middle and Late **Minoan**, using a name derived from the legendary King Minos.

The earlier excavations had been paid out of the so-called Cretan Exploration Fund to which various societies and friends had contributed, but Evans now wished not only to excavate but also to restore many parts of this Palace of Minos which was emerging, and in 1902 he determined that he must take over the financial responsibility for all this work.

The 1904 excavations were largely devoted to tombs, to the Late Minoan cemetery on Zafer Papoura and to the great vaulted royal tomb on Isopata about two miles north of the Palace, robbed of its precious metals but containing a fine series of vases in alabaster and other stones.

Hogarth had earlier excavated six **chamber tombs** on the west slope of Zafer Papoura. In 1904 Evans assisted by Duncan MacKenzie and by a Danish artist named Halvor Bagge started to explore this cemetery more thoroughly and uncovered sixty graves mostly of the Late Minoan III period (1400–1100 B.C.) including eighteen chamber tombs cut in the soft rock, twenty-five **shaft graves** and seventeen **pit graves**; of these the first group were family graves and the others devoted to single interments. These were largely graves of warriors and their families.

The royal tomb at Isopata at the north end of the same ridge was also excavated in 1904. The walled oblong chamber with a keeled vault was a more splendid version of the Late **Bronze Age** tombs later revealed at **Ras Shamra** in Syria.

In 1905 Evans continued his exploration of the little palace at Knossos where he discovered a fetish shrine erected in the re-occupation period after 1400 B.C. in a disused lustral area. In 1906 Christian Doll, the official architect of the excavations, built to Evans' order the Villa Ariadne to serve as his permanent headquarters in place of the dilapidated house of the Turkish Bey hitherto employed for that purpose. Evans himself, however, was too heavily employed in reorganizing the Ashmolean Museum to excavate in Crete.

In 1907 he returned to Knossos and also worked on the first volume of *Scripta Minoa*. In 1908, after Evans' return to Crete, his father died leaving to him his collection of coins, Roman glass and stone tools, and in the autumn he inherited a large fortune from his uncle whereupon he retired from his post as Keeper of the Ashmolean Museum to which he presented his father's collection of Anglo-Saxon and early Teutonic jewellery.

In 1910 Evans resumed his exploration of the "papoura" (flat-topped hill) of Isopata where he uncovered six Late Minoan chamber tombs, later published in *Archaeologia* (1914) under the title of "The Tomb of the Double Axes and Associated Group and the Pillar Rooms and Ritual Vessels of the Little Palace at Knossos". All these tombs had been robbed but each retained something of interest; tomb one a fine gold ring and good ashlar masonry lining both the chamber and the entrance passage, tomb two ("The Tomb of the Double Axes") a bronze double axe and a burial shaft shaped like such an implement, tomb three ("The Mace-bearer's Tomb") a fine breccia mace, and tomb five a fine pair of ritual goblets with polychrome designs on plaster, resembling fresco rather than ceramic technique. The following year Evans was busy in England, was elected President of the Hellenic Society, and was knighted by the King. Then the first world war interrupted the excavations at Knossos.

When the armistice was proclaimed in 1918 the Great Powers were inclined to favour Italy in their allotment of the Dalmatian coast. Evans went to Paris while the Peace Conference was in progress, conferred with the Slav leaders and advocated *coups de main* in the D'Annunzio manner by local Slav militias raised on the Adriatic islands to resist Italian aggression.

In 1926 Evans, back in Crete, became convinced that much of the damage to the ancient palace had been caused by earthquakes and, as he writes, "my own mind was full of past earthquakes when on June 26 last... the shocks began... the movement resembling a ship in a storm. A dull sound rose from the ground like the muffled roar of an angry bull..." (In a later passage he refers to the sacrifice of bulls in a room in a house destroyed by earthquake and now restored and quotes **Homer's** words that "the Earthshaker delighteth in bulls".) Much damage was done in the Museum including the destruction of the small "jewel fresco" but Evans' restorations in the palace stood the shocks very well.

In 1927 Evans finally presented his Cretan property to the British School at Athens and endowed the curatorship but, as Evans continued to excavate and Duncan MacKenzie became Curator, the Villa Ariadne was treated by visiting archaeologists as if it were still his own property.

In 1928 the second volume was printed on the Palace of Minos and when Duncan MacKenzie's health broke down he was replaced as Curator by J.D.S. **Pendlebury** for whom Evans later erected a new home known as the Taverna.

In 1930 Evans excavated the temple tomb and the same year published the third volume on the Palace of Minos, and carried out extensive restorations to the north-west area of the Palace. He also discovered the *enceinte* wall and the original west entrance to the Palace of Minos.

In 1934 Evans was awarded the Gold Medal of the Society of Antiquaries, and the following year saw the publication of the fourth volume on the Palace of Minos. The introduction to this contains warmly sympathetic references to the various scholars who had laboured on the subject of Minoan Crete especially to his friend and colleague Duncan MacKenzie, to Federigo Halbherr, the excavator of **Phaistos**, to A.H. Sayce, H.R. Hall, L.R. Farnell, the German von Buhn and the Frenchman Salomon Reinach.

In 1935 Evans visited Crete for the last time and was honoured by Herakleion, the inhabitants of which made him an honorary citizen and erected his bust by Gillieron in the West Court of the Palace, a scene witnessed by some 8,000 spectators and compared by Evans to the scene on the miniature frescoes of the Palace. During this visit he inaugurated several small trial excavations into tombs on the Acropolis, a cave shelter near the temple tomb, and a Roman villa with fine mosaics and a statue of Hadrian in the vineyard of the Villa Ariadne.

The following year the Jubilee of the British School at Athens was celebrated and Evans' personal collection formed a large part of the work exhibited at Burlington House.

In 1938 Sir Arthur's health deteriorated and he had to undergo an operation but in 1939 he was still active in the Ashmolean, where he supervised the arrangement of a new Minoan room furnished with antiquities he had presented.

The outbreak of war brought devastation to the countries he knew and loved in the Near East and he was saddened by false reports of the bombing of Knossos and the Herakleion Museum. He became ill and had to suffer a second operation. On his ninetieth birthday a deputation headed by Mr Leeds, the Keeper of the Ashmolean, presented him with an honorary scroll from the Hellenic Society; he died three days later. *See* plate 47, page 151.

Evolution of Man, *see* Primates, Prehuman Evolution of, *and* Fossil Man.

Eyasi Skull, *see* Africa, East.

F

Faience. Decorated earthenware pottery and porcelain.

Faiyum, the. The great natural depression of the Faiyum lies some fifty miles south of Cairo in Egypt, only a few miles from the western edge of the desert. In **Neolithic** times the level of the lake – lake **Moeris** – was 180 feet higher than it is today and hunters lived along its shores, where their refuse-pits have been excavated. It was the region of one of the earliest Egyptian cultures, the Predynastic Egyptians, who followed much the same kind of life as the Neolithic hunters before them.

During the Egyptian Middle Kingdom considerable schemes of land reclamation and irrigation were initiated and the interest of the twelfth dynasty in the area is shown by the choice of Faiyum sites for pyramids, notably at Hawara, Illahun, and Mazqhuna. The best-known is the great limestone mortuary temple of Amenemhat III (1842–1797 B.C.) singled out by **Herodotus** for his most extravagant praise. It was known to the Greeks as "the Labyrinth", and they included it with the Parthenon, in their list of the **Seven Wonders of The World.** The temple has now been almost completely destroyed by quarrying.

The Faiyum has an individuality of its own; it is the only part of Egypt where a visible slope in the agricultural land can be seen, and it is famous for its use of great water-wheels for irrigation purposes.

Fauresmith Culture, *see* Africa, Stone Age Man in *and* Africa, Stone Age Man in South.

Fertile Crescent. The name given by **Breasted** to that area of the world's surface in which civilization first began; it stretches from Egypt round the shore of the eastern Mediterranean through Palestine and Syria, then swings to the east in a great arc, and so down to Mesopotamia – "between the rivers" of Tigris and Euphrates.

Figurine. A statuette.

Flake. A **stone tool** of **Stone Age** times made by taking a **flint** and striking it so as to knock a flake off the **core**. The flake was then shaped by further strokes. The finest flake tools appear in the **Levalloisian** culture; here the required shape was carefully blocked out on the core before a skilled blow in just the right place detached the flake.

Flexed Burial. The burial of a body with the knees drawn up to the chin and, often, the hands together under the cheek; this is very much the position that the foetus assumes in the uterus.

Flint. An irregular grey lump of rock occurring in layers in chalk, or in gravels in chalk country, flint was used by early man when he discovered that it would, as a result of hammering, break into fragments with sharp edges and points. Further, two flints struck together will cause sparks and so produce fire; **Sinanthropus** (*see* plate 127, page 393) had learnt to control and use fire. The earliest **stone tools** were very simple ones; later, more specialized tools were developed such as the **hand-axe**, the chopper, and the cleaver. These were made from the core, the central lump after the outside had been chipped off. Later still, skill developed further and the flakes and points chipped off the core were deliberately designed for a specific purpose – knives, spear-heads, scrapers, awls, **burins**, and so on.

Flint Mine. Neolithic man sank mines in the chalk to extract **flints** for making **stone tools**. Such mines have been found in England and France. Twenty-foot-deep shafts were sunk, and galleries excavated in the flint layers. Flints were dug out with deer-antler picks and collected with shovels made from the shoulder-blades of oxen.

Flood, the. That the world had been destroyed by a Flood, as recounted in Genesis, **6–8**, was an article of faith in the western European world for many centuries, and led to **Boucher de Perthes** classifying man as "diluvial" (of the flood) and "antediluvial" (before the flood). The theory was destroyed by Charles **Lyell's** doctrine of the uniformity of nature, and it became widely believed that the **Sumerian** legend of the Flood (from which the Hebrews' version stemmed) had no basis in historical fact. Then Sir Leonard **Woolley** excavated **Ur** and discovered a bed of water-laid clay, over eight feet thick, which he dated to before 4000 B.C. "This deluge", he says in *Ur of the Chaldees* (1929), "was not universal, but a local disaster confined to the lower valley of the Tigris and Euphrates, affecting an area perhaps 400 miles long and 100 miles across; but for the occupants of the valley that was the whole world!"

Fluorine Dating. Fluorine is a gaseous element that in the form of fluorides is fairly widely distributed in nature. It occurs as a trace in most ground water, usually less than one part per million. When "atoms" (or rather ions) of fluorine come into contact with crystalline calcium phosphate, the mineral matter of bones and teeth, they enter the ultramicroscopic mesh of the crystals and become locked in.

If a bone or tooth lies for thousands of years in a moist gravel or sandy formation (or even in some kinds of clay) it gradually absorbs wandering fluorine ions from the percolating ground water. Once the ions enter the bone-substance they are not released (unless the soil is so acid that the whole bone dissolves). The process goes on continuously, and the fluorine content of the bone or tooth increases in course of time. This fact provides a neat means of distinguishing between bones of different geological ages occurring at the same locality and under similar conditions. It does not make it possible to date bones in years, because the rate of absorption is not uniform and varies considerably from place to place. Thus, bones buried in deposits where there is a fair amount of fluorine in the ground-water will obviously accumulate this element more rapidly than others buried where there is a very little. However, if one is merely concerned with separating bones of different ages at particular localities, estimation of their fluorine content may be very helpful. For example, when human bones are found in ancient river gravels, doubt sometimes arises as to whether they were embedded at the time when the gravel was laid down, or whether they were buried into the deposit at a later date through the activity of a grave digger. If fossil animal bones undoubtedly contemporaneous with the gravel are available for comparison, fluorine analysis may clearly differentiate bones which have been interred at a considerably later date. This method of relative dating is most effective at open sites where the enclosing deposit is permeable and where the ground is continually damp. It is of little use in very dry situations, or in cave deposits where layers of crystalline calcium carbonate (drip-stone, stalagmitic or stalactitic layers) prevent the free circulation of fluorine-bearing water.

Fluorine analysis was proposed as a means of dating bones as early as 1844, by an English chemist, James Middleton, at a meeting of the Geological Society of London. He was, of course, mistaken in believing that it provided a means of *absolute* dating. The French mineralogist Adolphe Carnot was the first to show, in the eighteen-nineties, its value for *relative* dating; but his work on the fluorine content of fossil bones (like Middleton's work before his) appears to have been forgotten until it was rediscovered during the second world war.

The application of the fluorine dating method to the Galley Hill Skeleton (found at **Swanscombe** in north Kent) provided a spectacular demonstration of its usefulness in certain circumstances.

The Galley Hill Skeleton had been the subject of controversy for over sixty years. It is the skeleton of a man of modern type but with a few so-called primitive traits, and was discovered in 1888 at a depth (it is said) of eight feet in ancient Thames gravel containing Palaeolithic flint hand-axes and remains of extinct elephant, rhinoceros and lion, dating from before the time of **Neanderthal** Man. In these same gravels the bones of the Swanscombe Skull were found in 1935–6 at a depth of twenty-four feet. The fluorine content of the Galley Hill Skeleton, of the Swanscombe Skull and of some twenty fossil animal bones from the same gravel was determined in 1948 by chemical analysis in the government chemist's laboratory. The results confirmed the antiquity of the Swanscombe Skull, and indicated that the Galley Hill Skeleton was an intrusive burial very considerably later than the gravel in which it lay. In 1954 the results were checked not only by redetermination of the fluorine content of the bones using the more refined technique developed in the course of the Piltdown research, but by measurement of their organic nitrogen content. The organic matter (mainly protein) in bones decreases in course of time, while their fluorine content increases. Therefore estimation of protein (or nitrogen) content serves as a valuable cross-check to fluorine dating.

TABLE I

	Fluorine %	*Nitrogen* %
Neolithic skull, Coldrum, Kent	0.3	1.9
Galley Hill skeleton	0.5	1.6
Swanscombe skull	1.7	nil
Bones of fossil mammals from Swanscombe gravels	More than 1.5	Traces or nil

These results indicate quite clearly that the Galley Hill Skeleton is much later in date than the fossil-bearing gravel in which it lay, but the question of how much later cannot be solved by the fluorine method (even in combination with the nitrogen test) since it is only a method of relative dating. Possibly one day it may be possible to determine the absolute age of the Galley Hill Skeleton by applying the **carbon fourteen** method to the traces of protein which have survived it.

Fluorine does not provide a means of very close relative dating, because a given bone or group of bones usually shows a certain range in fluorine content. Consequently, unless the difference in age between two lots of bones which are being compared is geologically appreciable (say 10,000 years), there is usually an overlap in the ranges of their fluorine contents. For this reason the method is unsuitable for differentiating clearly between, say, a **Neolithic** and a medieval skeleton, whereas it does enable one, as we have seen, to distinguish bones of Neolithic or later date from others of Early **Palaeolithic** age, at any rate when both occur under similar conditions at the same locality.

The attempt to solve the problem of the relative age of the **Piltdown Skull** (*see* plate 115, page 381) by fluorine analysis in 1949 led ultimately to the discovery that it was a forgery. The Early or Lower Pleistocene fossils recorded from the Piltdown gravel pit were found to contain over two per cent of fluorine, whereas the controversial cranium and jawbone showed only around 0.1 per cent. This was regarded in 1949 as proof that neither the cranium nor the jawbone was Early Pleistocene as had been claimed, but it did not show that they were recent or that they were forgeries. Indeed, an unquestionably fossilized hippopotamus tooth recorded from the same site also showed only about 0.1 per cent fluorine, and as hippopotamus lived in Britain during the early Upper Pleistocene, it seemed conceivable that this was the age of the "aberrant Piltdown Man" and that the low fluorine content was due to lack of this element in the local ground water since that date. When in course of further research on the Piltdown problem (in 1953–4), the nitrogen content of the various specimens was determined, and the fluorine content redetermined by means of a more refined technique that the jawbone was modern, that the cranium was slightly more ancient, and that the misleading hippo tooth was very ancient, having lost nearly all its organic matter. This last specimen had probably come from some limestone cave deposit where fluorine had not penetrated.

TABLE II

	% *F.*	% *N.*
Modern bone	0.03	4.0
Piltdown jawbone	less than 0.03	3.9
Piltdown cranium	0.1	1.4
Piltdown hippopotamus tooth	less than 0.05	0.1
Pleistocene hippopotamus tooth from cave in Malta	0.1	0.1

In retrospect it could be argued that the fluorine method was invalid at Piltdown because (as we now know) the various fossils had been taken there from widely separated sources. It was fortunate that the Lower Pleistocene fossils used in the hoax had been brought from regions where the fluorine content of the ground-water was higher than the average; for if they had been drawn from an area where fluorine was exceptionally deficient it is possible that the fluorine test of 1949 would have failed to differentiate the skull from the undoubted Early Pleistocene fossils placed with it and the whole problem might have remained unsolved for many more years.

Fluviatile. Found in, or produced by, rivers; used for instance, of geological deposits.

Folsom, New Mexico, *see* America, Early Man in *and* Amer-Indians.

Foote, Robert Bruce (1834–1912), geologist and prehistorian, was well named the "father of Indian prehistory". He came to India at the age of twenty-four and joined the geological survey with which he served for thirty-three years, mainly in south India. During this time, and in his subsequent work directing the geological surveys of Baroda and Mysore states, he used every opportunity his field work presented to collect archaeological specimens. In 1863 he discovered the first **hand-axes** to be recorded in India (other **stone tools** had been found more than twenty years earlier). In 1903 the Madras museum purchased all his collections and housed them in a special room. Foote spent his last years in arranging and cataloguing, and the resultant books, the *Catalogue Raisonné* (1914) and *Indian Prehistoric and Protohistoric artefacts* (1916), set out a brilliant account of Indian prehistory, and summarized the results of his years of work. His other archaeological writings consist of some twenty papers ranging in time between 1886 and 1898.

It has recently been asserted that up to 1945 there was scarcely a prehistoric site in India which did not owe its discovery to Foote. This is, of course, an overstatement but it is a very happy one. Although Foote relied upon field observations and surface collection, and made no use of excavation, he was able in an almost uncanny way to reconstruct accurately India's prehistory. Several of his brilliant deductions have only recently been proved true.

Fossil. Plant or animal remains preserved in **sedimentary rocks**; the soft parts disappear and only the hard parts remain, preserved by minerals infiltrating into them. (*See* **Fossil Man,** etc.)

Fossil Apes. Fossilized remains of apes, some as much as 35,000,000 years old, have been found; they were the ancestors either of man or of the present-day anthropoid apes. Among them – Parapithecus, Propliopithecus, Proconsul, Pliopithecus and Dryopithecus – Proconsul is the most famous. (*See* **Primates, Prehuman Evolution of.**)

Fossil Man. The expression "Fossil Man" is generally applied to remains of man dating from the Pleistocene or Palaeolithic period, that is to say more than 10,000 years old. The mere fact of bones being "fossilized" in the sense of having been altered or hardened by infiltration of mineral matter does not always indicate great antiquity. In the Natural History Museum in London there is a human skeleton embedded in limestone which was excavated on the island of Guadalupe in the West Indies. It is only a few centuries old, and represents the body of a native buried in a beach of coral sand which became cemented into rock by percolating water. On the other hand, the skull of a "fossil man" of the extinct Neanderthal type found in one of the caves of Monte Circeo in Italy lay loose on the cave floor and had been so little altered in 50,000 years that traces of organic matter (protein) can still be detected in the bone.

Sometimes when a human skeleton is unearthed there is doubt whether it is "fossil" or "recent". In such cases the problem can usually be settled by chemical analysis.

Using the term "Fossil Man" in the broadest sense, we may include in this category the remains of **Australopithecus** found in cave deposits nearly half a million years old in South Africa. These creatures apparently lived in open country (*veldt*), they walked upright and had teeth of essentially human type; yet their brains (average about 500 c.c.) were no larger than those of apes. It is generally agreed that these australopithecines were **hominids** (members of the same biological family as man, rather than members of the ape family known as **pongids**), but it has been largely a matter of opinion whether or not they should be counted as "human". Simple flaked pebble-tools have been found with Australopithecus at one of the cave sites (Sterkfontein), but there has been much uncertainty as to whether they were made by that creature or by a higher type who hunted the latter. The discovery in 1959 of a new Australopithecine (**Zinjanthropus**) on a lake-side occupation site at **Olduvai** in Tanganyika, in direct association with pebble-tools, has largely confirmed the view that these creatures were tool-makers and can be regarded as the earliest known man.

Living in Java at about the same time as the latest Australopithecines were undoubted men of the genus Pithecanthropus, with brains averaging about 1,000 c.c. in volume, but with great overhanging brow-ridges and receding foreheads. Remains of **Java Man**, including a thigh bone which indicated his upright gait (hence the specific name Pithecanthropus erectus) were first discovered in river gravels at Trinil in Java in 1891 by a Dutch scientist, Eugène Dubois. A related species occupied caves at **Chou-kou-tien**, south-west of Peking, about 400,000 years ago. Nearly a dozen incomplete skulls of Pekin Man were discovered between 1927 and 1937, as well as numerous fragments and isolated teeth, representing altogether nearly forty individuals. All this material was lost during the second world war, but fortunately good casts exist of all the more important specimens. The skulls had been broken open at the base, presumably to extract the brain. There is little doubt that these early men were cannibals. Associated broken animal bones indicate that they were successful hunters of many kinds of game, particularly deer. They made a fair variety of crude **flake**- and **core**-tools from pebbles of quartz and sandstone collected from river beds nearby. They regularly used fire.

Fossil human remains are exceedingly rare before the time when man began to bury their dead (about 50,000 years ago). The oldest human fossil in Europe is the lower jaw of **Heidelberg** Man (about 400,000 years old) found in a sand-pit at Mauer near Heidelberg in 1907. Next in age comes the Swanscombe Skull, assignable to Homo (the genus to which modern man belongs), discovered in gravels of the Thames dating from the second interglacial period (that is to say, about 200,000 years old). Three pieces of this skull have been found. The first two pieces (occipital and left parietal bones) were discovered in 1935–36 by Mr Alvan T. Marston, a dentist in Clapham; and the third bone (right parietal, fitting the other two perfectly) by John Wymer and Adrian Gibson in 1955. These bones lay more than twenty feet below the surface, in gravel of the so-called hundred-foot terrace, associated with remains of extinct animals such as elephant (Elephas antiquus) and Merck's rhinoceros, and with flint hand-axes of the type known as **Acheulian**. So far as it is preserved the Swanscombe Skull is not very different from that of modern man, but the brow region (which has not yet been found) may have ridges similar to those of the contemporaneous Steinheim Skull found in a gravel pit near Stuttgart.

Fossil men dating from the succeeding period show two lines of development, some approaching the extreme **Neanderthal** type (Homo neanderthalensis), with bun-shaped skull and prominent brow-ridges, others with domed brain-case and much reduced brow ridges. Neanderthal men attained their maximum development in north-west Europe in the early stages of the last **glaciation**

(70,000–50,000 years ago). In spite of their rather bestial appearance, due to receding chins, low foreheads and projecting brows, and their short stature (not more than five feet high), their brains were on an average larger than those of modern Europeans. They occasionally at least buried their dead with ceremony, and were skilful workers in flint (their industries are known as **Mousterian**). They hunted animals, including big game, with a fair measure of success. They were for the most part cave-dwellers, and regularly used fire. Towards the east and south-east they graded into the other branch of the developing human stock, leading to modern man who probably first emerged in south-west Asia. The most advanced of the neanderthaloids found in the Mount Carmel Caves, such as the skeleton known as Skull Five, are scarcely distinguishable from our own species.

The first representatives of the fully evolved Homo sapiens, the **Cro-magnon** race, spread across Europe between 40,000 and 30,000 years ago, completely replacing the specialized Neanderthalers. In Britain, the fossil **Cheddar Man** (*see* plate 35, page 139) is representative of the Cro-magnon stock. The Cro-magnons and related racial groups were responsible for the Upper **Palaeolithic** industries (e.g. **Aurignacian**, **Solutrean**, **Magdalenian**), distinguished by flint blade tools and by a remarkably varied and skilful use of bone, antler and ivory. They were responsible, too, for the cave art of France and northern Spain. The speed with which their culture developed suggests that they had some new means of communicating ideas. Possibly they were the inventors of the first fully articulate language.

Elsewhere in the Old World, man evolved along parallel lines. The beetle-browed **Rhodesia Man** flourished in southern Africa between 50,000 and 25,000 years ago, to be replaced by the locally emerging ancestors of Bushmen and Negroes. In Java Pithecanthropus appears to have evolved into a local neanderthal-like type known as **Solo Man**. Eleven fossil skulls, with bases broken open for extraction of the brain, were discovered in gravels at Ngandong in the Solo Valley.

There are indications that man migrated into the New World and into Australia during the later stages of the Ice Age, when the sea-level was low. The oldest human remains of unquestionable antiquity in America are from Midland, Texas, and date from about 9,000 B.C. The Keilor Skull found near Melbourne may represent the oldest known Australian aborigine; but there is still some doubt about its precise antiquity: recent estimates based on radiocarbon dating of charcoal in related deposits indicate an age of about 10,000 years.

Fossils, Living. The name given to certain animals which have survived unchanged from past ages. Examples are the tiny brachiopods, creatures of the sea-shore, preserved in the Ordovician rocks of 400,000,000 years ago, and found today on the shores of Japan, the East Indies, and northern Australia; and the coelacanth, a fish believed to have been extinct for over 60,000,000 years until dredged up off the coast of South Africa in recent years.

Frere, John (1740–1807). The name of John Frere is associated with the famous **Palaeolithic** site of **Hoxne**, in England where, in 1790, he found **stone tools** lying among the bones of extinct animals.

Frere was a country gentleman, with the liberal tastes and interests of the eighteenth-century man of means. He belonged to an old family settled in East Anglia. He lived at Roydon Hall, in Norfolk, and Finningham, in Suffolk. Born in 1740, at the age of twenty-six he became High Sheriff of Suffolk, and represented Norwich in Parliament in 1799. In 1768 he married the daughter of a rich London merchant, who brought him "rare gifts of intellect and disposition" as well as her dowry. They had seven sons and two daughters.

Frere's duties as Member of Parliament did not hinder his interest in the past. He was elected a Fellow of the Royal Society of Antiquaries in 1771, and was an active member. Only one year after he entered Parliament, he gave to the Society his memorable paper on the finds he had made at Hoxne.

There he had found flints which, he said, "if not particularly objects of curiosity of themselves, must I think be considered in that light from the situation in which they were found".

Frere in that one statement was anticipating the modern view that objects intrinsically worthless may be archaeologically valuable if found *in situ*. Considering the decades of romanticism that were to follow Frere's death, it is interesting to find such an outlook.

The paper describes in detail the different strata

uncovered by the workmen in digging brick-earth. Frere noticed that the flints were covered by deposits left by different "inundations". It is this feature which has made the site so valuable today for the study of the chronology of the British Pleistocene.

Frere could come to no other conclusion than that "the situation in which these weapons were found may tempt us to refer them to a very remote period indeed, even beyond that of the present world." But the temptation was avoided by his learned audience. It is noted that "Thanks were recorded to our worthy Member Mr Frere for this curious and most interesting communication". The inconvenient and disturbing implications of Hoxne were buried in *Archaeologia* (1800).

It is hard for the present generation of archaeologists to appreciate the dilemma of their pre-Darwinian forbears. They could only solve the problem of how to account for the presence of man (as shown by the tools) with animals demonstrably extinct by calling in the Deluge. This was used to try to bring the observed facts into line with Genesis, by assigning the gravels in which the finds were made to the time of the **Flood**. The toolmakers could then be regarded as "antediluvian".

Frere was a pioneer fettered by the limitations of scientific knowledge of his time. He should have lived when the work of Darwin and his contemporaries had burst open the chronology of Archbishop **Usher**, for his observations and his astute deductions would have brought him respect in any era from that of **Pitt-Rivers** to the present day.

Fu-nan was a kingdom of southern Indo-China. Its native name is unknown, but the Chinese characters are thought to transcribe a proto-**Khmer** form of the Cambodian word for mountain, *phnom*. This was probably originally an Indonesian kingdom in the Mekong Delta which at the height of its power controlled the whole of the mainland littoral from the Malay Peninsula to Cam Ranh Bay. Aerial photographs have revealed a number of large sites in the Delta area which are believed to belong to Fu-nan and a complex network of canals which furnish evidence for a large-scale irrigation and communication system. One of the sites, **Oc-eo**, has been partially excavated, and shows evidence for considerable trade between East and West, a fact which is substantiated by Chinese historical sources. Little is known of Funanese architecture, but one or two sites in the Delta area, but away from the coast, have been assigned to the later part of the Funanese period which seems to be from the second to sixth centuries A.D. These include certain buildings near Kompong Cham, Cambodia. The statuary assigned to this kingdom includes a few Buddhist images, and a number of figures of Vishnu and of Hari-Hara (a Siva-Vishnu composite). If these assignments are correct, it seems that Indian influences were still strong. (*See also* **Chen-La**.)

G

Gandhara. This name is applied to a region and also to an art form.

The region has been defined differently by both ancient and modern authorities. The definition most generally accepted extends from Jalalabad and the Kunar River in Afghanistan in the west to the Manikyala Stupa, a few miles east of Rawalpindi on the east. Though mentioned once in the *Rigveda* in connection with the sheep of the Gandharins, this people took no part in the Vedic Battle of the Ten Kings and are descended from the Druhyu who did. Many references occur in the *Mahabharata* where Shakuni, prince of Gandhara, using his loaded dice, wins his wife Draupadi from Yudhishthira. From this, events moved inevitably to the great battle of Kurukshetra, in which the Pandavas had their revenge, and Shakuni the gambler, aiding the Kurus with a Gandharan force, was killed.

The *Jatakas*, tales of previous incarnations of Gautama the Buddha, give Takshasila (**Taxila,** *see* plate 137, page 437) as the capital of Gandhara, though one of the Chinese pilgrims to India makes the river Indus the eastern boundary. Scylax, the Greek sea captain employed by Darius I, passed through Gandhara on his way to the Indus, and that monarch then invaded north-west India in the sixth century B.C., adding Gandhara to the Achaemenid Empire as part of the seventh satrapy (*see* **Satrap**). Lying on the main invasions route into India, Ghandhara was crossed in 326 B.C. by Alexander the Great and was occupied between 180 B.C. and A.D. 100 by successive incursions of Bactrian Greeks, Saka-Pahlavas and Kushans, the two latter being in fact mixed peoples displaced by events in central Asia during the final centuries before the Christian era.

Gandhara as an art form refers to the Romano-Buddhist school of art which flourished in Gandhara from early in the first century A.D. to the middle of the fifth century. This classification of the art of Gandhara is not a new fad, having been used by Vincent Smith in 1889. It is unrelated to the rule of the Bactrian Greeks and not clearly attributable to the influence of the philhellenic **Parthians.** The sculptures which are classed under the heading of Gandharan art are of schist, stucco and terracotta. Dating, particularly of what may be the earliest examples, is insecure. Among the earliest must be the stucco heads from the apsidal temple at Sirkap, Taxila, dating to early first century A.D. showing that good stucco work is as old as anything in stone.

The proposal to define stone as early and stucco as late, with a considerable hiatus between them, is unrealistic. It is the adoption of facile explanation which labelled all the more elegant stone pieces as Greek and early, and less well-fashioned ones as Indian, decadent, and late, that has produced this stone-stucco division to explain the merit of demonstrably late stucco work. This is doubly fallacious as much that is more Indian in appearance is early and derives from the same tradition as Bharhut, and much that appears inferior is due to the mass-production of sculptured decoration. The western influences in the art of Gandhara were due mainly to trade contacts with Rome in the early centuries of the Christian era. *See* plate 49, page 189.

Garstang, John (1876–1956). Like many archaeologists, Garstang early showed his love for exploration. When at Oxford studying mathematics and continuing to indulge in his hobbies of astronomy and archaeology, he worked on Roman Ribchester, on which he published a report in 1895 when nineteen years old. Four years later he joined Flinders **Petrie** at **Abydos** and thus began a long career in Egyptian archaeology, excavating also at el Arabah, Mahasna, Beit Khallaf, Beni Hassan, Hierakonpolis, and finally at **Meroe,** city of the Ethiopians, in 1910–14. The latter site was identified by his great friend, A.H. Sayce, through whom he had been introduced to the antiquities of Turkey. The geography of the land of **Hittites** was to be one of his lifelong interests. In 1907 Garstang visited the German excavations at **Boghazköy** under the direction of Hugo Winckler. While there Garstang witnessed the discovery of the cuneiform tablet bearing the text of a treaty made between the Hittite king Hattusil III and Ramses II of Egypt in 1269 B.C.

This rare enthusiast was able to maintain an interest in several fields of research at the same time. He was thus able to apply his early experience, gained under Petrie then developing his system of pottery-sequence dating which was tested at Gezer in Palestine, in a variety of ways and places. His journey in the Cilician plain and adjacent areas in 1907 drew his attention to Sakçe Gözü where work during two seasons (1908, 1911) uncovered monuments of both the Hittite and earlier levels. The earlier phases of Near Eastern civilization and culture always held a special fascination for him. The first world war temporarily halted archaeological work in Turkey, so Garstang readily accepted new opportunities when the British Mandate was founded in Palestine in 1919. He was the obvious choice both as first Director of the new British School of Archaeology and pioneer Director of the Department of Antiquities in Jerusalem, a post he held until 1926.

During this time he was able to lay plans for the Palestine Archaeological Museum and to encourage the development of systematic surface exploration. He himself made a number of soundings, including the site of Ashkelon. In 1928, backed by the support his enthusiasm always won readily, he examined sites connected with the entry of the **Israelites** into Canaan, always a subject of much interest to Bible students. In the course of this survey he examined the vast ruin-mound of Tel el-Qedah, the biblical **Hazor.** He identified the outer city as a **Hyksos** camp and, from the absence of **Mycenaean**-type ware, concluded that the Israelite occupation had to be dated not much later than 1400 B.C. This seemed to agree with his findings at Jericho, where he began work in 1930, and the results of years of exploration and thought were gathered in his *Joshua and Judges* (1931). This book remains a mine of information, even though his chronological findings have had to be revised in the light of the more recent Israeli work at Hazor.

Garstang's most widely-known work was done at **Jericho** where he led an expedition, backed by Sir Charles Marston and others interested in the site because of its biblical associations, from 1930–36. He worked down to **Neolithic** and earlier pre-pottery levels now better known from the later excavations there (1952–58) by the British School under Miss Kathleen Kenyon. Some fallen city walls (late fifteenth century B.C.) he assigned to the period of Joshua's attack, but this identification has been disproved by the finds of the 1952 season showing that they are to be dated at least three centuries earlier. But such revisions in the interpretation of Garstang's finds in no way diminish the permanent value of his work which was always meticulously published.

With the changing position in Palestine, Garstang turned once again to Asia Minor. In 1929 he had published *The Hittite Empire* to bring his *Land of the Hittites* (1908) up to date. Once again his aptitude for choosing the right place to dig, the mark of the master archaeologist in the ancient Near East with its more than fifty thousand known sites, stood him in good stead. He chose Yümük Tepe, near Mersin, where he was able to trace the development of the site from its Hittite fortifications down to the earliest Neolithic levels, known to him from his earlier work. The results appeared in his characteristically thorough *Prehistoric Mersin* (1953). Mersin was the site he revisited only a few days before his death in 1956.

The British Institute of Archaeology at Ankara, of which he was Director and, later, President, is but one permanent tribute to one of those rare British archaeologists who are able to combine both field and academic work in not one, but several, periods and places.

Geological Periods. The history of the earth extends back in time far beyond the ken of archaeologist and historian, back through more than 4,000 million years to a primordial cosmic origin almost completely shrouded in mystery. However, most of the present-day theories concerning this origin seem to agree on one fact, that the earth and other members of the solar system probably had birth in the condensation of a great cloud of interstellar gas.

The geological record, strictly speaking, began approximately 3,000 million years ago, when the earth had a cool exterior, continents and ocean basins had been established, and wind and rain had begun their ageless erosion of upstanding land masses.

The earliest, and by far the longest, stages in geological history can only be incompletely sketched, for the most ancient rocks have been largely destroyed by erosion, re-crystallised by metamorphic changes, or obscured by varying thicknesses of later-formed rocks. Subsequent chapters of earth history, covering the last 500,000,000 years, can, however, be reconstructed with increasing fullness of detail; the record is written in the stratified rocks, and in the fossilized relics of past life which these rocks contain.

The natural basis for subdividing geological history lies in the belief that recurrent disturbances of the earth's crust have broken the continuity of the record and marked off the major units of time so clearly that they can be recognized in all parts of the world. The most important of these disturbances; the so-called "crustal revolutions", have led to widespread changes in the distribution of land and sea, and have profoundly influenced the distribution and evolution of plants and animals. They serve to delimit the eras of geological time (Azoic, Proterozoic, **Palaeozoic**, **Mesozoic** and **Caenozoic**), each of which is represented by a group of strata in the idealized geological column.

Within each era there have been crustal movements less violent and widespread than revolutions, but nevertheless sufficiently great to cause well-defined "breaks" in the stratal and fossil records. Such episodes of crustal disturbances separate the *periods* of geological time. The strata formed during any one of these periods constitute a rock *system*, which can be often subdivided into *series*, with *epochs* as time equivalents.

The names of the periods (of time) and the systems (of strata) have generally been chosen to correspond with the geographical localities where the representative rocks were first studied. Thus the Cambrian and Silurian systems bear the Roman names for certain districts in Wales, where their rocks were first described (1833, 1835), although strata formed during the same intervals of time have since been found, and similarly named, in many other parts of the world. Likewise, the name Permian was first applied (1841) to a vast system of rocks, found in the province of Perm in central Russia. A few of the systems, however, were named before this custom had been established. Such are the Cretaceous (Latin *creta* – "chalk") and the Triassic (Greek *trias* – "three-layered").

The much simplified Stratigraphical Column in the following table shows the periods of geological history, their ages in millions of years, and their most distinctive forms of life.

Principal time units		*Idealized geological column (divisions not to scale)*	*Distinctive life*
Eras	*Periods*		
Caenozoic	Quaternary	Recent Pleistocene 1	Modern life evolves (including man)
	Tertiary	70	Mammals dominant
Mesozoic	Cretaceous	120	Spread of flowering plants; peak of dinosaurs before extinction
	Jurassic	145	Dinosaurs and reptiles dominant; first birds
	Triassic	170	Mammals and dinosaurs appear
Palaeozoic	Permian	210	Climatic extremes; spread of reptiles
	Carboniferous	285	Coal-forming forests widespread; reptiles and insects appear
	Devonian	310	First amphibians; plants highly developed
	Silurian	350	First evidence of land life
	Ordovician	410	First appearance of certain marine invertebrates
	Cambrian	500	Abundant fossils representing lower marine invertebrates
Eozoic	Pre-cambrian	2000	Algal life and soft-bodied creatures
		(Ages in millions of years)	

Gibraltar Skull. This was found in 1848, significantly before the publication of Darwin's *The Origin of Species* (1859). The existence of more than one species of man was not generally acceptable at that time, and the thick bone and strange appearance of the skull were attributed to a disease. It was, however, the first member of the **Neanderthal** species to be found. It lost the honour of giving its name to the species as a whole because it was only the controversy aroused by the finding of the skeleton at Neanderthal, in west Germany, in 1856, that led to the recognition of this distinct group of extinct men.

The Gibraltar Skull was found in the Devil's Tower rock-shelter. Excavation of the site in 1928 by Professor Dorothy Garrod resulted in the discovery of more Neanderthal bones, and **Mousterian** tools. These were found in a layer resting on the remains of an old beach nine and a half yards above the present sea-level. This beach was formed during the last inter-glacial period of the Pleistocene. This accords with evidence from other sites that Neanderthal men lived about 50,000 years ago at the beginning of the last **glaciation** (the Würm).

The Neanderthal species is easily distinguished from Homo sapiens by the characteristic shape of the skulls. The Gibraltar Skull is typical, with its thick bone, long pointed skull-back (occiput) and the great brow-ridge or torus above the eyes. Also, the orbits and nasal aperture are larger than those of Homo sapiens. However, in spite of their homogeneity as a species, the Neanderthals are thought by some anthropologists to have been divided into races. The Gibraltar Skull has contributed to this theory in that it is slightly different from French and Belgian skulls, which are again different from the Krapina remains.

Gigantopithecus (*G. blacki* von Koenigswald). The first diagnosis of this fossil was made as the result of the find of a number of giant teeth in Chinese druggists in south China. The material was the subject of much controversy, and Weinert improperly referred to it as Giganthropus, an improper change of name, whatever the status of the fossil. It was obvious that the provenance of the teeth was the southern provinces of China: this could be determined from the associated fauna which showed comparable fossilization and the same partial preservation – the roots of teeth are almost always destroyed by the gnawing of porcupine. All bore a similar yellow staining. The date, on faunal evidence, should be early Middle Pleistocene. (A number of other teeth suggest the presence in the same period of Australopithecinae.) Also present was a specimen of **Sinanthropus** officinalis. The find of a complete jaw which, from its dentition clearly belongs to *G. blacki*, has now established that we are here dealing with a giant form of ape.

Gilgamesh Epic, The. Not only is *The Gilgamesh Epic* the earliest considerable poem which has survived: it might also be claimed as one of the greatest. The form in which the poem has come down to us, that of an Assyrian recension, dates from the seventh century B.C. It was found, incised in **cuneiform** upon the fragments of a dozen clay tablets, in the ruins of the Royal Library of Ashur-bani-pal at **Nineveh** during the excavations of the last century. But the materials of which the poem is comprised are considerably older, and date back in substantially the same form to the beginning of the second millennium B.C.

Originally, Gilgamesh may have been a historical character: his name occurs in the **Sumerian** King List, where he is cited as the fifth king of the post-diluvian first dynasty. Conversely, there seems reason for believing that he was one of the **Kassites** who established an Elamite suzerainty at Erech (the Uruk of the poem). But whatever his historical origins, the Gilgamesh of the poem is essentially a folk-hero, as the poem itself is essentially a folk-myth.

The raw materials from which the epic was built seem to have been a series of disconnected poems, mainly Sumerian in origin. Many of them, no doubt, were as old as the third millennium and certain of them have been unearthed in the Sumerian excavations at **Nippur**, Kish and elsewhere. The process by which these fragmentary episodes came to be united into a single epic is now familiar to us, and has been examined at length by the Chadwicks in their work *The Growth of Literature* (1932).

The poem is written in short lines of four beats, not dissimilar from the four-beat line of alliterative Old and Middle English. The style abounds in repetitions of key passages and phrases, as do the Greek epics, and the whole is characterized by "heroic" manners and mannerisms. Of the estimated three thousand lines of the original, some two-thirds have survived wholly or in part, and the epic plan of the poem is clearly apparent in all but the ending. The work is divided into twelve books, of which the first eleven have obviously survived in their original form. The twelfth, on the other hand, has the appearance of a priestly addition (or substitution) and is merely a translation from a Sumerian original, remaining at odds and even at variance with the rest of the work. The original ending of the poem may well have been lost.

The subject of the epic might briefly be stated as man's conquest of his environment and his quest for the secret of immortality. Its hero is Gilgamesh himself, the Lord of Uruk, and his friend the beast-man Enkidu. The relationship between them is profoundly significant, and the death of Enkidu about halfway through the poem has suggested various parallels with prehistoric ritual and vegetation rites. It has also been pointed out that the division of the poem into twelve books parallels the division of the solar year. and many of the incidents have obvious zodiacal implications.

To the general reader, however, by far the most interesting feature of the poem is its inclusion of the Babylonian story of the **Flood**. Taken over as it was from Sumerian sources, the story was obviously drawn upon by the writers of Genesis. And, although the Old Testament version of the Flood story omits all mention of it, the onset of fire (with which the disaster commences in *Gilgamesh*) is still to be found in the pseudepigraphical *Book of Enoch*.

Since George **Smith** gave his translation of the Flood story to the world in 1872, the *Gilgamesh* tablets have continued to fascinate scholars and general readers alike. Accurate texts have been published and translations made into many languages.

Giza. This Egyptian site consists principally of three pyramids and a **sphinx**, but there is also a hill-side with innumerable tombshafts, some eighty feet deep. The three pyramids date from the fourth dynasty (about 2600 B.C.). The most important is the Great Pyramid of Cheops, or Khufu, which differs from any other pyramid in its internal arrangement, having a great number of passages and chambers, and the King's Chamber being entered by a vertical shaft in the floor. The work is very highly finished and the pyramid is constructed with remarkable precision. The second pyramid of Chephren, or Khafra, has two entrances, but neither chamber runs deep into the masonry, which appears to be solid. Part of the original outer casing of granite and limestone slabs remains. Nearby are the workmen's barracks, consisting of long chambers designed to house 4,000 men. The sixteen lowest courses of the third pyramid of Mycerinus or Menkanra are encased in red granite. Unlike the plain granite **sarcophagi** found in the other two pyramids, the sarcophagus in this one was ornamented with panel decoration; it was unfortunately lost at sea in 1838. The fourth dynasty Great Sphinx guards the entrance to the Nile Valley. 189 feet long, it is carved out of the solid rock. There is a shrine of Harmachis, the sungod, between its paws.

Glacial or **Glaciation.** The name given to a period of the earth's history when a large part of the

Photo: India Office Library, Commonwealth Relations Offices

PLATE 49. GANDHARA: statue of Bodhisattva from Peshawar district, Romano-Buddhist School. *(By courtesy of the Director General of Archaeology in India)*

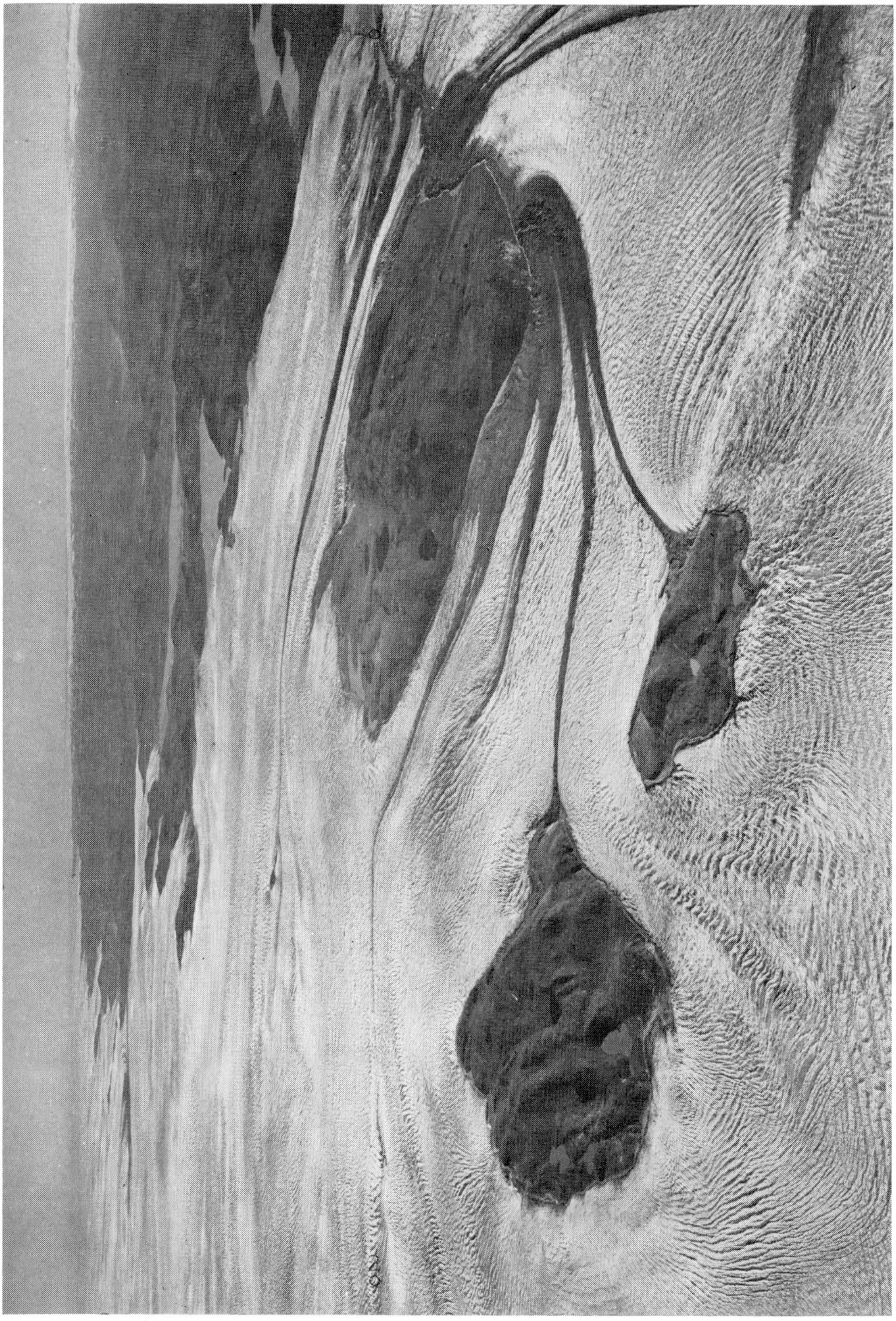

Photo: Geodetic Institute of Denmark, Copenhagen

PLATE 50. GLACIAL: the Greenland Ice Cap, similar to those to be found during the glacial periods in the earth's history.

Photo: *Exclusive News Agency*

PLATE 51. GREAT WALL OF CHINA.

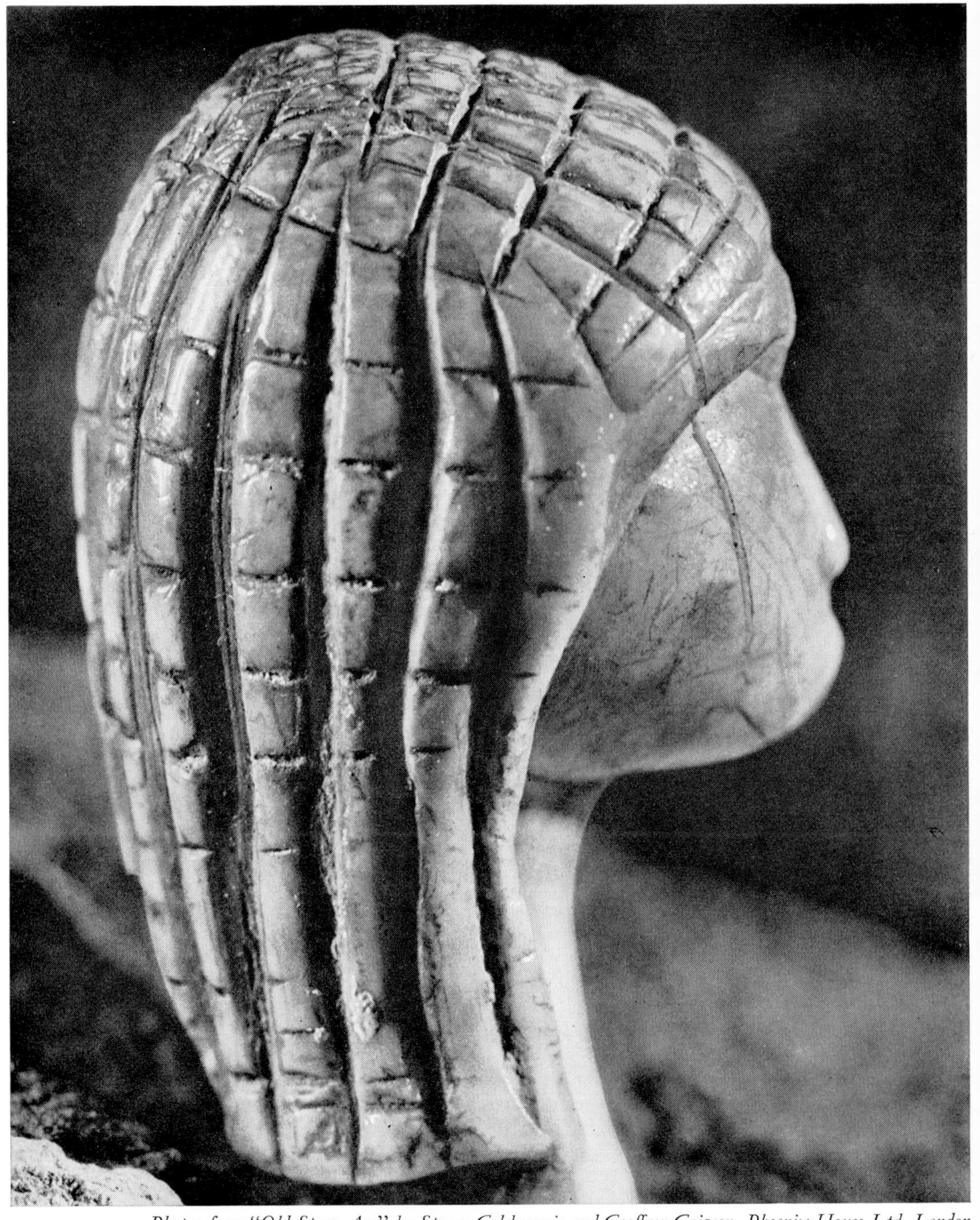

Photo: from "Old Stone Age" by Stevan Celebonovic and Geoffrey Grigson, Phoenix House Ltd, London

PLATE 52. GRAVETTIAN: head of a female figure carved in mammoth ivory.

Photo: British Museum

PLATE 53. HALLSTATT: bronze bucket from the Early Iron Age cemetery at Hallstatt, sixth century B.C. *(British Museum, London)*

Photo: Naturhistorisches Museum

PLATE 54. HALLSTATT: geometrically decorated bronze basin with the handle in the form of a cow and calf from the Early Iron Age cemetery at Hallstatt. The eyes of the cow are iron. *(Naturhistorisches Museum, Vienna)*

Photo: British Museum (Natural History)

PLATE 55. HAND-AXE: flint hand-axe from a gravel terrace of the river Thames near Maidenhead. *(British Museum (Natural History), London)*

Photo: from "Archaeology from the Earth", by Sir Mortimer Wheeler, Oxford University Press

PLATE 56. HARAPPA: burial of about 2000 B.C. showing outline of the wooden coffin.

Photo: Metropolitan Museum of Art

PLATE 57. HIEROGLYPHS: palette of King Narmer with a scene of the king hitting his enemy with a mace. *(Metropolitan Museum of Art, New York, Dodge Fund, 1931)*

Photo: from "Archaeology in China" by William Watson, Max Parrish and Co. Ltd, London

PLATE 58. HSING-LUNG HSIEN: iron mould for bronze socketed axe from Hsing-lung Hsien, probably fifth century B.C.
(By courtesy of the Britain-China Friendship Association)

Photo: John R. Freeman and Co

PLATE 59. INDUS VALLEY CIVILIZATION: steatite seals from Mohenjo-Daro.
(British Museum, London)

Photo: British Museum

PLATE 60. IONIANS: terracotta figure of a woman holding a dove, about 510 B.C. Height 10 inches. *(British Museum, London)*

Photo: British Museum

PLATE 61. IRAN: silver dish carved and engraved with a prancing animal, parcel gilt, Sassanian or post-Sassanian. *(British Museum, London)*

Photo: British Museum

PLATE 62. IRON AGE: cast bronze disc of unknown purpose, perhaps a sacral bowl, Irish, La Tène (Iron Age) style, second century A.D. *(British Museum, London)*

Photos: Exclusive News Agency

Plate 63. Jericho: pots found at Jericho.

Photo: Pierre Verger

PLATE 64. INCAS: the Fortress of Sacsahuana built by the Incas to protect Cuzco.

world's surface was covered by ice-sheets or glaciers. There have been four in the Pleistocene epoch (*see* **Quaternary Period**), and they are named after those parts of the Alps where their deposits are most clearly seen: Gunz (600,000 years ago), Mindel (450,000 years ago), Riss (200,000 years ago), and Würm (80,000 years ago). In America the four glacials are named after the four states where their deposits are most easily recognizable: Nebraskan, Kansan, Illinoian, and Wisconsin. It is possible that our own epoch, the Holocene, is an inter-glacial period, and that there will be another glaciation in the future; if so, a large part of the northern hemisphere will become uninhabitable, including most of Europe and America. *See* plate 50, page 190.

Glacis. A sloping bank built to make the approach to a fort more difficult.

Glyph. A carving, picture, or sign; a **hieroglyph** is a sacred (Greek – *hieros*) carving or picture, a petroglyph a carving on the living rock (Greek – *petra*).

Gordion, *see* Phrygians.

Gournia is a prehistoric **acropolis** site on the Gulf of Merabello in eastern Crete excavated almost completely by an American expedition under Mrs Harriet Boyd Hawes in 1901, 1903 and 1904, though only test-pits were sunk in the Late Minoan III (1400–1100 B.C.) settlement to the west.

Between the acropolis and the cove which formed an indifferent harbour were found some 20,000 sherds and a rock shelter with burials of the Early **Minoan** periods (about 2500–2000 B.C.), and some graves of the Middle Minoan periods (2000–1550 B.C.) indicating that this valley was occupied throughout the **Bronze Age.**

A small palace or princely villa erected in the Middle Minoan III period (1750–1550 B.C.) was situated on the crown of the hill, obviously aping its betters since the small theatral area is reminiscent of **Knossos**, but the **ashlar masonry** with its partly recessed façade and the alternation of square piers with round columns in the court is more reminiscent of the palace at **Mallia.** Round this building clustered houses of the Middle Minoan III period with small stones set in clay.

In the Late Minoan I period (1550–1450 B.C.) the palace was abandoned as such but around its ruins (turned into workmen's flats) there grew up a flourishing little industrial town with houses of at least two storeys. These often employ large boulders for the basement courses, and with narrow streets (stepped like those of modern Valletta) radiating from the crown of the hill and co-ordinated by an outer and an inner street at right angles to them of the kind that the Germans term "Ringstrasse". One house contained an oil-vat, another a complete carpenter's outfit including a double axe, balance-pan, saw, hook, five chisels, three small bars of bronze, a razor and half a pair of tweezers. Of the potter's wheel discs found in Crete no less than five were found at Gournia.

The town was burnt and completely destroyed at a date estimated by the excavator as 1500 B.C. Since, however, we now know that Late Minoan II pottery was peculiar to Knossos and that Late Minoan I wares continued in use on other sites throughout the following period, it seems not unlikely that Gournia, like Knossos, was destroyed about 1400 B.C., conceivably by fires following the earthquakes and by tidal waves that must have accompanied the great eruption that severed Thera from Therasia. There was little reoccupation of the town but the small shrine on the north crest of the hill (whether or not constructed originally, as some think, in the Late Minoan I period) has preserved for us a very interesting series of cult furniture of a town shrine of the household goddess in the fourteenth century B.C. The "altar vase" and the snake tubes were found in position. The figurines of the goddess and the clay doves were displaced but had presumably originally been set in the recess corresponding to the "raised dais" of the Hall of the Double Axes at Knossos.

During the main occupation of the town (1550–1450 B.C.) Gournia produced a fine series of painted vases including a splendid vase adorned with a life-like octopus, perhaps the first example of the Late Minoan marine style ever found in Crete. (*See also* **Minoan Civilization.**)

Gravettian. This upper **Palaeolithic** culture is probably a descendant of the **Châtelperronian** one in central France, presumably dating from the second phase of the last **glaciation.** Characteristic **stone tools** are blades more regular in outline and trimming than the Châtelperronian ones, later blades having tanged points for hafting. The Gravettians left cave paintings in France and were responsible for much of the painting in the **Lascaux** caves in the Dordogne. They are also famous for the female figurines of mammoth ivory, probably found in most places where the culture occurred. *See* plate 52, page 192.

Great Wall of China. A system of frontier defences came into existence before 300 B.C. in northern China to prevent sudden raids by Turkish and Mongol tribes. These provided the first fixed frontier between Chinese and non-Chinese tribes in the north, and also served as a focus for markets which took place there, as they did outside town and city walls. During the time of the Ch'in dynasty (256–207 B.C.) their rulers pushed the northern frontier farther outwards and this brought about a consolidation of the northern tribes under the Hsiung Nu. This formed a real threat to the Chinese and it was decided to form a permanent northern army and to consolidate the existing defences into a single, permanent wall. Accordingly under Ch'in Shih Huang Ti the Great Wall was constructed, being completed in its original form (about 450 miles) in 214 B.C. It consisted of a wall of stone and earth with a brick facing, about twenty to thirty feet high, with crenellated parapets flanking a road ten to thirteen feet wide on the top. Square watch towers were built at intervals to serve as signal-fire stations. The whole was carefully sited to conform with the landscape. Additions were subsequently made – it finally achieved a length of about 1400 miles – and it was extensively restored in the Ming period. It has been characterized as "the greatest and most monumental expression of the absolute faith of the Chinese in walls". *See* plate 51, page 191.

Grimaldi. In a cave at Grimaldi on the Italian Riviera two skeletons of the **Aurignacian** epoch of a distinctly Negroid type and with strongly projecting jaws were discovered in the early twentieth century. It has been suggested that these argue for the arrival in southern Europe in Aurignacian times of a Negroid race from Africa. In support of this, parallels have been drawn between details of Aurignacian cave paintings and the cave art of the modern **Bushmen**. The validity of the apparently Negroid characteristics has, however, been questioned.

Grotefend, George Friedrich (1775–1853), is the German classical scholar to whom is owed the first real success in decipering the **cuneiform** script. He claimed no special knowledge of Oriental languages but possessed an unusual facility for solving riddles. While he was studying philology under Heyne at Göttingen, his friends drew his attention to the curious wedge-shaped signs first copied by Niebuhr at the ruins of **Persepolis** in **Iran** in 1765.

As another basis for his work he had the memoirs on the antiquities of Persia published by De Sacy in 1793 in which some of the Pehlevi inscriptions at Naqsh-i-Rustam had been read. These were engraved above sculptures showing kings. The Persepolis texts were similarly associated with royal figures and Münter had already shown that they belonged to the Achaemenid period and that the writing was to be read from left to right. He had also decided which groups of letters should signify the royal names.

Grotefend inferred that the cuneiform inscriptions could have served as a model for the later Pehlevi monuments. He recognized that the recurring word of seven letters was "king" and that "king of kings" was to be found in two adjacent words. On the Pehlevi form he deduced, by comparing two similar Persepolis inscriptions beginning with different words, that two kings were mentioned, the one whose father was also named calling himself son of the king named in the other. He had thus found that "king Z" was son of "king Y" and that "king Y" was the son of "X"

The next step was to identify the three Achaemenid kings in question. Since the two names at the head of the inscriptions commenced with different signs they could not be Cyrus and Cambyses. Nor could they be Cyrus and Artaxerxes, because the names were of approximately similar length. Only the names of Darius and Xerxes remained. "X" who was not called a king fitted with Hystaspes of the Greek writers. Grotefend first transliterated the names of D-a-r-h-e-u-s-h and Kh-sh-h-e-r-sh-e, then the word for "king" on the basis of the known Zend word *khsheio* and finally Goshtasp or Hystaspes. Nine of the thirteen thus deciphered turned out to be correct.

On 4 September, 1802, Grotefend presented his findings to the Göttingen Academy. It is curious to note that at the same meeting Heyne first drew attention to the Greek inscription on the **Rosetta Stone** (*see* plate 119, page 385) from which the Egyptian **hieroglyphs** were later deciphered. By

1815 Grotefend had assigned values to thirty-seven cuneiform signs, twelve correctly. His attempts at translation of the complete inscriptions however, were not always so happy and some provoked well-deserved ridicule. His interest never flagged till his death in 1853, by which time others, building on his work, had overcome all the difficulties of the Persian alphabet and had gone far to understand the more complex Babylonian cuneiform script. (*See also* **Rawlinson.**)

Guanape, *see* Peruvians.

Gudea, *see* Lagash.

Gypsum Cave, Nevada, *see* America, Early Man in.

H

Haematite. A common iron oxide ore used by prehistoric man for colouring purposes; it is either red, brown, or blackish. (*See also* **Iron Age.**)

Hagia Triada. This is a prehistoric site in the Messara Plain near **Phaistos** excavated by the Italian Mission in Crete and deriving its name from a medieval chapel overlooking the remains of the Late **Minoan** palace. F. Halbherr excavated two round communal tombs of the type described as **tholos tombs** though only the smaller of these could ever have been completed by a dome of corbelled courses. The burials in these tombs covered a period from Early Minoan II to Middle Minoan I or II times (about 2300–1750 B.C.)

The palace was built in the transition from the Middle Minoan III to the Late Minoan I times (about 1550 B.C.), perhaps to replace the great palace of Phaistos then in decay because of earthquake damage, though Professor Banti only calls it a "sumptuous villa" and remarks that its occupation overlapped that of the second palace at Phaistos. The plan of the surviving structures is L-shaped with two wings facing north and west. The designers display the same partiality for the use of gypsum floors, dadoes and column bases as at **Knossos** but certain peculiarities such as the erection of peristyles (known but not common at Knossos) and the placing of light-wells in the middle of an important room (not at one of the narrower ends) indicate that the architect was a man of the Messara.

The chief residential quarter of the palace seems to focus on the north-west corner where three rooms opening out of each other form a unity slightly comparable to the Hall of the Double Axes at Knossos; the last room gives access to an open court flanked by a portico on two sides affording a glorious view of the gulf of Dibaki and the valley of the Ieropotamos. Accessible both to this complex and to the court were two square rooms of which the innermost was adorned with splendid frescos depicting a lady seated in a garden, two cats stalking a pheasant, and a leaping doe.

No lustral areas were found in this palace. East of the north-west complex of rooms lay a series of store-rooms and, beyond these, another series of elegant rooms with gypsum floors and bases all facing on to what the excavators termed the "Rampa dal Mare", a stepped road separating the palace proper from the small but well-built houses of the town. East of the palace lay the so-called "Piazza dei Sacelli" flanked by small household shrines containing conical bases for double axes.

About 1400 B.C. the city was overwhelmed by a catastrophe, presumably the same as that which destroyed Knossos. The palace was not rebuilt but two large houses were constructed on the ruins, the larger resembling closely the **megara** of **Mycenae** on the mainland and it seems probable that a Mycenaean Greek inhabited it. Some of the houses in the town, however, remained intact and others were reconstructed. The "Piazza dei Sacelli" was extended to the west now covering part of the old palace site. A new household shrine was constructed but the old ones seem to have remained intact. A shrine was provided with a higher floor-level, which obscured the magnificent fresco floor with marine designs of the Late Minoan I period (1550–1450 B.C.).

A row of what appear to be shops was erected in the north-west part of the town. The site was abandoned at the end of the Late Minoan III period (1400–1100 B.C.).

Halafian. Traces of this **Neolithic** civilization in its prehistoric stage were first found at Tell Halaf on the river Khabur in northern Syria. More remains were later found at **Nineveh**, fifty feet below buildings of the Assyrian Empire and others have been found at the neighbouring sites of Arpachiya and Tepe Gawra. A characteristic feature of the civilization was its hand-made burnished polychrome pottery decorated in a very lively way with animal designs and geometric patterns which are probably magic symbols. Halafian knives and tools were mostly of **flint** and **obsidian**. The Halafians were very skilled in small-scale craftsmanship, making objects such as serpentine stamp seals, amulets in the form of double axes and clay figurines. They built small mud-brick houses. Their more important buildings were circular in plan and were vaulted, with stone foundations. These were ancestors of the **tholos**, a type of building recurring more than a millennium later in Crete, Cyprus and other parts of the Mediterranean, often associated with religious symbols of Halafian type. The Halafians were a peaceful agricultural people. Traces of their culture have been found in Cilicia, Armenia and from the Mediterranean coast across north Syria to the Upper Tigris.

Hallstatt. The village of Hallstatt lies in the heart of the Salzkammergut in Austria thirty miles south-west of Salzburg itself. It is sited at the south-east end of the lake of that name on a narrow alluvial tract of the Mühlbach stream. Above the present village is the Salzbergtal, site of the famous salt-mines. Since the eighteenth century and the first reported finds by miners at Hallstatt and Dürrnberg, it has been clear that the salt workings of the region are of very great antiquity. The earliest prehistoric finds of any number at Hallstatt date from the later **Bronze Age** – a winged axe and a sword, plus fragments of cinerary urns found in the earliest graves in the nearby cemetery. Although, apart from a doubtful site at Steeg at the north end of the Hallstatt lake, there is no sign of the so-called **lake dwellings** or lake-side settlements of the **Neolithic** or indeed any other period, there can be little doubt that from an early date man followed in search of prey the animal tracks which led to the brine springs on the level Dammweise at the head of the Hallstatt Valley.

By the close of the Bronze Age the salt workings were a going concern involving complex mining systems with shafts of a total length of 1300 feet and techniques which were also used in the copper mines of the Mitterberg. In the Later **La Tène** period the use of the "lye" extracting method (excavating, flooding and boiling off the brine) involved a complex system of wooden troughs and channels as is evidenced by discoveries not only on the Dammweise, but also at the contemporary workings of Swäbisch-Hall where four such troughs were found employed as solar evaporation tanks. The damp at the salt workings resulted in the construction of "corduroy" roads of parallel-laid tree trunks. In both the Dürrnberg mines above Hallein and the type-site itself there have been found well-preserved corpses wearing the peasant smock and pointed skull-caps as depicted on the bronze buckets imported into the east Alpine region from northern Italy. The miners' equipment, wicker and hide carrying-panniers and pine torches no less than the wooden shovels and adze hammers of bronze and iron have all been retained through the preserving qualities of the salt itself; a similar series has been found in the nearby copper mines of Kelchalpe. The animal bones found in both the cemetery and mining regions enable us to reconstruct the economy of a herding community keeping cattle of both long- and short-horned variety, pigs, and mountain sheep or "mouflon". Dogs were also kept and not only is there evidence for the small breed of horse introduced already in the Bronze Age but also of a larger local "Noric" type. Hunting does not seem to have played a large part in the life of the Hallstatt community. The cultivation of apple trees is also proved by analysis of the miners' excrement preserved in the salt.

The only clues we have to the habitation of the early mining community is the discovery of two "log-cabins" found preserved beneath the alluvial clays in the area of the salt workings. One contained a bronze palstave of the true Hallstatt period. The construction of both huts recalls such extensive Hallstatt settlements as that of Wasserburg-Buchau on an island in the Federsee. Here a series of nine farmsteads with pitched roofs and gaps between the logs filled with clay were contained within a multiple palisade. Similar too is a copper-miner's hut on the Kelchalpe yielding just the same range of animal bones as at Hallstatt itself.

Itinerant smiths were attracted to the wealth of Hallstatt, and the bronze hoard found on the Salzbergtal in 1830 doubtless represents one such merchant's goods. It consisted of bronze sickles, daggers and a single sword amongst other objects, all belonging to the transition between the end of the Bronze Age and the true Hallstatt period.

The largest range of material evidence for the prehistoric peoples of Hallstatt comes of course from their cemetery. Some 3,000 graves have been uncovered but there has been a lamentable lack of really detailed examination until recent years.

The burial rites of the Early **Iron Age** graves are varied, with cremation tending to prevail in the earlier graves, linking them with the custom of the preceding Urnfield people.

Inhumations of up to five individuals in the same grave and double graves usually of a mother and her child are also known, as are mixed cremation and inhumation graves, and even partially cremated bodies. These last belong to the Later Hallstatt period. This later period followed the first stage of the true Hallstatt culture which began about 700 B.C. and lasted until 550. During the second phase, ending about 480 B.C., the culture spread as far as Brittany – there perhaps to boost the tin trade – and northern France and thence to Britain and Scandinavia, while the Celtic origin of many place-names in Spain suggests an even earlier expansion into Iberia in the wake of the Urnfield culture.

Some graves of the Hallstatt cemetery date back to the true Bronze Age, at the end of which bronze smithing had reached its height and sheet metal-working including such sophisticated techniques as lathe-cleaning had been mastered. The introduction of iron was a gradual process and the typical long tapering-bladed "antennae" sword inherited from the Late Bronze Age was still often made of bronze in the earliest phase of the Hallstatt culture. However, of the twenty-one swords known from the cemetery to be dated to the end of this phase, only four are of bronze. One of the iron examples from a cremation grave has a typical "Dutchman's cap" pommel with a zig-zag design of ivory set in amber. This use of geometric decoration is a typical Hallstatt motif inherited from the Urnfield peoples.

A parallel sword from Gomadingen-Sternberg, Württemberg, has a similar design inlaid in gold as has indeed a third example with a ritually bent iron blade from a cremation contained in a parallel-sided corrugated bronze situla of Italian origin found at Oss in north Brabant. This find on the edge of the Hallstatt region shows that imports were also making their way across the barrier of the Alps in the Later Hallstatt period, when the long sword gives way to a short broad knife-dagger with modified antennae hilt often of sweated-on bronze. The throwing spear also comes into its own, as does a new range of fibulae, mostly with long catch-plates showing links once more with northern Italy, and particularly the Villanovan site of Certosa, near Bologna.

At this Villanovan site was found one of a group of bronze shouldered buckets decorated with warriors and wild animals such as have been found throughout the east Alpine region. These, like the two bucket lids found at Hallstatt itself, and made of copper from the Kelchalpe mines, seem to have originated in the area of Este, home of an offshoot of the Villanovans, and like them and the Hallstatt groups to have sprung from the eastern Urnfield culture. The winged beasts on the Hallstatt lids are influenced from the Orient and ultimately the art of Luristan; while on the other hand a local version of the Oss ribbed pail from the cemetery has representations of the "duck and solar wheel" symbol inherited from Urnfield times and common also on the Villanovan-type bronze belt plates. All these objects foreshadow the Early La Tène art style.

The La Tène occupation of Hallstatt must be equated with that second wave of Celtic invaders of the Alpine territory who pushed on to sack Rome in 390 B.C. On the Turmkogel above the cemetery Late Hallstatt occupation material is overlaid by that of developed La Tène while it seems likely that the salt mines as on the Dürrnberg continued to be worked by the original inhabitants. In the latest section of the cemetery at the head of the valley, new pottery forms occur including beak-shaped flagons following the **Etruscan** pattern, metal examples of which, as at **Vix**, were imported west already in Late Hallstatt times. Of the metal-work from the La Tène graves one typical parallel-sided iron sword was contained within a bronze scabbard bound with a double dragon-mouthed chape and engraved with a procession of three spearmen bearing oval Celtic shields and four spear-carrying cavalrymen. The figured frieze of the Certosa bucket and a similar scabbard from Este itself show the continuity of trans-Alpine connections.

Definite evidence of habitation of Hallstatt in the Late Iron Age is as scanty as it was in the earlier period. Mention has already been made of the miners' hut, while the "lye" works on the Dammweise belong to Late La Tène, and the period of Caesar's conquests. Continuity is the keynote of the Hallstatt cemetery and the forming of the Roman province of Noricum by Tiberius is reflected in the prosperous Roman settlement around Lahn, immediately to the south of Hallstatt. Here imported *terra sigillata*, pillar-moulded and painted glass-ware, and even three bronze statuettes of

Osiris, no less than a pair of iron crampons, must surely reflect the continued exploitation of the salt-mines where now the miners would be of La Tène ancestry and economy.

But what of the origins and spread of the actual culture to which Hallstatt has given its name? The clue lies in the earliest finds of the site itself. For it is with the great unified expansion of the Late Bronze Age Urnfields in about 1000 B.C. that we see the beginnings of that warrior-chieftain society which was at the root of the Celtic world. The arrival during the eighth century in Hungary of a warrior horseman group is also evident in the very last stages of what we may term the proto-Hallstatt period. These peoples, with their improved horse-bits and bridle-mounts clearly had connections with the Scythian steppe chieftains, and indeed represent the first of a series of nomadic incursions into eastern Europe, bearing types of undoubted eastern origins. The nomadic element indeed continued side by side with Hallstatt and, later, La Tène offshoots in eastern Bohemia and the Balkans. Whatever the true origins of this group, it seems to have strongly influenced the manner of burial of the first Hallstatt chieftains found with their wagons under the barrows of Bohemia, Bavaria and Upper Austria itself. This chieftainly burial, often in a wooden lined chamber as seen in the Later Hallstatt graves of the forest of Haguenau and central France, as at Vix, was more typical of the period than the simple flat-grave cemeteries as at Hallstatt itself, and may not only have been influenced by the customs of the nomads but also by those of Etruria, while the great Hallstatt sword copies a type first found in Bosnia. This is the first of that series of links with the upper Adriatic which culminates in the Venetic culture of Este.

The positioning of fortified settlements on major trade routes reaches its peak in the later Hallstatt period, with not only various Jura sites, such as the Camp du Château and its Rhodian pottery imported by the upland routes from the south, but also the **Heuneburg** placed high above the Danube in Württemberg. The mud-brick walls and bastions of the second period of reconstruction and Greek black figure ware, show the strong links with the classical world and indicate a flourishing wine trade with origins in the Late Bronze Age. The Later Hallstatt period, which is marked at the type-site by a less warlike panoply, seems to have been one of unity and peaceful expansion. This is the world which is represented in the full at Vix.

The transalpine routes into central Europe were not only used by north Italian traders as we have already noted but also produced such finds as the seventh- or sixth-century B.C. Greek bronze hydria from Grâchwil in Switzerland. A scatter of late Greek coins in southern Britain, and an Italo-Greek statuette from Uffington in Berkshire, show the northernmost limits of early classical penetration no less than the evidence for cart burial in the New Forest offers tangible links with the retarded Hallstatt cultures of northern France which followed there immediately upon the Urnfields. This was the world described in the sixth century by Hekataius of Miletus who speaks of Celts in "Nyrax" (Noricum?) and by Pytheas the sixth-century Massiliote adventurer, a fourth-century A.D. version of whose voyage beyond the Pillars of Hercules records dealings with the inhabitants of Albion. *See* plates 53–54, pages 193–194.

Hamitic People. The term Hamitic as used at present includes certain peoples in north Africa, such as the Berber and Tuareg, and in north-east Africa, such as the Beja, Galla, and Somali, the former being the northern Hamites and the latter the eastern Hamites. It is now proposed that the term Hamitic should be abandoned, that the northern Hamites should be called simply "Berber" and that the eastern Hamites should be called Kushitic (Cushitic). Further, since there is a relationship (certainly linguistic and probably genetic) between the Hamites and the Semites, which has given rise to the term "Hamitico-Semitic", it has recently been suggested that "Hamitic" should be used instead of "Hamitico-Semitic" to cover both the Hamitic and Semitic languages, keeping Kushitic for the eastern Hamites. In modern ethnological and linguistic studies, the term Hamitic or Kushitic is used to describe the non-Negroid peoples of north-east Africa who do not speak Semitic (Ethiopic) languages and who are comprised in four zones: northern, central, eastern and south-western.

There are certain Negroid features in the Hamites, but these are scanty both in the peoples of the northern zone, suggesting that the Negroes did not penetrate so far north, and also in the Somali and Afar of the eastern zone, which suggests that by the time these groups entered Africa the Negroes had left the region. Though the dark skins of many Hamites are due to early Negro admixture, their hair is not normally woolly, and when woolly hair does occur it is due to comparatively recent mixture with Negroes. The Hamites are by inclination pastoral, with cattle or camels according to terrain, though agriculture has developed among them and they have ploughs of their own. (Outside the Hamitic areas, the plough was unknown in Negro Africa till introduced by Europeans.) While some, for example the Beja, Somali, and Afar, are Moslems, many, like the Galla and Sidama, worship a sky-god. Certain Hamitic features, such as the reverence for milk and the psychological importance of cattle, have spread outside the Hamitic area among the pastoral Negroids of east Africa; and many of the African Negroid stocks have Hamitic physical elements.

Hammurabi, king of Babylon in the earlier half of the eighteenth century B.C. (he reigned forty-three years, but his exact date is still not certainly fixed, 1792–50 B.C. being most generally accepted), was the sixth in a line of kings who made up the first dynasty of **Babylon.** There is little or no direct historical record of his reign, only the date-formulae of his years, supplemented by much incidental evidence from state letters, his laws, and also from private business documents.

In the letters there are the king's own orders to his local officers, which show him as taking an almost excessive interest in affairs of administrative detail, and somewhat over-anxious to please every suitor. There are many side-lights upon him from the archives of **Mari**; here he appears as a strategist and organizer, moving forces as strong as 10,000 men, asking for or sending reinforcements, contracting alliances, treating with ambassadors, and conferring honours. The undoubted supremacy which he exercised during the last ten years of his reign (before which the Mari records cease, for Hammurabi had captured that city) was certainly founded upon victory by arms, but the general picture of this king is predominantly that of an outstanding statesman.

Well suited to this character is the achievement for which Hammurabi is celebrated today, as the first-known and most complete legislator of the ancient world. His laws, inscribed upon sculptured pillars, of which one is now in Paris, were for long afterwards copied and studied. In form, his "code" (so-called, though by no means comprehensive) consists of a prologue and epilogue, with the laws, about 200 in all, between these formal pronouncements. While no description of their contents can be attempted here, it may be noticed that criminal, civil, and commercial laws are all included, and similar subjects are grouped, though without formal division; that many topics are omitted, being evidently left in the realm of customary law; that society is divided into three social classes, with corresponding rights and liabilities; and that corporal punishments are frequent and severe, often upon the principle of "an eye for an eye". Hammurabi was the last in a succession of lawgivers, fragments of whose work survive from several centuries before him, and much of their matter can be seen incorporated or amended in his own system.

Of his work as a builder of temples and opener of canals something is related by his inscriptions, but modern discovery has found little of his period remaining, not even in the ruins of Babylon, where the much later dynasty of Nebuchadnezzar has covered everything with its own vast constructions.

It is, however, indicative of Hammurabi's enduring greatness that his god Marduk, raised by him to the head of the pantheon, never again yielded that place until Babylon itself passed away, and that his laws have emerged again in the last century as one of the supreme cultural achievements of remote antiquity. (*See also* **Ur-Nammu.**)

Hand-axe. The characteristic **stone tool** or weapon of the **Palaeolithic** era, the hand-axe was a **flint** tool. Flakes were struck from the central core in such a way that one end of the core was given a point with sharp cutting edges leading down to it and the other end was left rounded so as to fit conveniently into the palm of the hand, hence its name. It was not until **Neolithic** times that man discovered how to fit the tool into a wooden handle. The knowledge of how to produce a hand-axe became gradually diffused over many parts of the world during the long Palaeolithic Age and **Abbevillian-Acheulian** hand-axes have been found in places as far apart as southern England, south-eastern India, and southern Africa. Different cultures produced their own characteristic type of hand-axe which, to the trained archaeologist, are instantly recognizable. *See* plate 55, page 195.

Hanging Gardens. The Hanging Gardens of Babylon were one of the **Seven Wonders of the World.** It is not known for certain what they were, but it is thought probable that they were ornamental gardens planted on the terraces of the **ziggurats** in **Babylon** and other Mesopotamian cities.

Haniwa. In about the third century A.D. the practice developed in Yamato, south-west of Osaka, Japan, of burying the more important dead in large graves inspired by the **tumulus** burials of southern Korea. The boundaries of these graves were demarcated by a row of terracotta cylinders, known as haniwa. In the fifth century the upper portions of these cylinders were decorated by human figures, usually of women or of warriors, or animals – horses, dogs, monkeys, deer. The practice was probably related to the use of stone figures placed by Chinese graves, but these haniwa, though of crude technique – being made by coil methods, and shaped with a knife or a bamboo spatula – have a lively appearance full of expression, and are the earliest form of Japanese sculpture.

Harappa. The great mounds at Harappa, lying on the old bank of the River Ravi, one of the "Five Rivers" of the Punjab, in the Montgomery district of West Pakistan, were first discovered in the eighteen-twenties by Sir Alexander Burnes and Charles Masson while they were travelling to Afghanistan, but their potential importance was not recognized until a century later. In 1921–22 excavations were started there almost contemporaneously with the discovery of the other great city site at **Mohenjo-Daro** (*see* plate 97, page 325) and the startling remains of the **Indus Valley civilization** (*see* plate 59, page 199) began to appear.

The most important mound is the Citadel (Mound AB) rising to a height of fifty feet above the plain. Its massive mud-brick ramparts were first recognized by Sir Mortimer Wheeler in 1946. In plan it is roughly a parallelogram some 460 yards long and 215 yards wide. To the east lies the straggling and much denuded Mound E which probably represented the main living area. North of the citadel were discovered a series of granaries, working floors for pounding grain, and lines of workmen's quarters. South of the citadel were two cemeteries, the first – R 37 – containing graves of the Harappan period and the second cemetery – H – containing graves from a post-Harappan date. The excavations, which have hardly been systematic and have as yet left large areas unexplored, brought to light quantities of structural remains and of antiquities which show a striking similarity to those from Mohenjo-Daro and other Indus sites. *See* plate 56, page 196.

Harpoon. Prehistoric man began to make harpoons towards the end of the Upper **Palaeolithic**, using antlers of deer or reindeer for the purpose. They became widely used in **Mesolithic** cultures such as the **Azilian.**

Haua Fteah, *see* Africa, North.

Hazor. The site of ancient Hazor was identified in 1926 by Professor J. **Garstang**, with the uninhabited mound, Tell-el-Qedah, which lies in Israel about eight miles north of the Sea of Galilee and five south-west of Lake Huleh. The site consists of two main parts; a city **tell** of approximately twenty-five acres extent, and, adjoining this to the north, a much larger area of about 150 acres with a beaten earth rampart on the uphill, or western, side. In 1928 Garstang conducted a brief investigation of the site, but no further excavation was done until 1955 when an expedition from the Hebrew University of Jerusalem under the direction of Dr Yigael Yadin, son of Professor E. L. Sukenik of **Dead Sea Scrolls** fame, selected the ruins as worthy of long term investigation. Though it is probable that earlier remains exist on the site, no level has been reached (1958) earlier than the Middle **Bronze Age** (about 2100–1500 B.C.), which is represented near the surface in the large northern area. This was a built city estimated to have been capable, with the tell proper, of accommodating up to 40,000 souls, but it was only occupied for about five centuries, having been destroyed, probably by Joshua, with considerable violence in the thirteenth century, and never thereafter inhabited. The tell proper was occupied before this lower city, and continued in use after its destruction. Excavations on the tell have revealed remains of the subsequent Israelite period, though the earliest belong to the time of Solomon, some two centuries after the time of Joshua. Soundings in three areas of the tell throw much light on the civilization of the Northern Kingdom, and the final destruction of the city at the hands of Tiglath-Pileser III in 732 B.C. (2 Kings 15, 29) is indicated by thick layers of ash and other signs of violence.

Hebrews. The name Hebrews is used of the people more correctly called the Israelites in ancient times, and later, the Jews. It may be that the name means "one from the other side [of the Euphrates]", but a view which perhaps finds support in the Bible (Genesis 11, 16–26) is that it signifies the descendants of the Patriarch Eber. While the primary source of information about the Hebrews is the Bible, it is possible that they are to be connected with a number of people mentioned in documents of the second millennium B.C. from the ancient world under what are probably variants of the name Habiru. These seem to have been troublesome migratory tribes, who sometimes settled in urbanized areas with menial status. This would accord with the Old Testament, where the descendants of Eber include many peoples other than the Israelites. Moreover, the Old Testament usage, whereby the name Hebrew is generally only used in contrast to other nations, rather than as a national name, and is indeed largely replaced by the name Israelite by the time of the monarchy, would agree with the picture of the Habiru as widespread and numerous, but mostly settled under different national names, or absorbed by other national groups by about 1000 B.C. The Israelites would thus be one group of wandering Hebrews, who under Abraham had left southern Babylonia to move to Palestine. A famine caused them to move to Egypt, but during a long sojourn there they descended to a status of servitude. Finally, led by Moses, the entire people escaped from Egypt, and after lengthy wanderings, took **Jericho**, then attacked and overran the Canaanite-inhabited region of Palestine, probably in the late thirteenth century B.C. After a period of consolidation, the rule passed to a series of kings, and under David, partly as the result of a period of decline in the great powers, the kingdom reached its greatest extent, with **Jerusalem** as its capital. Solomon benefited from this inheritance, but due to his unwise policy of self-aggrandizement and oppression, the northern tribes revolted from his son's rule, and set up the kingdom of Israel with its capital first at Tirzah, and then at Samaria. In 722 B.C. the **Assyrians** took Samaria, and the ten northern tribes, which formed Israel, were deported to other parts of the Assyrian empire. The southern kingdom of Judah, that portion of David's dominion which had remained loyal to Solomon's son, survived the Assyrian menace until Jerusalem was in its turn destroyed, and the elite exiled to **Babylon** by Nebuchadnezzar in the years following 587 B.C. The return of the remnant of what are now most conveniently called the Jews, (probably from the first syllable of *Ju*-dahites) took place when Babylon fell to Cyrus in 539 B.C. Persian rule was succeeded by that of Alexander, the Ptolemies, and the Seleucids; under the latter the Jews successfully revolted until, in 63 B.C., Pompey imposed Roman rule. It was under Rome that Jesus Christ lived and died, and the end of the Jews as a nation and the beginning of their dispersion throughout the world came in A.D. 70 when Titus sacked Jerusalem.

Heb-sed, or the *Sed*-festival, was in the nature of a jubilee celebrated by kings of Egypt from the earliest times. The circumstances under which it was celebrated are still obscure.

For the occasion a series of temporary buildings were usually erected. They are best exemplified for us in the *heb-sed* court of the step pyramid complex of Zoser at **Saqqara**. This court, oblong in shape, lies between the entrance to the complex and the pyramid itself. The east and west sides contain model or dummy shrines of the gods of Upper and Lower Egypt, consisting of solid masonry with a sculptured façade and small court. At the southern end a double throne was erected as a high dais beneath a canopy.

During the festival the king accompanied by priests went in a procession to the row of shrines and made offerings to the gods. Then, dressed in an archaic cloak, close fitting round the shoulders and reaching to the knees, the king would process to the throne, preceded by the emblem of the god of Siut, Wepwat. He was then crowned, first seated on one throne with the white crown of Upper Egypt and then on the other with the red crown of Lower Egypt.

In a subsequent ceremony the king appears dressed in the short kilt with an animal's tail attached to it; he ran a ritual course four times holding in his hands emblems of royal authority.

In the absence of contemporary written accounts the origin and explanation of the festival are uncertain, but it is thought that the ceremonies represent a ritual re-enactment of the union of Upper and Lower Egypt into one kingdom, traditionally by Menes, the first king of the first dynasty.

Heian. At the beginning of the Heian period in Japan (A.D. 781–1184) the court moved from **Nara**

to Heian, the present Kyoto. In the Nara period, the links with China had been maintained by Buddhist priests, but now it was the Japanese aristocracy who felt drawn to Chinese literature and art. Esoteric Buddhist sects, including also Shingon and Tendai, began to appear, with a complicated iconography which gave rise to new styles of painting and sculpture, based on late Tang styles. The Bodhisattvas, who were symbolic of spiritual power, began to be represented in large statues carved in a single piece of wood with heavy draperies. The gods of the national Shinto cult were depicted now in anthropomorphic form, instead of, as previously, by the symbols of the sword and the mirror. This was under the influence of the Bodhisattva cult, while the style chosen was that of the Tang period. But as the power of the Tang dynasty declined, in the tenth century A.D., the links with China weakened, and the aristocracy felt less inclined to rely upon foreign models. They took over the power from the emperor, made political decisions in his name and strongly influenced artistic development. (The period from the end of the ninth century to the middle of the twelfth century A.D. is known as the Fujiwara period, after the noble clan which effectively exercised power.) Art, during a period of some three centuries of isolation from China, developed along national lines. The cult of the god Amida or Amitabha became paramount, and in A.D. 1053 the Phoenix Pavilion was built as an earthly representation of the Western Paradise to which the followers of Amida would gain access. A group of fifty-two followers surround the gilt and lacquer figure of the Buddha Amida, the work of Jo-cho and his atelier. It was Jo-cho who introduced the practice of making figures from a number of pieces of wood, instead of a single large block, so as to leave open spaces between the different figures. The images were coloured and decorated with gold leaf, in the style of paintings. Plastic methods of expression gave way to an interest in details and decoration, and a more superficial graphic treatment. The same tendency can be seen in the graphic arts, and grace and refinement and an emphasis on decorative details in contrasting colours on a golden ground are common.

Wall paintings and painted screens were a feature of royal palaces and the homes of the nobility. These were often decorated with secular themes. Here two schools existed: one of Chinese origin, the other a Japanese school. There also developed a school of illustrative painting which went with the growth of a national literary style. The earliest versions of the *Genji Monogatari* are examples of this type of illustrated epic in a Japanese manner. Buddhist popular texts might also have secular illustrations, and schools of satirical art also developed which were to have a considerable impact on the subsequent history of Japanese artistic modes of expression.

Heidelberg Jaw. The discovery of the Heidelberg Jaw was due to the perseverance of Dr Otto Schoetensack of the University of Heidelberg. At Mauer, a village about seven miles away from the city, there was a great sand-pit. For twenty years he visited it constantly, feeling certain that there must be human fossils in such an enormous exposure of Pleistocene strata. The large mandible was found in 1907, eighty feet below the surface of the ground.

At the same level as the jaw were found animal fossils which included forms of elephant, rhinoceros and horse typical of the warm climate at the beginning of the Pleistocene. The deposits have been dated to the warm interglacial period between the first and second **glaciations**. This makes Heidelberg Man almost half a million years old, contemporary among the relics of **Fossil Man** with the **Pithecanthropus** finds in Java and Chou-kou-tien in China.

The teeth are perfectly human in appearance; large compared with those of modern men, but not big considering the size of the jaw itself. The canines do not project, but are level with the rest of the teeth. The teeth are arranged in a curve, not in the parallel-sided arrangement of the anthropoid apes.

The jawbone itself is massive. The lost skull must have had zygomatic arches much larger than those of modern men to support the masseter muscle which would have moved the mandible in chewing. The hind part of the jaw is wider, and the sigmoid notch shallower, than in Homo sapiens. There is also a complete lack of chin, the lump of bone at the front of the jaw which is found on all Homo sapiens skulls. But, on the other hand, there is no simian shelf, the bony thickening inside the jaw to which the tongue is attached in apes. The tongue of Heidelberg Man was attached to genial tubercles, as is that of Homo sapiens.

Heliopolis, the "city of the sun", the biblical On, was in ancient times the chief centre of the solar cult in Egypt. It was here, according to one Egyptian myth, that the sun god Ra first manifested himself. This ensured for Heliopolis and its priestly college an importance throughout the ancient period. The cult goes back to Predynastic times (before 3188 B.C.). Throughout its long history, the influence of the city seems to have been more religious than political.

Heliopolis continued as an important centre of religious worship and teaching during the Middle and New Kingdoms. The scale of benefactions to the Great Temple by Ramses III recorded in the Great Harris Papyrus is proof of its importance. By the Roman period this importance had disappeared, for Strabo speaks of Heliopolis as a deserted city. Its fame as a centre of religious speculation was, however, well known to classical authors.

Of the ancient site little is now to be seen. It lies a short distance north-east of Cairo, in the neighbourhood of the village of Matariah, and is marked by the surviving granite obelisk dedicated by Sesostris I (about 1950 B.C.) before the Great Temple.

Helladic. Of Greece in pre-Classical, that is, **Bronze Age** times.

Hellenic. Of Greece in Classical times.

Herodotus. The Greek historian, Herodotus, son of Lyxes, was born about 485 B.C. at Halicarnassus on the west coast of Asia Minor. Because of political troubles involving his family, Herodotus left home as a young man and settled in Samos; he then made a series of extensive journeys in **Egypt** (as far as the first cataract and the Red Sea), the Levant, down the Euphrates to **Babylon** (where he conversed with the Chaldaean priests and climbed the Tower of Babel), in Scythia (where he witnessed a royal funeral) and Greece. He lectured in Athens and Olympia; and from Athens he went to Italy as a colonist in Pericles' new foundation of Thurii (443 B.C.). He died sometime after 430 B.C. It is probably true to say that he was the most confirmed traveller in the ancient world before the Emperor Hadrian.

His published work was an *Exposition of History* (*historie* = inquiry or research), divided into nine books by later editors. The main theme was the struggle between free Greece and the Persian Empire (*see* **Iran**) which culminated in the ruinous expedition of Xerxes and Mardonius (480–79 B.C.). But he recognized that the object of his research was not only to record events for posterity and to preserve the memory of great deeds performed on both sides, but also to explain the causes of the struggle; and he sought for first causes far back in the past. In effect he gives a panorama of the rise and debacle of the Persian Empire.

Herodotus also recognized that a knowledge of the environment and habits of different races is essential to the understanding of them. For that reason he embraced in his study the geography of the known world, natural history, the customs and social organization, religious practices and mythology of all peoples. His work appears to have been preserved complete. Unfortunately there is no trace of the "Assyrian Discourses" to which he refers in his account of Babylon; presumably Herodotus never wrote them up for publication.

The principal topics are: the Lydian Kingdom and the Expansion of Persia under Cyrus the Great (book one); the conquest of Egypt, with the description of its history and marvels (book two); Cambyses' end and the Persian Empire under Darius (book three); Darius' failure to conquer Scythia (book four); the Ionian Revolt, with great digressions on Athens and Sparta, and the Persian invasion repelled at Marathon (books five to six); finally the grand expedition against Greece (books seven to nine).

Herodotus' treatment of this great subject is discursive. He draws upon an ample fund of stories and ranges the world from India to Cadiz (Tartessus) and equatorial Africa. Often his digressions are not strictly relevant to the narrative; but besides entertaining the reader they illuminate the whole course of human action. For example, the discussion of the inundation of the Nile (in which Herodotus gives three explanations and with good reason rejects the theory of melting snows that we now know to be the true one) will not appear to be irrelevant if we bear in mind that the life of Egypt depends on this annual event. Herodotus' *History* is thus unrivalled in its scope; and Herodotus was not only (as Cicero called him) the Father of History, but the founder of historical geography and anthropology also.

Quite apart from the history of the wars, the account of the Persian Empire is of outstanding value. Herodotus no doubt spoke Persian, and he seems to have had Persian friends of high standing from whom he obtained reliable information. The description of Egypt is lively and informative. Herodotus' first-hand observations here, as at Babylon and elsewhere, seems tolerably accurate. But in his account of the Egyptian kings and their works he was dependent on priests and guides who seem at times to have been bigoted and ill-informed. Thus his all-conquering king "Sesostris" is largely a figure of fiction, and his "Rhampsinitus" (i.e. "Ramses Si-Nit", "son of Neith") is an error of the Saite priests. He saw engraved on the Great Pyramid what he understood to be the grand total of the radishes, garlic and onions consumed by the workmen who built it; perhaps on this occasion he was the victim of a guide who did not care to admit that he could not read. The one grave blunder is the dating of the pyramid-building kings to the period following the eighteenth and nineteenth dynasties.

Herodotus recognized the importance of precise chronology, and is still the most valuable single authority for the framework of Greek and Middle Eastern history in the seventh and sixth centuries B.C. His error of six years (606 instead of 612 B.C.) for the date of the fall of **Nineveh** may be explained by a mistake in his arithmetic; and the Babylonian tablets show that his dates for the Median kings are at least substantially correct.

Herodotus wrote in an easy and fluent, though highly artistic, Ionic Greek prose which disguises the complex structure of his work. He is the most dramatic of ancient historians, searching for the clue to events in the characters and destinies of his chief actors, so that his Croesus, Polycrates, Cleomenes and Mardonius hold the stage like tragic heroes. Many of his stories have almost the force of parables. But he is alive to the momentous effect of unpredictable happenings. He recalls the little girl's words which prevented a Peloponnesian invasion of Asia, and the Spartan king incautiously counting the months on his fingers when he received the news of his son's birth (in consequence of which the son was later dethroned and sought vengeance by urging a Persian invasion of Greece). Another instance is the voice of the god at the oracle of Branchidae, who changed his mind and the fate of Ionia rather than be the loser in an argument with a mortal man.

As a historian Herodotus is impartial and generous in his judgements, and, for a Greek, extraordinarily sympathetic in his understanding of foreigners. He is called credulous by scholars who reject what is strange or unfamiliar; but modern archaeological and geographical discoveries show that he was very often better informed than his critics. He generally used sound judgement in accepting or rejecting stories that he was told. Among the wonders and curiosities that he relates are Scythian cannibals and were-wolves, Arabian sheep with trolleys to support their tails, bitumen and oil wells, the crocodiles of the Indus and the crocodiles and pygmies of central Africa, palm wine and beer, the great thickness of the Egyptians' skulls which he thought was caused by the sun. He tells of the circumnavigation of the Cape of Good Hope, but does not believe the sailors' statement that when rounding the cape they had the sun on their starboard side. Of northern Europe Herodotus knows next to nothing; he tells us that he could obtain no reliable knowledge of the tin islands or the sources of (Baltic) amber.

Heuneburg. The Heuneburg, in Saulgau, Württemberg, is one of the most important of the early **Iron Age** hillforts of south-west Germany. Overlooking the western bank of the Upper Danube some twelve miles east of Sigmaringen, it is of great importance because not only do the finds from the fortified camp and the neighbouring barrows demonstrate the importation of luxury goods from the Mediterranean world (compare with the finds from the Mont Lassois hillfort and the nearby **Vix** burial in eastern France), but the fortifications of the Heuneburg (in period four) themselves furnish a unique example of the influence of east Mediterranean ideas on the art of fortification in the early Celtic world in late **Hallstatt** times (sixth century B.C.).

The Heuneburg is a promontory fort of trapezoidal shape sited on a pear-shaped plateau, rising about 180 feet above the valley of the Upper Danube which flows by its eastern slopes, the apex of the pear being a spur projecting to the north-east. This plateau is about 350 yards long from north-east to south-west and just over 250 yards wide at its broadest point on the south side. The hill dominates the Danube Valley and the marshy plain on the east bank, while to the west lies more undulating and hilly country, dotted with barrow groups, from some of which (e.g. the Hundersingen group) have come rich finds of gold and a number of bronze vessels. One group of four barrows some 400 yards west of the camp seems to have been the principal burial place for the rulers of the Heuneburg: one of these barrows was undisturbed and, when fully excavated, was found to have contained a wooden mortuary chamber. Beneath the mound were found remains of an open settlement clearly related to period four of the fortified citadel.

The excavators working since 1950 distinguished four constructional periods in the fortification of the Heuneburg, period four being the earliest and period one the latest. In addition there is evidence for a pre-fortification phase of settlement (period five) of the early Urnfield culture (final Late **Bronze Age**), represented by a hearth and a scatter of isolated potsherds over the entire site.

The earliest period (four) in the history of the fortified camp begins in the first phase of Late Hallstatt times. A deep defensive ditch seems to have been cut from the main entrance on the western side across the plateau to the middle of the eastern slope. This was later filled in during the rebuilding and modification of the defences. At the same time, another deep ditch was dug right round the foot of the northern, western and southern sides of the plateau, defensive palisading was set up, part of the hillslope was dug away to make it steeper, and the area of the plateau within the defences was levelled off.

Not very long after the erection of the period four defences (still in the first phase of the Late Hallstatt) a new series of defensive structures (period three) was put up, though not apparently because the earlier defence works had been violently destroyed.

A new defensive wall was built to encircle the plateau top. One part, running for about 350 feet south-east from the main entrance on the south side and defending the most vulnerable approach on the landward side, was constructed in the native tradition. This section of wall was a heavy timber-laced structure consisting of three parallel lines of baulks running lengthwise, tied at regular intervals by cross-baulks, this framework being filled with stones and earth. The completed wall was over fifteen feet thick, but evidence for its exact height and the character of its upper works is lacking.

The other part of the period three rampart (on the north-west side and on the southern and eastern sides of the plateau top) is a wall of a kind quite unique for this period in Late Hallstatt west central Europe. So different is it in architectural conception, choice of materials and constructional technique that it seems to be the work either of some architect from the contemporary Mediterranean world or of a native who was very well acquainted indeed with its ideas on fortifications. The closest of the many parallels is the citadel of Larisa on Mount Hermos, built around 500 B.C., and if indeed the inspiration for the period three defences was from Greece, the rulers of the Heuneburg at that time must have commanded considerable local resources and had far-flung commercial and cultural connections to have been able to have so uniquely and exotically fortified their citadel.

The architect of these defences laid a footing of roughly squared limestone blocks, which were quarried some three miles west of the Heuneburg. This footing mortared with clay was ten feet broad and varied from two to three feet in height, its purpose being to even out irregularities in the terrain and provide a solid and level foundation for the upper courses of the wall. These upper courses were of large flat square-shaped bricks made of clay tempered with gravelly sand and chopped straw. These were all more or less of standard size sixteen inches square two and a half to three inches thick, half-standard bricks also being known. These bricks were not baked but sun-dried and the evidence from working floors near the ramparts suggests that they were mass-produced by setting down square wooden frames and pouring in the clay which was then left to set in the sun. The frames were then withdrawn and the process repeated.

This primitive technique of making mud bricks is still in use today in parts of southern Europe, Asia and Africa.

A wall of this type ran along the south side of the Heuneburg, then through ninety degrees to cover the eastern flank of the plateau. A further section covered over 350 feet of the north-western side and it was rendered even more imposing by the provision of a row of rectangular hollow bastions (measuring roughly twenty by twenty-five feet) which jutted out from the line of the rampart at regular intervals of about thirty feet. Ground plans of at least eight of these have been recovered: each was accessible from inside the citadel area and was occupied since they have yielded remains of hearths, cooking pots and a large stone quern. A golden spoon was found near one of these bastions and this perhaps hints that the chieftain's hall was nearby.

The best preserved sections of the clay brick wall are still over six feet in height and may originally have been up to ten to twelve feet and possibly topped by crenellated battlements and wooden protective works. The outer surface of the wall was faced with clay and at intervals horizontal courses of wood or stone slabs were let in to strengthen the middle of the wall.

The impressive defences of the period three citadel perished in a great conflagration. The fortifications of period two were put up afterwards and have been dated by associated finds to the end of the Late Hallstatt period. These include a number of features whose relationship is not clear. On the north-west side, a foundation trench and a double row of post-holes suggest a double palisade of upright logs; and on the south-east corner upright posts seem to have supported a wooden wall of horizontally running planks. These fortifications also perished by fire and associated sherds of Attic black-figure ware suggest that this was some time after 525–475 B.C.

The defences of period one were put up round about the transition from final Hallstatt to early La Tène times. They are rubble filled timber-boxwork ramparts, with stone outer facings and wooden upper works. Part of this wall on the north-west side was rebuilt within the existing rampart, but this, too, perished by fire sometime in the fourth century B.C. The hillfort was then finally abandoned and so ends the story of the Heuneburg as a stronghold in prehistoric times.

Hierakonpolis. During the Egyptian prehistoric period the capital of Upper Egypt was Nekheb, now represented by the ruins of El Kab, and the royal residence was across the river from it at Hierakonpolis. Finds at Hierakonpolis include a painted tomb with colour-washed brick walls from the prehistoric period, first and second dynasty ivory figures of men, women and animals, portrayed with simplicity and honesty and manifesting careful observation, and a very fine first dynasty syenite vase.

Hieratic. The term hieratic describes the ancient Egyptian **cursive** script which, from about 700 B.C. down to the second century A.D. was confined to rituals about funerary books; earlier it had had a much wider employment. Hieratic was in fact the form which **hieroglyphs** took when written with a brush, generally on **papyrus** or potsherds (ostraca), and it bore fundamentally the same relation to them as handwriting does to monumental inscription today. The classical period of hieratic dates from about 2000 B.C., and a rich series of literary papyri demonstrates the great beauty of which the script was capable. **Demotic** usurped its place in popular use from 700 B.C. onwards.

Hieroglyphs. The word "hieroglyph", often indiscriminately used in modern times to denote any picture sign, derives from the Greek expression *hieroglyphika grammata* "sacred carved writing", which was used specifically of the ancient picture writing of the Egyptians. This was the system of writing originally devised by the Egyptians to record their language, but by Greek times it had been superseded for all except monumental purposes by its **cursive** derivatives **hieratic**, and then **demotic**, and was understood by the priests alone. The name "hieroglyphic" thus accurately described the function of the writing in Greek times. The native term – used on the **Rosetta Stone** (*see* plate 119, page 385) and the **Canopus Decree** – *sh n mdw ntr*, "writing of god's words", had a wider connotation; it referred to the Egyptian belief that hieroglyphic writing and the language itself had been given to men by the moongod Thoth, who was the god of wisdom and writing. This belief largely accounts for its continuing in use from late Predynastic times (known to the Egyptians as "the time of the gods") down to the Roman period.

Hieroglyphic writing consists of groups of pictures, many of which had already assumed their final (conventionalized) forms in the earliest inscriptions we possess, dating from just before 3000 B.C. The direction in which the writing is to be read is determined by the direction in which the creatures depicted face, the rule being that one must read from the head towards the tail. All other things being equal, the Egyptians preferred to write from right to left; but in sculptured or painted scenes, of which hieroglyphs often formed a part, the direction of the writing was dictated by considerations of space and symmetry.

The hieroglyphic system in its fully developed form appears complicated because of the multiplicity of signs and their varied functions. In fact its principles are basically simple, and are rooted in the original pictorial character of the writing. The simplest way of writing a word is to draw the object it describes and certain words throughout Egyptian history were regularly written with a single picture sign (**pictograms**). But it is impossible to draw every word, particularly those of cognate meaning, and therefore signs came to have extended pictorial use (**ideograms**) and so finally to have a phonetic value (**phonograms**).

The Egyptians could thus express a word pictorially or phonetically; and in the majority of cases they chose to use both methods at the same time. They did this in order to make their meaning quite clear, and because writing to them was more than the means by which one conveys an idea – it was an artistic experience. As time went on they tended to use the alphabetic signs more and more, because of their convenience; and when it became necessary to transliterate foreign words and names, alphabetic signs alone were used and semi-consonants like *z*, *w* and *y* pressed into service to give some notion of the pronunciation of the vowels. It is not true, therefore, to say that the Egyptians never developed an alphabetic system. They did, but preferred to retain the ancient dual character of their writing; and this character was transmitted to the cursive scripts derived from the hieroglyphs for use on **papyrus.** *See* plate 57, page 197.

Hindu Art and Architecture. The earliest substantial remains of Indian architecture, after the **Indus Valley** sites, are of Buddhist origin, but there is no reason to think that they did not spring from a common sense of the appropriate form for religious architecture. In the fourth century A.D. through the emergence of free-standing architecture, in contrast to the rock-cut sanctuaries of earlier periods, Hinduism began to develop distinctive styles suited to the requirement of its rituals. The essential element was the provision of the house for the god, which in its simplest form consisted of a sancturary (*garba-griha*) preceded by a porch (*mandapa*). The next stage was the addition of a tower above the sanctuary, the *shikhara*, possibly an attempt to symbolize Meru, the world's axial mountain. This idea was probably also present in the type of temple in which the sanctuary was set in the middle of one or more enclosures, the entrance or entrances being set at the cardinal points to reinforce the cosmic theme. The enclosure space was soon filled with ancillary buildings, subsidiary temples for the god's *vahana* or sacred vehicle (the bull of Shiva, the *garuda* of Vishnu, etc.), for the goddess, for temple cars and so on, as well as housing for priests, texts and the temple treasures. Later developments are largely to be seen as complex developments from these simple features.

Hittites. This Indo-European people appeared in Asia Minor, probably from beyond the Black Sea, around the beginning of the second millennium B.C. and became, towards the end of the same millennium, a strong imperial power in the Middle East. They first occupied a considerable area of central Anatolia round the bend of the Halys River, making Hattusas (**Boghazköy**) their capital. About 1640 B.C. Labarnas extended the Hittite dominions within Anatolia and Hattusil I carried this process further and initiated a drive for the control of northern Syria and domination of the trade routes to **Assyria** and **Babylon**; this was to some extent achieved by his successor Mursilis I who captured Aleppo and made a spectacular raid down the Euphrates, capturing Babylon but not making any permanent occupation of it. Following a period of consolidation within Asia Minor, Shubbiluliuma achieved (about 1380 B.C.) a formidable extension of Hittite power, establishing control over many north Syrian cities, exerting a controlling interest in the dynastic affairs of the **Mitanni**, placing Hittite nominees as rulers in the city states of the Orontes Valley and seeking to detach cities of Phoenicia and southern Lebanon from their allegiance to Egypt. By 1350 B.C. Hittite power was at its height but the area of the empire was too wide and control over north Syria weakened. The Hittites came into conflict with Egypt over north Syria though finally friendly relations were established between the two powers. The downfall of the Hittite empire was sudden; records cease about 1230 B.C. and there is evidence of widespread destruction, possibly by one of the **Sea Peoples.** Elements of Hittite culture survived, however, and the Hittites entered their "Syro-Hittite" phase when they spread to Syrian cities where they mingled with the populations of other peoples.

The decipherment of the Hittite language was aided by the discovery at Boghazköy of several thousand clay tablets forming part of the royal archives. It was mainly Indo-European in structure and vocabulary. Two tongues appear to have been spoken: Nesite was the language of the ruling house, but Luvite, another language of the same family, was also widely used.

The Boghazköy texts are also a valuable guide to Hittite administration, religion and economy. In the administration the king was not only head of the state but also chief priest, leader in battle and supreme judge. The queen mother acted as regent during his absence. There was an advisory council of nobles and, in most provinces, governors, among whose duties were the provision of a contingent for the national army and maintenance of a permanent garrison. Surviving portions of law-codes indicate that the people were divided into freemen and slaves. Penalties were adjusted according to the offender's. Almost all subjects were compelled by law to work on public schemes.

Comparatively little is known of the Hittite religion though it is certain that the Hittite pantheon included gods of Syria and of the **Hurrians** and probably also contained local deities of Asia Minor. It has been shown that gods on the reliefs at Yazilikaya were largely Hurrian. Although the Hittites had temples, some religious ceremonies were held in the open air, often by streams.

The wealth of the Hittites came from their metals: they mined copper, lead and silver and developed an advanced technique of metallurgy. Possibly iron was first worked by them. Their life was based on agriculture and sheep-farming. Agriculture was protected by regulations in the civil code in which certain prices and the wages of certain artisans were also regulated.

Their cities were strongly built, with sturdy fortifying walls. Characteristics of Hittite building were the decoration of walls with slabs of carved stone reliefs and gateways with flanking stone **colossi**.

Hmawza is the site of a city near Prome in Burma, associated with the Pyu (Chinese P'iao), which has yielded a large number of Buddhist remains from the sixth century A.D. onwards and where considerable architectural remains are still to be seen within the walls of oval outline. Their kingdom seems to have extended over most of Upper Burma, and they appear to represent the first Tibeto-Burmese speakers in that country to have had anything more sophisticated than a tribal organization. The architecture shows three basic types: a **stupa** and two temple forms. The stupas (e.g. the Bawbawgyi) are of conical type resting on a five-fold terrace platform, and presumably crowned by an umbrella finial, since this last is shown on reliefs of stupas from the site. The temples are of a square ground plan. The first type (e.g. Lemyethna) has a substantial masonry central core in the middle of the structure, joined to the outer walls by a vaulted corridor. The images are placed against the central core and there are openings in the sides. The second type has an open ground plan with a door in one face, and windows in the other three sides (e.g. Zegu). A feature of these buildings is the presence of the true arch. It is from the nucleus of Pyu architecture, either directly or through the Mons, that **Pagan** (*see* plate 105, page 333) draws most of its architectural conventions. Although the art obviously derives from India, it shows a marked local development. Further excavation at the site may reveal an earlier phase, or this may remain to be found elsewhere, perhaps nearer the delta region.

Hoa-binh is the type-site for a **Mesolithic** culture of south-east Asia, in Tonkin, north Viet-Nam. The tools include oval, unifacial pebble tools which in Sumatra form ninety per cent of the finds (the so-called Sumatraliths), and semi-circular or ellipsoid stone adzes with straight-cut butts. These are sometimes found in association with polished **stone tools** of the **Bac-son** culture, a fact which suggests that the two were contemporary for at least part of the time. The Hoa-binh sites, however, contain neither pottery nor bone tools. The skeletal material is of a generally Melanesian type. Hoa-binh material has been found in Indo-China, Thailand, Malaya and Sumatra, where it appears to undergo a local development. So far as is known it does not occur elsewhere in Indonesia.

Holocene Epoch, *see* Quaternary Period.

Homer is the name given to the great epic poet of early Greece. According to the prevalent ancient tradition he was born at Smyrna and, having lost his sight, taught in Chios. But there was no general agreement among the ancients about the facts of his life; and his date was variously reckoned between the twelfth and ninth centuries B.C. (or even later).

Besides some lesser poems, the two great epics (*The Iliad* and *The Odyssey*) were almost universally attributed to him. *The Iliad* (in 15,693 hexameter lines) has as its tragic theme the Wrath of Achilles, and is limited in time to a few days of the tenth year of the siege of **Troy** by the **Achaeans**; but in fact it presents so diverse a range of episodes, personalities and digressions that a complete scene of wartime activity is unfolded. *The Odyssey* tells (in 11,670 lines) the story of the wanderings and home-coming of Odysseus (Ulysses) and is in effect the poem of the Complete Man who can rise superior to any situation or adversity.

Both poems are distinguished by nobility of diction, rapid and unerring command of narrative, and humanity. *The Odyssey* is the better constructed and more moral of the two; *The Iliad* is the more heroic in tone and excels in sustained grandeur. Most ancient and modern critics are agreed that *The Odyssey* (reputedly a creation of the poet's old age) is the later work of the two.

The existing text of Homer goes back to the scholars of Alexandria (third to second centuries B.C.). The first written edition was most probably made for the Athenian tyrant Pisistratus in the sixth century B.C. Before that time the poems seem to have been preserved orally by the descendants of Homer (Homeridae) in Chios, and may have been in a somewhat fluid state. Alphabetic writing was known in Greece before 700 B.C., and some scholars maintain that the poems were written down at the time of their composition; but the lack of skill in writing and of suitable writing materials at that early date would have made the inscribing of almost a million letters an impossible task without years of labour and the support of a princely bounty.

Homer's language was not that of common speech, but an artificial one. His dialect shows that he was an **Ionian**, the descendant of emigrants from the shattered kingdoms of **Mycenaean** (Late **Bronze Age**) Greece to the eastern Aegean; but it is not consistent, and contained much that was already centuries old. The stories are also largely traditional. The epic language evidently had a long history of adaptation to the special needs of sustained recital; and the lays must have gone through a process of fermentation for several centuries before reaching the stage at which they became crystallized in *The Iliad* and *The Odyssey* (and afterwards in supporting poems, now almost entirely lost, which were composed in imitation of Homer to complete the epic cycle).

Modern Homeric scholarship, which was for some generations concerned with dissecting *The Iliad* and *The Odyssey* into a series of disconnected lays, is now aligned to the belief that there was in fact a great poet called Homer, in whom the long development culminated; but some parts of both poems are commonly regarded as later additions, and many scholars still believe that the poems are works of two different poets.

The earliest date now assigned to Homer is the ninth century B.C., and the latest the seventh century. A date about the second half of the eighth century fits the archaeological evidence best.

The stories of Troy and the Achaean heroes must in the main hark back to **Mycenaean** times. The homes of Homer's Achaean chieftains have (thanks to the labours of **Schliemann** and others) been shown to coincide in geographical position with the Mycenaean citadels of Greece. Some of the objects described by Homer – the boar's-tusk helmet, for instance, or the inlay-work of Achilles' shield – seem certainly Mycenaean. Anachronisms are avoided; the post-Mycenaean settlements of the east Aegean are ignored, the weapons of the heroes are not of iron but of bronze, and their diet is unnaturally heroic; and the poet is at pains to contrast his own degenerate age with that of the heroes.

On the other hand, serious error results from uncritical acceptance of the Homeric background as being wholly Mycenaean. Much of Homer's geography seems to be the new knowledge of his own times. His dead are not (as in Mycenaean times) interred, but cremated. His cities, with their forums, temples and circuit-walls, seem to be more contemporary than Mycenaean; and the royal residences which he describes cannot be satisfactorily explained in terms of the excavated Mycenaean palaces.

In fact old and new elements are inextricably mixed in the poems, though *The Odyssey*, being less heroic, seems to reflect the poet's own times the more readily of the two, and Odysseus himself, despite his heroic environment, can perhaps be regarded as a contemporary ideal of manhood. Similarly, it is a serious mistake to regard the poet as an accurate historian. The tales of the heroes are poised between history and legend. Undoubtedly most of the principal heroes once lived, and undoubtedly Troy was besieged and fell. But different generations have been fused into one; no particular incident in *The Iliad* can be regarded as historical, and *The Odyssey* is largely compounded of folk-tale and pure fiction.

It is perhaps not unfair to sum up as follows: the epic machinery and the heroic saga derive from the Late Bronze Age; but Homer himself was essentially the child of his own age; he drew freely on his own experience of daily life and human nature, and in his knowledge of the world and his outlook on society and religion he was inspired by the Ionic Renaissance which gave birth to the humane civilization of classical Greece. In the following centuries Homer came to be recognized as the canon of Greek religious belief and of behaviour, and was the fountain head of Greek education.

Hominid. A general term for members of the biological family which includes Man and man-like fossils such as **Australopithecus**. The dividing line between hominids and **pongids** cannot be drawn by examination of the skeleton, or even of the brain-case for there seems to be no link between the size of the brain and intelligence. Prehistorians make the distinction that of "tool-making"; not "tool-using", for apes will use a tool for an immediate purpose. By "tool-making" is meant making a tool for use, not at the present moment, but to serve some future need.

The system of naming hominids is not very satisfactory at the present time; often a new genus and species is created for each find; what many people think is needed is a system of classifying hominids which will illustrate relationships between them according to their age, physical likeness, stage of development, and so on.

Homo sapiens, *see* Fossil Man *and* Cro-magnon.

Horizon. The limit of knowledge in a particular direction. Thus, the historical horizon in the Middle East is round about 3000 B.C., for it was at this time that the invention of writing made a system of dating by historical records possible; beyond that lies prehistory.

Horoztepe, *see* Alaca Höyük.

Hoxne. The **Quaternary** deposits at Hoxne, Suffolk, have been known since John **Frere** found **Palaeolithic** tools there in 1790. They have been exposed through the exploitation of the clay-mud to make agricultural pipe by the Hoxne brick works.

East Anglia and the lower Thames are regions which are studied in the attempt to correlate the Pleistocene deposits of the British Isles with those of the Continent. During the last two interglacial periods there were certain cool times which, while leaving geological traces, were not cold enough to produce an advance of ice. These "minor cold phases" are useful for correlation, and Hoxne is one of the few sites where traces of them are found.

Through borings and the study of exposed sections, it has been established that the significant deposits at Hoxne date to the Mindel-Riss (or penultimate) interglacial, about 300,000 years ago. A lake of over twenty acres formed in a hollow in boulder clay left by ice which corresponded to the Mindel **glaciation**. Through **pollen analysis,** it is known that the open ground round the lake was covered with sea-buckthorn, grass and sedges. The climate became warmer, and **Acheulian** people lived by the lake among oak forest, leaving many tools in the lake. During this time, the forest was burnt, and it would be interesting to know whether or not the fire was begun by human agency as hunting technique.

A number of other deposits covered the Acheulian settlement; some containing Acheulian flints that had been caught up from the lower levels. These gave rise to an earlier belief that there was a series of cultures represented at Hoxne, but in fact the tools cannot be separated stratigraphically. The importance of Hoxne is that an important series of Palaeolithic tools and lake deposits have been found in direct association with traces of an older glaciation.

Hsiang-t'an Shan. This, the only offering shrine associated with tombs which has survived from the Han period in its original condition, is situated in Shantung Province, China. It is fourteen feet long, seven feet deep and six and a half feet high, and consists of eight slabs of stone. The interior faces are smoothed and covered with intaglio cut reliefs with bevelled edges. The technique is that of the jade-cutter, a fact which is important for the history of relief carving. The evidence for ivory carvers as craftsmen for early **Buddhist** stone shrines in India is comparable.

An early visitor has cut the date A.D. 129 on one of the stones.

Hsing-lung Hsien. The importance of this site in Jehol Province, China, lies in the fact that it has yielded cast-iron moulds for the manufacture of bronze axes. The earliest cast-iron tools are from Ku-wei Ts'un, Honan, and date from between the fourth and the third centuries B.C., while the moulds are probably late fifth century B.C. The use of cast-iron in China, which has long been suspected from textual sources to antedate the Christian era, is thus confirmed, and it can now be asserted that cast iron was in use here for at least 1500 years before it played any significant role at all in western technology. *See* plate 58, page 198.

Huaca Prieta, *see* Peruvians.

Huaxtecs, *see* Mexico.

Hurrians. This people emerges historically early in the second millennium B.C., coming westwards from the region corresponding to modern Kurdistan and establishing itself on the Upper Tigris, while an offshoot, the Kingdom of Mitanni, was formed on the northern confines of Mesopotamia. The Hurrians overlap with the period of the **Hittite** Kingdom and figure in Hittite records as having attacked it during the reign of Hantilis I. As Hittite power increased, however, the Hurrians became Hittite vassals. There is evidence for the influence of Hurrian art and culture on those of the Hittites both during the period of the Hittite Empire and subsequently when the Hittites were expelled into the Upper Euphrates Valley and north Syria where they founded city states, many of them with Hurrian subjects. One of the most remarkable instances of this influence is the reliefs at the Hittite sanctuary at Yazilikaya, which represent some kind of religious ritual. Recent research indicates that it is largely the Hurrian pantheon which is represented here and that the ritual illustrated belongs to the Hurrian religion.

Hutton, James (1726–97), was the first to develop, in 1785, the theory that wind, rain and frost can, by a process of weathering the rocks and washing away the debris, produce all the known changes in the surface of the earth. It was not accepted at the time he stated it because Archbishop **Usher's** views held the field, but it was later developed and firmly established by Charles **Lyell.**

Hyksos. These were a group of Asiatic herdsmen who in 1800 B.C. swept over Syria and Palestine and imposed a foreign dynasty on Egypt. It may be that their moving force was a **Canaanite** or **Amorite** element. Some of their kings had Canaanite names and the deities they introduced into Egypt were largely Canaanite. They introduced superior weapons, metallurgy and, it was formerly believed, the use of the horse and the horse-drawn chariot. However, the discovery in 1959 of the skeleton of a horse at Buhen in Nubia throws doubt on this supposition, since the bones were found in an archaeological context which clearly antedates the Hyksos period. **Scarabs** with delicate spiral designs and a ware called Tell-Yahudiyeh, characteristic of the Hyksos, were widely traded, being found on many sites between Syria and the Nile. In 1580 B.C. Egyptian Ahmosis I crushed the Hyksos dynasty.

Hypaethral. Open to the sky.

I

Ice Age, *see* Quarternary Period *and* Glacial.

Ideograms. The earliest form of writing was by means of **pictograms** in which each picture represented an actual object. The next step was for the picture to represent an idea – an ideogram ("idea-writing") or a word; thus the circle which represented the sun was extended to mean "day" and then "hot". The Egyptian **hieroglyphs** were at first purely pictographic, later both pictographic and ideographic; for instance the stylized picture of a man's legs came to mean both legs and also "walking" or "running". Most systems progressed beyond this to the invention and use of **phonograms.** The use of ideograms means that the number of signs tends to increase continually; to read Chinese, which has remained an ideographic writing, entails learning some thousands of characters.

Incas. Like the **Aztecs** of Mexico, the Incas came upon the historical stage late, rose swiftly to power, established one of the world's greatest empires, and quickly succumbed to a band of Spanish adventurers. It was a true empire of the ancient Old World pattern, the only one of this type in pre-Columbian America.

Unlike Old World empires, however, ancient Peru left no contemporary historical records, for the Peruvians had no system of writing. Our only data are the traditions that were written down by Spanish chroniclers after the Conquest.

The first eight traditional emperors, Manco Capac, Sinchi Roca, Lloque Yupanqui, Mayta Capac, Capac Yupanqui, Inca Roca, Yahuar Huacac and Viracocha Inca, are legendary. The "guess date" for the first is about A.D. 1200. Two centuries later the Incas were, according to the best modern opinion, still merely one of many small tribes, with their centre at Cuzco and their conquests were in that immediate vicinity.

With the accession of Pachacuti Inca Yupanqui (about A.D. 1438) the Inca burst of expansion began. He and his son Topa Inca Yupanqui were the Philip and Alexander of America. By the time of the death of the latter in 1493 the Inca armies had subjugated all of the Andean and coastal peoples from Quito in Ecuador to south of Santiago in Chile. Topa Inca's son, Huayna Capac (1493–1525), extended the Inca Empire a little in Ecuador to the borders of present Colombia. At this time it stretched over 2,500 miles north to south, and embraced some 380,000 square miles, about equal in extent to France, Belgium, Holland, Luxembourg, Switzerland, and Italy combined.

Huayna Capac's sons Huascar and Atahuallpa battled for the succession. Defeated Huascar was killed on Atahuallpa's orders, and Atahuallpa was executed by Pizarro. Its master gone, the Inca Empire fell into the hands of the Spanish "army" of 180 men like a ripe plum.

The Inca state was an extraordinary blend of socialism, monarchy, and theocracy. The land and most of its products belonged to the state which partitioned them out to the people. Arable land was divided into three classes, for the state i.e. the the emperor, the church and the people. Each family was apportioned land according to its size and needs, but the people cultivated all lands, first those of the gods and the emperor, and then their own, communally. The harvests from the public lands were gathered into storehouses for the support of the priesthood, the nobility, the administrative officers, the army and a few state-supported persons, including the aged or infirm without family connections. The remainder was kept in storehouses as insurance against crop failure or similar great emergency. The state thus guaranteed its people against hunger and want, but kept them tied to the land and strictly regimented. Each man was also required to give a certain amount of service each year, in lieu of taxes, to public work such as employment on roads or bridges, in the mines, the army, or as couriers or servants; this was termed *mit'a*. Some craftsmen were excepted and statesupported; their work belonged to the emperor. The unit of population was the *puric*, the able-bodied man of middle age and head of a household.

At regular periods officials selected from among the people the most attractive boys and girls. The girls, "chosen women", were trained in weaving and other feminine accomplishments. Some were attached to temples and served the priests, though vowed to chastity; others became concubines of the emperor and the higher nobility. The young men, known as *yanacona*, served as servants at the court, temple attendants, and in other similar offices.

At the apex of the pyramid was the divine emperor, descendant of the sun, whose person was sacred. Beneath him were the royalty and nobility, governors known as *curaca*, and minor officials over groups of men in decimal numeration down to the foreman over ten *purics*. All of these had definite and recognized duties, and were severely punished if they imposed on the men under their charge. The emperor enjoyed the best of everything, including a very large seraglio; he ordinarily married his sister, and the office was hereditary. Censuses were regularly taken, the results recorded on knotted cords known as *quipu*, and forwarded to Cuzco for filing; this was the only system of record known.

One of the reasons for the relative peace in the Inca Empire was the practice of *mitima*, by which intransigent peoples were removed to other regions and their places filled by peaceful colonists who had become accustomed to Inca rule and customs. Also part of the population of overcrowded regions was often transferred to thinly occupied ones.

The Incas were pure **American Indians,** ancestors of the modern Quechua. Their language is not related to any Old World one. Cranial deformation was a usual practice. There was no formal education except for boys of the nobility. Polygamy was a privilege of the nobility, but only the first wife held her husband's rank; the others were little, if anything, more than concubines.

Excellent roads traversed the empire, over which armies marched and relays of couriers carried messages or packages with great speed; wheeled vehicles were unknown. The masonry, without mortar, was marvellous, and immense blocks were set in place; some of those in the great fortress of Sacsahuaman at Cuzco are estimated to weigh over a hundred tons.

Ancestor worship was of great importance, and the bodies of the dead were dried, carefully preserved, and taken out frequently for attention and worship. Priests were numerous, and constantly busy with calendrical ceremonies, divination, consultation of oracles, sacrifices, curing, etc.; human sacrifice was rare. The great deity was the sun, but the creator, Viracocha, Pachacamac, and a host of minor deities were worshipped. Every large centre had its sun temple, with its priests and "virgins of the sun". There were hundreds of sacred places known as *huacas*. Probably certain priests were primarily physicians and surgeons.

Remarkable surgical work was done, including **trepanning**, which was rather common. Illness was believed to be due to sin, for which confession and penance were the cure. *See* plate 64, page 204.

India. The Indian sub-continent comprises the modern political territories of India, Pakistan, Ceylon and Nepal. It is bounded on the north, north-east and north-west by the Himalayas, Hindu Kush, and other great mountain ranges. Geologically these are all of recent origin, sometimes still in process of formation. Within the mountain barrier the sub-continent falls into two major regions: the Deccan plateau which, in contrast to the Himalayas, consists of some of the most ancient rocks found anywhere on the earth's surface; and the great alluvial plains of the Indus and Ganges rivers. Rather more than half the Indian-sub-continent lies actually within the tropics, but owing to the mountain barrier which shields the low lying plains of northern India, summer temperatures are high throughout. Rainfall and humidity vary greatly from region to region but everywhere are seasonal, depending mainly upon the south-west rain-bearing winds (the monsoon) of the summer months. In the north and west rainfall is low and the seasonal variation in temperature is very great; eastward the rainfall increases steadily. In peninsular India the climate is generally more equable, with less marked contrasts between winter and summer or day and night, but the rainfall varies from over eighty inches to below twenty inches a year. The natural vegetation has been destroyed completely by cultivation over vast areas, but enough remains to show that it varies from tropical rain forest in the extreme north-east and along the western coastal strip, through the open woodland and dry savannah of the Deccan and central India, to semi-desert or desert in parts of Rajputana or Sindh. The greatest centres of population are today the areas of relatively high rainfall and deep alluvial soil, the Ganges basin, the Tamil plain, and Kerala. This has not always been so, for in prehistoric times these areas were sometimes thinly populated while the Indus basin carried a relatively high population (*see* **Indus Valley Civilization**).

The main Indian languages may be divided into two groups: those of the north, which belong to the **Aryan** or Indo-Iranian branch of the Indo-European family; and those of the south, constituting the Dravidian language family, which are not closely related to any other group. The oldest Indo-Iranian language recorded is that of the **Rigveda** (about 1500–1000 B.C.). From it were derived the classical Sanskrit and also the Middle Indian dialects out of which the modern Indian languages have arisen. The literature of the Dravidian language Tamil goes back about 2,000 years.

India's position as a peninsula has meant that she has, throughout her history, received fresh waves of settlers from the north-west who have become absorbed in the population. As one of the great civilizations of the world she has, for more than two millennia, been renowned for her religious and metaphysical thought. The simple hymns of the *Rigveda* are followed by the voluminous exegetic literature minutely describing Brahmanical rituals and sacrifices. Meanwhile the Upanishads contain mystical and esoteric teachings. The seventh and sixth centuries B.C. produced many great thinkers and teachers, among them the founders of Buddhism and Jainism. Buddhism soon spread throughout India leaving a host of monuments to testify to its glory. It also found its way to China, south-east Asia, and Tibet. The growth of Hindu sectarianism in the early centuries A.D., particularly of Vaishnavism and Saivism, the worship of Vishnu and Siva respectively, was probably a reaction (by the Brahmins) against the popularity of Buddhism.

An objective archaeological interest in India's

past is almost as old as European colonial interests in the country. Between 1500 and 1800 numerous travellers, Portuguese, English, Danish and French, described monuments they had visited. The foundation of the Asiatic Society of Bengal in 1784 under the influence of Sir William Jones opened a new period of interest and research. During the opening decades of the nineteenth century many British officers contributed: the remarkable Colonel Colin MacKenzie, who excavated at **Amaravati**; James Prinsep who first read the inscriptions of **Asoka Maurya** (*see* **Mauryan Empire**), and founded Indian numismatics; James Fergusson the founder of Indian architectural studies; and many others. In 1863 Sir Alexander **Cunningham** became first director of the Archaeological Survey of India. After 1902 it was reorganized and for the next thirty years was directed by Sir John **Marshall.** The last British Director-General, Sir Mortimer Wheeler made important changes during his short term of office, and, since Independence, the Survey, which has expanded steadily from 1900, has made notable advances in all branches of archaeology. Simultaneously many Indian universities have become flourishing centres of teaching and research.

India, Prehistoric. In the Indian sub-continent, as in Europe and Africa, three major divisions of the **Palaeolithic** or Old Stone Age are now recognized. These have been termed Early, Middle and Late Stone Age, and are discernible both by **typology** and **stratigraphy.**

Tools belonging to the Early Stone Age have been found at a number of sites, notably in Madras, Gujerat, central India and the Siwaliks. In general these belong to the great **hand-axe** tradition of stone working which extends with such remarkable uniformity throughout Europe, Africa and parts of western and southern Asia. Many of the pear-shaped hand-axes are indistinguishable from European and African examples. Their companion tool, the cleaver, is also found in proportions comparable to the Early Stone Age of Africa. Choppers and chopping-tools not dissimilar from those of south-east Asia have also been found in north-west India, but their relationship to the hand-axe industry is not clear.

Middle Stone Age tools have also been found at a number of sites, particularly in southern, western and central India. Little research has as yet been done on this period, but it seems clear that the tools bear a general relationship to those of the African Middle Stone Age and the European **Mousterian.** They consist chiefly of scrapers and occasionally of points, made upon **flakes** with faceted striking platforms which have been struck from carefully prepared cores. The cores are also found sometimes utilized as chopping tools.

The Indian Late Stone Age is closely comparable to that of Africa, and quite distinct from both the Upper Palaeolithic and **Mesolithic** of Europe. In common with all these cultures, however, it is marked by the appearance of the important technique of manufacturing parallel-sided blades and geometric forms (segments, crescents, triangles and trapeziums).

We also know that the people who made the Late Stone Age tools inhabited caves and rock shelters in many parts of India. These they decorated with pictures of animals and men, and with hunting scenes in a manner comparable to, and yet distinct from, that of the cave artists of Europe, Africa, and Australia.

The **Neolithic** or New Stone Age is represented in India by finds of ground stone axes from many parts of the continent, in a range of forms which suggests ultimate connections with the Middle East. In some areas, notably the **Deccan,** Neolithic settlement sites have been found and excavated. Here a characteristic range of hand-made pottery, and stone blades not unlike those of the Late Stone Age, have been found together with ground stone axes. In southern India the Neolithic is succeeded directly by the prehistoric **Iron Age** (*see under* **Arikamedu**).

In Maharashtra and Gujerat considerable **Chalcolithic** settlement sites have been excavated which yield painted pottery, stone blades and a small number of copper tools. The relationship of both these and the Neolithic sites to each other and to the **Indus Valley civilization** has yet to be established. West of the Indus in Baluchistan another series of sites has been found whose affinities are with southern **Iran.** These produce their own distinct varieties of pottery and terracotta figurines.

Indonesian. The term Indonesian refers essentially to speakers of Indonesian languages who are mainly concentrated in the Republic of Indonesia. They are also still represented on the mainland of Asia, in Malaya and in the Annamite Chain by the **Chams,** as well as in the mountainous region on

China's southern frontier, and also in the island of Madagascar which seems to have been peopled by Indonesian speakers in the early centuries of the Christian era. The Indonesian group seems, culturally, to derive from a fusion between a group in the process of change from hunting and collecting to simple forms of slash-and-burn agriculture and a more sophisticated culture, associated with Thai language groups, which had developed rice culture in south China. This hybrid group, which played a major part in the make-up of the people of **Yueh**, from whom the Viet-Namese derive, moved southwards along the coast of China and Indo-china, offshoots apparently making their way to Japan, and into the Indonesian islands, some by a western route across Thailand and the Malay Peninsula, others through the Philippines, and others from the coasts of southern Indo-China. It is probable that Neolithic axes of rectangular section are to be associated with the main spread of the Indonesians.

Indus Valley Civilization. Few archaeological events have been so dramatic as the discovery of the Indus civilization in India. Even in the instances of the most spectacular finds previously recorded, the excavators were as a rule searching for something to which they already possessed a clue. With the appearance of the **Harappa** (*see* plate 56, page 196) culture a whole quite unguessed civilization came into existence practically overnight. As a result of years of search it is now known that these people whom, after the name of one of their main sites, we call the Harappans, spread their dominion over the whole of Sind and much of the Punjab and south into Gujerat, an extent of a thousand miles, the colonization of which was a notable achievement. It had been known since the days of Sir Alexander **Cunningham** that strange seals with an unknown script had appeared on the mounds at Harappa in the Montgomery District, but not until these were excavated by D.R. Sahni in 1921 and similar finds made at **Mohenjo-Daro** (*see* plate 97, page 325) in the Larkana district of Sind by R.D. Banerji in 1922, was it evident that here were the remains of a people who antedated any known Indian civilization by hundreds of years.

In spite of the fact that there have been extensive excavations at the principal sites of Harappa and Mohenjo-Daro and test diggings at many other places, the origins of this culture are still unknown. As Sir Mortimer Wheeler has said, "It is legitimate to affirm that the *idea* of civilization came to the land of the Indus from the land of the Twin Rivers [Mesopotamia], indeed in spite of many differences in detail it is difficult to suggest any reasonable alternative". That the founding fathers of Mohenjo-Daro brought the knowledge of the elements of civilization by sea seems on the present evidence to fit the facts. A small settlement has recently been discovered at Kot Diji in Khairpur State in Sind, where a Harappan occupation is preceded by a small town which was burnt down. It is likely that this was a community that developed parallel to the Harappa culture and preyed possibly on the communications between Mohenjo-Daro and Harappa, and so had to be eliminated. The various elements which went to make up the total of the Indus civilization in its prime did not exist from the very beginning, but can be shown to have developed during the first 300 years of its existence in what may be called the Formative period.

The outstanding achievements of the Harappans lay in building and town planning. From the earliest times these people seem to have used burnt brick on a scale quite unknown elsewhere among their contemporaries. It has been provisionally accepted that the known life of this civilization is from about 2500 to 1500 B.C. and that its second or Great period coincided roughly with the Sargonid period in Iraq and covers about 2350–2100 B.C. All Harappan cities and towns show signs of competent administration, ensuring that building followed a definite plan and that adequate sanitation was maintained by a system of drainage far in advance of anything found elsewhere at that time.

Round about 2300 B.C. a citadel was built at Mohenjo-Daro which housed a vast granary and possibly religious establishments and the houses and administrative buildings of the ruling class. Shortly after this a similar citadel was raised at Harappa on a site previously occupied by peasant farmers; it was probably the earliest Harappan structure around which a new city was formed. In spite of these fortifications the Harappans do not seem to have been a particularly warlike people, though doubtless willing to fight to preserve their own interests. Spears, bows and arrows, axes, slings and daggers formed their equipment but, judged by contemporary western Asiatic standards, none of their weapons was at any time particularly efficient.

The economy upon which the Indus civilization was based was agricultural. To judge by the large granaries at Harappa and Mohenjo-Daro and the coolie-lines found near that of the former, grain crops and probably cotton formed the bulk of the exportable surplus. The presence of seals inscribed with the Harappan script at sites in ancient Sumer is evidence of commercial contacts between those cities and the Indus valley, and the presence of a Harappan trading centre at Sutkagen Dor on the Makran coast of the Persian Gulf is further evidence in favour of such trade. Transport both by sea and land must have been well organized, and the presence of cart models in terracotta and bronze at Harappan sites and of actual cart tracks at Harappa shows that the cart they used was identical in form and wheel-gauge with that found in Sind today. A boat depicted on a seal, probably a river craft, gives some indication that the art of building a good practicable small ship was known to them.

Of all the objects recovered from their houses the **seals** are by far the most unmistakably Harappan. Usually about an inch to an inch and a quarter square, they were sawn out of a block of steatite, smoothed, engraved with a picture and a line of script, and coated with an alkali which was baked on. Various animals including a type of prehistoric ox called the urus, elephant, buffalo, rhinoceros and tiger are shown on these seals and, occasionally, what may be regarded as a cult scene. Among hundreds of seals there are only two or three cases of duplicate inscriptions, so this item is probably personal in some way to its owner; the animals may be amuletic. Status as **amulets** is claimed for a class of small engraved copper tablets also bearing an inscription and an animal, but in this instance these are linked; for example, all hares have the same inscription, and it is probable that these were tokens used by merchants indicating a payment obligation.

As an indication of the stage of civilization reached by the Harappans one can instance their script, so far not deciphered, and the fact that they employed standard weights and measures. Their weights, polished cubes of chert, are on a unique system. The ratio of the low weights is by doubling – 1, 2, 4 up to 64, which is two-fifths of the next unit which is 160, upwards from which progression is in decimal multiples of 16, i.e. 320, 640, the highest weight being 128,000 or eight times 16,000, the unit being 0.8570 grammes. Two scales of measurement were found, and these, as shown by a series of measurements observed by Wheeler at Harappa and Mohenjo-Daro, are related to a system with a foot ranging from 13 to 13.2 inches and a cubit from 20.3 to 20.8 inches. Both seals and weights are rare in the lowest levels, even allowing for the smaller area explored, and it is doubtful whether the former were introduced before 2550 B.C. and the latter nearly a century later. The script, which bears no resemblance to any other, seems to have been an arbitrary product, the result of a knowledge of writing rather than an evolved one.

In the case of most ancient civilizations, religious or funerary monuments are by far the most imposing and durable. The Harappan cities, however, reveal little that can be recognized as unequivocally religious in its nature and purpose; in fact, without the help of the engravings on the seals, we would have very little from which to draw even a tentative picture of the Harappan religion. It is probable that the majority of the terracotta figurines found in considerable numbers have some religious significance. The male horned figures are without doubt gods and the female ones goddesses; the naked male figures and the women supporting a voluted object on their heads are almost certainly votaries; the many oxen and buffaloes are for the most part probably votive, though many must be toys along with the model ox-carts. Other animals may be **totemic** luck-bringers or toys. The men shown in the stone sculptures are as likely to be rulers as gods.

The seals reveal that the principal object of worship was a horned god either seated in a posture of yoga or framed by the branches of the clearly sacred pipal tree. This is the horned god of the figurines who appears also as a horned archer on the copper tablets. On the seals also are scenes of bull and buffalo sacrifice, bull-baiting and leaping; and as the last is connected with a shrine enclosing a sacred tree and incorporating a sacred pillar, parallels have naturally been drawn with the religion of **Minoan** Crete.

The Harappans do not appear to have been an artistic people; ordered administration and commercial enterprise seem to have been their outstanding characteristics. Stone sculptures are few and, where Harappan attribution is certain, of indifferent quality. It is for this reason that unhesitating support cannot be given to the idea that the two small limestone statuettes, the only stone sculptures to be found at Harappa, are relics of the

Indus civilization. By far the most artistic products are the small images in bronze, of which the figures of a dancing girl and a buffalo from Mohenjo-Daro are of considerable merit. On the seals also, which show very varying standards of competence, there are some excellent engravings of animals.

As craftsmen the Harappans were as competent as any to be found among their contemporaries. In planned building they were outstanding as the orderly streets of houses in well bonded burnt brick testify. But they built no very imposing structures, nothing having been found which can with certainty be identified as a palace or temple. The Granary and Great Bath at Mohenjo-Daro are the notable buildings, and the latter is of great interest as it embodies a water-tight layer of bitumen in its sides and floor, the idea of which probably came from Iraq but the mastic employed is a refined asphalt, shown by Forbes' analysis to be a local product.

The standard of metallurgy in copper and bronze was well advanced, and though many thin-sectioned articles such as knives, razors and spear-heads were chiselled from sheet metal, open mould casting was used for flat-axes and mirrors and closed moulds or the **cire perdue** process for the more elaborate bronze figurines. Household utensils were made by the method of "raising" for deep and "sinking" for shallow vessels, and the process of lapping was used for joins at bases or sharply carinated shoulders. The chemical reaction of copper articles preserved fragments of what proved to be the square-woven cotton cloth in which they had been wrapped. The articles of copper in household use were supplemented by long blades of cherty flint, used no doubt as the utility kitchen knife.

The pottery followed about six basic types each showing a small range of variants. This well-fired, pale pink ware was wheel-thrown and mass-produced. As already noted there were a considerable number of terracotta figures, mostly potter-produced to meet a general demand rather than objects of artistic merit, only a few carved terracotta, possibly from one hand or school, showing any skill or vitality. There are a fair number of painted pots, decorated in black on a polished red slip, the designs on which are for the most part crowded and inartistic, though some of the earlier black on cream ware and a few large jars with intersecting circle patterns are pleasing and effective.

Elaborate bead necklaces adorned the wealthier Harappan women, and though the more usual materials were steatite and faience, many beads of semi-precious stones such as agate, carnelian, jasper and amazonite from Gujerat, jade from central Asia or Burma and lapis lazuli from Afghanistan were found together with gold disk beads of a style found at **Troy** and **Ur**. Their clothing consisted of cotton loin-cloths and probably woollen blanket-shawls for winter. This rich and civilized people, who had succeeded the peasant farming communities in Sind, dominated north-west India for a thousand years, but their Great period was followed by phases of stagnation and decline. The high administrative standards grew more lax and many spacious houses were converted into huddles of tenements. At about 1750 B.C. invaders, mixed bodies of adventurers probably Aryan-led, came from the Iranian plateau seeking new lands, easily won and easily held. We see evidence of their passage in the sudden disappearance of the peasant farmers of Baluchistan. They attacked the Harappans and between 1700 and 1650 B.C. took all the less well defended townships in Sind. About 1600 B.C. Harappa, which shows signs of being on the defensive in its closing years, fell to the Ravi people whose shanties cluster on the summit of the citadel they had sacked. Mohenjo-Daro probably held out for some time, and there is evidence in the **Rig**veda and from the few weapons of western type found in the upper levels that for about 150 years the large cities effected a compromise with the invaders, who fought and squabbled among themselves with Harappan aid. By 1550 B.C., with the possible exception of such outlying settlements as Rupar and Lothal which may have survived a few more decades, all this great civilization was entirely swept away. Plate 59, page 199.

Inhumation. Burial in the ground, as opposed to cremation.

Inter-galacial, *see* Glacial.

Ionians. These people were recognized by the ancient Greeks as one of the four main branches of their race, the others being the **Dorians**, Aeolians and **Achaeans**. They derived the name from Ion, son of Zuthus; in its earliest form it was *Iāwones*, (later *Iōnes*), and this was the name by which the Greeks as a whole were known to some of their eastern neighbours (Hebrew *Javan*, Old Persian *Yauna*). According to legend they originally occupied parts of the Greek mainland; but in the period following the Dorian invasions (about 1100 B.C. onwards) they emigrated to the islands of the central Aegean and the coast of Asia Minor, leaving only Attica and Euboea inhabited by kinsmen.

In the classical period the name of Ionia was restricted to the Asiatic coast and offshore islands from Phocaea to Miletus; and more especially to the twelve cities which kept the festival of the *Panionion* at Mount Mycale (Phocaea, Clazomenae, Samos, Chios, Erythrae, Teos, Lebedos, Colophon, Ephesus, Priene, Myus, Miletus). Their trade prospered, and they founded numerous colonies, especially in the Black Sea area. In the sixth century B.C. Ionia came under foreign rule, first of Lydia, then of Persia, but was eventually freed, following the failure of the Persian invasions of Greece, in 479 B.C.

The kinship of Athenians and Ionians is confirmed by the similarity of their dialects. Together they formed the most active and progressive branch of the Greeks; the poems of **Homer**, as we have them to-day, are a product of Ionia, which was, too, the home of the earliest Greek philosophers and scientists. Plate 60, page 200.

Iran. When most of Europe was still under the influence of the Ice Age, Iran (formerly known as Persia) was undergoing a **pluvial** period. Between about 15,000 and 10,000 B.C. however, there began a dry period, which still prevails. The central Iranian plateau, now mainly a salt desert, was originally covered by an immense inland sea. When the plateau became habitable, prehistoric man settled there in cave-dwellings, as at Tang-i-Pabda in the Bakhtiari mountains, excavated in 1949. The oldest human settlement yet excavated in the Iranian plains is the mound of Siyalk near Kashan, south of Teheran.

The first settlers of Siyalk I in the fifth millennium B.C., were hunters who supplemented their livelihood by agriculture and stock-breeding. Soon their hut-like dwellings were replaced by small **pisé** structures; black hand-made pottery of Siyalk I type was also found in the cave of Tang-i-Pabda mentioned above. Siyalk I also produced painted pottery with decorations in imitation of basketry. Towards the end of this period copper objects appeared, but metal casting was still not known. A large quantity of stone and clay objects resembling spindles suggest that textiles were produced. Shell and stone ornaments, and bone-carving on knife handles reveal the artistic endeavours of the Siyalk people. These shells, a type found in the Persian Gulf, indicate trade between two areas 600 miles apart. The dead were buried in a contracted position under house-floors, red stains on the bones showing that corpses were covered with iron oxide powder.

During the fourth millennium B.C. Siyalk II showed progress in its material culture: larger mud-brick houses with interior walls in red, and with doors swinging open on sockets, replaced the cruder *pisé* structures. The use of a potter's wheel produced a finer ware, decorated with stylized animals in black paint on a red ground, remarkably skilful in execution for so early a date. Metal tools were in use in conjunction with the earlier types in stone, and carnelian and turquoise were incorporated in the jewellery. The village communities of Siyalk II were increasing, and in addition to domestic animals found in the earlier phase, greyhounds and the Przewalski type of horses were bred. Thus Siyalk II was an extension of Siyalk I, with some developments.

Siyalk III covered the greater part of the fourth millennium B.C. A new building material – rectangular bricks made in moulds – considerably improved the size and appearance of houses, which now had windows, though doors continued to be narrow and only three feet high. As a protection against damp, large potsherds were inserted into the thickness of walls. Building façades were ornamented with recesses, and interior walls had red paint. Potter's wheels and kilns with grates were significant innovations of Siyalk III, resulting in a greater variety of ceramic forms and colours. The decoration of the pots depicts animals in both a stylized and a realistic manner. Figurines of **dea mater** type were common. Copper was now smelted and cast, and both weapons and jewellery had richer ornamentation.

These three periods of Siyalk cannot be traced in all prehistoric Iranian sites. Qumm, Savah, Rayy, and Damghan have the two earliest phases; at Giyan, Tell Bakun and Susa, however, there are no settlements earlier than the end of Siyalk III.

The beginning of the third millennium B.C. sees the destruction of Siyalk III, and subsequent remains show evidence of an intrusive culture – that of **Susa**, which was much influenced by Mesopotamia. Because climatic conditions on the plateau imposed a nomadic life on the people, prehistoric Iran did not rapidly progress towards urbanism, except in Susiana, where in the third millennium the first civilized state of Elam emerged, and where during the second millennium a national dynasty was established.

The eastern branch of the Indo-European speaking people, the **Aryans**, entered Iran during the second millennium B.C. One of these nomadic tribes of warrior horsemen settled in the oasis of Kashan (Siyalk), and converted this prehistoric village into a fortified town. These newcomers buried their dead in cemeteries, and the grave-goods reveal a variety of weapons and ornaments; a significant type of spouted vessel, undoubtedly used in ritual, introduced a new style in pottery which spread to other sites in Iran. The sun and the horse, two Indo-European symbols, feature in the decoration of these spouted vases. Several **Assyrian** reliefs represent such Iranian towns with moats, triple enclosure walls, and stone structures with battlemented towers, and it was this period that inaugurated the true growth of urban Iran. In spite of its fortifications, Siyalk was finally sacked by the Assyrian army during the ninth and eighth centuries B.C.

Though bronze and iron objects from the tombs of Luristan in the Kermanshah district have been known for some time, these **tumuli**, often surrounded by stone circles, have never been scientifically excavated. The majority of these objects suggest that they belonged to warriors, who were both horsemen and charioteers, and the fact that there are no settled sites in the neighbourhood indicates that they were a nomadic people.

Highly stylized animal forms are very largely used in the decoration of most of the objects; another recurrent subject is the fertility goddess. As is general in the art of ancient Persia, the artist renders animals better than human forms (*see* **Persepolis** *and* **Ziwiyè**). Most Luristan bronzes indicate a highly composite art style, and may be dated between the eighth and seventh centuries B.C. The question of the origins of the Luristan culture raises highly complex problems and much as yet remains unresolved.

Assyrian annals of the ninth century B.C. mention various early Iranian tribes of which the Medes in the north of Iran were the first to form an empire. Little is known of Median history, but **Herodotus** mentions one Phraortes, who probably united the tribes, and then in about 670 B.C. succeeded in subjecting the Persians in the south. Ecbatana, modern Hamadan, as yet remains unexcavated, but classical sources describe the splendours of this Median capital, which housed the royal treasury. The Medes were frequently in conflict with the nomadic Scythians. Allied with the Babylonians, Cyaxares, the son of Phraortes, eventually took **Nineveh**, the Assyrian capital, in 612 B.C., and vastly extended the frontiers of his empire. The only archaeological remains which can really be regarded as Median are a series of rock-cut tombs. Their façades, with columned porticoes, represent the architecture of the period, an influence strongly visible in the subsequent style of Achaemenian buildings.

In 834 B.C., Assyrian annals mention the Parsua tribe, which had settled in the area west and south-west of Lake Urmiya. In the eighth century B.C. they migrated south and settled in the foothills of the Bakhtiari mountains. They called this new land Parsumash, and were ruled by chiefs who acknowledged Achaemenes as their eponymous ancestor. The architecture of Masjid-i-Sulaimān, north-east of Khuzistan, the capital of one of these Achaemenian chieftains, reflects the marked influence of **Urartu** with which the Persians were familiar before their migration south.

Cambyses I, one of the kings of Parsumash, married the daughter of Astyages, then king of the Medes; their son, Cyrus II, the Great, after a brilliant military career, defeated Astyages in 553 B.C., and thus became heir to the Median Empire. He established his main capital at Pasargadae in the heart of Pars. Though intended for a royal capital, Pasargadae resembles in its layout a nomadic camp, with widely scattered buildings, each surrounded by the typical Persian "paradise" (an enclosed park or pleasure-ground). The most remarkable monument of the site is the tomb of Cyrus the Great, a hut-like stone structure with gabled roof, set on a stepped plinth, which reflects an alien architectural style. The height of Achaemenian art and architecture was achieved by the successors of Cyrus II, and of their several royal capitals, **Persepolis** (*see* colour plate XII, plates 107–109, pages 335–337) today reveals the finest extant examples of a highly cosmopolitan and yet essentially Persian art.

Of the nine Achaemenid dynasts the first three

made outstanding contributions in different fields: Cyrus the Great (559–530 B.C.) used his military genius to establish the first Persian Empire; Darius I (522–486 B.C.) excelled as an administrator, when he had successfully subjugated the rebellious elements of the Empire; Xerxes I (486–465 B.C.), after the wars with the Greeks, spent much time and money on the completion of buildings which Darius I had commenced.

The Achaemenids were liberal rulers, and they permitted conquered peoples to keep their own religion and language. With so vast an Empire in which the Persians were only a small minority, a tolerant policy was undoubtedly incumbent upon them. The Empire was divided into provinces, with a *satrap* often of Persian royal blood, at the head of each. The commander-in-chief held high office, and the 10,000 "Immortals", a special royal body-guard, served under him. Treasurers maintained accounts of yearly tribute, which was stored in the treasure-houses of various Achaemenid capitals. The "King's Ears and Eyes" were inspectors who travelled widely, and reported to the Court on matters concerning the Empire and its outlying satrapies (*see* **satrap**). The Royal Road from Susa to Ephesus, 1,677 miles long, was well maintained, and excavations near Gordion have revealed part of it. With the increased trade and caravan traffic, its upkeep was vital. Though the **Lydians** were responsible for the invention of **coinage**, it was Darius I who first based the economy of his empire on a monetary rather than on a barter system. Several texts of Darius I on the **Behistun Rock** (*see* plate 25, page 95) and other monuments indicate that he had established a legal framework for his peoples. **Cuneiform** was employed in royal inscriptions, but the Aramaic script was in use for state business, and became the *lingua franca* of the Achaemenian Empire.

After the death of Alexander the Great in 323 B.C., the Seleucids ruled the Achaemenian Empire, but were replaced within a century by the **Parthians** who in turn ruled Iran from the third century B.C. to the third century A.D.

In about A.D. 220, Ardashir Papakan, a feudal lord of the Parthian king in Pars, revolted, and when, in A.D. 226, the last Parthian king died, the new dynasty of the Sassanians was established under Ardashir. Both he and his son Shapur were often at war with Rome, and the latter had a great victory over Valerian in about A.D. 260; this event is recorded frequently on Sassanian reliefs, as at Bishapur. The Roman prisoners were used by Shapur to build dams in Persia. Later Sassanian kings warred with the eastern Roman Empire; by A.D. 619 Chosroes (Khusrau) II's troops had reached the Bosphorus. But Heraclitus, the new Byzantine Emperor, invaded Iran in A.D. 628. After Khusrau II there followed a rapid succession of kings, and eventually the Sassanian Empire was destroyed by Arab invasion in A.D. 651.

The Sassanians were great town-planners. Ardashir built Firuzabad on the circular plan which the Parthians preferred. Bishapur, however, built by Shapur I, followed the western style and was rectangular in plan. Fortress walls had rounded towers. Rubble and plaster were the most common building materials of the period, and vaulted roofs, as at **Ctesiphon** (*see* plate 41, page 145), and cupolas on square plans were popular architectural styles. Stucco was largely used in structural ornamentation and it even influenced the style of stone carving. Building interiors were decorated with frescos and mosaics.

In art, the Sassanians favoured traditional Iranian rock-reliefs; their themes were mainly the chase, the king and his court and the celebration of victories. The investiture of Bahram I at Bishapur is a good example of the high quality of these large-scale sculptures. The later examples, however, were influenced by the technique of painting, as the style of the famous hunting relief of the grotto of Taq-i-Būstān suggests.

Because of its position between China and Rome, Sassanian Iran was influenced by the silk trade, and many fine textile designs are depicted in the details of sculptured reliefs. After the defeat of Syria, colonies of weavers were deported, and made to settle in Khuzistān.

The most illustrious periods of Iranian history, the Achaemenian and the Sassanian, belong to pre-Islamic times. Both saw the hegemony of Zoroastrian dynasties arising in the heart of the Persian homeland, and extending their influence over two of the most cosmopolitan empires of the ancient east. *See* plate 61, page 201.

Iraq. The country of Iraq claims to be "the cradle of civilization" and the home of many ancient peoples who have influenced their neighbours and successors and, through them, the West. The country is watered by the 250-mile-long twin rivers

Euphrates and Tigris and was thus formerly named "Mesopotamia" ("between the rivers"). Throughout its history, prosperity has depended on artificial irrigation from these rivers and their principal tributaries, the Habur, Zab and Diyala.

In the north lay the country called Assyria after Ashur, its ancient capital, on the Tigris; it was bounded by the Syrian Desert and Sinjar Hills in the west, the hills of southern Turkey in the north, the Kurdish mountains in the east, and in the south the low range of Hamrin hill. The terrain is rolling and well-watered, but dependent for its economic well-being on holding back the hill peoples and keeping open the mountain passes for trade.

In the south, the flat Mesopotamian plain is open along its entire western flank to the Arabian deserts and overlooked on the east by the Persian hills. The rivers meander through marshes and flow into the Persian Gulf. This is an area in which the coastline, like the climate, has changed little in historic times. Dry summers with short winters and spring rains are the lot of the whole area.

Early travellers, some drawn by the biblical references to the country, noted the principal upstanding ruins and **tells.** Attention was focussed on the ruins of Kuyunjik, opposite Mosul, which were described by such voyagers as Benjamin of Tudela (1160–73) and Ricoldo Pennini (1290). The identification of these ruins with **Nineveh,** doubted by **Layard** at first, was confirmed by his excavations there in 1847 and gave rise to much Western interest.

Babylon, described by Pietro della Valle in 1616 and identified by Niebuhr in 1761 as the biblical city of that name, was first explored by C. J. Rich in 1821. The collection of antiquities brought by the latter to the British Museum was probably the first from the country displayed in Europe. Pioneer excavations followed. The work of the Frenchman Botta at Nineveh and Khorsabad, and of Layard at Nineveh and **Nimrud** was followed by that of the less skilled. Interest was further quickened by the decipherment by **Rawlinson** and his colleagues, of the many **cuneiform** inscriptions discovered, and by the publication of the Assyrian royal bas-reliefs. Scientific excavation can be said to have begun in Iraq with the work of the Deutsche Orient Gesellschaft under **Koldewey** in Babylon in 1878–1914.

As a result of survey, soundings and excavation at more than 6,400 ancient sites in Iraq, its ancient history and culture are rapidly becoming better known. Each period is distinguished by its characteristic architecture, pottery, artifacts, seals and writings. These disclose the way of life of many different peoples who inhabited the country in ancient times; **Sumerians**, Semitic Babylonians, **Assyrians**, **Amorites** and invading non-Semites, Mitannians, **Hurrians**, **Kassites**, Persians and Mongols.

In the central Kurdistan Hills, lower **Palaeolithic** implements have been found at Barda Balka, while at Shanidar cave in the same range were **Levalloise-Mousterian** implements and a **Neanderthal** baby, the first human skeleton of Palaeolithic times yet found in Iraq. Upper Palaeolithic and Mesolithic **microlith** flints were found in adjacent areas. In Iraq the **Neolithic** revolution came soon after 10,000 B.C. The American excavations at Jarmo since 1950 have revealed the earliest village farming communities yet found, dated by **carbon fourteen** tests to 5000–4500 B.C.

Tools, houses and clay figurines found at Hassuna in the Tigris Valley are not unlike those from Jarmo, but the pottery shows gradually developing painted and incised forms. The change from a purely Neolithic camp site to full village life shown by the introduction of Hassuna wares may perhaps mark the advent of a new population. Similar wares have been found in Cilicia (Mersin), Syria (**Ras Shamra**) and Palestine (**Megiddo** and **Jericho**) as well as elsewhere in Iraq. The upper levels at Hassuna also yielded pottery of a better decorated type called Samarra after the finds made by the Germans in 1912–14 in the Abbasid capital.

The subsequent prehistoric period at Hassuna is marked by decorated pottery called **Halafian** from the Habur site where it was first found. The same pottery type was also unearthed at Arpachiya, Tepe Gawra and Chagar Bazar in the north, and somewhat similar at Eridu in the south. This was followed by a phase characterized by **Al Ubaid** pottery with its deep purple painted patterns, found both at the temple site of Al Ubaid, four miles to the north-north-east of Ur, at Ur and at sites in the north as far west as the Mediterranean.

The earliest dwellings at this time were reed and mat huts, daubed with mud, which were later imitated in mud brick. In the north, simple temples (Tepe Gawra) and **tholoi** (Arpachiya) were built, while in the south the first temple on a raised platform appears at Warka (Uruk, the biblical Erech).

In the south, an independent culture developed

with elaborately constructed temple areas which testify to the increasing wealth and political power of the new cities being founded in this late prehistoric age. The crude stamp seal was now gradually replaced by the introduction of the cylinder seal which, among other uses, was rolled upon clay tablets on which the earliest form of writing in **pictographs**, the most important invention of the age, now appears at **Uruk**.

The Early Dynastic period (about 3000–2350 B.C.) was one of increasing technological progress. Excavations in the Diyala region (Khafajah and Tell Asmar), and at Ur and other cities show the agricultural wealth of this time, a time when strong government secured that irrigation of the soil necessary to make the area one of the richest granaries in the world, comparable to modern Canada, and certainly as wealthy as it was later described by **Herodotus**.

Bitumen and surface oil deposits were worked and contemporary documents show there is no reason to believe that there has been any significant change in the climate of Iraq in the historical period. The magnificent finds of metal-work and other articles from the Royal Tombs at Ur, especially the **shaft grave** of Shubad, to be dated at the end of this period, show the wealth and culture at its best.

Control of the city-states by a few strong rulers continued in the **Accadian** period (about 2350–2150 B.C.). Men like Sargon of Accad, whose portrait-bust in bronze survives, and Gudea of **Lagash** carried their arms as far as Syria, Anatolia and Persia to win wood, precious stones and rare materials for embellishing their temples and stimulating trade. The French finds at Lagash (1897–1933) include many fine examples of sculpture in the round, and it is at this time that bas-relief work is first found.

Political power next passed to **Ur**, where the third dynasty (about 2150–2050 B.C.) under its vigorous founder, **Ur-Nammu**, rebuilt the city walls, **ziggurat** and temples. In his control of Sumer he undertook similar work at Eridu, Uruk and other southern cities. Trade and the arts flourished, the **stele** of Ur-Nammu representing his military exploits being a good example of the latter. Daily life can be reconstructed from the thousands of tablets found at Ur by Sir Leonard **Woolley** in 1922–34.

The coming of Semitic **Amorites** into the south resulted in their control of the principal cities with their capital at Isin, Larsa, and eventually **Babylon**. This period, often called "Old Babylonian" or first dynasty of Babylon (about 2050–1600 B.C.), is well-known from written documents, especially letters, which passed between the major rulers, and from many thousands of economic texts.

Unfortunately, little has been found at Babylon itself of this early phase, perhaps owing to the rising water-table there. The principal ruler, **Hammurabi**, united Sumerian and Semitic subjects by revised legislation known from inscribed diorite stelae originally set up in Babylon and other centres, but subsequently found at **Susa** to which they had been carried off. Hammurabi extended his kingdom as far north as **Mari** on the Upper Euphrates and thus came into contact with the rulers of Assyria (Shamshi-Adad I) and Aleppo, while nearer at home Eshnunna and **Elam** were his strong neighbours. The chronology of this period is still disputed, 1792–50 B.C. being now accepted by the majority of scholars as the date for Hammurabi himself.

After the **Hittite** raid on Babylon, the north was overrun by non-Semites and Hurrians whose presence is best known from the documents found at fifteenth century B.C., Nuzi (near Kirkuk) and at Ras Shamra and **Tell Atchana** in Syria. Further incursions came from the Kassites (about 1600–911 B.C.) whose occupation of Dur-Kurigalzu (Aqar Quf, near Baghdad) is known from Iraqi excavations there in 1942–4 and from the Kassite buildings at Ur and other sites. In addition to a revival of interest in the Sumerian literature, there seems at this time to have been an increased use of inscribed boundary stones (***kudurru***), a special form of title deed invoking divine protection on property.

The great days of the Assyrian Empire (about 900–612 B.C.) followed the revival of Semitic influence in the north. The Assyrian royal sites of Ashur, Nineveh, Nimrud (Calah) and Khorsabad were the first to be explored by the pioneer archaeologists. Subsequently, work at Ashur by the Germans and at Nimrud by the British School of Archaeology under Mallowan (1949–60) have greatly increased knowledge of the period. Palaces with their sculptured walls, streets, administrative buildings and army barracks with their contents and inscriptions, have been found. The finest carved ivories (originally furniture decorations) yet recovered from the ancient world have been found at Nimrud, from which came the oldest book yet discovered (715–711 B.C.) and unique inscriptions describing the rebuilding of the city in 879 B.C. and the treaties made by Esarhaddon with the Medes in 672 B.C. At Nineveh, the palace of Sennacherib (705–681 B.C.) has been cleared. He rebuilt the city and gave it a new water supply, and cut his inscriptions and reliefs in rock faces at Maltai and Bavian. He also introduced cotton-growing into Assyria. From the palace of Ashur-bani-pal (669–630 B.C.), the reliefs showing his lion-hunt are, perhaps, the best known. More than 25,000 tablets found here and in the Nabu temple library provide unique literary texts from one of the oldest libraries in the world and have been the major contribution to the understanding of Assyrian, Babylonian and Sumerian, languages and literature. These, with administrative texts, enable the study of the organization of the Assyrian army and Empire, and of the provinces which at one time included Assyria's great rival Babylonia, northern Arabia, Armenia, Media, Syria, Palestine and as far to the west as Egypt. The short-lived palace-site of Sargon II at Khorsabad was excavated by Botta and an American expedition (1928–35). Here were found particularly fine examples of **colossi** which guarded the gateways of the courtyards around which Assyrian palaces were planned.

The Medes and Babylonians combined to destroy Assyria in 614–612 B.C. and political power shifted once more to Babylon, where a Chaldaean dynasty was established (626–539 B.C.) Nebuchadnezzar II rebuilt Babylon (also Sippar, Borsippa, and Ur) on a grand scale as shown by Koldewey's work. However, increasing threats from Lydia and Persia curtailed the activities of his successor Nabonidus who introduced some unpopular religious reforms, reflected in changes in temple plans at Ur, which led to his exile in central Arabia. Hardly had he returned when Babylon fell to Cyrus in 539 B.C. This period is only partly known by building and other cuneiform inscriptions, including the Babylonian historical chronicle, for by this time Aramaic written on perishable papyri and leather was in common use.

The **Achaemenid** occupation of Iraq (539–331 B.C.) has left little archaeological trace, and is best known from inscriptions, isolated buildings at Babylon and Ur, many stone figures, finely-worked jewellery and seals.

The Hellenistic domination which followed is also known mainly from inscriptions, from coins which now appear for the first time, and from ruins at Babylon (a Greek theatre), and at Seleucia, the new capital. Hellenistic levels of occupation are found at most of the larger sites throughout Iraq.

The principal **Parthian** remains (248 B.C.–A.D. 226) are at Hatra (fifty miles to the south-south-west of Mosul) where the Iraqi government continued earlier German excavations, and at the imposing Palace and "Arch" of **Ctesiphon** (*see* plate 41, page 145) south-east of Bagdad. Miscellaneous grave-goods found with heavily glazed bluish-green slipper coffins from cemetery sites are characteristic of this period. Stamp seals and seal stones of this and the **Sassanian** era (A.D. 226–632) are common.

The antiquities of Iraq are well represented in the larger museum collections in the West. Thanks to the liberal encouragement of the Iraq Department of Antiquities (founded after the first world war by Gertrude Bell) expeditions of many different nationalities have worked in the country. There are excellent museums in Baghdad and also at Mosul, Babylon, and other sites where preservation work has been undertaken.

Iron Age. This, the last of the classic "three ages of stone, bronze, and iron", like its predecessor the **Bronze Age**, grew out of the natural resources and technical skill of the East. However iron ores are found not only in Egypt and Nubia, east Jordan and Syria, north-east Anatolia, Armenia, Caucasia, the Taurus and northern Persia, but also scattered throughout Europe in Britain, Spain, northern France and particularly in the rich deposits of Etruria and Elba, while in central Europe there are the ores of what later became the Roman province of Noricum. As with copper the new metal was used first of all as decoration or even amulets and the earliest datable finds of iron are of meteoric origin whose steel-like properties (due to a high nickel content) rendered their easy working beyond the simple skills of the copper-smiths. Indeed the **Sumerians** called the natural iron "heaven-metal" and the early Egyptians "black copper from the skies", while beads found in a late Predynastic tomb at Gerzah and in the Sumerian Early Dynastic royal tombs at **Ur** attest to these magical ascriptions. However, not much later than the royal tombs from such Mesopotamian sites as Tell Asmar, Chagar Bazar, and **Mari** of about 2500 B.C. we have evidence that man had mastered the reduction in a charcoal fire and production of simple objects from magnetite, haematite and other ores which are in fact much more widely distributed than copper deposits. A fine early iron dagger with a gold band in it comes from the Anatolian tombs of **Alaca Höyük.**

It is with the coming of the Hittite Kingdom that we come across a true iron industry stemming from the rich dependent region of Armenia, home of the Chalybes of the classical authors; wrought iron was being produced as early as 1900 B.C. By the second half of the second millennium B.C. the full techniques of the true "Iron Age" were being employed – carburizing, quenching and tempering. Although the new material at first produced in the Near East a temporary rise in corn prices, its general cheapness resulted in a gradual extension of economic benefits and a resultant drop in the cost of living.

At first the **Hittites** kept a tight hold on the market. Iron was a treasured gift for the brother kings of Middle Kingdom Egypt, where the new skills lagged behind the Anatolian foundries, carburizing of natural ores being introduced only after the time of the **Sea Peoples** about 1200 B.C. and a full technological Iron Age came into being as late as about 600. Thus the iron dagger blade with bronze cast-on hilt decorated with gold and rock crystal from the **Tomb of Tutankhamun** must represent just such a present from the Mitanni as are known from the somewhat earlier **Tell el Amarna** letters. Somewhat later still there is a letter from Hattusil III (1281–1260 B.C.) to Ramses II, the pharaoh of the Exodus, mentioning the gift of a dagger blade and also indicating the embargo on iron production outside Urartian Armenia. Nevertheless we know from the Old Testament that the Philistine allies of the Hittites had obtained the necessary skill to work the Syrian deposits (Judges 4, 3). One recalls, too, Goliath's spear head. From **Ras Shamra** of about 1300 is a Mitannian or Luristanian dagger with a high nickel content iron blade and cast-on copper hilt inlaid with gold in the style of the Tutankhamun example. By the close of the second millennium the downfall of the Hittite Empire and later the Thraco-Phrygian incursions opened up a wider series of workshops. Thus by 1180 B.C. we have at Gerar on the Palestinian border just such a great iron-working centre as is mentioned by Samuel. Later still Assyria took the Hittites' place as mass producers. In the palace of Sargon II (722–705 B.C.) were found, some 300,000 pounds of unworked iron ingots, and it is at about this time that Egypt was at last approaching an iron-using economy while the first steeled iron in India may been produced also, although farther to the east China was not to practise casting and forging of iron until the late fourth century B.C.

From **Urartu** to the Greece of Proto-geometric times came the use of iron, while farther west it is associated with the Urnfield expansion of about 1200 – the time of the Sea Peoples – when once more it appears as a precious metal in the form of inlay to bronze slashing swords. Round about 1800 in the metalliferous regions of central Europe we see the gradual employment of the new metal. Here too the skills originally evolved for the **Hallstatt** salt-mines and copper lodes of the Tyrol not only may have resulted in accidental blooming of iron ores but in a ready established economic system which in Roman times turned Noricum into what has been called the "Sheffield of antiquity".

At the Hungarian site of Velem Szentvid deep smelting hearths dating from the beginning of the Hallstatt period may represent direct Anatolian influence. In Scandinavia, however, a Bronze Age community lasts until well into the third quarter of the first millennium B.C. while in Britain the local Forest of Dean ores were not worked until the developed Belgic Iron Age. *See* plate 62, page 202.

Ise. The province of Ise on Honshu Island, Japan, is the centre of the Shinto cult and its shrines are of great importance. These are rebuilt every twenty years, but it is generally accepted that they represent the purest style of traditional and ancient Japanese architecture. This amounts to no more than the idealization of the thatched hut, set on piles and with a ridge pole crested by a decorative board above the thatch, terminating in gables. The shrine at Yamada is that of the sun goddess and houses the sacred mirror which is her emblem. The next most holy is that of a food goddess, Toyo-uke-hime, and there is reason to believe that some form of food deity cult is native to the area, the sun goddess being installed by the royal house as a political act. It is widely held that in the **Nara** period, when the imperial house was anxious to instal a central Buddha image for the kingdom in A.D. 742, permission was first sought from the Yamada shrine by a Buddhist monk acting as imperial envoy.

Photo: Percival David Foundation of Chinese Art

PLATE VII. KANSU: Kuan vase with crackled blue-grey glaze, bound with copper at foot and rim, Sung dynasty, tenth to eleventh centuries A.D. This vase represents the culmination of a ceramic tradition which begins in the Chinese neolithic period. (*Percival David Foundation of Chinese Art, School of Oriental and African Studies, London*)

Photo: Exclusive News Agency

PLATE 65. KARNAK: part of the avenue of sphinxes at the entrance to the temple enclosure.

Photo: from "Archaeology in China" by William Watson, Max Parrish and Co. Ltd, London

PLATE 66. KANSU: pottery urn decorated in red and black from Pai-Tao-Kou-p'ing, near Lan Chou, Kansu Province, Pan Shan and Yang-shao cultures.
(By courtesy of the Britain-China Friendship Association)

Photo: Radio Times Hulton Picture Library

PLATE 67. KARNAK: red Aswan granite columns bearing the cartouche of Tuthmosis III. The foreground column is the papyrus, the rear is the lotus, with turned sepals.

Photo: Editions Cahiers d' Art, Paris

PLATE 68. KNOSSOS: the stairway and corridor which led to the pillared hall.

Photo: Radio Times Hulton Picture Library

PLATE 69. KNOSSOS: the throne room, with the frieze of guardian griffons, restored by M. Gillieron.

Photo: by courtesy of the Ashmolean Museum

PLATE 70. KNOSSOS: amphora with plant design from Knossos, 1650–1580 B.C.
(Ashmolean Museum, Oxford)

Photo: British Museum

PLATE 71. LAGASH: statue of a royal personage or official who belonged to one of the families of non-Semitic origin which reigned at Lagash, before 2500 B.C. *(British Museum, London)*

Photo: Mansell Collection

PLATE 72. Austen Henry LAYARD (1817–94), photograph.

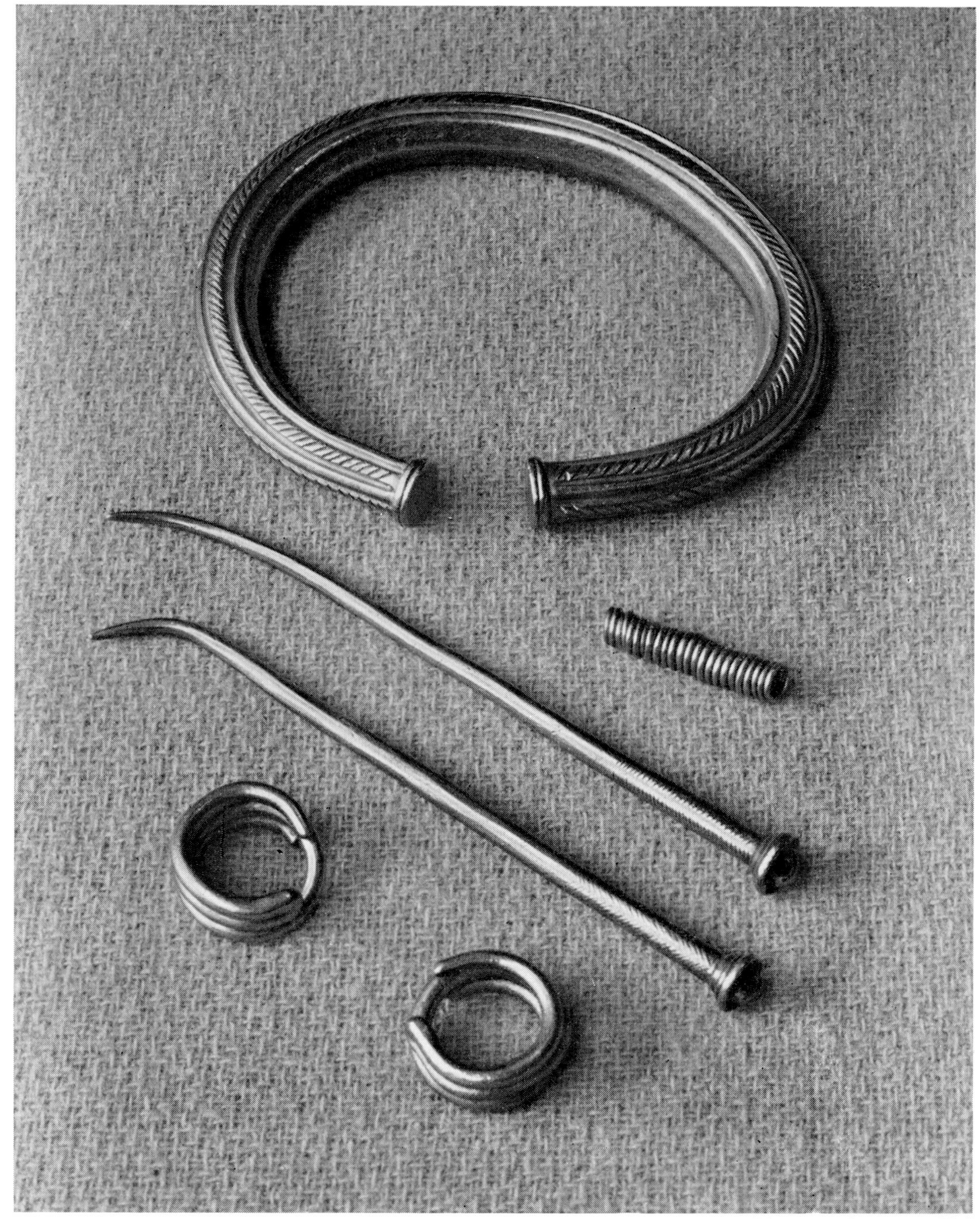

Photo: Landesmuseum, Halle

PLATE 73. LEUBINGEN: gold ornaments from the chieftain's tumulus – massive chased bracelet, spirally-wound hair ring, pair of loop-headed pins and a pair of recurved wire finger rings. Length of pins $3\frac{7}{10}$ inches. *(Landesmuseum für Vorgeschichte, Halle/Saale)*

Photo: Sam Waagenaar

PLATE 74. LUXOR: detail of carved relief.

Photo: Aerofilms Ltd

PLATE 75. MAIDEN CASTLE: an aerial view.

Photo: Nelson Gallery

PLATE 76. LUNG-MEN: imperial procession of the empress, limestone relief with traces of colour, about 522 A.D. northern Wei dynasty. *(Nelson Gallery – Atkins Museum, Kansas City, Missouri [Nelson Fund])*

Photo: from "Old Stone Age" by Stevan Celebonovic and Geoffrey Grigson, Phoenix House Ltd, London

PLATE 77. MAGDALENIAN: engraving of wounded hinds.

Photo: India Office Library, Commonwealth Relations Office

PLATE 78. MATHURA: an *ayagapata* with small figure of Jain Tirthamkara in the centre. *(By courtesy of the Director General of Archaeology in India).*

Photo: India Office Library, Commonwealth Relations Office

PLATE 79. MAURYAN EMPIRE: sculptured facade of the rock-cut polished cave of Lomas Rishi in the Barabar hills which may be Mauryan. *(By courtesy of the Director General of Archaeology in India)*

Photo: India Office Library, Commonwealth Relations Office

PLATE 80. MATHURA: railing pillars with dancing girls standing on dwarfs, Kushan period.
(By courtesy of the Director General of Archaeology in India)

Photo: *Ralph Morse—courtesy Life Magazine* © 1947 *Time Inc.*

Plate VIII. Lascaux: painting of bison, Gravettian period, about 1800 B.C.

Israelites, *see* Hebrews.

Italy, Prehistoric, *see* Mediterranean, The Western.

Iyateyet Site, *see* America, Early Man in.

J

Japan, Prehistoric. Recent studies of the **Palaeolithic** period in Japan have revealed the presence of **hand-axes**, blades and points in the loam layers. There is some indication that the points belong to a stage that succeeds the other implements, but the chronology is not yet entirely clear and it is difficult to ascribe satisfactory time periods to the pre-pottery material, as it has not yet been possible to collect samples for **carbon fourteen dating**. Its age, however, more than likely precedes the tenth century B.C.

The Jomon period, named after the cord-impressing on pottery, is known through the existence of numerous shell-mounds, camp and dwelling sites, and **cromlechs** of small stones in north Japan. These remains lie above the loam in the top layer of Japan's soil, a bed of black humus, and their date is probably at the earliest in the vicinity of 6000 B.C.

Thatch houses were built over a pit two to three feet deep and up to fifteen feet across, of circular, square or varying shapes, and were normally protected from water by ditches; they can also be identified by the marks of numerous holes for posts. By the Middle Jomon period communities of thirty or more houses were not unusual. All these **Neolithic** sites are impressive owing to the profusion of pottery fragments. Besides cord-marking, this hand-made pottery is embellished by a diversity of abstract designs, almost invariably visually remarkable, and fashioned in a great variety of shapes.

Clay figurines, at first extremely simple and usually zoomorphic in nature, take on human and often female characteristics with the passage of time, and must represent an incipient form of a cult that culminated in the worship of the sun goddess taken subsequently in protohistoric and historic centuries.

Neolithic **stone tools** include chipped axes, arrow-heads, tanged knives, scrapers and awls. In later stages ground and polished axes, shafts with bulbous tips, and, in north Japan, long and sometimes curved knives make their appearance. Stones of a magical nature, bone fish-hooks and harpoons, bone and antler ornaments, some **basketry** and **lacquering** are also among the remains.

Discoveries of human skeletons do not precede the Jomon period, and those of Jomon times are found almost exclusively in the shell-mounds where the dead were buried, often in a flexed position. The earliest physical types demonstrate relatively little consistency and probably represent groups from the north Asiatic continent, not distinctively Mongoloid. It is quite possible that the modern-day **Ainu** of Hokkaido are akin to the Neolithic peoples of Japan. It was the later arrivals from China and Korea in the Yayoi and protohistoric periods who provided the Japanese with their strikingly Mongoloid features.

These Mongoloid migrants to the island of Kyushu from the China coast and Korea in the third century B.C. brought with them many facets of continental life, changing the entire economic structure of south Japan. Thus, as rice-growing practices, the use of iron and bronze, the making of pottery with the aid of a wheel and other innovations took hold, the older Neolithic habits of hunting and gathering supplemented by inadequate methods of food production were superseded, except in north Japan where for centuries a primitive society continued to exist, of which the Ainu are a reflection.

This period is called Yayoi, after the name of a place in Tokyo where reddish pottery was first discovered in 1884. Yayoi pottery is often devoid of decoration, or bears horizontal incisions and a variety of combed patterns, and when found north of Shizuoka may be cord-marked. Large vessels were frequently used singly or doubly as burial urns in south Japan, sometimes in association with cist graves. Personal possessions were occasionally deposited with the dead, a practice that had its beginnings in the first or second century B.C. amongst the jar-burial people.

These new arrivals imported the earliest metal objects, as did others well into the first century A.D., but local copies were soon made and, as skills developed, Japanese types of socketed and tanged spear-heads, halberd blades, bells, and circular mirrors of bronze were produced for ceremonial purposes.

Houses were now built on the surface of the

ground and had assumed an appearance much like the wood and thatch dwellings visible in the countryside of Japan today. Storehouses with raised floors became the prototype for official dwellings and after that the earliest form of Shinto shrine.

According to the two eighth-century A.D. books, *Nihon Shoki* (Chronicles of Japan) and *Kojiki* (Records of Ancient Matters), a local group claiming descent from the sun goddess and led by the first emperor Jimmu Tenno began to emerge from the Kansai (Kyoto and Osaka) region, swallowing up lesser tribes. The dominance of the nobility is attested to by the thousands of tumuli that dot the landscape of central and south Japan and give the name to the period: Kofun (Old Tomb) period, or Protohistoric because of the later written records referring to this age.

The first of these tombs were constructed in the Kansai near the close of the third century A.D. In mature fifth-century examples, they are moated mounds of earth covering as much as eighty acres, containing a stone chamber, frequently one or more stone **sarcophagi,** and a dazzling array of grave-goods. In the sixth century some interior walls were carved and painted in simple symbolic designs. Most tombs are circular mounds, but one distinctively Japanese type is a rounded knoll with a projecting member that taken together resemble a keyhole in shape. Only a few of the largest have ever been excavated because of their attribution to individuals of the imperial family and the veneration in which they are held, but research has gone on in hundreds of smaller ones.

Grave deposits include grey Sue pottery in great quantities, body armour, long single-edged swords of iron, horse trappings, bronze mirrors, an assortment of personal ornaments, and other ceremonial objects. Clay replicas of human beings, animals and houses were placed on the exterior slopes.

Buddhism was, by tradition, brought to Japan in A.D. 552, and may be looked upon as a climax to events that virtually completed the continentalization of the country. The Buddhist practice of cremation and government decree combined forces to eliminate the tumulus mode of burial, but in outlying areas it persisted into the eighth century.

Java Man (Homo modjokertensis). In 1891 the Dutch anthropologist Eugène Dubois found in central Java portions of a skeleton of a type of man who became known as one of the now extinct genus **Pithecanthropus** erectus, which can be seen as one of the "missing links" between the ape and true man. In 1936 and during the following three years parts of three more skulls belonging to the same group were found in Java, including one of a child aged about two.

The skull structure of Java man is ape-like in its heavy prominent eyebrow ridges which form a continuous line running across the root of the nose, and in the backward slope of the forehead from the eyebrow ridge and the sharply pointed back of the skull. The brain-case is flattened and the jaws are massive and projecting. However, the fragments of limb bones found suggest that the limb structure was close to that of modern man, the thigh bone indicating that Java man walked erect. The brain capacity – approximately 900 c.c. – is about halfway between that of apes and modern man (1,350 c.c.). Java man was probably in existence as much as half a million years ago and lasted until the mid-**Pleistocene** era. He was skilled enough to fashion **stone tools** and this fact groups him rather as a **hominid** than as a member of the ape family.

Jemdet Nasr, *see* Sumerians.

Jericho. The city of Jericho was sited in a strategic position on the west side of the Jordan, commanding the crossing just north of the Dead Sea. It lay at the eastern foot of the mountains of Judah in the oasis produced by a spring, which was necessary for the city's existence in the hot valley 800 feet below sea level. There are three sites at Jericho today, as the position of the settlement has altered at different times in history. The present village has only been occupied since Byzantine times, when it was moved from a site about a mile to the west, Telul Abu el-'Alayiq, which represents the city of New Testament times. About one and a half miles to the north of the modern village stands the mound of Tell es-Sultan, the site of the most ancient city. This **tell**, which stands about sixty feet high and measures some 330 by 175 yards, is the site which has mainly concentrated the attention of excavators.

The first excavation on the site was made by Charles Warren in 1868, but this was only a small-scale affair, and nothing further was done for nearly forty years. From 1907, Ernst Sellin, assisted by Carl Watzinger, directed an Austro-German expedition on the site. The results, published in 1913, set a high standard, and also produced lively discussion on the question of the date of the Exodus, since any evidence of destruction which might be connected with Joshua would naturally have a definite bearing on this matter. An attempt to resolve the questions raised by Sellin's excavations was made in 1929 when John **Garstang** reopened the work, and continued each year until 1936. One of the main objectives of these campaigns was the dating of the city destroyed by Joshua (Late **Bronze Age**). This Garstang identified with the last of four successive cities, which he found to have been fortified with a double wall which had collapsed outwards, leaving signs of violent destruction. On the basis of Egyptian **scarabs** associated with these walls, and the absence of **Mycenaean** pottery, Garstang suggested a date not much later than 1400 B.C. In the last two years of his campaign at Jericho, Garstang drove a deep sounding through to the base of the mound, and revealed that the site was of extraordinary antiquity. After passing seventeen building levels he came upon a layer of deposit which he characterized as **Mesolithic**. Above this level he distinguished two phases of **Neolithic**, the earlier without pottery, followed by **Chalcolithic**, and then the Bronze Age levels known from other areas of the site.

The very early levels were of such importance for the general history of the Middle East, and the date of the fall of the Late Bronze Age city so involved in biblical chronology, that in 1952 a further attack was made on the mound, this time an Anglo-American undertaking, led by Miss Kathleen Kenyon, director of the British School of Archaeology in Jerusalem. Careful examination of the fortifications revealed that the double walls, whose fall the previous expedition had associated with Joshua, were neither contemporary with each other, nor of later date than the Early Bronze Age. It appeared moreover that the levels of the Late Bronze Age city, which would have been the one destroyed by Joshua, had been largely eroded off the mound, and lost in the modern cultivation which adjoins it. Thus the early date for Joshua's destruction of the city, which had militated against a body of other evidence, was no longer tenable.

The other main objective of the expedition, the early levels, was rewarded with remarkable discoveries. While no evidence was found of Garstang's Mesolithic level, the Neolithic was uncovered at the base of a deep trench through the western fortifications. The earlier phase of Neolithic, that without pottery, was discovered to have had two sub-phases, and in the earlier of these, the settlement had evidently occupied about half the area of the present tell. This settlement was protected by a fortification, which on the western side consisted of a rock-cut ditch eight feet deep and twenty-seven feet across, behind which stood a stone tower twenty-five feet high and thirty feet across. A **radiocarbon** test from this earliest Neolithic phase yielded a date of about 6800 B.C., much earlier than any hitherto attached to any other Neolithic site in the world. This produced considerable controversy, which devolves ultimately on the question of the reliability of the radiocarbon method of dating.

Thus, three major excavations have elucidated, in some degree, the history of the very ancient city of Jericho. From a substantial "town", with its beginnings perhaps in the early seventh millennium B.C., it passed through three main Neolithic stages. The Chalcolithic, of the fourth millennium, was not well represented, but during the Early Bronze Age a large city occupied the whole mound. This period ended with troubled times when marauding **Amorites** occupied the area. The Middle Bronze Age which followed was the period of **Hyksos** power, and it is probably to these conquerors that a series of massive fortifications, found on the western side of the tell, are to be attributed. The most remarkable remains of this period were a number of sealed tombs outside the mound, where household objects of wood, basketry and textiles as well as food were preserved from decay, to give an idea, unusual for Palestine, of the conditions of daily life. It seems that, during the earlier part of the Late Bronze Age, the site was deserted, being resettled perhaps about 1400 B.C., but the subsequent denudation of the site is such that very little can be concluded as to the date of its destruction at the hands of Joshua. The same is true of the **Iron Age** when, according to the Bible, the city was refounded in the time of Ahab, and little evidence is available until New Testament times, when the site was moved to the south. *See* plate 63, page 203.

Jerusalem. Ancient Jerusalem stood in Judah in **Palestine**, about fifteen miles west of the Dead

Sea, on two hills which project southward to form a triple fork at the head of a small valley. The three branches which thus united at the south-eastern corner of the city, provided a ring of declivity that separated the city from the surrounding hills on all but the northern side. The two main hills were themselves subdivided by smaller valleys, the western into a south-western (Mount Zion) and a north-western hill, and the eastern into a north-eastern, a central (Temple) and a south-eastern (Ophel) hill. This last, a narrow spur only about one hundred yards across, was the site of the original "City of David", and it was towards the north and west that the city expanded as time passed.

The first excavator at Jerusalem was Charles Warren, who dug (1867–70) a number of tunnels to examine what lay below the Islamic precinct of the Temple Hill. Both southern hills were excavated in 1894–97 by Fredericke Bliss and A. C. Dickie, and in 1913–14, Raymond Weill penetrated to the original rock on the south-eastern hill, establishing the pre-Israelite settlement of the area. In 1927 John Crowfoot and Gerald Fitzgerald dug a trench from the south-eastern to the south-western hill across the central valley, revealing that the valley had been much deeper in ancient times than today, an observation which has been found to apply to all the valleys.

The evidence from these and many other excavations and from the written sources show that the south-eastern hill was already occupied in the **Bronze Age**, being mentioned as Urusalim in the **Amarna** letters. Though Joshua sacked the city it remained in **Canaanite** hands until its capture by David who made it his capital. In the time of Solomon the city was extended northward to include the central part of the eastern hill, on which the temple was built. As the capital of Judah the city suffered several sieges, and it was while awaiting the approach of Sennacherib's army that Hezekiah had a tunnel hewn through the rock (commemorated in the famous Siloam Inscription), to bring water from the nearest external spring to the Pool of Siloam within. In 597 B.C. Nebuchadnezzar sacked the city, exiling part of the population to Babylonia, and eleven years later he utterly destroyed Solomon's Temple. The city was rebuilt under Persian patronage, but the Temple of New Testament times was only put up under Herod the Great (37–4 B.C.). The entire city was razed to the ground in A.D. 70 by Titus, and in the time of Hadrian became a Roman colony, Aelia Capitolina, to which the Jews were forbidden entry. In A.D. 638 the city fell into Moslem hands and, except for a brief dominion by the Crusaders (1099–1187), has so remained ever since. The present city walls, which exclude the south-eastern hill, are mainly of sixteenth-century date, though the Dome of the Rock, on the site of Solomon's temple, was largely built in the seventh century.

Jews, *see* Hebrews.

Jomon, *see* Japan, Prehistoric.

Jordan. The geographical situation and peculiarities of the country now known as Jordan always made it in the past something of a backwater. Isolated from its neighbours on the south and east by the great desert tracts, cut off from Syria on the north by the deep gorge of the Yarmuk and from Palestine on the west by the Jordan Valley, possessing no natural resources or riches of its own, lying on no particular highway, it did not attract the attention of the forces of Egypt and Mesopotamia in their frequent forays against each other through Palestine. Though it passed through the same cultural phases as its neighbours, the **artifacts** of these cultures shown slight differences from those of its nearest and most influential neighbour, Palestine.

The eastern part of the country is desert, and comprises nearly two-thirds of its total area; the desert slopes gently up to the fertile plateau that ends abruptly at the rim of the Jordan Valley, lying some 4,000 feet below the steep scarp. Through this mountain range four rivers cut their way: the Yarmuk and the Zerka (ancient Jabbok) in the north empty into the Jordan, while in the centre the Mojib (ancient Arnon) and the Hasa (ancient Zered) pour their waters into the Dead Sea. From the south end of the Dead Sea, some 1,200 feet below sea level, the valley rises steadily to sea level at Aqaba, the only contact Jordan now has with the sea.

In ancient times the country was divided into four districts or kingdoms, that of Edom in the south, stretching from Aqaba to the Wady al Hasa, Moab in the centre, from the Hasa to just north of the Mojib, Ammon from there to the Zerka, and Gilead, north of that to the Yarmuk. These divisions, however, appear fairly late in history, for Jordan was occupied by man from earliest prehistoric times; this early occupation was strikingly illustrated in 1956 by the discovery at Azraq of enormous quantities of **Acheulian hand-axes** and **flakes**, which had hitherto been found only sporadically about the country. Many of the earliest prehistoric sites are in the eastern desert, frequently on the edges of what are now mud flats but may have been lakes in these early times. In **Neolithic** times settlements begin to appear on the plateau and in the mountains, and a site of the pre-pottery culture has recently been discovered at **Petra**, while another of some size is known in the Wady Shaib a few miles west of Al Salt. The many **dolmen** fields scattered up and down the country and in the Jordan Valley are usually attributed to this period. In the following **Chalcolithic** period (about 4500–3000 B.C.), settlements seem to be thicker in the Jordan Valley than on the plateau, though some have been found there.

The Early **Bronze Age** (3000–2100 B.C.) is well represented in both places, and on the plateau a line of settlements stretches from the Yarmuk to Shobak, south of which no sites have yet been found. This line seems to represent a north–south road or trade route, and is the line of what is later described in the Bible as the King's Highway and still later the line of Trajan's great road. The Middle Bronze Age (2100–1500 B.C.), so rich a period in **Palestine**, is but little represented in Jordan; it is a period of invasions, first by the nomad **Amorites**, then by the **Hyksos** and the Egyptians, but except for the first of these, which destroyed the Early Bronze culture, Jordan seemed to be little affected. Some authorities consider the country was virtually uninhabited in this and the succeeding Late Bronze Age (1500–1200 B.C.), but evidence has recently come to light that Ammon at least was well occupied then.

It is about this time that the country begins to appear in the biblical narratives, and the divisions referred to were established. The Israelites in their journey from Egypt passed through Jordan, skirting most of Edom but cutting across a corner of it to attack and defeat the Amorites at Heshbon; they also occupied at least part of Gilead which remained under their control for some centuries. During most of the **Iron Age**, about 1200–330 B.C., the political aspect of Jordan changed hardly at all, with Edom, Moab and Ammon sometimes allied against the Jews, sometimes fighting each other. The Mesha stele found at Dhiban on the Mojib and dating from about 850 B.C. is the only known contemporary version of the other point of view to the biblical account of the war of Omri against Moab. Ammon at least came under the control of Assyria in the seventh century B.C., and of the Babylonians and Persians subsequently. The **Nabataeans** were pushing the Edomites out of their territory into south Palestine, later called Idumea, probably about the fifth century B.C., and from then on it became their kingdom.

The conquests of Alexander the Great in 330 B.C. started a process of standardization in the Middle East which was continued by the Romans. Greek became the language of culture in Jordan as elsewhere and remained so until the rise of Islam. The kingdoms of Moab and Ammon ceased to exist as such and the Nabataeans extended their control northwards until they in turn were absorbed into the Roman Empire in A.D. 106.

K

Ka, *see* Ba.

Kafuan, *see* Africa, Stone Age Man in South.

Kanam Jaw, *see* Africa, East.

Kanjera Skulls, *see* Africa, East.

Kansu is a north-western province of China. This was a main centre of a number of **Neolithic** cultures of importance in the early development of Chinese history, and possibly as a region providing links with cultures to the west. The sites were originally discovered by the Swedish archaeologist, J. G. Andersson who distinguished six groups, the best known being those of Pan-shan and Ma-ch'ang. Pan-shan is a burial area, with a number of cemeteries all situated on hill tops. There are plain wares and painted, as well as a number of pots decorated in relief. Some of the pots seem to have been made on the slow wheel, but most are built up of coils of clay. They have some affinities with Caucasian wares. The paste is a buff one, and about two-thirds of the upper body is decorated with painted designs in black, filled with red. In dishes and bowls only the interior is decorated. The pots were burnished before painting. The relief decoration was made by applying clay to the surface of pots of a greyish paste, apparently fired at lower temperatures than the painted wares. The Ma-ch'ang wares seem on the whole to represent a later and coarser variant of the Pan-shan. *See* colour plate VII, plate 66, page 240.

Karnak, a village on the eastern bank of the Nile, gives its name to one of the magnificent ruined temples once forming part of the ancient Egyptian city of **Thebes**. The great temple of Amun at Karnak was the work of many successive monarchs. The surviving remains are mainly of the eighteenth dynasty. The temple itself, largely erected by Seti I and finished by Ramses II, had a processional hall with massive columns and was profusely decorated with carving and brilliant colouring. Tuthmosis I and Hatshepsut erected great obelisks there; Amenhotep III set up the avenue of ram-headed sphinxes leading from the river to the main gate. The wall surrounding the sacred precinct at Karnak also enclosed a number of smaller temples dedicated to various deities. *See* plates 65, 67, pages 239, 241.

Kassites. The importance of this tribe lies chiefly in the part it played in the history of Babylonia. It was one of the **Elamite** tribes which inhabited the mountainous district east of **Babylon**. The Kassites are identifiable with the Kossaeans of Ptolemy and the Kissians of the older Greek authors. They are recorded as attacking Babylonia in the ninth year of Samsu-iluna, son of **Hammurabi** and in 1780 B.C. they overran it and founded a dynasty there, which lasted for over 570 years. During this period they were gradually absorbed by the Babylonian population: the kings took on Semitic names and married into the royal family of **Assyria.** A Kassite vocabulary has been handed down in a **cuneiform** tablet as well as a list of Kassite names with Semitic equivalents. Some Kassite deities were introduced into the Babylonian pantheon. It is probable that the Kassites introduced the horse, their sacred animal, into Mesopotamia.

Keilor Skull, *see* Fossil Man.

Khmer is the native term for Cambodian. It was probably included in the various ethnic terms subsumed in Chinese sources by the expression **K'un-lun.** The Arab writers use *kmr* and *krm* when referring to Khmer areas of south-east Asia. Linguistically, Khmer forms part of a group of languages extending from India to the borders of Cochin-china (Austro-asiatic) and perhaps as far as New Zealand (Austric). This group consists of a number of tribal languages and two languages of civilization, Khmer and Mon (in the Menam Valley and Lower Burma). There is evidence of significant if not genetic relationship between Khmer and **Cham** (which is basically Malayo-Polynesian). The Khmer seem first to have been a tributary people of **Fu-nan**, inhabiting a state called in Chinese **Chen-la**, centred about the upper portions of the Lower Mekong. At the end of the sixth century A.D. a rebellion brought Chen-la to the hegemony of the Fu-nan Empire and laid the foundations for the great Khmer expansion which was ultimately to control parts of Viet-Nam, Laos and Thailand, and the whole of Cambodia, and to produce the great buildings, such as Angkor Wat, in and about **Siemreap**, and to play a large role in the development of the modern states which once formed part of the Khmer Empire.

Khoisan Peoples, *see* Bushmen.

King Solomon's Mines. Much controversy took place in the nineteenth century over the site of the mines of Solomon, king of Israel in the tenth century B.C. It has now been established that these were at Aqaba, the ancient Ezion-geber, at the head of the Red Sea. Copper and iron ore is to be found in the neighbouring hills and a smelting-plant has been excavated; it is aligned so as to catch the full blast of the violent winds blowing down from the north, and thus to obtain a forced draught without the need for a bellows system.

Knossos in Crete is a site of paramount importance in the history of archaeology, because it has revealed the outlines of the very earliest European civilization. Hardly any traces of this civilization had been discovered until 1900, when Sir Arthur **Evans** began to make excavations here. The civilization was named by him the **Minoan**, because Minos had been, according to Greek historians, one of the early rulers of Knossos.

Knossos was occupied in Neolithic times and from about 2500 B.C., the period known as Early Minoan I, was characterized by incised and painted pottery which shows a strong influence from Asia

Minor. The next 500 years – up to 2000 B.C. – saw great advances in building, carving, painting and pottery. Then came the Middle Minoan period – roughly contemporary with the Middle Kingdom in Egypt – and it was then that the palace of Minos was built and though it was subsequently destroyed and rebuilt many times, the general plan was never changed from that of a succession of courtyards with blocks of buildings round them in a rather haphazard arrangement.

By the end of the Middle Minoan II age the palace had been destroyed by earthquake, not conquest, the proof of which is that the civilization continued to flourish without a break. By Middle Minoan III it had developed into an even more brilliant stage, but the forces of nature once more intervened. The palace had been rebuilt, but about 1550 B.C. was once more hurled to the ground and yet again reconstructed. Many houses have been found at Knossos almost as remarkable as the palace, and even though they have not been excavated on a large scale, models of them have been found showing their size and advanced design.

Pictures of the people of Knossos are numerous, showing their activities, their pastimes and their clothes. They seem to have written two kinds of linear script (*see* **Minoan Scripts**), now to be seen in accounts and lists of property. But most information about the civilization is to be gained from paintings. These throw a great deal of light on religion, which chiefly took the form of a worship of the powers of nature.

This interest in nature spreads itself to Minoan art, which is much more concerned with natural phenomena than most forms of ancient art. Landscapes in fresco have often been found, with birds, animals and plants as prominent features. Painting on vases shows flowers executed with great delicacy and charm. Seascapes are quite common, and there is a bathroom at Knossos with walls covered by pictures of dolphins.

Knossos reached its zenith between 1550 and 1400 B.C. There are many sites at and near Knossos which show the remarkable standards achieved, including some superb villas and a very wide range of frescos, pictures and stone houses.

In about 1400 the palace of Knossos was burnt down, and most of the other great buildings were destroyed. The city was no longer the centre of cultural advance, now that the power of **Mycenae** had spread all over the Aegean regions. The palaces of Knossos were restored, but the whole island of Crete rivalled them in prosperity and culture. There were still no signs of any marked departure from the typical Minoan civilization, until the Late Minoan period, which ended during the twelfth century B.C.

During the **Iron Age** the palace of Knossos lay in ruins, its site never again to be built on. The art of this later time still shows signs of the old Minoan tradition, but iron was now in use and the marked individuality of Minoan civilization begins to fade from the scene. Greek art from the mainland asserted itself, and in Knossos there are many superb examples of it, such as polychrome vases, figures and sculpture. These bear many traces of the old Minoan spirit, but they also show the marks of oriental influence and motives, such as were shown in the art of Greece herself.

The palace of Minos, as excavated by Sir Arthur **Evans**, will always remain one of the great triumphs of archaeology. It includes an elaborate drainage system, huge storage space for wine and oil, a great central courtyard, a pillared hall, a throne room and a vast number of apartments. The walls were of limestone, the columns of timber or limestone, and much of the palace was decorated with magnificent frescos. It must have made Knossos the most remarkable city of the age, and given it a precedence over all other cities which has perhaps never since been rivalled. (*See also* **Labyrinth** and **Minotaur.**) *See* plates 68, 70, pages 242–244.

Kofun, *see* Japan, Prehistoric.

Koldewey, Robert (1855–1925), was a German architect whose interest in classical archaeology and architectural history first took him to work with his American friend F.H. Bacon at the **acropolis** of Assos which he both planned and drew in 1862–3. His call to archaeological field-work was confirmed by working at Lesbos, an island south of Troas (**Troy**), for the German Archaeological Institute. His first visit to **Iraq** was in 1887 when he was sent to make soundings at Surghul and El Hibba on behalf of the Berlin Museum.

After working at Neandria, Koldewey was recalled to accompany von Luschan's expedition to Sinjirli (Sam'al) in north Syria. Here his architectural skill had full play and he was able to make both surveys, plans, drawings and reconstructions of the site. This work was interrupted by his journeys in

Sicily and southern Italy with Puchstein to record the Greek temples there. The publication of these took up many years, otherwise occupied by teaching at Gorlitz.

In 1897 the German Orient Society (Deutsche Orient-Gesellschaft) became anxious to select sites in Mesopotamia for systematic excavations by Germans, and was encouraged in this both by the success of the French and British undertakings and by the desire to acquire **cuneiform** tablets which by that time were coming to Western museums in large numbers from excavations and from dealers in Baghdad. Accordingly it despatched Sachau and Koldewey to make a survey; they covered most of the principal sites of Iraq and reported most favourably on Baghdad.

On 26 March, 1899, Koldewey began the excavation of the ancient city of **Babylon** which was to occupy him, with but few interruptions, for eighteen years. His expedition was well equipped, being the first both to use a light railway to move the earth clear of the site and also to employ more than 200 men. He developed a system of wall-tracing and simple **stratification** which can be said to have inaugurated the era of scientific excavation in Iraq. However, his architectural interests, for which he had been chosen to lead the expedition, meant that the results, hard and slowly won and published only in sections year by year, did little to stimulate support. He was thought also to be too prone not to search walls and foundations for their hidden foundation records lest the buildings be disfigured. It must be remembered that he worked at a time when most Middle Eastern excavations were prized either for the antiquities they could send back to museums or for the inscriptions they could provide for the Assyriologists, and his expedition had no trained linguist with it. With the commencement of work at Qalah Shergat (Ashur) in 1903 some of his ablest German colleagues, including Andrae, were moved north and after five years of continuous work on the difficult site his health broke down. Before this Koldewey had explored Borsippa (Birs Nimrud) where the **ziggurat** drew his special attention. He made successful soundings at Fara and Abu Hatab (Kisurra). At the former **Jemdet Nasr** pottery, archaic inscribed tablets, tombs, seals and remains of buildings rewarded his decision to reopen a site judged of little value by Hilprecht only two years earlier.

Koldewey did not merely bring an architect's skill and classical experience to work in Babylonia and then develop a technique suited to the local conditions. His work at the vast site of Babylon revealed for the first time to both scholars and laymen an ancient oriental city, hitherto known only from the Bible and classical authors, with its massive fortifications, and its complex street and royal buildings, and he made the great city of Nebuchadnezzar II come to life in a new way. His work, which ended with the advance of British troops up the Euphrates in 1917, was to prove a standard and inspiration for renewed efforts at other sites by scholars of many different countries.

Köln-Lindenthal is a site on the western outskirts of the modern Cologne map, once inhabited by a race of peasants of the Danubian culture. It is the only one of the prehistoric settlements of Europe which archaeologists have now completely excavated and is therefore of outstanding importance.

It was found that houses and other buildings had utterly disappeared but enough traces of the settlement could be identified for a complete plan of the whole to be made. This was possible by taking careful note of all the discolourations in the subsoil which were caused by the filling-in of holes into which posts had been driven, and of ditches and other man-made hollows.

The reconstruction of the whole plan finally showed a number of dwellings of no very precise uniform arrangement, with floors scooped out of the earth and walls and roofs of light material. There were rectangular barns as much as thirty-six yards or more in length and a number of small buildings raised on piles, which were probably used to store grain. They were sited close to the dwellings.

Over a period of two or three hundred years, the settlement had been occupied on four separate occasions. Every now and then it had been abandoned by the inhabitants so that they could cultivate fresh areas of land, in a way that was quite normal for agricultural practice of the time. The original settlement seems to have had no defences and occupied a roughly circular stretch of ground on either side of a shallow valley. The second settlement appears to have been inhabited by some 300 people and was surrounded by a small ditch, which was also planned to divide the village into two parts.

The third settlement covered only the southern side of the whole site and was considerably smaller in size, having space for only some seventy persons.

The fourth and last settlement was better defended than any of the others. The houses and grain stores were surrounded by a ditch which also had an inner palisade, and the site was certainly able to accommodate more people. They may have numbered up to some 300.

Excavation of the site has shown that all the four communities must have been mainly self-supporting. There are, however, traces of pottery being traded up and down the Rhine and of some green material for axes brought from the Taurus Mountains.

The system of agriculture was that common to the whole Danubian civilization, as it spread through Poland, Galicia, Moravia, down to the mouth of the Vistula, and over Germany to the Rhineland. It depended on the burning of recessive patches of forest land, which could then be cultivated until the potash obtained from the charcoal was exhausted. The site was then abandoned, fresh forest trees were planted, and the whole process was repeated.

This necessitated not only the frequent moves from one cultivated plot to another, but also the shift of the whole population of the settlement, complete with its buildings.

The Danubian I culture lasted from about 3000 to 2500 B.C. and covered part of the **Neolithic** stage of European pre-history. The Danubians at this stage spread very rapidly over eastern Europe and Köln-Lindenthal marks one of the furthest eastern points that was reached.

Korea. Although Korean sources claim a long and venerable history for their country, this is not yet confirmed by other means. There is evidence of tribal cultures and settlements, and a probability that both **Yueh** and even **Ainu** strains were present in the **Neolithic** period, and some influence from China in the first millennium B.C. is observable. But the most important developments took place with the expansion of the Han Empire when colonies were established in north-west Korea, from one of which, Lo lang (Lak lang), Japanese archaeologists, excavating a necropolis, revealed Han objects of outstanding merit and interest. In addition to **lacquer** objects, of great importance for the early history of this technique, bronze mirrors, jewellery, images, etc., testify to the wealth and culture of the Han. From these colonies Chinese influence spread into Manchuria and to southern Korea. In the south two native kingdoms developed, Silla and Paekche, and the introduction of rice-cultivation by hand-tillage provided a staple crop which served as a basis for expansion. Confucianism and Buddhism were both introduced from China. With the end of the Han dynasty, and the collapse of the colonies, Silla expanded until in Tang times and with Tang support it ruled almost the whole of the present Korea. Kyongju became a cultural centre of great importance (the observatory there, built in the sixth to seventh centuries A.D., is one of the earliest in the world.) Korea played a significant role in the history of the Far East because its position between China and Japan enabled it to serve as a cultural intermediary. Its sailors seem also to have played an important part in east–west trade in the centuries before the development of ocean-going Chinese shipping.

Kra, Isthmus of. This narrow neck of land across the Thai-Malay Peninsula affords an easy land connection, "a few hours' ride on a bicycle", from the Bay of Bengal to the Gulf of Thailand, thus enabling early voyagers to avoid the long passage through pirate-infested waters of the Malacca Strait. It seems that the towns of Takua-pa (probably the Takkola of Indian texts) and Ch'aiya were the important termini. It has indeed been claimed that the latter was a key centre for the dissemination of Indian culture to the countries of south-east Asia in the early centuries of the Christian era. The Wat Na Pra Tat at Jaya seems to be a seventh-century foundation which has some affinities with early Indo-Javanese temples. From this area too are a number of important Hindu and Buddhist images dating from the ninth and tenth centuries and there are similar finds from Takua-pa perhaps slightly earlier in date.

Krater. A mixing-bowl for wine.

K'un-lun. This word, found in Chinese texts relating to south-east Asia, is an ethnic term which seems to apply to a number of peoples who are characterized by a "black" skin and frizzy hair. Their habitat was essentially a littoral one, and there is reason to think that they were, in the widest sense, Indonesians, although their kingdoms were generally on the mainland of the region. Their geographical location and their maritime skills made them important contributors to the cultural history of south-east Asia and south China. (There are also pointers to a connection with the Kao-li of Korea.) By association, and as a conventional Chinese transcription, the term k'un-lun is also applied to the **Khmer.** Later, by extension, because of physical resemblances, the term was used by Chinese writers for African Negroes. The connection with the Khmer was also justified because of the parallel between the mythical K'un-lun Mountain of Chinese cosmology and the mountain cult, assimilated with the Indian Meru, of the Khmer kingdoms. The position of the original Indonesian k'un-lun kingdoms on the coast gave them an important position in early east-west maritime trade and the establishment of ports and markets in their territories led to contacts with foreign cultures, notably those from India, which were disseminated into the interior of the south-east Asian mainland. (It was by such means that the Khmer, the successors to the first K'un-lun, obtained their indianized culture.) The Chinese sources seem to suggest that the first three or four centuries of the Christian era were the period in which this k'un-lun culture played a decisive role in the development of south-east Asian history.

Kuyunjik, *see* Nineveh.

L

Labyrinth, *see* Minotaur.

Lachish. In 1890, when Flinders **Petrie** first went to **Palestine**, he excavated at Tell el-Hesi, supposing it to be the site of ancient Lachish, a city of considerable importance in biblical times. However, the suggestion made by Albright in 1929 has been confirmed by more recent discoveries, and the city is now identified with Tell ed-Duweir, a mound lying some twenty-five miles south-west of Jerusalem. The first full scale excavation of the site was undertaken under the leadership of J.L. Starkey from 1932 until it came to a premature end with his murder in 1938. The summit of the **tell** occupies some eighteen acres, and owing to the fact that a considerable time was devoted to clearing areas off the summit to justify their later use as dumps, only a relatively small area on the tell has been excavated. Due to this the Early **Bronze Age** is only represented by a number of cave dwellings outside the city wall, but though the tell seems to have been deserted in the earlier part of the Middle Bronze Age, fortifications typical of the **Hyksos** appear later. During the Late Bronze Age (about 1500–1200 B.C.) the city expanded and a small temple, now given the name of the Fosse Temple, was built over the older fortifications. It is probably to Joshua that the violent destruction of this temple, in about 1220 B.C., is to be attributed. The mound seems to have been deserted for about two centuries after this and, while there are traces of building of perhaps the time of David, the main **Iron Age** fortifications were probably built by Rehoboam, Solomon's son. These consisted of a ring wall round the summit of the mound, and another, over fifty feet down the slope, with a gate on the west side, protected by a bastion. This was probably the form of the fortifications at the time of its capture by Sennacherib in 701 B.C., an event depicted on bas-reliefs from his capital at **Nineveh**. The neo-Babylonians were the cause of the next destruction. Nebuchadnezzar had partially destroyed Lachish in 598 B.C. but this was far exceeded in violence by the final sack in 589 B.C., when there are signs of a fierce conflagration. It is to the period shortly before this destruction that the most famous finds at Lachish, twenty-one **ostraca** inscribed in Hebrew, belong. Some of these are dispatches to the governor of the city from an outpost some miles away, concerning the troubled state of the country under Babylonian attack. The great importance of these ostraca is due to the fact that they represent about a hundred lines of readable Hebrew from the time of Jeremiah, and therefore provide valuable linguistic material for comparison with the contemporary Bible books, which are only preserved to us in relatively late manuscripts. Following the destruction by the Babylonians, there was a long period during which the mound was virtually abandoned, and the last major structure uncovered was a palace of the Persian period, being perhaps one of the residencies of "Geshem the Arabian" (Nehemiah **6,** 1), governor of the province of Idumea.

Lacquer. The basis of lacquer is a gummy sap obtained from a variety of trees. Originally grey in colour, the sap hardens in moist air to a jet black solid. (Sunlight and temperatures inhibit the hardening process.) The natural colour can be modified by the addition of various dye-stuffs: sulphide of mercury (cinnabar) yields red; arsenic sulphides (realgar and orpiment) produce yellow and orange; the addition of indigo to these produces green. Silver dust can also be used as a colorative, and gold-leaf can readily be applied as a surface decoration.

Lacquer forms an impermeable surface, and its original use may have been to produce water-proof containers; the application of lacquer to basket-work by filling the interstices is in fact the basis of all lacquer techniques. A framework is constructed from horse-hair or split bamboo, and the major gaps are filled with a suitable filler: clay in the case of coarse work, fine vegetable ash for work of fine quality. Layer after layer of the gummy substance is applied to this base and each layer is allowed to harden, either in an underground cellar or by being buried, before being polished prior to the application of the next layer. The base colour is usually black. The process is a lengthy one and a fine piece may take six months or more to complete. Decoration is by incision, the lines being filled with various colours, gilding or embossing.

The earliest surviving specimens are from **Korea** where they were found in tombs of the Han period and date from about 50 B.C. to A.D. 50. Some of these pieces have inscriptions indicating that they were made near Cheng-tu, Sze-chwan. It seems likely therefore that lacquer was originally a non-Chinese technique which achieved international fame and distribution after the Chinese absorption of the area of its original manufacture. From here it spread, through Chinese conquest and cultural influence, throughout the mainland of Further Asia. In addition to its use for the manufacture of containers of every sort, it was used as a general surface fixative – for example, in the gold-leaf industry – and as a water-proofing medium for such things as boats and umbrellas.

Lagash. This city was the centre of one of the oldest cultures of **Sumerian** civilization. The site, first discovered in 1877 by Ernest de Sarzec, French consul in Basra, and subsequently excavated by him, is three miles east of Shatt al Haï and ten miles north of the town of Shatra.

Its era of greatest importance was in the fourth millennium B.C. when it was ruled by independent kings, while later, under Sargon and his successors, it was governed by dependent rulers known as patesis. It remained a great centre of artistic development, however, its art reaching a high peak under the patesi Gudea (about 2700 B.C.). Gudea's records also indicate great commercial activity during his reign: they recount that cedars were brought from the mountains of Amanus and Lebanon, diorite from eastern Arabia, and copper and gold from central and southern Arabia and Sinai. After Gudea, Lagash apparently lost its importance; nothing more is known of it until the construction of a Greek or Seleucid period fortress on the ruins, when it seems to have belonged to the Greek kingdom of Characene.

Much material of great interest has been excavated on the site. Among early works are the famous Stele of the Vultures (*see* plate 90, page 284) and a great silver vase decorated with the Lagash "coat of arms". From a later period are numerous statues of Gudea and bas-reliefs of outstanding quality. Excavations of what had been palace and temple storehouses of the earliest Sumerian period have revealed vessels, weapons and sculpture and a great diversity of other objects. De Sarzec also discovered about thirty thousand clay tablets – the temple archives – recording minute details of temple administration. *See* plate 71, page 245.

Lake Dwellings. Prehistoric man often built dwellings at the side of lakes on marshy ground. Such dwellings have been found on the edges of Swiss and German lakes; they date from **Neolithic** times, about 2800 B.C. On the Federsee Lake in Germany both Neolithic and **Bronze Age** settlements have been found. Similar settlements of **Iron Age** times in the British Isles are called **Crannogs**.

Lamma Island, Hongkong. Investigations here, notably by Father D. J. Finn, have revealed a series of cultural remains with a surprisingly wide range of affinities. The material seems to represent two main traditions, one a Neolithic one, with soft pottery, the other bronze with a much harder ware; but there is some evidence to indicate that these are in part contemporary and that one has to deal with different cultural traditions and possibly different ethnic groups, rather than with any major interval in time. Although some of the objects found may belong to an earlier period, the bulk of the objects seem to be of the Ch'in or Han periods, approximately the last three centuries B.C. and persisting for a little into the Christian era. There are traces of connections with the **Yang-shao** culture of the Chinese Neolithic, and also with the Shang material from **Anyang**, but these should probably be seen as southern survivals, being perhaps derivatives. The decoration of the pottery seems to belong to a bronze tradition, probably of southern origin, perhaps to be associated with the kingdom of Ch'u. The stone adzes from Lamma are all of the rectangular or square section type, and should therefore belong to Heine Geldern's group of Austronesians, who, in his view, moved from south-west China to south-east Asia and from Malaya spread in two groups, one through Sumatra and Java to Papua and Australasia, the other through **Borneo** and the **Philippines** to Japan. He places these movements in the second millennium B.C., but the Hong-kong evidence would argue for a considerably later date. Other finds include bronze adzes (one has forty per cent iron in the alloy) and moulds made from local fire-clay, arrow- and spear-heads in stone and bronze, stone rings, bracelets, discs and a number of swords and daggers of various types which include the Chinese *ko* or dagger-axe which was mounted as a halberd. The finds show that Hong-kong and its vicinity was a meeting point for cultures with connections to the Eurasiatic steppe, China proper, Indonesia, Indo-china and the Polynesian islands of the Pacific.

Laos. The relative neglect of Laos in archaeological research programmes is unfortunate, for its position places it upon a main migration route for Thai-speaking peoples, and what is known of its prehistory suggests that it had earlier experienced both palaeo-Melanesian and Indonesian cultural influences.

The prehistoric material from Laos falls into two categories. From the neighbourhood of Luang-prabang come crude **stone tools** of a **Hoa-binh**ian type. It seems likely that the material from Khammouane province belongs to a later stage of the south-east Asian **Neolithic**. The skeletal material from the caves of Mahaxay was accompanied by axes which are comparable with **Bac-son**ian finds. There is also material which suggests a comparison with the coastal kitchen-midden sites of central Viet-Nam, and marine shells in the Laotian sites prove the existence of trade routes across the Annamite Chain. The next prehistoric phase is represented by the **megalithic** cultures of the Tran-ninh Plateau. (These sites seem to belong wholly to a period after the introduction of metal into south-east Asia and were apparently in use as burial places, perhaps by others than their original founders until at least the tenth century A.D.) The most characteristic feature is the use of large stone burial urns, a fact which may link the Tran-ninh culture with that of **Celebes** and also with the Pyu of Burma. Finds include glass beads, ceramics (some of Chinese origin), bronze and iron objects, the latter probably manufactured locally. Some of the stone objects have clearly been worked by metal tools. There is evidence to suggest that the use of stone urns gradually gave way to rock-cut graves and earthenware urns.

The earliest historical cultures of Laos show connections with the south, with **Chen-la.** The most important site is that of Wat Phu in Champassak, a region which seems to have come under more sophisticated cultural influences in the sixth to seventh centuries A.D. These higher cultures reached Vientiane by the tenth to twelfth centuries A.D. and Luang Prabang by the twelfth to fourteenth centuries A.D. There is evidence, from the region of Keng-kok, Savannakhet, of direct **Cham** influences. Wat Phu, some nine miles from Bassac, is a mountain temple which probably dates from the sixth century A.D. and was originally dedicated to Siva, apparently as some form of royal linga (phallic symbol) cult. This association of linga, mountain and royalty is a fundamental concept of Khmer kingship and may have achieved architectural expression for the first time at Wat Phu. The shrine was apparently associated with a spring. Additions were made to it in the eleventh and twelfth centuries. As the result of major collapses of part of the structure a considerable rebuilding scheme was begun, but before it was completed the Khmer power waned and the temple passed into the hands of the Laotians who turned it into a Buddhist shrine with a monastery. (*See also* **Khmer.**)

Lascaux, in the Dordogne department of France, ranks with **Altamira** as one of the two richest painted caves of the Upper **Palaeolithic**. Sealed and hidden for thousands of years, its paintings wonderfully preserved in the stable atmosphere, the cave was not discovered until 1940. An up-rooted tree had left a hole in the ground on a scrubby hilltop above the Vézère River and the small town of Montignac. A dog fell into the hole; one of a party of boys who were rabbiting slithered to its rescue and found himself in a gallery bright with colours.

No district is so prolific in habitation sites and decorated caves. The valley of the Vézère running between cliffs gave shelter from the winds of the last **Ice Age**. Strung along the river below Montignac are the famous sites of Le Moustier (**Mousterian** culture), Laugerie Basse, Laugerie Haute, and **Cro-Magnon**. The carved horses of Cap Blanc and the decorated caves of Rouffignac, La Mouthe, Les Combarelles, Font-de-Gaume and Bernifal are not far away.

The last named cave at Bernifal offers an analogy helpful in describing Lascaux. When he discovered this little cave deep in the woods, the explorer climbed in by a shaft which cannot have been the original entrance. Afterwards he found the original entrance, which had been blocked, or so it appeared, by the men who had frequented Bernifal; the inference being that caves were not so much open temples as secret places of occasional resort for religious rituals. One is reminded of the "family caves" shown to Thor Heyerdahl on **Easter Island** – caves carefully covered and concealed, the whereabouts of which were liable to be forgotten.

A crowd of tourists eagerly waiting in the intense sunshine outside the concrete steps and concrete portal of Lascaux rather destroys such an impression of the secrecy of religious awe. The impression returns when the doors are shut behind the visitor and he finds himself in the main hall, in the presence of huge bulls and cows. The cave is by no means enormous, the roof is not very high, the passages are not very wide or very long. Lascaux, in fact, is a miniature system compared with some of the other caves which contain decorated chambers – for instance, Niaux, or Les Trois Frères, Pech Merle, or the nearby Rouffignac. None the less, Lascaux was a long while in use, is crowded with animals, engraved, drawn and painted, and must have served important groups of the cattle and horse hunting people of the neighbourhood.

Predominantly the Lascaux animals are oxen, horses, and red deer – with some ibex and bison. Style, species and **carbon fourteen dating** combine to affirm a much earlier date for Lascaux than for the flamboyant polychromes of Altamira. The Altamira bison are late **Magdalenian**. Most of the Lascaux animals are western **Gravettian**, painted somewhere about 18,000 B.C.; the work, that is to say, of those immigrant hunter peoples of Homo sapiens stock who came to the west from the eastern steppes and the plains and adapted themselves to a less open milieu, where they added painting and engraving on the freely available limestone surfaces to their older accomplishments in sculpture. The later Magdalenian hunters of France and Switzerland and Germany (though not the Magdalenians of Spain) were specialists adapted to hunting reindeer. The western Gravettians of Lascaux enjoyed a less bitter climate, hunting animals of brush-steppe and semi-woodland.

Neighbouring caves give pictorial evidence of the change to a colder climate. In Bernifal there are well-drawn mammoths, in Font-de-Gaume mammoths, reindeer and woolly rhinoceros, in Rouffignac mammoths by the score and family parties of rhinoceros. All these are tundra creatures. The woolly rhinoceros walked with head down, a species adapted to grazing low tundra vegetation. In Lascaux in the celebrated group of drawings in the "Well", there is one rhinoceros with head raised and differently set – Merck's Rhinoceros, it has been suggested, a species preceding the woolly rhino of the tundra and differently adapted for feeding on loftier vegetation.

The art of Lascaux is of mixed quality. The huge oxen, for example, have a lumpy, ungainly quality. Red deer are drawn or engraved with a grace and an elegance proper to their kind, particularly in the frieze of "Swimming Deer", a series of heads depicted above a horizontal cleft in the rock in such a way as to suggest that they are swimming a river. Wild horses are drawn and painted with a particular sprightliness and calligraphic freedom.

The paintings show direct evidence of hunting. Rectangles drawn by the feet of oxen can most reasonably be interpreted as tread-traps. Feathered spears stick in the flanks of horses. If the frieze of antlered deer is rightly interpreted, that also may be evidence of hunting, on the supposition that Upper Palaeolithic huntsmen, like hunters of other times, liked to attack fast moving animals when a river slowed them down. In several cases – suggestive again of ritual use and long frequentation – animal images in Lascaux are painted one over another, as if the ritual importance lay in the act of painting an animal, rather than in the painted image after it had been finished.

All in all, Lascaux impresses one with its sheer

amount of *life* – lively sensitive creatures of an ancient and scarcely conceivable world preserved here by acts of man's imaginative power and the intimacy of his knowledge. The effect here is richer than at Altamira, where the more gorgeously coloured animals are concentrated on a roof which it is awkward to examine. Here the animals stretch left and right along the walls, some of them at eye-level. They are designed with less elaboration; so their reds, browns, yellows and blacks – their earth colours – attack the eye with a more immediate insistence. There is, after all, more sense of an important shrine inside Lascaux than inside any cave. Though it has been denied, it seems likely that many of the paintings will fade in years to come. *See* colour plate VIII.

La Tène, *see* Tène, La.

Layard, Austen Henry (1817–94). Sir Austen Layard's boyhood was spent in France, Italy, Switzerland and England and he early showed a love for travel and adventure. In 1839 after six years confined to a solicitor's office in England he set out with a friend to go overland to Ceylon where his father had served. In his travels through Iraq and Persia he noted many ruins and on being forced to go back to Constantinople in 1842 he there interested the British Ambassador, in whose temporary employ he was, in his scheme to explore the ruins of Assyria. Sir Stratford Canning gave Layard sixty pounds and he rode to Mosul. From 1845 to 1847 Layard, with only the assistance of Hormuzd Rassam, directed the local Arabs in excavation at **Nimrud** (which he first thought to be Nineveh) and later at **Nineveh** (Kuyunjik).

Layard's return to England in 1848, and the publication of his *Nineveh and Its Remains*, and *Illustrations of the Monuments of Nineveh* in 1848–49 did much to arouse public interest in Assyrian discoveries and to encourage further excavations by the British Museum. In 1849–50 he continued exploration, sending many cases of antiquities to England from Assyria, and from Babylonia where he made soundings at Babylon, Borsippa, Nippur and other sites. Thanks to Layard the British Museum has the first collection of Assyrian antiquities in the Western World. Moreover, stacked a foot deep in one room at Nineveh, Layard came upon tablets inscribed in the **cuneiform** script which were found to be part of the royal library of Ashur-bani-pal. These texts, together with the copies of the monumental inscriptions still standing, enabled **Rawlinson** and others to progress rapidly in the decipherment and reading of the **Accadian** and **Sumerian** languages.

From 1851 onwards Layard turned to politics, being for a time Under-Secretary of State for Foreign Affairs and Ambassador to Constantinople. He never lost his interest in the East and after retiring to Venice he wrote up from his journals his *Early Adventures in Persia, Susiana and Babylonia.* This classic of travel literature was re-issued after his death in 1894. *See* plate 72, page 246.

Le Moustier, *see* Mousterian.

Lepsius, Karl Richard (1810–84), was born at Naumburg-am-Saale in Germany on 23 December, 1810, the son of a state official. He studied classics, philology (including Sanskrit) and archaeology at the universities of Leipzig, Göttingen and Berlin. Then followed three years in Paris during which he broadened his education and mastered the craft of lithography, wrote his first musical composition, invented a standard alphabet for writing foreign languages in Roman script, and, encouraged by Baron von Bunsen (1791–1860), began in 1834 to study **Coptic** and Egyptian **hieroglyphics.** Between 1836 and 1842 he visited all the main European collections of Egyptian antiquities, making paper-squeezes of a large number of inscriptions and copying papyri. He interested himself particularly in chronology and in funerary texts, to which he gave the name **Book of the Dead.** He also discovered the canon of proportions in Egyptian sculpture, but did not develop fully his discovery. On returning to Berlin he obtained, through Baron A. de Humboldt, the financial support of Frederick William IV of Prussia for an expedition consisting of himself and nine artists and technicians to visit Egypt, Nubia and Sinai in order to record all possible historical and religious inscriptions and to collect antiquities. The results of the expedition were published in twelve large volumes with 894 plates, entitled *Denkmäler aus Ägypten und Äthiopien* (1849–59). While in **Nubia** he learnt the Nubian language, of which he published a grammar, in the vain hope that it would provide the key to the decipherment of Meroitic. On his second visit to Egypt in 1866 he discovered the **Canopus Decree,** a bilingual text in Greek and Egyptian, second in importance only to the **Rosetta Stone** (*see* plate 119, page 385).

He was appointed Keeper of the Egyptian Collection in Berlin in 1865 and Director of the National Library in 1873. Apart from the *Denkmäler* he published nearly 150 books and articles, mostly on Egyptology. He died in Berlin on 10 July, 1884.

Lerma Points, *see* America, Early Man in.

Leubingen, near Sömmerda, Thuringia. The tumulus near Leubingen is one of a group of outstandingly rich burials in the Saale region of the sixteenth century B.C. These represent the taking over of the first true **Bronze Age** types by nomadic warriors using battle-axes and cord-ornamented pottery. The bronze users spread from the east along the Elbe and crossed over into the Saale basin. The tumulus itself (one of the largest in Thuringia), excavated at the end of the nineteenth century, originally had a diameter of thirty-seven yards, a height of nine and a half yards and a circumference of 157 yards. Three different layers were shown in the excavation, the uppermost containing Slav burials. This was followed by a sterile earth layer, almost five yards thick, while under this was a cairn more than two yards high which covered the primary burial. The surface of the ground had been carefully paved with stones set in the clay subsoil, around which a ditch of twenty-two yards diameter served as a boundary for the cairn, and under this was a rectangular wooden lean-to in the form of an inverted v. The ridge of lean-to was supported at the southern end by a heavy upright, while seven lighter posts supported each side with another four serving to carry the planks which closed the south end of the chamber, the northern end being left open. The planks which formed the sides had been made by splitting small tree trunks, the gaps between them being filled with clay. Over all was a layer of thatch, while around the whole area covered by the tumulus, there were traces of burning, indicating that ceremonial fires had been built before the construction of the grave – a habit in evidence from **Neolithic** times.

Inside the mortuary house and lying on a floor of boards was the extended skeleton of an old man. Across him at right angles was found another skeleton, that of a girl of about ten years old. By the man's left side were found the fragments of a pot surrounded by a setting of stones which owing to the scarcity of building material in the region must have been brought from some considerable distance away. Other fragments of pottery seem to give evidence for a funerary feast. Near the urn lay a hone and a perforated stone adze of serpentine resembling in form the grubbing axes of the Late Neolithic Danubian farmers. The man had originally held in his right hand a bronze halberd fixed in a wooden haft, a form manufactured in quantity by the first bronze-smiths of the copper-rich south of Ireland. Nearby were found three round heeled daggers, a type ancestral to the earliest daggers of the British **Bronze Age**, and exported from central Germany to the comparable warrior chieftains of Wessex. The Leubingen daggers had originally had handles of wood, while one had been contained in a sheath of oak bark, the other two in leather sheaths. Other bronzes included two axes with low side flanges and three bronze chisels. With the girl were found two gold pins with bent ends, eye heads and zigzag ornaments on the upper part, a type typical in bronze in the Unetice culture of central Europe, whose spread into central Germany was the impetus for the metal-using chieftains of Saxo-Thuringia. Also found were a pair of recurved wire finger rings, and a spirally wound hair ring, as well as a massive chased bracelet also of gold and also typical of the Unětice culture.

The wealth of the Saale/Elbe region seems to have been based on two factors, first the local salt and secondly its advantageous position at the crossing of the long distance trade routes, one of these being the amber route from Jutland to the Adriatic and on to **Mycenaean** Greece, while westward as we have seen, the continental bronze-smiths influenced Britain and Ireland from whence must have come at least some of the gold, copper and tin as well as actual objects themselves.
See plate 73, page 247.

Levalloisian. This **Palaeolithic** culture, named after its type-site, a suburb of Paris, dates back to the third **glaciation** (approximately 230,000 years ago). It was located in both France and England. Levalloisian Man made great advances in the manufacture of **stone tools**, principally in the form of **flakes**. It is characteristic of the culture that the **cores** from which the flakes were struck were carefully prepared first so that the ultimate shape of the flake could better be controlled. At some stages of the culture large broad flakes predominated; at others, narrow blade-like ones. Late Levalloisian points were intended for mounting as spear-heads and were probably the earliest implements to be treated like this.

Ligor. This site, at Nak'on Sitamarat, south Thailand, on the east side of the peninsula in a bay which could serve as a port for trade across the Gulf of Thailand and farther east, seems to have formed part of the Further Asian trading system from perhaps the second century A.D. Its importance was probably due to its function as a point of trans-shipment for goods which were taken by land across the peninsula to avoid the long haul around the south with the ever-present threat of piracy in the narrow waters of the straits. During the eighth century A.D. it formed part of the commercial empire of Srivijaya which seems to have been centred upon Sumatra, perhaps with its capital near Palembang. An inscription from Ligor dated A.D. 775 is crucially important for the history of Sumatra and for that of the Sailendra dynasty of Java. Finds from Ligor and its vicinity testify to its importance as a centre of Mahayana Buddhism, and suggest that the entrepôt trade was an important aspect in the spread of Indian religions through south-east Asia.

Linear A and B, *see* Minoan Scripts.

Lingua Franca. The common language of an area or empire, whose peoples speak a number of different languages.

Lipari, *see* Mediterranean, the Western.

Lopburi on the Menam River, north of Ayuthia, in Thailand was probably the largest **Khmer** city outside Cambodia proper, with the exception of Pimai on the Mun River near Korat. Two cultures are represented here: that of the Khmer Empire and that of the Kingdom of Dvaravati. This should probably be associated with speakers of the **Mon** language, now confined largely to Lower Burma. The surviving buildings at Lopburi belong either to the Khmer period, or later when Thai kings seem to have encouraged the use of Khmer styles in official buildings. It is noteworthy, however, that the Khmer style as exemplified at Lopburi is clearly of Cambodian origin, but the forms which it takes owe much to a distinctive Lopburi school whose origins are to be traced to the Dvaravati period which is best represented at such sites as Nakom Pra, Pathom. The connections between the delta and Lopburi are attested by a large number of terracottas which testify to a school of native art of a non-Indian tradition, and an amount of statuary which predates the eleventh century A.D. when this region became part of the Khmer Empire. Prehistoric tools of **Hoa-binh** type have also been found at Lopburi, but there is no evidence of a continuity of occupation until the beginning of the sixth century A.D. The earliest known Mon inscription (seventh or eighth century A.D.) also comes from Lopburi.

Lost Wax Process, *see* Cire Perdue Process.

Lotus. The lotus flower was, in ancient days, a symbol of Upper Egypt. Representations of both the white lotus (*Nymphaea Lotus L.*) and the blue lotus (*Nymphaea caerulea*) have been found on Old Kingdom monuments. The white lotus was believed to have cooling properties and people wore them on their foreheads and carried them in their hands. Both species were used for making garlands, decorating banqueting rooms, wearing on festive occasions, and giving as tributes to the dead.

The lotus was widely used as a motif in art and architecture throughout Egyptian history. Capitals of columns were made in the form of lotus buds and flowers (*see* plate 67, page 241). **Faience** beads, used during the New Kingdom and later for floral collars, were made to look like single blue lotus petals, or sometimes complete flowers.

Lung-men is a series of caves, about ten miles south of Lo-yang, north Honan, which had become the capital of China in A.D. 495. The sculptors of the period cut Buddhist cave shrines into the limestone cliffs, the oldest being that of Ku-yang. The style is a development of that from the sandstone caves of **Yün-kang**, but greater experience and a more satisfactory material enabled the artists to achieve work of a greater distinction, the main Buddha image of the Pin-yang cave (completed about A.D. 523) being one of the finest examples of the early style of Buddha image surviving in China. It is probable that this image, perhaps in a smaller bronze copy, provided the pattern for certain seventh-century Japanese images at Horyuji. In addition to the Buddha on the main wall of the shrine,

Photo: *Fiona Wilkie*

PLATE IX. LUXOR: the temple, built by Amenhotep III and completed by Tutankhamun and Horemheb.

Photo: Exclusive News Agency

PLATE 81. MAURYAN EMPIRE: lion capital on pillar erected by the Emperor Asoka.

Photo: British Museum

PLATE 82. MAYA: lintel from house "G" at Menche, Guatemala. It shows a penitent kneeling before a priest and mutilating his tongue by passing a roep of thorns through it. Height 3 feet 7 inches. *(British Museum, London)*

Photo: British Museum

PLATE 83. MAYA: stela "F" from Quirigua.
(British Museum, London)

Photo: Rijksmuseum

PLATE 84. MAYA: the Leyden Plate, a carved jade pendant, the earliest dated object from the Maya area, A.D. 320. Found near Puerto Barrios, Guatemala. *(Rijksmuseum voor volkenkunde, Leyden)*

Photo: Sam Waagenaar

PLATE 85. MEDINET HABU: detail of temple.

Photo: Museo Arqueológico Nacional

Plate 86. The Western Mediterranean: alabaster figure of a Punic divinity, seventh century B.C. Found in a tomb in the Iberian necropolis of Galera in the province of Granada. (*Museo Arqueológico Nacional, Madrid*)

Photo: Oriental Institute, University of Chicago

PLATE 87. MEGIDDO: statuette of Canaanite god, bronze overlaid with gold leaf, about thirteenth century B.C. Found at Megiddo.

Photo: British Museum

PLATE 88. MEMPHIS: funerary stela of Jehuty-mes, chief of "the keeper of the gates" at Memphis. Above, the dead man followed by a sister and brother adores Osiris and Isis: below, the son pours out a libation to Jehuty-mes. Eighteenth dynasty, about 1450 B.C. *(British Museum, London)*

Photo: Oriental Institute, University of Chicago

PLATE 89. MEROE: south wall of pyramid XII.

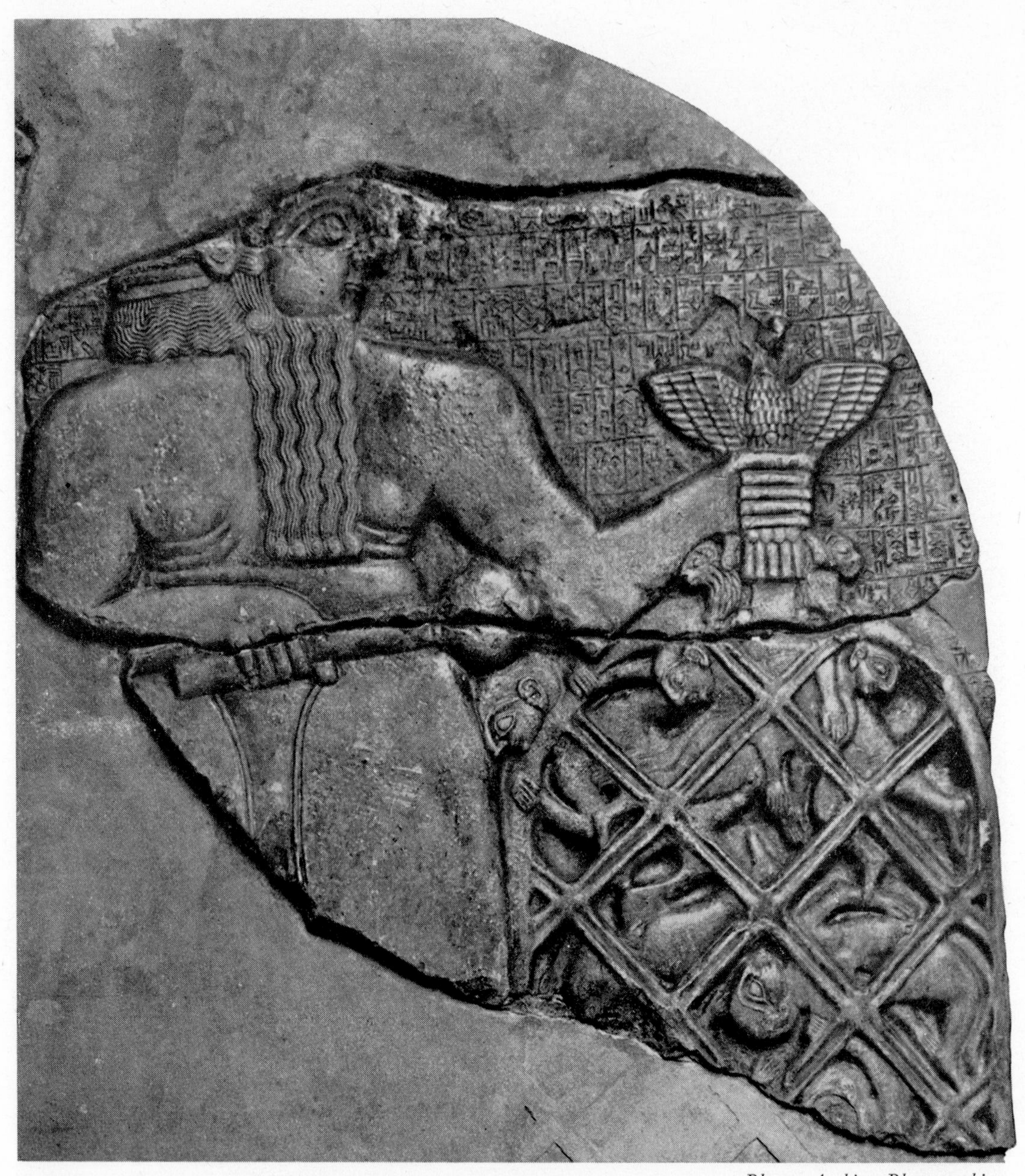

Photo: Archives Photographiques

PLATE 90. MESOPOTAMIAN SCULPTURE: the Stela of the Vultures, mythological side, about 2500 B.C. *(Louvre, Paris)*

Photo: British Museum

PLATE 91. MEXICO: ceremonial jade adze with the poll carved in the form of a feline monster, Venta culture, Vera Cruz. Height 12 inches. *(British Museum, London)*

Photo: British Museum

PLATE 92. MEXICO: Zapotec funerary urn from the Province of Oaxaca, probably about thirteenth century. Height 2 feet 2 inches. *(British Museum, London)*

Photo: by courtesy of The Ashmolean Museum

PLATE 93. MINOAN CIVILIZATION: pottery storage jar from Knossos, about 1580–1450 B.C. *(Ashmolean Museum, Oxford)*

Photo: *Ewing Galloway*

PLATE 94. MEXICO: pyramid of the sun at Teotihuacán.

Photo: by courtesy of The Ashmolean Museum

PLATE 95. MINOAN CIVILIZATION: impressions from three Late Minoan seal-stones from Crete – (left) veined agate signet ring from Lyttos with chariot drawn by goats; (right) a piece of agate with a Minoan *genius* harnessing a cow; (bottom) a piece of green jasper from Knossos with water birds in a papyrus swamp. *(Ashmolean Museum, Oxford)*

Photo: Exclusive News Agency

PLATE 96. MEGALITHIC REMAINS IN MINORCA: the Taula Torrauba.

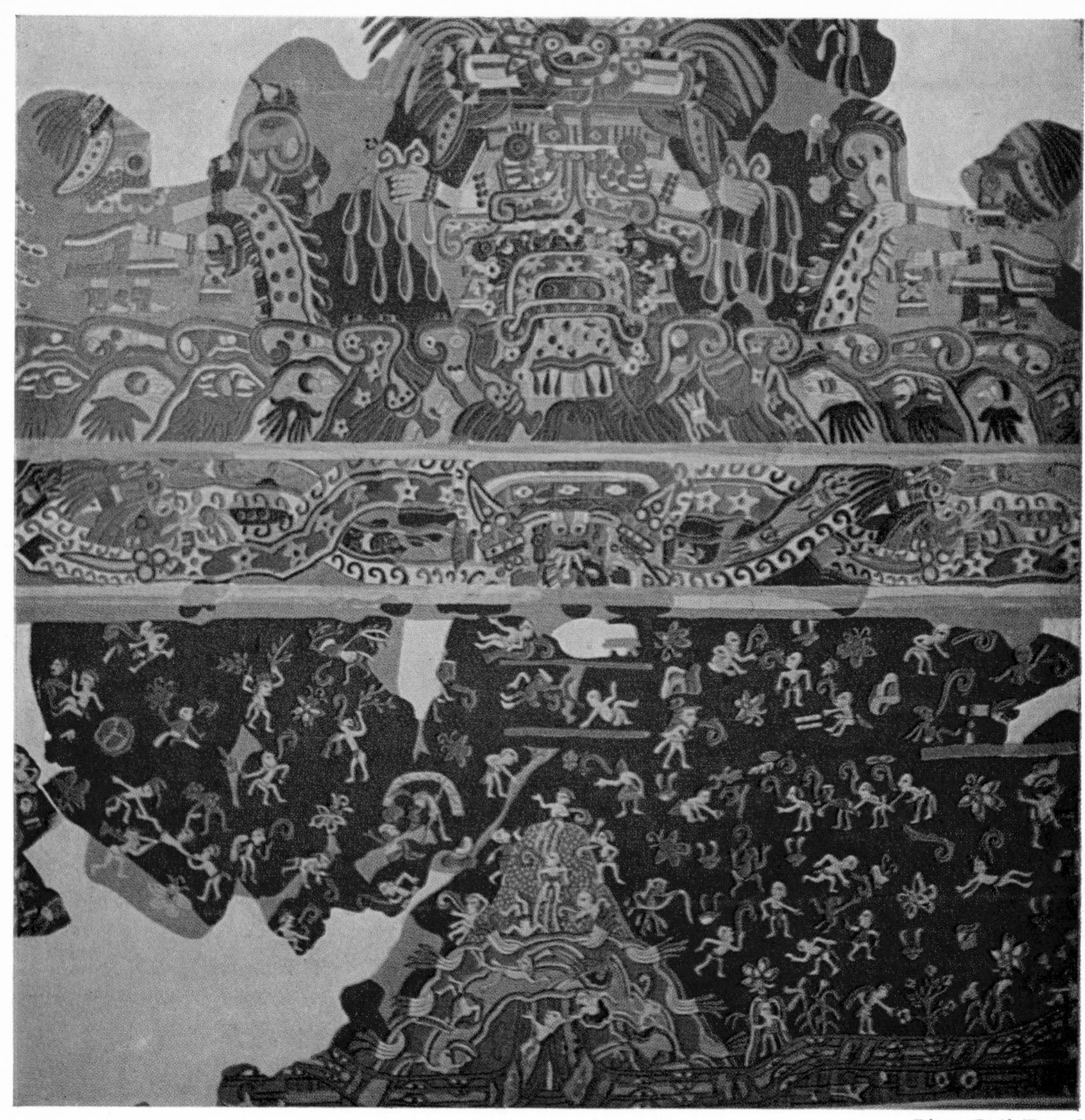

Photo: Gisèle Freund

PLATE X. MEXICANS: wall painting of heaven found in a house at Teotihuacán.

with his acolytes, there are Buddhist trinities on the side walls, separated by adoring figures and, forming a sort of dado for the whole shrine, a baldachin surmounted by flying figures surrounding a great lotus in the ceiling. The front walls bear figures of monsters, surmounted by imperial processions of the emperor to the left and the empress to the right. Above these again are *jataka* scenes, and above these again **Bodhisattvas** in debate.

The statuary is extremely formal, the figures being treated with a rigid verticality: the reliefs on the walls show, by contrast, a noticeable naturalness in treatment, deriving no doubt from the courtly art of the Han period, instead of from an Indian iconography which had become hieratic in its passage through central Asia which, it was thought, could not to be changed without a risk of invalidating the efficacy of the Buddhist images. *See* plate 76, page 250.

Lung Shan is a Neolithic site in north China, near Ch'eng Tzu-yai, Shantung, whose upper levels belong to the historical Chou period. Below this level, and separated from it by a stratum of sand and silt about one and a half feet thick, with very few **artifacts,** is a **Neolithic** level which contains a remarkable black ware of a finely levigated clay with a repertory of about thirty shapes, almost all wheel-made, and with an average thickness of about an eighth of an inch. The finest specimens are less than a twenty-fifth of an inch thick. Small cups and bowls are hand-modelled. These wares are among the finest earthernware articles ever produced in any culture in their fineness of execution and their accuracy of shape. Cruder vessels, in grey and black wares, more rarely in white and red, show a number of forms which belong to the bronze vessels of early historical times. The smaller ones are hand-made, while most of the others are wheel products, a few being moulded. Associated with this pottery are certain other culture traits, including the construction of walls in pounded earth, the working of jade, the practice of scapulomancy (a method of divining by the cracks and lines made in a shoulder blade when placed in fire), by the heating of deer and ox bones. Sites yielding material of this culture are found in Manchuria, Shantung, Honan, Shansi and Anhwei. It is probable that influences from the Lung Shan culture played some part in the synthetic Shang-Yin culture as revealed at Anyang where many of these traits are also found.

Luristan Culture, *see* Iran.

Lustral. A term used in connection with ceremonial purification, usually with water, made before worship.

Luxor is a town, properly known as El-Aksur ("The Castles"), situated in Upper Egypt on the east bank of the Nile, 450 miles south of Cairo. The Temple of Luxor, one of the greatest monuments of **Thebes,** was built by Amenhotep III on the south-west side of the town and is nearly 300 yards long. Its decoration was completed by Tutankhamun and Horemheb. The axis of the temple runs from south-west to north-east. An avenue bordered by recumbent rams leads to the temples of **Karnak** (*see* plates 65, 67, pages 239, 241).

Ramses II added an extensive court, embellished with scenes of his victories over the **Hittites** and Syrians, and containing several **colossi** and a pair of obelisks – one of which is now in the Place de La Concorde in Paris. The sanctuary was rebuilt by Alexander the Great. Luxor's chief religious festival was that of "Southern Opi", when the sacred ships bearing the gods were conveyed in procession from Karnak to Luxor and back again. Scenes of these festivities are found on the walls of the Great Colonnade, which is the most striking feature of Luxor. Later, Christian churches and a mosque were built within the temple. Clearance and restoration are still in progress. *See* colour plate IX, plate 74, page 248.

Lycians. It was this people which gave its name to the area on the south coast of Asia Minor between Caria and Pamphylia. Though they called themselves *Trmmili,* they were known to the Greeks as *Lukioi,* and to the Orient (**Amarna** Letters) as the people of the "Lukku Land". A number of inscriptions in the Lycian language are known, written in a script clearly derived from the Greek alphabet, and dating from the fifth and fourth centuries B.C. Most of these come from the area of Xanthos, the ancient capital, which has been excavated, first by Sir Charles Fellows from 1834–44, and now since 1950 by P. Demargne and H. Metzgar. In the fourteenth century B.C. they are mentioned in the Amarna Letters as raiding pirate bands in the eastern Mediterranean. They appear again in the thirteenth century among **Sea Peoples** invading

Egypt in the reigns of Ramses II and Merneptah. That some of them became absorbed within Egypt itself is shown by a reference to a Lycian butler in a twentieth dynasty harem conspiracy. At the time of the Persian invasion, the Lycians of Xanthos put up a determined struggle, preferring rather to perish than to suffer domination.

Lydians. This people gave its name to the area on the western coast of Asia Minor, which was consequently known to the Greeks as Ludia and to the Assyrians as Luddu. A number of native inscriptions are known, of the fifth and fourth centuries B.C., written in an alphabet clearly derived from the Greek, but the language is not well understood. The ruins of Sardis, source of most of these inscriptions, were excavated from 1910–14 by H.C. Butler of Princeton University, but the actual site of Lydian Sardis remained undetected until 1958, in which year another American expedition under G.M.A. Hanfmann and A.H. Detweiler seems finally to have located it. In the seventh century B.C. Lydia became an important middle-state between the Greek colonies of the Aegean coast and the oriental civilizations, the trading opportunities proving so lucrative that the name of the last king, Croesus, has become proverbial of wealth. It appears that it was in this milieu that coined money was first developed, culminating in the establishment by Croesus of a standard gold and silver currency. The eastward expansion of Lydia caused a clash with Cyaxares the Mede which ended when Croesus suffered the destruction of a "great empire", his own, as the Oracle at Delphi had predicted, when he unwisely challenged Cyrus the Persian.

Thenceforward Lydia became a part of Persia, and Sardis the most westerly point on the famous **Royal Road.**

Lyell, Charles (1797–1875). Lyell was an Englishman who was led to the study of geology by the lectures of Dr William **Buckland**, but far outstripped his teacher. His book, *The Principles of Geology* (1830–3), followed the views of James **Hutton** and established the principle of uniformity – that the forces of wind and weather had, over millions of years, slowly altered the shape of the earth's crust – and dealt the death-blow to the "catastrophic theory" of Baron **Cuvier**. (*See also* **Geological Periods**.)

Lynchet. When the sides of a hill are ploughed one result of the disturbance of the earth is to cause the soil to creep slowly downhill under the influence of gravity helped by rain, and it tends to collect in sloping banks which are known as lynchets. This effect is particularly noticeable in the case of **Celtic fields**, perhaps as a result of the methods of cultivation or of delimiting the fields, and has led to their identification in hitherto unsuspected sites.

M

Machu Picchu. This well-preserved late **Inca** city is sited to the north-west of Cuzco in Peru and rendered almost inaccessible by being at the top of precipices over 1,000 feet high; it was thus unknown to Spanish chroniclers and only discovered in 1911 by Professor Hiram Bingham. It contains fine examples of stone-masonry, and structures there include house-compounds, temples, shrines and a complicated system of stone water-basins. It has, too, a number of stone staircases, necessary because of the unevenness of the ground.

Macrolith. A large **stone tool**, about a foot or so in length. (*See also* **Microlith**.)

Magadha, *see* Mauryan Empire.

Magdalenian. This Upper **Palaeolithic** culture named after remains found at la Madeleine in France, superseded the **Aurignacian** in western Europe, flourishing in the last **glaciation** in a climate of arctic severity and probably lasting until the end of the **Pleistocene** era. Surviving Magdalenian tools and **artifacts** reflect a society made up of communities of fishermen and reindeer-hunters. The prevalence of reindeer is indicated by the increased use of reindeer antlers to make such characteristic implements as harpoons, lance-heads and spear-throwers. Typical stone implements are **burins**, much used for working antlers, blades, occasionally of great length and fineness, indicating the perfecting of blade-making techniques, and microliths – small blades with blunted backs, sometimes only half an inch long and an eighth of an inch across, used to barb wooden points or hafted in rows to form a cutting or sawing edge. These latter form the beginning of a tool tradition dominant in some **Mesolithic** cultures. The continued practice of cave painting in this culture culminated in such fine examples as the painted caves at **Altamira** (*see* plate 8, page 58) and Font-de-Gaume. *See* plate 77, page 251.

Maglemosian. The name Maglemose, signifying in Danish "big bog", is now generally applied to the **Mesolithic** culture which spread over the north European plain between 6800 and 5000 B.C. The name refers to the fact that Maglemose sites are always in low-lying places, under 600 feet above sea level, often in bogs or fens, or on small islands or peninsulas by lakes and rivers. The well-known Zealand sites of Mullerup, Svaerborg and Holmegaard are bog sites. Many sites, like Duvensee in Germany, must have been inhabited during the dry season only. In this period, the whole area from the lowland zone of Britain as far east as Poland and Russia and as far north as southern Sweden, formed one single plain unbroken by water or mountains but probably thickly forested. The greatest density of Maglemose people was probably in the centre of this area, in Denmark and southern Sweden, especially the island of Zealand. Maglemose tools dredged from the North Sea also point to heavy settlement in this area, whilst stray finds and sites are found as far apart as Poland, Estonia, Belgium, Picardy and south-eastern Britain. In addition to the sites from Zealand the main sites include, in England, Broxbourne, Kelling Heath, Newbury, Thatcham, Skipsea; in Estonia, Kunda; in Germany, Calbe, Dobbertin, Duvensee; and in Sweden, Istaby, Åmossen, Sandarna, Stora Dode Mose, Bare Mose and Horninge Mose.

Their economy appears to have been based on fishing, fowling and hunting and the sites are rich in pike, edible waterbird, and wild animal remains, with auroch and elk predominating. Great quantities of hazelnuts have also been found at Duvensee and Holmegaard. The Maglemose folk were not agriculturalists, for no carbonized grain nor sickle-flints have been found. They had no domesticated animals except the dog, and they made no pottery. The size of the communities must have been small, since such an economy would not support large groups, and this is confirmed by their small settlements. It is probable that they migrated annually, for the known sites show that these were inhabited only in summer and autumn. No Maglemose burials are known, but the presence of human bones strewn haphazardly in habitation debris suggests cannibalism.

The material equipment was designed to deal with the forest and water environment, and many perishable objects of wood, bone and antler have survived in the damp conditions of the low-lying sites. Holmegaard has produced four ends of wooden rods pointed and hardened in fire, a wood plaque and a willow paddle rudder. Another paddle rudder comes from Duvensee, whilst part of a dug-out canoe of Scottish fir was found under ten feet of estuarine silt at Perth in Scotland. In Finland, fragments of a fishing-net of plant fibre were found with sink-stones and pinebark floats. Antler was widely used both as sleeves for the hafting of flint axes and adzes, and as axe and adze blades. Fine points were made from antler tines; pieces of antler were decorated with geometric engravings, and awls and needles were made of bone. Barbless bone fish-hooks were common, but the most typical piece of equipment of the Maglemose culture was the bone or antler point which is found in a great variety of forms. These include plain sharpened points, but many have one side carved into a row of barbs varying from simple irregular notches to large recurved barbs. Some have two rows of inset flints, some are tanged and a few are curved. Though often called harpoons, there is evidence that most of them were more probably hafted in pairs as fish-spears ("leisters") or in groups as bird-catchers. Different forms of point have been found together as units of a single implement, and single points were hafted in wooden shafts as javelins.

The Maglemose people made great use of flint **artifacts. Microliths** form an important element on all the settlement sites, though some of the minute geometrical shapes are lacking. The commonest Maglemose microlith is the simplest form, blunted obliquely or all down one edge. Some triangular, crescentic and trapezoidal forms occur, but more characteristic is the fine, narrow **flake** and the **core** showing scars of these flakes. **Burins,** micro-burins and scrapers also occur. Very characteristic is the "heavy equipment" for dealing with the forests. This includes the flint axes, adzes and core-chisels mounted in wooden or antler sleeves into which a wooden handle was inserted. Flake axes, called "tranchet axes", also existed but have never been found mounted. These flint artifacts were not polished. Stone was used for pebble hammers and axes, for perforated adzes and mace-heads.

Maglemose art consists mainly of engraving on small objects, usually implements of daily use, including antler hafts, axes and adzes, bone points, pieces of polished antler, and, in four cases, amber pendants. The engravings were made by incision or pricking with a sharp point, or by boring, probably with a bow-drill. The patterns were mainly geometric, many of them apparently based on net motifs, though barbed lines, linear chevrons and chequer patterns also occur. There is little attempt at naturalistic rendering.

The Maglemose culture is very homogeneous over the whole North European plain; few regional variations occur in the industries or in the art, except in the later part of the period in Britain which was by then almost cut off by the North Sea. The earliest phase of the culture is mainly represented by **Star Carr.**

Certain elements of the Maglemose culture can be traced back to the Upper **Palaeolithic** period. The microlithic industry derives probably from the Upper Palaeolithic of north Africa, whilst the art and certain forms of bone point seem to have developed from the Late **Magdalenian.** The axe and adze forms have their immediate origin in the Lyngby culture and evolved in response to the forest environment; similarly, the fish-hook, line and net were devised in consequence of Maglemose man's habitat.

With the isostatic rise of the land following the retreat of the glaciers at the end of the last **glaciation,** the Maglemose groups were pushed back into the centre of the Scandinavian peninsula by new cultures settling along the coastline. The Maglemose was not, however, obliterated, but formed an underlying stratum to the new cultures and continued to flourish in the peripheral regions.

Magosian. This is a Stone Age culture whose type-site is in the eastern African area. The culture is also present in South Africa. It is characterized by small triangular leaf-shaped and lozenge-shaped points finely worked, sometimes on one, sometimes on both faces. It is not known what type of man created this culture.

Magosian, South African, *see* Africa, Stone Age Man in South.

Maiden Castle is a prehistoric hill-top fortification, two miles south-west of Dorchester in Dorset, England. Situated on a long low hill about two-thirds of a mile long, its massive defences dominate the surrounding countryside.

Excavations carried out in the years 1934–37 under the direction of Sir Mortimer Wheeler showed that its development was a slow one, continuing intermittently from 2000 B.C. to A.D. 70.

The earliest occupation on the hill-top could hardly be termed a fortification, but was a cattle corral (**causewayed camp**) belonging to the first farmers to arrive in this country who formed part of the Windmill Hill culture of the Early **Neolithic** period. It consisted of two roughly circular interrupted ditches one inside the other, covering about ten acres, the ditches being some five feet deep and flat-bottomed. About a dozen or so of these causewayed camps are known scattered over the south of England. At Maiden Castle tools of flint and bone and blackish round-bottomed pots were found, both in the ditches and in the rubbish pits. Their pottery and a chalk idol connects them with similar farming communities in France.

Soon after this corral was abandoned an enormous Long Mound or Bank Barrow of religious function was constructed across it by people of the same culture. It was sixty feet broad, at least six feet high, and one-third of a mile in length. It was bordered on each side by parallel flat-bottomed ditches twelve feet wide and six feet deep, the ends of this enormous mound being rivetted by a palisade. Perhaps the most surprising feature was the burial of a man about thirty years old whose body had been hacked to pieces and whose brain had been cut out and eaten. Ox bones nearby suggested some kind of ritual feast. Such cannibalism is also attested from other Neolithic sites in Britain, and other similar bank **barrows,** although very rare, are known from the same county.

This hill seems to have been occupied from time to time by Late Neolithic (Peterborough) and Early **Bronze Age** peoples, who finally abandoned the site about 1500 B.C.

It was not until about 250 B.C. that the first "castle" of about sixteen acres was built by **Hallstatt** peoples from north-east France, who already had a certain admixture of **La Tène** folk (Early **Iron Age** A). They must have chosen, perhaps by chance, the site of the deserted causewayed camp on which to build a single wall-like rampart of earth twelve feet wide and supported on each side by vertical timber posts. Seven feet in front of this was a ditch with a v-shaped cross-section. This was a typically Hallstatt type of defence but it did not last long, however, and as the timber rotted it was replaced by more permanent dry-stone walling. Inside there was a village settlement complete with metalled streets. The inhabitants lived in wooden rectangular huts and stored their grain, water and other produce in large pits below the ground, which were finally used as rubbish pits when the contents had gone sour. Their pots had a characteristic polished surface coloured red by the use of **haematite**. The excavation was not extensive enough to obtain an overall view of the village economy.

These peasants lived a quiet, self-sufficient but prosperous life as is witnessed by the paved cattle market with wooden stalls outside the eastern gate. Clad in cloth woven on their own looms and possessing few luxuries except some personal ornaments (most of which had been handed down) including a few out-of-date La Tène brooches, they did, however, increase in numbers so much that the ramparts had to be extended to the west, and a new type of double funnel-like entrance (barbican) added to give much more protection to the double gates. Now enlarged some three times this small "town" had new ramparts (**glacis** type) which presented a long steep slope to the attacker rather than an unscalable wall as previously.

This state of affairs seems to have continued until about 56 B.C. when we find Maiden Castle indirectly involved in the great political upheaval caused by Julius Caesar's campaigns in Gaul. The Veneti, a powerful tribe living in southern Brittany, organized an unsuccessful rebellion against Caesar which was very harshly repressed. Having already extensive trade contacts many of the Veneti fled to southern Britain bringing with them their own method of warfare, the sling, and an anti-sling device – multiple ramparts which were designed to keep the attacking slinger just out of range. These Veneti were La Tène peoples and when they settled down in Wessex they formed part of the British Early Iron Age B group. At Maiden Castle they greatly increased the defences, and gave this Early Iron Age town the massive appearance it has today. The defending slingers had stone platforms well sited between the ramparts with reserves of sling pebbles beside them – in one case as many as 20,000! Their pots had a characteristic "bead" rim probably imitating the rolled rim of metal vessels. Maiden Castle had now become one of the mightiest of all the Early Iron Age citadels in Britain.

Following on the Veneti, the next inhabitants were the Belgae coming originally from north-eastern Gaul. They were forced to move westward into Dorset from east Hampshire about A.D. 25, since they had there come into conflict with the expanding kingdom and political domain of one of the most powerful of the British kings, Cunobelin. These Belgae were responsible for the general repair of the ramparts, streets and buildings.

Some eighteen years later, about A.D. 43 or 44, Maiden Castle was one of the twenty "towns" which the future emperor Vespasian in command of the Second Augustan Legion stormed and captured as part of the Roman Imperial policy for the subjugation of the south of England. Excavation has shown that the main attack was at the eastern gate and it has been possible to reconstruct this in some detail. An initial volley of iron-headed ballista-bolts killed a number of the defenders, one of whom was later buried with a bolt still lodged in his spine. A charge was then made which got as far as some huts just outside the gate; these were then fired and, in the confusion, the gate was stormed and taken.

A war cemetery, the earliest known in Britain, bears eloquent witness to the defence and the slaughter following the defeat. Near the east gate thirty-eight bodies had been hastily bundled into shallow graves, sometimes three to a grave which should have held one. Even in haste the customary grave-goods had not been forgotten. Sword gashes on the head showed how many had met their death.

The great period of this Early Iron Age fortress-town had finished, although life continued under Roman occupation until about A.D. 70 when the Belgic inhabitants were "Romanized" and transferred to an organized town in the valley. Three centuries later a small Romano-British temple was built within the eastern gate but the site was, by then, virtually deserted. *See* plate 75, page 249.

Majapahit, east Java. From about the eleventh century A.D. the centre of power in Java tended to lie in the east of the island, perhaps because of the existence of another, rival power in the west of Indonesia and Malaya. After the death of Erlangga in A.D. 1049 – a fine mortuary image of the king as Vishnu was found at Candi Belahan – there is a gap in our knowledge of over 200 years, when a new kingdom emerged with a distinctive art and architectural style, best exemplified at Singha-sari, from which some fine statues can now be seen in the Leiden Museum. The Buddhist centre at Candi Jago is interesting because the reliefs are clearly akin in style to the cut-out figures used in the *wayang*, or shadow puppet theatre. There is a freedom of representation, and a tendency towards the humorous, even grotesque, which testifies to the emergence of a native school of art based, unquestionably, upon Indian cultures, but with certain elements which seem to throw back to the megalithic period and tradition, and with a considerable degree of new invention. At the end of the thirteenth century A.D. the capital was transferred to Majapahit, which was to become the centre of an empire which exercised considerable control over the whole of Indonesia, as well as parts of the Philippines and Malaya. Brick architecture became more general, though the great complex of Panataran, a collection of unrelated buildings from the period about A.D. 1320–1450, is in stone. Here the style of the carvings and the decoration must be called Javanese: Indian influences have disappeared although the texts which are illustrated are Indian in origin. By the beginning of the fifteenth century A.D. Malacca in Malaya, a Muslim foundation, began to replace Majapahit as the great centre of south-eastern Asian trade, but the crystallization of Javanese culture which reached its peak under the Majapahit Empire was sufficiently strong to withstand even Islam, and modern Javanese art and literature are the products of this crystallization.

Mallia. This site on the north coast of Crete to the west of Mount Lasithi, shows traces of **Neolithic** occupation and was probably a port for inland Neolithic settlements. It is rich in traces of **Minoan civilization.** From the Early Minoan period (about 2500–2000 B.C.) dates pottery decorated with reddish brown painted patterns using such motifs as the double axe and "butterfly". The palace dates mainly from the Middle Minoan era (about 2000–1500 B.C.) and follows the same general scheme as that at **Knossos.** Of this era too is the very fine rectangular ossuary lying between the palace and the sea, whose site was called by peasants "pit of gold" because of the number of gold ornaments dug up there. The finest achievements in metal work of this period are also from Mallia: a great bronze sword a yard long, with a hilt of gold-plated ivory and a pommel of crystal, was found with a dagger also originally hilted with gold and an axe-head of brown schist, the butt carved to represent a springing leopard and the blade decorated with spiral designs; these were probably part of the regalia of the king of Mallia. A gold pendant of this era in the shape of two hornets is decorated with remarkably fine granulated work.

Signs of fire and destruction found also at many other sites indicate that a catastrophe put an end to Minoan occupation of the site.

Malta, *see* Mediterranean, the Western.

Mammoth. The mammoth is probably the best known of all prehistoric animals. It was similar to the Indian elephant, standing some fourteen feet high, with long curving tusks, and a thick woolly coat to protect it from the cold. During the fourth **glaciation** it roamed in herds along the Thames Valley in southern England, which was at that time enduring a tundra climate similar to northern Russia today. In Siberia, mammoth have been found frozen, perfectly preserved by the climate as if in a deep freeze, so that their flesh is still found eatable by dogs, 20,000 years after they met their end.

Manetho was an Egyptian priest, who lived during the reign of Ptolemy Philadelphus (285–246 B.C.). His writings, preserved in a fragmentary state in later historical works, form a valuable source of information about Egyptian history. It is difficult to discover precisely what Manetho wrote because all that remains today are copies and extracts from his books which have been altered and commented upon by Jewish and Christian polemicists to give weight to their own arguments.

The principal chroniclers who quoted Manetho were three. Josephus, the Jewish historian who was born in A.D. 37, wrote a treatise *Against Apion* in which he sought to prove the antiquity of the Jewish race and referred to events in Egyptian history as related by Manetho in his *Aegyptiaca* to help to prove his case. Josephus quoted Manetho at length on the invasion and expulsion of the **Hyksos** and identified them with the Jews of the Exodus. The Christian writers, Julius Africanus (third century A.D.) and Eusebius (fourth century A.D.) both made use of an Epitome of Manetho in their own World Histories.

Manetho wrote in Greek for a Greek public and

dedicated his work to the king. The material available to him must have included king-lists and royal annals such as the Turin Papyrus and the **Palermo Stone**, for the surviving evidence shows that the ancient Egyptians had kept their own historical records from the earliest times. All that remains, however, of his historical writings is the framework – the divisions into dynasties which have proved to be a workable system. These lists give the number of years the kings ruled and sometimes a remark about them or a note on some important event during their reigns; this information, however, is not always accurate.

Manetho also wrote works on Egyptian religion, parts of which have been preserved in Plutarch's essay on Isis and Osiris as well as in later writers.

Man, Evolution of, *see* Primates, Prehuman Evolution of *and* Fossil Man.

Man, Fossil, *see* Fossil Man.

Mannians, *see* Ziwiyè.

Mari. Tell Hariri, site of ancient Mari, the tenth city to exercise kingship after the **Flood** according to the **Sumerian** King List, stands on the west bank of the Euphrates near Abu Kemal on the Syria-Iraq border. It first attracted attention after the discovery of a headless statuette of Sumerian Early Dynastic style by Arabs in 1933. A concession to excavate was granted to the French Musées Nationaux and Ministère de l'Education, on whose behalf Professor André Parrot began work the same year. Six seasons were conducted up to 1938 and subsequently three more from 1951–54.

Information about the earliest occupation at Mari was obtained by a **stratification** pit to virgin soil (below the Early Dynastic temple of Shamash). Pottery from this pit showed analogies with the earliest finds at Chagar Bazar and **Nineveh** v, especially a grey incised ware. No buildings earlier than the Late Protoliterate (the period of earliest written records) were examined.

During the Early Dynastic period Mari rose to great heights of prosperity and power. The city was adorned with a **ziggurat** and numerous temples of which those of Ishtar, Ninhursag, Ishtarat, Shamash and Ninni-zaza have been identified. At last, however, Mari suffered a violent destruction following the entry into the city of a conqueror, perhaps Lugalzaggisi of **Uruk** or Sargon of **Accad**. In the temples, especially those of Ishtar and Ishtarat, many statuettes of devotees, including royal personages, as well as other votive objects were found shattered and strewn about.

Nevertheless, Mari apparently recovered rapidly during the Sargonid period. Two inscribed bronze vessels from a hoard discovered in a house near the temple of Ishtarat reveal that Naram-sin installed two of his daughters in Mari, probably as high-priestesses.

Belonging to the Isin-Larsa period is the foundation of a temple to Dagan by Ishtup-ilum. From the entrance to the sanctuary were recovered two bronze lions with inlaid eyes, similar to the guardians of the Early Dynastic temple at **Al Ubaid**. Isolated inlay eyes suggest that there were forty more lions. The palace, undoubtedly the most remarkable complex of buildings excavated at Mari, was also begun at this time. In the days of its last occupant, Zimri-lim, opponent of **Hammurabi** of **Babylon**, it covered the enormous area of six acres. Enclosed by a wall with but a single gateway, it contained at least two hundred and sixty rooms and courts, numbering in addition to the royal apartments a chamber of audience, administrative offices, archives (from which some thousands of diplomatic and economic tablets have been recovered), scribal school-rooms, chapels, workshops, kitchens and stores. Many painted frescos depicting ritual scenes were found. In the thirty-third year of his reign Hammurabi conquered Mari. When the city revolted two years later, he caused the magnificent palace to be systematically pillaged and burnt.

Late in the second millennium, Mari was a quiet Assyrian garrison town guarding the river-crossing for the caravans plying between the Mediterranean and the Persian Gulf. By neo-Babylonian times there remained only a village.

Mariette, Auguste Ferdinand François (1821–81). Mariette Pasha was the founder of the Egyptian Museum in Cairo and Director of the Service des Antiquités from 1858 until his death. He was born at Boulogne-sur-Mer in France, the son of the head of the Marine Department. On leaving school he went into his father's office but soon left, first, to be a drawing master at a private school in Stratford-on-Avon, and then to be a teacher at the College of Art at Boulogne. He was active as a journalist and essayist and much interested in art.

His first introduction to Egyptology was through his cousin, Nestor Lhote, who had been a pupil of **Champollion**. He died in 1842 leaving Mariette as his executor. When he read through the Egyptological papers of his cousin Mariette was fascinated by the writing and the language. "The Egyptian duck", he wrote later, "is a dangerous animal. A peck of his beak, he injects you with his poison and you find yourself an Egyptologist for life." Mariette studied all the available books on Egyptology, particularly the *Description of Egypt* compiled by Napoleon's savants. Having taught himself **hieroglyphs** as well as he could, he began to learn **Coptic**. His first Egyptological publication was a *Catalogue of the Egyptian Objects in the Boulogne Museum*. Every vacation from the College of Art of which he had been made director, he went to Paris to study at the Louvre Museum and in 1849 his friend, the Vicomte de Rouge, offered him a post in the Louvre with a very small salary. He eagerly accepted this offer and the following year the Ministry of Public Instruction sent him on a mission to Egypt to collect ancient manuscripts. The priests in charge of the various monasteries were very courteous, but not at all anxious to show him their treasures; and so he occupied his time and the money intended for the purchase of manuscripts with excavations at **Saqqara**. He uncovered a long avenue of sphinxes leading to the **Serapeum**, the burial place of the sacred Apis bulls. The tombs of these bulls had been richly furnished with gold and other valuables and extended in time from the nineteenth dynasty to the reign of Nectanebo.

Mariette persuaded the French Government and the Louvre to give him enough money for two more years' work at the Serapeum and his promotion in 1855 to the rank of Conservateur.

His ambition was to found a museum in Cairo to preserve the antiquities which had been discovered and to prevent the wholesale removal of works of art from Egypt. In 1858 Said Pasha, the viceroy of the Ottoman emperor, agreed to his plans. The Antiquities Service was formed and excavations at a number of important sites began on a large scale. The local *moudirs* were ordered not to destroy or remove any antiquity. This law greatly angered the dealers and foreigners who were stocking their own collections.

The excavations at Saqqara produced many Old Kingdom statues for the Museum, among them the diorite seated statue of Chephren and the striding figure of the Sheikh el Beled. The beautifully decorated fifth dynasty tomb of Ti was excavated by Mariette at Saqqara, and his subordinates were also engaged upon work at **Abydos** and **Tanis**.

Sometimes the treasury of the viceroy was full and he could offer Mariette large sums of money for excavation and publication, but often these benefits could not be kept up and Mariette was continually accused of failing to publish his discoveries.

The Museum at Boulak, built in the Moorish style, was opened in 1863 by Ismail Pasha who had succeeded on the death of Said Pasha. Mariette found it more difficult to combat the attacks of his enemies under the new regime; and Ismail was liable to give away to importuning foreign royalty the antiquities which Mariette was so painstakingly preserving for Egypt. Five years later a severe flooding of the Nile destroyed part of the Museum and its collection, but Mariette reassembled and rebuilt his work. His books describing his work at Saqqara, Abydos, Dendera and in Nubia were at last beginning to appear in print.

Marshall, Sir John Hubert (1876–1958). Director-general of Archaeology in India from 1902–31, Sir John Marshall was appointed to this important post on the initiative of Lord Curzon, at that time the British Viceroy of India. His years in office witnessed substantial advances in almost all aspects of Indian archaeology. His first task was to reorganize the archaeological department to make it comprehend many activities till then only partly covered. From the beginning he set about recruiting Indians themselves and for this purpose created several scholarships. The listing and preservation of monuments occupied much of his attentions, but the expansion of museum services and publication of inscriptions in no way diminished. Besides all this he and his officers undertook a wide programme of excavation of early historic sites. These included city sites at Charsadda, in the **Gandhara** region, Bhita, Patna, Vaisali and **Taxila** and Buddhist religious centres at **Sanchi, Sarnath,** Kasia, and Sravasti. It is not surprising that one aspect should have been neglected at this time: it was prehistory, both Stone Age and later, for which almost no provision was made. In the last decade of his service this omission was somewhat rectified by the large scale excavation which Sir John directed at **Mohenjo-Daro** (*see* **Indus Valley Civi-**

lization). He was responsible for the publication of a vast quantity of reports, but it is particularly with his two final reports, *Mohenjo-Daro and the Indus Valley Civilization* (1939), and *Taxila* (1951), that his name will be associated.

Maspero, Gaston Camille Charles (1846–1910). Maspero was one of the great French directors of the Service des Antiquités in Egypt. He succeeded **Mariette** Pasha in 1881 and continued his work of preserving ancient standing monuments from the depredations of stone robbers, dealers and natural decay, as well as conducting fresh excavations.

Maspero, an Italian by birth, was educated in France and became de Rouge's assistant at the École des Hautes Études and Professor at the Collège de France. His special interest was in the language of ancient Egypt, particularly in trying to find out how words were pronounced by comparison with living languages.

His work in Egypt was a continuation and expansion of that of Mariette Pasha. He opened the pyramids of Unas, Pepi II and Teti which were all inscribed with previously unknown texts. A discovery of great importance was made in June 1881 when one of the members of the Abd el Rassoul family, which had been engaged for many years in illicit excavation and dealing in antiquities, revealed to the authorities the whereabouts of their "treasure". At Deir el Bahri, priests during the twenty-first dynasty had hidden the bodies and funerary equipment of thirty-four kings whose tombs were being robbed, and it was this secret burial place which was now disclosed to Maspero. He continued the excavations at **Saqqara** and ordered the removal of sand from the Great **Sphinx** at Giza which had been excavated in 1869 (as part of the celebrations of the opening of the **Suez Canal**) but had become partly covered again. In 1886 he retired from the Service and devoted himself to publishing the results of his work; the translation of the texts he had found in the pyramids at Saqqara and several general books including a three volume *History of the Ancient Peoples the Classic East* (1894–1900).

Three years later, Lord Cromer invited Maspero to return to the directorship of the Service des Antiquités and of the new Museum which was being built in Cairo to replace Mariette's house at Boulak which had suffered from flooding. Maspero wrote a Guide to the collection which was designed to serve both the tourist and the expert. He engaged specialists to compile catalogues of the various branches of the collection.

Maspero was anxious to make a complete record of the buildings and inscriptions at **Philae** (*see* plate 114, page 380) and other Nubian temples which were threatened with submersion by the construction of the Aswan Dam. Egyptologists working under his direction published their results in a series entitled *Les Temples immergés de la Nubie* (1911).

The antiquities laws needed to be rigorously enforced and Maspero tried to win government support for preventing random excavation, but he did not succeed until 1912. By setting up museums in other parts of Egypt he hoped to encourage a wider scientific interest in antiquities and to prevent their sale and export from the country.

In 1912 he retired and two years later died while addressing the Académie des Inscriptions et Belles Lettres of which he was secretary.

Mastaba Tomb. A type of ancient tomb found in Egypt; it had sloping sides and a flat roof. ("Mastaba" is the Arabic for "bench".)

Mathura, an ancient city on the River Jamuna in the Uttar Pradesh (formerly United Provinces) of India, is renowned for its traditional association with the hero Krishna and with the war which forms the central theme of the great Indian epic, the *Mahabharata*. The earliest settlement so far discovered at Mathura is of the period of the painted grey ware (first half of the first millennium B.C.), but earlier settlements may well be discovered among the many mounds. Little is known of the archaeology of Mathura before the first century B.C. when it became famous as the capital of invaders of central Asian origin, Sakas and Kushans. The Kushan dynasty culminated under Kanishka (flourished about A.D. 78–100) who held sway over all north-west India and across the Hindu Kush into central Asia. Mathura was celebrated for its sculptors' workshops (hence Ptolemy's "Mathura of the Gods") and during the first five centuries A.D. vast quantities of sculpture were made there and exported to distant places, such as the Buddhist site at **Sarnath** (*see* plates 122, 124, pages 388, 390), near Benares. The work was mainly religious, sometimes architectural, and includes Jain, Buddhist and Hindu icons; royal portraits of the

Kushan rulers are also known. It is thought that the Buddha icon originated in Mathura. The Kushan period was one of intense commercial activity and it is not surprising that the sculpture of Mathura, though to a lesser extent than that of **Gandhara** shows western influences. It should be recalled that Roman contacts were then at their height. Nevertheless, as with the sculpture of **Sanchi** (*see* colour plate XIV, plates 31, 121, pages 101, 387), that of Mathura is peculiarly Indian. *See* plates 78, 80, pages 252, 254.

Mauer Jaw, *see* Heidelberg Man.

Mauryan Empire. The Mauryan Empire succeeded for the first time in integrating into one political unit the far-flung regions of the Indo-Pakistan sub-continent. It was established soon after the return of Alexander the Great, who had advanced right up to the River Hyphasis (the modern Beas) in the Punjab and had stopped at the frontier dividing the old Persian empire of the **Achaemenids** from the rising north Indian kingdom of the Nandas with its centre in Magadha (south Bihar). This Magadhan kingdom had embraced the whole of the Gangetic Valley and stood face to face with the Persian provinces in the Indus Zone. Alexander's conquests upset the balance of power in this part of the world. His ambition to integrate his Indian conquests into a new Hellenic empire was dashed to the ground by the machinations of an audacious youth, Chandragupta, belonging to the Kshatriya (warrior) Maurya clan, which gave its name to the empire. Chandragupta was destined to lay the foundation of a new political force uniting for the first time the Gangetic Valley with the Indus Zone and pushing farther through the Malwa Plateau and Gujerat into peninsular India. Later (305 B.C.), his firm stand against Seleukos Nikator, Alexander's successor in western Asia, brought an addition to the empire of the outlying provinces of Kabul, Kandahar, Herat and Baluchistan, areas which had long been under the Achaemenian dominion and influence. Nearer home Chandragupta's grandson, Asoka, marched through the densely-forested routes along the eastern coast and conquered Kalinga (modern Orissa and north Andhra). This extensive area, from the Hindu Kush to the very borders of the Kaveri Valley in south India and from the Bay of Bengal to the Arabian Sea, became united under the authority of the Mauryan Emperors for nearly a hundred years.

Politically, the Mauryan empire brought to a successful climax the aggrandizement of the Magadhan power; culturally it inherited not only the Indian tradition of monarchy, but also most of those ideas and artistic traditions of the Achaemenians which had for long been implanted in their eastern provinces, now under the aegis of the Mauryas. Socially, it created a new outlook for a pattern of life in which the diverse cultures of the sub-continent found their due place under a common religious code. Throughout the country, where civilization was largely confined to the river valleys and the secluded forest regions were backward, fresh routes were developed, connecting the valleys and the new centres of population.

The Magadhan monarchy was built up by a succession of royal dynasties, all following an expansionist policy of absorbing the neighbouring kingdoms under one sovereignty. It was with the growth of this new state that the Indian conception of a *Chakravarti* (paramount ruler) was gradually unfolding. He was authority incarnate. The whole administrative machinery centred round the personality of the king who was an upholder as well as an executor of law. The system developed a social policy peculiar to India, while the king increased his status not only by the heroic deeds of his conquests but also by absorbing the many royal titles and ceremonies of the Achaemenian kingship.

The fortune of Magadha dates from the foundation (fifth century B.C.) of the new capital of Pataliputra (the modern Patna in Bihar) at the junction of the Ganges and the Son, which gave to the rulers a dominant position in the Gangetic valley and also opened up easy means of communication. This city, as rebuilt by the Mauryas, had a wooden palisade for defence – a framework of a double row of wooden uprights bonded together by a floor and roof of cross timbers obviously meant to hold rammed earth. This archaeological evidence is elaborated by Megasthenes, the Greek ambassador to the Mauryan court, who says that "the city has been surrounded with a ditch in breadth six *plethra* [606 feet], and in depth thirty cubits [a cubit is about twenty inches]; and that its wall has 570 towers and sixty-four gates". This wooden fortification is a great contrast to the massive stone walls of the older capital of Magadha at Rajgir.

The Magadhan Empire had the advantage of easily accessible raw materials for tools and weapons in the copper and iron mines of south Bihar. As soldiering was no longer a monopoly of the Kshatriya caste, it was necessary that the king should work these mines in order to provide arms for his professional warriors. The iron-tipped arrows of the Indian soldiers, so early mentioned by **Herodotus**, lay at the root of the Magadhan expansionist policy, and it appears that the Mauryas took full advantage of this metal and spread its wider use through the length and breadth of the sub-continent. Though no worthwhile examples have so far been made available from the Mauryan cities, yet the appearance of iron weapons in Indian cave paintings of a slightly later date as well as the abundance of iron tools in the grave complex of southern India, were not isolated phenomena. They were parts of a common Iron Age tradition generally associated in peninsular India with a typical pottery called red-and-black ware.

Like the professional warriors, the Mauryan administration had regular officials whose pay was graded in terms of *panas*, silver coins better known as *karshapanas*, (the term being formed with the addition of the Persian word *karsha*). This fuller name was due to the fact that the silver currency of India was brought, at least in the north-west, into metrological relationship with the Achaemenian weight system, though the metal pieces were stamped with local punches since they were meant for local circulation. This silver currency became gradually popular in India with the standardization of the punch marks and the readjustment of the weight system, in line with that prevalent in the heart of India. The traditional method of hoarding in the form of ingots of gold, as associated with the Nandas, is no longer heard of, and the fact that silver, a metal so rare in India, became so widely current, suggests an extension of the practice of issuing silver coinage, already known during the Achaemenian rule in the Indus Zone, by a successor government like that of the Mauryas. The punch-marked coins survived after the disappearance of the Mauryan empire in a debased silver and copper currency.

The imperial necessity also demanded the adoption of a uniform script and language. As evidenced by the Inscriptions of **Asoka**, two scripts – the Kharoshthi in the Indus Zone and the Brahmi in the other parts of the empire, both based on the alphabetic system evolved by the Sanskrit grammarians – were regularly used, and the language that finally became universal was a form of Prakrit illustrated by these inscriptions. The Asokan Brahmi survived longer and became the ultimate source of all the subsequent scripts that developed in India and the neighbouring countries, while the Prakrit remained as a court language for some centuries more until it was superseded by the sophisticated Sanskrit.

Side by side with the adoption of these new measures must be mentioned the imperial style in arts and letters. The most remarkable literary remains of this type are the Asokan Inscriptions, which are engraved on rocks and monolithic sandstone pillars in the same fashion as the Achaemenian emperors engraved their records on rocks. The likeness is further traceable in some common modes of expression as well as in the use of the Persian word, *Lipi*, or *Dipi*, for writing in the Asokan Inscriptions.

The pillars of Asoka introduced a new tradition in Indian art. Their workmanship, as evidenced by their rounded shape, fine grinding and high polish, is far removed from the wooden architecture that was for long practised in this country. The new stone-masons who designed and chiselled these pillars added further from their own tradition of art motifs and stone sculpture. Here, for the first time since the destruction of the **Indus Valley civilization**, are found sculptured figures either in round, as in the case of arranged back to back lions, or a single bull surmounting the capital of the pillars, or in high relief, as seen at the abacus of the same pillars. The design of the pillars with bell-shaped motif, floral patterns and volutes is a new creation in Indian art. Except for this artistic tradition, the pillars follow the Indian conception, in this particular case related to the Buddhist religion and mythology.

The high polish is also seen at the caves on the Barabar hills in Bihar, which were excavated during the reign of Asoka and presented by him to the religious sect known as Ajivakas. These are the earliest artificial caves known in India. Later in the north-west Deccan, numerous caves, like those at **Ajanta**, were excavated and given over to the Buddhists, but the art of polishing is no longer traceable there.

The traces of polished pillars have also been found in the remains of a building at Pataliputra, which formed a part of the Mauryan Palace. The building was a pillared hall, only eight rows of ten pillars each having been so far traced. On one side were found timber sub-structures obviously to support a platform, the whole complex resembling an Achaemenian audience hall.

The construction of an audience hall in the Achaemenian fashion, the issuing of the edicts, the erection of monolithic round columns, the use of high polish, the excavation of caves and the sculptural tradition and motifs, all these illustrate the imperial style of Mauryan art. In its formation there is no doubt that Achaemenian craftsmen had a direct hand. It was the patronage given to them by the Mauryans that led to the creation of naturalistic art in India. But no sooner did they die out than the naturalism also vanished for good. However, the students that they left behind continued the sculptor's art, and it is not difficult to see their hands in the later art treasures of **Sanchi** (*see* colour plate XIV, plates 31, 121, pages 101, 387), **Mathura** (*see* plates 78, 80, pages 252, 254), **Sarnath** (*see* plates 122, 124, pages 388, 390), Bharhut, Bodhgaya and the **cave temples** of the Deccan.

This imperial style of art is traceable only in those places where direct Mauryan patronage was available. This was the court art, far above the cultures that existed in different regions of the sub-continent. The regional cultures varied materially from one to the other. Unfortunately the available materials are not clearly definable. In general the iron age tradition was widely spread, but its associated red-and-black ware proves that it started much earlier than the Mauryan period. In the upper Gangetic Valley, and also spreading westward, has been found a culture characterized by painted grey ware. Its terminal date may fall within the Mauryan epoch, but how far back it goes is difficult to say. Many sites in north India have produced potsherds of a type termed "northern black polished ware". The fragments represent mainly three types of pots: a flat plate for eating "dry rice", an incurved bowl for taking "wet rice" and a shallow dish for curry. In a few places the northern black polished ware has been found to overlie the painted grey ware, but in the majority of the sites in the lower Gangetic Valley it forms the lowest occupational level. The evidence is clear that this ware survived right up to the beginning of the Christian era, but its lower limit is ill defined. In no case can these cultures be termed "Mauryan", which is a political term and is hardly applicable to the material cultures that transcend the limits of political boundaries in time and space. One can only rightly speak of Mauryan art, as applied to the imperial style that developed under the Mauryan patronage.

Mauryan influence is noticeable to a greater degree in the Indian society of the time, which consisted of numerous segregated tribes and races. For the first time they were all brought together under Mauryan political authority. In order to maintain them together it was found necessary to create a spirit of respect for common morality. This new basis was attempted by Asoka in his promulgation of a religion of piety *(Chamma)* as is known from his edicts. He got the inspiration from Buddhism, a sectarian religion of Bihar which marched forward to absorb the heterogenous mass of the peoples. The popular element caught the attention of Indian society and even broke the seclusion of the Brahmanical order. Asoka inaugurated Buddhist art by founding **stupas** and monasteries and set the pace for a popular religion in which the mass of the non-Aryans found a refuge along with the Aryans. The change was fundamental, and the rise of new peoples within India to which it led was one of the chief causes of the collapse of the Mauryan empire, but that led on to the dawn of the "heroic age" by collecting the whole tradition of popular mythology and heroic deeds in beautiful epic narrations, the *Mahabharata* and the *Ramayana*, as a religion of the masses. *See* plates 79, 81, pages 253, 275.

Maya. The most brilliant ancient civilization of the New World, and one of the most amazing of the entire past world, was that of the Maya people.

These **"Stone Age"** people amongst other achievements produced a form of **hieroglyphic** writing, and without scientific instruments compiled extensive astronomical data, and produced a calendrical system with a solar year and a leap year correction that was more accurate than our present Gregorian calendar.

The ancient Maya occupied the greater part of what is today known as Yucatán, Campeche, Tabasco, Chiapas and Quintana Roo in southern Mexico, and Guatemala (except the plain on the Pacific coast), British Honduras and small western sections of Honduras and El Salvador in northern Central America. This is an area very roughly the same size as the British Isles.

The Maya civilization flourished during the fourth to the sixteenth centuries A.D. and was at its height long before Columbus and the Spaniards invaded the continent of America. However, the whole story of the Maya, from their origin to their collapse, extends over a period of just over two thousand years starting at about 500 B.C.

Maya history has been divided into several periods, and different classifications and dates have been given by various scholars. New discoveries can change previously accepted ideas overnight and as archaeological work continues in Central America the Maya story and its place in the overall pattern of other early civilizations in the same area becomes clearer.

Until only a few years ago most authorities considered that the Maya civilization grew in isolation at its very beginning, and that other Central American civilizations emerged subsequently from contact with the embryo of the Maya. Some brilliant archaeological work since the second world war has now been analysed and the findings indicate a different picture, namely that several cultures appear to have emerged independently and more or less at the same time.

The main periods of the Maya story in this new light have been classified by the eminent British archaeologist J. Eric S. Thompson, who has spent many years of his life on excavation and exploration in the Maya area.

The Formative period, the beginning of which is very uncertain, is thought to have begun about 500 B.C., and to have continued until about A.D. 325. During this time the Maya people developed the culture which distinguished them from the other American Indians who inhabited that part of the world. Archaeologists have found very little, save pottery remains, by which to identify the Maya of this time with those who followed. No stone monuments, architecture, hieroglyphic writing or other datable remains have been found; there must have been monuments and buildings bearing inscriptions during this period but, as they were almost certainly made of wood or stucco, they have not survived the weather and the jungle. The reason for this certainty is that evidence is available of hieroglyphic writing on stone monuments, together with other proof of cultural and intellectual maturity, dating from the beginning of the fourth century of the Christian era. Naturally this maturity could not have been attained overnight, and such advances must have taken many many years. It is with regret that we feel reasonably sure that we shall never find relics, which will reveal more to us of the Formative period. The climate of the Middle East has helped the Egyptologist by preserving relics, but the student of the Maya is faced with the fact that the area of his interest is probably one of the worst, climatically, for the survival of such things as wood, cloth, and other perishable materials.

The second period is known as the Classic and lasted until A.D. 925. It was during this era of their history that the Maya reached the height of their achievement in art, architecture and other intellectual matters, a level never gained by any other people of pre-Columbian America, and never again attained by them. It was right at the close of the Formative and beginning of the Classic period that stone was first used by the Maya for the creation of their buildings and **stelae** on which they inscribed dates and other details in hieroglyphic writing. Many of these have been found, the earliest of which was a pyramid at Uaxactún, in the department of Peten in Guatemala. Amongst the many other important things discovered in Uaxactún by the late Sylvanus Morley and his colleagues of the Carnegie Institution of Washington, was the old stela known as Stela Nine, on which was carved a date in Maya hieroglyphics corresponding to A.D. 328.

A vast amount of information on the Maya achievements in the fields of agriculture, mathematics, calendrical systems, hieroglyphic writing, astronomy and architecture has been obtained from these early remains. It is indeed fortunate that the Maya wood-carvers were attracted at this time to use stone as another medium, and to become the originators of a long line of some of the finest stone masons the world has ever known – masons whose implements were simply of stone, wood or bone, because the Maya, for the whole of their history, were without metal tools.

Between the years A.D. 800 and 925, one of the mysteries in ancient American history took place. The Maya gradually abandoned one by one the work of their ceremonial centres and cities in the central region of their "Old Empire". In some cases the cessation was so sudden that buildings in the course of erection were left unfinished. Because of this, many authorities considered until quite recently (in fact, some still do) that there had been a wholesale exodus by the population from this area. However, modern archaeological excavations have convinced most people that this was not the case. Many ideas have been put forward during the last fifty years in attempts to explain the reason for this supposed exodus. Many theories about the cause of the migration of the population to the north and south have been advanced. They include disease, earthquakes, climatic conditions, invasion and even an interpretation by the priests of the command of the Maya gods. Some explanations have been pure fantasy, others scholarly works, the products of clear thinking and an appreciation of the facts available. However, no one reason has gained, or is likely to gain, general recognition as the evidence available is insufficient, and hypothesis must inevitably form part of the story. Nevertheless, the Maya did abandon the work on their ceremonial and religious centres, and a number, but not the whole of the population, did move away. The most probable explanation is that the peasants revolted against the hierarchy, a revolt brought about by reasons often repeated in other pages of the world's history – the inequality of rights between the two classes growing greater until the masses called a halt. This cessation in ceremonial city life and the things of aesthetic value that attended it, was a contributory cause of the decline and final close of the Classic period of Mayan history. There were other causes, one of which was the infiltration of Mexican influences from the west, influences which were gaining momentum at the close of the Classic period.

This Mexican intrusion continued for approximately the next hundred years, and from architectural remains, particularly those at the ancient city of **Chichen Itzá** (*see* plate 40, page 144) in Yucatán, it is apparent that these invaders were the Toltecs from an area north of modern Mexico City. Apart from the first fifty years (A.D. 925–75) which is classified as the "Interregnum", the next period of Maya history following the Classic is known as the Mexican period and lasted until A.D. 1200.

The Maya were influenced by the Toltecs to the extent that the Maya ruling groups incorporated Quetzalcoatl (the Feathered Serpent) and other Mexican gods into their existing pantheon. This caused the Maya to become far more militaristic than they had been in the past, for the religion of the Mexicans demanded intensive human sacrifice to sustain the gods. Warfare was therefore necessary to obtain extra victims for these sacrifices. A considerable amount of "popular" literature has been issued, aimed at appeasing the macabre taste of a portion of the public, highlighting these human sacrifices in ancient America: tales of how the hearts were torn out of living victims by blood-stained priests anxious to appease the gods. Such things were practised by the Maya throughout their history but never on such a large scale as, say, their neighbours, the **Aztecs**, with whom it became an all-consuming religious mania.

The worship of Quetzalcoatl and other Mexican influences gradually declined as the Toltec characteristics were slowly absorbed into the Maya way of life. Warfare, however, continued.

Many other civilizations in the past have collected and retained significant influences from foreign invaders. Language, religion and even physical characteristics have been changed to a marked degree and have differed so completely from the days before the foreigners came that the pre-invasion way of life has been unrecognizable from that which succeeded it.

The Maya, however, between A.D. 1200 and 1540 completely reversed the usual pattern of events. They shed their Mexican culture and all it entailed, the invaders themselves taking up the Maya way of life. This last period of the ancient Maya story is therefore known as that of the Mexican Absorption. The cultural decline continued and was reflected in nearly everything, especially in art and architecture. Internecine wars broke out and the Maya civilization came to an abrupt halt with the Guatemala was completed in 1525 and in 1541 Yucatán was enslaved. Only a small number of Maya, the Itzá, driven from Chichen Itzá, retained their independence on the small island of Tayasal in Lake Peten until 1697.

The Spaniards, with their desire to convert the "heathen" Indians to Christianity, together with their lust for gold, rapidly set about destroying everything Maya. This they performed with great skill, for all but three of the ancient Maya "books", the codices, were destroyed. These were made from a bark which was pounded to a cloth-like thickness and then covered with a thin sizing of lime to form a surface on which the hieroglyphics and illustrations were made. We have learnt much from these three codices, Codex Dresden, Codex Madrid, and Codex Paris (their names are derived from the places where they are now conserved): for example,

Förstemann, the German archaeologist, first obtained from the hieroglyphics in the Codex Dresden a considerable amount of information concerning Maya chronology – a truly brilliant piece of work. Undoubtedly many years of labour would have been saved for the students of the Maya if more codices had survived.

It was to a Spaniard, however, that we owe much of our knowledge of the last period of Maya history. Bishop Diego de Landa, arrived in Yucatán as a Franciscan friar just after the conquest, and in about 1560 produced his *Relación de Las Cosas de Yucatán* – the history of Yucatán. This book contains abundant information on the Maya and without it there is much we should never have known.

The physical characteristics of the ancient Maya have been portrayed to us from the many carvings, sculptured remains and the few murals that have been discovered. In addition it has been possible for exact details to be found out from skeletal remains unearthed by archaeologists in ancient burial grounds. It has been established therefore, that the ancient Maya was very similar to his modern descendants who now live in the Yucatán Peninsula and other adjacent areas. Similar that is in appearance only, for the present-day Maya has retained very little of the intellectual capacity of his ancestors, an intellect that was admittedly limited to the priests and noblemen. Many Maya (especially the women) still wear a form of dress that has changed little since pre-Columbian times. Their food, chiefly maize, is very much the same and very faint traces of their old religion have been incorporated (unofficially!) into their Christian form of worship. Well over a million Maya are now populating parts of Central America, mainly in Yucatán, British Honduras and Guatemala. It is impossible to know what the population was in the old days, and estimates have ranged from one to thirteen million. The modern Maya have been studied intensely by anthropologists and interesting comparisons made with their predecessors. They are short, stocky, usually *café-au-lait* complexioned people with high cheek bones, little facial hair and very broad heads (the average head width is over eighty-five per cent of the length). We know that the ancient Maya were very similar.

It is neither possible, nor intended, to give in these notes on the Maya more than a brief synopsis of their ancient civilization. The brilliant achievements of the ancient Maya have been briefly referred to above, and it is interesting to know that these intellectual achievements were nurtured, cultivated and given impetus by the Maya's fascination for the passing of time. The days, the months and the years, were all carefully named, symbolized, celebrated and recorded. Altars and stelae were erected to mark the close of certain periods and the hieroglyphics recorded the appropriate dates, the ruling gods and corresponding astronomical data. Their sacred year, *Tzolkin*, was a period of 260 days, and this determined the individual's and community's behaviour in the ceremonial and religious life for every day of this period. It was the ancient Maya's horoscope and contained rules for the day, and strict deference was paid to everything connected with it. There was also the normal calendar year or *Haab*, which was approximately 365 days. This was synchronized with the sacred "year" and the mathematics were such that future days for religious and other ceremonies could be calculated with absolute accuracy. Much of the sacred calendar dealt with the agricultural life of the Maya, the cultivation of Indian corn – maize, which was their "life blood", their staple diet. The Maya civilization evolved round this food, and it was their main concern in life. Many offerings were made to the gods – especially the corn god, to ensure that a successful harvest took place.

Maya hieroglyphic writing is very complex, and so far only about one third of the known signs have been deciphered; all of them have a mathematical, or astronomical, significance bound up with religious matters. It is one of the earliest forms of ideographic writing, that is, one in which the characters are **ideograms**, representing ideas rather than pictures. The work of decipherment continues, but it is impossible to forecast what progress, if any, will be made. There is no **Rosetta Stone** available to the student of the Maya.

The arithmetic of the Maya is remarkable for they were the first people to make calculations involving the use of the quantity zero. It was a vigesimal system, a progression by units of twenty, as compared with the decimal system. Two different forms of representing numbers were employed (as we ourselves use two: Roman numerals and Arabic notations). One method was a dot, equalling one, and a bar, equalling five. By the various combinations of these two symbols the Maya were able to perform their arithmetic, and record it in their inscriptions. The second method was the use of a symbol of a different type of human head (the heads were patron deities) for each number.

A little-known fact is that one of the finest collections of Mayan objects outside Mexico is in the British Museum. Here it is possible to see examples of their jade work, ceramics, stelae, hieroglyphics and carvings. Many of these objects were obtained late in the nineteenth century by Alfred Maudslay, the British archaeologist, who was one of the first men to make a serious and prolonged study of the ancient Maya. Other specimens in the collection were obtained by an expedition of the museum representatives in 1930. In the last fifty years the bulk of the archaeological and other research work on the Maya has been most ably performed by American institutions, in particular the Carnegie Institute of Washington.

There are still many pieces missing to the Maya jigsaw, and some will probably never be found. The picture that is portrayed to us today is sufficiently intriguing to ensure that the searchers will not relax their efforts. *See* plates 82–84, pages 276–278.

Medes, *see* Iran.

Medinet Habu. An Egyptian temple situated on the west bank of the Nile, on the edge of the desert near **Thebes**. It forms part of a long row of temples, including those of Seti I, Amenhotep III – to which are attached the famous colossi of "Memnon," at least sixty-four feet in height, – and the Ramasseum, which contains an enormous seated **colossus** of Ramses II in black granite. At Medinet Habu also is the temple of Ramses III, which is carved with interesting scenes of his wars in Syria and Lybia, and with scenes from religious festivals. The temple is chiefly remarkable for its unique entrance tower, which originally probably formed part of the royal palace. *See* plate 85, page 279.

Mediterranean, the Eastern. The term eastern Mediterranean is used here to cover Greece and Crete, the Greek islands, the western coast of Asia Minor and the island of Cyprus.

Interest in the antiquities of this region began with the revival of interest in Classical Greek civilization at the Renaissance. By the seventeenth century the agents of aristocratic collectors were searching these lands for remains of Greek sculpture and architecture, and it was the enthusiasm for Classical culture which ultimately led to the revelation of the prehistoric civilizations of the area.

In the nineteenth century the successful businessman Heinrich **Schliemann** was led, through his enthusiasm for the poems of **Homer** and a conviction (in opposition to the views of most contemporary scholars) that they were based on fact, to give up his profession in early middle age and devote the rest of his life to seeking archaeological proof of his idea. Schliemann's spectacular success, first at **Troy**, and then at **Mycenae**, began a brilliant era of research on east Mediterranean, and particularly Aegean, prehistory. Schliemann revealed the Mycenaean civilization of Greece which lay behind that of the Classical period and formed the background of the Homeric poems, but in 1900 Arthur (later Sir Arthur) **Evans** began to excavate the remains of a palace at **Knossos** in Crete and discovered the **Minoan civilization** which lay behind that of the Mycenaeans. Since then continuous and ever more intensive research has broadened the bases of our knowledge, and pushed back further and further in quest of the earliest human societies who inhabited the area. Much more surely remains to be discovered, but it is already possible to piece together the main outlines of this fascinating story.

Very little is yet known of the activities of man in the east Mediterranean during the Old **Stone Age**. Stone implements belonging to almost all the main phases of the **Palaeolithic** have been found in Asia Minor, but scarcely any have yet come to light in Greece, and none are known as yet from the islands of Crete and Cyprus.

At present, then, the story begins with the arrival of people in a **Neolithic** (or New Stone) stage of culture, who knew the arts of food-producing and were therefore able to lead a settled life in permanent villages instead of wandering in search of game. The arts of farming and stock-breeding which these people brought with them had been invented in western Asia some time previously, and it was almost certainly the search for new land to cultivate which brought the first settlers to Cyprus and the shores of the Aegean.

The earliest farmers known in Cyprus and northeast Greece were still at a stage when they did not use pottery, but in Cyprus at any rate they could make excellent stone bowls, and they no doubt also used containers made of other perishable materials. Very soon, however, pottery came into use all over the area. In Greece and Cyprus, and at a recently discovered site in western Asia Minor this earliest pottery was painted with patterns in red on a light background, and has close relations with the early painted pottery of western Asia generally. In Greece a rougher type of pottery, decorated by means of impressions made in the soft unbaked clay with a stick, finger-nail or shell-edge, was used by some early groups. This type also resembles some of the earliest pottery found on sites in western Asia.

The houses in the early villages were often built of mud-brick, and the remains of successive rebuildings of these form mounds which are easily recognizable, and show that the same sites were inhabited for many generations. This means that the Neolithic people knew how to maintain the fertility of their fields by manuring, and it may also imply that they cultivated fruit trees, though we have no direct evidence of this until a later phase of the Neolithic. They grew cereals, however, and bred cattle, sheep, goat and pig. Probably they practised transhumance, like some modern communities in the same region.

The early settlements were generally small, rarely exceeding 108 by eighty yards in area. In Cyprus houses were circular in plan and beehive-shaped. Round houses were known also in Greece, but rectangular ones were much more common. Houses were often of mud-brick on a stone foundation, but timber-frame houses covered with wattle and daub have recently been recognized in Thessaly. A house-model from a site there shows that they were sometimes gabled.

The early Neolithic people seem to have been peaceful. Their settlements are generally undefended and weapons are rare. Only the sling was known, and used probably in hunting. There was some trade, but the communities were in most ways self-sufficient. Little is known of their religious beliefs. No temples and scarcely any graves are known, but small models of houses, chairs, tables, vases, animals and human beings, chiefly women, may have some religious significance. Probably they had some sort of fertility cult, like those of the early farmers of western Asia.

In the later stages of the Neolithic and the commencement of the **Bronze Age** the picture changed and societies became definitely more warlike. A new culture appeared in the north whose settlements, often on the same sites as the older villages, were heavily defended by stone walls. These new people owned a material culture which shows connections with that of Neolithic people in the Balkans, and also perhaps with that of the first city of **Troy**.

A culture very like that of Troy II has been found on the Cilician Plain at the beginning of the Bronze Age, and the Early Bronze Age culture of Cyprus shows close similarities to the Cilician and Trojan culture. In the various islands of the **Cyclades** too, local cultures developed which owed much to the Troadic and Cypriote cultures, though they also have links with those of other parts of Asia Minor. The first Bronze Age culture of mainland Greece, known as Early Helladic, also seems to be due to immigrants from the Troad and other parts of western Asia Minor, so closely does it resemble the remains from these areas.

From the beginning of the second millennium B.C. Crete took a leading part in developments in the east Mediterranean. The Neolithic culture of Crete is still very imperfectly known, but its dark-faced, incised pottery seems to have more links with the early culture of central Asia Minor than with those of mainland Greece. Towards the middle of the third millennium B.C. influence and possibly immigrants from Asia Minor and north Africa combined with the earlier culture to produce the Early **Minoan** culture.

Cretan power and prestige were founded on trade and mastery of the sea. They had bases in the Cyclades and Rhodes, and they perhaps dominated part of the Greek mainland. Their pottery has turned up in Egypt and Syria, and pictures of Minoans appear on frescos in Egyptian tombs of the eighteenth dynasty. They influenced Egyptian art in the New Kingdom period, and it also seems likely that they penetrated into the central Mediterranean, influencing particularly the art of the still Neolithic inhabitants of **Malta**.

The apogee of Cretan civilization was attained in the Late Minoan I period (about 1550–1400 B.C.), after which it seems likely that the island fell under the domination of mainlanders. By 1400 B.C. power in the Aegean had passed to the Mycenaeans. Inscribed clay tablets of the Late Minoan II period (1450–1400 B.C.) from Knossos are written in an early form of Greek, identical with the language now known to have been spoken by the mainland Mycenaeans, and quite different from the Cretan language (*see* **Minoan Scripts**).

Soon after 1200 B.C. Mycenaean power collapsed under pressure from without. The last centuries of the second millennium B.C. are a time of chaos and crisis all over the east Mediterranean. Barbarian war-bands ranged far and wide, burning and looting towns and cities. Some of them, known to the Egyptians as **Sea Peoples** even got as far as attempting to invade Egypt, but were repulsed. In Crete the population retreated to inaccessible fastnesses and everywhere standards of living fell disastrously. Only Cyprus seems to have escaped to some extent, and there a culture of Mycenaean tradition long persisted. In mainland Greece the "Dark Age" which followed the end of Mycenaean civilization gradually gave place to a new synthesis which ultimately produced Classical Greek civilization.

Mediterranean, the Western. This article will touch on the prehistory of the following countries: Italy and the Italian islands, Malta, north Africa, Spain and the Balearic Islands, and the Mediterranean coast of France.

Knowledge about the prehistoric cultures of this region has grown only slowly, and at an unequal rate in different countries. Although some of the lands included contain striking monumental remains of prehistoric times, such as **megalithic** and rock-cut tombs, megalithic temples (as in Malta) and Cyclopean towers, as the *nuraghi* and *talayots* of Sardinia and the Balearics, all of which early attracted the attention of travellers and antiquaries, the field of prehistoric research was for long comparatively neglected through excessive preoccupation with Classical antiquities.

In the later nineteenth century, however, much good work was done by devoted scholars, both amateur and professional, in various parts of the area, of which that of the brothers Siret in south-eastern Spain, Pigorini in Italy, and Orsi and the brothers Cafici in Sicily achieved notable results. During the present century work has gone on in a more intensive fashion, particularly since the end of the last war, and it has now become possible to see the main outlines of prehistoric development in the area fairly clearly, though much still remains to be cleared up. Vital to the interpretation of west Mediterranean prehistory has been the work of discovery and systematization carried out by Dr L. Bernabò Brea in recent years in Sicily and the Lipari Islands. Beneath the medieval **acropolis** of Lipari itself his excavations have revealed a magnificent stratified sequence of remains covering the whole of prehistoric times from the Neolithic onwards.

In the west Mediterranean – unlike the east – the **Palaeolithic** is well represented. Abundant remains of the **flint** implements used by man in the earlier parts of this period have been found in Spain, southern France and Italy, and numerous finds of skeletons of **Neanderthal** men who made the Middle Palaeolithic **stone tools** have also been made in these areas. In the Upper Palaeolithic north-west Spain was included in the area of the hunting societies who produced the brilliant naturalistic paintings and engravings of animals well known in the caves of France, the Pyrenees and the Cantabrian Range. The influence of this art extended to central and eastern Spain also, where engravings of similar type have been found. Recently a rather similar art has been found in Sicily.

In late Upper Palaeolithic and **Mesolithic** times, however, a somewhat different type of art developed along the east coast of Spain; this depicted vigorous scenes of the life of groups who specialized in hunting with bow and arrows (as against the harpoons used in the north-west), and who sometimes used them in fighting among themselves. Pictures in a similar style have again recently come to light in Sicily.

At the beginning of the **Neolithic** period, however, cultural influences began to come from the east rather than the west and north, and southern Italy and Sicily became for a time the focus of progress. The earliest Neolithic societies in the West Mediterranean were small groups of primitive farmers who used pottery decorated with patterns impressed in the wet clay with a stick, finger or shell edge before firing. This pottery has close affinities with very early pottery from the Balkans, Greece and western Asia, and it indicates pretty clearly the direction from which its makers probably reached the west. This pottery is also known from the **Sudan** and parts of north Africa, and it is possible that a separate stream reached Spain from this direction and mingled there with the one which had followed the northern coast of the Mediterranean. The spread of the users of this pottery over large areas may be accounted for by the primitiveness of their agriculture. They were probably ignorant of techniques of preserving the fertility of the soil and so were forced to move on every few years in quest of new land. Remains of the users of impressed pottery have been found in south-eastern Italy, Sicily, Malta, northern Africa, Spain, southern France and north-western Italy. Their remains have also come to light on the Tremiti islands, off the east coast of Italy, and to reach these and Malta they must have had boats. They are never found far inland, and it may be inferred that much of their coastwise spread was by sea. They cultivated cereals and were stock-breeders, but in many cases they also supplemented this by hunting and collecting shell-fish, activities which they perhaps took over from the older Mesolithic inhabitants, just as they also adopted some of the latter's equipment of pigmy flints. Perhaps because of their still semi-nomadic mode of life, their settlements did not form mounds like those of the earliest farmers in the eastern Mediterranean.

After the initial uniformity produced by the spread of the impressed-pottery peasants, local groups soon emerge and diverge more or less rapidly from each other. In southern Italy and the Lipari Islands impressed pottery was soon superseded by more attractive painted pots whose shapes and patterns recall those used by early farmers in Greece and the Balkans. In southern Italy the makers of painted pottery lived in villages of farmsteads surrounded by rock-cut ditches. Villages may contain up to a hundred circular enclosures, each between six and a half and twenty-two yards in diameter, and delimiting a small farmyard. Apart from the ditch which encloses the village or farmstead, there is generally an outer one which takes in a much greater area, and may have surrounded the fields and pastures. More than 200 such sites have been identified on aerial photographs on a plain in northern Apulia which is only fifty miles long and thirty broad. Little is known, however, about the religion or burial practices of these people; such burials as have been found were generally in rubbish pits.

The fashion of making ditched enclosures around settlements spread to Sicily, but otherwise the impressed pottery culture continued there, though a certain amount of painted pottery was made or imported. The earliest painted pottery in Italy was of a very simple type, but later more elaborately decorated styles appeared. Finally, however, at the end of the Neolithic period, fashions changed, and a monochrome red pottery came into use in southern Italy, the Lipari Islands, and even in north-eastern Sicily. By this time the Lipari Islands had become an important centre for the export of the volcanic glass, obsidian, which was much prized for the manufacture of tools and weapons, such as arrowheads, and of which almost inexhaustible supplies existed on the islands.

At the beginning of the **Bronze Age**, probably soon after 2000 B.C., new influences, and probably also colonists, reached Sicily and Lipari from the eastern Mediterranean. It is significant of changing social and economic conditions that settlements, which had been generally on flat ground and often undefended in Neolithic times, are now found more and more in inaccessible, easily defensible, though often uncomfortable positions. Trade and commerce were developing rapidly, and with increased wealth and the interdependence of communities came the accompanying scourges of war and piracy. Sicily was colonized by various groups of people who used different types of painted pottery with eastern Mediterranean affinities. Their settlements are found on small rocky acropolises, and their cemeteries are nearby, often in the rocks below the settlement. They introduced the rock-cut burial vault which was such a common form of burial in the east Mediterranean. These occur in groups of up to about thirty, corresponding to the settlements, which are already the nuclei of urban agglomerations. In Lipari the Early Bronze Age people used unpainted pottery, which was decorated with incision, and has strong affinities with the Early Helladic pottery of Greece. By the mid-sixteenth century B.C. Lipari, at any rate, had come within the orbit of Aegean traders, since fragments of **Minoan** and **Mycenaean** pottery ranging in date from about 1550 to 1400 B.C. have been found among the local remains.

Meanwhile in other parts of the west Mediterranean various cultures had arisen, all characterized by the use of monumental rock-cut or megalithic collective tombs. In Malta there are rock-cut tombs and megalithic temples, the latter resembling tombs in plan, but actually used for the celebration of a cult of ancestors and of a fertility goddess. In its later stages this culture was strongly influenced by the Minoan/Mycenean civilization but to the end it seems to have been without metal.

Along the eastern and southern coasts of Spain small metal-using communities of semi-urban type sprang up and flourished throughout the first half of the second millennium B.C. They appear to have had wide contacts with Africa, Italy and the eastern Mediterranean. In south-east Spain they buried their dead in beehive-shaped tombs (*see* **Tholos Tombs**), along with an elaborate paraphernalia of symbolic and ritual objects, and pottery, both plain and decorated with religious symbols. Another type of pottery often found in these tombs is the so-called Bell-Beaker (*see* plate 24, page 94), which is also found in northern Italy, Sardinia, southern France, north-east Sicily, and even north Africa. This type of drinking vessel is also widespread in central and north-western Europe at about the same time, where it seems to be characteristic of a people of pastoralists and traders.

By the fourteenth century B.C. Italy and Sicily had been drawn fully into the orbit of Mycenaean commerce, while copper ingots of Mycenaean type have been found as far afield as Sardinia. The people of Lipari and eastern Sicily now used a new grey pottery; in Lipari this is found in villages of up to twenty-three oval huts, ruled by chiefs who had larger huts and used imported Mycenaean pots, while in Sicily it comes from large cemeteries of rock-cut tombs on the coast. Probably the settlements were on the flat ground nearby, but nothing is left of them. These people used metal freely for jewellery, tools and weapons, some of the latter being of an already outdated Aegean pattern. They also had metal vessels which they perhaps imported. Mycenaean traders also supplied them with blue paste beads, which are found at this time in Malta, south-east Spain, France and many other parts of Europe as well.

In Malta, the temple-builders had disappeared by 1400 B.C. and had been succeeded by metal-using people from south Italy, who were themselves supplanted shortly after by new colonists from Sicily. In south-eastern Spain, too, the older culture was replaced by a new one which discarded the old ritual equipment and substituted single burial, in **cists** or large jars, for collective interment. These new people were extremely warlike, living in inaccessible settlements on hillsides or small plateaux, but they were competent metallurgists, using bronze freely for tools and weapons.

In mainland Italy, however, metal long remained scarce, except in the vicinity of the Po Valley. This region was occupied in the Neolithic period by people of Balkan affinities, but later communities appeared who created a local bronze industry based on that of central Europe. They lived in villages of timber-frame houses walled with wattle and daub. In their later phases these were often raised on piles to avoid the consequences of floods which became more frequent with the worsening of climate which took place in the latter part of the second millennium in this region. The rest of Italy was inhabited in the Bronze Age by tribes who also lived in hut villages, but their economy seems to have been more pastoral.

The troubles which brought about and followed the collapse of Mycenaean power about 1200 B.C. had their repercussions in Italy. The Middle Bronze Age villages of Lipari were violently destroyed by people from the mainland who then settled there. This event may be recalled in a legend preserved by the Greeks about the conquest of Lipari by Liparos the son of Auson from the mainland. Other traditions recorded by later Greek colonists speak of the crossing of the Sikels from Italy to Sicily, and this too may be reflected in the abandonment about the same time of the coastal settlements there in favour of rocky fastnesses some distance inland. These settlements were, however, of truly urban size, and the dead from them were deposited in cemeteries of rock-cut tombs, which often number several thousand. Though there are no more Mycenaean imports, the whole culture is permeated by recollections of Mycenaean civilization. In a settlement at Pantalica the ruler even lived in a palace modelled on the Mycenaean **megaron**. Several stages of this culture have been distinguished, and it survived until the arrival of Greek colonists in the eighth century B.C.

The cause of the invasion of Lipari and eastern Sicily may well have been the arrival in Italy of bands of invaders belonging to the so-called "urnfield cultures" of central Europe. These may have been the first speakers of Indo-European languages in Italy. They brought with them their burial-rite of cremation, which had a vogue in Italy, though later the inhabitants of many areas switched back again to inhumation. Cremation, however, continued to be the rule in northern Italy during the Late Bronze and Early Iron Ages, and a fine industry of beaten bronzework following central European models developed in this area. In the late eighth century B.C. the Early **Iron Age** culture of Tuscany was transformed, partly through the influence of Greek and Phoenician merchants attracted by the rich iron ores of the area, and perhaps also partly by immigrants from Asia Minor, according to the tradition preserved by **Herodotus**, into the brilliant **Etruscan** civilization.

A similar transformation was effected in eastern and southern Spain in the culture of the natives by **Phoenicians** operating from bases like Carthage, which they had established among the backward peoples of northern Africa, and the Greeks, who colonized the Spanish coast from their older colony of Massilia, in southern France. The result was the creation of the Iberian culture with its attractive sculpture and painted pottery. Farther inland, however, Spain was now occupied by the descendants of Urnfield people, who were almost certainly already Celtic in speech.

In the west Mediterranean islands local cultures long continued to flourish. In Sardinia and the Balearics the population lived in villages dominated and defended by the massive stone towers called *nuraghi* and *talayots* respectively and built stone towers known as "giants' graves" in Sardinia and *navetas* in the Balearics (*see* **Minorca, Megalithic Remains in**). This way of life continued down to, and even after, the Roman conquest. The Sardinians produced a remarkable art featuring particularly rather spindly figures of men and animals in bronze, which has influenced some modern sculptors. In Corsica, where a similar culture probably existed, a series of huge stone monoliths carved to represent figures has recently come to light. *See* plate 86, page 280.

Megalith. Megalithic (from the Greek for "large stone") is the term applied to **Neolithic** and **Chalcolithic** monuments, built of great blocks of stone; a typical example is **Stonehenge** (*see* colour plate xv). Many long **barrows** contain a megalithic burial chamber. Also megalithic are the long avenues of **Carnac** (*see* plate 29, page 99) in Brittany and the famous monuments of **Minorca** (*see* plate 96, page 290).

Megaliths are found all round the coast of western Europe, from which it may be assumed that the people who were responsible for them were seafarers.

Meganthropus palaeojavanicus. The type specimen is a fragment of a lower jaw with first molar and two premolars in position, from central Java. The jaw is that of a giant ape-man, comparable in size with that of an adult gorilla, but without the typical large canines. Other specimens have subsequently been found, but the exact status of Meganthropus in the history of human evolution remains in dispute. It probably represents an early collateral form.

Megaron (plural – megara). A room in the shape of a narrow hall with a porch at one end and no exit at the other, and often with an open hearth in the centre. The name comes from the resemblance of the plan to **Homer**'s description of the hall of Odysseus.

Megiddo. The ruin of ancient Megiddo, the Armageddon (Hebrew *har-megiddo*, "Mount of Megiddo") of the Apocalypse, which stands nearly seventy feet high and has an area on the summit of over ten acres, is today called Tell el-Mutesellim, and lies on the north side of the Carmel Ridge, commanding the strategic opening of the best pass from the coastal plain of Palestine to Esdraelon. A German expedition excavated there from 1903 to 1905, but the major work was done by Chicago University from 1925 to 1939. They made a deep sounding through twenty levels to an early fourth millennium settlement. By Middle **Bronze Age** times the city was strongly fortified, but even so it was evidently destroyed frequently in this period, culminating in a great devastation, probably due to the Egyptian conquest of **Palestine** which marks the end of the Middle Bronze Age. The evidences of violence are less frequent in the Late Bronze Age, and the culture of Palestine in this period of Egyptian domination reflects the Canaanite civilization to the north. Though there are signs of destruction towards the end of the twelfth century, after the end of the Bronze Age and the arrival of the **Israelites**, the people who resettled the mound seem still to be **Canaanites**. The cultural influence from the north continued and is seen in a cache of over 200 carved ivories of a type well known later from as far afield as Assyria, but showing **Phoenician** design and workmanship. The earliest known Israelite remains belong to the period of Solomon, to whom are attributed some commodious stables capable of accommodating about 450 horses, and a triple-piered gate almost identical with one discovered at **Hazor.** Megiddo was probably destroyed in 733 B.C. by Tiglath-Pileser III, when it became the capital of an Assyrian province, but its subsequent history is of minor importance. *See* plate 87, page. 281.

Memphis. The capital of Egypt in the earliest times, Memphis is mentioned several times in the Old Testament and is situated on the west bank of the Nile fourteen miles south of Cairo, at Bedreshen. It was the chief seat of worship of the god Ptah. Its rise to importance began when Menes made it the capital of the united kingdoms of Upper and Lower Egypt. It remained the centre of government and the largest city in Egypt until the New Empire (1570 B.C.) when the worship of Amun replaced that of Ptah, and **Thebes** took the place of Memphis, which underwent rapid decline, accelerated by the rise of the arabic city of Fustat on the opposite bank of the Nile. Its ruins were used as a quarry for the building of Fustat and Cairo, with the result that only a few heaps of rubble remain to mark the position of the city, its royal palaces, temples and the Dwelling of Apis. But the necropolis of **Saqqara** was protected by blown sand, and forms part of a chain of **pyramids** and **mastaba**, extending for twenty miles, from **Giza** to Dashur.

Among the chief monuments at Memphis are the Sepulchre of Apis, which was discovered by A. F. F. **Mariette** in 1861, and the Coptic Monastery of St Jeremias, found in 1905 by J. E. Quibell, which contains remarkable frescos and sculptures. An important series of terracotta heads of Greek workmanship and dating from the time of Persian rule down to the Ptolemaic period was discovered by Sir Flinders **Petrie**. *See* plate 88, page 282.

Mendoza Codex, *see* Aztecs.

Menhir. A tall upright single stone, believed to have been erected as a monument. Particularly common in western England, they are also to be found in Europe, Africa, and Asia.

Merimde. This is a site on the borders of the Libyan desert, thirty-two miles downstream from Cairo. Excavations made here by H. Junker disclosed the remains of a large **Neolithic** settlement, consisting of light huts made of branches, arranged on either side of a main street. The foundations of the dwellings were of pounded earth. Inside these were hearths. A primitive sort of silo was also discovered here, consisting of trenches some twenty inches deep, lined with straw basket-work daubed with clay. Wheat-grains were found in them. Large, buried jars were also found, which were probably used for storing food. Graves of the women and children were found inside and outside the huts. The bodies were buried facing east, in a contracted or foetal position – with the knees drawn up to the chin. The long-bones of hippotamuses have been found here, stuck upright in the ground, probably representing some sort of religious monument. The village seems to have been abandoned when the invasion of the desert sands became intolerable.

Meroe. The main southern bastion of Egyptian influence, the city of Meroe was the southern capital of the kingdom of the Ethiopian kings of Napata from 700 to 300 B.C. Extensive ruins remain on the east bank of the Nile in the Egyptian **Sudan**. Meroitic sites extend over a wide area, as far up the Blue Nile as Roseires. Remains have recently been found 200 miles south of Khartoum.

The city of Meroe was surveyed by **Lepsius** in 1844. It consists of an enclosure containing royal palaces, the later ones having baths attached, and other buildings, dating back to Aspaluta (about 590 B.C.). A head of Augustus, now in the British Museum, was found here. Outside the enclosure are several temples, including those to Isis, the lion-god Apiremak and the sun. Two miles south is a shrine with stelae of Queen Candace and Akiniras, containing a reference to Augustus.

More distant cemeteries and pyramids were excavated by G. **Reisner** in 1921–23. There are two main groups of **pyramids**. The southern group dates from the eight to the third centuries B.C. Three kings were buried here. The northern group dates from the third century B.C. with a pyramid of thirty kings and queens. A great cemetery of nobles was found one mile west of the city.

Iron was smelted north of Khartoum from 400 B.C. Workings have been found on an island in the Nile north of Khartoum and in the region of Lake Chad.

The main inscriptions that have been found are not only in Egyptian **hieroglyphics**, but also in Meroitic scripts and are modelled on debased Egyptian. Fragments of Greek inscriptions have also been discovered. *See* plate 89, page 283.

Mesolithic. Mesolithic ("middle stone") is that part of the **Holocene epoch** which lies between the **Palaeolithic** of the **Pleistocene epoch** and the **Neolithic** and links the two together. It may be said to begin round about 10,000 B.C. From the point of view of material prosperity it was largely a continuance of the Palaeolithic, but it also marks the beginning of the food-producing, as opposed to the food-gathering and hunting, period. A characteristic **stone tool** of the Mesolithic Age is the **microlith** of the **Azilian** culture (*see also* **Stone Age**).

Mesopotamia, *see* Iraq.

Mesopotamian Sculpture. Statuary on the large scale is not an art in which the people of ancient Mesopotamia excelled, partly because they had no good stone, and preferred to work with precious materials, but mainly because their talent was for drawing figures in scenes of action, depicted on flat surfaces. These were mostly paintings on plastered walls and consequently have nearly all perished by decay.

Human forms in the round are nearly always of small size, being designed to stand in temples before the presence of the god's effigy so as to keep him continually in mind of the dedicators. A deposit of archaic figures, both men and women, was found at Tell Asmar near Baghdad; they are stark and angular, their eyes inset crudely with white shell giving a dark spot for the pupil. In strong contrast with these appear (about 2000 B.C.) the celebrated Gudea statuettes, all (with one exception) being much smaller than life. These are not only of fine style and finish, but they depict the governor of different ages, and are worked in different carefully-selected stones which, he tells us, were specially imported. The sudden excellence of these figures is unexplained, for they have no known forerunners, and no subsequent statuary (rare in any case) preserves their remarkable qualities.

In the art of bas-relief on stone several ages of Mesopotamian history have left notable examples. At the height of Sumerian civilization, about 2500 B.C., there are the famous reliefs on the "Stele of the Vultures", in the Louvre. Still more accomplished is the great sculptured monument, also in the Louvre, of Naram-Sin, of about 2300 B.C.

Best known of all Mesopotamian sculptures are the Assyrian reliefs, belonging to the ninth to seventh centuries B.C. These storied slabs, which have to be imagined as brightly coloured, lined the chambers, courts, and passages of the palaces which successive kings of Assyria built for themselves. The lion-hunt sculptures of Ashur-bani-pal in the British Museum, with their combination of splendid animal-studies and inexhaustible detail, are of unsurpassed interest among extant works of ancient art. *See* plate 90, page 284, and plate 17, page 87.

Mesozoic. An era of the earth's history lasting for some 120,000,000 years and comprising the geological periods of Triassic, Jurassic, and Cretaceous. It was preceded by the **Palaeozoic** and **Archaean** eras, and succeeded by the **Caenozoic** era. It is sometimes called the Secondary era.

Mexico. Few countries in the world provide such a rich field for the archaeologist as Mexico. Some two thousand sites have been recorded by the Mexican authorities, including pyramids, architectural remains of various kinds, temples, houses, tombs and fortifications. This is partly because with few exceptions, the monuments of the many cultures which flourished before and up to the Spanish conquest were allowed to decay naturally, while the books of picture-writing of the Indians were deliberately destroyed by the Spaniards. Only three codices, as these books are called, survive (*see* **Maya**). Consequently everything in Mexico which would in Europe be regarded as medieval history must be treated archaeologically.

The beginning of Mexican archaeology goes back to about 15,000 B.C. This early period was a hunting and food-gathering phase, comparable to the Middle or Upper **Palaeolithic** in Europe. The first inhabitants were nomads who had crossed into America from Asia by the Bering Strait, and filtered down through America. Naturally their remains are few, and only two sites are worth serious consideration. At the first, Tepexpan, the fossilized skeleton of a man was found face downwards in lake sediment of the **Pleistocene** era – about 10,000 B.C. The interpretation of this find has been questioned, and it has been suggested that the skeleton represents an intrusive burial. The second find, at Santa Isabel Iztapan, consisted of stone **artifacts** associated with the bones of a **mammoth.**

The first settled communities, and the cultivation of maize, a phase comparable to the **Neolithic** in Europe, can be dated to between 1500 B.C. and 1200 B.C. This period, known variously as the Archaic, pre-Classic, or Formative, lasted up to between A.D. 200 and 300. It is best known for its little, solid, hand-modelled figurines, variations of which are found all over Mexico and the area to the

the south. This culture has been studied most thoroughly in the Valley of Mexico. The Early Formative Period is represented by El Arbollilo, Zacatenco, and Tlatilco. In the Middle period Tlatilco had grown into a sizable village, and other sites in this period were Copilco and Coatepec. There was a great advance in the pottery of this period and jade figurines have also been found. As far as we can tell, the Olmec, or La Venta people of the Gulf Coast were the most advanced at this time. They will be described later. The Late Formative period, represented by Cuicuilco, saw the development of a regular priesthood. A large circular mound, in three terraces, surmounted by a small temple, could only have been produced after a high degree of social organization had been achieved. The period held the germs of all the principal elements of the Classic period, the Golden Age of Mexican archaeology, which was to follow it. The transition was a gradual one, and several of the great cities of the Classic period had their beginning in the Formative.

Probably the Classic period began somewhere between A.D. 200 and 300. In the Maya area, it is somewhat arbitrarily supposed to have begun about A.D. 320, the date of the earliest surviving inscriptions. It was a period of large cities, great cultural advances, and regional specialization, but one of regular intercourse between the various areas, pottery of obviously Teotihuacán manufacture, for example, being found as far south as Kaminaljuyu in Guatemala. Technically, however, it still remained a **Stone Age** culture.

The period is very complicated, and we can treat it best by considering the various regions separately. They were the highlands of central Mexico, the State of Oaxaca, the Gulf Coast region, the Maya area including the States of Tabasco, Chiapas, Campeche, Quintana Roo, and Yucatán, and finally the north and west of Mexico which are not so well known archaeologically.

On the Gulf Coast, the most advanced culture at the beginning of the period was that of the Olmecs. It was also a culture which seems to have had a great influence on the development of other areas. The earliest find of importance was the Tuxtla Statuette, discovered in 1902. It represents a man wearing a beak-like mask, and is inscribed with a date which if interpreted correctly would correspond to A.D. 162. This would place it in the Formative period, but it is relevant to the Classic period because of a number of carved **stelae**, one of which bears an even earlier date, found at Tres Zapotes by Matthew Stirling in 1936. These monuments, and especially the dates inscribed on them, may well have been the forerunners of the calendar system which spread all over Mexico, reaching its highest development among the Maya. The principal Olmec sites were Tres Zapotes, Cerro de las Mesas, and La Venta. Tres Zapotes consists of a number of mounds extending over a distance of about a mile and a half. The jaguar was one of their gods, often represented by ceremonial axes. These are carved with ferocious faces with snarling lips and beetling brows. They also made colossal monolithic stone heads, and naturalistic pottery and jade figurines, all characterized by a mouth drooping at the corners.

The Huaxtecs, living farther north in Vera Cruz, San Louis Potosi and Tamaulipas, were a warlike people who kept their identity not only through the Classic period, but also through the troubled times of the post-Classic. Serious excavations have been undertaken in the area by Du Solier, Ekholm, and Garcia Payon. The whole area is very rich in remains. The most characteristic feature of their architecture is perhaps the combination of rectangular and circular structures in the same building. Their sculpture is bold and simple. They practised cranial deformation and tattooing. Their pottery in the Late period was generally painted with a white slip and further adorned with heavy complicated patterns in black. Spouted vessels rather like teapots, used for chocolate, are the best known shape.

Also in the centre of the state of Vera Cruz was the so-called Totonac, or Tajin culture. This too survived into late post-Classic times. The data of its origin is uncertain, but it is almost certain to have been later than the Olmec culture. The most important site is Tajin, where there are many pyramids and mounds and no less than three ball-courts, covered by a deep layer of tropical vegetation. Only some of the buildings have been explored. Among these is the unique Pyramid of the Niches, a building of seven terraces, each delimited by a well-marked cornice. The top is reached by two stairways and the face of each terrace is lined with a row of rectangular niches. There are altogether 364 of these, and they may have some connection with the length of the solar year. With one more, possibly in a temple on top, there would be one for each day.

Tajin style sculpture is of a high order. Very typical are palmate stones, U-shaped yokes, and thin axe-like stones, carved in the form of human heads. Relief carving is characterized by tight scrolls and double outlines. Many examples of Tajin sculpture have been found in the Maya area.

While the great advance into the Classic period seems to have been initiated by the people of the Gulf Coast, the heart of the period was undoubtedly in the highlands of central Mexico. For this area Teotihuacan is the best example. It was the leading city in the Valley of Mexico, and has been the subject of many excavations, on which Batres, Gamio, Linne, and Armillas have worked. It had its origin in the Formative period, and dominated the area until its final decay, apparently before the Toltecs at the end of the Classic period. There are two huge pyramids, one of the sun, the other of the moon, the Temple of Quetzalcoatl, a long ceremonial road, as well as numerous other buildings. The Temple of Quetzalcoatl is a stepped pyramid with alternate representations of Quetzalcoatl, the feathered serpent, and of the rain god Tlaloc. Other gods they worshipped were a large female deity whose attributes are uncertain, and Xipe Totec, the flayed god, whose victims' skins were worn by the priests who sacrificed them. The influence of Teotihuacán spread far and wide, and examples of her pottery were traded as far south as Kaminaljuyu in Guatemala. Her figurines show a progressive elaboration from the simple hand-modelled types of the Formative period to very complicated, mould-made, and far less pleasing, mass-produced articles of their last period. Pottery showed considerable variety. The best known shape is a cylindrical vase with slab-like tripod feet. Decoration was commonly achieved by cutting away the burnished outer skin to reveal the lighter paste from which the pot was made. Another remarkable ware was ornamented by a coating of coloured stucco applied like **cloisonné**.

Just as the influence of the Olmecs is traceable in Teotihuacán, so is that of Teotihuacán to be seen all over Mexico. This is particularly true of the province of Oaxaca, where the Zapotecs, situated between the Teotihuacanos and the Maya, received strong influences from both, and also from the Olmecs. The best-known Zapotec city is Monte Alban, where the whole of the top of a hill has been levelled off to form a huge plaza bordered by the customary mounds and terraces. Their development also began in the Formative period and the well-known early figures, called Los Danzantes, the Dancers, show the typical drooping Olmec mouth, and caps not unlike those of the colossal stone heads of the Olmecs. They worshipped chiefly a god known as Cocijo, a rain god comparable to the Tlaloc of central Mexico. Other gods included a corn goddess, a general agricultural god and Xipe Totec. Human sacrifices were offered to all of these. They had, like the Maya, a bar and dot system of numeration, and a calendar derived from the Maya. Important people were buried in tombs, with urns modelled in the forms of their gods. Certain very rich tombs contained quantities of gold ornaments, probably made by the Mixtecs. The Mixtecs seem to have become the dominant power in Oaxaca towards the end of the Classic period, but they do not seem to have subjugated the Zapotecs completely because the two tribes were both resisting the Aztecs at a much later date.

The most interesting, and most studied, people in Mexico were the **Maya**. They, too, were influenced by the Olmecs. They are best known for their calendrical knowledge which they recorded on stone monuments. Many of their centres were in Chiapas, Tabasco, Quintana Roo and Yucatán. Their greatest development, however, took place in the Peten which is in Guatemala. Two Mexican sites are of paramount importance. At Palenque, Alberto Ruz discovered a tomb built into a pyramid, containing the burial of an important chief, and very rich in grave-goods. This has given rise in some quarters to speculation, which does not seem to be really justified, of connections with ancient Egypt. At Bonampak, an American photographer, Giles Healey, found a number of wall-paintings preserved under a coating of lime, which can be made transparent by the application of paraffin. The study of these has thrown much light on the ceremonial and ritual life of the Maya. At the end of the Classic period all building and astronomical activity ceased in southern Mexico and the Peten, though in Yucatán the Maya remained to be subjected to Mexican domination in the Late Classic period. This period is marked by the rise of Tula, the abandonment of Teotihuacán and the upheaval among the Maya already described. The home of the Toltecs is the great city of Tula, where for a number of years excavations have been carried out under Mexican government auspices by Jorge R. Acosta and others. They have shown that **Chichen**

Itzá, in Yucatán has many remarkable similarities; feathered serpent portals, Chacmool (rain-god) figures, and the same sequence of colour bands on buildings. The Mexicans who intervened in the quarrels of the Maya cities of Yucatán must have been Toltecs. The Toltecs themselves later suffered under an invasion of barbaric hunting people, the Chichimecs, bands of whom spread into the Valley of Mexico. They gradually adopted the culture of the cities already established there. One of these tribes, the **Aztecs**, was the dominant tribe at the time of the Spanish conquest.

The problems of the archaeologist in Mexico are complex and varied. One of the most interesting is exactly what lead to the break-up of the Classic period. The difficulty in solving this lies to some extent in the wealth of sites needing excavation and the limits which have to be set to the resources available. The Mexican authorities have done wonderful work, and solutions to the problems of the Classic and Late Classic period are only a matter of time. The same is true to some extent of the Formative period, but the chances of learning very much about the early hunting period are not so good. *See* colour plate x, plates 91–92, 94, pages 285–286, 288.

Microlith. Microliths ("small stones") are tiny **flint** tools which are principally found in **Mesolithic** settlements and camps such as those of the **Azilian** culture. They are very small **flakes** about an inch long, skilfully chipped and carefully shaped.

Midden. A refuse-dump, onto which prehistoric man threw all his discarded objects, chiefly bones and shells. Since much of what **archaeology** has discovered about the past is based on what man has discarded, lost, or thrown away as no longer useful, middens are a very valuable source of material to the archaeologist.

Middle Stone Age, *see* Mesolithic *and* Stone Age.

Midland Man, *see* America, Early Man in *and* Fossil Man.

Miller, Hugh (1802–56). For long an ordinary quarry-worker, Hugh Miller developed a passion for geology aroused by the specimens he uncovered in the pits where he worked along the shores of the Moray Firth in Scotland. He eventually achieved fame as a geologist and his book *The Old Red Sandstone* (1841) became a classic.

Minnesota Man, *see* America, Early Man in.

Minoan Civilization. From about 2400 B.C. to 1400 B.C. Crete was the centre of a splendid civilization, all trace of which then disappeared, except for the legends recorded by the Greeks of classical times. It fell to Sir Arthur **Evans** to prove that the legends were based on fact. By his brilliant excavations on Crete, principally at **Knossos** (*see* plate 68, page 242), he proved the existence of a civilization centuries older than that of the classical Greeks. He called this civilization Minoan, naming it after the legendary King Minos, and he divided it into three periods – Early, Middle and Late.

The Early Minoan civilization lasted from about 2500–2000 B.C. This was followed by the Middle Minoan period, in which the island became extremely wealthy through commerce. A brilliant civilization was created, and the rulers who emerged at a few centres in the fertile central part of Crete built themselves large labyrinthine palaces, the largest of which is the one at Knossos excavated by Evans. These palaces were several times destroyed, probably by earthquakes, and each time rebuilt on traditional, but more splendid, lines. They were surrounded by populous and extensive towns, whose two-storied houses are pictured for us in a mosaic found at Knossos, and whose richer inhabitants evidently lived in considerable luxury. Accounts and inventories were kept in a system of writing adapted and modified from the methods used by the Egyptians and Syrians with whom the Minoans traded. However, there is no linguistic link between Egyptian and Babylonian writing and the **Minoan Script** Linear B. Pottery was now made on the potter's wheel and wheeled vehicles were in use. Vases, sometimes eggshell-thin, were painted with attractive patterns, and the palaces and large houses were adorned with brightly coloured frescos depicting landscapes, fish, birds, animals, and scenes from Cretan life. Many other arts, such as seal-making, carving in ivory and stone, metal-working and jewellery reached a high level.

The Cretan palaces and villas are collections of rectangular rooms, lit by light-wells and equipped with excellent drainage systems. The palaces were furnished with long rows of magazines in which stocks of oil, wine and grain were stored in huge jars. The rulers of Crete were priest-kings, and their palaces contain various ritual installations, such as lustral baths. They probably also presided over displays of bull-leaping performed by specially trained youths and maidens, which were public spectacles, but also had their religious side, since the bull was important in Minoan ritual. The complex plan of the palaces and the association of the priest-king with bulls almost certainly gave rise to the Greek legend of the labyrinth and the **Minotaur.** The bull-leapers themselves may well have been the children of subject people abroad sent to Crete as tribute. The Minoans also worshipped a fertility goddess, who was associated with wild animals and snakes, in cave sanctuaries, and built pillar-shrines crowned with "horns of consecration". Their dead were buried in a great variety of ways.

The Late Minoan period began about 1550 B.C. and saw the climax of Cretan civilization. About 1400 B.C. the palace of Knossos was violently destroyed and supremacy in the Aegean area passed to the people of **Mycenae.** *See* plates 93, 95, pages 287, 289.

Minoan Scripts. Sir Arthur **Evans** coined the term **Minoan** as a label for anything typical of the great prehistoric culture of Crete. His earliest researches disclosed the existence of a **pictographic** script found chiefly on engraved seal-stones, dating from the first part of the Middle Minoan period (2000–1550 B.C.); this he termed, after the early Egyptian script, **hieroglyphic**. His excavation of the palace of **Knossos** produced abundant evidence of writing, mostly on tablets of unbaked clay inscribed with a sharp stylus while the clay was moist. The analysis of these documents revealed two variant forms of the script, descended from the hieroglyphic, but replacing the pictorial signs with bare and often unrecognizable outlines. These Evans named Linear A and Linear B.

Another member of this family was recognized in the **Bronze Age** script of Cyprus, called Cypro-Minoan. The earliest example of this so far known is dated to the fifteenth century B.C., and in varying forms it continued in use, both in Cyprus and in the Syrian city of Ugarit (**Ras Shamra**), down to about the eleventh century. Examples are still relatively few and poorly preserved, and the full history of the script is not yet known. Although direct evidence of continuity is lacking, this script must have been the origin of the Cypriot syllabary of the classical period (sixth to third centuries B.C.). This was used for inscriptions in Greek, and also in an unknown language usually called Eteo-Cyprian. It was deciphered by means of bilingual texts during the latter part of the nineteenth century, the first steps being due to the English scholar George **Smith.** It differs in some details of its structure from Linear B, and only signs of the simplest form can be equated in the two systems. The direction of writing is normally from right to left, and in this it differs from the Bronze Age Minoan scripts which all run from left to right.

Linear A has been found inscribed on clay tablets and religious articles of stone and metal, and painted or scratched on pottery from a large number of sites in Minoan Crete. Although some potters' marks from sites outside Crete (Melos, Lipari) may have affinities with this script, no true inscriptions have yet been found anywhere else. The largest collection of clay tablets (about 150) is an archive from the palace of **Hagia Triada**, near Phaistos in the south of Crete; but similar tablets have been found at **Phaistos**, Knossos, **Tylissos**, Palaikastro, Zakro and **Mallia.** It was clearly in extensive use throughout Crete in the Middle Minoan period, probably continuing into the first part of the Late Minoan period (roughly 1550–1450 B.C.); the exact chronological limits are disputed, and it is doubtful whether or not it overlapped with Linear B.

The clay tablets consist almost exclusively of lists of what appear to be names, followed by amounts or numbers of various commodities. Numerous attempts have been made to interpret the inscriptions, in particular since the decipherment of Linear B; but despite great advances in the understanding of their contents, little progress can be made at present in identifying the language, since very few of the sign-groups appear to represent vocabulary words. A Semitic connection has been proposed, but has not yet been conclusively demonstrated.

The relationship between Linear A and Linear B is now clearly seen not to be so close as was believed by Evans, who thought the later script was due to nothing more than orthographic reform. Significant differences in the metric systems were observed by Emmett L. Bennett Jnr. in 1950, and the demonstration that Linear B concealed the Greek language made it certain that the change corresponded to the adaptation of the script to write a different language. The common origin is, however, beyond question; more than half the signs are recognizably the same in both scripts; but Linear A remains obscure, and is likely to be so until more material is available for study.

Linear B was first found on clay tablets at Knossos in 1900, where it was in use in the Late Minoan Palace, destroyed about 1400 B.C. But it is not yet recorded at any other site in Crete. It was identified on the mainland of Greece on Mycenaean jars found at Thebes and **Orchomenos** in Boeotia, at Eleusis in Attica, and at **Mycenae** and **Tiryns** in the Argolid. It was not until 1939 that clay tablets in this script were found on the mainland, in the Mycenaean palace at **Pylos** in Messenia (a site called Epano Englianos, a few miles north-west of the Bay of Navarino). The tablets appear to date to about 1200 B.C. Further tablets of the thirteenth century were found at Mycenae in 1952 and later years, in buildings outside the citadel walls. The total number of tablets known to date is about 5,000, but this includes a very large number of small fragments.

The script consists of ninety syllabic signs (some very rare ones may be variants rather than separate characters). These are used in groups of from two to eight signs, separated into words by a small vertical stroke. Single syllabic signs are often used as abbreviations. The numeral system is self-evident; it is decimal in character, the number of units, tens and so forth, being indicated by repeating the sign the appropriate number of times; upright strokes are units, horizontal bars tens, circles hundreds, circles with rays thousands. The numerals are regularly accompanied by **ideograms**, single signs denoting objects, commodities etc., many of them sufficiently pictorial to be clearly recognizable.

Each syllabic sign represents a whole syllable; either a vowel (*a e i o u*) or a consonant plus vowel (*ma me mi* etc.). The range of consonants is restricted, and one series of signs serves to represent *k*, *kh* and *g*; likewise *p*, *ph* and *b*; and *t* and *th*; *l* and *r* are confused in a single series. On the other hand two consonants unknown to later Greek are used: *w* representing the archaic Greek letter *digamma* (Ϝ), which is found in some early alphabetic inscriptions; and *q* standing for the "labio-velar" consonants which are partially preserved in Latin (as qu*is ning*u*it*), but had been eliminated from all later Greek dialects. There are also a number of rare signs conventionally transcribed pa_2, ra_2, ra_3, (or *pá*, *rá*, *rà*) etc.; these are probably not real doublets, but represent slightly different values; ra_2 for instance is often to be read *ria*, ra_3 as *rai*.

The script is ill-suited to the writing of the Greek language. As a result the gap between spelling and pronunciation is much wider than in alphabetic scripts. Consonants coming together are noted by the addition of extra vowels (*ko-no-so* = *Knōs*(*s*)*o*(*s*); *ku-ru-so* = *khruso*(*s*) "gold"). But final consonants (only *n*, *r* and *s* in Greek) are omitted, and *m*, *n*, *l*, *r*, and *s* are also omitted at the end of a syllable before another consonant (*pa-ka-na* = *phasgana* "swords"; *ka-ko* = *khalkos* "bronze"); *pa-te* = *pantes* "all" or *pater* "father"). In addition *i* as the second member of a diphthong is omitted at the end of a word or syllable (*po-me* = *poimēn* "shepherd", *ko-wo* = *korwoi* "boys"); but is represented by the consonant *j*, if a vowel follows immediately (*i-je-re-ja* = *hiereia* "priestess").

The ambiguities inherent in this system have given an opportunity for attacks on the correctness of the decipherment; but it must be borne in mind that these ambiguities only appear so to us, and the correct reading would have been instantly apprehended by the Mycenaean reader; in any case the tablets are all of the nature of memoranda or lists, which were probably never intended to be read by anyone other than those concerned in their writing.

The language of the tablets is a very archaic form of Greek, which is otherwise known only from alphabetic texts of the seventh century B.C. onwards. The closest relatives surviving into the classical period are the dialects of Arcadia and Cyprus, which have long been believed to be relics of pre-**Dorian** Greece. The areas where tablets have been found were inhabited in classical times by speakers of the Doric dialect, which is significantly different from Mycenaean; these peoples are believed to have caused the collapse of Mycenaean civilization by their invasion about 1200–1100 B.C.

Despite its unfamiliar forms there is no doubt that the Mycenaean dialect is properly described as Greek. It shows sound-changes which are characteristic of Greek; and its vocabulary contains numerous words which are known only in Greek. Some of these may be loan-words from a pre-Hellenic language of the Aegean area; but others which are not loan-words already show exactly the same form as they have in classical Greek. The decipherment has in many respects confirmed previous theories about the early stages of the Greek language, and the lack of surprises is yet another proof of the validity of the decipherment.

The decipherment was the single-handed achievement of Michael **Ventris.** Numerous earlier attempts had failed owing to the lack of sufficient material; his was the first which was able to make use of the newly published Pylos tablets. Much sound and valuable work had, however, been done by Evans himself, the Finnish scholar J. Sundwall, and the Americans Alice Kober and Emmett L. Bennett.

No bilingual texts are known. The decipherment had therefore to begin by a statistical analysis of the frequency of signs in different positions and combinations. The number of signs indicated that it was a syllabary of simple type, probably, like the Cypriot, consisting of signs for the consonants with each of the vowels. This work revealed the presence of inflected forms, words having the same stem but different endings. Variant spellings of the same word were also detected by this means. Two genders were distinguished by inflexional variation in words accompanying the ideograms for man and woman. These pairs of words could then be used to give information about the probable relationship of the signs; some pairs were associated as sharing the same consonant, others as sharing the same vowel. A long period of testing these links enabled Ventris to build up what he called a "grid": a table of signs in which those in the same horizontal line had the same consonant but different vowels, those in the same vertical column had the same vowel but different consonants. Most of the common signs were placed on this grid before values were assigned to any. A possible clue was the resemblance between the simpler signs of Linear B and the Cypriot script; but although this was a tempting lead, the similarities were in all but a few cases hard to decide, and Ventris dismissed this as a starting point, though it may have influenced him unconsciously. Instead he took a group of words which had been pointed out by Miss Kober. Identifying them as Cretan place-names, Ventris tried to match them with likely place-names known from historical times, being guided by the requirements of the grid. The names of Knossos and Amnisos were identified by this means, and the determination of six signs in these two words gave values in three vertical columns and five horizontal lines of the grid. These allowed further guesses to be made about some of the vocabulary words, which began to show resemblances to Greek. Although far from believing in a Greek solution, Ventris experimented with Greek interpretations, being driven to elaborate the system of abbreviated spellings outlined above. The result was the rapid identification of a number of Greek words which gave plausible sense in their contexts.

From that point the decipherment became a matter of applying knowledge of the Greek language to the data. Ventris began to work on this with John Chadwick, and together they developed the theory to the point at which it was accepted by other scholars, who in turn added their contributions to the increasing stock of knowledge about it.

The most striking confirmation came just a year after Ventris had taken the first steps. Professor C. Blegen, the excavator of Pylos, started testing the experimental values on the new tablets which he had found the previous summer. He quickly noticed a large tablet with **pictograms** of various pots. The text of this transliterated with Ventris's values yielded clear Greek words: tripod cauldrons were described as *ti-ri-po-de*, and a series of vessels called *di-pa* (Homeric *depas*) and epithets recording the number of their handles; and these numbers could be verified from the pictograms, in which the handles appeared as loops attached to the rim. Several similar cases have since been found where a pictogram has an annotation which is an appropriate Greek description; and this proof of the decipherment has been accepted by all but a handful of scholars.

Although it was soon possible to translate coherent phrases and some whole tablets, many difficulties remained, some of which are probably beyond the reach of a solution. This is particularly true where we have to deal with technical terms which did not survive, or survived only with altered meaning, into historical times. Even more difficult than the problems of translation are those of interpretation. The tablets were written by scribes for their own use, or at least that of their immediate colleagues and superiors; they were never intended to be intelligible to strangers. Thus we often find that even when we can give a complete translation, we are still far from understanding what were the circumstances in which the record was made. Careful analysis and comparison with similar records found in other cultures (e.g. at **Ras Shamra,** Nuzi, **Tell Atchana** etc.) have enabled some progress to be made.

The graphic system prevents certain identification of more than a small fraction of the personal names which make up the bulk of the records. It is however, clear that a large proportion of these names were Greek, though some are apparently of foreign origin, especially in Crete. More than fifty names can be identified with names in the text of **Homer**, the most remarkable being Hector and Achilles. None of these names can be referred to any actual person mentioned by Homer or the other legends.

The geography of the tablets is equally obscure. The numerous place-names recorded at Pylos include a few which can be identified on a map; there is no doubt that Pylos was the Mycenaean name of the site. Internal evidence suggests that the kingdom was restricted approximately to the area of the classical Messenia, though it is tempting to locate some place-names outside that area. In Crete about a dozen names can be placed on a map; these cover almost the whole island, but none appears to belong outside Crete.

The contents of the Linear B tablets are very dull; we should not give them much thought if we had anything better; but in default of all other sources of information we have to recover all we can from these bare lists and inventories. Both Knossos and Pylos were the centres of monarchies; there was also an important person called the *lawagetas*, who may have been a military commander; and various other titles and officials are known, though we know little of their powers or functions. A large number of men are referred to by their occupations, and although many are natural and expected (bakers, cowherds, wood-cutters, potters), many are specialized craftsmen (goldsmiths, bow-makers, perfumers). Slavery was certainly known, though under what conditions we cannot say; it is likely that the Palace of Pylos controlled a female labour force of some six hundred slaves; not all in one place, but scattered in various parts of the kingdom. Many of these women are described by their occupations (corn-grinders, bath-attendants, carders, spinners, weavers, etc.).

The dominant impression given by the tablets is of the strength of the Mycenaean bureaucracy. Not a jar of oil or a pot of honey left the palace stores without a clerk making a note of its destination. It is unfortunate that the clerks made many of their notes in abbreviated form. Moreover, they do not seem to have kept records for any length of time; the tablets recovered at both Knossos and Pylos apparently deal only with a single year. It is ironic that the more important records may have been kept on a perishable material (papyrus or skins?), and that what we have left are only the rough day-to-day notes.

However, it seems fairly certain that literacy was not very widespread, for not a single inscription in Linear B has been found on stone or bronze; no buildings or tombs bear the name of their builders. Thus any hope of recovering a Mycenaean literature is vain; if, as is likely, there was already a tradition of Greek poetry, it was an oral tradition, and the poems were recited, not written down to be read. It may be doubted if the Linear B script would have been adequate for that purpose, even for Mycenaeans.

Minorca, Megalithic Remains in. The megalithic remains in Minorca in the western Mediterranean are unique. There are three types, the talayot, the taula, and the naveta.

The talayot is a circular building constructed of unmortared stones, usually built solid as if for the foundation of a superstructure, but occasionally containing a small chamber at ground level. Talayots occur in groups, rarely singly. Their use is still conjectural, but possibly they were the foundations of houses. There are upwards of three hundred still standing in different parts of the islands.

The taula (*tabula*) stands to the south-east of a group of talayots, and is enclosed with them in an encircling wall, suggesting a walled village. A taula is never a solitary monument but is always in close proximity to the largest and most important talayot of the group. A taula consists of a thin stone slab set upright with an oblong stone block laid horizontally across the top. This upper block, being much longer and wider than the shaft, overhangs on every side, giving the appearance of a table. The supporting shaft is often the cap of an outcrop of limestone, which has been split off and the edges squared by hammer-dressing, the flat sides being left in their natural roughness. In contrast with the shaft the upper stone is always carefully worked, all the angles are sharply defined, the top is flat and smooth, and the sides are bevelled downwards and inwards so that it overhangs the shaft by one to two feet all round. In some cases the upper stone has a groove on the under side which fits over the top of the shaft as a mortise-and-tenon joint. In other cases the upper stone is merely balanced on the top of the shaft and remains in position by its own weight. There appears to be no standard of proportion between the shaft and the upper stone, or between the height and width of the shaft. The measurements of the taula of Trapuco are as follows: total height sixteen feet; shaft, width nine feet, thickness one foot to one foot six inches; upper stone, twelve feet four inches by five feet seven inches by two feet one inch. A taula faces south and stands well to the west of the centre of a circular or semi-circular **temenos**, of which the limits were indicated by narrow stone slabs set upright like pillars at intervals all round. At what appears to have been a later date a wall of unmortared stones was built outside the "pillars". The entrance, which is never opposite the taula, is to the south-east, and is by steps and through massive gate-posts. There is no trace of a temenos having been roofed, whether by flat stones or by corbelling.

A naveta is a boat-shaped structure, pointed at one end and square at the other, like the bow and stern of a boat. The only naveta which is still almost complete shows that it represented an overturned boat. A naveta always stands at a distance of about 433 yards from a group of talayots, and was part of the same complex. Its use was as an ossuary. The grave-goods from the primary burials appear to have always been taken with the bones and put with them into the naveta. The grave-goods consist of pottery of the Early **Bronze Age** and objects of copper and bronze. No iron or late pottery has ever been found in a naveta.

The three main megalithic sites in the island are: (1) Torre d'en Gaumes, near Alayor, which is the largest and contains at least three taulas; (2) Son Carlá, near Ciudadela, also a large site; (3) Trapucó, near Mahón, once probably as large as the others but now partly destroyed by modern buildings. *See* plate 96, page 290.

Minotaur. In Greek legend the Minotaur was a monster, half man, half bull, which fed on human flesh and was kept in a maze called a labyrinth at Knossos on Crete; the Athenians had to send every ninth year seven youths and seven maidens as food for the Minotaur. This continued until Theseus killed the monster, finding his way out of the labyrinth with the help of a ball of string given to him by Ariadne.

Until 1900 historians believed there was no truth in this tradition. Then Sir Arthur **Evans** excavated **Knossos** and proved the existence of the **Minoan civilization**. Here the name of the dynasty was Minos and a bull (Greek – *tauros*) was an object of worship by ritual dances in which young men and women seized the horns of a charging bull and turned back-somersaults over his shoulders. Nor was this all. The symbol of the royal power in Minoan days was a double-headed axe called a *labrys*; and Sir Arthur Evans suggests that the royal palace at Knossos was named the "labyrinth" because it was where the "labrys" was kept; certainly it is clear, from its ground-plan, that it was such a maze of rooms, halls and passages that a visitor could only too easily lose his way in it.

Miocene Epoch. Named from the Greek *meion* – less; *kainos* – recent, the Miocene epoch marked the mid-point of **Tertiary** times, and, with a duration of 20,000,000 years, drew to a close only a little more than 16,000,000 years ago. From the point of view of modern world geography the epoch was perhaps the most important of the period in geological history.

The outstanding feature of Miocene times was the final upheaval of the Alps and Himalayas by powerful crustal movements which squeezed and buckled the sedimentary strata of the Tethyan geosyncline (large degression of the earth's surface) to form highly complex mountain chains (*see* **Eocene** and **Oligocene epochs**). The ancient Tethys "Ocean" was reduced to mere lagoons and inland seas, some of which eventually survived as the Mediterranean. During this period Asia finally became united to Europe, and was for a short time also linked with north Africa and North America. Britain formed part of a land area undergoing erosion; the principal fold structures now present in the strata of south-east England merely represent the northern fringe effects of the Alpine mountain-building movements.

After Oligocene times the cooler and more arid climate of the Miocene epoch led to further shrinkage of wooded areas in many parts of the world; the continued spread of carpet vegetation, such as grasses and flowers, stimulated the evolutionary development and multiplication of herbivorous mammals, and the flesh-eating types which preyed upon them. Most of these mammals belonged to families which have persisted to the present day.

Miocene horses, like Prothyppus and Merychyppus, had smaller lateral toes, and teeth with higher crowns than their more diminutive Oligocene ancestors. Elephants of varied types and increasing size spread from Africa into Europe and Asia (Trilophodon), and finally to North America (Gomphotherium). Rhinoceroses and camels of different kinds had also become widely distributed. Amongst the commonest carnivores were small sabre-toothed "tigers", but probably the most fearsome beast was the "bear-dog" Amphicyon. Amongst the primates were the primitive anthropoid apes known as **Proconsul** which flourished in parts of east Africa. These ape-like creatures may have contributed to the stock from which man was to evolve.

Mison. This site, on the banks of the Song Thu-bon, south of Tourane in central Viet-Nam, appears to have been especially favoured by the **Chams**, and it was the religious centre of the kingdom, it appears, wherever the capital was situated. The earliest surviving building dates from the sixth century A.D., but an inscription says that this was erected to replace one in wood which was destroyed by fire. There are the remains of some sixty-seven buildings on the site, all in brick and dating from between the sixth and the thirteenth centuries A.D. The contrast with **Khmer** architecture is marked especially by the complete absence of any attempt to integrate the buildings into a complex. Although some of the smaller structures must clearly have been associated with their larger neighbours, they are not interrelated architecturally into a single plan. The bulk of the statuary from Mison is now in the museum at Tourane. Although the themes are Indian, the treatment is clearly local, and has some affinities with certain Javanese styles. Other finds from the site, in addition to large numbers of inscriptions in both Sanskrit and Cham, include some remarkably finely worked golden jewellery, and examples of silverwork. The reliefs bear witness to music and dancing as Cham entertainments, and there are numerous representations of religious scenes and of animals treated in a most naturalistic and attractive manner. The Cham sculptors were also skilled in the devising and representation of mythical beasts which served as caryatids and to accent architectural features.

Mitannians, *see* Hurrians.

Mlu Prei. This area, to the south of the Dangrek Mountains in Cambodia has been the centre of metal-working for many centuries, apparently conducted by tribal peoples known as Kuy. Archaeological investigations have revealed the existence of a **Neolithic** culture in the region, with a considerable corpus of **stone tools** of various methods of manufacture: flaking, polishing, sawing and drilling. The forms, which all have off-centre cutting edges, and many of which are adzes, include also chisels and gouges, and are of lenticular, trapezoid and rectangular cross-section. Polishers, sharpeners, bark-cloth beaters, potter's tools, knives and points have been found, as well as bracelets and drilled beads. There are also a number of moulds for bronze casting. Bone objects include pins, combs and points. The bronze material includes simple axes with asymmetrical edges, adzes and chisels, knife-blades, and sickles, as well as bracelets. There is considerable evidence for iron-working on the same sites. There is an extensive ceramic corpus, though there is no trace of slip or painting, and all the wares are relatively low-fired. The decoration is either incised or in low relief. Some of the designs seem to have been made with cords or bamboo devices. There is a marked absence of handles and lids. The material has some affinities with that of Samrong Sen, farther south, but possibly its real connections are with the Eurasiatic steppe cultures, perhaps by way of Yunnan.

Moche or Mochica culture, *see* Peruvians.

Moeris, Lake. Moeris is the classical name for the great lake of the **Faiyum** in Egypt. It lies about 130 feet below the level of the Mediterranean, and is approximately thirty-four miles long and six and a half miles wide at its broadest point. Classical authors attribute the construction of the lake to a King Moeris; but the word probably derives from the Egyptian expression *Mi-wer*, the name both of a town on the lake (possibly Ghurob) and also of the canal connecting the lake with the Nile. The lake is in fact a natural reservoir fed by the Bahr Yusuf, a natural arm of the Nile leaving the main stream in the neighbourhood of Asiut. The level of the present lake is one hundred and eighty feet lower than that of **Neolithic** times.

Mohenjo-Daro. The site, on the banks of the river Indus in the Larkana district of Sind (West

Photo: J. Allan Cash

PLATE 97. MOHENJO-DARO: street showing covered drain.

Photo: from "Old Stone Age" by Stevan Celebonovic and Geoffrey Grigson, Phoenix House Ltd, London

PLATE 98. MOUSTERIAN: balls of flint which may have been used as bolas stones, from the type-site at Le Moustier.

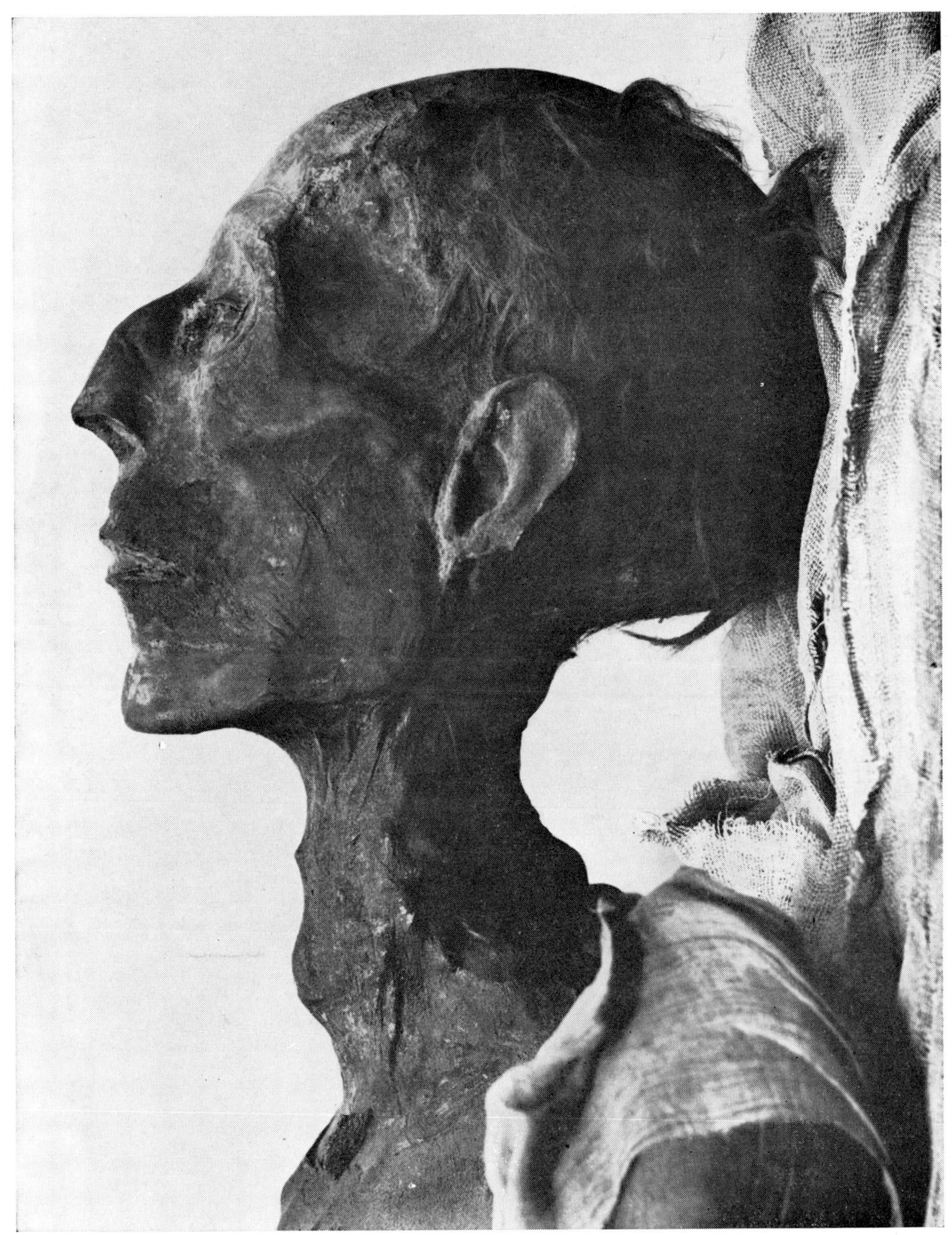

Photo: Service des Antiquités, Cairo

PLATE 99. MUMMIES: mummy of Ramses II.

Photo: British Museum

PLATE 100. MYCENAE: goblet, Late Mycenaean, about 1250 B.C. The cuttlefish is painted in black, and white over black. *(British Museum, London)*

Photo: British Museum

PLATE 101. NINEVEH: guardians of a doorway from the palace of Sennacherib at Nineveh. *(British Museum, London)*

Photo: Richard Harrington

PLATE 102. NUBIA: colossus of Ramses II wearing the double crown of Upper and Lower Egypt at Abu Simbel, over sixty-five feet high. The smaller figures are his wife, princes and gods.

Photo: A. F. Kersting

PLATE 103. OBELISK from Heliopolis.

Photo: Arborio Mella

PLATE 104. MYCENAE: the Lion Gate.

Photo: Anthony Christie

PLATE 105. PAGAN: in the 250 years before its fall in the face of the Mongol armies in A.D. 1287, Pagan was the centre of a great period of religious building. In this time more than 5,000 temples and monasteries were erected. Of these one of the most famous is the Ananda, shown here.

Photo: Exclusive News Agency

PLATE 106. PALMYRA: carving in the form of acorns and oak leaves.

Photo: Oriental Institute, University of Chicago

PLATE 107. PERSEPOLIS: capital of column, formed of animals back to back.

Photo: Oriental Institute, University of Chicago

PLATE 108. PERSEPOLIS: Darius seated on his throne with Xerxes behind, relief from Persepolis.

Photo: Oriental Institute, University of Chicago

PLATE 109. PERSEPOLIS: Xerxes's "Gateway of All Lands" flanked by *lamassu* (statues of winged bulls regarded as guardian spirits).

Photo: Hunting Aerosurveys Ltd

PLATE 110. PETRA: aerial view.

PLATE III. William Matthew Flinders PETRIE (1853–1942).

Photo: British Museum

PLATE 112. PERUVIANS: two pottery stirrup-mouthed vases, Mochica culture, about A.D. 600. Both represent priests wearing deerskins, possibly representing nature gods. *(British Museum, London)*

Photo: Gerald Cubitt

PLATE XI. MYCENAE: tholos tomb known as the Treasury of Atreus, the finest of the tholos tombs at Mycenae, before 1330 B.C.

Pakistan), was one of the two great city centres of the **Indus Valley civilization**. It lies some 400 miles to the south of the second city of **Harappa** (*see* plate 56, page 196) and was first brought to notice in 1922 by R. D. Banerji of the Archaeological Survey. It was made famous by the excavations of Sir John **Marshall**, and later of E. J. H. Mackay and Sir Mortimer Wheeler, and not only was it found to be better preserved than Harappa, but also greater in extent. There is a striking similarity between the layout of both cities. At Mohenjo-Daro the citadel stood to the west of the main habitation area and when first investigated was crowned by the remains of a Buddhist **stupa** dating from the beginning of the Christian era. Beneath lay a remarkable complex of buildings surrounding a great bath or tank, thirty-nine feet long and twenty-three feet broad, built of brick set in gypsum mortar and bedded in a thick bitumen damp-proof course. It has been generally agreed that this bath served some religious function. Nearby were the massive brick foundations of what must have been a great granary, not dissimilar to that found at Harappa. A large part of the extensive gridiron of streets and houses in the lower city, to the east, was at least partly excavated. They revealed a high degree of architectural skill, the bath-room and drainage systems being particularly noteworthy. *See* plate 97, page 325.

Mojokerto. This site in eastern Java is the name-site of Homo modjokertensis, the specimen consisting of a child's cranium belonging to a stratum which is clearly of Lower **Pleistocene** date. This dating is determined by the faunal association which was first established at Djetis which is the neighbourhood of Mojokerto. The whole region is of a deltaic nature in which mammalian beds are found with interposed strata containing molluscs of marine origin which testify to a number of marine transgressions in east Java in the Lower Pleistocene. Homo modjokertensis is thus contemporary with **Pithecanthropus** robustus and **Meganthropus** palaeojavanicus. The skull is five and a half inches long, lacking teeth and the facial portion. The fontanelle has just closed, a condition in modern man which occurs towards the end of the second year. The brain capacity is considerably less than in Homo sapiens of the same age. The brow is without the frontal overhang found in adult pithecanthropoids, but though there is no supra-orbital ridge, there is marked post-orbital constriction. Dubois, the discoverer of the original Pithecanthropus erectus, objected to the skull which has clear affinities with Homo sapiens being included in the Pithecanthropus series, since by 1936, the time of its discovery, he was of the opinion that his find did not belong with Homo sapiens. There can, however, be little doubt that Homo modjokertensis belongs to thepit hecanthropoids, and that its infant facies has remarkably affinities with Homo sapiens.

Montezuma, *see* Aztecs.

Mound-builders, *see* Amer-Indians.

Mousterian implements of the Middle **Palaeolithic** have been found in western Asia, north Africa and Europe (but not in the British Isles). They are made from **flakes** struck from a **core,** and worked into two main implements: the scraper and the point.

These are very consistent in form. The D-shaped side-scrapers are large, about three inches long, and many are shaped to fit comfortably into the hand for dressing skins. The worked edge along one side was made by the "stepped flaking" technique. Recent experiments have shown that small facets can be removed to reproduce the Mousterian effect by striking inwards with a hammerstone against the edge of the flake.

A triangular point was fitted into the split end of a wooden spear, and bound into position. These spears were the main weapons with which Neanderthal men hunted the mammoth and woolly rhinoceros, and they must have been supplemented with great ingenuity and courage. Points were made from flakes about three inches long, trimmed round the edges.

By studying the conservative techniques used in making **flint** tools, it has been worked out that basically the Mousterian industry was derived from the Lower Palaeolithic **Clactonian** flake tradition. There was also an admixture of **Levalloisian** and **Acheulian.** At Le Moustier, the rock-shelter in the **Dordogne** in France from which the industry takes its name, three superimposed Mousterian levels were found. The middle layer contained small, finely-worked **hand-axes** (between three and four inches long), but these were not found in the layers on each side.

Mousterian tools have been found everywhere associated with the bones of **Neanderthal Man.** The earliest finds have been dated to the third interglacial period, and the latest to the last **glaciation,** during which the industry and its makers yielded to the Upper Palaeolithic blade cultures of Homo sapiens. *See* plate 98, page 326.

Moustier, Le, *see* Mousterian.

Mummies. The term mummy derives from an Arabic root meaning "bitumen" and was applied to the embalmed bodies of ancient Egypt as the result of an early erroneous belief that bitumen was the preservative used.

The practice in Upper Egypt during the Predynastic period of burying the body in a shallow grave dug in the porous sand on the desert edge resulted, owing to the dry and hot climate, in a natural dessication of the body and its consequent preservation. Doubtless the observation of this phenomenon was a formative element in the Egyptian belief, held throughout the dynastic period, that the continuation of the deceased's identity depended upon the preservation of his body and features by mummification.

The process began with the extraction of the brain by means of a metal instrument through the nostril, usually the left one. The cavity was then irrigated. The removal and preservation of the viscera followed (*see* **Canopic Jars**). The next stage of the operation was dessication, the removal of the surplus water-content of the body. There has been some difference of opinion on the method employed. The probability is that the body was placed in a wooden coffin or on a mat on the ground and packed with dry natron crystals which acted both as a purifier and as a drying agent. When it had been thoroughly desiccated, the body might be coated with resin and then bandaged and the face covered by a mask with an idealized representation of the features of the deceased.

The Egyptians also mummified animals, and great cemeteries, mostly of the Roman period, for sacred animals have been found (*see* **Serapeum**).

The mummified crocodiles of the **Faiyum** have been a rich source of **papyri,** which was used as packing. *See* plate 99, page 327.

Mycenae. The Mycenaean civilization succeeded the **Minoan civilization**. It developed under Cretan influence out of the Middle **Bronze Age,** or Middle Helladic culture of Greece, which began soon after 2000 B.C. Its creators, who probably came from various parts of Asia Minor, began by destroying the Early Helladic settlements, but often settled on the same sites. They may well have been the first people to speak a form of Greek in Greece. Gradually a number of centres of power and wealth grew up, of which the first to emerge, somewhere about 1600 B.C., was Mycenae. The rulers lived in a citadel on a heavily fortified hill, having their palace on the very top, whilst "suburbs" of villas belonging to prosperous merchants and craftsmen grew up on neighbouring hills. The kings were at first buried in rectangular pits, or shaft graves, of which one group was found by **Schliemann,** who believed it to be the Tomb of Agamemnon, and another very recently by Greek archaeologists. Later they favoured large beehive-shaped chambers with a large entrance corridor (*see* **Tholos Tombs**). The Mycenaeans seem to have dominated, besides Crete, the **Cyclades** and Rhodes, and they colonized **Cyprus** very heavily. They were extremely warlike, but they also built up a vast trade with the countries of western Asia and the central Mediterranean. There is also good evidence that they traded more indirectly with the barbarians of western and northern Europe. Mycenaean civilization drew much of its inspiration from that of Crete, but it has many special features, and cannot be considered a mere reflection of Minoan civilization as was once thought. Towards the end of the twelfth century B.C. Mycenae was burnt and destroyed, possibly by the invading **Dorians.** (*See also* **Mediterranean, The Eastern.**) *See* colour plate XI, plates 100, 104, pages 328, 332.

N

Nabataeans. The first historical record of these remarkable people is in a list of the enemies of Ashur-bani-pal, king of Assyria in 647 B.C., when they seem to have been a nomadic Arab tribe of some size and importance. They were then inhabiting the neighbourhood of Taima and Madain Salih in northern Sa'udi Arabia, which was apparently their native country. The territory they then controlled included an area through which passed the important ancient incense and spice route from the Hadramaut in the south to the markets of Syria and Palestine. At first they probably contented themselves with plundering occasional caravans and making off with the booty, but in time they seem to have found it more profitable to levy a toll for safe conduct through this area. They grew rich on this commerce and settled down into towns and villages, and at Madain Salih started carving their great rock-cut tomb façades for which **Petra** (see colour plate XIII) is now so famous. Their power and ambition grew with the centuries, and they began to extend their area of control. Eventually, perhaps in the fifth century B.C., they drove the Edomites out of Edom in southern **Jordan** and occupied their territory, including the site of Petra. Here they settled themselves, and proceeded to build up a small empire with its capital at Petra, making the city into the great emporium of the incense trade and turning it into one of the wonders of the world with its great rock-cut monuments, tombs and houses. They evolved types of architecture, sculpture, pottery and stone-dressing peculiar to themselves, and if the ancient writers report at all correctly, had a democratic monarchy unique in the Semitic world.

The architecture as represented in the façades of rock-cut tombs both at Petra and Madain Salih is a combination of Hellenistic and Babylonian or Assyrian, and the most characteristic feature of their early work is the "crowstep" design which crowns many of the monuments, rather like an enlarged battlement. For stone-dressing they used a single-ended pick and ran the cutting lines at an angle of forty-five degrees across the face of the block, column, rock-face or whatever it was they were shaping, whereas all other peoples dress their stones either horizontally or vertically. In sculpture they developed many individual traits, such as the treatment of the eyes, and the frequent use of busts in wall decoration, but comparatively little of their work has as yet come to light. The pottery was perhaps their most remarkable achievement, though it is the commonest **artifact** and was obviously held in but little esteem by them. It is of a fineness and thinness seldom equalled and never surpassed in the common pottery of other lands, its only equal being some of the best Roman moulded ware. But the Nabataean pottery was all thrown and turned on the wheel, not moulded, and the commonest form is a shallow open bowl, the inside of which is always decorated with a delicate pattern in black or dark brown. Owing to its extreme thinness not a single intact specimen is known to have survived, but many have been reconstructed from fragments.

They had their own script which was related to the north Semitic group of alphabets, whereas all other inhabitants of the Arabian Peninsula used forms from the south Semitic group. It bears some resemblance to the contemporary Hebrew, but the letters are curiously elongated vertically. Recent excavations at Petra have shown that they also had a **cursive** form of the script, which has a startling resemblance to Arabic; and indeed the Arabic script developed from the Nabataean, which can be traced through some texts found in the Jebel Druze region where the script is half-way between Nabataean and Kufic. Their language was a mixture of Arabic and Aramaic, and personal names were almost entirely Arabic.

Nachikufan culture, *see* Africa, East.

Nag Hammadi. Nag Hammadi is a small town in Upper Egypt about sixty miles from **Luxor**. Here, in 1945 or 1946 (the exact date is not known), some peasants found a jar in one of the tombs of an old cemetery. Inside the jar were thirteen **papyrus** books in **codex** form, comprising a library in the **Coptic** language of more than forty Gnostic treatises. (Gnosticism is an unorthodox form of Christianity in which the believers claimed a special "knowledge" – Greek *gnosis* – revealed to them alone.)

Of the books the most interesting to the western world is Codex III, for it contains a work called *The Gospel of Thomas*; the title is not strictly accurate, for the work is not a Gospel but a collection of 114 sayings of Jesus. To the astonishment and delight of biblical scholars it has proved to be the complete work of which certain fragments, the so-called "Sayings of Jesus", had been discovered at **Oxyrhyncus** at the turn of the century. The Oxyrhyncus fragments gave a mutilated text of a few sayings; these had been completed by scholars to the best of their ability but, as the originals now showed, their suggestions were somewhat wide of the mark.

The sayings of Jesus in *The Gospel of Thomas* have been classified into four groups: sayings which are already known from their inclusion in the four New Testament Gospels; sayings which are variations of Gospel ones; sayings known from ancient sources other than the four Gospels; and completely new sayings. There are about forty of the last-named group. Some are definitely Gnostic in outlook and have obviously been edited by a Gnostic sympathizer; others possibly, though not certainly, are new sayings of Jesus which have escaped the net of the four New Testament Gospels.

Nara. Chinese culture in the Tang period (A.D. 618–793) had a profound effect upon Japan and by A.D. 710 a new capital was laid out at Nara on the chequerboard pattern of the Tang capital at Chang-an. During this period Buddhist influences became predominant, and great efforts were made to ensure that a Buddhist temple was to be found in every town. Many of these housed large images; that in the Todai-ji in the capital was of the Buddha Vairocana and was eighteen and a half feet high. Bronze, wood and clay were used for these figures, as well as *kanshitsu* or dry **lacquer.** The model was that of Tang sculpture, but there is a greater naturalness and variety of expression. Both benevolent and frightful forms of the deities are portrayed.

The wall paintings of the Kondo of the Horyu-ji show clearly, both in the line and in the use of colour, that they stem from Indian originals which reached Japan by way of China and Korea in the Sui and Tang dynasties. Paintings on silk show clear Chinese influence. It is in the Gigaku masks, made for performers in religious plays given in temples, that the tendency to caricature which characterizes Japanese art from the earliest periods can best be seen. The minor arts of the Nara period have been preserved especially in the collections of the **Shosoin.**

Natufian. Palaeolithic and Mesolithic men were food-gatherers, dependent on such animals as they could hunt and such vegetable food as they could find. Neolithic men became food-producers, growing corn and tending flocks and herds of domesticated animals. This fundamental change in economy has been called the **Neolithic** Revolution; but, like all revolutions, it had its roots in the past. The Natufian is a **Mesolithic** culture which, while basically food-gathering, has some indications of food-production. Finds of transitional cultures of this kind will ultimately throw more light on the problem of where the Neolithic adoption of food-production took place.

The Natufian culture was identified by Professor Dorothy Garrod in **Palestine,** in the cave of Shuqbah in the Wadi-en-Natuf, from which it takes its name.

The Natufians did not make pottery, or polish stone axes, nor did they domesticate animals; but the Neolithic activity that they seem to have pursued is the collection of the seeds of "noble" grasses (Triticum dicoccoides, **emmer wheat,** grows wild in Palestine). They may even have sown it deliberately. The evidence for harvesting is the presence of straight bone sickles, with a slot in which **flint** teeth were inserted. That these were used for cutting corn-stalks is shown by the gloss on the cutting edge of the flints, imparted by the silica in the stems.

Other Natufian **stone tools** include long barbed bone points, and scrapers, gravers and borers made from flint blades. These, and naturalistic sculptures in antler and stone are **Palaeolithic** in origin. Typical Mesolithic elements are the **microliths** – battered-back blades, segments of circles and micro-gravers. These resemble the **Capsian** industry.

Over one hundred Natufian skeletons have been found at the cave of Shuqbah and at another site, el-Wad. The skulls are dolichocephalic (long from back to front), with projecting jaws and slight chin eminences.

Naveta, *see* Minorca, Megalithic Remains in.

Nazca Culture, *see* Peruvians.

Neanderthal Man. This quite distinct type of early man, named after the cave near Düsseldorf in Germany where the earliest described remains were discovered, existed, according to the evidence afforded by the type of **stone tools** found with the bones, during the Mousterian **Palaeolithic** era. Remains showing the same general characteristics have been found in widely scattered sites: in Gibraltar, at Spa in Belgium in association with typical **Mousterian** implements and the bones of mammals, and a particularly well-preserved example, from which the structure of the whole skeleton could be observed, at La Chapelle-aux-Saintes in south-western France. They have also been found at sites in Croatia, the Channel Islands, Italy, Palestine, southern Russia, Siberia and north Africa, and remains of very similar type have been discovered in Rhodesia and Java.

The skull of Neanderthal Man was large and the cranium thick. It was characterized by massive brow ridges, a receding forehead, a flattened brain-case and strongly developed ridges to which the neck muscles were attached; the skull projected backwards and had a prominent upper jaw; the palate was broad and the teeth large. The limb-bones were clumsy with very large extremities, the general limb structure indicating a stooping posture. The size of the skull indicated a large brain, with an average capacity of about 1,450 c.c., as compared with the 1,350 c.c. average for modern man. It was thought until recently that Neanderthal Man represented an ape-like stage in the main line of evolution to modern man, but this theory has now been dropped. Since a type of man much closer to Homo sapiens existed, in Homo pithecanthropus, long before Neanderthal Man, in the early **Pleistocene** era, it seems likely that Neanderthal Man represents a "side-line" development. This idea is further supported by the fact that the Neanderthal characteristics appear to become more extreme during the period in which this type of man flourished rather than coming closer to Homo sapiens, and the fact that no remains have been found which indicate a transitional step between Neanderthal man and Homo sapiens.

Thus it seems probable that Neanderthal Man represents a separate line of development which became extinct at the end of the Middle Palaeolithic period.

Negative Confession, *see* Book of the Dead.

Negroes, Origin of the. It has been held that the Negro originated somewhere in southern Asia and occupied parts of India, Malaysia, Indonesia, and some of the Pacific islands. This is a facile theory, but when applied to the African Negro it assumes a movement across Persia, Mesopotamia, and Arabia, ending with a crossing of the Red Sea. Moreover, the Negro of Africa is physically so different from other human types that this theory is unlikely, and an origin in tropical Africa is more probable, though it should be realized that in actual fact we do not know where the Negro came from. Though there are peoples in Asia with Negro characteristics, they are not "Negro" but "Negroid", that is, "Negro-like". Even in Africa itself all the people with dark skins and woolly hair are not "Negroes", though many of them may legitimately be classed as Negroids. The Negro type, with its very dark skin, woolly hair, thick and everted lips, and projecting jaws, seems to be a dominant one, and among African peoples a mixture with Negroes quickly imposes the dark skin colour and woolly hair.

How long ago the Negro stock came into being we do not know. There is a certain amount of historical evidence taking it back to the third millennium B.C. from Egypt (on slate palettes of about 3200 B.C.) and Nubia (burials of about 3000 B.C.), but the Negro may well have been in existence long before this. The absence of skulls of very early date definitely attributable to this stock can be explained by the widespread African custom of laying out the dead to be eaten by hyenas, which leave nothing. From the ethnological evidence at present available, it is possible to suggest that the Negro stock arose somewhere in central or eastern central Africa, and moved into the Horn of Africa at a time when conditions there were much better than they are today. Here was their main concentration until they were displaced by **Hamitic peoples** from Arabia who began to push them westwards across the continent.

These Hamites intermixed with the Negroes, with the result that successive waves of Hamitic immigrants can be distinguished by the greater or lesser amount of Negroid physical characteristics which they show. (This, however, does not make the Hamites either Negro or Negroid; they are essentially Europoid.) The Negro was gradually pushed across to west Africa, which is now the home of the true Negro, but he has left his mark on the other inhabitants of what is often called "Negro Africa". Apart from the present Negro concentration in west Africa, a few isolated groups remain in the southern Sudan-Ethiopian frontier region.

Neolithic ("new stone") is the name given to that part of the **Holocene Epoch** which follows the **Palaeolothic** and the **Mesolithic** and is itself succeeded by the **Bronze Age** and the **Iron Age.** The Neolithic has been dated as beginning about 2500 B.C., but this is a relative dating and true only of, say, Britain and Germany. In Egypt and Mesopotamia it had ended a thousand years earlier, whereas Captain Cook found the Maoris of New Zealand still in the Neolithic period. (*See also* **Stone Age.**)

New Stone Age, *see* Neolithic *and* Stone Age.

Niah caves, *see* Borneo.

Nimrud, the ancient **Assyrian** military capital of Kalhu (the biblical Calah of Genesis 10, 11), lies near the River Tigris twenty-two miles south-east of Mosul in **Iraq.** A.H.**Layard** began the first serious British excavations in that country in 1845. In his first month's work on the citadel he discovered three royal palaces; that of Ashur-nasir-pal II (883–859 B.C.), the despoiled centre palace of his son Shalmaneser III (859–824 B.C.) and the south-west palace of Esarhaddon (681–669 B.C.). The early discoveries of massive stone bull-colossi, sculptured wall-reliefs (*see* plate 17, page 87), carved ivories and **cuneiform** inscriptions encouraged the British Museum to sponsor further work. The initial excavations had been undertaken at Layard's own initiative and expense, save for sixty pounds given by Sir Stratford Canning at Constantinople.

Work continued on the ruin-mound intensively for three years but thereafter was but a subsidiary to Layard's main efforts at **Nineveh** until 1851. At first he had thought that at Nimrud itself lay the ruins of that famous city. Layard and his assistant Hormuzd Rassam cleared part of the **ziggurat** and of the temples of Ninurta and Ishtar which lay nearby. In uncovering three wings of the north-west palace they found five rooms lined with reliefs. Two other rooms appeared to have been used as stores for the loot taken by Sargon II, and bronze bowls, furniture and utensils were found, some hidden down a disused well. Some of these finds were shipped by raft to Basra and thence to England where, with the contemporary discoveries from Nineveh, they formed the basis of the famous Assyrian collection in the British Museum.

Among the reliefs were a **stele** depicting the submission of Jehu of Israel to Shalmaneser III in 841 B.C. and scenes from the wars of Tiglath-Pileser III (the biblical Pul). The publications of Layard in 1849–61 aroused widespread interest in Assyrian art and history.

Until 1878 the work at Nimrud was mainly left in the hands of Rassam with brief periods of excavation by **Rawlinson** (1852) and George **Smith** (1873). Loftus in 1854 followed up the initiative of Layard in exploring the south-east part of the mound and found many ivories.

In 1949 the British School of Archaeology in Iraq under the direction of Professor M.E.L. Mallowan reopened the excavations. Using modern techniques the expedition had by 1958 revealed additional wings of the vast north-west palace and cleared its northern façade (now restored as a national monument). Near the entrance to the throne-room was found a stele inscribed with details of the ceremonies at the opening of the palace in 879 B.C. when Ashur-nasir-pal feasted 69,574 people for ten days. In the very well partly excavated by Layard further bronzes were found together with writing-boards of which one, set in ivory and bearing a series of astronomical omens written for Sargon II about 715 B.C., is the oldest "book" or **codex** yet found.

Other discoveries included the Palace of Adad-nirari III (about 810 B.C.), the city governor's residence, many administrative buildings and private houses, the citadel defences and gateway, and the quay-wall, as well as a large complex of buildings around the Nabu Temple with its library. The largest and most diverse collection of ivories yet found in the Middle East was enriched by whole sections of ivory furniture fittings found in the barrack rooms of Fort Shalmaneser in the south-east corner of the outer town.

The many discoveries at Nimrud now enable the history and daily life of this city to be traced from its foundation in the thirteenth century B.C. to the destruction by the **Medes** in 612 B.C. and its subsequent sparse occupation in the Hellenistic days as recorded by Xenophon.

Nineveh, the capital of **Assyria** in its most flourishing days, is now a vast tumbled site with little habitation, for most of its people have migrated across the River Tigris to the medieval city of Mosul. The ruins of Nineveh are covered by two principal mounds, Kuyunjik to the north-west, containing the royal palaces and the temples, and Nabi Yunis to the south-east. This is a much smaller mound where stood the storehouses of the Assyrian kings but is dominated today by the mosque reputed to contain the burial of the prophet Jonah (Yunis), the sanctity of which has prevented exploration of this locality. The greater mound, Kuyunjik, is about ninety feet high and is now a mile distant from the river which, at the crisis of its final siege, carried away part of its walls. From Nabi Yunis it is separated by the Khosr, a small tributary stream.

Prehistoric settlements of great antiquity have

been revealed by digging in the depths of Kuyunjik and a succession of pottery evidence connects these with other early sites in Mesopotamia and Syria. Not until the eighteenth century B.C. did Nineveh become a capital, the residence of Shamshi-Adad I, a king of remarkable character and ability, who outshone, while he lived, even his contemporary **Hammurabi** of Babylon, and has become almost intimately known through his letters discovered at **Mari**, many of which are dated from Nineveh.

In the vicissitudes of Assyrian supremacy and decline Nineveh had no leading part, and Sennacherib (704–681 B.C.) was the first to set himself to make Nineveh into an imperial centre, to outmatch even the ancient glories of **Babylon**. The centre of his new creation was his vast and magnificent palace, one of the first Assyrian monuments to be explored by modern diggers. The king's copious inscriptions give detailed accounts of its building by hordes of enslaved captives, also of the extensive works of fortification, town-planning, water-supply, cultivation, and general embellishment carried out by craftsmen directed by a monarch who was himself a notable inventor, with an exceptional interest in technique.

The last Assyrian emperors continued the perfecting of this great city, and the Palace of Ashur-bani-pal (668–626 B.C.) has been a second source of the Assyrian works of art now in museums of the western world. But the end of all this was sudden and fearful; in 612 B.C. the mighty city fell before the onslaught of **Medes** under Cyaxares, of Babylonians under Nabopolassar. Its last king perished, a remnant escaped to the west, and the place itself was "turned into mounds and ruins" as it has ever since remained.

So enormous is the mound of Kuyunjik that it has never been possible to excavate the whole, and therefore no plan of the ancient city has yet been drawn. Its two cardinal points as now known are the palaces of Sennacherib in the south-west and of Ashur-bani-pal to the north of the site. Both were discovered in the middle of the last century, and even they are far from completely disengaged. Sennacherib's palace alone was so vast in area that its limits have never been reached. It contained a multitude of courts and chambers, the walls of which were lined with stone slabs carved with bas-reliefs illustrating in detail the king's widespread campaigns and scenes of court-life. Writing in 1853 A. H. **Layard** reckoned a total of nearly 10,000 feet of such sculptured walls which he had uncovered. Most of these sculptures had suffered grievously by the fierce conflagration of 612 B.C. as well as by decay underground in the succeeding ages. The best of what was preserved can now be seen in the British Museum. At the other end of the mound the north palace of Ashur-bani-pal is even less known, for not only is its ruin more complete, but even what remained (mostly sculpture) of the area explored was partly lost afterwards in transport, as also were the drawings made of these subjects. Nevertheless a wonderful series of hunting-scenes, also in the British Museum, reveals that Assyrian art had reached its height only those few years before its final extinction.

Towards the middle, between these palaces, have been unearthed remains of two temples, those of the goddess Ishtar and of the god Nabu, the former having a stately approach lined with sculptures of the king proceeding to worship there, drawn in his wheeled chair and accompanied by a splendid procession of officers, guards, and musicians. Much of the ground, however, seems to have been clear of buildings and was perhaps given up to royal parks and gardens, which figured prominently in the planning of Sennacherib, for he was interested in the acclimatization of exotic plants, and especially in the introduction of cotton. The adjacent country still has many remains of the boldly engineered water-system constructed by this king for the support and amenity of his capital. *See* plate 101, page 329.

Nippur (modern Nuffar), about one hundred miles south-east of Baghdad, is one of the most impressive ruins in **Iraq**. As a religious centre, the seat of the **Sumerian** god Enlil, it was frequently rebuilt between Early Dynastic and **Parthian** times (between about 3000 B.C. and A.D. 226).

The site was first noted by Loftus and Churchill in 1849 and briefly sounded by **Layard** in 1851. Following a survey by Ward in 1884 the Babylonian Expedition of the University of Pennsylvania was formed and thus began the first major American excavations in Iraq, led initially by J. P. Peters, and later by H. V. Hilprecht who dug there from 1888 to 1896. The **ziggurat** and E-Kur temple of Enlil were cleared as well as many Parthian buildings.

The site was reopened by the American Schools for Oriental Research in 1948 and many new architectural features traced. The most spectacular discoveries include an Early Dynastic II temple of Inanna, another dedicated to Ishtar, goddess of love and war, by Shulgi, king of **Ur** about 2000 B.C., and remodelled by his **Babylonian** and **Kassite** successors. A Parthian temple with remains standing twelve feet high was cleared in 1958.

In every season's work inscribed tablets have been found, mostly in the Tablet Hill; the total of about 80,000 includes the sole surviving copies of Sumerian literary texts, school-texts and the reference works of master-scribes as well as the well-known archives of Murashu and Sons, a business and finance house active in the reigns of Artaxerxes I and Darius II, that is, between 464 and 405 B.C.. The discovery of architect's plans including one of the temple area and city walls enables the results of the modern excavations to be checked by the original town plans.

Nome. A territorial division of ancient Egypt.

Nubia is the name commonly given to the land south of the first cataract of the Nile from Aswan to the neighbourhood of Khartoum. This stretch of land was referred to by various names in the Egyptian language, the most common from the time of the Middle Kingdom being Kush (the biblical Cush). In the classical authors the term Aethiopia is used. The first cataract formed a natural boundary between Egypt proper and Nubia from at least the time of the first dynasty but there is some evidence that in the predynastic period the boundary lay more in the region of Gebel Silcilah, and to this day the country south of Deirut is marked by the use of the Nubian dialect and domed roofs in the villages.

The Nubians were in ancient times a people of similar stock to the Egyptians, and the earliest culture is similar to the predynastic cultures of Upper Egypt. The general impoverishment of the graves corresponding to the time of the Old Kingdom suggests that Egyptian exports to the region may have been perishable goods, possibly grain. In return the Egyptians imported ivory, ebony, cattle, sheep, goats, panther skins, incense. From the Middle Kingdom, but not apparently during the Old, great quantities of gold were imported in the form of rings, ingots and dust.

During the Second Intermediate period Nubia regained its independence; and at one time was in contact with the **Hyksos** kings of the Delta, along the oasis route. It was reconquered by the eighteenth dynasty and the Egyptian frontier pushed south to Napata, almost to the fourth cataract. In spite of occasional revolts, usually at the beginning of a new reign and easily suppressed, Nubia was firmly held until sometime after the twenty-first dynasty. Nubia became thoroughly Egyptianized, and a number of temples was built in Nubia by the pharaohs. The most impressive of these is the great rock-cut temple of Ramses II between the first and second cataracts at Abu Simbel, which is dominated by four huge colossi-statues of the king flanking the entrance, over sixty-five feet in height and hewn out of the solid rock, on which are found graffiti in Greek, Carian and Phoenician, carved there by mercenary troops on later campaigns. The hypostyle hall, carved from the rock, is fifty-four feet wide and fifty-eight feet deep and rises to a height of thirty feet.

The Egyptianization of Nubia is shown by the Kushite (Aethiopic) Invasion. The unsettled state of Egypt which followed the twenty-second dynasty provoked the intervention of the Nubian king Piankhi around the year 730 B.C. which resulted in his conquest of Egypt and the founding of the twenty-fifth dynasty (730–663 B.C.). The account of his campaigns and the defeat of the Delta prince Tefnakhte, is contained on a **stele** found at Napata and now in Cairo Museum.

The Kushite power in Egypt was ended by the Assyrian invasion of 671 B.C., but the Kushite kingdom continued to thrive in Nubia, where the successors of the twenty-fifth dynasty were buried in **pyramids** with such traditional Egyptian funerary equipment as **ushabti**-figures. Cut off from Egypt, however, and later split into rival kingdoms centred at Napata and farther south at **Meroe**, the cultural influence of Egypt declined, and the emergence of a more native culture was marked by the adoption of a peculiar script (Meroitic) written alphabetically with signs derived from **demotic.** *See* plate 102, page 330.

Numismatics. The study of coins or **coinage.**

Nutcracker Man, *see* Zinjanthropus.

O

Obelisk. The word obelisk is of Greek origin. It means literally "spit" or "dagger" and was applied to the long narrow shafts of stone, usually granite, with pyramidal shaped tops set upright on bases in pairs before the entrance to Egyptian temples. The obelisk in London (Victoria Embankment), popularly called Cleopatra's Needle, originally formed, with the New York obelisk, a pair before the temple at Heliopolis dedicated by Tuthmosis III (about 1500 B.C.) and containing also an inscription of Ramses II (about 1250 B.C.). The temple of Hatshepsut at **Thebes** contains scenes of the transport, by water, of obelisks and an inscription on the base of the obelisk at **Karnak** records the completion of the work of quarrying within seven months. *See* plate 103, page 331.

Obsidian. A volcanic glass, much prized in prehistoric times for the manufacture of **stone tools** and weapons such as arrow-heads.

Oc-eo. This site, lying in the Mekong Delta in Cochin-China, south Viet-Nam, seems to have been a port for **Fu-nan**. The finds include a number of objects of western origin: grylli, a gold coin of Antoninus Pius dated A.D. 152, and Sassanid seals. Other seals seem to have affinities with Alexandrian examples. Indian material from the site includes seals which date from the third century A.D., other examples being of later date. There is a large rectangular enclosing wall, and all the evidence points to a town of considerable size, with buildings in stone, as well as numbers of wooden houses on piles. Spindle whorls and net-weights have also been found, and the outlines of a canal system linking Oc-eo with sites in the interior can clearly be seen on air-photographs. It is certain that Oc-eo must represent one of the ports and entrepôts lying on the main east–west trade route which is hinted at in the periplus for the region beyond the Ganges, and for which confirmation is found in the Chinese historical sources.

Oldoway, *see* Olduvai Gorge.

Old Stone Age, *see* Palaeolithic *and* Stone Age.

Olduvai Gorge. The archaeological importance of this famous site is that an extraordinary sequence of **Palaeolithic** cultures has been revealed by erosion. It is in Tanganyika, in the Serengeti steppe, a plateau formed from sediments laid down during the **Pleistocene** period (the time of the Ice Age in Europe). The Olduvai River has cut a gorge more than three hundred feet deep through the plateau. The strata revealed in the sides of the gorge consist of black volcanic basalt in the lowest levels; above this a layer of bright red sediment over one hundred feet thick, and more grey sediment, on top of which is the recent steppe-limestone which forms the present ground-surface.

Many remarkable animal fossils have been collected near the Gorge. They show that the conditions that prevailed in the Serengeti steppe during the Pleistocene allowed a number of **Pliocene** species to go on living there, when they had become extinct in other regions. The three-toed horse, for example, persisted alongside its descendant, the modern single-toed horse. An elephant similar to the modern Indian elephant was found with two much older forms, the Mastodon and the Dinotherium.

Well down in the sides of the Gorge, among the fossils of the oldest elephants, humanly-shaped **stone tools** have been found. They are pebbles which have been given a cutting edge by blows directed first from one side, then the other. They are more primitive than any tools yet known, and might have been dismissed as natural were it not for the numbers that have been found. These forerunners of the hand-axe have been named the Olduvan culture, after the Gorge. Above the Olduvan level are nine more strata containing **hand-axes**, which show the development of this tool from the crudely-pointed **Abbevillian** to the finely finished artifact of Late **Acheulian** times. (*See also* **Zinjanthropus.**)

Oligocene Epoch. The 10,000,000 years which followed the close of Eocene times, about 45,000,000 years ago, constitute the shortest of the **Tertiary** epochs, the Oligocene, so-named after the two Greek words meaning "few recent" (as applied to forms of life).

The most important geographical changes of the Oligocene epoch were probably caused by widespread crustal movements, many of which continued into **Miocene** times and eventually gave rise to the world's main mountain systems – the Alps, Himalayas, Andes and Rockies. The development of the Alpine System, for example, began during Oligocene times with the compression of the thick deposits of **Mesozoic** and early Tertiary sediments which had accumulated on the floor of the "Tethys Ocean" (*see* **Eocene Epoch**), and their gradual upheaval in a series of island ridges. Meanwhile marine, fresh-water lacustrine and fluviatile sediments were being laid down in many parts of the world. Volcanic rocks were also formed over widely separated areas, including central France, Haiti, northern Britain and north-western America.

A gradual cooling of the climate began in Oligocene times and led to the spread of grasslands and temperate forests before the retreating tropical and sub-tropical forests. The distinctive feature of Oligocene life under these conditions was the great development of herbivorous mammals, such as the three-toed horse (Mesohippus) from a four-toed Eocene ancestor (Eohippus), and the appearance of early forms of camel (Poebrotherium), pig (Archaeotherium), and deer-like cud-chewer (Protoceras). The giants of the Oligocene were, however, the Titanotheres, an American group of ponderous plant-eaters which became extinct before the close of Oligocene times. Brontops, a small-brained, horned beast of more than fourteen feet in length, was one of these animals. Small, tusked creatures with short probosci (Moeritherium and Palaeomastodon) were forerunners of the present-day elephant. Some primitive types of carnivorous animals, such as the creodonts, were rapidly disappearing, but recognizable ancestors of dogs, cats and bears had begun to appear.

Olmecs, *see* Mexico.

Olorgesailie is an African site of **Palaeolithic** date forty miles south-west of Nairobi on the road to Magadi soda-lake. Hand-axes were discovered here in 1921, but the chief site was discovered in 1942 by Mrs Leakey, who has since made it into a museum. The site has yielded thousands of **Acheulian** culture **stone tools** dating from the period when the **hand-axe** technique had reached its peak. Seventeen levels have been excavated, yielding **artifacts** of different stages, including **flake** tools, choppers, cleaners and hand-axes. Other finds include twelve sets of stone balls in groups of three and many isolated balls which are thought to be either hunting bolas, such as those found in South America, or possibly grindstones or anvils.

Olympia. This, the greatest Pan-Hellenic sanctuary, was built at the confluence of the Alphaeus and Cladeus near the southern extremity of Greece. Zeus was the chief deity of the sanctuary which was only of local importance before the establishment of the Olympic Games (traditionally started in 776 B.C.). The games were held every four years at full moon, alternately in August and September. All freeborn Greeks, and later Romans, were eligible to compete. The games lasted five days, the central event being the sacrifice to Zeus on the morning of the third. In the fifth century B.C. the winning of the chariot race conferred the highest distinction on the city of the victor. Later the games became increasingly the sphere of the professional but remained the highest test for athletes until their suppression in the fourth century A.D.

The sacred precinct at Olympia, called Altis, was originally a grove. The Heraeum (about 640 B.C.), is the oldest building in it and also the oldest surviving Greek temple of importance; the Hermes of Praxiteles was found inside it. To the south of this is the great Temple of Zeus (468–456 B.C.) largely destroyed by an earthquake in the sixth century A.D. Built mainly of stuccoed limestone, it was one of the largest temples in Greece and had magnificent marble pediments. East of the Temple stood Paionios of Mende's statue of a winged goddess of victory (425 B.C.). Excavations on the stadium were begun in 1936, but the Hippodrome, scene of horse and chariot races, has vanished.

Ophir. The site of the biblical Ophir, from which King Solomon obtained cargoes of gold and precious stones (1 Kings 10, 11) has been much disputed, without any agreed answer being obtained; guesses have ranged from the Arabian coast to Ceylon or the Malabar coast.

Oracle Bones. Certain **Neolithic** sites in north China provide examples of tortoise-shell and bone which seem to have been used for a type of divination, the application of heat to the objects producing cracks which could then be interpreted by the diviner. In the Shang dynasty, as exemplified by the finds at **Anyang**, a more sophisticated version of this technique involved the inscription of questions on pieces of bone. These inscriptions are written in the earliest known forms of Chinese characters, forms which on the whole are more obviously **pictographic** than the later characters.

Their value is thus double, for in addition to their importance for the study of the early history of the Chinese script and language, they also afford evidence for the types of vessels, weapons, tools, vehicles of the Shang period, some of which have been verified by archaeological finds.

Oranian. A **stone tool** culture peculiar to north Africa, similar to and contemporary with the **Capsian.** It dates from the close of the **Pleistocene** era and persists after the introduction of **Neolithic** traits into the area. Distribution is mainly centred round the coastal areas of Tunisia, Algeria and Morocco. As in the Capsian culture, sites are occasionally found in caves and rock-shelters, but traces are more normally found in large **middens,** which are all that remain of the open camp dwellings of these peoples. **Artifacts** found include a variety of **microlithic** tools, backed blades, points, scrapers, gravers or **burins** and simple bone implements all very similar to those of the Capsian culture, but generally smaller in size.

Orchomenos. Situated at the north-west corner of Lake Copaïs in Greece, this ancient city of Boeotia was the capital of the kingdom of the Minyae and a member of the Boeotian confederacy. It was very prosperous and, until the end of the second millennium B.C. when supremacy passed to Thebes, controlled the greater part of Boeotia. Orchomenos was continually in conflict with Thebes – its government was aristocratic whereas Thebes was a democracy – and in 379 B.C. it sided with Sparta against Thebes. This resulted in 368 in the destruction of the town by Thebes and the enslavement or extermination of its people. Rebuilt by Philip of Macedon as a bulwark against Thebes, it never regained its former power. In 1880 **Schliemann** excavated there the "Treasury of Minyas" – a royal beehive or **tholos tomb** slightly smaller than the "Treasury of Atreus" at **Mycenae** (*see* colour plate XI).

Oreopithecus is the name which has been given to an animal of either the late **Miocene epoch** or the early **Pliocene epoch**, dating, that is, to some 12,000,000 years ago. Numbers of skeletons have been unearthed in the strata of the soft coal mines of northern Italy. Oreopithecus has been classified as a **hominid,** although this claim has been disputed by some palaeontologists. If the claim is true, then Oreopithecus is a hominid far older than **Australopithecus,** and is a pointer to the truth of the theory that man did not evolve directly from the apes, but that both had a common ancestor in the **Oligocene epoch** and then split into two groups – hominids and apes.

Ossuary. A receptacle for storing the bones of the dead.

Ostrace or **Ostracon** (plural – ostraca). A piece of pottery used for writing purposes.

Oxyrhyncus was the Greek name of the ancient Egyptian city of Pemdje, which was a district capital in late times. The site of the town, partially covered by the dwindling modern village of Behneseh, lies on the edge of the western desert eight miles north-west of Beni Mazar, and about 120 miles south of Cairo. The town ruins, about one and a quarter miles by half a mile in extent, have been extensively cut away by fellahīn digging for lime and manure, and the adjacent cemeteries have all been plundered. The fame of the place rests on its rubbish mounds, from which Bernard Grenfell and Arthur Hunt in five campaigns between 1896 and 1906 extracted by far the greatest body of **papyri** ever recovered from any site. The papyri range in date from the first century B.C. to the tenth century A.D., and were mainly found in the upper parts of the mounds, the lower levels being ruined by water. The vast majority of the documents are in Greek, and their publication has already filled twenty-five volumes. A proportion are literary, and have provided unknown works by Pindar, Sappho, Bacchylides, Euripides, Theopompus, and other authors, as well as early texts of many known works, which are of the greatest value for literary criticism. Less numerous are theological texts, since these were not so likely to be thrown away; fragments of previously unknown gospels and of the "Sayings of Jesus" (*Logia Iesou*) have aroused great interest and controversy. A complete version of the latter, *The Gospel of Thomas,* has recently come to light at **Nag Hammadi**. The bulk of material, however, consists of documents, legal and personal, of the most varied description, which give a unique picture of life in a provincial city of the Roman Empire. Similar documents in Arabic from the seventh to tenth centuries provide the next largest bulk of material; later Arabic texts on paper were also found. Latin papyri were far less common, but contained some literary pieces of interest; there were a few scraps of vellum. **Coptic** documents were surprisingly few, while **hieratic** and **demotic** papyri were a rarity. This shows that the literate native population of Oxyrhyncus cannot have been great in the Roman and Byzantine period; though it must be remembered that most Coptic literature was religious and therefore unlikely to be thrown on rubbish heaps.

P

Pagan. This site in central Burma on the left bank of the Irrawaddy, some eighty miles south-east of Mandalay, was the capital of much of Burma from about the middle of the tenth century A.D. until its fall to the Mongols in 1287. It was the centre of the area in Burma where the Burmans came to predominate at the expense of the Pyu and the Mon. During the 300 years of its existence it was the scene of a vast activity of building, all of it either religious or immediately connected with the court, though all traces of secular buildings, being of wood, have more or less disappeared. There remain some thousands of temples, pagodas and monasteries in various states of preservation, all but two of them, the Nan-paya and the Nat Hlaung Kyaung being Buddhist foundations. The two exceptions are Hindu. The evolution of Burmese architecture can be traced in the surviving buildings, and it can be seen that a number of traditions went to its making. Both Pyu and Mon influences are clear – Burmese tradition tells of a campaign to the south which led to the coming of Mons to Pagan – and a number of foreign elements are also to be seen. The fact that Mon and Pyu rather than Burmese are used in the early inscriptions at the site shows how strong these outside influences were in the first period. The building material was brick, stone being almost unused, and the walls, both inside and out, were covered with plasterwork, that over the doorways and windows being worked into flame-pattern arcades of great beauty. Mural paintings covered much of the interior, but it doubtful whether any surviving specimens belong to a period before the Mongol attack. Terracotta plaques, often glazed and moulded with Buddhist scenes, are a favourite form of decoration, inset into the walls. There are two patterns of buildings, the **stupa** and the temple, the former to house relics, the latter to enshrine a Buddha figure. In addition there are monasteries, some two-storied, and libraries. Among the best-known of the monuments are the Ananda, probably modelled on a temple at Paharpur in eastern India, and dating from the eleventh century, the Shwezigon, which also houses a *nat*-shrine, (*nats* are non-Buddhist spirits generally held in some considerable veneration), the Hti-lo-min-lo (1218) a two-storied temple decorated with glazed sandstone, the Maha-bodhi (about 1220) modelled on the shrine at Bodhgaya, and the Mingalazedi (1284), a stupa on a high platform with very fine terracotta tiles. A fine gateway set in part of the surviving city wall has also survived, flanked by a *nat*-shrine at either side of the outer face. Much statuary has also been found and a fine hard-fired red pottery decorated with embossed designs. There are also some remains of **lacquer** ware, the production of this remains a local industry. *See* plate 105, page 333.

Palaeobotany. The study of ancient (usually fossilized) plant life.

Palaeo-Indian, *see* America, Early Man in.

Palaeolithic, ("old stone") is the name given to the old cultures of the **Pleistocene** epoch. It is divided into Upper, Middle and Lower, so called because **stratigraphy** shows that it is at these levels in an excavation that their **artifacts** are found. The Lower Palaeolithic is therefore the oldest, dating from about 600,000 B.C. and is occupied by such **cultures** as **Chou-kou-tienian, Clactonian, Abbeville-Acheulian**, and **Levalloisian,** which were developed by such predecessors of Homo sapiens as **Heidelberg Man, Java Man** and **Pekin Man.**

The Middle Palaeolithic began about 220,000 B.C. and is represented by **Neanderthal Man** and the **Mousterian** culture.

The Upper Palaeolithic lasted from about 75,000 to 10,000 B.C. and sees the appearance of Homo sapiens – **Cro-magnon Man, Grimaldi Man.** Typical cultures of this period are the **Aurignacian, Solutrean,** and **Magdalenian.**

The Palaeolithic age was succeeded by the **Mesolithic**, but certain peoples of the world – the Arunta of central Australia and the **Eskimos** of the Arctic region, for example – had a Palaeolithic economy until very recent times.

Palaeolithic, Further Asian. Old Stone Age material from the countries of the Far East tends to fall into a single morphological group within which local types, distinguished by methods of manufacture and raw materials used, can be defined. The general characteristics include a preference for forms other than the **hand-axe,** and a typical asymmetry of the cutting edge, which may either be offcentre or a full adze form. The cultures have been described as forming a chopper-chopping-tool complex. The main divisions are **Chou-koutienian** (China), Patjitanian (Java), Tampanian (Malaya), **Anyathian** (Burma), Bhan-kao-ian (Thailand). The Soan industries of India also belong to this complex, but the Madrasian of south India does not, having its affinities rather with more westerly Palaeolithic cultures.

Palaeontology. The study of extinct organized beings.

Palaeozoic. An era of the earth's history lasting for some 325,000,000 years and comprising the geological periods of Cambrian, Ordovician, Silurian, Devonian, Carboniferous and Permian. It was preceded by the **Archaean** era and succeeded by the **Mesozoic** era.

Palembang, Sumatra, Indonesia. It is convenient to refer under this heading to various finds from southern Sumatra which belong to the historical period, and are probably to be associated with a kingdom of Srivijaya, known mostly from Chinese historical sources, which seems to have built up a powerful position in the western part of south-east Asia because of its ability to command the trade routes passing through the straits between Sumatra and Malaya. The position of its capital is unknown but it is believed to have been in the neighbourhood of Palembang. It seems to have begun to emerge as a power at the end of the seventh century A.D. and to have remained as a major force, though with diminished realms, until the thirteenth century. A considerable **megalithic** culture had flourished in Sumatra, at about the beginning of the Christian era with **menhirs, dolmens,** (probably erected as memorial stones), stone troughs, terrace graves and stone cist graves. Their contents included bronze objects, gold and glass beads, and in one case, paintings on the inner walls, a series of remarkable carvings of men riding buffaloes, and carvings in relief of men carrying bronze drums of the **Dong-son** type. In later times Sumatra seems to have come under Indian influences, and to have been a notable Buddhist centre. The archaeology of Sumatra is still largely unknown, but the finds in and about Palembang include both Buddhist and Hindu remains, some of which show clear affinities with material from Java of the eight to tenth centuries A.D. Some of these are of very large size; a Bhairava figure (a form of Siva) stands fourteen feet four inches high including the base. Few buildings have survived, except in a very ruined state, but remains indicate the presence of extensive temple sites. The bronze images testify to the presence of skilled metal-workers in the island, a tradition which persisted until modern times.

Palermo Stone. So called because it has been since 1877 in the possession of the Museum of Palermo, this is the largest and best preserved of six fragments of black basalt originally emanating from Egypt; they are about two and a half inches in thickness and all bear inscriptions which are related in content. How this object reached Sicily is uncertain, but it is believed to have been taken there as part of a ship's ballast and cast ashore. Four of the other fragment are in the Cairo Museum and the sixth fragment is in the Petrie Collection of University College, London.

Nothing is reliably known about the provenance of any of these six fragments, and it is impossible to say whether or not they all belonged to one inscription. Copies of so important a text may have been placed in several different temples so that the surviving fragments may have come from more than one source.

The inscription, carved on both sides of the stone, consists of horizontal lines of **hieroglyphic** text, each line after the first being separated from the one above by a narrow space. In the first line were given the names of the kings who ruled over Upper and Lower Egypt before the two lands were united under one crown by Menes. Only seven of these names are completely preserved. The second and subsequent lines refer to the reigns of the dynastic kings, whose names are written in the appropriate positions in the spaces between the lines. Each line is divided into a series of compartments, the number of compartments under the name of every king corresponding with the number of years in his reign. The last king to be mentioned is Neferirkara, the third king of the fifth dynasty, and consequently it may be deduced that the list was written soon after his time. Within each compartment for the first and second dynasties is mentioned some notable event after which the year in question was named, e.g. "The Year of Smiting the Troglodytes". Most of the years were named after some religious festival celebrated during the course of it or in commemoration of the making of a statue of a particular deity. A somewhat different system of naming was introduced in the third dynasty and was maintained, with slight variations, for the rest of the period covered by the Stone. Alternate years were called "The first, second, third, etc., occasion of the census of gold and fields". From the beginning of the fifth dynasty the biennial census was changed to one of cattle.

The importance of these fragmentary records of royal annals lies both in the events which they record and in the assistance which they give in determining the length of the reigns of the early kings. In later times kings numbered their regnal years on their monuments so that historians are able to deduce at least the minimum number of years in any reign from the highest date found on the monuments. While the years were merely named and not numbered this information can only be obtained from consecutive name-lists such as those on the Palermo Stone.

Palestine. A country of this name no longer exists, for the area once called Palestine is now divided between Jordan, Israel and Egypt. The word Palestine, however, still means a geographical area to many and its boundaries are usually thought of as being the River Jordan and the Dead Sea in the east, the Sinai desert in the south, a line drawn roughly from just north of Acre to the headwaters of the Jordan at Banias in the north, and the Mediterranean in the west. Within that small area there have occurred events which had, and still have, a great effect on the whole world.

The area can be divided into three parts; the flat coastal plain of which the principal cities are Haifa, Tel Aviv and Gaza, a mountainous strip in the centre in which are **Jerusalem**, Nablus and Hebron, and the Jordan Valley, the most low-lying district in the world, nearly 1,300 feet below sea level at the Dead Sea. In ancient times, the Philistines occupied the coastal plain, the **Hebrews** and other biblical tribes the mountain district, and nomadic tribes the Jordan Valley.

Palestine has been occupied by man since earliest prehistoric times, some 100,000 years ago, and excavations in various parts of the country have brought to light remains of the **Palaeolithic, Mesolithic** and **Neolithic** cultures. In the latter period (about 7000 B.C.) it would seem, from the excavations at **Jericho**, that the Jordan Valley at least was leading the rest of the world in its cultural development. In the following periods, the **Chalcolithic** and the Early **Bronze Age** (about 4000–2000 B.C.), the absence of natural resources and difficulties of agriculture caused the country to lag somewhat behind its wealthy neighbours, Syria in the north, Mesopotamia in the east, and Egypt in the south. In the Middle Bronze Age (about 1900 B.C.) the **Hyksos** swept through the land on their way to conquer Egypt; a few centuries later they were sweeping through again in the opposite direction, hotly pursued by the Egyptians, who then incorporated the country in their Empire. Some time just prior to the first Hyksos invasion Abraham had arrived with his family from **Ur** and settled in the Hebron district, and during the Egyptian domination more Semitic tribes were infiltrating, culminating in the arrival of Moses and the Israelites from Egypt about the end of the fourteenth century B.C. (Late Bronze Age). This federation of tribes occupied Palestine until united under David and Solomon, about 1000 B.C., but split into two main sections, Israel and Judah, on the death of Solomon. The next thousand years saw much coming and going of the armies of the great powers, Egypt, the **Hittites**, the **Assyrians, Babylon**, the Persians and the Greeks. During the brief lulls in between being overrun by outsiders, the people of the country took the opportunity to have some private wars of their own. Yet out of all this seeming chaos came two of the world's greatest faiths, Judaism and Christianity; while a third, Islam, has close affinities in the country, Jerusalem being the holy city to them, second only to **Mecca**.

Palestine has produced no ancient wonders like the royal tombs of Ur or of **Tutankhamun**; it has no **Towers of Babel** or Great **Pyramids**, yet its close association with the three great faiths and their prophets and patriarchs make it still a world focal point. And one of the most important archaeological discoveries of the century, which has aroused world-wide interest, is that of the **Dead Sea Scrolls** (*see* plate 39, page 143), the oldest known manuscripts of the Old Testament, found in a cave not far from Jericho.

Palmyra, the Latin name of a place always known locally as Tadmor, is a ruined city lying in the midst of the Syrian Desert, about half-way to the north-east between Damascus and the River Euphrates. A city-wall built by the Emperor Justinian (A.D. 527–65) encloses a space about one and a quarter miles in width and five-eighths in depth, which is evidently less than the area covered by the city in its most flourishing days (third century A.D.). This space contains the principal edifices which, even in their present fallen condition, are one of the most impressive remains of the ancient world, enhanced by their position at the foot of a chain of desert hills dotted with tower-tombs and dominated by an Arab castle.

Tadmor was a very ancient place, for its inhabitants are cursorily mentioned in **cuneiform** inscriptions of the nineteenth and eighteenth centuries B.C. and early in the eleventh century Tiglath-Pileser I of **Assyria** launched an attack upon the Aramaeans who lived there. Two biblical passages (1 Kings **9**, 18 and 2 Chronicles **8**, 4) as well as local tradition aver that Solomon himself (tenth century B.C.) built at Tadmor, but this is perhaps a mistake caused by confusion of names. It was not until the establishment of the Roman Empire that Palmyra rose to a great height of importance and wealth, derived from the carriage of goods between the east and the west. This traffic proceeded by way of the Persian Gulf, up the rivers Tigris and Euphrates, and across the desert by caravans of camels and asses. Much of the commerce was articles of luxury. From the east came the silk of China, precious stones for jewellery, rich clothing, and the incense of Arabia; from the west came the purple-dyed wool of Tyre, fine glass vessels, and Syrian wines. The profits of this trade were vast, and the governments, both imperial and local, took care to share amply in them by means of taxation.

In the principate of Hadrian (A.D. 117–38) the city had already reached the height of its commercial prosperity and most of its principal buildings were completed. But its greatest days in history were reserved for the third century A.D. when the enfeeblement of the Romans amid the assaults of western barbarians and the struggles of usurpers left the distant outpost at liberty to become a virtually independent power. Udainat (Odenathus), son of a leading family, became governor of Syria by appointment of the Emperor Valerian, and when the latter had been defeated and captured by the Persian King Sapor I in the year A.D. 260 Udainat attacked the Persian in his retreat, and afterwards carried his arms up to the walls of the Persian capital, **Ctesiphon** (*see* plate 41, page 145), on the Tigris. The wife of this heroic ruler was Zenobia, celebrated alike for her military prowess, her beauty, and her magnificence. When Udainat was assassinated in A.D. 267, Zenobia assumed the rule with her son Wahballat, and defied Rome by assuming the Imperial titles and inscribing them on her own coinage and by sending an expedition to conquer Egypt. But Aurelian, who had been made Roman emperor in A.D. 270, soon moved against the East, conquered Asia Minor, defeated the general of Zenobia at Antioch and Homs, and laid siege to Palmyra itself. Zenobia escaped to the Euphrates on a swift dromedary, hoping to bring back aid from the Persians, but she was captured, and the city surrendered (A.D. 272). In the next year it attempted revolt, and this time Aurelian, returning in wrath, gave it over to fire and pillage. Zenobia, weighed down with gold and jewels, was the principal figure in the splendid triumph of Aurelian. In the long centuries succeeding this disaster Palmyra never rose again.

Among the buildings at Palmyra the most imposing, even in ruin, are the Temple of Baal, the great colonnade of the principal street with its monumental arch, and the tower-tombs on the neighbouring slopes. The temple stands in a walled and paved court about 250 yards square. On the north, south, and east sides this space was lined with porticos supported by double lines of Corinthian columns. On the west was a triple portal approached by broad steps. The temple itself has its entrance in one of its long sides (the west), and two sanctuaries occupy the north and south ends; there were probably cult-places also upon the roof. Leading north-west from this temple, a great colonnade flanked the main street on either side, originally backed by continuous walls, and these, with the columns, supported raised terraces above the street. Half-way up each column was a sculptured corbel, upon which stood bronze statues of distinguished citizens, as attested by many surviving inscriptions. At the east end of the street the great and lofty arch still stands impressively, with its main parts preserved.

A strange solemnity belongs to the tower-tombs, peculiar to Palmyra. Each of these has several stories and around the walls are rows of niches each designed to receive a corpse, belonging to the family which owned the monument. Mainly from these and other tombs are derived the sculptured figures in high relief, portraits of deceased persons, but also of gods and religious scenes, which are the best-known representatives of Palmyrene art. They are highly-accomplished works in a characteristic style combining western and eastern influences, and they are accompanied by frequent epitaphs in the Aramaean language, written with a local variety of the alphabet. The same is found, with figured impressions, upon the so-called "Palmyrene tesserae", clay tokens giving admission to ritual banquets which followed the offering of sacrifices. *See* plate 106, page 334.

Palstave. A bronze **celt** fitted into a handle of split wood.

Papoura. A flat-topped hill.

Papyrus. The papyrus plant *(Cyperus papyrus)*, which belongs to the sedge family, once grew abundantly in the marshy districts of Lower Egypt; today it is not found in its wild state anywhere in Egypt. It was used anciently by the Egyptians for many purposes, but principally for making sheets of writing material.

The stems, which can measure from about ten to twenty feet in length, were probably first cut into more convenient pieces before being stripped of their outer rind. The pith was then cut into thick slices and arranged in overlapping rows, both vertically and transversely. That done, the whole was pounded and pressed into one homogeneous sheet. Despite the sere and friable appearance of ancient papyrus, when freshly made it is almost white in colour and easily rolled.

Though the size of the sheets varied slightly from time to time, the number to a roll seems to have been standardized at twenty. These were pasted together so that all the horizontal fibres were on one side (the "recto") and all the vertical on the other (the "verso"). The sheets were then rolled with the horizontal fibres inside and the vertical outside to avoid the strain on the latter which compression into the cylinder would produce.

When writing, the scribe sat cross-legged with his kilt drawn tightly over his knees to form a firm support for the papyrus. He held the roll in his left hand and released it as he needed it, writing with a brush on the inside from right to left, either vertically or horizontally according to the nature of the document.

It is not known when papyrus was first used as writing material. An unused roll was found in a first dynasty tomb at **Saqqara** (about 3000 B.C.), but the earliest inscribed fragment we have comes from the fifth dynasty (about 2500 B.C.). Papyrus rolls imported from Egypt were used by the Greeks from the seventh century B.C. until the second or third century A.D. when the vellum **codex** took their place, but in Egypt and other parts of the Arab world they continued in use until after A.D. 1000.

Paracas Culture, *see* Peruvians.

Parthians. These were a semi-nomadic Iranian people who lived in the third century B.C. to the south-east of the Caspian Sea. About 250 B.C. Arsaces established the independence of Parthia, once part of the Seleucid Empire, and rapidly expanded his power. At its height, Parthia controlled all of modern **Iran** and **Iraq**, and most of Afghanistan. Its original capital was the town of Arsak (classical Rhagae), in Parthia proper; under Mithradates I (about 170–138 B.C.), however, it was established at **Ctesiphon** (*see* plate 41, page 145) on the middle Tigris. The Parthians, often in conflict with the nomads on their north-east borders, had later to face the attacks of the Romans. Their most famous victory was at Carrhae (the Harran of Genesis) in northern Mesopotamia, in 53 B.C., when the troops of Crassus were practically annihilated by the forces of Orodes II. Though the Parthians later suffered reverses, and Ctesiphon was more than once occupied by the Romans, they set a limit to Roman expansion. The Parthian Empire, however, was never tightly controlled, and its links weakened with time. In A.D. 224 it fell to Ardashir, a local ruler of Fars (south Iran), who rose in revolt, slew King Artabanus V, and established the **Sassanian** Empire.

The Parthians were not an original or inventive people, and the world owes little to them. Their

Photo: R. E. *Dixon, Barnaby's Picture Library*

PLATE XII. PERSEPOLIS: carving of one of the great kings.

military successes were mainly due to their armoured lancers *(cataphracti)* and mounted archers, and it was largely as a result of the defeat at Carrhae that cavalry was introduced into the Roman army. Perhaps the roots of the feudal order of medieval Europe are in part to be traced back to the Parthians.

The chief archaeological sites of the period are Darabgerd (Iran), and Ctesiphon and Hatra in Iraq. The latter were originally fortress-towns on the frontier between the empires of Rome and Parthia; their circular town-plan followed an old west Asiatic tradition, seen also in Assyrian military camps. Of the two styles of domestic architecture, the best Parthian examples are at Dura-Europos, Ashur and Hatra; of these the first typifies the Mesopotamian style of courtyard architecture, while the buildings of the two other sites favour the Iranian *iwan* (columned portico), as at **Persepolis.** Walls were generally built of rubble and **ashlar masonry**, though at Hatra blocks of hewn stone were mainly employed. Moulded stucco and murals were used as architectural ornamentation, and at Hatra masks were carved on stone façades.

The arts of the period reflect the fact that culturally Parthia was much influenced by Hellenism. The kings styled themselves "Philhellenes", and used Greek motifs and inscriptions on their coinage. The most typical example of the Parthian style of sculpture is at Nimrud-Dagh in north Syria – the tomb of King Antiochus I of Commagene (69–34 B.C.). Though this is a Seleucid-Parthian example, it well illustrates the true Parthian style of bas-relief, which elsewhere is found in a poor state of preservation. The Parthians also maintained the Iranian tradition of rock-carving, and the **Behistun Rock** (*see* plate 25, page 95), with the inscription of Darius I, also bears badly-damaged Parthian figures of 80 B.C., carved in strict frontality and in flat relief. Perhaps the most impressive art object of the period is the bronze statue of a male figure from Shami (ancient Elymais), of the mid-second century B.C.; unlike the **Achaemenians**, the Parthians seem to have favoured free-standing sculptures.

The Parthian religion was chiefly the worship of Iranian divinities in fire-temples, with some influence from the Mediterranean world. Zoroastrianism was in existence, but it is doubtful if it was ever the official cult of Parthian kings.

Patjitanian, *see* Palaeolithic, Further Asian.

Paviland Cave. The Paviland Cave is on the Gower Peninsula in south Wales. It is now thirty-five feet above sea-level but some 60,000 years ago was on the sea-shore. Here Dr **Buckland** found a human skeleton as well as animal bones in 1822. Mindful of Archbishop **Usher**'s chronology, he declared the human skeleton to be a man of Roman times. It has since been identified as **Aurignacian** and the bones as those of the woolly mammoth and other animals. Buckland identified the skeleton as that of a woman and it was called the "Red Lady of Paviland" because the bones are stained red as a result of the body having been buried in a shroud of red ochre, perhaps because it was reminiscent of blood and its life-giving powers; it is now known, that the bones are those of a young man.

Pebble Tools, *see* Stone Tools *and* Olduvai Gorge.

Pekin Man, *see* Sinanthropus *and* Fossil Man.

Pendlebury, John Devitt Stringfellow (1904–41), was born in London in 1904 and educated at Winchester and at Pembroke College, Cambridge. Even as a schoolboy he displayed great interest in the classics and in Egyptology. In 1927 he became a student of the British School at Athens and the following year married Hilda White, a fellow student, and attended the excavations he was later to direct at **Tell el Amarna** in Egypt. During 1928–34 inclusive he was Curator at **Knossos** for the British School at Athens, and travelled on foot over the whole island of Crete of which he knew almost every nook and cranny. He and his wife, apart from their work at Tell el Amarna, also excavated at Knossos and almost completely cleared the post-Minoan refuge city of Karphi in eastern Crete.

In 1932 he published *Aegyptiaca*, a survey of all Egyptian antiquities he found in Greece, and in 1939 his *Archaeology of Crete*, which is still the best general survey of this subject.

In 1940 he was appointed as an extra British Vice-consul in Crete, and when Greece came into the war was gazetted with the acting rank of Captain as a liaison officer to the British Military Mission in Crete and given the task of preparing for guerilla warfare if the island should be invaded. On 21 May, 1941, when the first German parachute attack was delivered against Herakleion, Pendlebury was wounded in an attempt to break through to Krousonas to organize his guerrillas and was killed by a German parachutist the following day.

Perigordian. A term which is sometimes used to cover both the **Châtelperronian** and the **Gravettian** cultures.

Persepolis is the principal site of **Achaemenian** Persia, and its monumental structures have been consistently excavated. The Greeks had no very clear knowledge of this royal capital until Alexander the Great's invasion and sack of Persepolis in 330 B.C. Darius the Great planned this palace-fortress as his spring capital; work commenced on the site soon after his accession in 522 B.C., and continued under the later Achaemenids.

Located at the foot of an isolated rock, Persepolis lies in the plain of Marv Dasht in south-east **Iran**. Named Parsa after the Persian homeland, the capital was planned to cover an area of approximately 135,000 square yards of virgin rock. The site was backed by a mountain for added defence; the natural outline of the Persepolis terrace, roughly oblong, was surrounded by mud-brick walls, with rectangular bastions at regular intervals. On the west side of the terrace a monumental stairway of double flights leads to a gate-house and to Xerxes' "Gateway of All Lands", flanked in the Assyrian fashion by *lamassu* (statues of winged bulls looked on by the **Assyrians** as guardian spirits and therefore placed at the gates of Assyrian palaces).

Persepolitan architecture illustrates two varieties of structures – the residential and the administrative. Similar units are characteristic of both, for style does not vary to suit structural function. The essential ground plan consists of a columned *iwan*, or portico, leading to a spacious hall. Wooden roofs are supported by tapering columns with fluted shafts, terminating in capitals formed of animals back to back, a feature unique to this period of architecture. Some of these columns are more than twenty yards tall, and certain halls of administrative buildings contain as many as 121 of them. Despite clerestories and the occasional use of windows, Persepolitan buildings must always have been dim because of their many-columned halls.

Locally quarried limestone was the chief medium of construction. The vast blocks were secured by dry joining, and by the insertion of metal clamps. Though colour was widely used in the interiors, the main ornamentation was on the façades.

The sculpture at Persepolis must be regarded as "architectural art", for it is an integral part of the architecture. Objects in the round were little favoured by the Persepolitan artist, whose genre was carving in low relief. The range of Achaemenian art is limited to the purely ceremonial and royal; it lacks the quality of narrative portrayal and thus provides no scope for the study of social history. A rigid application of set conventions makes the art of the period highly stylized; its repertoire is limited and the subjects are confined to horizontal registers separated by ornamental borders. The reliefs are highly decorative, and great attention is paid to minute detail. There is a taboo on the representation of women in royal art; neither does the chase, a much-favoured sport in ancient Persia, appear on the sculptured reliefs. Instead of battle or siege, the artist prefers to record foreign conquest by tribute-laden processions (as on the great staircases of the Apadana), rather than by the carnage of the conquests themselves. In this the art of Persepolis shows a distinct break from the earlier Assyrian tradition.

The Achaemenids employed foreign craftsmen at Persepolis as a matter of deliberate policy; this is mentioned in an inscription of Darius I at **Susa** recording the employment of artisans from several satrapies (provinces) of the Empire, which extended from Asia Minor to the borders of India. This has given a cosmopolitan character to Persepolis, for Mesopotamian, Greek, Egyptian, Elamitic and other influences can be traced in its remains. Indeed, this new Persepolitan style reflects the achievement of the Achaemenids as the builders of a world empire. *See* colour plate XII, plates 107–109, pages 335–337.

Persia, *see* Iran.

Peruvians. To the average reader, the ancient Peruvians were the **Incas**, but the Incas were only the last in a long succession of peoples of different cultures in Peru, about whom much has been learned in the last few decades through archaeological investigations.

In few regions of the world are found such great diversity and contrast in natural conditions as in Peru. The Andes rear their snow-capped peaks within, relatively, a few miles of the Pacific coast, and the waters from their east slopes form the sources of the great Amazon, which flows some

3,000 miles to the Atlantic. At the foot of their eastern slopes are the great tropical lowland rain-forests, populated today, as they were in the days of Pizarro and the Inca emperors, by Indian tribes of relatively low culture. These are not the real Peruvians, and with them we shall not be concerned.

The Pacific coast of Peru is one of the most arid regions in the world; good rains are years apart and in some places rain is unknown. The sandy wastes are as bare as the Sahara, with not a blade of vegetation, not even cactus. But in the valleys of the short rivers, fed by the Andean snows, the desert springs to life with verdant cultivated fields and dense populations. Here are the modern cities and towns, and here from time immemorial have lived the Peruvian peoples, once differing considerably in customs in each widely separated valley. The great systems of irrigation, begun by the earliest populations, use the life-giving water to its maximum possible extent, so that the populated lower valleys cover considerable areas.

In the highland valleys, on the other hand, rainfall is greater and, especially by the use of extensive terracing, the native Indians raise crops sufficient to support a large population, as did their ancestors. Here also there are llamas and alpacas, native American cameloids which are specially abundant on the high grassy treeless *punas*. Many Indians live at an altitude of 13,000 feet or more; the highest habitation is said to be at 17,400 feet.

The native Peruvians are, and were, pure **American Indians** without any apparent or proved mixture from Europe or Asia. Those in the highlands developed a physique peculiarly adapted to the rarefied air. In early days many different languages, some entirely unrelated, and dialects must have been spoken, especially on the coast, but most of these were replaced in later times by Quechua, the language of the Inca Empire. The cultures and customs were also basically those of the American Indian, though it is coming to be believed that a few practices may have been introduced from across the Pacific at different times.

Though varying local conditions naturally compelled deviation from the norm among certain groups, nevertheless the history of Peruvian cultures followed more or less that of other great world civilizations. Developing or adopting agriculture, formerly sparse hunting-and-gathering peoples became sedentary in scattered, small, peaceful communities. The leisure time between sowing and harvest favoured the development of culture, arts and crafts, a priesthood, and the erection of great temples and other public enterprises. With technical improvements the population increased rapidly and soon competition and wars ensued. Later, great urban centres developed, the capitals of "kingdoms", which vied for supremacy. Finally one of these, impelled by lust for power, overcame all others and established a great empire. In Peru the victors were the Incas.

The earliest known agriculturists in Peru were coastal peoples who combined fishing with rudimentary agriculture. The type-site is at Huaca Prieta at the mouth of the Chicama Valley in northern Peru. They raised a kind of bean, bottle gourds, squash, chilli peppers, and cotton, but maize was unknown. Most of their food, however, came from the sea. Strange to say, pottery was entirely unknown, but considerable weaving was done, mostly by the twining technique. All implements were rude, and decorative art almost absent. **Radio carbon** provides dates of about 2500–1300 B.C.

Nothing is known of the development of Peruvian civilization in the thousand or more years following Huaca Prieta. Population increased, the people came to depend more and more on agriculture, arts and techniques improved. In the next period of which we have any knowledge through archaeological excavations, pottery and maize had been introduced, but the life of the people had not changed greatly. This period is best known at Guanape in the Virú Valley and dates from about 1250–840 B.C.

The earliest known of the great civilizations of Peru – and a remarkable one for this early period – apparently had its centre in the northern highlands, at Chavín de Huantar, just across the divide from the Callejón de Huáylas. Here are many buildings of admirable stone dry masonry, some with three floors, ventilation shafts, and other elements of a highly perfected architecture which must have developed over a long period of time. As indicated by its art style, in which prominence was given to a stylized jaguar, its influence was widespread, extending over most of coastal Peru, and possibly even more widely. The art is best known not at Chavín but on the northern coast, especially in the graves at Cupisnique in the Chicama Valley. Most Peruvianists believe that this influence represented not a political or ethnic entity, but the ramifications of a religious cult. The estimated date for the Chavín-Cupisnique period is 850–500 B.C.

About 500 B.C. there began a very dynamic period during which many new techniques were developed; this period is generally known as the "Experimental". Now archaeological investigations reveal early cultures, though probably not the earliest, in other parts of Peru: the highlands and the southern coast. It should be remembered that we know nothing of these people but what archaeological excavations disclose. These investigations have been few and scattered; each one reveals a **culture** different from any other, and there must have been many more of these than are now known. They are generally named from the place where the excavations were made, and frequently differentiated from later periods at the same site by the type of ceramics made, **pottery** being our best criterion: Salinar and Gallinazo occur on the north coast, Chancay white-on-red on the central coast, Paracas Cavernas and Ocucaje on the south coast, Huaraz white-on-red in the northern highlands, Chanapata in the central highlands, and Chiripa in the southern highlands.

Agriculture, with extensive irrigation and terracing, had been greatly developed in this period, and hunting and fishing were of slight importance. New food plants had been introduced, and llama herding was extensive. One of the characteristics was a widespread "horizon style" of pottery, painted white on red. There are varying estimates as to the length of this period, but it certainly lasted for several centuries following about 500 B.C.

Somewhere about the beginning of the Christian era – various estimates place it several centuries before or after – Peru entered upon its Golden Age. In it, Peruvian culture practically reached its apogee. Later periods saw change, political strivings, but little betterment. Craftsmanship in textiles, ceramics and metallurgy attained a high level, great feats of engineering were performed, enormous pyramids erected in some regions, and religion was highly organized. The centres of highest culture seem to have been, as before, on the coast, but this may be merely because the evidence is better preserved there. The arid coastal deserts, as in Egypt, preserve, sometimes perfectly, the remains of objects that have disappeared completely in the rainier highlands.

The two outstanding cultures of the period were the Moche or Mochica of the north coast and the Paracas and Nazca of the south coast. The former constructed immense irrigation ditches, one of them said to be seventy-five miles long, and erected the enormous temple substructures known as the *huacas* of the sun and the moon, the former estimated to contain some 130,000,000 adobe mud bricks. The Moche are also famous for their naturalistic modelled pottery vessels, many examples of which are found in most large museums. Representations of Moche life, people, animals and objects afford us much knowledge of their customs. Erotic scenes and elements, rare in American Indian art, are a famous feature of this ceramic.

The Moche were obviously well along the road to "civilization" in social and political matters as well as in technological and economic ones. There were apparently great social distinctions between aristocracy, nobility or plutocracy on the one hand, and peasants, serfs, servants or slaves on the other. Wars must have been frequent, and possibly the "empire" was spread and maintained by force, for figures of warriors are very frequent in the pottery.

On the south coast, evidences of two apparently different cultures were discovered about 1925 on the Paracas Peninsula just south of Pisco, one in some deep **shaft graves** known as Paracas Cavernas, and one in a nearby cemetery called Paracas Necropolis. Graves with Cavernas type of pottery have also been found at Ocucaje in Ica Valley, but nothing more is known of these people, not even the sites of their towns and fields. While they may have been contemporary, the standard belief is that Cavernas was older, and it is sometimes put in the preceding period. In the Necropolis in 1927 Dr Julio C. Tello unearthed 329 **mummy** bundles. Many of the smaller ones are still unopened, but the larger ones contained some of the most magnificent textiles known, many in perfect condition. Outstanding are the beautiful mantles, averaging eight by four and a half feet in size, covered in embroidery in which small figures, very stylized in a characteristic way, are repeated in many different colours in alternation. Other plain cloths as large as eighty-four by thirteen feet were found.

About a hundred miles south of Paracas was the centre of the better-known Nazca people, probably slightly later than those of Paracas Necropolis, for some of the exotic designs on Nazca pottery vessels are very similar to those on the Paracas mantles, and the debris of Nazca occupation is underlain by many feet of refuse similar to that of Paracas. While the life of the people was doubtless very similar to that of the Moche they erected no great pyramids, though their houses were, like those of the Moche, of adobe mud; they may have been more democratic and less warlike.

Extensive engineering features are also missing. The graves contain exquisite textiles showing admirable workmanship, and quantities of beautiful pottery vessels. These differ completely from those of the Moche, being of simple shapes but painted with designs, often of stylized natural objects, in harmonious pastel colours, with as many as eleven tints on one vessel.

The cultures of the central coast at this period are known as Intermediate, Interlocking (from the decoration on the ceramic), and Early Lima. The city of Cajamarquilla and the immense temple mound of Pachacamac were probably begun about this time; both are mainly of adobe mud. In the northern highlands much massive but rude stone sculpture was made and, following the Chavín tradition, two- and three-storey stone temples with subterranean rooms and galleries. A negative-painted pottery known as Recuay was typical. In the south the site of Pucára with its characteristic excellent stone sculpture and pottery style was important as foreshadowing the later Tiahuanaco culture. This "Florescent" period lasted at the minimum for half a millennium, but opinions vary as to the exact dating. From 300 B.C. to A.D. 500 is probably the best estimate, but some authorities place it much later, from A.D. 400 to 1000.

The next period, "Expansionist" or "Fusion", was dominated by the culture whose ceremonial centre was at the great site of Tiahuanaco, east of Lake Titicaca in Bolivia, one of the most famous archaeological sites in America. In spite of the altitude of 13,000 feet, good crops of potatoes and of other highland food plants are raised there, and the llama and alpaca are in their native habitat. The major monuments occupy about a sixth of a square mile, with lines of monoliths, terraces, and building foundations. There are few walls and none of any height. The stones are **megaliths**; the famous monolithic gateway has been calculated to weigh about ten tons; other blocks have been estimated at about a hundred tons. The nearest quarries are three miles away. The stone carving is admirable, with smooth faces, the blocks fitting tightly together. Stone statuary, one monolith being over twenty-four feet high, is also an important element.

The influence of the Tiahuanaco culture, particularly as evidenced by the art style, spread all over Peru, highland and coast; it was a "horizon style". On the coast it is known as "Epigonal". This culture was probably an element of a religious cult, the spread of which was possibly accompanied by some loose political force: a Tiahuanaco "Megalithic Empire" is no longer credited. It is believed that Tiahuanaco was a sacred site rather than the cultural centre from which the influence spread; Huari in the province of Huanta, Ayacucho, is a more likely source. The period lasted for a few centuries, various authorities estimating its final phases as from A.D. 1000 to 1300.

The Peruvians had by now reached their apogee. All the techniques of weaving, metallurgy and other crafts had long since achieved their practical maximum, agricultural and engineering methods were on a high plane, all the food plants later known had been domesticated, and so had llamas and alpacas. But the population had also probably reached its maximum and tended to congregate in great urban centres; this period is therefore known as the "Urbanist". With large cities, social stratification naturally developed with autocratic rulers, and small nations that might be called kingdoms came upon the scene. These warred until some vanquished others and formed small empires.

The outstanding people of this period were the Chimu who controlled a number of the valleys of the northern coast. Their capital was the great city of Chanchan near Trujillo. Its ruins, all of adobe, are an impressive sight, with a rectangular street plan, high walls, reservoirs, pyramids and temples; they cover over eight square miles, and almost no excavation has been done there. Craftsmanship was at a high level, but standardized for quantity production, and uninspired.

The Chimu kingdom lasted until it was conquered by the Incas in about 1470, and therefore much of the history of the later dynasties was remembered in Inca traditions. Their language was entirely different from that of the Incas. The cultures, nations, or "kingdoms" in other parts of Peru at this period, especially those in the highlands, are not so well-known, but were probably of a character and quality comparable with the Chimu. The great temple of Pachacamac and the large city of Cajamarquilla, both near Lima, probably belong to this era. Characteristic types of pottery are found in each region; those on the central and southern coasts are known respectively as Chancay and Ica, from the localities where they are found in greatest abundance.

The last chapter in the history of pre-Columbian Peru pertains to the **Incas.**

The Peruvian farmer made invaluable contributions to world economy. He developed potatoes, lima beans, and peanuts, and also certain species of maize, kidney beans, sweet potatoes, squash, pumpkins, chilli peppers, and tobacco (all of them unknown in Europe before Columbus), as well as many lesser-known food plants. He made masterpieces of art in metal and ceramics, and his wife wove textiles that have never been surpassed for technique and beauty. She employed practically every technique known to the modern textile manufacturer, and made fabrics of finer yarns than are made today by the best mechanical means. *See* plate 112, page 340.

Petra as the capital of Edom was called Rekem or Arkem; in Hebrew, it was Sela (rock), a name which continued in use under the Crusaders until the Moslem Conquest. Petra was the name given by the Greek traders who visited the site, and was also used by the Romans.

The site is a large deep glen or valley situated in the precipitous western side of the limestone plateau of Jordan. It owed its importance partly to its perennial springs of water, partly to its position as a convenient halting place for caravans carrying the Oriental trade from Aqaba to the sea-port of Gaza in the west or to Damascus in the north, and partly to its innumerable caves which provided habitations for man and beast, and warehouses for goods in transit. It became famous about the third century B.C. when Greek traders brought home accounts of its fabulous wealth and luxury.

Petra was then the capital of the Nabataean Kingdom. The **Nabataeans** were an Arab tribe, originally nomad shepherds; they became caravan-guards, and finally traders. Their reputation for honesty made Petra a great commercial centre and the Nabataeans for three centuries the most powerful nation of the Middle East. When Rome became the ruling power the Oriental trade was shifted to the Persian Gulf and passed through **Palmyra**, and the traders then deserted Petra and moved to Palmyra. Later on the Crusaders fortified Petra, and held it till the Moslem conquest drove the Franks out of the Middle East. Petra was then so completely abandoned that the very site was lost, and it became a legend and a dream city.

The main entrance into Petra is through a mile-long water-worn cleft in an otherwise impenetrable rock-barrier. Under the Nabataeans the cleft, now called the Sik, was widened to an average of twelve feet, and the roadway was levelled and paved with limestone flags. This paved road continued into and across the Petra Valley, whence other paved roads led in various directions. The rocks on either side of the Sik rise to a height of three hundred feet, and are profusely carved with the emblems of the god Dusares. The Sik ends abruptly at the transverse gorge of the Wady al Jarra. On the side of this wady, immediately opposite the mouth of the Sik, the façade of a temple is sculptured in the rose-red rock. The contrast between the twilight of the Sik and this brilliant piece of architecture is startling in the extreme. The Arabic name of this temple is Khazneh al Faraún – "Pharaoh's Treasury".

The Petra Valley is dominated by the great mass of Umm al Biyara, "Mother of Cisterns", which dwarfs all the surrounding hills. The general colour of the rocks is a brownish-red, varying to dull crimson or rose-pink, and in places striped horizontally with white, yellow and dull blue. In all parts of Petra every available rock has been worked to a vertical face, sometimes left plain, but more often sculptured as the façade of a temple, a shrine, a palace, or a dwelling. Behind each façade is a large chamber hewn in the rock and entered through a tall rectangular doorway. Early travellers, without real evidence, called these chambers tombs; most of them, however, were certainly dwelling places.

Among the surrounding hills are the remains of the skilfully contrived channels and cisterns of the system of water-supply and water-conservation constructed by the Nabataean engineers. In the efficient management of water the Nabataeans rivalled and even surpassed the Romans.

The Roman remains consist of a large rock-cut amphitheatre, with thirty-three rows of seats, holding approximately three thousand spectators; and a built temple known as Kasr al Bint Faraún, "Palace of Pharaoh's Daughter". Ruins of Crusader forts crown several of the hills.

Nabataean sanctuaries were open to the sky and simple in plan, a rock-cut courtyard with an altar and stands for offerings also cut out of the rock. One or more pillar-emblems of the deity marked the sacred place. Under Egyptian and Greek influence temples and shrines were hollowed out in the hill-sides with elaborate façades. Little of the ritual is known. Human and animal sacrifices were offered, and round about every shrine the ground is strewn with fragments of bowls made of the finest pottery painted with designs of ivy or vine leaves. The great mass of these potsherds suggests that part of the ritual was the breaking of the vessel in which an offering was made.

The chief deities of Petra were the goddess Al Uzza, "The Mighty", and her son Dhu-l Shara or Dusares, "The Lord of Seir" (Shara = Seir), both represented by stone blocks, cut as cubes or rounded like the shaft of a pillar, but the most usual form is a quadrangular tapering and truncated pillar. Two such pillars stand at the chief sanctuary, their respective heights being twenty-three feet and twenty-one feet; they probably represent both deities. Another emblem of Dusares is a pyramid.

Nabataean inscriptions are numerous; mostly votive and addressed to Dusares. The Nabataean script is sufficiently like the Hebrew and Aramaic to make decipherment easy. The language was a dialect of Aramaic with an admixture of Arabic. A few Greek, Latin, and Arabic inscriptions also occur.

The present inhabitants of Petra are the Bdul ("The Changed Ones"). Their origin is unknown; they are probably the descendants of a defeated tribe who took refuge in this "nest in the rocks". *See* colour plate XIII, plate 110, page 338.

Petrie, William Matthew Flinders (1853–1942). Petrie was the only child of William Petrie and Anne, daughter of Captain Matthew Flinders of Australian fame. In his early manhood young Petrie travelled, always on foot, over most of the southern counties of England in order to visit, measure, and survey ancient earthworks and stone circles. In 1877, at the age of twenty-four, he published the result of these surveys in a small volume entitled *Inductive Metrology*, a book which marked a new era in the accurate study of the past. In 1866 Piazzi Smyth, the Astronomer Royal for Scotland, published his *Our Inheritance in the Great Pyramid*, in which a theory was propounded founded entirely upon measurements of and in the pyramid. This book turned Petrie's attention to Egypt, and in 1880 he went to Egypt to verify Smyth's measurements. His *Pyramids and Temples of Gizeh* (1883) demolished Smyth's theory, bringing him to the front as an archaeologist, and he then joined the newly founded Egypt Exploration Fund, by which he was sent to the Delta with instructions to look for new sites for excavation, and to excavate at **Tanis.** This was the beginning of his life's work unravelling the past. In 1893, with a bequest of Miss Amelia B. Edwards (a nineteenth-century novelist) a Chair of Egyptology was founded at University College, London. This is still the only Chair of Egyptology which is primarily for the study of and the training of students in the archaeology of Egypt rather than the ancient language. Petrie was appointed the first Edwards Professor, and his famous Egyptological collections were used for the training of the students. Those collections now belong to University College, and are unrivalled for teaching purposes. In 1897 he married Miss Hilda Urlin, by whom he had a son and a daughter. In 1923 he received the honour of knighthood. In 1924 a "Petrie Medal for distinguished Work in Archaeology" was founded in the University of London. Petrie himself was the first recipient, and Sir Aurel **Stein** and Sir Arthur **Evans** were among later recipients. In 1926 the Antiquity Laws in Egypt were made so rigorous that excavation became impossible, and Petrie transferred his work to south Palestine, "Egypt over the Border" as he called it; he never worked in Egypt again.

In 1933 he retired from the Professorship and went to live in Palestine where his work on the **Hyksos** threw much light on the culture of those people. At the age of eighty-nine he died at Jerusalem, where he is buried.

In order to understand the effect of the impact of Petrie's genius on the intellectual world, the conditions then obtaining must be understood. The discovery by **Boucher de Perthes** of man-made **flint** implements of a date before 4004 B.C., which was the accepted date for the Creation, affected only a very small group. But the storm over **Darwin** was still raging, and to the majority of educated people the Bible, as the Word of God, had to be believed "from cover to cover". Only slightly inferior to the Bible for the study of the past were the classics. Nothing could be accepted that was not confirmed by documentary evidence; to judge the date of an object by style was a matter for scepticism and scorn.

Excavation everywhere was in the nature of treasure-hunting. The earth was shovelled out in spadefuls, and never sifted; objects, then known as "relics" or "curios", were not kept unless the excavator happened to know what they were; if kept, their relative positions in a group and the levels at which they were found were not noted. Of the few that were kept, some might end in a museum, but it was not uncommon for them to pass into private hands, and, when the owner died, to be thrown away with "other rubbish". The importance of related groups was not recognized; each object was exhibited as a separate item, seldom placed in its chronological sequence. Petrie, as the pioneer of the recognition of the value of small and often apparently insignificant objects, suffered so much at the hands of ignorant curators, that he stigmatized museums as "the charnel-houses of murdered evidence". It was not until this century that museums began to employ experts to repair and preserve the "curios".

His experience at the **pyramids** showed Petrie that his life's work was to fill the blanks in the history of Egypt. The archaeological problem was very different from that already begun in Europe. There, flint implements having been first found in a geological connection, the search for them was strictly controlled by the methods of that science, and the implements when found had no monetary value. Petrie set himself to study this new subject, especially the exact methods of dating objects, and of excavating so that no information should be lost. Though he was never permitted to excavate the most important sites in **Egypt**, his work altered the whole conception of archaeology in general, and Egyptology in particular. The excavations which were most important in effecting this great change were few in number but startling in their outcome.

In the Delta he excavated Naucratis and Daphnae (1883–6), thus widening the horizon of classical archaeology and bringing new information into the scanty records of the late period of Egyptian history. His new method of excavation had brought to light the knowledge of the life of the people of each period, and showed an aspect of archaeology which had never before been realized. Though a certain amount had been already learned, mostly from pictorial evidence but a little from the language, Petrie's finds and his interpretation of them gave facts about which there was absolute certainty. His was concrete evidence which could not be disputed.

The excavations in the **Faiyum** (1887–90) were equally important. The workmen's town of Kahur, which was absolutely dated to one reign, showed clearly the life of the builders and craftsmen of the time, while the objects found there were of great dating value. Here the value of potsherds was demonstrated, for the pieces of painted pottery found in the town and identified by Petrie as Aegean, were later proved by Sir Arthur Evans to be Cretan in origin, and the Cretan find could thus be dated by the Egyptian evidence. The excavations in the Faiyum covered many periods, and at the end Petrie was able to say, "I have now really outlined the greater part of the long blank of hitherto undefined history of domestic and personal objects of the eighteenth and twelfth dynasties, which had been such an attractive unknown region".

The discovery of the famous **Tell el Amarna** tablets took Petrie to that site (1891–2). It was this excavation which made him famous far beyond the narrow circle of archaeologists. For here was a religion and an art that the man in the street could understand and appreciate. To the archaeologist the Amarna culture was a revelation, to the technician the remains of the glass factory came as a surprise.

The greatest of all his finds, and the one that had the most far-reaching results, was at Naqada (1904–5). It was here that he found that bewildering mass of graves of a people hitherto entirely unknown and unsuspected. These were finally proved to be earlier than even the still legendary first dynasty, and were soon recognised by Petrie as belonging to two distinct **cultures**. He worked out a simple system of sequence dating, by which a predynastic object can be placed in its correct chronological sequence even though the actual intervals of time cannot be ascertained. Later work brought other predynastic cultures to light. These were found by Petrie's assistants working with him. The Badarian pot-sherds were first noted by J. L. Starkey; and the site was excavated by Gertrude Caton-Thompson, and published by her and Guy Brunton. Petrie followed the system of all European prehistorians by naming the culture after the sites where the most characteristic pieces had been found. The Egyptian cultures, in chronological sequence, are Badarian, Amratean, Gerzean, and Semainean.

The excavations at **Abydos** (1899–1901) filled

the blank between the end of the predynastic period and the beginning of the Old Kingdom. This was perhaps his greatest achievement, for it was only by his archaeological method and knowledge that anything was recovered from the miserable wreckage of the plundered and ravaged royal tombs. Though the plunderers had overlooked some fine objects, including the bracelets of King Zer, it was from the bits and pieces that Petrie recovered the names of all the kings of the first dynasty and could place them in their correct chronological order. Much of the second dynasty was also recovered. Yet he had little to work on except broken stone vases, the clay sealings of wine-jars, pottery, and other objects which the plunderers had thought worthless.

Thus in less than twenty years he had filled in the blanks and had traced the history and civilization of Egypt from a remote antiquity till its end under the Romans, so that now there is hardly any object that cannot be placed in its right period and cultural setting.

The less spectacular excavations were often of importance, for every site that he worked yielded something new, interesting, and often vital, no matter how unpromising both site and material might have appeared. These single finds were sometimes of value to the whole world, sometimes to Egyptology only. Foundation deposits, first noted at Naucratis, are clearly connected with the ceremony of founding a temple; the name of the royal founder is always inscribed on some of the objects, and so the exact date can be obtained. And as the deposits were placed at every angle of the external walls and at every junction of the internal walls, the ground-plan can be recovered even if the whole superstructure has disappeared. The **stele** inscribed with the Triumph Song of Merneptah gives the name of "Israel", the only mention of that nation in the whole of the Egyptian records; the discovery of it roused world-wide interest. The pottery heads of foreigners found at **Memphis**, with the casts of the heads of foreigners sculptured on the walls of temples, form an unrivalled collection of early ethnological material. His work on weights and measures proves the many trade connections of Egypt and foreign countries, and also shows the kind of produce that was exchanged.

He set a standard for the treatment of workmen in an archaeological excavation. He trained his men till they became experts in archaeological digging. He never allowed a workman to run a risk to life or limb; if there were a risk he took it himself; therefore he never had a fatal nor even a serious accident among his men in all the years of his active work. He allowed no interference by local authorities between him and his men, thus warding off the bloodsuckers who usually made a wage-earner their prey. He instituted a sytem of *bakhshish*, paying dealers' rates for any objects found on the work. More than one lucky worker was thus able to return to his village at the end of the season with enough money in his pocket to buy himself a wife or even a camel. But if a man were idle or found to be selling the finds to dealers, he was summarily dismissed with the money due to him and never employed again.

Petrie was the first to have the material of all objects identified; metal to be analysed by a metallurgist, botanical specimens submitted to a botanist, and so on. He was the first to show that **pottery** was one of the chief essentials for dating purposes; and that knowledge of the clay, the method of firing, the characteristic shapes of a country, and the types of decoration, was indispensable. In tracing the growth of archaeology, there is hardly an aspect of the subject or a method of identification of an object that was not first introduced or indicated by Petrie. It was the truth that he aimed at, and he refused to accept any theory, however brilliant and plausible, unless founded on proved facts.

He revolutionized the ideals and methods of archaeology, making the past live, and proving that an accurate knowledge of the past is of vital importance in the understanding of the growth and mental development of the human race. *See* plate 111, page 339.

Phaistos, one of the most important centres of **Minoan civilization**, was situated in southern Crete overlooking the Messara Plain and many finds have been made attesting to the wealth of its culture. It was already occupied in **Neolithic** times. Pottery dating from the Early Minoan era (about 2500–2000 B.C.), mainly of grey clay with simple painted decoration has been unearthed there. The Middle Minoan (about 2000–1550 B.C.) palace, built on the brow of a steep hill, was a loose collection of buildings with courts to the west, north and in the centre, and underwent much transformation later on. To the Middle Minoan period belongs intricately patterned pottery, one of the finest examples being a fruit-stand with a design of petals in the bowl and a frieze of petals and lozenges on the stem. The use of a quick potter's wheel evidently accounts for cups of an egg-shell fineness which were often decorated with wavy lines and rosettes. With a find of Late Middle Minoan (about 1750–1550 B.C.) vases a clay disk was discovered on which was an inscription spiralling from the rim to the centre. The characters on this have no resemblance to **Minoan scripts**: certain elements illustrated, such as a plumed head-dress, are reminiscent of the **Sea Peoples** and other elements indicate that it is of Anatolian origin.

The period of about 1550–1400 B.C. was one of great brilliance at Phaistos but, as at **Knossos** and other Cretan cities, in fire and destruction.

Philae, a small island in the Nile to the south of Aswan about 500 yards long and 160 yards wide. contains some of the best preserved temple buildings of Egypt ranging in date from the reign of Nectanebes I (about 378 B.C.) to the reign of the Emperor Trajan (died A.D. 117). They are important for their scenes and inscriptions of religious and mythological import. The great temple was dedicated to Isis, whose worship continued to the time of the Emperor Justinian (sixth century A.D.). The island and temples now lie submerged from April to December beneath the water stored by the Aswan Dam. *See* plate 114, page 380.

Philippines. Although parts of the Philippines at least formed part of the empire of **Majapahit**, and there is some evidence to suggest that Indo-Javanese influences reached the islands, no monuments have survived, any traces having been destroyed by the Spanish when they occupied and christianized the islands. Nonetheless, excavations, up till now on a very limited scale, have revealed that in pre-Spanish times the Philippines formed a part of the general south-east Asian cultural sphere, and that it was incorporated into the Chinese trading system as can be clearly seen from the large quantities of Chinese ceramics found in the islands. (A Chinese source recounts how successful these were as trade goods.) The work of H. Ottley Beyer has done much to demonstrate the continuity of Philippine culture from the **Palaeolithic** period onwards, and it is clear that most of the cultures found in south-east Asia and in China are also represented in the islands, from which area some of them at least seem to have penetrated into the Pacific Ocean islands. Palaeolithic material, though rare, has been found in late **Pleistocene** contexts, and these seem to be followed by a **Hoa-binh**ian culture, scantily represented in Luzon, and a much more widely distributed microlithic culture. The **Neolithic** facies is well represented with round axes, shouldered axes, a ridged axe, and a tanged type which in its Philippino type spread into the Pacific. Highly polished rectangular axes probably reached the Philippines from the south, while a cultural phase with much use of jade seems to have spread from Indo-China. Some of these Neolithic culture phases were probably coeval with an iron-using period, and it seems likely that the islands first came to the notice of the Chinese as a trading area in pre-Tang times. Tang and Sung ceramics are found but the great period for Chinese contact was late Yuan and Ming.

The occurrence of wares from kilns in Thailand and Indo-China points to trade with the south-east Asian mainland, and contacts with Indonesia and Malaya are historically attested. Local traditions seem to record raiding by **Cham** pirates from the Indo-china coast. An interesting problem is posed by the famous terraced rice cultivation of Mountain Province in north Luzon where terraced fields, based on a complex system of stone walls and long irrigation trenches, some of which run for many miles, are associated with head-hunting tribes who seem to represent, in a much diluted form, an early **megalithic** culture. Even earlier is the surviving culture of the negrito tribes who still live largely by food-gathering and forest nomadism. Scientific and intensive field-work in the Philippines is likely to throw much light upon the pre- and protohistory of a considerable area of southern Asia, for the islands seem to have served as a refuge zone and also as a transit area, both north and south and between Asia and the Pacific.

Philistines, *see* Sea Peoples.

Phoenicians. The history of the ancient Semitic peoples called by others Phoenicians, but by themselves at first probably **Canaanites** or "merchants", is little known. There has been but scant excavation at their principal cities, Tyre, Sidon, Berytos (Beirut) and Arad, all situated on that part of the eastern Mediterranean coast now known as Lebanon. The origin of these seafarers is obscure, though they were traditionally thought to come from the Red

Sea (perhaps via Bahrain) and to have founded Sidon.

Egyptian reliefs of the fifth dynasty (about 2500 B.C.) show ships of **Byblos** (Gubla) where, according to excavation, the Phoenicians may have settled as early as 3000 B.C. Trade with **Egypt** was certainly carried on extensively by the sixteenth century. Two centuries later the rulers of Phoenician cities are among the Palestinian correspondents with the pharaoh at **Tell el Amarna.** This close link with Egypt and the supply of "Asiatic" luxuries resulted in considerable influence on Phoenician art. Egyptian methods of glazing, mounting of jewellery, and motifs were freely taken over and adapted to local materials and ideas.

By the early second millennium B.C. colonies had been founded at Joppa, Acre, Dor and Ugarit. The French excavations at the latter port (**Ras Shamra**) are of particular interest as showing the daily life of the Phoenicians and the mixed population there. In addition to the "Canaanite" myths and literature, tablets were found which show an early **alphabet** (of thirty letters) using a modified **cuneiform** script. About the same time there appears another less cumbrous "Phoenician" alphabet, perhaps adapted from the Egyptian **hieroglyphs** via the Sinaitic script into a simple **cursive** alphabet of twenty-two letters no longer associated with their **pictographic** original. This, and the invention of the abacus for counting, were influential aids to a developing trade. Yet another form of script is known from Byblos (from which the word *biblia* or Bible – "books" – is derived). It is sad that the "Phoenician" literature including the mythology of Sanchuniathon of Byblos and the history of Menander of Tyre have not survived.

About 1200 B.C. the **Sea Peoples** destroyed Ugarit, Arvad and Byblos. The Sidonians fled to **Tyre** which now became the chief city and free from Egyptian domination. It was from Tyre that the colony of Utica was founded, according to tradition round about 1100 B.C., but traceable by archaeology only to the tenth century. The Phoenicians occupied many natural and easily defended harbours throughout the Mediterranean. From inscriptions they are known to have settled at Carthage in the ninth century B.C. and in Sicily (Motya), Sardinia (Nora, Tharrosi), Tunisia, east Cilicia and the Taurus Mountains (Sam'al and Karatepe) by the eighth century. By the following century they had a firm hold on Cyprus (Kition) and the central Mediterranean (Malta). Such colonizing activity was partially due to difficulties in the home ports.

Under Hiram I of Tyre (970–936 B.C.) Phoenicia enjoyed a golden age. By treaty with Solomon of Israel he gained port facilities at Ezion-geber on the Red Sea from which his fleets reached **Ophir,** Arabia and east Africa. His architects, craftsmen and materials were used to build the Temple at Jerusalem where they employed distinctive Phoenician motifs, using bronze-work, and two free-standing pillars before the porch as in the temple of Melqart of Tyre.

When the **Assyrians** intervened on the Mediterranean coast the economies of the ports declined. Eluleus of Tyre withstood sieges by Tiglath-Pileser III in 734 B.C. and by his son Shalmaneser using ships captured at Sidon and Acre. The Assyrian annals name many Phoenician towns and villages at this time. Tyre alone retained its independence until it was sacked by Esarhaddon in 677 B.C. and again by Ashur-bani-pal in 665. Although, with the decline of Assyria after 630, Phoenicia regained its independence, by that time the founding of the Greek trading-centres in Egypt and the increasing economic power of their Punic kinsfolk in the western Mediterranean had drawn off much of the Phoenician trade.

Tyre itself was besieged for thirteen years by Nebuchadnezzar II of **Babylon** (586–573 B.C.) and so weakened that even under the freedom of Persian rule it never regained its position as a trading power. The naval victory of the Carthaginians over the **Etruscans** off Sicily in 535 B.C. finally closed the western Mediterranean to them. Tyre was finally sacked by Alexander in 332 B.C. In the seventh to fifth centuries B.C. Carthaginian (Punic – Phoenician) colonies were founded in Algeria (Djidjelli), the Balearics (Iviza), Spain (Cadiz and Gibraltar) and along the Moroccan coast. It was from these sites that the Phoenicians, in their search for raw materials, reached the Azores, west Africa and the coast of Cornwall.

The Phoenicians will be remembered, as they were indeed well-known to their contemporaries, as sea-traders. They exported silk, wool, linen and cloth, some of it embroidered and called "Tyrian purple" from the dye extracted from the local *murex* shell-fish. From the timber of Lebanon, also exported, they carved furniture and rich objects, some decorated with carved (Syrian) ivory. Their jewellery, glass, copperware and, more latterly, their coinage are found at coastal sites throughout the Mediterranean. The returning convoys brought raw materials needed to sustain the Phoenician trade. Thus a cluster of small city ports became the gateway through which many of the ideas both in writing and in art reached Greece and her neighbours and thus the Western World.

Phonograms. Writing began with **pictograms** and advanced into the use of **ideograms.** The next step was for the writing to become phonetic with each written symbol representing an actual spoken sound, at first a syllable (the best known examples of which are **cuneiform** and modern Japanese), and then a letter. Ideographic writing entails the multiplication of characters; the use of phonographic writing reduces this sharply until the modern **alphabet**, of some two to three dozen characters according to the language, is finally arrived at. The first alphabetic script is believed to have been developed by the **Phoenicians** and to have come into existence by 1500 B.C.

Phrygians. The *Phrugioi* of the Greeks, who gave their name to the area of west central Asia Minor to the east of **Lydia**, are possibly the *Mushki* people of the **Assyrian** inscriptions (assuming the identity of Mita of *Mushki* with Midas of Phrygia), but this cannot be certain. Knowledge of these people depends mainly on references in Greek and Persian sources, and on the results of archaeological excavation. By about 1000 B.C., they were established as the main successors to the **Hittites** on the Anatolian Plateau, with their capital at Gordion on the Sangarius River. The site of Gordion, modern Yassihöyük, was identified in 1889 by the Körte brothers, but the significant modern excavations, under the direction of Dr R. S. Young of the University of Pennsylvania, were begun in 1950. The Phrygian levels lay above Hittite remains and below Persian and Graeco-Roman, and this **stratigraphical** situation is confirmed by recent excavations at **Boghazköy**, Kayapinar, Kültepe and Fraktin, all well to the east of Gordion. These various sources suggest that the Phrygian kingdom consisted of a warrior aristocracy of Indo-European speech, who established themselves as rulers over an indigenous agricultural population of higher culture; their kings bore the name, or title, of Midas and Gordias.

The Phrygian people came under Persian rule when, in 547 B.C., Cyrus came to Gordion in the course of his conquest of Lydia, and recent excavations have shown that the famous **Royal Road** of the Persians ran past the city on its way to Sardis from **Susa.**

Phylakopi, *see* Cyclades.

Pictograms. The oldest form of writing was by means of pictures; it is called pictographic ("picture-writing"), and a single character is known as a pictogram or pictograph. The picture represented the actual thing, whether it be the sun, a man, or an animal. The most well-known form is the Egyptian **hieroglyphics.** The pictures soon became standardized in what might be called a shorthand form; thus a simple circle would represent the sun. From this the next development of writing was by the use of **ideograms.**

Piltdown Skull. The so-called Piltdown Skull was reported as being found in a gravel pit near Barkham Manor, Piltdown, near Fletching, Sussex, England, in 1911–12. The fragments found included pieces of a thick human brain-case and a very ape-like jaw bone. For many years it was thought that these pieces belonged together and represented a genuine missing link between apes and man which had lived about half a million years ago. Then in 1953, to the world's astonishment, evidence was found that the skull was a fake.

Why was the authenticity of the Piltdown Skull accepted when it was first investigated? Why did suspicion fall on it eventually? What methods were used in proving that it was a forgery?

It was accepted in the first place because it was found in circumstances which seemed to exclude all suspicion. The finder, Mr Charles Dawson (who died in 1916 at the age of fifty-two), was a highly respected country lawyer, and an amateur geologist well known to the authorities at the Natural History Museum in London as the discoverer of many genuine fossils in Sussex. He was a personal friend of Dr Smith Woodward, then Keeper of Geology at the Museum. In 1912 Mr Dawson brought fragments of the skull to Dr Woodward saying that he had recovered them in the Piltdown gravel pit, together with some fossil animal remains such as the tooth of an extinct type of elephant, which suggested an age of about half a million years. All these specimens were of the same rusty colour as the gravel itself. Dr Woodward was very interested and went to Piltdown to dig with Mr Dawson. While they were excavating together Mr Dawson unearthed the famous lower jaw which was so very ape-like. The teeth however were worn in a way found only in man, so it was natural to associate this jaw with the bits of thick human skull found within a few feet of it. Dr Woodward described the remains as the skull of an ape-man, which he called Eoanthropus ("Dawn Man"), a strange mixture of man and ape. Some scientists even in 1912 thought that Dr Woodward had made a mistake, that there were really two creatures represented by a man's skull and an ape's jaw. But no one at that time suggested or thought (as far as we know) that it was a question of fraud. The hypothesis that the remains represented a single creature, a missing link, seemed entirely reasonable at that time. Darwin had predicted that just such an intermediate type had once lived. Another reason why Dr Woodward's interpretation was accepted as reasonable was that there were scarcely any specimens with which the skull could be compared in 1912. There was the **Java** skull cap, and the **Heidelberg Jaw**, but the fact that they were different could be due to their being off the main line of evolution or of another age. So "Piltdown Man" got into all the textbooks and popular books on early man. Indeed this skull was generally accepted as one of the most important specimens bearing on human evolution that had ever been found. But as the years passed, the skull became more and more difficult to understand. It did not fit in to the picture that was emerging as a result of other discoveries. Fossil human skulls of about the same presumed geological age were found in various parts of the world after the first world war. There was Pekin Man, and more remains of Java Man and the skulls of the nearly-human Australopithecus of South Africa. All these other fossil men had jaws that were fully human while their braincases had ape-like brow-ridges. The Piltdown Skull was quite otherwise; the braincase was fully human without brow-ridges, while the jaw was ape-like. All the new finds supported the theory that man and apes trace their descent from a common ancestor, but Piltdown Man did not appear to fit in.

A crucial question was the age of the skull. In 1949 Dr K. P. Oakley in collaboration with staff in the Government Laboratory was trying a new method of dating fossils, not in years but relatively, by the amount of **fluorine** they have absorbed from the ground. When they tested the Piltdown Skull and jaw they found that neither of them contained more than a small trace of fluorine, whereas the fossil elephant tooth reported from the same site contained a high percentage of fluorine. Thus it became apparent that the Piltdown Skull was much more recent than the extinct elephant; it could not be older than the latter part of the **Ice Age.** That made it even more difficult to understand. Neither an ape nor an ape-man was to be expected in Britain in the later part of the Ice Age. All manner of possibilities were considered and dismissed for lack of evidence. Then in 1953 Dr J. S. Weiner, an anatomist in Oxford University, became interested in the teeth of the Piltdown jawbone. The one feature that seemed to link the jawbone with the human braincase was their flat wear. Dr Weiner experimented and found that it was possible to reproduce the appearance of the Piltdown teeth exactly by artificially grinding modern ape's teeth. With Sir Wilfrid Le Gros Clark, Dr Weiner studied this question closely, while Dr Oakley, in collaboration with colleagues, explored the problem of how to prove conclusively whether or not the jawbone was modern. Between them they showed that the Piltdown mandible was that of a modern orang-outang that had been artificially treated to make the teeth appear human and the bone to appear fossilized. They found too that the fragments of human braincase were ancient, but had been brought from some other site and artificially stained to match the gravel. These bones may not be older than medieval. **Carbon fourteen** tests in 1959 indicated that they were less than 500 years old. Their unusual thickness is due to disease.

The investigators proved in 1953 that the jawbone was modern by refining the fluorine method, and by applying other tests. They found that the jaw contained as much organic matter (protein) as modern bone, while the bones of the braincase contained only a trace. By means of the electron-microscope, which gives an enormous magnification, it was possible to detect the actual protein fibres in the jawbone.

When they turned their attention to the fossil animal remains and **artifacts** found at the same site they found that these too had been fraudulently introduced. The Piltdown "bone implement" was fossil elephant bone that had been whittled with a steel knife. The "flint implements" were **Neolithic** wasters that had been artificially iron-stained.

We now know that uranium, like fluorine, is absorbed by bones buried in the ground, so that the radioactivity of bones at a particular site is a rough measure of how old they are. The Piltdown elephant tooth proved to contain ten times more uranium than fossils of the same age from other English gravels.

The investigators compared it with fossil elephant teeth from all over the Old World, and only in north Africa were examples found that contained as much uranium. It seems that the Piltdown elephant tooth was a foreign, probably African, fossil that had been artificially stained and placed in the Piltdown gravel to suggest that the bogus skull was of great antiquity.

Everything reported from the Piltdown gravel pit has proved to be fraudulent in one way or another. But at any rate in uncovering this remarkably skilful and elaborate hoax new techniques were developed that will be of value not only in preventing the repetition of such a fraud in the future, but in dating genuine fossils.

Already some of the same tests have been applied to the **Swanscombe**, **Rhodesian** and other fossil human skulls. The results not only show that they are genuinely ancient, but have helped to establish their geological antiquity more precisely. *See* plate 115, page 381.

Pisé. Clay or earth (and sometimes gravel) beaten down until it is solid, and used as building material.

Pit Graves. These were shallow graves cut usually in rock; at **Mycenae** they represent the graves of the common people as opposed to **shaft graves**, **tholos tombs** and **chamber tombs** which were for the ruling class. Sometimes, however, pit graves are found at Mycenae on the floors of tholos and chamber tombs roofed over with slabs of limestone or conglomerate.

Pithecanthropus. The first specimen of this group, Pithecanthropus erectus, **Java Man**, was discovered by Eugène Dubois at Trinil, central Java, in 1891–93. At first there was much opposition to the status implied by the name, the ape-man who walked erect, but it became generally accepted, though Dubois himself finally changed his mind and said that he had discovered a giant ape. No further specimens were found until 1936 when G.H.R. von Koenigswald made the first of a series of discoveries in a programme designed to make more material available. As a result, a number of other specimens of Pithecanthropus erectus are known, as well as Homo modjokertensis, an infant of this group and the only example known from the Lower **Pleistocene**, the others being middle Pleistocene. At least two species of Pithecanthropus appear to have existed, the other being Pithecanthropus robustus. It is probable that the differences between the material from Java and that from **Chou-kou-tien** are insufficient to warrant a generic distinction and that the Chinese material should be referred to the Pithecanthropus genus also, specifically distinguished, in view of their more advanced characteristics. The Java skulls of four adults and one infant show, in the case of the three which can be analysed, a mean cranial capacity of just under 900 c.c. (rising to just over 1000 c.c. if the Chinese material is included). The skull shows marked supra-orbital ridges, a post-orbital constriction and a massive occipital torus. There is little forehead, and the skull is very low. There is no doubt that these creatures made and used tools, and no indications against their being capable of speech. Their status in the history of human evolution is, however, disputed. Weidenreich held that they were in the main line, while Le Gros Clark places them in a collateral line.

Pitt-Rivers, Augustus Henry (1827–1900). Lieutenant-general Pitt-Rivers was born at Hope Hall, Yorkshire, in England, as Augustus Henry Lane-Fox, and assumed the surname of Pitt-Rivers in 1880 on succeeding to the estates of his great-uncle, the second Lord Rivers.

A brilliant archaeologist, he has sometimes been called the "father of British archaeology" and the "prince of excavators", mainly because of the high standard of excavation, recording, and publication which he set up well in advance of his contemporaries. Much of what he did remains an outstanding example even to this day.

His scientific career may be divided into two parts. Firstly, from 1845 to 1880, when he received a commission in the Grenadier Guards, soon after which he began to study the evolution of firearms which led him to consider the development of primitive arts and crafts all over the world. Ethnographical and archaeological material may be classified, not according to region, but in an evolutionary series showing a development from generalized forms of primitive cultures to specialized forms of higher cultures. It followed from this that it was typical specimens which were important and not only those with an artistic or exotic value. In this, like Sir Flinders **Petrie**, he ran counter to the general nineteenth-century trend, as they both stressed a sociological rather than an art-historical approach to archaeology. Naturally influenced by Darwinian evolution, Pitt-Rivers was not, however, blind to phases of degeneration. Although not the first to classify **artifacts** in a series, he approached the problem from an ethnographic and quite independent point of view.

During this period he published *Primitive Warfare* (1867–69) and built up the collection which was to form the Pitt-Rivers Department in the University Museum, Oxford.

The second phase of his career was from 1880 to 1900, the period of his greatest archaeological activity. This began on his succession to estates rich in archaeological remains and his appointment by Parliament as the first Inspector of Ancient Monuments. A spate of excavations based on his new seat at Rushmore, Wiltshire, produced in 1887 the first volume of his famous privately published *Excavations in Cranbourne Chase*. Thereafter the next three volumes followed at intervals of a few years up to his death. These contain accounts of his famous exploration of the Romano-British villages of Woodcuts, Rotherley, South Lodge, Handley Hill, and Martin Down. Defensive earth-works naturally appealed to one who had fought in the Crimea and, as well as camps, he made sections through Wansdyke and Bockerly Dyke. His excavation of Wor Barrow, Handley Down, Wiltshire was until very recently one of the few outstanding long **barrow** excavations in this country.

He still had time to devote to historical and anthropological work, publishing *Locks and Keys* (1883), *King John's House, Tollard Royal* (1890) and *Works of Art from Benin* (1900).

Pitt-Rivers did not invent the whole of excavation technique; he was, in fact, continuing the more scientific work started by earlier excavators such as William Cunnington and Sir Richard Colt Hoare; but he brought a touch of genius and many new ideas. He was the first to have three-dimensionat recording on the site, and one of the first to use **stratification** and to excavate domestic sites. He insisted on the importance of recording the smallest detail; on accurate plans, sections, and models; on an adequate staff, full publication, and graphs; and he stressed the distribution of similar forms.

Plainviews, *see* America, Early Man in.

Pleistocene Epoch, *see* Quaternary Period.

Pliocene Epoch. This was named from the Greek words *pleion* and *kainos*, meaning "more recent". With a duration of approximately 15,000,000 years the epoch brought the **Tertiary period** to a close, and left little more than 1,000,000 years of **Quaternary** time for the final completion of geological history.

The uplift and depression of some land areas, which still persisted after **Miocene** times, gradually gave the continents and oceans their present-day configuration. The large land-locked sea which stretched across the Danube Basin to southern Russia was gradually reduced to a series of lakes and inland seas, of which Lake Aral, the Black Sea and Caspian Sea are survivors. In north-west Europe the North Sea was formed by gentle subsidence. Meanwhile earlier formed mountain chains were being rapidly dissected by agents of erosion, under climatic conditions not very different from those of the present day. Towards the end of Pliocene times cooler temperatures heralded the onset of the Pleistocene "Ice Age".

In general aspect, Pliocene plant life closely resembled present-day vegetation. Marine life also appeared to have achieved a stable pattern, although a number of Pliocene species, together with a few genera (including the toothed whale Balaenodon), are unrepresented in modern seas.

Amongst the land animals, mammals were less varied than their predecessors of the Miocene epoch, but more diverse than modern forms, a trend which suggests that their decline had perhaps already begun. Elephants, true horses, oxen, giraffes and large deer made their first appearance. Elephants, including Doinotherium, and the more progressive mastodons such as Tetralophodon, were especially numerous, and more widely distributed than in any other period of geological history, whilst the first true horses, such as Hipparion and Pliohippus, had become single-toed. Man-like apes probably evolved before the close of Pliocene times; the South African **Australopithecus** ("southern ape") is thought to have been an early member of that family of hominids to which man also belongs.

Plough. Estimates as to when **Neolithic** Man, in his change from a food-gathering to a food-producing economy, first began cultivating plants range from 8000 to 4000 B.C. In Britain the earliest known agriculture dates from about 2400 B.C.

A pointed stick or branch was probably the first farm tool. Deer antlers were also used, and **stone tools** fitted with a handle. In some parts of the world a foot-plough was invented and used. A form of this, called the caschrom, was used in the remoter Scottish isles until very recently, and may indeed still be in use.

The first really great advance in agricultural techniques came with the invention of the ox-drawn plough, for with it a man could cultivate a far larger area than could a woman with a hoe. This meant that a bigger crop could be grown, more people fed, and, perhaps most important of all, a surplus produced which could be used for trading purposes. Specialization in crafts became possible, for carpenters and potters no longer needed to grow their own food but could barter their products against the grain produced by other families over and above their own needs. The invention of the plough was one of the factors which made civilization possible.

The earliest form of plough was made of wood but, with the coming of the **Iron Age**, the share was tipped with iron so as to make it last longer.

That the earliest ploughs were made of wood means that they have not survived, for wood perishes with the passage of the years, so it is not possible for archaeologists to discover when the plough was first introduced; they can only state that the finding of models in tombs, or the mention of ploughing in the earliest written documents, indicate that the plough must by then have been in use for a long time.

From such evidence it is possible to state that the plough was in use at either end of the **Fertile Crescent** by 3000 B.C., and probably had been used for as much as a thousand years before that date. Similarly, it is known that the plough was in use in the **Indus Valley civilization** in India well before 2500 B.C., and by 1400 B.C. it had superseded the hoe in northern Europe. In Africa, outside the area of the **Hamitic People**, the plough was unknown until the Europeans came.

These ploughs scratched at the soil and stirred it up; they did not turn it over so as to bury the surface vegetation beneath the furrow. The modern type of plough with its coulter to cut the sod in front of the share and its mouldboard to turn the earth over, was not developed until much later. It was first used in northern Europe, where the Mediterranean plough was useless in the heavy clayey soil, some two centuries before Christ, and brought to southern Britain in the first century B.C. by the Belgae, the Germanic successors of the **La Tène** culture.

Pluvial. A period of heavy rainfall.

Points, *see* Flint.

Polished Axes, *see* Stone Tools.

Pollen Analysis. Flowering plants reproduce themselves by pollination, a method in which the microscopic pollen containing the male reproductive cells is brought into contact with the ovules containing the female reproductive cells so that fertilization takes place.

Pollination can be brought about by the action of birds or insects transferring the pollen from one part of the plant to another or, where the male and female cells are on separate plants, from one plant to another. It sometimes occurs by the action of the wind carrying the pollen through the air and, with a certain amount of luck, depositing it in the right place. This last is a risky and wasteful process, and wind-pollinated flowers produce large quantities of pollen, most of which falls to the ground without achieving its object.

This "pollen rain", as it is sometimes called, usually decays, but may be preserved if it happens to fall in a suitable place, especially one where there is an oxygen-deficiency – such as mud or a peat-bog. It then, when sufficient time elapses, becomes fossilized and can in years to come be identified under the microscope by the palaeobotanist (one who studies the botany of the ancient past).

This method of pollen analysis can be used to decide what the climate was in the past. Many trees are wind-pollinated and, if a layer from a peat bog is examined and found to contain only pollen from pine and birches, this suggests that the climate was a cold one. A warmer climate would show pollen from oak, elm, and other deciduous trees. The

Photo: Michael Cubitt

PLATE XIII. PETRA: rock cut temple.

Photo: Museum National d'Histoire Naturelle

PLATE 113. QUATERNARY PERIOD: exhibition of quaternary carnivores – (left to right) cave hyeana, three cave bears, two cave lions and a cave wolf. *(Museum National d'Histoire Naturelle, Paris)*

Photo: A. F. Kersting

PLATE 114. PHILAE: the temple (Ptolemaic).

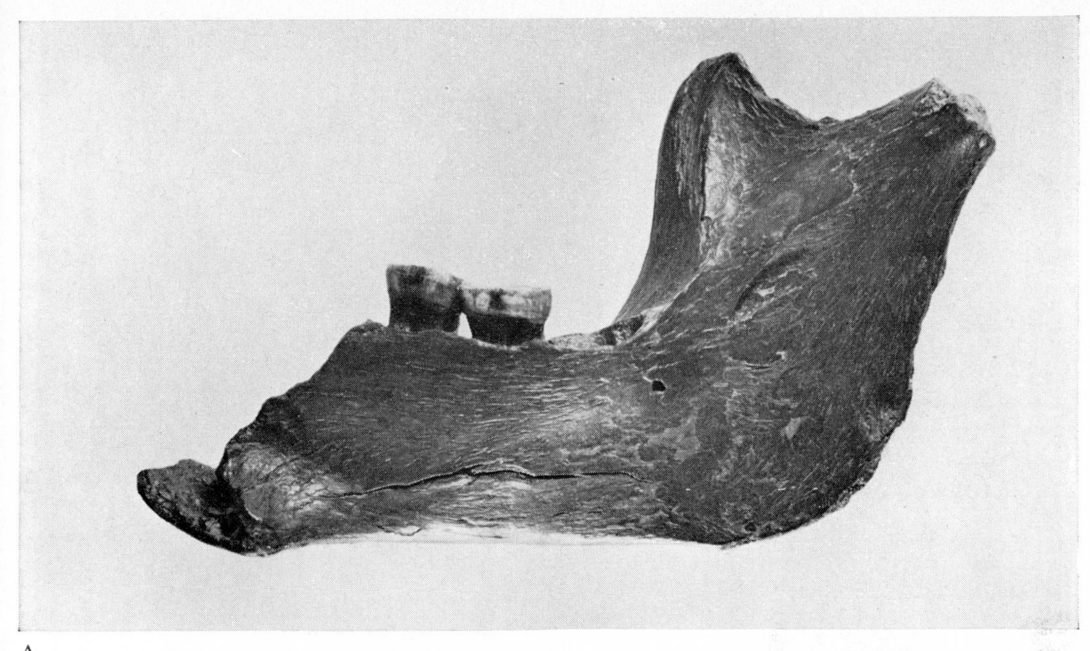

A

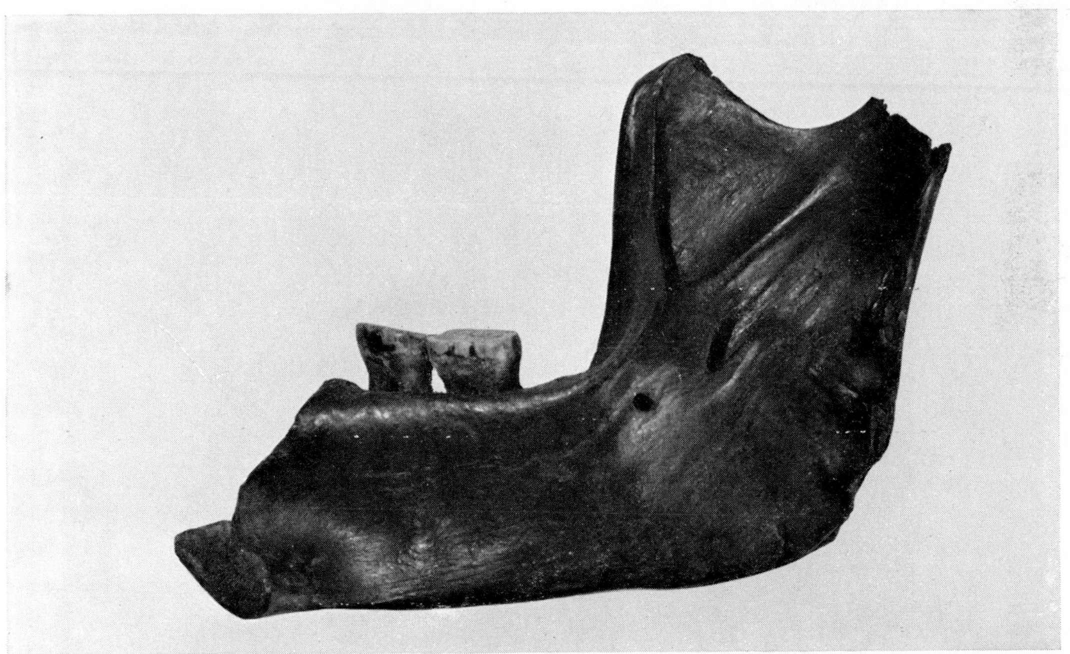

B

Photo: British Museum (Natural History)

PLATE 115. PILTDOWN SKULL: (A) Piltdown mandible (B) Mandible of orang-outang jaw ground down and stained. *(British Museum (Natural History), London)*

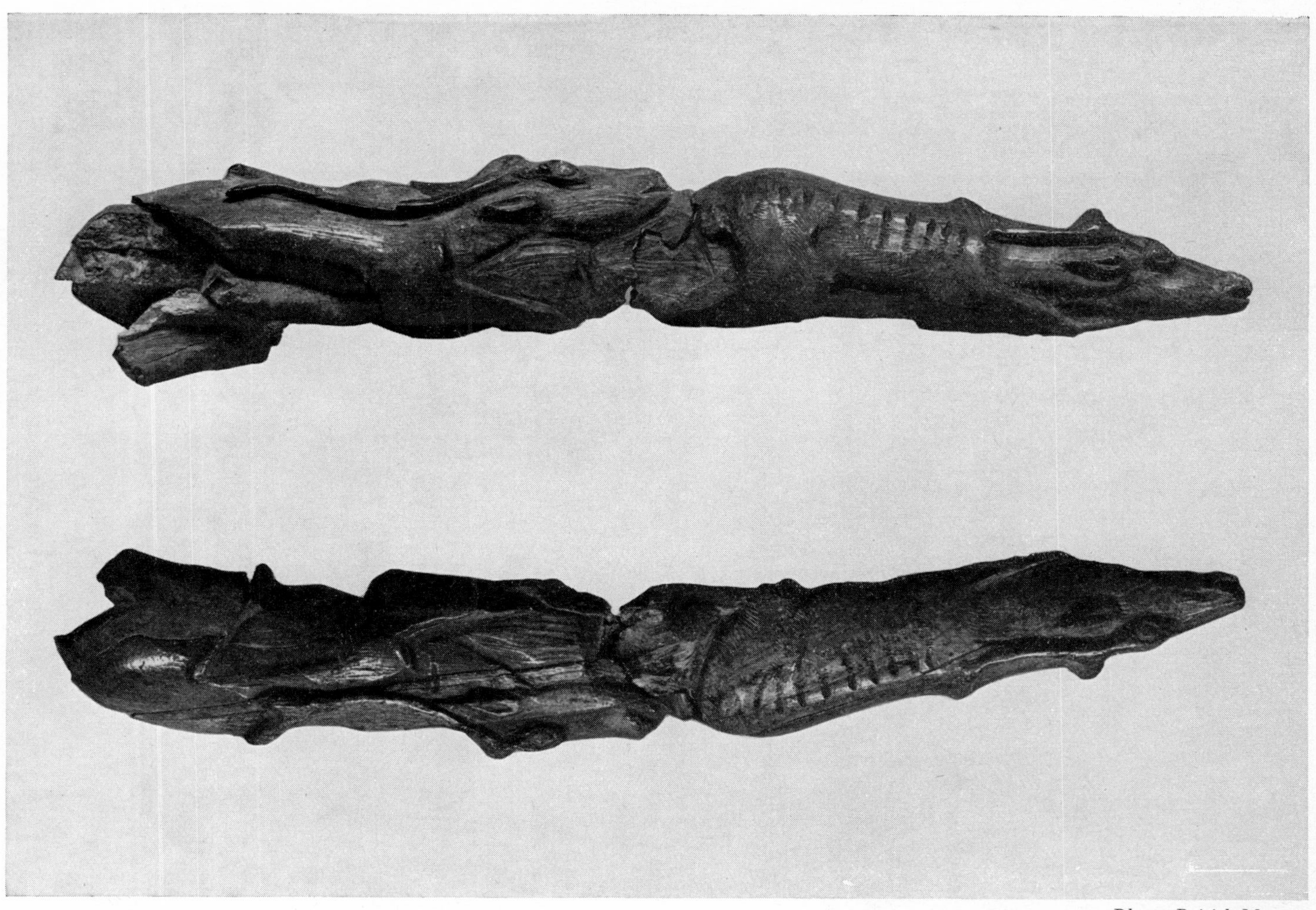

Photo: British Museum

PLATE 116. PREHISTORIC ART: reindeer carved on a point of a mammoth tusk, Magdalenian, from Monastruc.
(British Museum, London)

Photo: Museum, Tromsö

PLATE 117. PREHISTORIC ART: a bear, part of a rock carving from Nordland, northern Norway. The whole carving consists of seven figures drawn in ground and polished line in granite – three reindeer, two seals, one little whale and one bear, probably between 6000/5000 and 2000 B.C. *(Museum, Tromsö)*

Photo: Mansell Collection

PLATE 118. Henry Creswicke RAWLINSON (1810–95), photograph.

Photo: British Museum

PLATE 119. ROSETTA STONE: a slab of black basalt found near Rosetta in the western delta of the Nile, bearing a decree passed by an assembly of priests at Memphis written in hieroglyphs, demotic and Greek which gave scholars the key to Egyptian hieroglyphs. *(British Museum, London)*

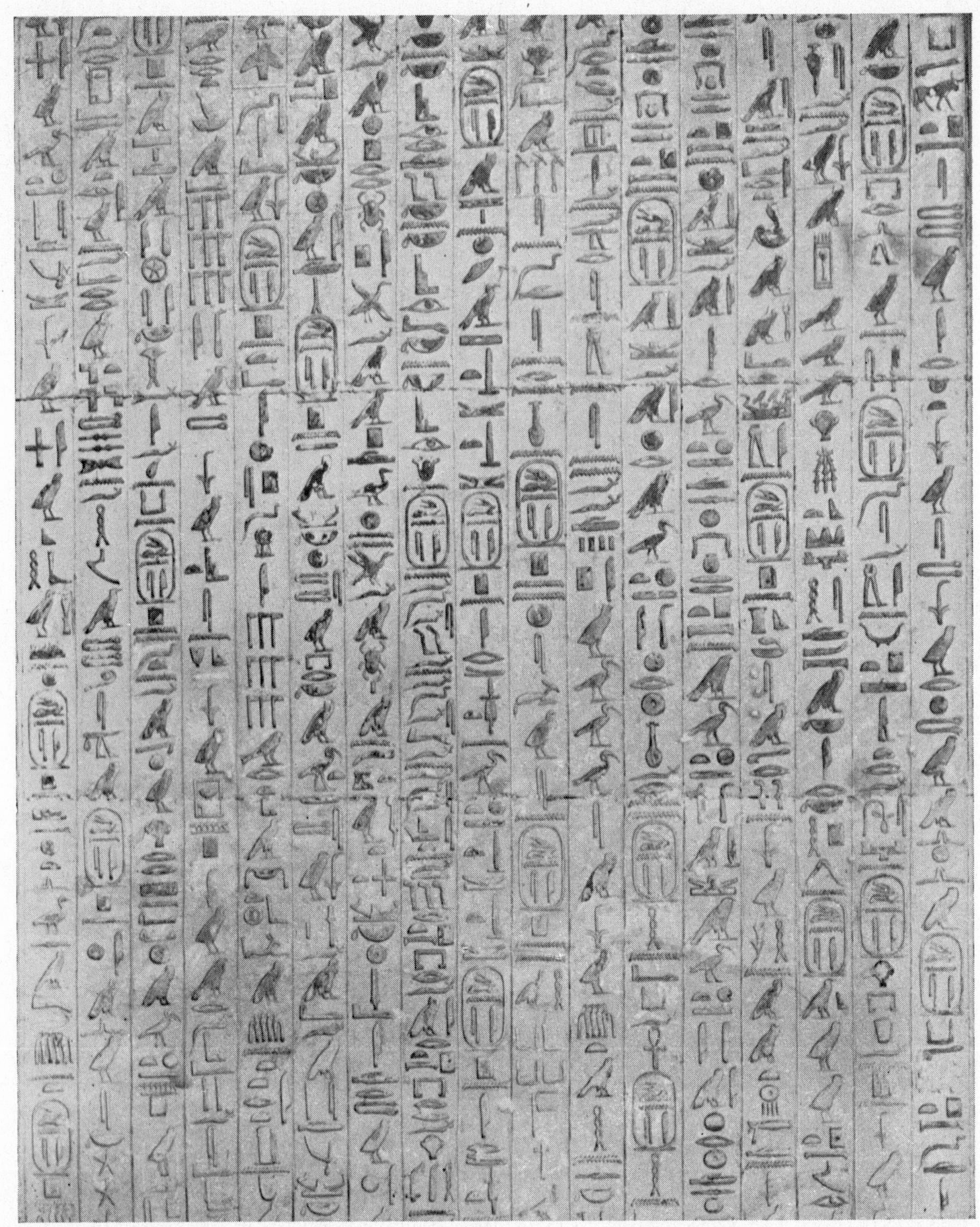

Photo: A. F. Kersting

PLATE 120. SAQQARA: detail of the pyramid texts in the tomb chamber of the pyramid of Unas at Saqqara.

Photo: Mansell Collection

PLATE 121. SANCHI: great stupa, back view of north gate.

Photo: J. Allan Cash

PLATE 122. SARNATH: the Dhamekh Stupa, the largest surviving stupa at Sarnath, stone and brick. Height 150 feet.

Photo: Mansell Collection

PLATE 123. Heinrich SCHLIEMANN (1822–87), photograph.

Photo: J. Allan Cash

PLATE 124. SARNATH: carvings on walls of the Dhamekh Stupa.

Photo: Radio Times Hulton Picture Library

Plate 125. Siemreap: relief of a battle scene from Angkor Wat.

Photo: from "Archaeology in China" by William Watson, Max Parrish and Co. Ltd, London

PLATE 126. SHIH CHAI SHAN: bronze drum. Some twenty tombs, recently excavated near Kunming, have revealed a flourishing Bronze Age culture of a non-Chinese type, which dated from the first two centuries B.C. *(By courtesy of the Britain-China Friendship Association)*

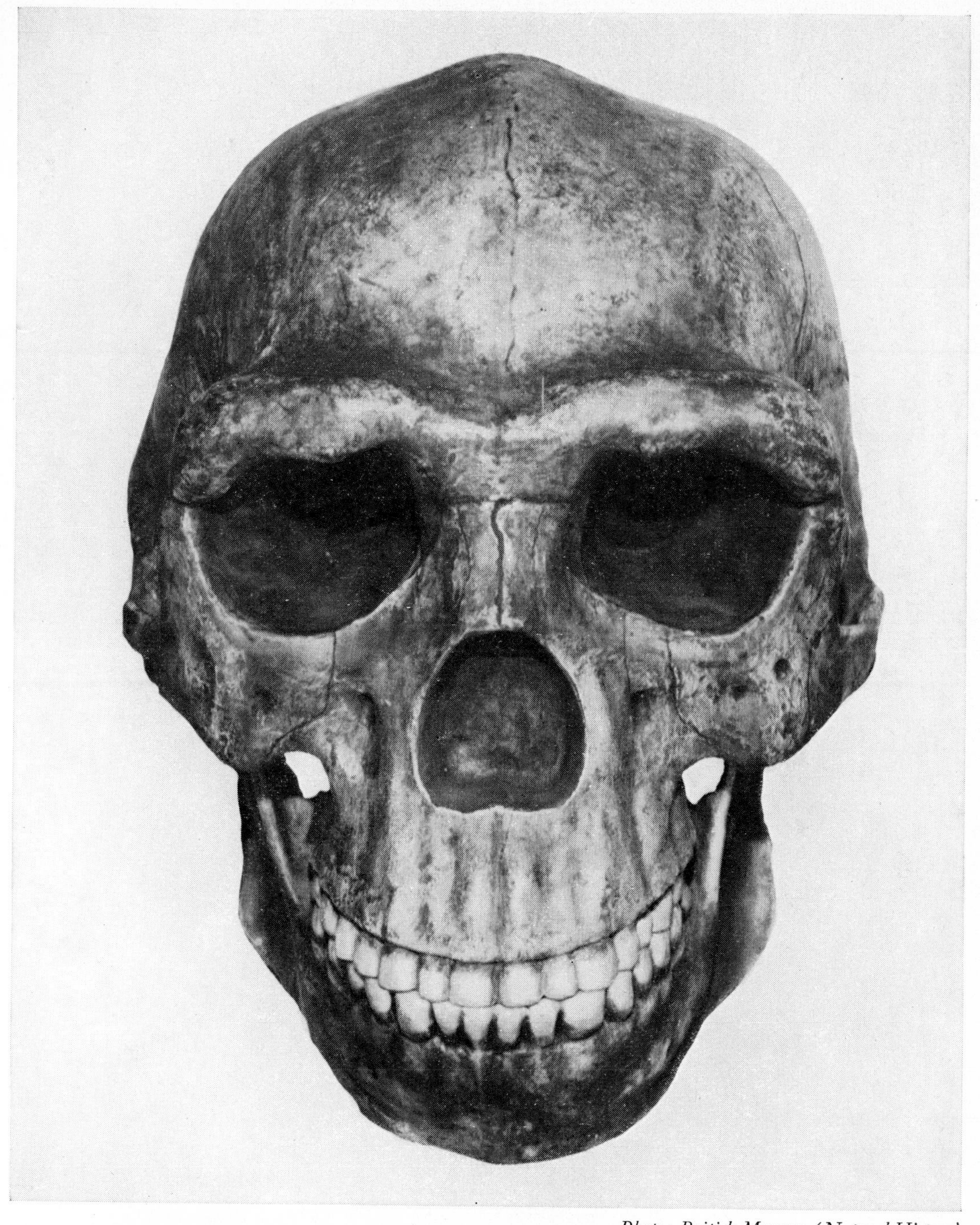

Photo: British Museum (Natural History)

PLATE 127. SINANTHROPUS: model of restored skull of Pekin Man from cave deposit at Chou-kou-tien. Restoration by F. Weidenreich. *(British Museum (Natural History), London)*

Photo: J. Allan Cash

PLATE 128. SKARA BRAE: interior of a house showing the drystone construction of the walls and the use of stone for furniture – for the hearth, the cupboard and even for the bed.

Photo: R. E. Dixon, *Barnaby's Picture Library*

Plate XIV. Sanchi: the Great Stupa from the south-west showing the west gateway.

method can also be used to determine the type of grass present, though not the smaller flowering plants since few of these rely on wind-pollination for purposes of fertilization.

The process of dating the retreat of the glaciers by **varves** can be cross-checked by pollen analysis, and the presence of tree-pollen on nearby prehistoric sites can sometimes help to link these with the accurate dating that varves can give.

As with **carbon fourteen** dating, the process is expensive; it is also slow, for it involves the examination of numerous slides and the laborious counting of the grains present in the specimen.

Polonnaruwa, Ceylon. As a result of continuous raids by Tamils from south India, the capital at Anuradhapura was abandoned and from A.D. 781 to 1290 the capital of Ceylon was at Polonnaruwa. Many buildings were constructed here, but the great period of building was that of King Parakrama Bahu (1164–97), who is sometimes thought to be represented by a great standing figure of a sage reading a palm-leaf book, some eleven and a half feet high and carved from a granulitic rock overlooking Lake Topawewa. The group of images at the Gal Vihara also belongs to his reign. These include an image of the Buddha in the Parinirvana (recumbent) attitude, almost fifty feet long, a portrayal in giant form of a typical Anuradhapura icon. A standing figure of Ananda (twenty-five feet high) shows more originality and invention. Other notable features include a group of temples and viharas in the so-called Great Quadrangle which date from the period 1198–1207. These include a pyramidal building, the Sat Mahal Pasada which seems to have south-east Asian affinities, and the Hata-da-ge, a fine **ashlar** building with delicate low-relief carvings of hamsa. The Wata-da-ge, Tooth Relic **Stupa,** which dates from the time of Parakrama Bahu is one of the finest of Singhalese stupas and seems originally to have had a wooden roof. (Both these buildings seem to derive from originals at Anuradhapura, and it is noteworthy that the whole effect of Polonnaruwa is of a conscious archaism.) A group of Hindu temples, the main intention of the site being Buddhist, belong to a period of Cola suzerainty when the raiders occupied this area in the first quarter of the eleventh century.

Pongid. A term for the biological family which includes the apes, but not man who is a **hominid.**

Pong-T'uk. This site on the Kanburi River in Thailand about forty miles from Bangkok revealed the foundations of a number of buildings and Buddhist images of Gupta style, as well as a bronze Buddha image which is said to belong to the **Amaravati** school, perhaps between the second and fourth centuries A.D. though it may be later in date. (Similar early images, this time Hindu, were also found at S'i Tep on the Nam Sak which are probably to be dated to between the fifth and sixth centuries A.D. or even later, while an early Buddha figure from Korat may belong to the Amaravati school.) There was also found at Pong-T'uk a bronze Roman lamp which has been identified as of a Herculaneum type from the second century A.D. but which may be rather later in date. This last may well have reached Thailand as a secondary export from India, though the famous mission to China of musicians and jugglers from "Rome" in A.D. 120 or the self-styled Roman embassy from Marcus Aurelius, A.D. 166, may have left some evidence of their passing.

Pottery. The making of pots is one of the arts which were first developed in **Neolithic** times. The need for pots arose out of the changeover from a food-gathering to a food-producing economy, for the cultivation of cereal crops meant that the produce had to be stored for future use. **Basketry** had its uses for this purpose, especially when lined with clay, and it may have been the accidental burning of a clay-lined basket which led to the crucial discovery that clay, soft and malleable when wet, becomes hard and set when heated sufficiently for the water to be driven out of it. A further discovery was made, that the burnt clay could be heated over a fire without harm being done to it; thereby the possibilities of cooking became enormously extended. The early history of pottery is, in fact, the history of cooking-pots.

The making of good pottery is a skilled process. The clay must not be too gritty, or it cannot easily be modelled and shaped, but it must contain some grit – sand, shells pounded to a fine dust, chopped straw, and so on – or it will not keep its shape when worked, and will crack on being fired. The modelled clay must be dried out before it is fired, and the heat of the fire must reach a certain critical temperature, now known to be at least 600°C, or the result will not be permanent.

With the possible exception of the **Natufian**

culture in Palestine, all these discoveries were almost universally made in Neolithic times, and pots, or potsherds, have been found in large numbers on the sites of Neolithic cultures.

Each **culture** developed its own form of pottery and, such is the conservatism of man (or woman, for the earliest potters seem to have been the women), the shapes develop into a characteristic form which changes little as the years go by. Flinders **Petrie** was the first to realize the importance of this, and to show how valuable it can be for archaeologists. He demonstrated that pottery can be one of the chief essentials in dating a site. Pots are easily broken, but potsherds thrown away by the exasperated owner can be excavated centuries later by the archaeologist and fitted together again; things made of wood, leather, skins, or cloth may rot and perish, but pots remain – hence the archaeologist's reliance on them for dating purposes.

Pottery can also provide a method of showing the contacts between prehistoric cultures or, in later times, the extent of a civilization's trade. For instance, pots exported from **Crete** in the eighteenth century B.C. have been found on the mainland of Greece, on Cyprus and the islands of the Aegean Sea, on sites along the Syrian coast, and in Egypt, thus demonstrating the wide trading contacts of the **Minoan civilization** in that area; and for every example of such pottery which has survived there were probably scores, or even hundreds, which have long since disappeared. Again, discoveries of Greek vases have shown that, round about 400 B.C., they were being exported as far afield as the steppes of south Russia, southern Germany, and northern France; from their distinctive trademarks it has been calculated that there were at least one hundred potters, some employing several workmen, producing these pots.

The earliest pots were made laboriously by hand, either by being moulded or by being built up. Small pots can be made by the first method, but larger ones, especially anything with a neck, have to be built up. This was done by the ring method. The base was moulded, and rings of clay prepared and placed one on top of another, or a spiral of clay coiled upward from the bottom. The process is lengthy, for the lower rings have to be allowed to harden before the upper ones are added.

The invention of the potter's wheel, a wheel spinning horizontally, transformed the manufacture of large vessels, for it meant that these could be made in a few minutes instead of as previously, several days. It also transformed the craft of pot-making. Women had hitherto been the pot-makers; when the making of pottery became mechanized, it passed into the hands of men. Specialization began, and the expert potter became a travelling craftsman, selling his pots wherever the demand was greatest.

The Chinese have claimed that they invented the potter's wheel, but it seems more likely that the invention was first made in the area of the **Fertile Crescent**; wheel-made pottery found at **Ur** may be five thousand years old. The potter's wheel is found in **Assyria** in the **Chalcolithic Age**, in Siyalk III in **Iran**, and appears in the **Indus Valley Civilization** in India by 2500 B.C. Surprisingly, it is not always contemporary with the **wheel** as used for transport, though it might have been expected that the two would develop side by side.

Pots were nearly always decorated on the outside even from the earliest times. Some of the oldest-known pots appear to have been made either in imitation of baskets or by being moulded inside a basket. Finger-nails, a pointed stick, the bone of a bird are all things which seem to have been used in the making of patterns.

Prambanan. The temple groups in the Prambanan area of central Java include both Hindu and Buddhist remains, as well as one complex, Ratu Baka, which, although probably belonging nominally to these systems, clearly owes much to an older, native, **megalithic** tradition. The earliest dated building is Candi Kalasan, dedicated to the Buddhist Goddess Tara (an inscription is dated A.D 778 but the temple which shows signs of considerable rebuilding may be an earlier foundation), and a very large complex, Candi Sewu, with 250 subsidiary chapels, probably dates from much the same time. Candi Sari is a two-storied building in which apparently the ground floor served for purposes of the cult and the upper story as a lodging for priests and monks. The main Prambanan group of a Hindu foundation was dedicated to the Hindu trinity with Siva as the principal deity. The main enclosure houses three large shrines, the largest central one housing the image of Siva and those on either side Brahma and Vishnu. Opposite these are three smaller shrines for the sacred beasts on which the gods were believed to ride. Various other minor shrines are found in and about the enclosure. Very fine carvings in low relief decorated the outsides of the main temples and related legends connected with Siva and Vishnu. The area has yielded numbers of bronze figures of Hindu and Buddhist deities and is still held in veneration by the local villagers, although they are Muslims, and is generally referred to by the local name of the goddess Durga, Loro Jonggrang, who is thought to grant the boon of children.

Predmostian. An Upper **Palaeolithic** culture of east and central Europe, roughly contemporaneous with the **Aurignacian** and **Magdalenian** cultures of France. The name-site is Predmost in Moravia, where an enormous **midden** containing the bones of more than a thousand mammoths has been uncovered, for the men of this time were very expert hunters. Excavations at similar sites in Russia have revealed the half-buried houses in which the people lived – half-buried because the climate was very cold at this time, the end of the last **glaciation.**

Prehistoric Art. No one knows when **Stone Age** Man first began to express himself by means of art, for it is certain that the earliest preserved examples of Stone Age art do not represent the beginnings of such art.

Long before man had reached the stage of painting recognizable animals on the walls of his caves and rock shelters, or of engraving pictures by means of stone **burins** upon rock faces and upon bones and pebbles, he must have made many cruder and less durable attempts at artistic expression. In all probability the earliest forms of art were drawings which, under normal circumstances, would not survive more than a few hours. Fortunately a few rare examples have, in fact, survived to prove that this form of art did exist in prehistoric times. On the ceiling of one of the chambers of the Pech Merle cavern in France is a patch of natural clay upon which can still be seen drawings, made with the finger tips, by Stone Age Man some 20,000 to 30,000 years ago. The entrance to this cave was blocked up by a fall of rock soon after prehistoric man had used it for painting and engraving (in addition to the mud drawings on the ceiling there are beautiful paintings and engravings on the walls) and it was only in recent times that a new entrance was accidentally cut into the cavern and these examples of early art discovered, together with a few footprints of the former Stone Age occupants.

There is another line of evidence that makes us sure that Stone Age Man indulged in art long before the date of the earliest known paintings and engravings. This is the recent discovery, at **Olduvai Gorge** in east Africa, of lumps of red ochre on a living floor of **Abbevillian** Man. This living floor dates back to about 400,000 years B.C. and yet, at this very remote time, man sufficiently appreciated colour to carry lumps of red ochre to his living sites from a distance of more than fifty miles. Since there was no rock surface upon which he could paint at this site, we may suppose that he used his colour to daub his body as the ancient Britains used woad.

The earliest known example of Stone Age art belongs to the Upper **Palaeolithic** period, and dates to some 30,000 years ago. This prehistoric art reached its zenith with the **Magdalenian** culture about 15,000 years ago, and then gradually became degenerate and formalized.

Most of the preserved prehistoric art consists of paintings or engravings upon the walls of caves and rock shelters. In addition there are rare examples of modelling in clay (*see* plates 18, 20, pages 88, 90) – such as the wonderful clay bisons at the Tuc d'Andubert in France, and of bas-relief sculpturing such as the friezes at Anges sur Angelin and Cap Blanc, also in France.

Yet another form of prehistoric art was painting or engraving upon small objects, such as slabs of stone, pebbles, and fragments of bone, or else upon bone, antler and ivory tools (*see* plates 52, 77, pages 192, 251).

There has always been a great deal of controversy as to the reasons which prompted Stone Age Man to paint animals upon the walls of his caves and shelters, or to engrave rock slabs and movable objects, or make carvings out of antler. Some believe that almost all Stone Age art was of magical or religious significance. They point to the fact that a very large part of it was executed in deep, dark, damp caverns, where the artist must have had to work by the feeble light of simple Stone Age lamps and where the results of his labours could not be seen, or appreciated, except by the very few who penetrated to the spot with similar lamps. They also point out that most of the paintings represent the same types of animals that occur as bones and teeth in the rubbish dumps of Stone Age Man of the same period. It is therefore suggested that most prehistoric art was performed in secret for magical purposes linked with some sort of fertility cult designed to increase the number of animals available for hunting.

There may well be some truth in this interpretation, at least for a part of prehistoric art, but it does not seem to cover all the known expressions of such art. Some of it, indeed, must be regarded as representational, for example, the paintings of hunting scenes or of dances, while the writer believes that much of it must have been art for art's sake, as in the case of some of the paintings on the walls of rock shelters which were used as living sites.

In Europe the majority of prehistoric art is to be found in France and Spain. In Africa it is very widespread indeed, except in the great forest zones. Outside these two areas, prehistoric art is rare.

Most of the African art (*see* colour plate I, plate 5, page 55) is to be found on the walls of rock shelters and not in deep caves, and would seem to be far more representational and less magical than its European counterparts. In Europe, moreover, except in the eastern Spanish zone which has many close affinities with Africa, it is very unusual to find a painting which shows the human face. We may even note that it is normal to find animals drawn with naturalistic faithfulness, accompanied in the same scene by human figures which are little more than caricatures. This fact suggests some very strong taboo against depicting fellow man in a recognizable form.

Turning from the art itself to the techniques by which it was produced, the painting was executed by different methods. Close examination with high-powered lenses reveals evidence of brush work, of application of paint with a palette knife, of daubing with lumps of moss or animal fur, and also of spray painting, presumably with the lips. We know, from analysis of scraps of the actual paints used, and from lumps of colouring matter found during excavations at prehistoric painted sites, that Stone Age Man's chief sources of colour were such minerals as **haematite** and red ochre, and that he also used substances of vegetable origin such as charcoal for black and wood ash for white. We do not know much about the medium with which he mixed his paint. Presumably it was of organic origin, and such substances as animal fat, vegetable juices and urine have all been suggested as possibilities, but owing to their organic origin time has removed all evidence.

For engraving, prehistoric man made a wide variety of special burins or engraving tools, and these are found in quantities at sites where prehistoric art of this form is seen.

It must not be assumed that the prehistoric paintings which we know of represent all the art of the period; far from it. It was only under very exceptional circumstances that early prehistoric art was preserved at all, and for every painting or engraving known to us we may postulate thousands of other examples that have perished. Most of the paintings and engravings were on rock faces, and rock disintegrates and crumbles easily, and as it does so destroys the works of art. Fortunately, under certain conditions, the action of silicates forms a film over ancient paintings and preserves them, as well as hardening the surface of the rock itself. Similarly, falls of rock that have blocked the entrances to caves where art was once practised have, from time to time, excluded air currents – which are very destructive agents – and also temperature changes which often cause disintegration, and have so contributed to the preservation of a number of magnificent prehistoric art sites.

The fact that sites such as **Lascaux** (*see* colour plate VIII) in France, **Altamira** (*see* plate 8, page 58) in Spain, Cheke in Tanganyika and Nswatugi in Rhodesia, are visited and studied by such a constant stream of visitors, bears witness to the great interest which modern man takes in the art of his forefathers. *(See also* **Africa, Prehistoric Art in.**) *See* plates 116–117, pages 382–383.

Prehistory. The name given to the period of man's evolution and development before the invention of writing and an accurate calendar enabled written records to be kept and a sequence of dating established.

Primates, Prehuman Evolution of. It is not so very many years ago that scientists believed that the prehuman ancestors of man were creatures having many outward features in common with one or other of the living great apes of today – the gorilla, the chimpanzee, the orang-outang and the gibbon. In particular, scientists expected that prehuman ancestral stock would exhibit massive overhanging brow ridges, long arms, and that the jaws would have simian shelves (a curious ledge of bone linking the two halves of the lower jaw in apes and monkeys).

Such a view was, perhaps not very surprising since the great apes do have so much in common with man structurally, and are clearly not very distant cousins.

There were always a few scientists who were a little worried by this view because, if it were true, it would mean that there had been major reversals of evolution. Everyone has long been agreed that if we go back in time beyond the stage where the great apes themselves made their appearance, we should find that the common stock of the higher primates was a monkey-like creature which had not yet developed the enormously long arms, combined with short legs, which are so marked a feature of the living great apes. This character is linked with the peculiar manner by which apes move about and which is called **"brachiating"** because the long arms play such a large part in it. Those who support ed the old theory felt that man, in his prehuman stage, had passed through a "brachiating" phase, and that subsequently, as he learnt to stand and walk upright without the help of his arms, these fore-limbs had gradually grown shorter again. Similarly they believed that the simian shelf had gradually been lost and replaced by a chin.

This belief, that man, as we know him today, had been derived from a prehuman ancestral stock with many ape-like features, led scientists to put forward a theory known as "paedomorphism" which can be interpreted as meaning "the retention of the juvenile characters of ancestral forms into adult life."

Underlying this theory is the fact that in the young of apes, monkeys, and also certain extinct types of "near-men" and men (such as **Australopithecus, Pithecanthropus** and **Neanderthal Man**), the brain case is fairly rounded and without massive brow ridges, while the face is relatively short and not snout-like. This is regarded as evidence that the ancestral stock from which present-day man came was of the ape and/or Pithecanthropus type, and that gradually present-day man retained the characteristic child-stage characters longer and longer until they were still present in adult life.

During the past fifteen years, however, new discoveries have come to light which make an alternative explanation seem more probable, and suggest that man's prehuman ancestors may have evolved from a four-footed monkey-like stage direct to an upright stage, in which the arms are not unduly lengthened, but even shortened, without ever having passed through a brachiating stage, such as is seen in the great apes.

Moreover, the new evidence also suggests that present-day man's relatively smooth forehead and absence of beetling brow ridges represents a retention of early and truly ancestral adult characters, rather than the paedomorphic theory which considers that it represents the retention of the juvenile characters of ancestors.

Among the discoveries which have had a major bearing upon this re-orientation of the views of scientists about the evolution of man is the finding of quantities of fossil remains of very ape-like creatures in Lower **Miocene** deposits in Kenya Colony and also the finding of parts of the limb bones and skeleton of the south African "near-men" or Australopithecines. The Kenya discoveries are those of a creature known as Proconsul which is represented by three distinct species. Proconsul was an ape, in the widest sense of that word, in that it had already evolved the type of dentition which we associate with apes and men, rather than with monkeys. In a very great many other ways Proconsul retained resemblances to his still earlier ancestors, which must have broken away from the monkey stock.

Proconsul lived about 30,000,000 years ago. His teeth proclaim him a hominid, or member of the ape and human branch of the Primates, rather than a Cercopithecoid, or member of the monkey-baboon stock. But Proconsul has not got the long brachiating arms of the later great apes. He was still quadrupedal in his gait, with more or less equal length of arm and leg. He was a climbing quadruped, however, with some obvious monkey characters in his limbs, and others which foreshadow the form seen in the apes. His forehead, when adult, did not have huge massive beetling brows, but was smooth and rounded, and of the form which we see in man. Moreover, in Proconsul the lower jaw has no trace of a simian shelf, which is the hallmark of the modern great apes and of monkeys, as well as of many fossil members of these families. Instead, the form of the lower jaw is intermediate and capable of evolving either towards the chin structure of man or to the simian shelf structure of the apes.

Proconsul was, in fact, in adult life, a creature

not unlike the juveniles of more recent forms. Instead, therefore, of postulating paedomorphism we may, with equal probability, regard present-day man as retaining many of the early adult characters of the ancestral stock, while creatures such as gorillas, the Australopithecine near-men, and the Pithecanthropus stock of man represent very over-specialized side branches which, in their adult form, disguise the ancestral characters by the growth of such specializations as simian shelves (in the apes), beetling brow ridges, and long arms.

The discovery of parts of the limb bones and skeletons of the Australopithecines, or near-men, of South Africa, has shown that these little creatures were already capable of standing, walking and running fully erect like man, and not with the help of their arms as in the apes. To this extent they certainly must be regarded as standing much closer to the common stock from which man was evolved than does any ape, and, indeed, most scientists today class them as hominids, or men, rather than as pongids, or apes, while not yet accepting that they had full "human" status. That is why they are often referred to as "near-men".

The Australopithecines had also reached a stage of evolution in which their teeth were very much more like those of man than those of any ape. The canine or eye-tooth is small, and the first lower milk molars have truly human characteristics.

The jaws, however, as well as the faces and the brow ridges of the adults of the Australopithecines all point to the fact that the group (as we at present know it from fossils of **Pleistocene** age) represents a specialized side branch, which left the main stock leading to man and became over-specialized and thereafter extinct.

On the other hand there seems little doubt that only a little further back in time there must have existed a somewhat similar group, having close resemblances to the Australopithecines in respect of teeth and body structure, but with less specialized brow ridges, facial structure and jaws. Such a stock could, very reasonably, be regarded as the potential ancestor of mankind.

Since it is in Africa that we have the great wealth of Miocene fossil hominids – as well as still earlier members of the family in Egypt during the **Oligocene** epoch – and since it is also in Africa that we see the development of the near-men or Australopithecines, we may, with some confidence, predict that it will also be in Africa – probably in **Pliocene** deposits when such come to light – that we shall find the stock which was the common ancestor of the Australopithecines and of modern man, and descended from the Proconsul group of Miocene primates.

Proconsul, *see* Primates, Prehuman Evolution of.

Pueblo Culture, *see* Amer-Indians.

Punt is a land that lay south of Egypt and was reached by way of the Red Sea. Voyages to it are first mentioned on the **Palermo Stone** for the reign of Sahure (fifth dynasty). The most notable account of travel there are the temple reliefs of Hatshepsut at Deir el Bahri. The people are depicted living in beehive-shaped houses, ruled over by an amazingly fat queen. From Punt came gold, and incense and other goods for religious practices. The exact location is uncertain but to judge from the products it must have been somewhere in the neighbourhood of Somaliland.

Pylos. Nestor, a legendary hero of *The Iliad*, was king of Pylos in ancient Greece, but the site of his palace was disputed in classical times. It was, however, identified with a fair degree of certainty in 1939 by a joint Greek-American expedition (Blegen and Kourouniotes). The site, today known as Epano Englianos, commands a superb view of the surrounding country and overlooks the Bay of Navarino (Messenia) to the south and is about five miles from the sea to the west.

The foundations that are in the course of being uncovered have presented the most complete plan of a Mycenaean palace known so far, not excluding **Mycenae** and **Tiryns**. The buildings are ranged round a central court which is dominated by the royal residence on the north-west side. This is of the **megaron** type, a great pillared hall, forty-three feet by thirty-seven, approached by a shallow vestibule of the same width as the hall, and this in turn is preceded by a two-columned porch of the same dimensions as the vestibule. The roof of the great hall, the throne room (for there was a shallow dais for the throne of the king on the right of the entrance to the august chamber), was supported by four fluted columns of wood on round plinths of stone. These were arranged symmetrically round a great central hearth measuring no less than thirteen and a half feet in diameter. Fragments of a massive terracotta chimney were found on the hearth. As at Mycenae the surround of the hearth was in stucco and was painted with running spirals on its upper surface and with a flame pattern on its vertical sides. The room in all its glory must have presented a fabulous picture with its frescoed walls painted with griffins, lions, and warlike scenes, but unfortunately only fragments survive, and these mostly in an unrecognizable state, such were the effects of the ferocious fire that consumed the palace in the twelfth century B.C., a destruction which is associated with the Dorian invasion.

The approach to the palace was by a massive gate-house (propylaeum) to the south-east of the central court. In this building there was an archives room. Here were found the greater number of the famous Pylos tablets that have contributed so largely to the decipherment of the script known as Linear B (*see* **Minoan Scripts**).

To the south-west of the central court were reception rooms. To the north-east of it a porch with two fluted wooden columns led to the residential quarters of the royal family, which included a replica of the throne room on a smaller scale with hearth, columns, and chimney. Nearby was a bathroom with a well-preserved, painted terracotta bath. A special feature of the palace was the pantries adjoining the megaron. In one of these 2,147 drinking cups were found, which had originally been stacked on shelves.

The palace was built in the thirteenth century B.C., but what was undoubtedly an earlier palace, perhaps of the fourteenth century, was situated to the south-west of it. Its plan is poorly preserved, but it also seems to have had a throne room, which was approached through a great hall with three columns asymmetrically placed.

Within a radius of about ten miles of the palace there are numerous **tholos tombs** which confirm the importance of this site. Two found close to the palace date from the sixteenth to fifteenth centuries B.C. **Chamber tombs** in the immediate neighbourhood are of the palace period.

Pyramids. Though buildings of pyramidal shape exist in several parts of the world, the oldest and most magnificent are those of Ancient Egypt. The earliest known pyramid was built by Zoser, the first king of the third dynasty (about 2800 B.C.), at **Saqqara**, in Lower Egypt, near modern Cairo. The last to be built in Africa were at **Meroe**, in the Sudan. They were built about A.D. 300 by Ethiopian kings who had inherited some of the funerary customs of the ancient Egyptians.

Since the fifth century B.C., when **Herodotus** and other Greek visitors made them fashionable, the famous "Giza group" of pyramids has attracted most attention, especially the so-called "Great Pyramid" erected by Cheops (Khufu) at the beginning of the fourth dynasty (2720–2560 B.C.). This concentration on three admittedly splendid examples of pyramid-building tended to obscure the fact that the Great Pyramid is only one of scores of such monuments, some of which almost equal it in size, and all of which served a funerary purpose.

The outstanding figure of modern pyramid-study was Sir Flinders **Petrie** who, between 1880 and 1882, made the first accurate mathematical survey of the Great Pyramid.

His original purpose was to test the truth of Piazzi Smyth's theories, which he soon found to be false. He went on to examine, survey and excavate many other pyramids. From his researches, and those of his successors, a vast corpus of knowledge has been accumulated; not only of the methods by which the pyramids were built, but of how and why they were built.

Since some pyramids have been completely destroyed it is not possible to estimate how many once existed, but there were certainly more than eighty, stretching in a discontinuous line from Abu Roash in the north to Hawara at the mouth of the **Faiyum**. There were also pyramids at **Thebes,** nearly five hundred miles south of Abu Roash. All were royal tombs, designed to protect the bodies of the pharaohs in accordance with the Egyptian belief that, unless the body was preserved from decay and violation, the spirit could not survive. The bodies were buried either within the main structure or in rock-cut chambers beneath it.

We do not know why the pyramidal shape was chosen. Some authorities believe that the straight-sided pyramid evolved from the simple **mastaba** but it seems more likely that the stepped form had some significance of its own, probably religious.

During the fourth dynasty (2720–2560 B.C.) pyramid-building reached its zenith. Cheops' pyramid took twenty years to build, and, as completed, rose to a height of 481 feet. It contained nearly two and a half million blocks of stone, each averaging two and a half tons in weight. Almost completely solid, save for two granite-lined chambers within the masonry, it is built with incredible precision. The orientation of the building is so accurate (the maximum error is one-twelfth of a degree) that compass errors can be checked against it. The four corners are almost perfect right-angles, the maximum deviation from ninety degrees being one-twentieth of a degree, and this in a building measuring 755 feet along each side at the base.

Galleries connect the inner chambers with the narrow entrance, which is on the north side. There is also a subterranean chamber beneath the pyramid which may have been intended originally as the sepulchre of the king, but evidently there was a change of plan during the construction. The sarcophagus rests in the upper chamber, within the pyramid, but it is not known if it ever contained a body. Like all the other Egyptian pyramids, Cheops' tomb was plundered in remote antiquity.

The mouth of the gallery was sealed by massive but accurately-fitting "plug-blocks", each weighing several tons, and the entrance concealed behind the smooth outer limestone casing. All Egyptian pyramids were originally so covered, but in most instances the casing has been removed by the Arab invaders in the sixteenth and seventeenth centuries and used in the building of Cairo.

The fifth dynasty kings built their pyramids at Abusir, between **Giza** and **Saqqara**; those of the sixth dynasty (2420–2294 B.C.) at Saqqara, near the monuments of their dynasty predecessors. Though small and ill-built compared with the pyramids of the fourth dynasty these sixth-dynasty tombs are of great archaeological importance, as their inner chambers are inscribed with texts which give us a valuable insight into the religious beliefs of this remote age.

Between 2294 and 2132 B.C. there came a Dark Age in Egypt's history. No great monuments were built, and it was not until the eleventh dynasty (2132–2000 B.C.) that royal power revived again under a line of kings ruling from Thebes, in Upper Egypt. Three of these were named Menthuhotep, and one, Neb-hepet-Ra Menthuhotep, built a great funerary temple at Deir el Bahri, on the west bank of the Nile opposite modern **Luxor**. This columned temple was built in tiers and was crowned by a pyramid.

Pyramid-building began again in earnest during the reigns of successive kings of the twelfth dynasty (2000–1777 B.C.) who seem to have regained at least nominal control of the whole country, and thus could deploy a greater labour force. Two of them, Amenemhat I and his successor, Senusret I, built pyramids at Lisht, a little to the south of Dashur, in Lower Egypt. These, though not as large or as well-built as those of the fourth dynasty, are still impressive, with their granite-lined burial chambers approached by elaborate "puzzle-passages" designed to foil the tomb-robbers. Senusret II, another twelfth-dynasty king, built his pyramid at Illahun, still further south.

With the end of the Middle Kingdom (about 1700 B.C.) the age of pyramid-building was virtually at an end. With the rise of the eighteenth dynasty (1573–1350 B.C.) the pharaohs gave up building pyramids, and sought another method of preserving their bodies; instead of a huge, conspicuous monument, visible for miles around, they chose secret, rock-cut tombs hollowed out of the Theban hills in a remote valley, the **Valley of the Kings,** which could be easily guarded.

Pyramid texts, *see* Book of the Dead.

Q

Quartz. A mineral sometimes used by **Palaeolithic** Man, when **flint** was not easily available, for the making of **stone tools** and weapons. It was the finding of quartz in the deposits of **Chou-kou-tien** which led to the discovery of **Pekin Man.**

Quaternary Period. Quaternary time, the beginnings of which date back little more than a million years, is very short when compared with preceding periods of geological history. Though hardly ranking as a distinct period, Quaternary time has nevertheless been divided into the Pleistocene epoch, and an incomplete recent or Holocene epoch, which spans the last 10,000 years and merges with the history of archaeologist and chronicler.

Pleistocene history has been called the "Great Ice Age", as large continental areas of the northern hemisphere were mantled by ice-sheets which formed during long intervals of climatic cooling. In the so-called "interglacial intervals", however, warmer conditions prevailed, and the ice was reduced in extent; four "**glacial**" and three "interglacial" episodes have been widely recognized in the Pleistocene of northern parts of Europe, Asia and North America. Changes in sea-level were caused by the removal of water to form the ice-caps and glaciers, by the return of water when they melted, and also by crustal movements in areas affected by varying weight of overlying ice. Such changes in sea-level are indicated by raised beaches, drowned valleys, and the submerged forests of many coastal regions at the present day, whilst stages in the advance and retreat of the ice are written in glacial deposits ("drift"), and in ice-moulded landscape features, only little modified by Holocene erosion since the last glacial retreat 10,000 years ago.

Most of the present-day mammal species came into existence during Pleistocene times, although their distribution was greatly affected by fluctuation of climate. Some extinct forms, such as the great cave-bear, the **mammoth** and the woolly rhinoceros, were specially adapted to the harsh climate of the Ice Age. By the beginning of Holocene times, true man, or Homo sapiens, had appeared. He may have evolved from earlier ape-like stocks, including **Sinanthropus,** Pithecanthropus, and the even more primitive and ape-like **Australopithecus,** remains of which have been found in early pleistocene deposits of Africa. Other authorities, however, suggest that these species are "side tracks" and that Homo sapiens evolved from a move direct line linking him with **Proconsul.** *See* plate 113, page 379.

Quern. A hand-mill for grinding corn into flour. The simplest form was a small stone rubbed round and round on a larger one. The harder the stone, the better the quern, because the less grit there would be in the flour. The saddle quern is shaped, as its name indicates, like a saddle. The **Iron Age** saw the introduction of the rotary quern – two stones fixed one above the other, with the upper one revolving when a handle was turned.

Qumran, *see* Dead Sea Scrolls.

R

Radio Carbon, *see* Carbon Fourteen Dating.

Ras Shamra (ancient Ugarit). The mound of Ras Shamra is situated on the Syrian coast only a short distance inland from the natural harbour of Minet el-Beida and about ten miles north of Latakia. Interest was first attracted to the area in 1928 when an Arab ploughman at his work struck the remains of a tomb near Minet el-Beida. In the following year a French archaeological mission directed by Dr C.F.A. Schaeffer began excavation and soon discovered that Ras Shamra marked the site of the ancient town of Ugarit. Work continued annually until 1939 and was subsequently resumed in 1948. Schaeffer has distinguished five main phases extending from the **Neolithic** to the Late **Bronze Age,** which he has designated I–V from the top downwards.

Deep soundings which provided the evidence for Levels V (Neolithic) and IV (**Chalcolithic**) revealed at bed-rock the hearths and flint and bone implements of the first occupants of the site. Schaeffer prefers to ascribe these people to a "pre-pottery" Neolithic stage of development since they were apparently ignorant of pot-making. Sometime later another group of early farmers arrived who used both stone and pottery vessels, some fragments of which are comparable to the earliest wares at Chagar Bazar and Sakçe Gözü. In Level IV the finely made and attractively painted **Halafian** ware was found.

The early history of Ugarit was not without its episodes of violence. During the course of Level III in the latter half of the third millennium B.C. the settlement was destroyed by fire and occupied by people using the so-called Khirbet Kerak ware. In Level II we find Ugarit expanding rapidly into a rich commercial centre. Her princes were engaged in close diplomatic and economic relations with twelfth-dynasty **Egypt** perhaps from the reign of Sesostris I down to Amenemhet III or later. Although it is uncertain whether Egypt exercised any direct control over Ugarit at this period, Schaeffer has discovered Egyptian statues bearing the inscriptions of kings, royal persons and officials. These statues had been smashed and mutilated by enemies of Egypt when Ugarit was ransacked sometime after the end of the twelfth dynasty. A period of decline followed this upheaval.

However, by about 1450 B.C. Ugarit had fully recovered. Schaeffer's excavations have brought to light the remains of the town's fortifications, temples and in particular the palace, which has as yet been only partially cleared. In this palace archives were discovered containing **cuneiform** documents not only in Accadian, Hittite and Hurrian, but also in a hitherto unknown language allied to

Hebrew and **Phoenician** and written in an alphabetic cuneiform script of twenty-nine characters. When deciphered a number of these new documents proved to be fragments of epic and mythological poems recounting stories of the god Baal and the goddess Anat, of a King Keret and of Aqhat, son of King Daniel.

This brilliant phase was of but short duration and ended in catastrophe when the town was brought down in ruins by an earthquake and fire broke out. Nevertheless a new town was built, which survived until Ugarit was finally overwhelmed and destroyed by the **Sea Peoples** at the beginning of the twelfth century B.C.

Rawlinson, Henry Creswicke (1810–95). The nineteenth century produced a great number of regular army officers who became famous as scholars and orientalists; among these was Sir Henry Rawlinson. He first went to India in 1827 as a cadet under the East India Company, and after six years as a subaltern was sent to Persia with some other English officers to reorganize the Shah's troops. Here he became interested in antiquities and particularly in **cuneiform** inscriptions, then unreadable, and applied himself to their decipherment. He was also a keen student of ancient oriental languages. The great cuneiform inscriptions on the **Behistun Rock** (*see* plate 25, page 95) engaged his attention, and it was not long before he overcame the immense difficulty of reaching the inscribed surface and making a copy and squeeze of it. Dr **Grotefend** had already been working on the decipherent of cuneiform and had succeeded in finding the key to a number of signs, but Rawlinson, unaware of this work, set himself independently to the task of finding the key to cuneiform. As, unlike Grotefend, he possessed a good knowledge of Zend, which is cognate with the Old Persian language of the cuneiform texts, he was able to carry the solution of the problem to its end, and in two years succeeded in transcribing the greater part of the text. But at this point friction between the Persian court and the British government caused the departure of the English officers, and in 1840 Rawlinson became political agent in Kandahar. At his own request he was subsequently transferred to Turkish Arabia and settled in Baghdad, where he devoted all his spare time to cuneiform studies.

His actual discovery of the key to cuneiform rests largely on a happy guess. He had found near Hamadan in Persia two short texts each in the trilingual form already observed at Persepolis, the three scripts being Old Persian, Babylonian and Susian cuneiform. The Persian is a simplified alphabetic form of the Babylonian, which is itself extremely complex and non-alphabetic, while Susian lies between the two. When the two texts of the simplified Persian version were set side by side, it was found that they were identical except in two places. In line twelve of text A was a word, which we will call x for convenience, whereas in text B at the same place was a different word, y. In line nineteen of text A was yet a third word z, whereas in text B the word x reappeared. Rawlinson worked on the assumption that these three words were the names of kings, and that the texts themselves were proclamations of successive kings who in the course of their inscriptions referred both to themselves and to their fathers; and that therefore the name of the king in the earlier text would appear in the place assigned to the king's father in the later one. Such a theory could be tested by trial, for all that was necessary was to find three successive kings whose names fitted the alphabetic characters. The requirements were fulfilled in the case of Hystaspes (y), Darius (x) and Xerxes (z) in their Old Persian form, and this identification gave Rawlinson fourteen characters of the alphabet of forty-three signs. With his knowledge of Zend, extension of the decipherment to cover the whole ground of the simplified form of cuneiform, now found to be Old Persian, was only a matter of time.

There remained the two more complex forms still to be deciphered. The Behistun trilingual inscription was a long one, and so offered valuable material for comparisons; owing to the nature of its contents it contains many proper names, which are the first things looked for by anyone attempting to elucidate an unknown script. Having succeeded in obtaining a copy of the great text, Rawlinson began work on it in 1835–7, and continued intermittently until in 1847 he was able to publish a complete translation, with full grammatical notes and analyses, of the Old Persian text. He then proceeded on to the Babylonian text with immediate success, and was soon followed by other scholars. The discovery that Babylonian was a Semitic language akin to Hebrew greatly facilitated matters.

In order to check that the various scholars were in fact correctly translating the texts, a final test was announced in 1857, when the Royal Asiatic

Society issued a challenge to scholars to produce for official comparison and without collaboration, a translation of the long inscription on the recently found cylinder of Tiglath-Pileser I. Rawlinson, Hincks, Talbot and Oppert each submitted translations which, when they were unsealed and compared, were so close in substance to each other that the President of the Society could state that no doubt whatever could exist that the true key to cuneiform had been found. *See* plate 118, page 384.

Red Lady of Paviland, *see* Paviland Cave.

Reisner, George Andrew (1867–1942), was born in 1867 at Indianapolis. His parents were not wealthy but they sent him to Harvard University. At first he studied law but soon turned to Semitic languages. His success in the examinations for a doctorate won him a travelling scholarship and he went to Berlin. There his teacher was the great German Egyptologist, Kurt Sethe. Four years later he returned to Harvard where he was given a lectureship in the School of Semitic Languages.

Until that time Reisner had never been to Egypt but in 1897 he was invited to join the team of scholars compiling the catalogue of objects in the Cairo Museum. He edited the catalogues of amulets (1900), and of models of ships and boats. Once in Egypt he lived there for the greater part of the rest of his life. He began in 1905 the series of excavations for which he is famous. Financial backing came from Mrs Phoebe Hearst, until the University of Harvard and the Boston Museum of Fine Arts agreed in 1905 to sponsor his work. Five years later he became Curator of the Department of Egyptian Art at the Boston Museum.

Reisner was a very methodical excavator who prided himself on the detailed record which he kept of the work. His first excavations were at Qift, Deir el-Ballas and Naga ed Deir where he explored the predynastic and early dynastic cemeteries. When he obtained the support of Harvard and Boston he transferred his activities to **Giza** where he explored the enclosure of the Third Pyramid (describing his discoveries in his book entitled *Mycerinus*, 1921), and also some of the **mastaba tombs** near the Great Pyramid many of which were published in his last work *A History of the Giza Necropolis* (1942). During these excavations he discovered statues of King Mycerinus, the builder of the Third Pyramid, which show him with various **nome**-gods and with his wife. As an outcome of his excavations he wrote the *Development of the Egyptian Tomb to the Accession of Cheops* (1936).

His expedition's most sensational discovery was the burial place of Queen Hetepheres, the mother of Cheops, which contained a quantity of decorated furniture, the wood of which had decayed, but he and his assistants were able to reconstruct much of it by noting how the gold foil and faience inlay had fallen.

He explored the pyramids of **Meroe** (third century B.C. to third century A.D.) in the Sudan from 1916 to 1923, and also excavated the tombs of the twenty-fifth dynasty kings and the temple at Napata. The Archaeological Survey of **Nubia**, undertaken in 1907 when the Aswan Dam was raised, was placed under his direction but only volume one of the report was published under his authorship. He excavated Middle Kingdom sites at Kerma (Dongola), publishing a report in *Harvard African Studies* (1923), and the fort of Semneh on the second cataract.

In 1909 he conducted an excavation at Samaria in Palestine but otherwise his whole life was devoted to work in Egypt.

Apart from the publication of his excavations he wrote many articles for scientific journals and edited in 1905 the *Hearst Medical Papyrus*.

Reisner died in Cairo in 1942 after suffering from increasing blindness for many years.

Repoussé. Designs on metal made by hammering the metal from the reverse side, so that the design stands out in relief.

Rhodesia Man. All that is known of Rhodesia Man is a skull which was found in the lead mines of Broken Hill, Rhodesia, and marks its owner as being a near-contemporary of **Neanderthal Man.**

Rigveda is the name of the oldest work of the Indo-**Aryans**. Along with three other texts it makes up the most sacred literature of the Hindus, called the *Veda* (knowledge) or *Sruti* (revealed), and consists of 1,017 hymns (*Rik* or *Rig*, hence *Rigveda*) of unequal length, divided into ten *mandalas* (sections), all in praise of various deities dear to the Hindus. The hymns are truly lyrical poems adapted to the purpose of ritual.

The *Rigveda* is a collection of family traditions

concerning different rituals which played an important part in the life of the Aryans. In their references to daily life these ritual hymns go beyond their religious significance and produce before us a picture of the Aryans as they lived in the country of the *Sapta Sindhu*, the seven rivers – the Indus and its eastern and western tributaries. The Rigvedic culture stands in great contrast to the city life of the **Indus Valley civilization**. The fair-skinned Aryans, who were themselves divided into numerous tribes often at war with one another, are depicted as constantly fighting with the darker non-Aryans, the Dasas, the Dasyus and several others who were rich in material wealth and had a culture of their own. The Aryans appear as new settlers, the pastoral economy still dominating their mind, though agricultural settlements had far advanced, with villages founded on a family basis as the nucleus of society. The tribal chief was a hereditary war leader. The strength of the Aryans lay in their swift-running horses, which they harnessed to war chariots with spoked wheels, as well as in their offensive weapons made of metal (*ayas*), probably bronze. Their victory was also due to their hereditary soldiers. Indeed, specialization had already gone far in Indo-Aryan society. We not only hear of the priestly class (the Brahmins) and the nobility (the Rajanya), but also of metal workers and carpenters, who, along with the farmers, merchants and others, formed the general mass (*Vis*) of the Aryan society. In the course of succeeding centuries this simple class division hardened into caste groups based on the principles of heredity and superiority. The very name, *Arya*, meaning a nobleman, suggests the sense of superiority with which they viewed the non-Aryans. In due course it affected also their own caste groups. But whatever distinctions might have existed in society, the culture of the Rigvedic Aryans was a mixed product. Its main difference from the local non-Aryan cultures was not so much material as in their concept of nature gods and their peculiar sacrificial (*yajna*) rites to appease those gods. We read of Indra, the mighty god of rain, destroying the non-Aryan enemies, the sky-god Varuna, infusing the spirit of orderliness, and the all-consuming Agni (fire) receiving the oblations. All these gods were conceptual but related to the practical life of the Aryans.

Rosetta Stone. This was found by French troops in August 1799 in the neighbourhood of Rashid, or Rosetta, in the western delta of the Nile in Egypt. It came into British possession in 1801 when the French army in Egypt surrendered and many important antiquities, including the stone, were ceded by treaty. In February of the next year it was sent to England and placed in the headquarters of the Society of Antiquaries for a time, before being transferred to the British Museum, where it has been ever since.

The Rosetta Stone is a slab of black basalt three feet nine inches long, two feet four and a half inches wide, and eleven inches deep. It is inscribed in Egyptian and Greek in the following order: (1) **hieroglyphic**, or picture writing; (2) **demotic**, a **cursive** Egyptian script; (3) Greek, cut in ordinary **uncials**. The stone is much damaged, particularly in the case of the hieroglyphic text.

The importance of the Rosetta Stone was recognized from the start; it lay in the fact that one of its inscriptions is in a known language, that is to say, in Greek. With the exception of **Coptic** (a late phase of the Egyptian language which used an alphabet of Greek letters supplemented by native symbols), all knowledge of ancient Egyptian was lost soon after the end of the fourth century A.D. It was therefore assumed that when the Greek was translated it would provide the key to the decipherment of the Egyptian scripts – if the subject-matter of all three texts was the same, which seemed likely. Egypt's monumental writing in particular had teased the minds of men since the Renaissance, and the discovery of the stone offered a unique opportunity for the recovery of her ancient language and literature.

The Greek was soon translated and its subject-matter proved to be a decree passed by an assembly of priests held at **Memphis** on the occasion of an anniversary of the coronation of Ptolemy Epiphanes. The benefits the king had conferred upon Egypt were recorded and the honours due to him in return enumerated. The decree could be dated to 27 March, 196 B.C., by modern reckoning.

Probably chiefly because of the damaged state of the hieroglyphic text, though doubtless also because of the erroneous belief that hieroglyphic writing was purely symbolic in character, the demotic was the first of the Egyptian scripts to be attempted. Silvestre de Sacy, a French orientalist, and Jan David Åkerblad, a Swedish diplomat and a good Greek and Coptic scholar, were the first in the field. By comparing the Greek and demotic texts, Åkerblad succeeded in elucidating all the proper names in the latter which were mentioned in the former, and in addition he recognized one or two nouns occurring in their Coptic forms. The words he identified had been alphabetically written and, due to a mistaken belief that demotic was exclusively alphabetical, he made no further progress.

Several years later, in 1812, a copy of the Rosetta Stone came into the hands of Dr Thomas Young, the eminent physicist. Dr Young was a man of considerable learning and wide interests, and the stone presented him with the sort of challenge he most enjoyed. It would be fascinating to trace in detail the method he pursued in seeking to decipher the ancient writings, but it is not possible in so short an article. All one can do is to make a short list of the most important of his discoveries. These were: (1) that demotic contained many signs that could not possibly be alphabetical, (2) that at least some of the demotic characters were derived from hieroglyphic writing, and (3) that the **cartouches**, or "royal rings" occurring in the hieroglyphic section contained the name (and titles) of Ptolemy. Although it had long been suspected that the cartouches contained the names of the kings and queens of Egypt, Young was the first to prove it. There is only one cartouche on the Rosetta Stone (five times repeated), and as Ptolemy is the only royal name mentioned in the Greek text, Young assumed that this would contain his name and, furthermore, the Egyptian characters would have the sounds of Greek letters. These he identified, sign by sign.

It was ultimately through the comparison of the cartouches of other kings and queens of Egypt, and in particular of those of the Greco-Roman period (which could be checked), that the greater part of the Egyptian alphabet was recovered. But although the discovery of correct alphabetic values served the purposes of transliteration, translation required a considerable knowledge of Coptic. In this respect no one was better equipped than Jean François **Champollion**, a brilliant young French scholar. Born in December 1790, Champollion's interest in Egypt had been aroused at a very early age, and while still a youth he had applied himself to the study of Coptic and other alphabets and systems of writing which might lead him to the decipherment of Egypt's ancient scripts. Unfortunately he too was hampered by the conviction that hieroglyphic writing was purely symbolic, and for many years he made no real progress. But once he had grasped the fact that hieroglyphs consisted of both sense-signs (**ideograms**) and sound-signs (**phonograms**), he made tremendous strides and soon outstripped his contemporaries in this field. In his *Précis du système hiéroglyphique*, which appeared in 1824, he gave the first continuous translations of Egyptian texts, and in his dictionary and grammar, published posthumously, showed conclusively how the principles of Coptic grammar could be applied to the ancient texts. Subsequently, his work was to some extent neglected, and certain of his interpretations have had to be revised, but he is now generally acknowledged to have been the greatest single figure in the decipherment of hieroglyphs.

Though both Young and Champollion concerned themselves with demotic, no real progress was made with this script till the publication in 1868 by the German Heinrich Brugsch of his great *Hieroglyphisch-demotisches Wörterbuch*, a book which finally demonstrated that demotic words could be successfully transliterated into hieroglyphs. *See* plate 119, page 385.

Royal Road. The Royal Road of the Persian Empire at the height of its power ran from **Susa** in southern **Iran** to **Sardis** in western Asia Minor. At intervals there stood inns where the royal couriers could obtain fresh horses as they carried their mes sages along its course. The journey of 1,677 miles could be covered in about thirteen weeks. **Herodotus** used it to visit **Babylon.**

S

Saddle Quern, *see* Quern.

Sais (Sa el-Hagar) lies on the western or Rosetta branch of the Nile Delta; it was the chief city of the fifth lower Egyptian **nome** and one of the principal shrines of the goddess Neith whose fetish, two crossed arrows over a shield, formed the **hieroglyphic** writing of the name of the nome. Neith, identified by the Greeks with Athene, is usually represented as a female figure wearing the red crown of Lower Egypt.

The city did not become politically important until the Late period. Under the leadership of Tefnakht it formed one of the most vigorous of the opponents to Piankhy's conquest of Egypt (about

730 B.C.) and seems to have retained a measure of independence throughout part of the Ethiopic dynasty. About 663 B.C. its prince, Psammetichus, took a leading part in the expulsion of the **Assyrian** garrisons from the Delta and reunited the whole of Egypt under his rule. The dynasty which he founded, the twenty-sixth, is commonly called "Saite" after the new capital. It is the last of the strong native dynasties and gave to Egypt a period of prosperity before the Persian Conquest, characterized by a high artistic achievement deriving its standards from the study of earlier monuments, particularly those of the Old Kingdom.

The rise of Sais coincides with the decline of **Tanis** and represents a shift in the direction of trade. The contact which developed from the seventh century between Egypt and Greece was by way of the western Delta to the great benefit and prosperity of Sais. Close by lay Naucratis which became a privileged city in which Greek merchants settled under the protection of the Saite kings. Little now survives of the ancient city of Sais; its mounds, much denuded by illegal excavation, are rarely visited. No royal tombs of this dynasty have been identified, though **Herodotus** says that the kings were buried within the temple enclosure.

Sanchi, a small sandstone hill in the Madhya Pradesh (Central Province) of India, contains some of the most remarkable sculptural remains in the whole country. The site lies on the northern edge of the jungles of the Vindhya hills, probably on one of the ancient trade routes to the west coast ports around Bombay and to the Deccan; when it was rediscovered in 1818 it was concealed by undergrowth. Since that time it has been the subject of much research and is now carefully preserved; there is a small museum on the site.

Although Sanchi has no known association with the life of Buddha (died about 486 B.C.) the whole foundation is of the religion which he created. The earliest monuments of which there is evidence belong to the time of **Asoka Maurya** who caused an edict to be inscribed upon a polished sandstone pillar here. Tradition associates the nearby city of Vidisa (modern Bhilsa) with his wife and suggests that his son Mahendra stayed here for a time on his journey to Ceylon as head of a Buddhist mission. The pillar stands beside the Great **Stupa** which was probably founded in Asoka's time, but few other monuments can be assigned to this date. The stupa is in origin a burial mound which came to be associated with relics of the Buddha. The earliest examples, whether of brick or stone, have a low hemispherical or sub-hemispherical dome, but during the early centuries of the Christian era the dome and the plinth upon which it stood became more and more elevated, until the height many times exceeded the base diameter – for example the Dhamekh Stupa at **Sarnath** (*see* plates 122, 124, pages 388, 390). The outer surface of the dome was plastered and even decorated with garlands, etc. At Sanchi the Great Stupa was first made of brick (about third century B.C.) and probably was surrounded by a wooden railing of which no trace remains. On several occasions during the succeeding centuries it was enlarged and modified. First the dome was enlarged and given a stone facing, then a circumambulatory path and stone railing were added, and finally, probably in the first century B.C., four monumental gateways were constructed. Two other stupas, numbers II and III, though a little smaller than the Great Stupa, and of slightly later foundation and less complex design, bear witness to roughly parallel stages of development. The railings and gateways of these three stupas bear the sculptures which are the peculiar glory of Sanchi. They are for the most part reliefs, their motifs deriving largely from the Buddha's life and from the story of his previous births, but their treatment is such that it reveals a wealth of detail of Indian life at the turn of the Christian era. The "cheerful busy realism" and the exuberance of the work convey a vivid impression upon the visitor. They form a link between the Mauryan courtly art style and the art of **Mathura** (*see* plates 78, 80, pages 252, 254) and **Amaravati** (*see* plates 9–10, pages 59–60).

The many other remains at Sanchi may be classed either as smaller stupas, as *chaitya* halls, originally apsidal and evidently connected with communal worship, or as monasteries, quadrangular rows of cells around a central courtyard. Nearly all of the surviving monuments of these classes date from the fourth to tenth centuries A.D. *See* colour plate XIV, plate 121, page 387.

Sandia, New Mexico, *see* America, Early Man in.

Sangoan. This culture, formerly known as the Tumbian, dates from the beginning of the **Mesolithic** period. Distribution covers a wide area of equatorial forest country in central Africa, in the basins of great rivers and round Lake Victoria. Three basic elements in the manufacture of **stone tools** are: firstly, the core biface technique; secondly, the prepared core or faceted platform technique; thirdly, the bifacial retouch of implements made by these two techniques, resulting in characteristic spearheads. **Artifacts** found include picks and adzes made on bifacially flaked cores, tranchet type axes, **hand-axes** of developed **Acheulian** form, massive side-scrapers and many elongated bifacially flaked points, sometimes as much as a foot long, probably serving as lances or spear-heads.

Saqqara, the great necropolis of the ancient capital of **Egypt** at **Memphis** and one of the most important sites, lies some twenty miles south of modern Cairo on the west bank of the river and occupies a vast expanse of the low limestone plateau above the cultivated areas, stretching about four and a half miles. Its name derives probably from Sokar, the titular deity of the necropolis, later assimilated with Ptah. It is dominated by the six stages of the Step Pyramid of Zoser (Neterkhet), founder of the third dynasty (about 2800 B.C.). This **pyramid** is built of the local nummilitic limestone and encased in the fine white limestone of the Tura quarries. It is the oldest stone monument in existence. Tradition ascribes its planning to Imhotep, later deified by the Egyptians and honoured as a wise man and the patron of medicine, identified by the Greeks with Asklepios. In its original form the monument was designed as a **mastaba tomb** but after two successive enlargements, the architectural plan was radically altered to achieve a four-staged stepped pyramid, subsequently enlarged by the addition of two more stages. The pyramid in its final form rose to a height of 204 feet and measured at its base approximately 411 feet from east to west and 358 feet from north to south. Beneath this massive structure lies the granite burial chamber of the king, at the foot of a shaft ninety-two feet deep, access to which was gained by a tunnel running in from the north. Transverse corridors leading off from the main tunnel open out into underground chambers and subsequent tunnelling by tomb robbers has resulted in a veritable maze beneath the surface. Apparently it had been the intention to cover the walls of the underground rooms and corridors with small blue glazed tiles in imitation of reed mats. Of the rich funerary equipment that must have accompanied the burial, little has survived except a vast number of stone vessels which constitute one of the highest achievements of the Egyptian craftsmen.

No firm explanation can be given for the adoption of the stepped pyramidal form. Henceforward until the end of the twelfth dynasty, the pyramidal form was the privilege of the pharaoh, only occasionally extended to his queens. The radical nature of the change of design which introduced it, suggests that its adoption was not the accidental resulr of piling mastaba on mastaba to achieve greatet security for the burial but was the expression of a religious symbolism, the meaning of which in the absence of contemporary written texts can only be guessed. The most likely explanation seems to be that the design was intended to represent some physical connection between the earth and the sky to which the dead pharaoh ascended.

The Step Pyramid is the most dominant feature of a large complex of buildings which have been largely recovered in recent years. At the northern end of the pyramid is a mortuary temple and close to it a small enclosed chamber (*serdab*) in which was discovered a seated limestone statue of Zoser which could look out through two openings made at the level of the eyes upon an open court. At the southern end of the complex lies a small mastaba tomb; other buildings are models of religious buildings connected with important ceremonies, including the **heb-sed**. Behind their façades of finely carved limestone lies only rubble masonry. The whole complex was enclosed by a high crenellated stone wall with fourteen imitation bastions, thought to imitate the wall of Memphis. Entrance was by means of a narrow passage at the south-eastern end of the wall and gave access to an imposing colonnade in which columns, deriving their inspiration from Egyptian plant life, are joined to the wall by cross abutments. There are no free-standing pillars in the complex. Though this feature and the small size of the blocks used suggest a certain hesitancy in the use of stone, as if the full technical potentialities of stone architecture had not yet been realized, it is possible that the reason is simply desire from religious conservatism to imitate in stone architectural forms derived from the old brick and reed constructions.

In selecting Saqqara as the site of his tomb, close to the capital of Memphis, Zoser was following the practice of his predecessors. A little to the north of the Step Pyramid, on the edge of the plateau, large brick-built mastabas of the first dynasty have been uncovered. In their size and the wealth of material recovered from them, and in the elaborate layout of the complex, these impressive monuments of the Egyptian brick architecture are probably the burial places of the kings of the first dynasty and members of their families, the **Abydos** monuments of the first two dynasties being **cenotaphs**.

Close to the Step Pyramid of Zoser, on the south-western end, lies a similar monument, never finished. It was discovered by the late M. Zakaria Goneim. Two stages of a stepped pyramid were completed and then work apparently abandoned with the construction ramps still left in place on all four sides. A stone enclosure wall, similar to Zoser's, but using large blocks, has been uncovered and it remains to be determined whether other buildings were planned. Goneim found the entrance to the pyramid, still sealed, in 1954, but the magnificent alabaster **sarcophagus** in the burial chamber was empty, though the presence of botanical specimens suggest that some ceremony had been performed in the burial chamber. This unfinished pyramid is attributed to Sekhemkhet, otherwise unknown except for a rock tablet at Sinai. He was probably Zoser's immediate successor.

The remaining kings of the third dynasty seem to have favoured sites a little to the north or south of Saqqara: but in the fifth and sixth dynasties further pyramids were constructed at Saqqara: true pyramids with a mortuary temple at the northern side and a covered enclosure leading down to a valley temple. Some of the reliefs decorating the causeway of Unas, the last of the fifth-dynasty kings, have recently been recovered. They show the transporting by boat of granite columns from Aswan, a market scene, and a unique stone depicting the victim of a famine. The earliest known copies of the **Pyramid Texts** are from these later pyramids of Saqqara.

Unlike the great cemetery of **Giza**, the pyramids at Saqqara have not the same formal layout of mastaba tombs of officials; but high officers of the government and priests of the mortuary cult are found buried in stone mastabas around the pyramid of the king they served. From one, that of Hesy-re, came a remarkable series of wooden panels carved with representations of the deceased, now in the Cairo Museum. It is probably approximately contemporary with the Zoser monument. The stone mastabas of the fifth and sixth dynasties at Saqqara are large, many-chambered and in the richness of the scenes, delicacy of relief and survival of colour are among the most interesting of this type of monument. Particularly noteworthy are the tomb of Ti, of the vizier Ptahhotep, and Kagemni of Mereruka, the latter containing no less than thirty-two sculptured chambers.

Saqqara ceased to be a royal necropolis after the collapse of the Old Kingdom, but it continued to be the cemetery of Memphis and contains tombs of all periods down to Roman times. The most important of the later tombs is probably that of Haremheb constructed before his accession to the throne. Though the tomb itself has been destroyed sculptured slabs have survived in a number of museum collections and are of particular interest for their evidence of the "Amarna style" of relief. From the later period comes the burial place of the Apis bulls, the **Serapeum**, the discovery of which by **Mariette** in 1850 first drew attention to the importance of Saqqara as a whole. Close by the Serapeum were discovered an interesting series of statues of Greek philosophers arranged in a hemisphere, while the former monastery of Apa Jeremias, passed as one climbs up from the cultivation to the Step Pyramid, is a reminder of the importance of early Christian remains in Egypt. *See* plate 120, page 386.

Sarcophagus. A stone coffin, such as those in which the Egyptians and others placed their **mummies.**

Sardinia, *see* Mediterranean, the Western.

Sarnath. Originally Saranga-natha, Lord of the Deer, a title of Buddha, Sarnath is renowned as the site of the Deer Park outside Benares, itself one of the holiest cities of India, where Buddha preached the first sermon to his disciples proclaiming the Noble Eightfold Path to Nirvana.

The Deer Park lies four miles north of the city. Since early times it has been a revered place of pilgrimage and thus contains many examples of the art and architecture of ancient India. The earliest surviving monuments belong to the period of the Mauryan Empire and include an inscribed pillar of **Asoka,** from which the noble lion capital has been chosen for the seal of independent India. The pillar stood beside the main shrine, which in its present form is of later date, and was described by the Chinese pilgrim Hiuen Tsang (early eighth century) as about two hundred feet high. A short distance south is the base of the great Dharmarajika **Stupa** also probably founded by Asoka. Farther east stands a second great stupa, the Dhamekh (sixth to eighth centuries), still standing to a height of one hundred and fifty feet. All around are many smaller stupas. Outside the central courtyard are the remains of many monasteries mainly of the early centuries A.D. The final period of construction dates from the twelfth century shortly before the Muslim sack of Benares. Sarnath is justly famous for its superb sculptures; the finest belong to Kushan and Gupta times (second to sixth centuries), but many are both earlier and later. *See* plates 122, 124, pages 388, 390.

Sassanians, *see* Iran.

Satrap. The title given to the governor of a satrapy, a province in the ancient Persian Empire.

Scarabs. Various forms of **seal** and seal-**amulet** were used in ancient Egypt. These included the cylinder seal, which has been found on predynastic sites; the button seal, of Old Kingdom date; the scarab, which first appears in the sixth dynasty, and its later derived forms; the scaraboid, cowroid and plaque. Although in the eighteenth dynasty all these objects, including the cylinder seal, shared the amuletic character of the scarab, only the scarab began by being a potent **amulet** in its own right, for it was a replica of the scarab beetle (Scarabaeus sacer) which, from the earliest times, was associated in the minds of the Egyptians with the rising sun, Khepri; it symbolized the power that drove the sun across the sky and, like the sun, was believed to be self-begotten.

Until the eleventh dynasty scarabs were purely amulets, buried with the dead, or strung on necklaces and worn to protect the living. By the twelfth dynasty the fine seal-scarab had come into its own, and royal and private names (with and without titles) were cut on its base. From the twentieth dynasty onward a gradual deterioration in quality led to the nondescript scarabs of the Late period, until their revival under the twenty-sixth (Saite) dynasty. The last scarabs certainly known are Ptolemaic, and these are purely funerary and without the seal base.

Schist. Rock formed, as a result of great heat and pressure in past ages, into a new structure of leaf-like layers.

Schliemann, Heinrich (1822–87). The son of a Protestant clergyman, Dr Schliemann was born at Neu Buckow in Mecklenburg-Schwerin in Germany in 1822. His father used to tell him tales of **Troy** and the Homeric heroes and before he was eight had given him a copy of G.L. Jerrer's *Universal History* with an engraving depicting Aeneas' escape from Troy. Despite his father's assurances that the city had been completely destroyed the young Heinrich became both convinced that "vast ruins of them must still remain" and determined that one day he would excavate them. He received no encouragement except from the two daughters of a local miller named Meineke, with one of whom, Minna, he fell in love. He was separated from her in 1829 when her mother died. After a few years schooling during which he learnt enough Latin to write an essay in that language on the Trojan war he became apprentice for five years in a small grocer's shop at Furstenburg where he worked from five in the morning till eleven at night. Here he encountered a drunken apprentice named Niederhoffer who could recite the poems of **Homer** in the original by heart. "Although I did not understand a syllable," writes Schliemann, "the melodious sound of the words made a deep impression upon me, and I wept bitter tears over my unhappy fate. Three times over did I get him to repeat to me those divine verses, rewarding his trouble with three glasses of whisky, which I bought with the few pence that made up my whole fortune. From that moment I never ceased to pray God that by his grace I might yet have the happiness of learning Greek."

After further years of hardship including a shipwreck, years when his Trojan dreams seemed quite unattainable, Schliemann procured a post under F.C.Quien, the consul-general of Prussia at Amsterdam. Here he applied half his annual salary of thirty-two pounds to the study of languages, successively mastering English, French, Dutch, Spanish, Italian, Portuguese and Prussian. In January 1846 he was sent by his firm as their agent to St Petersburg and felt that he now had sufficient money to apply for the hand of his childhood's love, Minna Meineke. To his distress he learned that she had just been married to another.

In January 1856 Schliemann set to work to learn first modern, and then ancient Greek with the aid of two Greek friends. Two years later he travelled in Europe, Egypt and Syria and in 1859 visited Smyrna, the Cyclades and Athens.

In 1863 he retired from business and spent the next two years travelling extensively, finally settling in Paris to study archaeology in preparation for his work at Troy. In April 1868 he set off via Rome and Naples for the Ionian Isles and there conducted his first excavation, some trial pits on the so-called "Castle of Odysseus" in Ithaca. He visited the Peloponnese including **Mycenae** where the upper part of the **Cyclopean** walls and the Lion Gate described by Pausanias in the second century A.D. were still partly visible. He visited Bournabashi in the Troad, rejected the then popular theory that it was the site of Troy, and decided that the prehistoric site must have been at Hissarlik which Strabo had called New Ilion and where a hoard of silver coins of Antiochus III had been found. In his first publication *Ithaque, le Peloponnèse et Troie* (1869) he announced his intention to excavate Hissarlik. In the winter of 1868 he was contemplating the dissolution of his first unhappy marriage and wrote to his old friend Vimpos, the Archbishop of Athens, with a request to find him a Greek wife, beautiful, poor but well-educated: "She must be enthusiastic about Homer, and about the rebirth of my beloved Greece". Vimpos sent back a photograph of Sophia Engastromenos, a beautiful girl eighteen years old, and the following year Schliemann married her.

In 1871 Schliemann and Sophia with eighty-five men (increased to one hundred and fifty the following spring) began the excavation of Hissarlik. The great trial trench cut through the debris of nine cities of which the excavator identified seven – but which was the city of which Homer had sung? Several of these settlements were obviously prehistoric but there was as yet no criterion for dating the pottery and other objects of pre-Hellenic date. Schliemann's great trial trench cut ruthlessly through the upper remains, including portions of the Greek Council Chamber and Temple of Athena, though the depths of whole vases or other objects were recorded and there is still much information that is recorded by Schliemann and often disregarded in the later reports.

In 1872 Schliemann uncovered a large bastion with double walls which he termed the Great Tower and west of that in the following spring a well-paved street with two large gateways in the city wall twenty feet apart, and inside this the remains of a large building. The excavator announced that he had found the Scaean Gate and the Palace of Priam which according to Homer should have stood inside. For this optimism Schliemann was bitterly attacked, especially in Germany, by many scholars who had doubted even the existence of Troy and resented this intrusion of a rich amateur. Schliemann, despite his enthusiasm, was discouraged and decided to stop digging on the 15 July, but the day before he noticed a gleam of gold in the soil near what he termed "the Scaean Gate". He dismissed his workmen and, aided only by Sophia, excavated the golden ornaments which he named "Priam's Treasure" though actually their date was much earlier than the reign of that king. It included two diadems, six bracelets, a bottle, sixty ear-rings, 8,700 rings as well as prisms, buttons and ornaments of gold, an electrum vase, others of silver and bronze and many bronze weapons.

The permission to excavate had been granted by the Turkish Government on condition that half the find remained in the country, but Schliemann, convinced that the Turks would melt down the gold regardless of its historic value, smuggled the whole treasure out to Athens. This act also alarmed the Greek authorities who not only searched, unsuccessfully, his house in Athens but refused to grant him permission to excavate at Agamemnon's old capital, Mycenae. Later, however, he obtained permission with exclusive publication rights for three years provided the finds remained in Greece. He fought and lost a lawsuit against the Turkish Government, but sent them five times his fine to obtain their goodwill and finally in 1876 obtained permission to re-open excavations at Troy. Two months previously, however, the Schliemanns had opened their excavations in **Mycenae.**

Here his literary guide was not Homer but Pausanias who had described the Lion Gate as he saw it in A.D. 123 and had stated that whereas Agamemnon and his murdered companions had been interred inside the city walls the bodies of their murderers, Clytemnestra and Aegisthus, had been buried outside. Some of the circular **tholos tombs** with beehive vaults regarded by Pausanias as "Treasuries" were also still visible and recent travellers had looted objects from the so-called Treasury of Atreus. The British Museum still retains the half-columns looted by Lord Sligo and the gypsum reliefs and other objects taken by Lord Elgin.

Schliemann started first to clear the Lion Gate and the area immediately inside it, clearing away with his usual impatience any walls that seemed to be later than the Homeric period.

Stamatakis, the Greek official appointed to supervise the excavations had a difficult time and complained in a letter to his superiors, "If we find Greek or Roman vases he looks at them in disgust and lets them fall... He treats me as if I were a barbarian... If the Ministry is not satisfied with me I beg to be recalled". But if Schliemann was impatient he certainly produced results. Inside the Lion Gate he found a double circle of upright slabs originally roofed with capstones, eighty-seven feet in diameter, enclosing a level space with upright sculptured slabs and a square altar furnished with a well-like opening. Schliemann identified this space as the Agora or city centre of Mycenae, the horsemen on the slabs as Homeric heroes and prophesied that graves would be found underneath. More sculptured slabs appeared and finally a gold ring. As at Troy the workmen were dismissed and the Schliemanns and Stamatakis successfully excavated five **shaft graves**, a sixth being uncovered later by Stamatakis outside the Grave Circle, (as the ring of slabs came to be known). In these shafts, which had originally been roofed, were found the remains of nineteen persons. The men had worn gold masks and breast plates, bronze swords and daggers inlaid with gold, silver and nickel, and had drinking cups of gold and silver. The women had gold toilet boxes and pins and wore clothes adorned with embossed discs of gold leaf. The two children were wrapped in gold sheeting. Grave One had the remains of a boar's tusk helmet like the one Meriones gave to Odysseus, Grave Four a golden cup with doves on the handles reminiscent of "Cup of Nestor". Well might Schliemann think that he had found the grave of Agamemnon and his followers. This was indeed Homer's "Golden Mycenae" though it is now known that the actual graves were some three hundred years earlier than Agamemnon.

In 1877 Schliemann made a triumphal tour in England where he was honoured by thirty learned societies and where the Prime Minister, W.E. Gladstone, wrote a preface to his book *Mycenae* published in English in 1880. In 1878 Sophia bore him a son and Schliemann built a splendid house in Athens. After a short excavation in Ithaca he returned to Troy where he discovered a smaller treasure not far from the site of "Priam's Treasure". In March 1879 he was reinforced at Troy by the assistance of Professor Rudolf Virchow, a distinguished German pathologist, and by M. Emile Burnouf, Director of the French School at Athens.

In 1880 Schliemann was active in Boeotia excavating the beehive tomb at **Orchomenos**, described by Pausanias as "The Treasury of the Minyae". The following year he was back at Hissarlik, this time assisted by Wilhelm Dörpfeld, a young German architect who had worked under Curtius on the **Olympia** excavations and who came to the conclusion that the sixth settlement, not the city of the treasures, had been the one described by Homer.

In 1884 Schliemann and Dorpfeld excavated at **Tiryns** where the former had sunk a few trial pits in 1876 and where the Cyclopean walls described by Pausanias were still visible. Here the two archaeologists found no golden treasure but the ruins of a palace with a **megaron**, or hall, resembling that of Odysseus as described by Homer.

In 1883 Schliemann applied to the Turks for permission to excavate the site of **Knossos** and in 1886 landed in Crete and even sank a trial trench on the Palace site, but when he discovered that the owner of the site was trying to cheat him he broke off negotiations.

The following year he returned to Germany for an operation on his ear but on his way back to Athens was taken ill at Naples and died on 26 December, 1887. *See* plate 123, page 389.

Scottsbluff, *see* America, Early Man in.

Scraper. A **stone tool** manufactured by **Stone Age** Man for the purpose of scraping hides and skins preparatory to using them for clothing or shelters.

Sculpture in Mesopotamia, *see* Mesopotamian Sculpture.

Seal. The first seal was probably a development from the **amulet**. An engraved gem or bead would be used to produce a copy of itself by pressing it on to soft clay. In this way some of its virtue or protective power would be transferred to the impression. A clay stopper over the mouth of a jar would, if stamped by an amulet, be thought to possess some of the amulet's magical power; anyone tempted to break open the jar and steal its contents would be halted, at least temporarily, by fear of the evil that might follow for him.

This seal would also be a proof that the jar belonged to a particular person, the one who could produce the amulet which had made the impression on the seal. So the seal became a mark to distinguish one's own property, and it cannot have been very long before it came to be restricted to that use alone. Seals of this kind are to be found in **Neolithic** settlements in Mesopotamia.

The earliest seals were flat ones which were stamped on to the clay and are consequently known now as stamp seals. A later development was the cylinder seal; this had the symbols carved on the outside of the cylinder and these left their impression when the seal was rolled on the wet clay.

Seals have been unearthed in quantity at sites throughout south-eastern Europe and the Near and Middle East from Greece and Egypt through to Iran. In Genesis **41**, 42 it is recorded that the pharaoh, on appointing Joseph as his vicegerent, gave him a ring as a sign that authority had been transferred to him; this would have been a signet ring with which Joseph could mark the royal property or seal documents. Many Egyptian seals were in the form of a **scarab**.

The earliest symbols on the seals would be geometric patterns, representations of a **totem** or some magical object, or animal figures. When writing was invented the seal would incorporate the owner's name. A typical example is a seal unearthed at **Megiddo** in 1904. It was made of jasper and bore the representation of a roaring lion and the words "of Shema, the servant of Jeroboam", the words "The seal" or "The property" being understood at the beginning of the inscription. It dates from about 750 B.C.

Sea Peoples or Sea Raiders are names given to the tribes invading Syria, Canaan, Cyprus and Egypt by sea from about 1200 B.C. onwards. One of these – the Danaana – is thought to have overthrown the **Hittite** Empire around 1200 B.C. and then moved southwards against the Egypt of Ramses II. Among names of ethnic groups making up the Sea Peoples which are preserved in Egyptian sources are some which seem philologically connected with those of people appearing in the first millennium B.C. in western Mediterranean lands. Such are the *Shrdn*, linked perhaps with the late Sardinians; the *Tshkl*, possibly forerunners of the prehistoric Sikels of Sicily; and the *Trshw* who may be ancestors of the Etruscans. If these connections are correct, there may have been among the Sea Peoples groups that were ancestral to western peoples, still in a migratory stage before their settlement in western lands.

Only one major tribe of the Sea Peoples settled permanently in Palestine – the *Prsht*, or Philistines, who probably came from Crete and occupied the coastal strip between the Carmel Peninsula and Gaza. Archaeological data support the theory of an Aegean origin for the Philistines; their wares, for instance, are closely similar to late **Mycenaean** ware. The Philistines introduced iron into everyday use in Palestine.

Sedimentary Rocks. Wind and frost are continually at work breaking up the exposed surfaces of the rocks; rain washes the debris into streams, then into rivers, and finally carries it down to the sea where it is deposited as a sediment on the bottom. Over millions of years the sediments solidify into new rocks which are often, by the movement of the earth's crust, thrust again above the surface of the sea to form new lands, when the process begins all over again. In past ages sea animals died, and their bodies fell into the sediment to be overlaid by succeeding sediments; the same thing happened to land animals and birds which died in river mud or on the sea shore. The soft parts of their bodies decayed but the skeletons remained, preserved as **fossils** in the rocks.

Serapeum is the name given to the huge underground burial places of the sacred bull of Memphis in the **Saqqara** necropolis in Egypt, to the northwest of the Step Pyramid of Zoser. The cemetery was first discovered and identified by Auguste **Mariette** in 1850. It had been in use as early as the middle of the eighteenth dynasty (about 1400 B.C.) for the burial of the bulls in separate tombs with individual chapels above ground. In the nineteenth dynasty the burials were effected in side chambers off a gallery driven through the rock for a distance of over one hundred yards. These chambers are now inaccessible but under Psammetichus I (663–609 B.C.) a more impressive gallery was driven at right angles to the old one and subsidiary galleries were subsequently added under the Ptolemies. These may still be entered; the main gallery is about ten feet wide and seventeen and a half feet high and runs for a total length of over 1,100 feet. The mummified bulls, richly accoutred and buried with a magnificence which can have been surpassed only by that of the pharaoh himself, were placed in huge **sarcophagi**, usually hewn of a single monolith of granite. A number of **stelae** recording the date of the death of individual bulls are a valuable addition to our knowledge of late chronology.

The bull was worshipped at **Memphis** from at least the beginning of the dynastic period (about 3100 B.C.) in association with the cult of Ptah. In Egyptian the bull was known as Hapi, from which derives the Greek form Apis. The mummified bull, the "Osiris-Apis" (Usor-hapi), became popular with the Greek settlers in Memphis who worshipped it under the name of Osorapis. This latter was chosen by Ptolemy I to be a god in the worship of which Greeks and Egyptians could combine. In deference to Greek convention the god was given a human form and termed Serapis. The original Serapeum was a temple in the Greek style for the worship of Serapis at Alexandria. The name was also applied to the temple built above the catacombs at Saqqara; it was approached by a long avenue of sphinxes, and became one of the most famous of Egyptian cult centres in the Ptolemaic and Roman periods. A considerable number of Greek and Semitic **papyri** have been recovered from the Serapeum; they include petitions to the god, and an interesting series throwing light on the institution of the *Katachoi*, the recluses who retired to the precinct of the god, erroneously thought by some to have been the origin of the **Coptic** monasticism.

Seven Wonders of the World. The Greeks listed seven great works of art. The lists vary, but the seven generally accepted wonders of the world are as follows: the Colossus of Rhodes, a hundred-foot-high statue of the sun-gold Helios which stood beside the entrance to the island's harbour; the four-hundred-foot-high Pharos (light-house) of Alexandria, the port of Egypt; the Mausoleum, the tomb of Mausolus at Halicarnassus in Asia Minor; the forty-foot-high gold and ivory Statue of Zeus at **Olympia**, made by the sculptor Phidias; the Temple of Artemis, or Diana, at **Ephesus**; the **Hanging Gardens** of **Babylon**; and the **Pyramids** of **Egypt**. All except the Pyramids have been destroyed, though some sculptures from the Temple of Artemis and the Mausoleum are to be seen in the British Museum in London.

Shaft Graves were rectangular oblong trenches with vertical sides, cut deeply into the earth and roofed in with stone slabs at a fairly low level, the shaft above the slab then being filled in with earth.

At **Mycenae** the shaft sides were lined with rubble up to a level of about three or four feet; wooden beams were then placed across from rubble wall to rubble wall to support the thin stone-slab roof. The bodies were laid in the empty area at the bottom of the shaft, not covered with earth. At Mycenae shaft graves as a rule contained two to five bodies, and the presence of the graves was indicated by **stelae** or other grave markers. At Mycenae these were graves for members of the ruling class.

Shaft-straightener, *see* Arrow-straightener.

Shang Dynasty, *see* Anyang.

Shih Chai Shan. This site, some nineteen miles south of Kunming in Yunnan, China, ranks in importance with the famous finds at **Anyang** in north China which first revealed the material culture of the Shang dynasty. Some twenty tombs have been excavated, belonging to the ruling group of the kingdom of Tien, at the time of the Chinese expansion south-westwards into Yunnan at the time of the western Han, in the period 206 B.C.–A.D. 24. The finds from the tombs show that the earlier period was considerably less under Chinese influence than the later, and that a number of cultural elements had gone to the make-up of this Yunnanese kingdom. Some of the material is comparable with the bronzes of the Eurasiatic steppe, though it is notable that whereas these tend to be two-dimensional, the Yunnan artists produced a truly three-dimensional version of the same motifs. Other finds belong to the same tradition as those from the **Dong-son** culture, though the precise relationship is still to be determined. There are other features which seem to be connected with the non-Shang elements from Anyang, perhaps by way of Sze-chwan, while yet others seem to belong to the Ch'u tradition of the Yangtze Valley. Others again are Chinese. An important find is of the Chinese seal, bearing the inscription "Gold Seal of the King of Tien", which is known from the Chinese historical text, the *Shih chi*. The material from the tombs includes a number of remarkable bronze drums, with figures in the round set on the upper surface arranged in a variety of scenes: a battle, and a sacrificial scene by a long-house are among these. Other drums have animals on top. The weapons from the site include spear and arrow-heads, and some daggers with decorated blades. There are also Dong-son type drums with modifications which make it clear that they are of local manufacture. One bronze model suggests that some form of bull-fighting was practised in Yunnan. Two distinct groups are represented in the glyptic in addition to the Chinese. *See* plate 126, page 392.

Sicily, *see* Mediterranean, The Western.

Siemreap. The main concentration and best known of the **Khmer** sites are situated in and about Siemreap in Cambodia. This is probably because the Siemreap River which runs into the north end of the Tonle Sap is never dry, even in the hottest seasons. The first remains here date from the seventh century A.D., but the great period of building begins in the ninth when at Roluos, near Siemreap, the first signs appear of the grouping of a number of shrines on a single terrace. At the end of the ninth century we find the first of the great complexes located about a central temple, in this case Phnom Bakheng, inside a moated and walled enclosure, with sides of almost two miles, which serve as a capital and as a microcosm, the central temple being envisaged as Mount Meru, the axial mountain of the cosmos in Indian cosmological schemata, and the moat as the encircling ocean. The central temple which lies at the intersection of four avenues leading to the main gates of the city consists of five terraces built about a small natural hill, with five towers on the topmost, and lesser towers on the lower stages. The importance lies in the grouping of individual towers on the pyramidal base. (Later the towers were to be linked by cloister and galleries, as at Angkor Wat itself.) Another style of treatment is to be seen at Banteay Srei, to the north of the main Angkor group. Its name, Temple of Women, is modern, but pays tribute to its reduced scale and the general delicacy of treatment in the carving, and the elegance of the whole. Here the individual towers are each treated as a pyramidal mountain, the three being grouped on a single base, and enclosed, together with ancillary buildings, within an elegant wall with gopuras. The niches house figures of deities and heavenly beings, the pediments illustrate Hindu myths, but the treatment, as in the case of Ravana, imprisoned beneath Mount Kailasa, is far removed from the spirit of the *Ramayana* and has been compared to that of an elaborate ballet rather than of an epic poem.

Before turning to the best known of the monuments of Siemreap, Angkor Wat, it is useful to consider the last of the major monuments which form the centre of the last capital, the city of Angkor Thom with the Bayon as its centre. (There is a celebrated account of this city by a thirteenth-century Chinese visitor.) Here the walls of the city were decorated with beasts, and the approaches to the gateways were flanked by mythological figures engaged in the churning of the Ocean of Milk, a Hindu creation legend, the moat being Ocean. The gates themselves are treated as monstrous carvings of deities and the central temple is Meru, the mountain which in the story was used for the churning. In fact, although a temple, it is best considered as an exercise in sculpture rather than in architecture, each tower being carved in the form of a four-faced image of the **Bodhisattva** Lokesvara, perhaps conceived of as the king Jayavarman VII (A.D. 1180–1220), in his capacity as divine ruler and guardian of the Khmer Empire. The building is covered with carvings, illustrating texts and depicting scenes within the empire. This tradition is older than the Bayon, and seems to have achieved its higher form at the time of Angkor Wat.

This monument, due to Suryavarman II (1112–52) was at once a temple of the royal palladium, the linga (a phallus, worshipped among the Hindus as a symbol of the God Siva) and a tomb for its founder. It is laid out with a western orientation in a rectangle, surrounded by two and a half miles of moat. A causeway entrance leads to a monumental portal which leads into the enclosure of the temple proper. This stands on an enormous stone-flagged platform, each side being more than 3,000 feet long. A cloistered gallery with almost half a mile of reliefs surrounds the main temple complex. This consists of a square with galleries and four open courts, which is reached by a staircase. Another staircase leads to a large courtyard with colonnades and towers at the corners. At the centre of this is the main block, a pyramidal mass, with four very steep staircases, one to each face, supporting the central temple which is linked by a cruciform system of arcades to surrounding galleries, with temples at each corner. The top must have originally attained a height of over 200 feet. A shaft 120 feet deep was under the central image, and a gold foundation deposit at its bottom.

In addition to figures of nymphs, of which there are over 1700, and delicately carved decorations based on vegetation, with birds and beasts, the great series of reliefs which cover the walls of Angkor Wat testify to the skill of Khmer carvers. These reliefs are almost wholly vaisnavite, and even the king is shown in a vaisnavite context. (A few saivite scenes which do occur are based on vaisnavite texts.) There is some evidence to suggest that the reliefs are of different dates, one set at least, those on either side of the north-east corner, being considerably later in date than the completion of the monument.

No account of the monuments of Siemreap would be complete without some reference to the enormous scale of hydraulic works which are to be seen there. The great moats which surrounded the capitals, and the two great artificial reservoirs, the eastern and western Baray, the latter about one and a quarter by five miles, to say nothing of more than a thousand smaller tanks and reservoirs, and a vast complex of linking channels, canals and conduits, testify to the skill of Khmer hydraulic engineers, of which the first traces, though perhaps of pre-Khmer origin, are to be seen in the territory of **Fu-nan.** Most of the larger works at Siemreap are linked by a sluice system to the Siemreap River, but the smaller tanks depended wholly upon the capture of surface water from the monsoon rains.

Dates of some Khmer buildings: Seventh century A.D.: Sambhor Prei Kuk. Eighth century A.D.: Ak Yom. Ninth century A.D.: Temples of Mount Kulen. A.D. 881: Bakong. A.D. 893: Lolei. A.D. 967: Banteay Srei. A.D. 1108 Phimai (near Korat, Thailand). Twelfth century A.D.: Angkor Wat. Thirteenth century A.D.: Bayon. *See* plate 125, page 391.

Sigiriya, Ceylon. The rock fortress of Sigiriya, Lion Rock, was built by King Kassapa I (A.D. 511–29). The remains of the palace foundations can still be seen, and the walled access gallery, with a façade in the shape of a seated lion. Two rock pockets contain paintings which seem to belong to an Andhra style of painting. They show two celestial women with their attendants, veiled in cloud below the waist, an indication of their non-mortal nature. The physical features are Singhalese but the manner of painting clearly owes much to India. The colours used are reds in various shades, yellow, green and black. The drawing and colouring are strong: the brush-strokes are used to form surface patterns.

Silbury Hill. About a mile from **Avebury** in England is the huge 130-foot-high artificial mound called Silbury Hill. How old it is, and why it was built (excavation has yielded no information), are questions which remain unanswered.

Simian Shelf. A thickening of the lower jaw to which the tongue is attached; it is found in apes and monkeys, but not in man.

Sinanthropus. In 1921 a Swedish geologist, Dr Anderson, found quartz in the deposits at **Chou-kou-tien** in China, and made a famous prophecy that fossil man would be found there. When a large wrinkled molar tooth was unearthed in 1927, Dr Davidson Black, Professor of Anatomy at Peking, took the bold step of naming a new genus of fossil man on the basis of this one tooth – Sinanthropus (Man of China).

Bones representing more than forty individuals have now been found. They consists of five more or less complete skulls, fourteen jaw-bones, 152 teeth, and parts of limb-bones. The fragmentary nature of the finds shows that they do not represent carefully buried skeletons but the remains of cannibal feasts, thrown away among animal bones and other refuse.

From the length of the thigh-bone, or femur, the Sinanthropus male was probably a little over five feet tall, the female about five inches shorter. The femur itself was straight, not curved as in anthropoid apes, indicating the upright posture of man.

The skull is thick, and the forehead only slightly developed. The top is flattened, and has a pointed back with a large area for the attachment of powerful neck muscles. The size of the brain is remarkably varied. The brains of the five skulls measured from 850 c.c. to 1,300 c.c. (the brain of Homo sapiens is about 1,350 c.c.) Across the eyes is a massive browridge or torus. The jaws project, and there is no chin, but the teeth are human in their arrangement in an even curve. The canines do not project.

There are so many similarities between Sinanthropus and the bones of **Java Man (Pithecanthropus** erectus) that many anthropologists include both in the one genus and refer to Sinanthropus as Pithecanthropus pekinensis (the ape-man of Peking), but in some respects the Chinese specimens are less primitive. *See* plate 127, page 393.

Singa Skull. The skull of a pre-Bushmanoid male found at Singa, on the Blue Nile in the Sudan. It is almost identical in shape with the **Boskop Skull** from south Africa, except that the Boskop Skull is much longer. The Singa man was apparently middle-aged when he died. The mastoid processes are short and narrow. This region and the temporal bone show paedomorphic or infantile characteristics similar to those of modern **Bushmen.**

Sirkap, *see* Taxila.

Siyalk, *see* Iran.

Skara Brae is situated in the Orkney Islands, which lie to the north of Scotland, and stands on the shore of the Bay of Skaill, seven miles to the north of Stromness. In 1850 storm waves exposed some buried houses there and these were partially excavated from time to time during the next eighteen years. A full excavation took place in 1927–30 under the direction of the late Professor V.G. Childe. Proving to be one of the outstanding village sites of the **Neolithic** period in Europe, its marvellous preservation was, like Rinyo (also in the Orkneys), due to stone, rather than wood, having been used for the houses and furniture, and to sand enveloping the site.

There were at least three villages, one on top of the other. Of the first and second very little is known, mainly owing to the lack of adequate excavation in these earlier levels. The four houses belonging to the second village so far located were not as solidly constructed as those of the last village. Seven houses of the last village remain, connected by very narrow slab-roofed lanes, only four feet high. The whole village had a low artificial mound of refuse built up around it, even covering the roofs of the lanes so that it was, in a sense, underground. The reason for this must have been to gain added protection from the weather or from intruders. A drainage system existed, although the village seems to have been in a rather filthy condition. A very severe sandstorm caused it to be finally abandoned.

The houses were of a rather peculiar type of unknown origin and of essentially the same design throughout the occupation. Both flagstone and shale were used in the drystone construction, exposed walls being plastered with clay. The internal house-plan was a rectangle with rounded corners up to fourteen by twenty-one feet. Externally, however, they had no plan, the four-foot-thick walls being modified so that they all fitted together into one compacted mass of houses and passages. The walls were at least ten feet high and slightly corbelled. The roof seems to have been of whalebone rafters with a skin covering or it may be possible that the corbelling was carried right over. In either case a large central smoke-hole must have been left. The door was a mere hatch less than four feet by two feet and could be closed with a stone slab held by a wooden bar. All the furniture was of stone slabs including a central hearth, wall-cupboards, a dresser, tanks, and male and female beds on opposite sides of the hut. Chambers in the wall may have been used for storage or as privies. The occupants sat on the edge of the bed facing the fire, the beds themselves being filled with rubbish and personal belongings.

Their self-sufficient economy was based solely on pastoralism supplemented by shell-fish. Clothes of cowhide and sheepskin were ornamented with strings of home-made bone beads and red, yellow and blue body paint. No separate cemetery was found, and flexed inhumation seems to have taken place amongst the houses.

These people belonged to the Rinyo-Clacton group of the British Secondary Neolithic, although they had mixed origins including a strong Circumpolar **Stone Age** and **Mesolithic** influence. Good at stone and bone-work, they were bad at pottery which, together with some pins, they had acquired from somewhere along the Atlantic Coast route. Their houses were of native design. In date the settlement was probably occupied during most of the first half of the second millennium B.C. *See* plate 128, page 394.

Sledge. The sledge is the earliest form of vehicle known to have been invented by man. It probably developed through man in **Palaeolithic** times laying his kill on the branch of a tree and dragging it home behind him. He then only had to keep the branch for use again, shaping it to suit its purpose better, or to tie a couple of branches together, to form a very primitive sledge. By **Mesolithic** times the sledge was a fully developed vehicle; sledge-runners of this period have been found preserved in bogs in Finland. The next step, which probably took place in **Neolithic** times, was to harness oxen to draw the sledge behind them; it is possible that dogsleighs were in use before ox-drawn sledges, for man tamed the **dog** long before he domesticated cattle and sheep. The sledge served mankind well until it was superseded by the invention of the **wheel.**

Smith, George (1840–76). At the age of fourteen George Smith was an apprentice engraver who stinted himself to buy books on the new discoveries in **Assyria** and spent every available holiday and dinner-hour studying the antiquities in the British Museum in London. His enthusiasm and knowledge were rewarded by his subsequent employment as a "repairer" of the numerous fragmentary **cuneiform** inscriptions from **Nineveh** reaching the Museum about 1861. His flair for the script and facility in identifying texts resulted in his quick promotion to Assistant in the Department of Oriental Antiquities for which he prepared Assyrian inscriptions for publication under the direction of **Rawlinson.**

In his spare time Smith wrote the first detailed Assyrian history of Ashur-bani-pal, drew up a list of signs and even deciphered Cypriote inscriptions. His greatest success came on 3 December, 1872, when he read a paper on his discovery of an Assyrian account of **the Flood** before a distinguished audience. There was widespread interest and an immediate clamour for the renewal of excavations at Kuyunjik (Nineveh). The *Daily Telegraph* promptly offered 1,000 guineas, provided that Smith himself undertook the work. After delays for a permit from the pasha, Smith reached Mosul on 2 March, 1873, and a week later had the remarkable good fortune to discover a fragment bearing seventeen missing lines of the Flood story.

A further journey in 1874 resulted in the recovery of several hundred more cuneiform tablets and this encouraged the Trustees of the Museum to send Smith on yet a third journey for which, with his impractical nature and ignorance of the Arab language and customs, he was ill-equipped. Lengthy and frustrating delays meant that he reached Mosul in July 1876 too late to dig. He unwisely insisted on crossing the desert by day and, suffering from dysentery, collapsed and was carried to Aleppo where he died, aged thirty-six.

Smithfield Culture, *see* Africa, Stone Age Man in *and* Africa, Stone Age Man in South.

Solo. It is in the Solo River system in central Java that some of the most significant finds for the history of human development have been made. The type specimen of **Pithecanthropus** erectus was discovered at Trinil in 1891, and a number of other skulls has subsequently been unearthed in the vicinity. At Ngandong in 1931–2 a series of eleven skulls was found, all without teeth or lower jaws, together with some 25,000 other bones. The presence among these of a heron whose normal habitat is north of the Hwang-Ho in China points to a period of maximum **glaciation** as the date of the Ngandong beds, a fact which is confirmed by other faunal evidence. There can be little doubt that the skulls, some of which show a typical artificial enlargement of the *foramen magnum*, had been opened for the brain to be extracted, perhaps for food. The fact that the skulls were all together suggests a camping site or meeting place for hunters at a point where animals approached the river to drink. The exact status of the material is still under discussion, but there can be little doubt that Solo man is a member of the **Neanderthal** group, and it has further been suggested that he is linked with the Tasmanians through the later specimens from Wadjak in south-east Java. Also from the Ngandong site were a number of stag horns which showed some signs of use, some rather doubtful bone tools, a few sting-ray spines, perhaps used as spear or dagger points (a bone copy is known from another site of the same period at Ngawi), and a number of round balls made of volcanic stone, similar to those found with Neanderthal remains at La Quina, France, and from Rhodesia.

Solutrean hunters entered Europe from the east during the Upper **Palaeolithic**. Their place of origin is unknown. Their sites form a narrow band across Europe, and they have been traced from Hungary to France and across the Pyrenees to

Cantabria. Some of their "laurel-leaves" have been found in Britain. Enormous numbers of bones of wild horses are found in Solutrean levels, and this exclusive choice of quarry may have been due to its being a tribal **totem.**

There were three phases of Solutrean development. The Lower Solutrean levels contain **stone tools** in the form of blades worked on the upper face only, the smooth bulbar face being untouched. **Flint** end-scrapers and gravers are found, and bone spear-heads, with a single bevel or a pointed base.

The Middle Solutrean layers are distinguished by the thin, deadly "laurel-leaf" spear-heads. These were made very thin by the skilful application of pressure, and both sides were worked. They vary in size from a foot to two inches. Most of them have been found broken, and on many sites the halves could not be fitted together. This suggests that half the blade remained in the quarry. This may have been human as well as animal, for the Solutreans ousted their **Aurignacian** and **Gravettian** predecessors from many caves, as the superimposed levels show. Bone-work in this phase was poor. Flint end-scrapers were made with some flat retouching on the upper face.

In the Upper Solutrean, narrow single-sided "willow leaves" are found. Shouldered points, with a single shoulder, were made by notching a willow leaf at one side of the base. The bone industry became more important; javelin heads and awls occur, and, an important advance for women, the bone needle with an eye.

Some cave art has been attributed to the Solutreans, notably the frieze in high relief at the rock-shelter of Le Roc. They were succeeded by the **Magdalenians.**

Somme-Bionne is situated about half-way between the sources of the Rivers Bionne and Tourbe in the department of Marne, France. It is one of the most outstanding of a series of rich **La Tène** chieftains' graves, notable also for its imports from the classical world which have been invaluable in helping to date the contents of such graves.

These burials, complete with an aristocratic chariot, extended from central Europe into western France and even as far west as Britain.

This grave was excavated in 1873 by an amateur archaeologist Léon Morel and the contents are now to be seen in the British Museum. A large rectangular pit about nine and a half feet by six feet by four feet deep was dug into the chalk. In this was placed a chariot, and two further recesses were cut in the bottom to accommodate the two wheels. The chariot pole and yoke projected beyond this pit and were therefore buried in a connected T-shaped trench. Beside the yoke lay a double harness, but the horses had not been included in the burial. The warrior had been laid out on a bier resting on the chariot platform, or possibly lying underneath it. Lying with his head at the rear, he was facing the direction in which the chariot had travelled in the funeral procession. Beside him lay his equipment, a long sword by his right hand, a dagger and a bunch of throwing spears at his left, a bracelet still on his right arm, and costly imported vessels and a local pot at his feet. His sword belt was decorated with large round bronze studs. The chariot itself was an elegant and light two-wheeled affair compared to the earlier and heavier four-wheeled **Hallstatt** carts such as that found at **Vix**, but it was similar in construction. Open in front, the wheels being guarded only by semi-circular wickerwork panels, the warrior and his driver both had to stand on a small square platform. The total length was not more than twelve and a half feet and the two horses which drew it were little more than ponies. The wheels, three feet in diameter, were shod with a single piece iron tyre, and they may have been deliberately broken when placed in the grave. This burial pit was surrounded by a circular ditch seventeen and a half yards in diameter and three feet wide and deep. A very similar burial to this was found at La Gorge Meiller, Somme Tourbe, in the same department.

This burial, however, only formed part of a larger cemetery of four other "royal" graves (destroyed) and at least eighty belonging to commoners. In this latter cemetery, the graves were cut into the chalk, the body lying in an extended position facing east. Belief in a life after death was testified by joints of pork and mutton as well as beads of amber and glass attached to ear-rings and bracelets. A rare possession must have been branches of imported pink coral. Other grave-goods included brooches and open-work bracelets. Evidence for the custom of **trepanning** may be seen in a piece of a human skull cut into a trefoil shape. This may have been made from a roundel removed during the operation. Such roundels frequently had a magical significance. Pear-shaped pedestalled urns were the most common pottery type.

The rich grave furnishings are, however, what makes this chariot-burial so outstanding. Imported **Etruscan** gold jewellery decorated the person of the chieftain, consisting of a repoussé diadem and a finger ring.

He also had a beautiful native belt-hook in bronze open-work, with a pattern of stylized griffins – very similar to one coming from the Ardennes. His sword was almost a yard long and had a bronze scabbard decorated with bronze disks and inset red corals. Most remarkable of all was the imported drinking set placed not on the bier but at the foot of the grave and partly under the chariot pole. This consisted of two splendid Etruscan bronze beak-flagons used for pouring out wine and a rather third-rate Attic cup used for drinking it. In life, these were used for banquets and they were obviously intended for a similar purpose in the after-life, as chemical analysis has shown similar vessels to have been filled with a resinated wine. Pairs of vessels are frequent in rich Celtic graves and the dead man evidently expected to drink with a companion.

Of the chariot, only various metal parts survived. The iron-shod wheels have rings and linchpins and the harness for the two small horses which would have drawn it, including the bits and horse brasses of fine openwork, some with coral inlay. The splendour of the bedecked horses, originally an Eastern custom, must have added to the richness of the whole funeral procession.

Why was this man buried with his chariot? Simply because it was an even older Hallstatt tradition and also an Etruscan one in the seventh to sixth centuries B.C. Making a chariot was a specialized affair and they seem to have been made in regional workshops, although they all shared a common tradition of design and technique.

About what time was the Somme-Bionne chieftain buried? Here the imported luxury objects are of great value. The Greek cup was painted about 420 B.C., the flagons made in the workshops at Vulci about 500–450 B.C. Only the pieces of Etruscan jewellery were made earlier than this. It is obviously a problem to know which of these objects has been recently acquired and which handed down. Supposing the latest object, the Attic cup, to have been kept for, say, a generation then the funeral might have taken place as late as 390 B.C.

Finally, the imported objects imply trade; these were mainly wagon-loads of wineskins, sent by Etruscan exporters across the Alps via the Little St Bernard and eastern passes of the Alps. Along with the wine came the fashionable things (according to the classical world) with which to drink it, and coral also. The return trade no doubt consisted of slaves and raw materials.

South African Chelles-Acheul, *see* Africa, Stone Age Man in South.

South African Magosian, *see* Africa, Stone Age Man in South.

Spain, Prehistoric, *see* Mediterranean, The Western *and* Altamira.

Sphinx. From the Greek *sphingein*, "to draw tight, or squeeze", sphinx is the name for a compound creature with a lion's body and a human head. It probably originated in Egypt (the Great Sphinx at **Giza** dates from the fourth dynasty). Other examples are found at **Thebes**, where the temple avenues are lined with sphinxes, rams and criosphinxes (ram-headed sphinxes). Greek sphinxes differ from Egyptian sphinxes in that they are winged, as is the mythical sphinx at Thebes in Boeotia. Sphinxes are also found in the art of Assyria, Phoenicia, Asia and Cyprus, and on Persian jewellery. They are also common in **Minoan** art, carved in ivory and bone and on glass and gold plates. Other sphinxes were to be seen on the throne of Apollo at Amyclae, on the metopes at Selinus, on the statue of Athena in the Parthenon and on the throne of Zeus at **Olympia**.

Stadium. As a measure of length, about 200 yards, the distance of one circuit of the stadium in a foot-race.

Star Carr. This **Mesolithic** site was the first in England to yield a **flint** industry associated with organic remains of recognized **Maglemosian** character, together with data enabling a reconstruction of the way of life and of the ecological conditions prevailing at the time of occupation. The site is five miles south-south-east of Scarborough in Yorkshire. The settlement was built on a platform of birch brushwood, stones and clay on the edge of a former Mesolithic lake. Because of the damp nature of the site, many organic remains have survived. There were no piles to stabilize the platform nor any hut remains, though skin tents or reed huts may have rotted away. This settlement belongs, both in time and culture, to the earliest phase of the Maglemosian (proto-Maglemosian) in Europe and forms a link with the Upper **Palaeolithic**. The only known sites of this earliest phase abroad are those of Klosterbund in Jutland, and Vig in Zealand.

The area of this settlement was about 240 square yards. Habitation debris varied from six to eighteen inches in thickness, but charcoal layers indicated that the site was abandoned and reoccupied at least once. Evidence points to occupation in winter and spring over a number of years by a small group of four or five families. There were no signs of cultivated plants or domesticated animals, the economy being based on plant-gathering, hunting and fowling. Remains of red deer and roe deer were plentiful; elk, ox and pig were also eaten, as were water-birds.

Flint-knapping was carried out on the site, and waste **flakes**, found sometimes with their parent **cores**, formed the bulk of the archaeological material. Of almost 17,000 **stone tools** found only seven per cent were finished forms. The worked flints are unabraded being protected from damage when covered by the mud; none were polished or ground. Of 248 **microliths**, 126 were simple obliquely blunted points, forty-five were triangles, forty-five elongated trapezes and fifteen micro-burins. Other forms included saws, awls, 446 scrapers, 334 burins, seven core axes and adzes.

From the animal materials utilized by the community, only antler and bone have survived. Red deer antler was abundantly used in the manufacture of barbed points, which were removed from the beam by "groove and splinter" technique using flint burins. The points, 191 of which were found, were probably mounted on wooden shafts as spearheads. Tines had their tips obliquely bevelled for use in skinworking. Elk antlers were perforated and mounted on wooden handles as mattocks; part of one wooden handle was found still in the perforation. Small elk bones were fashioned into bodkins while elk bone was made into skin-working tools. Amber, shale and animal teeth were worn as pendants or beads.

Numerous tightly-wound rolls of birch-bark which occurred may have been net-floats or a source of resin for mounting arrow-heads and spearheads. The only wooden **artifact** found was a birchwood paddle with a long narrow blade, the earliest navigational appliance known. There were no remains of dugout boats so skin canoes were probably used.

Stag frontlets, still bearing the antlers, were fashioned into headdresses with holes made for fastening-straps. Excavation uncovered twenty-one of these remarkable objects which must have been worn for deer-stalking or for ritual dances.

What was the date of this settlement? The archaeological material of the site was incorporated in organic mud of the early post-**glacial** period. A **radiocarbon** test on a sample of birchwood has given an age of 9488 $\pm$350 years or 7538 $\pm$350 B.C.

Steatite. A soft, easily-worked stone, sometimes called soap-stone.

Stein, Mark Aurel (1862–1943). Explorer and archaeologist, Sir Aurel Stein was born in Budapest. He served in India as head of the Lahore Oriental College from 1888 to 1899 and, after taking British nationality, as Inspector-general of Education for the North West Frontier Province. In 1903 he took a temporary post in the archaeological survey of India and later became superintendent of the N.W.F.P. Circle, serving until his retirement in 1929. His interests turned to archaeology from history; while at Lahore he had edited the Kashmir chronicle and had attempted to relate it to the historical geography of Kashmir. Between 1900 and 1916 he made his three great expeditions into central Asia, centred upon Chinese Turkestan. His work was almost as much geographical as archaeological and he regarded the two as interdependent. His first aim was accurate field observations, but, as at Khotan, Niya or Miran, he sometimes resorted to excavation. He collected large numbers of documents and objects of all kinds, ranging from **Neolithic** stone tools to textiles and grave-goods of the eighth century A.D. He brought back to India, where they are housed today in the central Asian Antiquities Museum in New Delhi, a large number of stucco wall paintings, mainly of the sixth to tenth centuries A.D. The results were published in the eleven quarto volumes of *Khotan* (1907), *Serinidia* (1921) and *Innermost Asia* (1928). About this time his interests turned towards Iran and the origins of Indian civilization and between 1926 and 1936 he made two further expeditions to Baluchistan and south Persia.

Stela or **Stele** (plural – stelae). A sculptured monument, usually in the shape of a tablet or a pillar. *See* plate 83, page 277.

Stellenbosch. An obsolete term for the culture now called **South African Chelles-Acheul.**

Step Pyramid of Zoser, *see* Saqqara.

Stillbay Culture, *see* Africa, East.

Stone Age. The Stone Age is the name given to that immensely long period (certainly over half a million years) when man used **stone tools** and weapons. It is divided into three main periods: Old, or **Palaeolithic**; Middle, or **Mesolithic**; and New, or **Neolithic**; and was succeeded by, first, the **Bronze Age**, and then the **Iron Age**.

The earliest known forms of stone tools are **eoliths**; they are so primitive that it is uncertain whether they are definite **artifacts**, or naturally fractured stones collected by the near-men who lived on earth half a million years ago. Slowly these wandering hunters learnt to make proper **flint** tools and to tame and make use of fire; as if satisfied with their achievements they remained at this level of development for many hundreds of years, and it is not until modern Homo sapiens (first known to us in the person of **Cro-magnon Man** and his relatives) displaced **Neanderthal Man** that there appears the wide variety of stone tools which is the precursor of Stone Age Man's ability to produce many and varied inventions.

The Middle Stone Age saw this tendency developing, with man inventing **boats** and **sledges,** but it was during the New Stone Age that the really great advances took place: the **domestication of animals** and stock-breeding, the cultivation of grain crops, **flint-mining**, the making of **pottery**, **weaving**, the growth of settled villages. The characteristic tool is the celt or polished stone-axe fitted into a handle, as opposed to the **hand-axe** (*see* plate 55, page 195) of previous times. Villages were not always permanently occupied; if the land became exhausted the people would move on; in later times another group might move in, on discovering that the land had recovered its fertility; **Köln-Lindenthal,** the Neolithic village near Cologne in Germany, is a typical example of this.

Stone Bowl Culture, *see* Africa, East.

Stone Circles. A circle of standing stones, usually of **Bronze Age** times and believed to have been erected for religious and ceremonial purposes; examples are to be seen at **Avebury** and **Stonehenge** in England.

Stonehenge is situated on Salisbury Plain in Wiltshire, England, eight miles north of Salisbury and some two miles west of Amesbury. As a prehistoric **megalithic** monument it is unique not only in Britain but in all Europe.

This monument was not built at one time but consists of at least three different monuments built at different times on the same site.

The first phase, dated by secondary **Neolithic** pottery to 1900–1700 B.C. (and by **carbon fourteen** to 1848 B.C. ± 275) consisted of a circular earthwork 320 feet in diameter. A low bank twenty feet wide by six feet high was surrounded by a shallow ditch. Just inside the bank were fifty-six small roughly circular pits (called "Aubrey Holes" after the seventeenth-century antiquary). More than half of these have been excavated and were found to contain the bodies of individuals who had been cremated, some with grave goods, such as bone pins, pots, stone maceheads. Their original purpose is, like much of the structure at Stonehenge, unknown. An undug causeway formed an entrance to the north-east and this seems to have been flanked by some sort of timber gateway. Just outside the entrance stood a standing stone ("The Heelstone") surrounded by a circular ditch. Nearby lay the Greater Cursus, perhaps used for funereal games, some 3000 yards long and more than a hundred yards broad, running roughly east to west. Another smaller cursus, of unknown date, lies nearby.

The second phase dated by A or B1 beaker pottery to 1700–1550 B.C., consisted of a double concentric circle of bluestones (no longer visible) arranged in thirty-eight pairs, which was built inside the older earthwork. (Their sockets are known as Q and R holes.) Bluestone is a collective name here for dolerite, rhyolite and volcanic ash. The entrance in this circle corresponded to the former one, and leading from it a zig-zag avenue 600 yards long, almost fifty feet broad, bounded on either side by a bank and ditch, leads down to the River Avon.

This avenue must have had a religious processional function. Similar avenues of upright stones leading to stone circles are by no means uncommon and occur, for example at Stanton Drew, Somerset, and also approach henge monuments as at Avebury.

The second phase bluestones were dismantled and their sockets filled in before the third was begun. Dated to 1500–1400 B.C. this consisted of a much more imposing and costly structure. High stones were now required, and the local sandstone ("sarsen") was used. This third phase represents what most people think of as "Stonehenge", and seems to have been carried out in three stages. Still within the bounds of the earthwork of period I, a massive circle of thirty sarsen uprights almost one hundred feet across was constructed. Each upright was eighteen feet in total height, seven feet broad, twenty-six tons in weight and had entasis (slight convexity) to correct perspective! Lintel stones ten and a half feet long joined the tops of these uprights into a continuous circle. Stability was maintained by means of mortise-and-tenon joints rather reminiscent of timber jointing. The inner and outer edges of the lintels are cut so that each one forms one-thirtieth part of the circumference of a circle. Only five of these lintels now remain in position. Within this circle is a horseshoe-setting, open to the north-east, of five massive sarsen trilithons. Each trilithon consists of two uprights connected by a lintel, but in this case the lintels are not continuous. An upright pillar (the "Altar Stone") stood on the axis of the horseshoe, and two sarsen pillars were erected, one on either side of the entrance of the phase I earthwork (one of these is the "Slaughter Stone"). The sarsens known as "the Four Stations" were also erected. On the line of the Aubrey Holes two of them are within barrow-like structures. Since a diagonal line connecting each pair of stones intersects at the centre of the main sarsen structures, they are probably contemporary with this third phase.

The next stage in phase III was to dig some sixty holes (the so-called Y and Z holes) outside the massive sarsen circle in order to re-erect some of the dismantled bluestones of phase II; the plan was changed and a bluestone circle and a horseshoe were set up each within the sarsen circle and sarsen horseshoe respectively. Thus the main features in sarsen were echoed in bluestone. Some of these bluestones were "secondhand" and had been brought from another, unknown lintelled monument (Bluestonehenge) which may have been nearby. The date of this phase is about 1500–1400 B.C., about the same date as objects, British flat axes and a Mycenaean dagger, carved on the sarsens. This type of dagger went out of fashion in Greece about 1500 B.C.

Stonehenge was obviously a temple used for a religious purpose. What this religion was is unknown, beyond the fact that it had certain astronomical elements in it. The "Four Stations", for example, could have been used to observe sunrise at the summer solstice and sunset at the winter solstice and the commencement of the four seasons. It is difficult, however, to go beyond certain basic facts in the lay-out and much that has been written about the astronomical meaning and religion is of very doubtful value. The Heel Stone is, for example, half an hour too late in marking midsummer sunrise! Stonehenge has nothing to do with the **Druids** although this mistaken connection is still reflected in the fanciful names for some of the stones and in the activities of Druid societies.

The wonders of Stonehenge III, both technical and economic, only increase with a closer inspection. 1500 men would have taken ten years merely to transport the sarsens! Whilst the bluestones were brought, mainly by water transport, from the Prescelly Mountains of north Pembrokeshire! All this must have meant great social unity, whether organised on a voluntary basis or not. Technically, Stonehenge III implies **Mycenaean** influence and it could only have been built by the Wessex culture princes, whose rich graves demonstrate east Mediterranean contacts, and who had the requisite social power at that time. *See* colour plate XV.

Stone Tools. *Development:* We define man today as "Man the Tool-Maker", and treat those **hominids** that did not make tools as only protohuman, simply because this makes a convenient label. Moreover, when we say "Man the Tool-Maker" we tend to think of stone tools as being the earliest tools that man ever made. In point of fact, it is more probable that before man made use of stone for tool-making he used other, softer materials; but this cannot, as yet, be proved. Such softer materials as may have been used have either perished in the course of time, or they show only inconclusive evidence of having been made into tools by very early man. Before we consider stone tools, however, we must, in fairness, refer to the fact that Professor Dart of Johannesburg believes that he can prove very early bone tool-making, even if many of his colleagues do not accept the evidence.

Since stone is hard and relatively imperishable it is natural that it forms the material of the first undoubted humanly made tools.

Before man started making cutting tools of stone, he was limited in his food to such vegetable matter as leaves, fruit, nuts, berries and roots, probably augmented by insects, other invertebrates such as snails, and small vertebrates such as rodents, baby-birds, and lizards, which he could catch, kill and eat without sharp tools. Without a cutting tool access to the wider field of meat supplies, represented by the larger mammals, was denied to man, because neither his finger nails nor his teeth were adapted to tearing through the thick skin of antelopes, or to cutting off chunks of raw meat from a large carcass. In this respect man was less well equipped by nature than such carrion feeders as hyenas, jackals, or even vultures, let alone such predators as leopards and lions.

The earliest and simplest stone tools of which we know are the so-called "pebble tools" which were used in the Lower **Pleistocene** and the earliest part of the Middle Pleistocene. These pebble tools consist, simply, of a water-worn pebble taken from a river gravel or a beach. From such a pebble three or four flakes were detached by knocking with another stone, the resulting jagged edge making a most effective cutting tool.

It is not always easy to distinguish between genuine pebble tools made by very early man, and the products of nature. Under certain conditions nature can, and does, produce specimens that look like humanly-shaped pebble tools, and therefore most scientists will only accept pebble tools as genuine when a group of them is found together, or when they are made of a material which is not local to the site where they are found, or under other similar conditions which preclude natural agencies. In the later stages of the pebble tool culture quite large concentrations can be found.

From these earliest and simple pebble tools the earliest stages of the **hand-axe** culture evolved. To start with, pebble tools remained the common tool, and only a very few of the more specialized pointed hand-axes were made. Gradually these became more common, but the simple pebble chopping-tool can be found as a survival in almost any stage of the hand-axe culture. The hand-axe, (*see* plate 55, page 95) a fairly carefully trimmed tool, pointed or sometimes oval in shape, was accompanied, during the latter stages of the culture, by the cleaver, a specially designed skinning tool with a sharp cutting edge at right angles to the long axis. At the same time, hand-axe man developed the use of stone balls and polyhedric stones, varying in size from tennis balls to large "bowlings woods". These were probably used in part to make bolases, and in part simply as hurling missiles and as club heads.

Hand-axe man was, in fact, far better equipped with a variety of different tool types than his pebble tool making predecessors.

It must be stressed that in addition to his tools of a special pattern, such as hand-axes, cleavers and stone balls, hand-axe man made a large variety of tools from the flakes which he knocked off in making his more specialized tools. These very early flake tools of hand-axe man do not follow any set pattern or shape, as they do in later **Stone Age** cultures. They are, therefore, all too often overlooked by prehistorians.

It has, indeed, been common to speak of the hand-axe culture as a "core-culture" to distinguish it from cultures such as the **Clactonian** and **Levalloisian** where the vast majority of the tools are made from relatively small flakes. Such a distinction is not, however, justified. The hand-axe culture people often used flakes, just as the Clactonian and Levalloisian cultures often used **cores** in addition to their more common **flake** tools.

There seems little doubt that the makers of the Clactonian and Levalloisian cultures were, at one time, contemporary with the hand-axe makers, the latter being predominantly a people of the African continent who did, however, invade south-west Europe and also the Near East, Middle East, and part of Asia, while the Levalloisian and to a lesser extent the Clactonian were essentially European cultures which did, however, invade parts of Africa and also the Near East.

In Africa and south-western Europe, where the two cultures overlapped, there was much borrowing of ideas, so that, in fact, the makers of the later stages of the hand-axe culture, in Europe were making side scrapers of the Levalloisian type, while the Levalloisians were making and using a limited number of hand-axes.

Another later development, which may derive mainly from the Clactonian culture, was that known as **Mousterian**, a culture characterized by "triangular points" and by side scrapers, and made, in the main, by **Neanderthal Man**.

In the latter stages of the Old Stone Age man

became a very specialized tool maker, and made a wide variety of stone tool types, such as knife-blades, skin scrapers, chisels, lance-heads, arrow-heads, spokeshaves, and tools for other special purposes. Many of these were tools which enabled him to make good tools and weapons from other materials such as wood, ivory, antler and bone, and also to make such things as beads and carvings. In most cases, too, these tools of the latter part of the Old Stone Age were very small, since man had discovered that a small, well-made tool with a sharp edge was just as effective as a large tool, and could be carried about more easily.

In the closing stages of the Stone Age man made the discovery that it was possible to grind and polish the edges of his tools on sandstone blocks, and thus produce a far finer and tougher cutting edge than he could do by chipping alone. The polished axes of the last part of the Stone Age are, indeed, capable of being used to cut down trees of six to eight inches in diameter, and this enabled man to start hut-building on a large scale, and to become a settled community dweller, no longer forced to live where nature provided him with rock shelters, or else in rough booths in the open country.

Manufacture: Since we cannot travel back into the past and watch Stone Age Man at work, we can only form an opinion by deduction as to how he made his stone implements. In this detective work we can, on the one hand, make use of what we know about primitive hunters of the present day, such as the Australian aborigines and the South African **Bushmen**, and, on the other hand, study the actual objects made by Stone Age Man to see what they tell us. Then, having reached tentative conclusions on the basis of these two lines of approach to our problem, we can test them out and see if they are, in fact, possible. If they are, we may feel that they are not too wide of the mark.

By applying the method outlined above we may say that the first conclusion to be drawn is that Stone Age Man must have had relatively little time on his hands for tool making. The task of perpetually finding enough food for himself and his family must have occupied the greater part of his time and energies at nearly all seasons of the year, so that we may guess that he had evolved techniques of tool-making which required the absolute minimum of time.

To some extent this was less true in the very last phases of the Stone Age when man had learnt to grow crops and to domesticate animals, and was, therefore, less dependent upon hunting, trapping and wild-food gathering, but even in this so-called **Neolithic** stage of life, the products of the domestication of plants and animals were probably insufficient to do more than supplement the results of his hunting, fishing and berry gathering, and these must still have been activities that occupied many hours a day. By this later time, however, man had fire (and, in some cases, simple lamps) so that tool making could have been carried out by artificial light when the daily activities were over.

The study of the actual types of tool which Stone Age Man made and the application of experimental methods to the fracture of stone show us that there are only a very limited number of ways in which stone can successfully be worked, and by which large and small flakes can be detached in the process of shaping a stone tool from a lump of rock.

The first and most simple technique consists of knocking one stone against another. If this is done in such a way that the angle at which the impact takes place is correct, a flake will be detached. If the angle is incorrect the result of hitting two stones together will either be a shattering of the smaller of the two, or else no fracture at all.

Stone Age Man seems to have learnt to use this technique, and to strike at the correct angle, at the very beginning of the Stone Age. It was indeed this discovery which was responsible for turning the prehuman animal into true man. He found, moreover, that he could apply the same principles in two different ways. Either he could hold the piece of stone which he wished to shape in one hand, and in the other hold a smaller stone and use it as a hammer. Or he could hold the piece of stone he wished to shape in one (or both) hands and knock it (at a suitable angle) against a projecting point of a stone on the ground. The first method is called the "hammer-stone technique" and the second the "anvil technique".

A third supposed variant of the first method of detaching flakes is sometimes described in books. This is the "pendulum technique", but experiment suggests that this method was too difficult to control accurately and too wasteful of material to be a probable Stone Age method of doing things.

The second major technique of flaking stone in the course of tool making is that which has come to be known as the "cylinder hammer" technique.

Photo: Oriental Institute, University of Chicago

PLATE 129. SUDAN: left side of sandstone steps in the west precinct of Temple "A" at Napata.

Photo: Oriental Institute, University of Chicago

PLATE 130. SUDAN: roof, architrave and Bes-pillar in east half of hall III of Temple "A" at Napata.

Photo: Oriental Institute, University of Chicago

PLATE 131. SUMERIANS: cult statues of the Lord of Fertility and the Mother-goddess from the Square Temple of Abu at Tell Asmar.

Photo: British Museum

PLATE 132. SUMERIANS: impressions from cylinder seals – (top to bottom) seal of Ibil-Ishtar with hunting scene, about 2250 B.C.; hero and animals, about 2750 B.C.; liberation of the sun god, about 2250 B.C. *(British Museum, London)*

Photo: Archives Photographiques

PLATE 133. SUSA: stela of Sargon of Accad. *(Louvre, Paris)*

Photo: Archives Photographiques

PLATE 134. SUSA: life-size bronze statue of Napir-Asu, wife of Untash-Uban who was king of Susa from 1265–45 B.C. *(Louvre, Paris)*

Photo: British Museum

PLATE 135. TELL ATCHANA: statue of Idri-mi, king of Alalakh, limestone and originally painted, north Syrian, fifteenth century B.C. Found at Tell Atchana. *(British Museum, London)*

PLATE 136. SUTTON HOO: Byzantine silver from the ship burial at Sutton Hoo.

Photo: Exclusive News Agency

PLATE 137. TAXILA: monastery of Mohra Moradu.

Photo: Exclusive News Agency

Photo: British Museum

PLATE 138. TELL ATCHANA: pottery bottle of "Nuzi" ware from Tell Atchana, late second millenium B.C. *(British Museum, London)*

Photo: British Museum

PLATE 139. LA TÈNE: bronze collar with embossed ornament including human faces, from Courtisols, Marne, La Tène style, about 250–100 B.C. Diameter $6\frac{1}{5}$ inches. *(British Museum, London)*

Photo: National Museum

PLATE 140. LA TÈNE: silver cauldron from Gundestrup (north Jutland), first century B.C. The panels round the cauldron are moulded with relief half-length figures of gods and goddesses, some holding human figures and others holding fabulous beasts. Diameter of

Photo: Aerofilms Ltd

PLATE 141. THEBES: the "Colossi of Memnon" (actually Amenhotep III).

Photo: British Museum

PLATE 142. LA TÈNE: bronze flagon with coral inlay from Basse-Yutz, Moselle, early fourth century B.C. Height 15 inches. *(British Museum, London)*

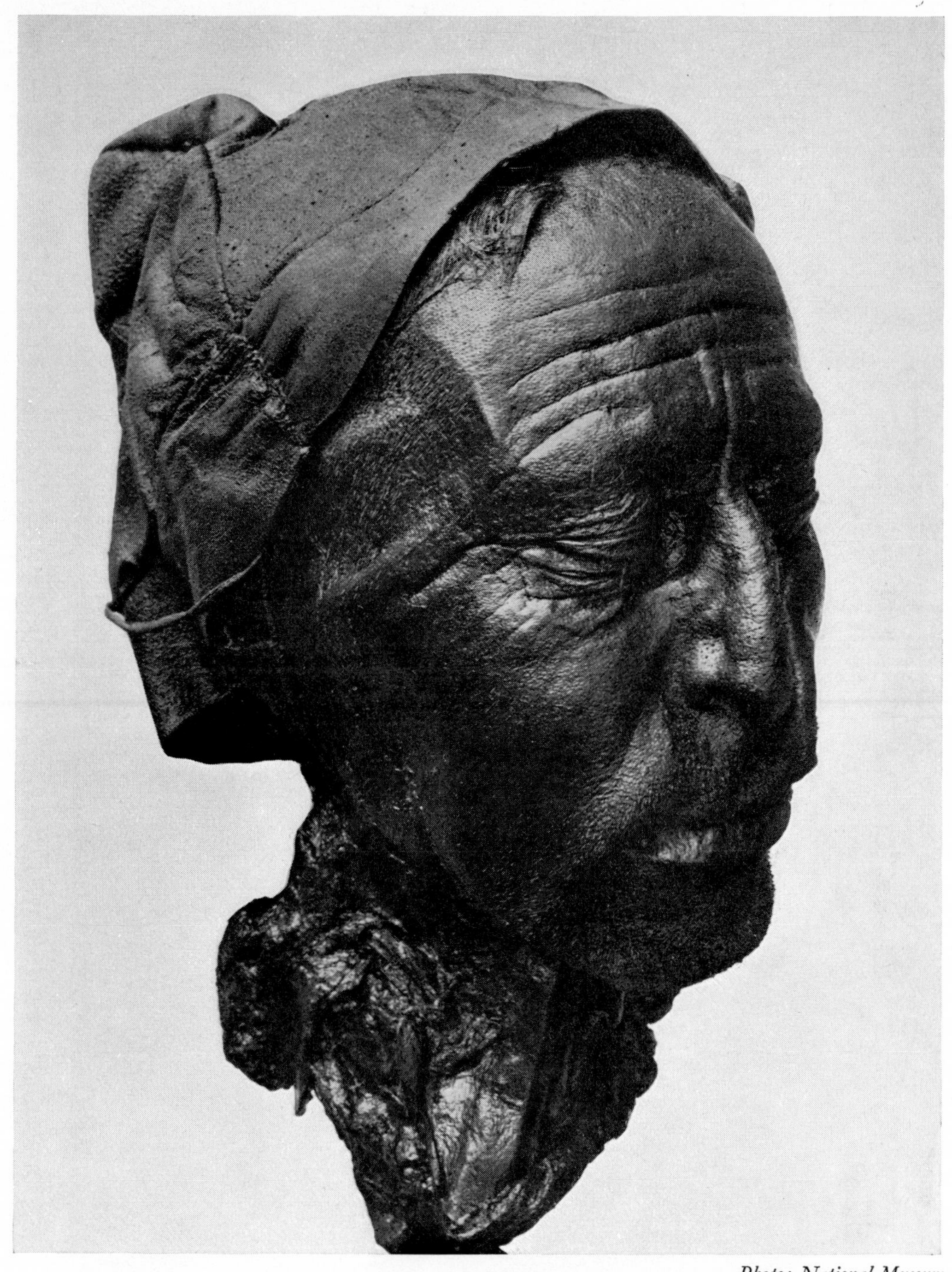

Photo: National Museum

PLATE 143. TOLUND MAN: head. *(National Museum, Copenhagen)*

Photo: Exclusive News Agency

PLATE 144. TIRYNS: the walls of the acropolis.

Photo: Radio Times Hulton Picture Library

PLATE XV. STONEHENGE: the circle of massive stone uprights, each weighing twenty-six tons, joined by lintel stones of which only five are still in position.

This technique was formerly called the "wooden hammer technique" because it was thought that it was the "woodenness" of the cylindrical hammer that was the essence of the technique. Experiment, however, has shown us that it is rather the cylindrical factor that is important in the technique and that a cylindrical hammer of bone or stone will work equally as well as a wooden one.

In point of fact, it is not even necessary to have a cylindrical object to use as a hammer to achieve success. The real essential is a curved side. For example, the lower surface of the jaw bone of a zebra or giraffe will serve very well indeed for the hammer in practising this technique.

Small flakes are detached from the larger flake or block of stone which is being hammered by hitting with the rounded edge of the "cylinder hammer" instead of with the point of a stone hammer. The impact of the blow is imparted along a narrow arc and the resulting flake scar when the flake has been removed is quite different from that resulting from the use of a hammer-stone.

The third major technique of flaking stone may be termed controlled flaking, and there are several minor variants. Its essence is to strike the blow with a very fine-pointed hammer, or a punch, in a very precise manner and with what is called "follow-through". At the same time the outer edge of the block or core from which the flake is to be detached is held firmly against the knee or a block of wood, or else embedded in clay or dug into a hole in the ground. In this way pressure is applied to the outside of the block from which the flake or flakes are to be detached, while the detaching blows are being struck.

This technique, in one or other of its many variants, is needed to obtain long narrow blade flakes, of regular width, such as are to be found in many Upper **Palaeolithic** and later cultures. It is also the technique which is employed by the flint knappers at Brandon in Suffolk, England, to make the long flake blades which they use in their gun flint industry.

Fourthly, there are a number of variants of what is termed "pressure flaking". With this method, flakes are pushed off and not struck off the specimen that is being trimmed and shaped. Pressure flaking is normally only used for the removal of very small flakes. The term was originally applied only to one particular variant of pressure flaking, namely that of pushing off narrow, parallel flakes – as in the making of **Neolithic** and **Bronze Age** arrow-heads, **Solutrean** leaf-shaped tools, some Egyptian specimens, and modern Australian aboriginal tools.

For this type of pressure flaking a bone or ivory point, or the jaw of a rodent with the incisor teeth, can be used, and the tool may be hafted or otherwise. Sometimes two people work together, one holding the specimen and the other exerting the controlled pressure. Sometimes the work can be done by holding the specimen in one hand and the pressure-flaking tool in the other. Or again the specimen to be flaked can be held in both hands whilst the pressure is exerted by pushing the long handle of the hafted fabricator with the chest.

But there are other variants of pressure flaking which are not always referred to as pressure flaking. Among these variants are the use of so-called "triangular section fabricators" of stone to push off flakes in the making of small backed blades and **microliths**. In both these variants the fabricator is used to crush off the edge of a flake in order to blunt it.

Indirect percussion flaking is yet another technique and was especially used for detaching very thin and narrow flakes from the side of a blade in the process of making burins or chisels. It is possible to detach burin facets by means of a small hammer-stone, but the method is unsuitable and results in battered fingers and thumbs and in many failures. The indirect percussion technique avoids these difficulties. To make a burin by this technique the point where the little flake from which a small spall is to be detached is held lightly against an anvil and the opposite edge of the blade flake is then tapped with a piece of wood. This tap forces the other edge against the anvil at the correct point and, if the angle is correct, a very small narrow flake is removed. The so-called "tortoise core" or "prepared core" technique which was used by the **Levalloisian** culture makers in Europe, by the **Sangoan** and other cultures in Africa, and later by many Neolithic peoples, is a variant of the stone-hammer technique combined with the controlled flaking technique. The flake to be struck off ultimately is first of all "blocked out" on the face of the core, by removing a number of smaller flakes from a number of different directions and the finished tool is then detached by a single blow. If the preliminary work has been well done no secondary re-trimming is necessary, or, at the most, the barest minimum.

The principal facts that emerge from the study of stone tool techniques are that the knowledge of the right methods and of the right direction from which to apply the blow or the pressure is more important than brute force, and that since there are so few ways in which stone can be successfully flaked it is likely that any of the given techniques may have been independently invented in different places at different times and that, therefore, the use of an identical technique does not necessarily imply "culture contact".

Strandlopers, *see* Africa, Stone Age Man in South.

Stratification or **Stratigraphy.** The method of defining and describing the ages and limits of the different strata in the rocks or soil, the principle being that the latest in date are at the top and the oldest at the bottom *(see* **Archaeology**).

Stratum (plural-strata). A layer; in geology, a layer of the **sedimentary rocks**, in archaeological excavation, a layer containing the debris of one period of occupation.

Stupa. An Indian burial mound *(see* **Sanchi** *and* **Anuradhapura**).

Sudan. The Sudan actually extends from the Red Sea to the Atlantic south of the Sahara. This article is restricted to what was until recently the Anglo-Egyptian Sudan, and mostly to the northern part. This is archaeologically a southern extension of Egypt. Geographically this Sudan consists of the Nile Valley above Egypt, including the Red Sea hills and littoral as far as **Ethiopia**, and is bounded by Kenya, Uganda and the Belgian Congo in the south. It includes Darfur in the west, and is there roughly bounded by the Nile-Congo divide.

From the Old **Stone Age,** man's earliest **pebble tools** occur in high gravel near the second cataract. **Hand-axes** of the **Acheulian** culture occur sporadically to about fifty miles south of Khartoum. South of that, much of the topography may be recent and the Old Stone Age levels far below the present surface. The Acheulian is followed by, and hybridized with, the **Levalloisian**, and it develops into a culture called in east Africa **Sangoan** (originally named Tumbian). The earliest fossil skull is that of a proto-Bushman from **Singa** on the Blue Nile associated with Levalloisian tools.

In the Khartoum area during the last wet period, about 8000–5000 B.C., Negro hunters and fishers had a **Mesolithic** culture with **stone tools** related to the **Capsian** of north Africa and the **Wilton** of east and South Africa, and the earliest pottery known. This culture has been traced from Kassala to Borkou in the west, more than 1000 miles away. It is followed by a **Neolithic** era in which the pottery is burnished and sometimes has the black top decoration characteristic of predynastic Upper Egypt, with other features (stone "gouge" and amazonite beads) shared with the **Faiyum** Neolithic (and perhaps derived from Tibesti).

About 3000 B.C. King Jer of the first dynasty of Egypt recorded near the second cataract his conquest of that area, and Egyptian imports of that period occur there in tombs with a fine native pottery that also occurs near Khartoum.

Rock pictures occur along the Nile between the first and third cataracts and sporadically elsewhere. Some representing wild animals are prehistoric, but all historic periods are represented.

During the Old Kingdom, Egypt at first raided the north Sudan, no doubt destroying the earlier civilization, thus accounting for absence of sites from this period. Under the fifth and sixth dynasties, raids were replaced by trading expeditions into the interior, recorded by caravan leaders on their tombs at Aswan. They brought back ivory, leopard skins, etc., and at least one dwarf.

After the collapse of the Old Kingdom, a cattle-owning people with black pottery, making flat-topped stone tombs, settled in the Nile Valley between the second and first cataracts. In the Middle Kingdom, Egypt occupied the north Sudan, building massive mud-brick forts, the three most southerly of which held the frontier at Semna, fifty miles above the second cataract. The best preserved of these forts is at Buhen just below that cataract. At the same time Egypt established a trading station south of the frontier at Kerma, the home of the chief of Kush, where they developed local industries, including the making of fine burnished black-topped red pottery and ivory-handled copper daggers. Nile flood levels were recorded on the rocks at Semna. These show that the Nile was then twenty-six feet higher in flood than now. The forts were burnt when the **Hyksos** were expelled from Egypt.

The eighteenth dynasty then re-occupied the Sudan as far south as the fifth cataract where they left a boundary inscription and traces of a fort at Kurgus. It was all incorporated in Egypt under the viceroy of Kush, and many stone temples were built, the finest at Sulb by Amenhotep III, and one at Sesibi by Amenhotep IV, dated exactly by foundation deposits giving his name before he changed it to **Akhnaton.**

Towards the end of the New Kingdom, the viceroy of Kush played an increasing part in power politics in Egypt; but after 1000 B.C. we enter a dark period during which Egypt lost control of Kush. During the New Kingdom, exiled priests from **Thebes** had set up a religious centre at Napata near Jebel Barkal at the fourth cataract. There Piankhi, about 725 B.C., built the great Temple of Amun. He and his successors were buried under small pyramids at Kurru. Taharqa, the greatest king of the dynasty, built several temples in the Sudan, and cut four colossal figures of himself on Jebel Barkal. A disastrous clash with the **Assyrians** whose army had new weapons of iron, led to his evacuation of the Sudan. A temporary reoccupation by his successor failed in 661 B.C. Taharqa started a new royal cemetery at Nuri for his large masonry pyramid. The dynasty continued to reign at Napata until 591 B.C., in which year Psamtik II sent a force of Greek mercenaries with iron weapons which destroyed Napata, to remove any fear of reoccupation of Egypt by the Sudan. Thereafter **Meroe** near Shendi, the southern sub-capital, became the capital, although kings were buried at Nuri till about 300 B.C.

At Meroe the royal burials continued under **pyramids,** at first of well-built stone masonry with chapels decorated in Egyptian style, but gradually degenerating, by the fourth century A.D., to tiny monuments in red brick or rubble. A few contacts with the external world help to fix the chronology, as when a Roman army sacked Napata in 23 B.C. on failing to recover a colossal bronze statue of Augustus raided from Aswan. The head of this statue, now in the British Museum, was found under the floor of a palace by **Garstang** when excavating Meroe, 1909–14. He uncovered foundations of several temples and palaces, much damaged by rainfall and stone-robbers. The large mounds of iron slag found there have led to Meroe being described as the Birmingham of north Africa, and indicate its importance for the history and archaeology of Africa; for thence knowledge of iron-working spread both south and west. The kingdom of Meroe was overrun by its trade rival Axum about A.D. 350, and a dark period begins; then a small kingdom appears in the north with its capital near Napata, and its rulers buried under large mound graves; this is probably that of the Nobatae, who occasionally appear with the Blemmyes in the history of Roman Upper Egypt. Farther south many similar but smaller mound graves stretch along the river to south of Khartoum. *See* plates 129–130, pages 429–430.

Suez Canal. The modern Suez Canal, an artificial waterway about one hundred miles long connecting the eastern Mediterranean with the Red Sea by way of Lake Timsah and the Bitter Lakes, was opened in 1869, but the idea of a water connection between the Red Sea and the Nile Valley can be traced back to the sixth century B.C. A passage in **Herodotus** describes how the Pharaoh Necho (609–594 B.C.) desisted from the work of construction after a warning from an oracle that it would benefit only the Persians. The projected canal was completed by Darius, the Persian King, and probably followed the course of the present sweet water canal through the Wadi Tumilat. It could take two triremes (galleys with three ranks of oars) abreast.

Sumatraliths, *see* Hoa-binh.

Sumerians. Mesopotamian history before the Babylonian period is a recent study. About fifty years ago, the Sumerians were only known through the texts of **cuneiform** tablets, while the archaeological materials of the period remained unknown. By 1931 several excavations established the three periods which preceded the dynastic history of Sumer, named after the sites where evidence for each phase was first discovered – the Al Ubaid, Uruk and Jemdet Nasr.

The Al Ubaid excavations indicated that the first inhabitants of Sumer (the biblical Shinar) originally came from the highlands of **Iran;** they had settled in southern Mesopotamia by about 4000 B.C., and this Al Ubaid period lasted for at least 400 years. The area occupied by them was at the head of the Persian Gulf, which was then much higher than its present level. Much of the land was once submerged, but later the Gulf began to recede, and silt was brought down by the two rivers, thus converting it into marshland. Eventually parts of these swamps dried out, and habitable "islands" emerged, which were occupied by the Proto-Sumerians of Ubaid.

The material remains of these Al Ubaid farmers suggest a Copper Age settlement of the type found in Iran or Syria. **Woolley** discovered evidence of the reed huts and painted pottery of these early settlers. Boats were used for netting and harpooning fish; animals were hunted with slings and stone-weighted clubs, and wild fowl also formed part of the diet. Though subject to periodic flooding, these swamps, when drained, produced a fertile soil, which was tilled with flint-headed hoes while sickles of very hard-baked clay were employed in reaping the grain. Wild date palm also grew in profusion on the delta soil.

The second cultural phase was revealed at Warka, the site of one of the earliest Sumerian cities – Uruk, the biblical Erech. The material remains, more advanced than those of the first marsh-dwellers of Al Ubaid, indicate a foreign influx of mountaineers from Anatolia, who dispersed over both north and south Mesopotamia. With the Uruk period comes the invention of writing; cylinder-**seals** were now introduced, probably mainly to guarantee the authenticity of written messages. A further innovation of this time was the potter's wheel, resulting in a change of ceramic style. The **plough** and chariot were used, as were the bow and metal-tipped spear. The prehistoric peasant villages now developed into towns, which continued to remain mainly agricultural. Social life centred round the temple precincts, each town being dedicated to a special deity. The "White Temple" of Warka, built on an elevated platform, illustrates the advance made in mud-brick architecture since the earliest shrine at Eridu of the Al Ubaid period. Building façades were ornamented with buttresses and recesses, and interiors were decorated by cone mosaics in colour.

In the succeeding period of Jemdet Nasr, the cultural advance of the Uruk period was both absorbed and furthered. In the field of art, for instance, sculpture in the round appears in addition to bas-relief, the life-size stone head of Warka being a good example of the former style. The stone vase of Warka of the Jemdet Nasr period is of special interest because its decoration portrays probably the earliest representation of the Sumerian people. Vessels of copper, lead and silver were found among grave-goods and temple treasures, and the process of separating silver from lead was known. Prolific trade was carried on in raw materials with neighbouring areas, and in manufactured articles as far east as the **Indus Valley**.

In every Sumerian chronicle, the first landmark of great significance was **the Flood**; this event divides king lists into two parts, the first of which ends with the Flood. Excavations in lower Mesopotamia established the historicity of the Flood at **Ur** and other Sumerian cities. The Royal Assyrian Libraries at **Nineveh** produced inscribed tablets which described the Chaldean story of the Flood as dramatically as the much later Genesis.

Sumerian chronology begins with the third dynasty after the Flood, known as the first dynasty of Ur. An inscribed foundation tablet at Al Ubaid confirmed the truth of the tradition, and shows that this dynasty was inaugurated by king Mesanni-padda (about 2900 B.C.). At this period Ur was the prosperous capital of southern Mesopotamia. In architecture, this Early Dynastic period is characterized by the use of plano-convex mud-bricks which, among other uses, were employed in arches over doorways of houses.

In 2350 B.C. the **Accadians**, a Semitic-speaking people, established the dynasty of Agade under Sargon, and ruled over both Sumer and Accad, a federation of city-states. Inter-state warfare was a common occurrence, the use of irrigation water being often the cause of internal strife.

Under **Ur-Nammu** (about 2050 B.C.) and his successors, the third dynasty of Ur controlled a vast area from the Persian hills to the Mediterranean. However, Sumer was later conquered by the **Elamites**, who established their capital at Larsa. With the rise of **Hammurabi** (probably about 1792–1750 B.C.), the Babylonians reigned supreme, and the glory of the Sumerians was soon eclipsed. (*See also* **Ziggurat**.) *See* plates 131–132, pages 431–432.

Susa was the capital of ancient Susiana, a region in south-west **Iran**, referred to as Elam in the Bible. Geographically this area formed a natural extension of the neighbouring plain of lower Mesopotamia.

Since 1897 the site has been excavated by French archaeologists, and the largest collection of Susian remains of all periods is to be found in the Louvre. Today this **tell** has three mounds which span a vast period of time.

At a depth of about twenty-seven yards the earliest settlements of Susa were revealed in the citadel mound. There are two archaic levels, separated by about twelve yards with distinct styles of extremely fine painted pottery. The earliest culture (Susa IA) begins in the latter part of the fourth millennium B.C. with a well-populated village, and the excavations have revealed a cemetery of about 2,000 graves. A high level of technical achievement is revealed in the quality of the grave-goods; copper was in use, and the skilled manipulation of the wheel indicates that potters formed a specialized group of craftsmen. This early pottery was produced in Susa when the Ubaid ware was being discontinued at the beginning of the Uruk period in Mesopotamia (*see* **Sumerians**).

Ancient Susiana employed the undeciphered proto-Elamitic writing, a semi-**pictographic** script, in use before 3000 B.C. Though this script originated under Mesopotamian influence, it was distinct from it; from Susa it penetrated to the heart of the Iranian plateau, where it was employed for many centuries.

According to Sumerian records the most important Elamite city in about 2670 B.C. was Awan and not Susa. The latter was merely of commercial significance. During the **Accadian** period Susa was much influenced by Mesopotamia. Sargon of Accad must have captured Susa in about 2360 B.C., for his **stele** was excavated at the site; later, in Naram Sin's reign, the king's viceroy or *ishakku* governed the city. Monuments bore Naram Sin's inscribed bricks, and at Susa the Accadian language supplemented the native Elamitic.

For 400 years after **Kassite** rule in Mesopotamia, the history of Elam remains obscure. With the thirteenth century B.C., however, a new dynasty was established, during the rule of which Susa acquired great importance. The reign of Untash-Uban (1265–1245 B.C.) was significant for Elam's advance in material culture; the life-size bronze statue of Queen Napir-Asu, wife of Untash-Uban, weighing about two tons, reveals great skill in early metal-casting.

The zenith of Susa's greatness was reached in the reigns of Shilhak-Inshushinak (1165–1151 B.C.) and his successors. The numerous sanctuaries erected at Susa were further embellished by trophies of war, such as the Victory Stele of Naram-Sin, the stone bearing the code of **Hammurabi**, the obelisk and statues of Manishtusu from Kish, and the images of Marduk and the Lady of Uruk.

With the reign of Nebuchadnezzar I of **Babylon**, however, the Elamite Empire began to disintegrate. For the 300 years that followed Elam entered a dark age, and suffered in consequence.

When Cyrus the Great conquered Elam, Susa became part of the **Achaemenian** Empire. Classical sources frequently mention the splendours of the city, which became the administrative centre of the empire, and contained many of the royal treasures. Archaeological records of Achaemenian art and architecture at Susa do not fully reflect this splendour, for Susa was sacked by Alexander the Great, and later by Shahpur II, who completely destroyed the city and rebuilt it as Nishapur. However, the fragmentary remains of columned halls and figured friezes in glazed brick indicate the richness of ornamentation for which the Achaemenian palaces of Xerxes (the biblical Ahasuerus) were justifiably renowned. *See* plates 133–134, pages 433–434.

Sutton Hoo is immediately east of Woodbridge in Suffolk, England, on rising ground on the opposite bank of the River Deben. This famous ship-burial was one of a group of eleven barrows. The excavation of the highest barrow, (some nine feet in height) began in 1939 and an outline of iron nails still in position was soon recognized as belonging to a large ship. Although the timbers had completely decayed, their outline could be clearly traced in the sand and the size of the ship led the excavators to think that it was a Viking ship-burial similar to those which have been found in Norway. It soon became apparent however that the burial was of Anglo-Saxon date and contained the richest treasure ever to be unearthed in Britain, as well as giving most important archaeological information about the migration period of the Teutonic peoples in Europe.

About eighty feet long, this ship was in fact a huge rowing boat requiring some thirty-eight oarsmen. It had a beam of fourteen feet and its depth amidships was four feet six inches drawing only two feet when unloaded. It fitted neatly into a trench cut into the ground surface and then covered with an oval barrow of turf. The ship had already been well used when it was buried. The grave-goods were laid on the bottom in an H-shape and in the gabled wooden burial chamber, some seventeen feet long, constructed in the middle of the boat, was found some astonishingly rich gold jewellery including a great gold buckle five inches long, decorated with an interlacing animal pattern and large plain bosses. No light ornament, it weighed nearly a pound. This buckle was different in design from the rest of the lively polychrome jewellery, richly inlaid with garnets and coloured glass and very much like ornaments from the earlier Swedish boat-graves. A magnificent purse lid had a jewelled gold frame decorated with seven ornamental plaques and ivory studs and at the bottom of the lid a gold tongue engaged with a sliding catch. In the purse were forty Merovingian gold coins and two plain gold billets. The rich personal jewellery also included a pair of curved gold clasps used to attach two parts of a garment together by fastening at the shoulders. These are unique objects in type, shape and decoration, being hinged and decorated with garnets, mosaic-glass and filigree; the rectangular panels were filled with a **cloisonné** carpet-like pattern and surrounded by interlacing, a design unique in pagan Saxon times which seems to be a prototype of motifs occurring in manuscripts some fifty years later. At either end of each clasp was a design of interlocking boars with tusks and crested backs.

One of the most important items of the warrior's panoply was a sword with a golden pommel and jewelled crossguard. On the hilt are two gold filigree mounts and the sheath is decorated with two jewelled scabbard bosses which are themselves a further link with Sweden. The silver in the grave was a very mixed collection from eastern Europe or the Near East. These pieces were probably acquired by way of trade, as the workmanship was too poor for them to be political presents. Of the Byzantine silver only the Great Dish, called the Anastasius Dish, can be well dated. It has minute and fussy incised ornament which is of a late antique style and datable to the years A.D. 491–518. Other notable pieces of the silver treasure were a fluted bowl of late classical style and a set of nine decorated silver bowls dated to about A.D. 600. These objects bear out the description of the burial of Scyld in *Beowulf* who was buried with "many treasures and ornaments from distant lands".

Lying at the west end of the burial chamber along the wall was a remarkable standard of iron six feet four inches long with a spiked base and surmounted by a well modelled bronze stag with spreading antlers. It was probably a personal standard and treads at the bottom would have made it easy to push into the ground. Nearby lay an impressive ceremonial four-sided whetstone. Extremely heavy (weighing over six pounds) and carved on each base and at both ends with human masks, it had attached to both extremities a shallow bronze cup. Obviously this was a ceremonial and not a functional object. A large circular shield almost three feet across was decorated with stylized animal-head mountings and a large iron boss. This shield with its several repairs was probably a family heirloom and is very like early Swedish types from the Vendel cemetery. Old weapons were very often passed on with great pride and it is known from texts that heirlooms could be as much as two centuries old. Nearby lay a heavy bronze bowl with drop handles and a large hanging bowl which was placed inside it, and this in turn contained a small harp. Alongside lay a bundle of seven-foot-long spears.

Perhaps the most outstanding object amongst these peoples, from the point of view of prestige, was the helmet. The Sutton Hoo burial contained an iron helmet having a silver covered metal crest, silvered bronze eyebrows, an iron visor with gilt bronze nose and moustache, hinged iron cheek-pieces and a projecting neck-guard. Encircling the helmet were a series of panels depicting battle scenes. The design of this helmet is derived from a late Roman type and it is very close to helmets from the Swedish sites of Vendel and Valsgärde and is indeed very probably a Swedish import. Another helmet of this period is known from Britain from Benty Grange but this is of a different type. The Sutton Hoo helmet gives a vivid picture of the splendour of the Saxon warrior-aristocracy.

All this very beautiful jewellery shows a high level of craftsmanship in Saxon art, and the Scandinavian, Frankish, central European and Byzantine contacts of an Anglo-Saxon royal house in the seventh century are somewhat surprising.

Both the absence of a body and of personal objects tend to prove that the grave was a **cenotaph**. The grave-goods were merely intended for the use of the deceased in the after-life and, according to pagan belief, these needs would be very similar to that of everyday life. The absence of a body simply means that it could not be recovered for burial; perhaps the dead monarch lost his life at sea. A royal burial is obvious from the richness of the grave-goods, and the ten other barrows clustered around it suggest a traditional family burial ground.

Who was the person for whom this cenotaph was constructed? This is not certain but authorities seem to think that it was for the East Anglian king, Aethelhere, killed in late A.D. 655 or early 656, as he is the only likely East Anglian king at about this date, although recent examination of the purse contents suggests that the coins were collected together after 650 and that the burial is more likely to be nearer A.D. 670. Although Aethelhere reigned only one year, he was a man of personality and action. He was killed, probably drowned, on a northern battlefield, that of Winwaed in Yorkshire; perhaps this is why the ship burial contained no body.

The whole of this treasure can now be seen in the British Museum in London. *See* plate 136, page 436.

Swanscombe Skull, *see* Fossil Man.

T

T'ai. Speakers of T'ai languages are found today from Hainan Island to the Shan State of Burma, and in parts of south China as well as throughout Laos and Thailand where they form the overwhelming majority of the population. It seems likely that their home was in southern China where they developed an agrarian culture based on the settlement of valleys and the cultivation of rice. It is probable that a mixture of T'ai and Yao cultures, the latter a people of the Chinese interior who by the third millennium B.C. were changing from a hunting and collecting economy to one of clearing and shifting agriculture, gave rise to the **Yueh** culture which was associated with the rectangular section *Neolitic* axe and a large component of which moved south to occupy the islands of Indonesia. If the cultivation of rice is rightly associated with the T'ai, their importance in the subsequent history not only of south-east Asia but also of China will readily be appreciated.

Tajin Culture, *see* Mexico.

Takshasila, *see* Taxila.

Talayot, *see* Minorca, Megalithic remains in.

Tampanian, *see* Palaeolithic, Further Asian.

Tanis. The ancient mounds of Tanis, the biblical Zoan, lie at the mouth of the eastern branch of the Nile Delta in Egypt by the modern village of San el Hugar. It was the chief city of the fourteenth Lower Egyptian **nome** and one of the most important cities in Egypt from the time of the nineteenth dynasty (about 1300 B.C.). Though blocks inscribed with the names of kings of the Old and Middle Kingdoms have been found there, it is uncertain whether they come from contemporary buildings at Tanis or have been brought there from elsewhere for re-use during the extensive building operations of the nineteenth dynasty. The Great Temple constructed by Ramses II was one of the most impressive in Egypt, to judge from the size of the complex, though little remains of the actual buildings beyond the collapsed granite columns, isolated architectural fragments and pieces of statuary. The site has been successively excavated by **Mariette** in 1860, **Petrie** in 1884 and by P. Montet in successive seasons from 1929.

The city retained its importance in spite of the collapse of the Egyptian empire and sea power at the end of the twentieth dynasty. It was the chief port of Egypt for trade with Syria and Semitic merchant houses were settled at Tanis. It was the capital of the twenty-first dynasty and although during the twenty-second dynasty Bubastis rivalled Tanis in importance, some of the kings of that dynasty were buried in crypts beneath tomb chapels constructed within the complex of the Great Temple. Though mean in scale and workmanship compared with the great royal tombs of **Thebes,** the tombs at Tanis, discovered by Montet, have proved unexpectedly rich in metal-work. Particularly noteworthy is the gold mask of Psusennes (about 1000 B.C.), the silver outer coffin of King Shishak and a group of gold, silver and bronze vessels. This fine metal-work is indicative of the contact between Egypt and Syria during the tenth and eleventh centuries B.C. before the decline of the city set in with the rise of **Sais.**

Tardenoisian. This **Mesolithic** culture is found in Spain, France, Belgium, Britain, southern and central Germany, Poland and Russia and was probably introduced into Europe by tribes from north Africa. It is characterized by the use of **microliths** of standardized geometric forms. In Britain, Tardenoisian **stone tools** are of two kinds, indicating two waves of arrival: first, small blades of regular proportions, followed by geometric microliths in shapes such as trapezes, crescents and triangles. These microliths were undoubtedly mounted – a triangular one has been found embedded in the vertebrae of a Tardenoisian skeleton from the island of Téviec off south-west Brittany, indicating that it had been used as an arrow-tip.

Tassili Frescos. The Tassili is a sandstone plateau in the Sahara. On the sides of the deeply eroded canyons are enormous numbers of rock carvings and paintings (*see* colour plate I) covering in time, it is estimated, a period of over 8,000 years. Giraffes, rhinoceroses, elephants, oxen and hunters riot and sprawl over the walls of the canyons in unbelievable profusion.

Taula, *see* Minorca, Megalithic Remains in.

Taxila is for a variety of reasons the best known of any of the cities of ancient India. Situated on what was from **Achaemenid** times onward the main route into northern India and lying forty miles east of the Indus, it vied with Pushkalavati as chief city of **Gandhara.** Takshasila, the Indian name, is mentioned in the *Jatakas* as a seat of learning. Though often spoken of as a university, teaching must in fact have been similar to that of the Greek philosophers by discussion groups of pupils; and young men frequented the city as a place where sages lived and dispensed their learning. Panini, the great Sanskrit grammarian, was supposed to have attended these classes, also Kautilya, minister of Chandragupta Maurya and compiler of the *Arthasastra*. Pukkusati, king of Takshasila and contemporary of Bimbisara (about 500 B.C.), seems to have been an historical character, and **Asoka** as crown prince was sent by his father Bindusara to quell a rebellion at that city. Alexander the Great paused here in his invasion of India to rest his army and receive tribal envoys. Though included between 175 and 75 B.C. in the realm of various Indo-Greek kings, it altered little in character under their rule. While in Parthian hands, legend associated it with visits by St Thomas the Apostle to Gondophernes and of Apollonius of Tyana to Phraotes. It is clear that by tradition the names of many famous people are linked with Taxila.

Three city sites and various monasteries cover the history of Taxila from about 420 B.C. to A.D. 500. The oldest site is that known as the Bhir Mound. Its remains are in four phases of which the last two, about 200–70 B.C., clearly overlap the first three of an adjacent new city now known as Sirkap, everything recovered tending to this conclusion. Hoards containing single fortuitous coins of Philip Aridaeus of Macedon and Diodotus II of Bactria were found at the Bhir Mound in an archaeological context suggesting their concealment about 170 B.C., when the Indo-Greeks were obtaining their first foothold across the Indus and times were disturbed. Sirkap was enlarged and fortified by Azes I about 55 B.C. and became a Saka-Pahlava city of some size, wealth and importance. Eventually it fell to another central Asian tribe, the Kushans; the upper three of seven archaeological levels at Sirkap are mainly Kushan and bring the life of the city up to about A.D. 100, some time previous to which a new fortified city had been founded nearly at Sirsukh, possibly by Wima Kadphises towards the end of his reign.

Close by these cities are the temple of Jandial, an enigmatic building with Greek features including two Ionic columns; the Dharmarajika **Stupa,** a huge Buddhist monument surrounded by a monastery; the monasteries of Jaulian and Mohra Moradu with a wealth of fine stucco sculpture; and the Giri fortress. This whole complex was virtually brought to an end by total destruction during the invasion of the White Huns in A.D. 460. Wide excavations by Sir John **Marshall** have recovered an immense number of articles of jewellery and household goods which help to bring to life the people of ancient Taxila. *See* plate 137, page 437.

Tell. A tell is a raised mound marking the site of an ancient city and caused by new mud-huts being built on top of the ruins of previous ones. At **Ras Shamra** the tell is sixty-three feet deep, twenty-three feet of which cover the period 3000–500 B.C.

Tell Atchana lies in the Amq plain by the eastern bank of the Orontes north of the modern frontier between Syria and the Turkish vilayet (province of the Turkish Empire) of Hatay. In antiquity it commanded the intersection of two important trade routes by which numerous products and materials entered the Middle East from Europe, Anatolia, the Aegean and the eastern Mediterranean. Its chief source of wealth was the export of cedarwood, felled on the slopes of the Amanus Mountains to the north-west.

Between 1937 and 1949 Sir Leonard **Woolley** conducted six seasons of excavation at Atchana in the interests of the British Museum. He distinguished seventeen main occupation levels, designated I–XVII from the top downwards. Since Level XVII lay below the water-table little was learned of the earliest settlements, save that their inhabitants were an early bronze-using people who introduced wheel-thrown pottery undiscovered outside the Amq. They apparently forcibly dispossessed the existing population who used a ware named after the Palestinian site of Khirbet Kerak. There was perhaps a temple from the beginning at Atchana. By Level XVI this was an extensive building with a courtyard containing an altar for burnt offerings and a brick bench-like structure with a "false-door". Part of this "bench" covered a brick-lined shaft filled with stones. The ritual which inspired these features is unknown.

To Level XII belongs the first palace. It is notable for a brick colonnade, architecturally unique in Syria at this date (2700–2350 B.C.) and doubtless copied from a Mesopotamian example such as that in the Early Dynastic palace at Kish. From the Level VII palace and temple come our first **cuneiform** documents revealing that the town was called Alalakh and belonged to the Amorite kingdom of Yamkhad, of which the capital was Aleppo. Yarim-lim, a contemporary of **Hammurabi** of Babylon, was the most powerful king of Yamkhad during this period and probably ruled from Alalakh since the town boasted an elaborately planned palace besides a strongly fortified citadel and main gateway. In the palace were found painted frescos similar technically to those in the Palace of Minos at **Knossos** but over a century older.

After the destruction of Aleppo by Mursilis I of Hatti, Alalakh passed through a period during which she was by turns the vassal of Egypt and the **Hurrians.** The most interesting document of these times is the autobiography of King Idri-mi inscribed on his statue found buried under the floor of the Level I temple annexe. After the defeat of the Hurrians by Shubbiluliuma of Hatti, Alalakh became a **Hittite** military strong-point. Nevertheless a revolt followed Shubbiluliuma's death and the Hittite "Hilani"-style temples of this level (III) were burnt down. The construction of a new defence system followed the restoration of order (Level II). At this time "Atchana ware" appears, a local variant of the Hurrian "Nuzu ware", bearing a painted floral design seemingly derived from an earlier Cretan motif. Towards the end of Level I Alalakh again revolted, but after a brief independence the town was destroyed by the **Sea Peoples** in 1194 B.C. *See* plates 135, 138, pages 435, 438.

Tell el Amarna is a collection of ruins and rock tombs in Upper Egypt, near the east bank of the Nile, 190 miles above Cairo. The ruined city of Akhetaton was built there by Amenhotep IV in 1360 B.C., as the new capital of his empire in place of **Thebes,** when he devoted himself to the worship of the sun and changed his name to **Akhnaton.** On his death, the court returned to Thebes and Akhetaton became uninhabited after only fifty years of existence. The lines of its streets and the ground plans of its houses are still traceable. The chief ruins are those of the Royal Palace and the House of the Rolls. Little remains of the Great Temple. In the Palace are four pavements of painted stucco, found by Sir Flinders **Petrie** in 1891. Three hundred clay tablets were found in the House of the Rolls inscribed in **cuneiform** characters. These are letters and documents addressed to Akhnaton and his father from neighbouring kings and governors, and have proved invaluable in the reconstruction of the history of the period.

Hewn out of the sides of the hills to the east are two groups of tombs of this period, the most important being that of Meri-Ra, high priest of the sun. Later the tombs were inhabited by Copts, who converted one of them into a church. In one building, known as the House of the Sculptor, a series of plaster masks taken from dead and living faces was found. Here also was found the famous coloured stone head of Queen Nefertiti, which illustrates the new impulse towards freedom and naturalism in art encouraged by Akhnaton, but which was soon overcome by the old stylized conventions.

Temenos. An artificial raised platform found in the plains of southern **Iraq**; in ancient Greece, a sacred enclosure.

Tène, La. The Swiss **Iron Age** type site of La Tène ("the shallows") lies at the east end of Lake Neuchâtel near the village of Marin, some five miles from the town of Neuchâtel itself. Originally the site lay at the mouth of the River Thièle, which, now canalized, runs out into the lake slightly to the east of its original course. Although 1858 is the first recorded mention of the site, the major finds at La Tène came when, as a result of the rectification of the Jura waterways from 1868 to 1881, the level of the lake fell by some feet. Between 1907 and 1917 a special commission was at work excavating the old river bed. The structural features revealed were of considerable interest; in a rough triangle spread across the original line of the river for some five hundred feet was found a mass of piles bounded at the north and south by two causeways carefully constructed with jointed sleeper beams, iron nails and clamps, and horizontal planks.

From within this area came a mass of finds, wood being preserved no less than metal by the alluvial silt which covered everything. Most spectacular and interesting among the wooden objects was a complete ten-spoked chariot wheel some three feet in diameter, bound with a sweated-on iron tyre. Of the two yokes discovered, each for a pair of light horses, one made of oak was complete and measured three feet nine inches. A parallel is shown on the Pergamon reliefs amongst the booty of the Galatae. Parts of what seem to be a pack saddle were also found, while smaller objects connected with traction include bronze horse-bits and other horse trappings. Other wooden objects include turned bowls (simple domestic pottery was very rare at La Tène), part of a long bow and oval shields, some with the pointed oval bosses and metal arm grips which evolved at the close of the Early La Tène period, and occur as far abroad as in the more or less contemporary ship burial of Hjortspring in Denmark, and a third century B.C. mercenary's grave at Kasir el Herit in the **Faiyum** – eloquent evidence of the widespread wanderings of the early Celts. Other warlike finds from La Tène include no less than 166 swords and 270 spear-heads, many in virtually mint condition. Several of the swords were contained within bronze sheaths, decorated with a curvilinear style, often incorporating strange sea-horse and dragonesque beasts, a style evolved in eastern Europe and incorporating nomadic elements. What appear to be smiths' marks decorate the iron blades themselves. Several of the spears have a graceful undulating edge, echoing the patterns on the sword scabbards. Amongst other objects, five amber beads show the continuing popularity of this long favoured import, while amongst other non-military metal-works was a whole range of axes, reaping hooks, scythes and shears and a small cauldron with a suspension chain. A few metal- and wood-working tools were also found. This mass of metal-work evidently belongs to what is known as the Middle La Tène period, the time of the great Celtic migrations. Important for dating are not only the form of the swords, long parallel-sided blades with blunted points and scabbard tops, but also the large number of fibulae only some dozen of which do not have the bent-back foot attached to the highest part of the bow by a separate collar which is another trade mark of Middle La Tène. Eight Celtic gold coins of about the third century B.C. copy a coin of Philip II of Macedon showing obverse a head of Apollo and reverse a quadriga, which was to remain a model until well after the Roman conquest of Gaul, being introduced into Britain in about 150 B.C. The lower date for the site is indicated by a few Late La Tène swords which, signs of burning suggest, may perhaps belong to the period of the incursions of the Germanic Cimbri at the close of the second century B.C.

As to the purpose of the site, it was clear from the earliest investigations that it could not represent a normal **lake dwelling** or lake-side settlement, the absence of pottery being one significant factor. On the other hand, a second suggestion, that La Tène was a customs or trading centre on the communication route with the Italian markets via the St Bernard Pass and the Swiss rivers is hardly possible in the absence of any exotic goods which mark the rich chieftain's grave of the early period, for instance at **Somme-Bionne,** or imported wares as in the latest levels of occupation at the **Heuneburg** However, the nearby finds from Port and the north-east end of Lake Biel on the Nidau-Büren Canal offer a clue. Here, in contrast to La Tène itself, much of the material belongs to the latest phase of the La Tène culture, as does a sword bearing a punch mark (copied in all likelihood from a classical cameo) and the Celtic name "Korisios" in Greek characters. The blade, like many from somewhat later bog deposits in Denmark, had been intentionally bent and this, with the few skeletons found at La Tène and the report of a corpse with a noose of hemp round its neck, once more recalling Denmark, suggests that they formed Celtic votive deposits like those mentioned by classical authors. Strabo, for instance, writes of treasure having been amassed by the Volcae Tectosages "in sacred precincts and ... pools" in the region of Toulouse, and there was the mass of objects found at Llyn

Cerrig Bach in Anglesey – Mona, the site of the last-ditch stand in A.D. 61 of the Celts and their **Druid** leaders. Further, the squatting bovine stamped on another sword from Port (a reminder of the importance of the bull in Celtic myth and symbol) together with the power ascribed to flowing water, clinch the verdict that La Tène is a great votive centre of the middle period to which it gives its name, with nearby Port as a possible successor of the Late La Tène period.

To fill in the picture of La Tène as a material culture, a concept first used in 1872 by H. Hildebrand, we must go farther afield; to the same Rhineland/Elbe area which produced the rich **Hallstatt** burials of Vilsingen and Kappel-am-Rhein. Here in the later fifth century B.C. the continued imports from the classical world and the introduction of the two-wheeled chariot – again perhaps under the influence of Etruria – coincides with the birth of the characteristic La Tène art style which at first relied mainly on Greek motifs derived from the retarded designs of Italy. This response to the needs of a warrior chieftain society and their inhumations supplies the richest material for this first phase of La Tène. Klein Aspergle in Württemberg contained not only an **Etruscan** *stamnos* but two poor though undoubtedly genuine Attic drinking cups of about 450 B.C. date, both broken in antiquity and carefully repaired by a Celtic craftsman with a gold leaf overlay decorated in imitation of the classical palmette design. The same grave contains a Celtic bronze copy of the **Etruscan** *oinochoe* or beaked flagon and gold sheep's head terminals for a drinking horn. All these objects made up a drinking set for the chieftain and his companion. The Celtic thirst for wine was the incentive to the Alpine traders and Massiliote middlemen in contact with the barbarian world. The idea of the funerary feast continues in the archaeological record into the later Iron Age of the north at the beginning of our era, when it was no longer Greece but Rome which supplied the necessary luxuries.

In the region of the Marne, Somme-Bionne and other rich chariot burials show that there too the Hallstatt tradition is not superseded but rather gradually evolves in the new wealth of early La Tène. On the other hand, the flat cemetery of Münsingen near Berne gives a good picture of the less exotic objects of the period: short two-edged swords evolved from the late Hallstatt dirks, broad-bladed knives as found in the Marne and in southern Britain (where the type offers some of the first clues for La Tène penetration), the first torcs or sacred neck rings of the Celts, influenced through the nomadic world from the East and fibulae in which the foot is free from the bow, unlike the Middle La Tène type, are all common. In the Low Countries a few rich graves represent the last resting-place of adventurous chieftains pushing westwards. At Eigenbilzen in Belgium a cremation in an Italic bronze cordoned bucket recalls the Hallstatt burial at Oss. The pair of Celtic bronze and coral inlaid beaked flagons said to have been found with a pair of Etruscan *stamnoi* at Basse-Yutz on the Moselle offer a trade mark for the skill and receptiveness of the early Celtic craftsmen who used an admixture of animal design stemming from the all-important nomadic art of eastern Europe and beyond.

Early La Tène is also the period of the first of the great Celtic migrations. By the beginning of the fourth century B.C. the Celts had not only swept down into Italy, sacking Rome in 390, but had actually settled in the north of the peninsula, while late in the period in Bohemia and Moravia, a cremating culture in the mixed Scytho-Hallstatt tradition, continuing the Italic and Etruscan imports, gave way to a new rich group of warlike inhuming agriculturalists. These used pottery recalling Marnian forms, and a new "plastic" zoomorphic style of metal-work, products of which reached far and wide. An example is the great bronze cauldron from Braa in Jutland which with its zoomorphic fittings is a find far beyond the true Celtic frontier. Farther afield a chariot burial inserted in a late **tholos tomb** at Mezek in Bulgaria lies on the route which led in 279 to a lightning raid against Delphi itself and finally to the settlements in Asia Minor. These raids proved such an embarrassment as to necessitate Attalos I's subjugation of the Galatae in about 240, commemorated in the temple sculptures of Pergamon, most famous of which is the "Dying Gaul".

In Britain, certainly by the second half of the third century B.C. if not before, a group of Marnian warrior chieftains had settled on the Yorkshire wolds, as is evident from numerous chariot graves. In Italy the Celts were checked only by the Battle of Telamon in 225 B.C. though they remained in virtual control of Cisalpine Gaul until 192. Among the Italian lakes, Middle La Tène cemeteries show continued links with the north Italian workshops while several Celtic weapon burials, including the typical pointed oval shield bosses, are sited at Este itself. In the south of France the fortress of Entremônt contains sculptured depictions of a Middle La Tène sword and shield boss, plus elements of the "plastic" style which demonstrates that the local population, though not fully of the La Tène culture, absorbed elements therefrom. Entremônt was destroyed by the Romans some time after the battle of Aquae Sextiae and the founding of Gallia Provincia in 124–3 which roughly coincides with the beginning of the last period of La Tène society. On the continent this is the period of the hill-top settlements, or *oppida*, where the material of late La Tène is remarkably uniform; swords have even longer and heavier blades than in the previous period, while fibulae feet are cast solid with the bow. Mont Auxois – Alesia where Caesar defeated Vercingetorix and the Helvetic confederacy about 52 B.C. – shows the intermingling of the middle and late periods while at other Gallic *oppida* Italic amphorae and sherds with Celtic names inscribed in Greek characters illustrate the continued encroachments of the classical world. In Britain the period before the conquest is one of tribal organization and enlarging of hill fort construction, as in the latest native phase at **Maiden Castle** (*see* plate 75, page 249), partly as a result of the migrations of the cremating Belgae, who were mentioned by Caesar as a Celtic speaking people of trans-Rhenish origin.

But it was not only the relentless spread of Rome which led to the decline of La Tène society, but also pressure from those northern tribes, such as the Cimbri and Teutones, who, as we have seen, were a ready market for goods manufactured by the Celts. Indeed the great silver cauldron found in a bog at Gundestrup – manufactured in all likelihood in the silver-rich middle Danube region and decorated with a mixture of Celtic life and mythology – recalls Strabo's record of the Cimbri's presentation to Augustus of "their most sacred cauldron". *S*ee plates 139–141, 142, pages 439–440, 442.

Teotihuacán, *see* Mexico.

Tepexpan Man, *see* America, Early man in.

Tertiary Period. The **Caenozoic** era, the era of modern life, covers the last 70,000,000 years of geological history, and is most conveniently divided into two unequal periods, Tertiary and **Quaternary.** With a duration of approximately 69,000,000 years, the earlier Tertiary period has been subdivided into four epochs, the **Eocene**, the **Oligocene,** the **Miocene** and the **Pliocene**, according to well-defined increases in the proportions of modern shelled invertebrates in their faunas.

Although in some parts of the world rocks of Tertiary age appear to show uninterrupted passage from older strata, the period in which they were formed was generally one of widespread earth movements, mountain-building, and volcanic activity. The principal mountain systems of our world, including the great Alpine-Himalayan system of Europe and Asia, and the Rocky Mountain-Andean system of America, were uplifted during Tertiary times, whilst associated with these mountain-building movements were readjustments of the earth's crust which, in some areas, had expression in outbursts of vulcanicity. Such vulcanicity is seen in vast outpourings of lava in every continent of the globe. Crustal movements continued to modify the distribution of land and sea, but by the close of Pliocene times the main land masses had acquired the broader outlines of their present-day configuration.

Rapid changes in animal life followed the extinction, at the close of the preceding Cretaceous period, of the marine and terrestrial **dinosaurs** and flying pterodactyls. In the absence of such formidable competitors the lowly mammals swept into dominance throughout the world. At first they were small and feeble, but their spectacular evolution soon eclipsed all other animal groups; by the end of Tertiary times forms had developed which closely resembled modern species. Some of the earliest known ancestors of man must have also appeared before the close of the Tertiary period, for crude **flint** implements (**eoliths**) have been found in late Pliocene deposits of eastern England.

Tessera (plural – tesserae). Either a small block used in the making of mosaics, or a small square of bone, clay, etc., used as a token or a ticket.

Thebes was the capital of Upper Egypt from the time of the eleventh dynasty. In ancient times the city lay on the east bank of the Nile and the necropolis on the west bank. The main part of the town, grouped round the temple of **Karnak** (*see* plates 65, 67, pages 239, 241), dated back to prehistoric times. It reached the height of its supremacy in the seventeenth and nineteenth dynasties and tombs of this period reflect its wealth and artistic and architectural magnificence. After Ramses II, however, Thebes became only one of several capitals and in the reign of Augustus it was finally destroyed after various sieges and rebellions. It still offers the greatest collection of ruined monuments in the world. At Karnak is the great state temple of Amun-Ra with its vast columns, its hall of Ramses II and its obelisks of Hatshepsut and Tuthmosis II. There, too, are the temples of Mut, Khousu and **Luxor** (*see* colour plate IX), all of which are interconnected by avenues of sphinxes and rams. In front of the necropolis is a long row of temples including that of Amenhotep II which contains the colossi of Memnon, and the Ramasseum containing the colossus of Ramses II. Nearby, in the foothills, is the Ptolemaic temple of **Deir el-Medinah** and the terrace temple of Queen Hatshepsut at Deir el Bahri. Also at Thebes are the Tombs of the Queens and the Tombs of the Kings – which include the tombs of Seti I and Ramses III, and, most important, that of **Tutankhamun** (*see* colour plate XVI, plate 145, page 465). *See* plate 142, page 442.

Tholos Tombs. The term tholos (plural – tholoi) is used loosely to describe a circular building; when applied to tombs it refers specifically to the great burial vaults that were constructed throughout the whole of the Mycenaean period (about 1580–1100 B.C.). About fifty such tombs have been excavated in Greece to date, but there must be many more as yet undiscovered. They are almost invariably situated in the coastal area where the great Mycenaean centres flourished. At **Mycenae** there are no less than nine such tombs and they show very clearly the development from the comparatively modest vaulted construction of the late sixteenth century B.C. to the sophisticated architectural wonders of the fourteenth century known as the "Treasury of Atreus" (*see* colour plate XI) and the "Tomb of Clytemnestra".

As a rule they were excavated in the side of a hill (at Mycenae invariably so), but in certain cases they were built above ground (Euboea, Messenia), and in one instance, in Messenia, the tomb was constructed underground in the plain. At Mycenae a great circular shaft was sunk into the side of the hill and within this was built a corbelled vault in the shape of a beehive, having a diameter roughly equal to its height. The vault was packed round with earth and a mound raised over it, the top of which would show above ground. The approach to the tomb was by a long open passage way, or dromos, cut straight into the hillside. The monumental doorway was of great depth and capped with lintels of colossal proportions. To relieve the tremendous pressure of the superstructure on these lintels, the masonry above them was constructed on the corbel or cantilever system to leave a hollow triangle, known as the relieving triangle. But this was not visible as it was concealed by a casing veneer, elaborately decorated in the "Treasury of Atreus". The dimensions of this last-named tomb may give some idea of the grandeur of the later monuments. The diameter of the tholos was about forty-eight feet. The doorway, eighteen feet high and nine feet wide, was flanked by two half-columns, carved in relief. The inner lintel weighed about one hundred tons. The dromos was lined with **ashlar** blocks of considerable size and was 120 feet in length.

These tombs were royal mausolea built during the lifetime of a king. On the occasion of each death in the immediate family the tomb would be reopened and closed after the obsequies, the doorway being walled up and the dromos filled in with earth. The tombs were nevertheless conspicuous and almost all were plundered in ancient times. The only exceptions are the tombs of Dendra (Argolis) and Routsi (Messenia), both partly plundered, and a small tomb of the sixteenth century near the palace of **Pylos** (Messenia) discovered in 1957, as yet unpublished. Judging by the first two named examples, the grave-goods placed in them must have been incredibly rich.

The origin of the tholos tomb is unknown. Related structures of about the same date are known in the western Mediterranean (Spain, Portugal) and in the British Isles (New Grange in Ireland, for instance), but the connection is not clear. In Greece they seem to be indigenous. The oldest tomb known so far is the underground tholos in Messenia mentioned above (early sixteenth century B.C.). They may have been derived from the **chamber tombs** which in Messenia are sometimes circular in plan and like miniature tholoi.

Tiahuanaco, *see* Peruvians.

Tiryns is a prehistoric site in the Argolis in Greece, traditionally the capital of the legendary Kings Proitos, Perseus and Eurystheus. Proitos was said to have employed the Cyclops (mythical one-eyed giants) to construct the walls, famous even in the days of **Homer,** consisting of huge, uncut, limestone blocks with a filling of smaller stones and rubble, which have given the name of Cyclopean to this type of masonry of which the Tiryns walls are perhaps the finest example.

The Mycenaean palace on this site was first uncovered by Heinrich **Schliemann** and supplementary excavations were conducted by Kurt Müller.

Trial trenches indicated that the site was occupied in the Late **Neolithic** period and abundant pottery was found of the Early Helladic period (2500–1900 B.C.) from which dated the stone and mud-brick foundations of a large round tower quite unparalleled in this culture, though it might be regarded perhaps as only a palatial development of the round houses at Orchomenos.

Shortly after 2000 B.C. probably the site was occupied, like most of southern Greece, by the first influx of the people (almost certainly Greek-speaking) who used the grey wheel-made or moulded pottery knows as Grey Minyan. These people were addicted to narrow, draughtless halls entered through a porch at one of the narrower ends, with no exit at the opposite end and often furnished with a central hearth. This form of room is known to archaeologists as a megaron because it bears a strong resemblance to the megaron or hall of Odysseus as described by Homer. It used to be considered that the megaron was a northern type derived from central Europe where it was popular but it now appears that the oldest examples are to be found in Anatolia.

Only the northern portion of the high southern part of the mound was occupied during the Middle Helladic period (1900–1600 B.C.); practically no structures survive from that period and very little from the succeeding Late Helladic I and II periods (1600–1400 B.C.).

The earliest Mycenaean palace, the plan of which seems largely to have determined that of its successors, was only constructed early in the fourteenth century B.C. A strong entrance gate protected by square towers on the south-east corner of the upper mound gave access to an outer ward flanked by secondary buildings; from this a gateway opened on to an inner courtyard with the main domestic quarter on the north side of it. Nothing remains of that except the interior wall but since the plan of this coincides with that of the third palace we may assume a somewhat similar plan for the earliest domestic quarter. The southern part of the mound, at least, was already protected by a great Cyclopean curtain wall of the kind that gives Mycenaean fortresses the appearance of robber barons' castles. The second palace on the same site was dated about 1300 B.C. by Kurt Müller but Georg Karo considered that the new gateway at the head of the ramps, modelled on the contemporary Lion Gate at **Mycenae** (*see* plate 104, page 332), could not be much later than 1350 B.C. The southern half of the upper mound was now included in the palace proper and terraced up so as to allow palatial rooms at approximately the same level over double the area. The new outer and inner gateways at the head of the entrance ramps, which had presumably been constructed to allow horsemen and chariots to enter the palace, rendered useless the old fortified gate into the outer ward and this was therefore destroyed. Little remains of the actual structure of this palace, even though Müller identified two later phases which he labelled II A and B, but some fragments of frescos survived from the second palace. Most of the existing remains belong to the third palace which was erected early in the thirteenth century B.C. and occupied the higher part of the mound to the south. The northern part was left empty but was contained by the great curtain wall of Cyclopean masonry, to the north-west corner of which was added a square tower protecting a long curving bastion that masked a sally-port. Store-chambers were added on the south-east side (with corbelled vaulting) and at the southern end. On the site of the old strong gateway into the outer ward (swept away by the architect of the second palace) there was now erected an ornamental propylaeum (entrance) with columns.

The third palace, like its predecessors, was strongly influenced by the **Minoan** art of Crete, especially in its decoration, in the painted frescos, the shapes of the wooden columns and the decorative friezes. That this was no Minoan building, however, but the palace of a Greek king was emphasized by the presence of the long megaron with its central hearth and the secluded private suite for the ladies of the royal household.

The fresco fragments preserved included some that appeared to be copies of earlier ones at **Knos-**

sos, such as a miniature reproduction of the shield fresco from the grand staircase of the Palace of Minos, a toreador fresco like that from Knossos, and one of women bearing gifts like those of Knossian Corridor of the Procession. There were other subjects, too, not paralleled in the surviving frescos from Crete, such as the two young princes (sometimes identified as women because of their white skins), a horse-drawn chariot and the spirited boar-hunt.

The palace was sacked and destroyed like that of **Mycenae** about 1150 B.C. and it has been assumed that this was due to the infiltration into the Argolis of the Doric-speaking Greeks, associated in Greek folk memory with the return of the sons of Herakles. The site was not completely deserted, however. A Mycenaean megaron like that at Korakou was constructed in the ruins of the palace megaron (supposed by the German excavators to have been the foundations of an early Greek temple, but the right identification was made by C. W. Blegen). However, an archaic Greek temple did exist somewhere in the vicinity since the excavator found an archaic Doric capital and terracotta revetments of a seventh-century temple.

Tiryns was a small town of no great importance in the sixth century but it did send a contingent of eighty men to fight the Persians at the battle of Plataea in 479 B.C. In 468 B.C. its tyrannical neighbour Argos destroyed it along with Mycenae. *See* plate 144, page 444.

Tolund Man. Tolund Mose is the name of a narrow bog set amongst high hills not far from Aarhus in Jutland, Denmark. It was here in 1950 that Professor Glob excavated the body of a man in a most remarkable state of preservation. Discovered in the course of peat cutting it lay at a depth of seven feet in a slightly contracted position, the only clothing remaining on the body being a leather belt and a skull cap. The man had been hanged and part of a braided leather rope still encircled his neck.

The great interest aroused by this bog-burial lay partly in the evidence of violent death, but even more so in its wonderful preservation, the body being tanned by action of the peat. This enabled a series of unusually accurate statements to be made about circumstances before death. The stomach contents, for example, showed that he had eaten no meat for three days and that his only food had been a rather poor quality "porridge" of grain and wild plant seeds. This same period of poor feeding coincided with a three-day-growth of stubble on his chin.

This discovery was soon followed by another, made at Graubelle a few miles away. In this case the man had had his throat cut. In Schleswig-Holstein the bodies of a fourteen-year-old girl, blind-folded, and of a man, strangled with a hazel-wand, were also discovered.

These bog-burials were, however, no new thing; some hundred had been found previous to that of Tolund Man, with a very limited distribution mainly in Jutland and Schleswig-Holstein. They had been thrown into already-existing peat-cuts, naked or with a few clothes thrown in afterwards, but without any laying-out of the body or any grave-goods, and they had all met with a violent death. Their date should come within the bracket 300 B.C.–A.D. 300.

They were therefore executed, some as criminals, but perhaps mainly as sacrifices. It was a basic Celtic religious practice to put offerings in bogs or to throw them into water. Tacitus refers to such customs, and it is possible that Tolund Man was a prisoner who had been sacrificed in the course of a religious ceremony. *See* plate 143, page 443.

Tomb Robbery Papyri. These are a series of Egyptian **hieratic** texts reporting official investigations conducted towards the end of the twentieth dynasty (about 1100 B.C.) into thefts from the royal tombs and other sacred places on the west bank at **Thebes.** These papyri do not contain a systematic account of the robberies but some of the incidents and guilty parties are mentioned in more than one document. They give us one of our rare insights into Egyptian legal practices and are our most substantial body of documentary evidence for that despoliation of royal and private tombs which is so familiar to the excavator. The verbatim records of the examinations, the familiarity of the scene, the information on social and economic conditions at Thebes, make them one of the most absorbing and human of our ancient records.

At the time at which the papyri were written, the necropolis area on the west bank of the Nile formed a separate administrative area known as the "West of Thebes" under its own "mayor" who was independent of the "mayor" of Thebes proper. The earliest group of texts refer to incidents in the sixteenth year of the reign of Neferkare Ramses IX, but before this date plundering had occurred in the necropolis, at least among the private tombs. In one of the depositions a thief boasts that he has only been doing what everyone had been in the habit of doing. It is uncertain what brought matters to a head in year sixteen; it is likely that the robberies had become an open scandal and jealousy between the two "mayors" played its part. Certainly the initiative in the affair of year sixteen was taken, not as one might expect, by Pwero the "mayor" of the "West of Thebes" but by his colleague Pesiur, "mayor" of Thebes, whose reports resulted in the setting up of the Great Tribunal within the precincts of **Karnak** on the east bank, headed by the vizier Khaemwese, other members of the palace and Pesiur himself.

As a result of the investigation an inspection of the pyramids, graves and tombs was undertaken by the commission. The itinerary of the inspectors can still be traced (Abbott Papyrus): from the river they went up to the seventeenth-dynasty royal tombs on the plain before Dra Abut Naga, and to a number of private tombs a little to the north. The commission found that some of the tombs alleged to have been robbed were still intact, but that of Sekhemre Sebekemsaf, a king of the sixteenth dynasty, was found plundered. So also was the tomb of Isis, a queen of Ramses II. Certain parties were arrested but not all were convicted. The report of the commission was considered by the necropolis workers of the "West of Thebes" as a great victory: and the papyrus preserves some of the banter which the rejoicing crowd hurled at the discomforted Pesiur.

The incidents in the story present certain unresolved problems; it is possible that the acquittals were due to bribery. Certainly the general air of satisfaction was not borne out by subsequent events. Among tombs plundered after year sixteen were the tombs of Seti I and Ramses II, two of the most powerful of the nineteenth-dynasty pharaohs.

Though no other texts contain such a detailed glimpse of the background of the investigations, we read of examinations of alleged thieves, lists of spoil and many condemnations. The last of the series is dated to year six of the "Repealing of the Births", a new system of dating initiated in the reign of Ramses XI, heralding apparently the official policy of a vigorous restoration of public order. The robberies however did not cease and it was considered necessary in the twenty-first dynasty (about 1050 B.C.) to move the royal mummies from their tombs in the **Valley of the Kings** and bury them devoid of jewellery in wooden coffins in secret caches. It was from one of these, that at Deir el Bahri, that the magnificent series of royal mummies now in the Cairo Museum was recovered.

The parties to the robberies were drawn from the artisans and minor officials in the employment of the estate of Amun connected with the great mortuary temples. Later some of the workmen of the village of **Deir el Medinah** who constructed the tombs were also involved. The robbers worked in small gangs, penetrating into the tombs by forcing passages through the limestone. The chief objective was the metal (gold, silver, bronze, copper) which formed part of funerary equipment and in their attempts to gain it the robbers regularly burnt the woodwork to which it was attached. The metal was melted down or broken up into small pieces and divided into shares. Though there was no stamped coinage in Egypt at this period, goods were regularly evaluated against a weight of metal and the metal could be used in commercial transactions. We read in the depositions how the metal was disposed of by the gangs, for instance to purchase bread or land, or a slave. Undoubtedly the scale of the robberies reflects the declining prosperity of Egypt after the death of Ramses III and the consequent economic hardship and sharp rise in the price of grain. The circulation of the stolen metal must have assisted in the general inflation and this probably as much as anything is the reason for the vigour of the investigations.

The method of examination was simple: an accused brought before the court, if he did not confess, was subjected to torture, either by heating the soles of his feet or by twisting his arms. The application of these methods usually induced a change of mind on the part of the culprit. He would call out, "Stop, I will tell all". If his subsequent statement was not considered satisfactory, further torture was administered with the result that usually the accused not only fully confessed his part in the incident but also disclosed the names of his confederates and his share and disposal of the loot. Occasionally one reads the laconic entry that an accused was examined, found not guilty and released. The records do not contain the sentences passed upon the guilty; but the defendants swear to tell the truth on pain of banishment to **Nubia**,

Photo: F. L. *Kenett*

PLATE XVI. TOMB OF TUTANKHAMUN: under the entrance to the tomb of Ramses VI.

Photo: Radio Times Hulton Picture Library

PLATE 145. TOMB OF TUTANKHAMUN: alabaster objects from Tutankhamun's tomb: Vase with cover mounted on a stand and bearing the names of the king and queen. Figure in the form of a lion, representing the god Bes, protector of sheep etc. Below is a base. Base of vase, in the form of an ibex, the horns, one of which is missing, are natural. Two vases inlaid with faience and stone.

Vase with side ornaments representing the sign of life on a papyrus column. Group representing the Nile-god holding a vase.

Photo: Exclusive News Agency Ltd

PLATE 146. UR: fragments pieced together which tell how the building of the Ziggurat was undertaken.

Photo: Radio Times Hulton Picture Library

PLATE 147. Charles Leonard WOOLLEY (1880–1960), photograph.

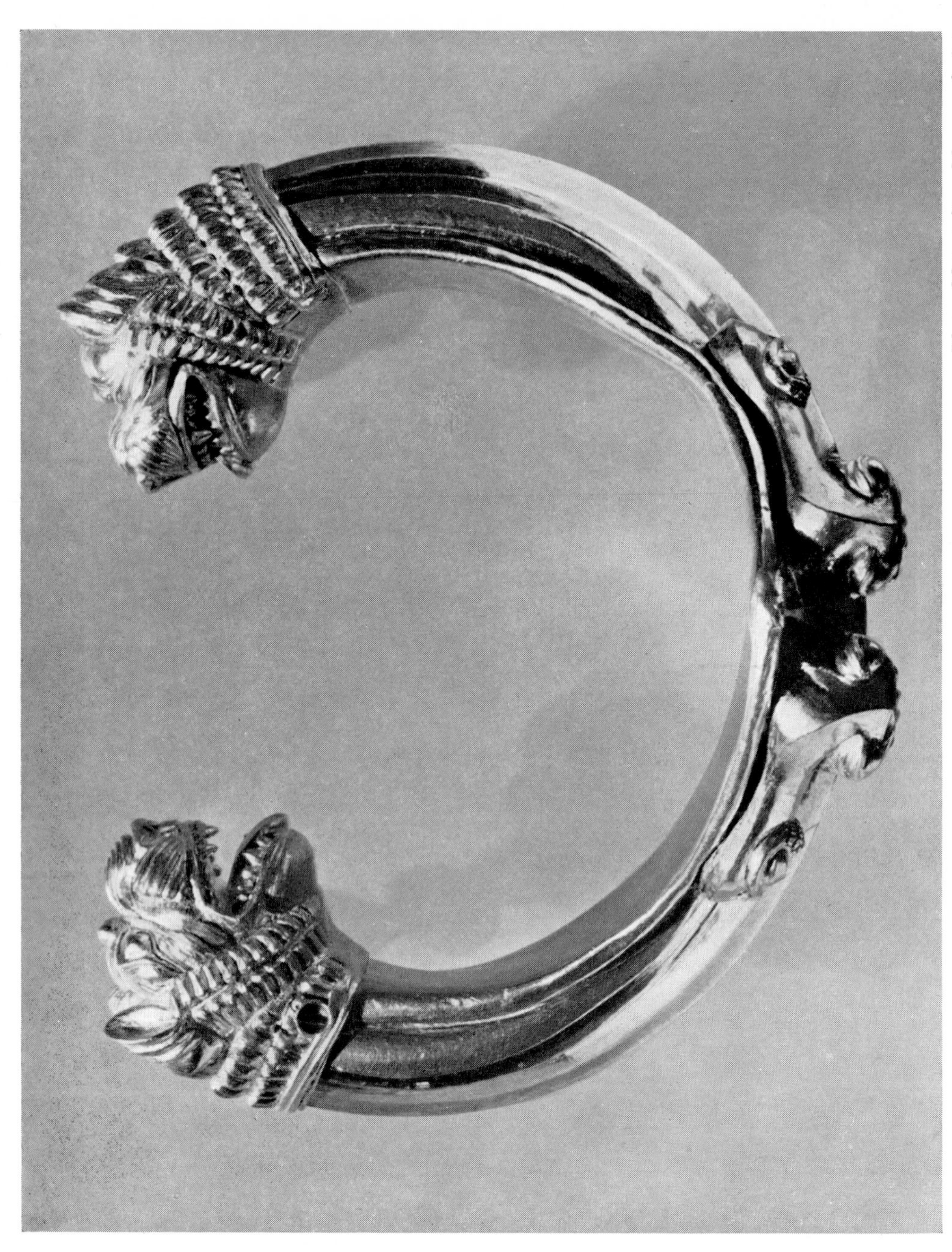

Photo: Metropolitan Museum of Art

PLATE 148. ZIWIYÈ: gold bracelet with lion head terminals, from Ziwiyè, about 700 B.C. *(Metropolitan Museum of Art, New York, loaned by Alistair B. Martin)*

Photo: Exclusive News Agency

PLATE 149. ZIMBABWE: the walls of the western temple showing the round turrets and one of the monoliths which alternated with them.

Photo: The Aircraft Operation Co of Africa Ltd

PLATE 150. ZIMBABWE: aerial view of ruins.

PLATE 151. AFRICA: map showing principal sites mentioned in text. See also map of Early Man·

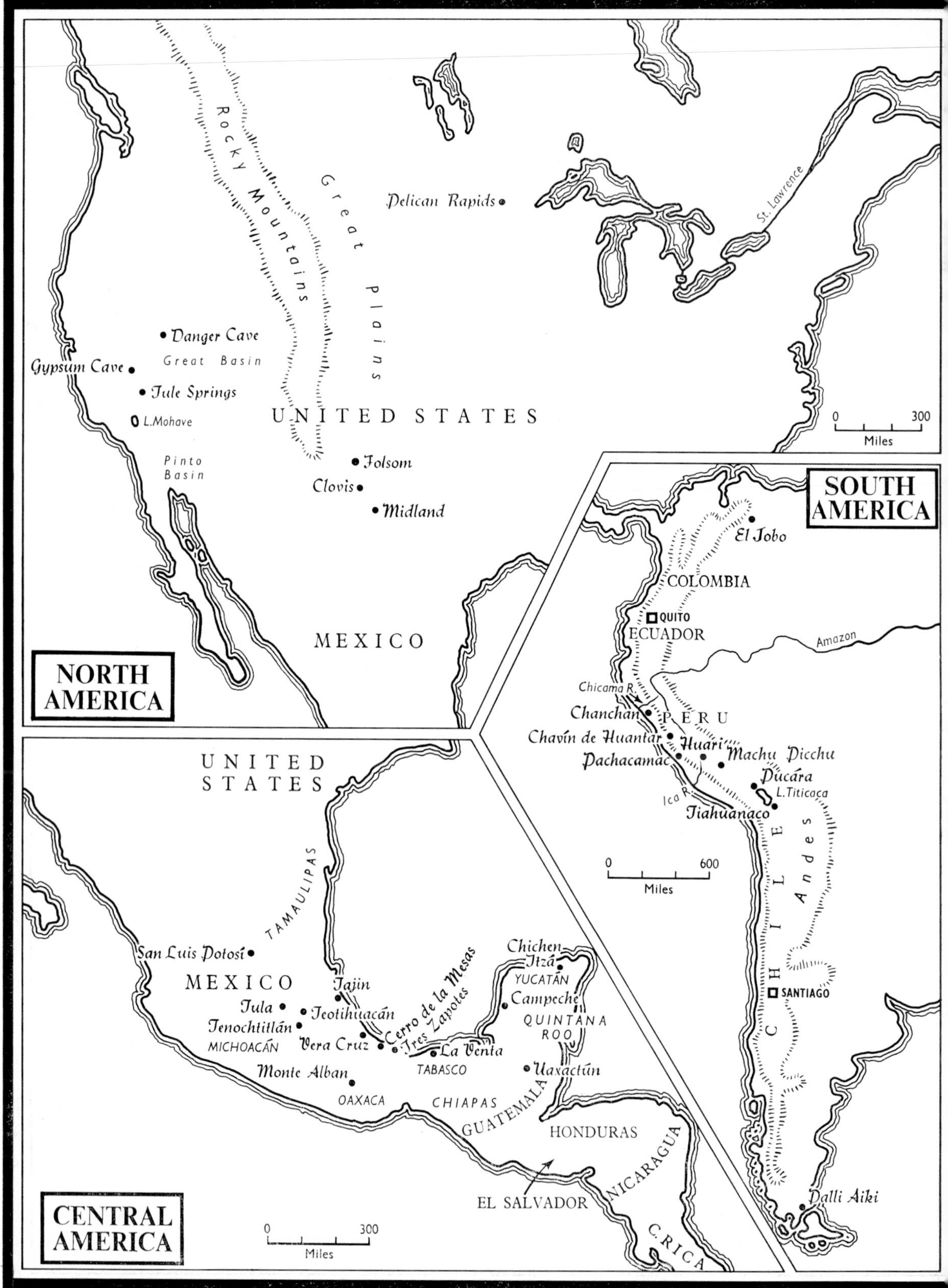

PLATE 152. AMERICA: map showing principal sites mentioned in text. See also map of Early Man.

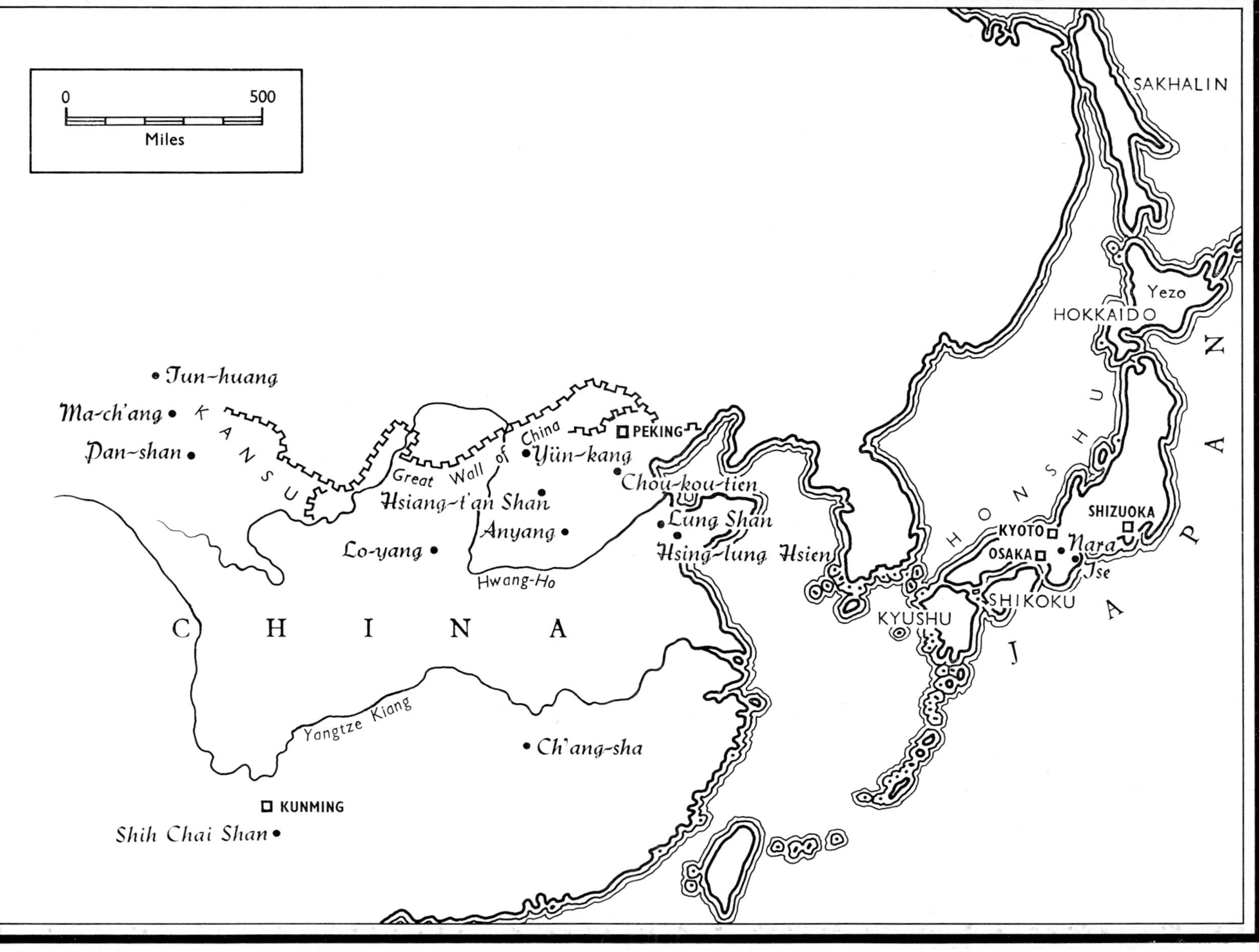

PLATE 153. CHINA AND JAPAN: map showing principal sites. See also map of Early Man.

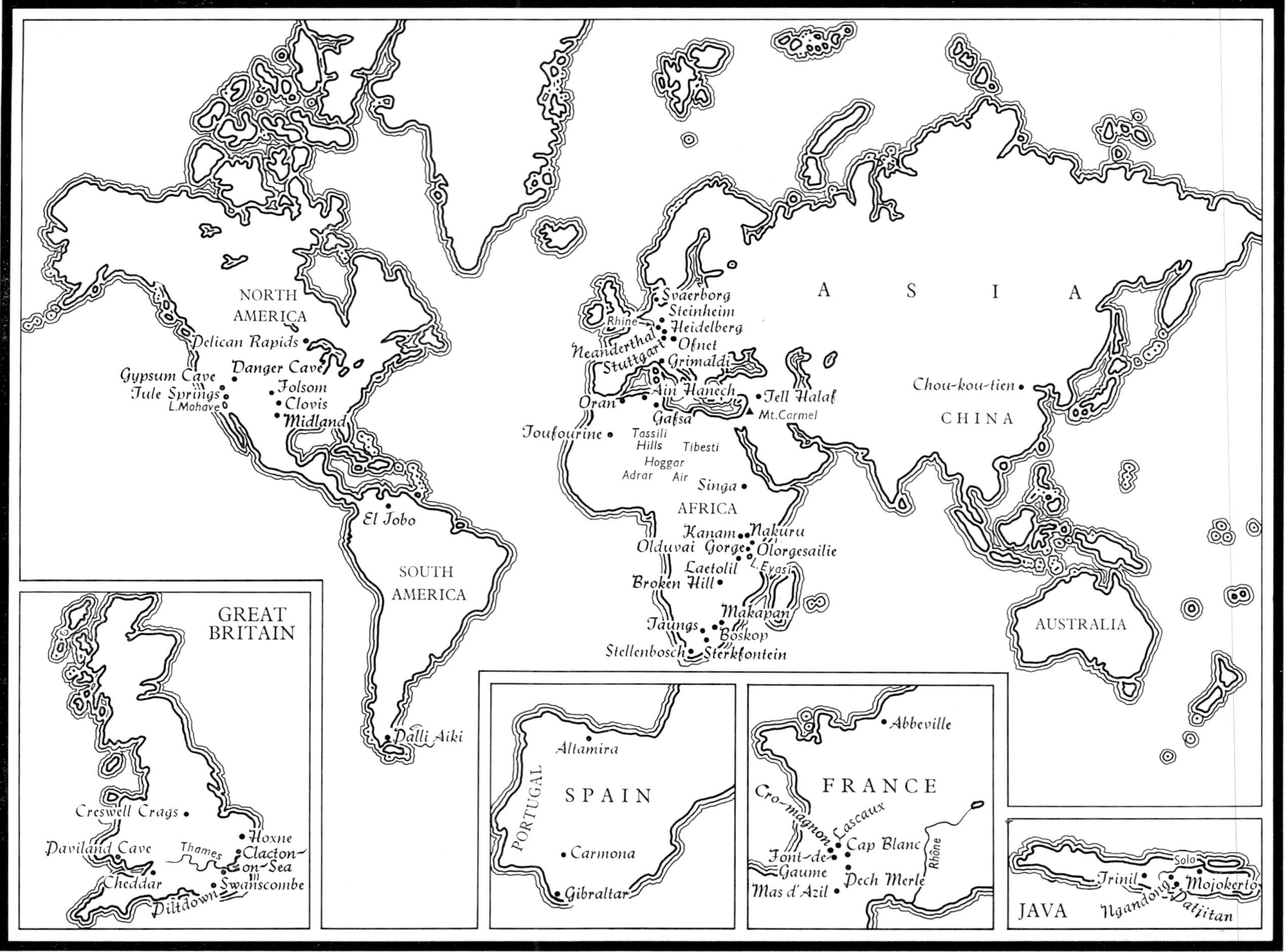

NORTH AMERICA
Pelican Rapids
Gypsum Cave
Danger Cave
Tule Springs
L. Mohave
Folsom
Clovis
Midland
El Jobo
SOUTH AMERICA
Palli Aiki
ASIA
Svaerborg
Steinheim
Rhine
Heidelberg
Neanderthal
Ofnet
Stuttgart
Grimaldi
Oran
Ain Hanech
Tell Halaf
Mt. Carmel
Gafsa
Toufourine
Tassili Hills
Tibesti
Hoggar
Adrar
Air
Singa
AFRICA
Kanam
Nakuru
Olduvai Gorge
Olorgesailie
Laetolil
L. Eyasi
Broken Hill
Makapan
Taungs
Boskop
Stellenbosch
Sterkfontein
Chou-kou-tien
CHINA
AUSTRALIA
GREAT BRITAIN
Creswell Crags
Hoxne
Paviland Cave
Thames
Clacton-on-Sea
Cheddar
Swanscombe
Piltdown
PORTUGAL
SPAIN
Altamira
Carmona
Gibraltar
FRANCE
Abbeville
Cro-magnon
Lascaux
Cap Blanc
Font-de-Gaume
Pech Merle
Mas d'Azil
Rhône
JAVA
Solo
Trinil
Mojokerto
Ngandong
Patjitan

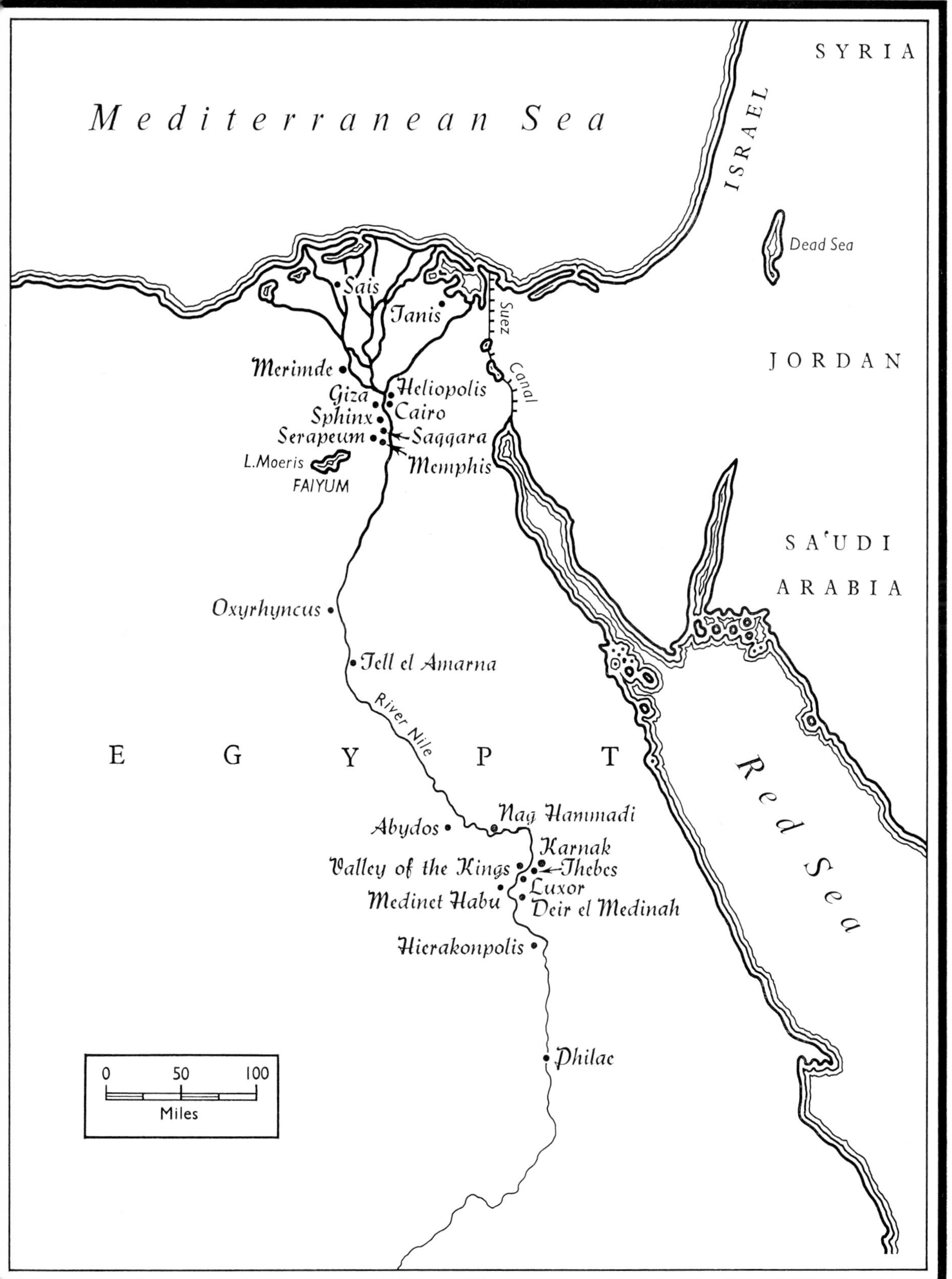

Plate 155. Egypt: map showing principal sites.

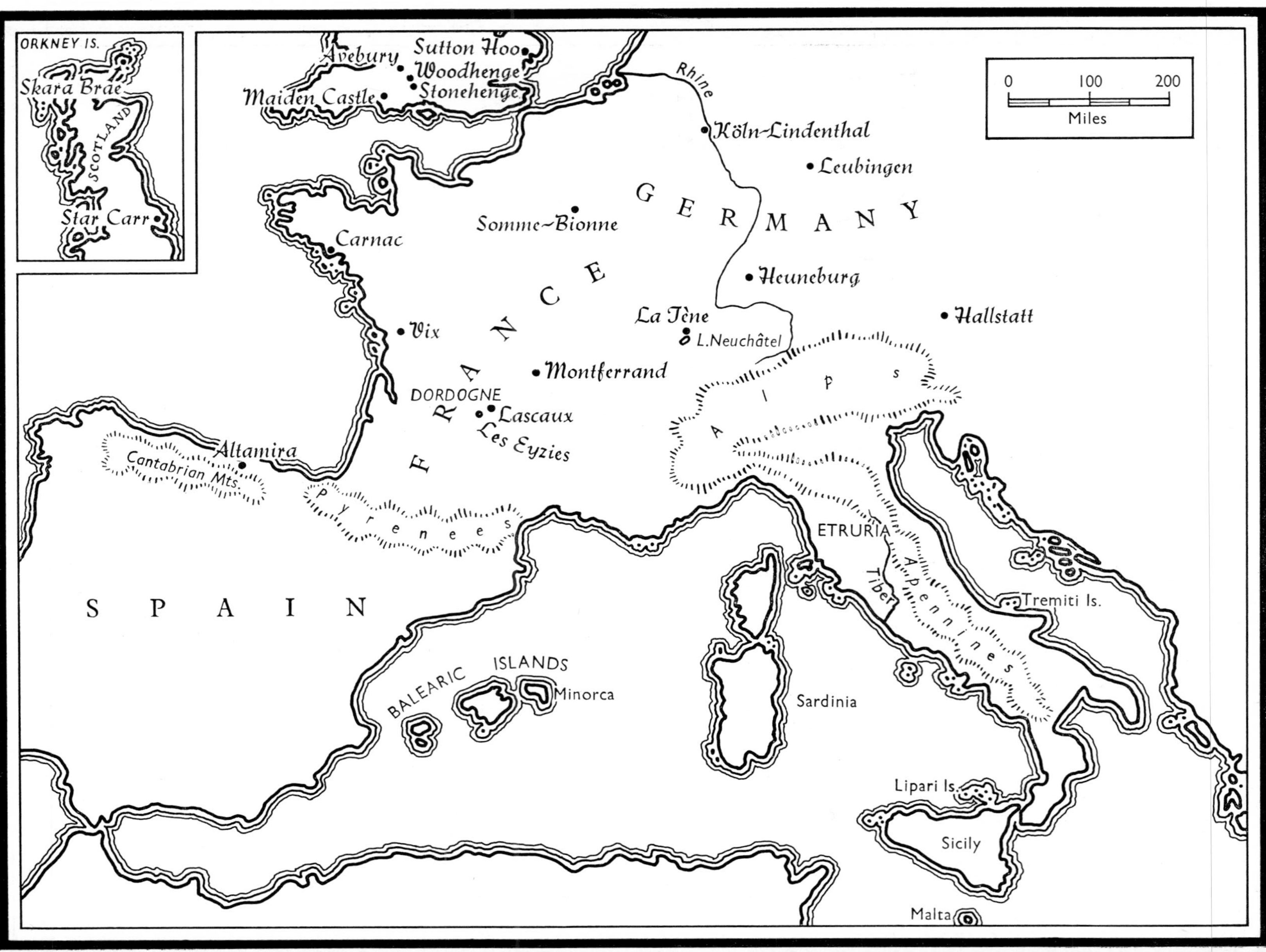
ORKNEY IS.
Skara Brae
SCOTLAND
Star Carr
Avebury
Sutton Hoo
Woodhenge
Stonehenge
Maiden Castle
Rhine
Köln-Lindenthal
Leubingen
0 100 200
Miles
GERMANY
FRANCE
Somme-Bionne
Carnac
Heuneburg
Hallstatt
La Tène
L.Neuchâtel
Vix
Montferrand
DORDOGNE
Lascaux
Les Eyzies
Alps
Altamira
Cantabrian Mts.
Pyrenees
SPAIN
ETRURIA
Tiber
Apennines
Tremiti Is.
BALEARIC ISLANDS
Minorca
Sardinia
Lipari Is.
Sicily
Malta

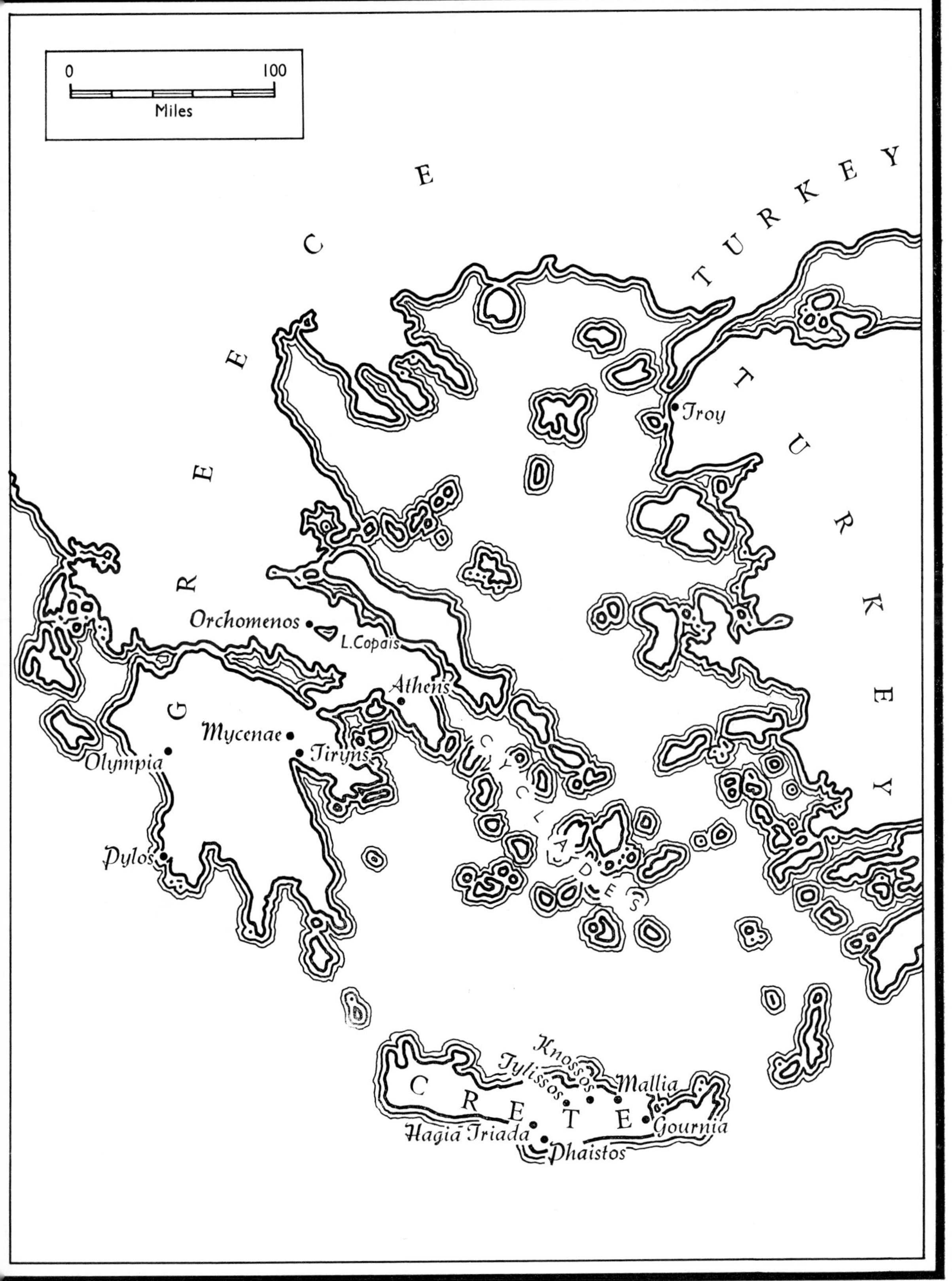

PLATE 157. GREECE AND THE EASTERN MEDITERRANEAN: map showing principal sites.

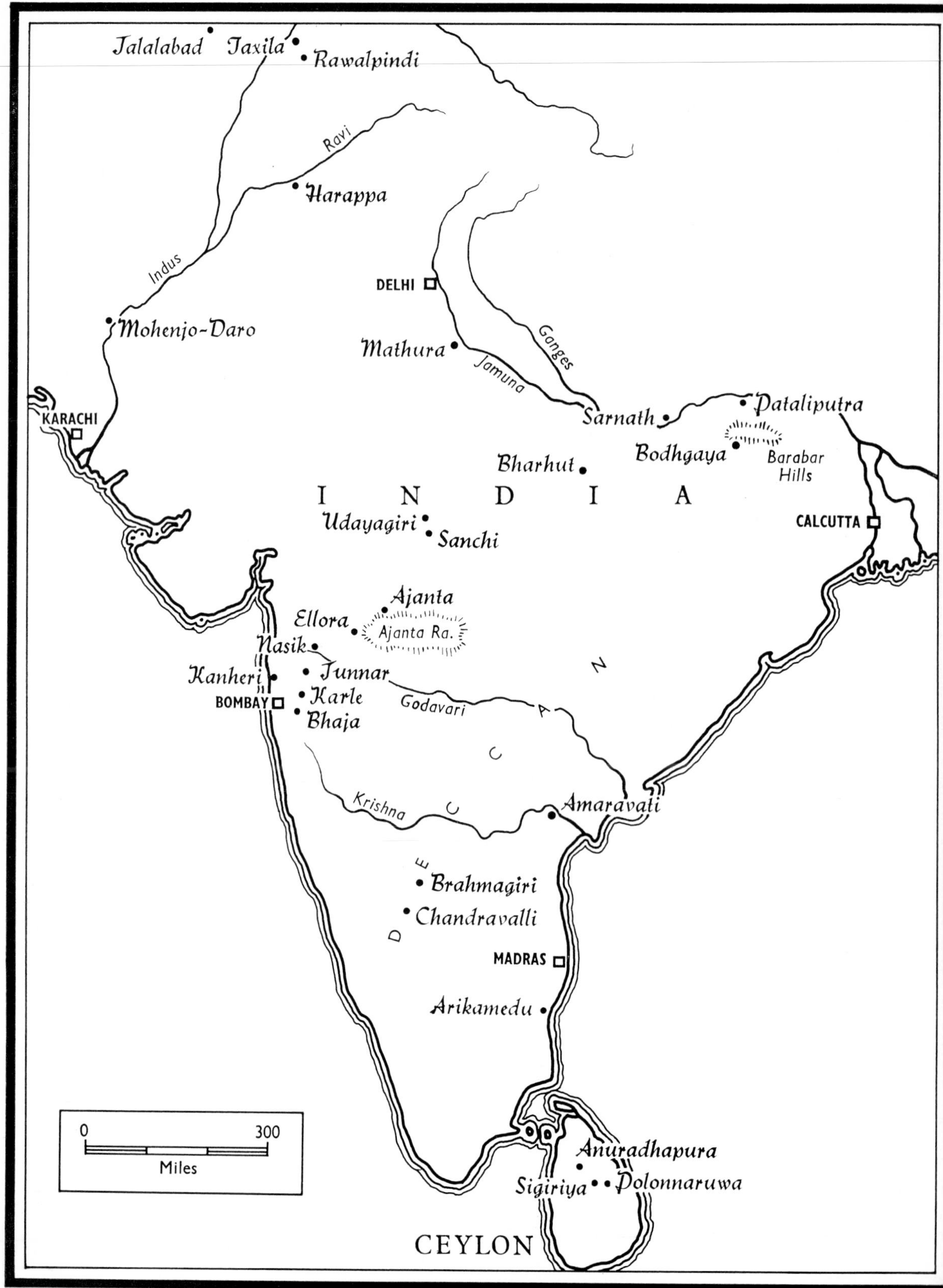

PLATE 158. INDIA: map showing principal sites.

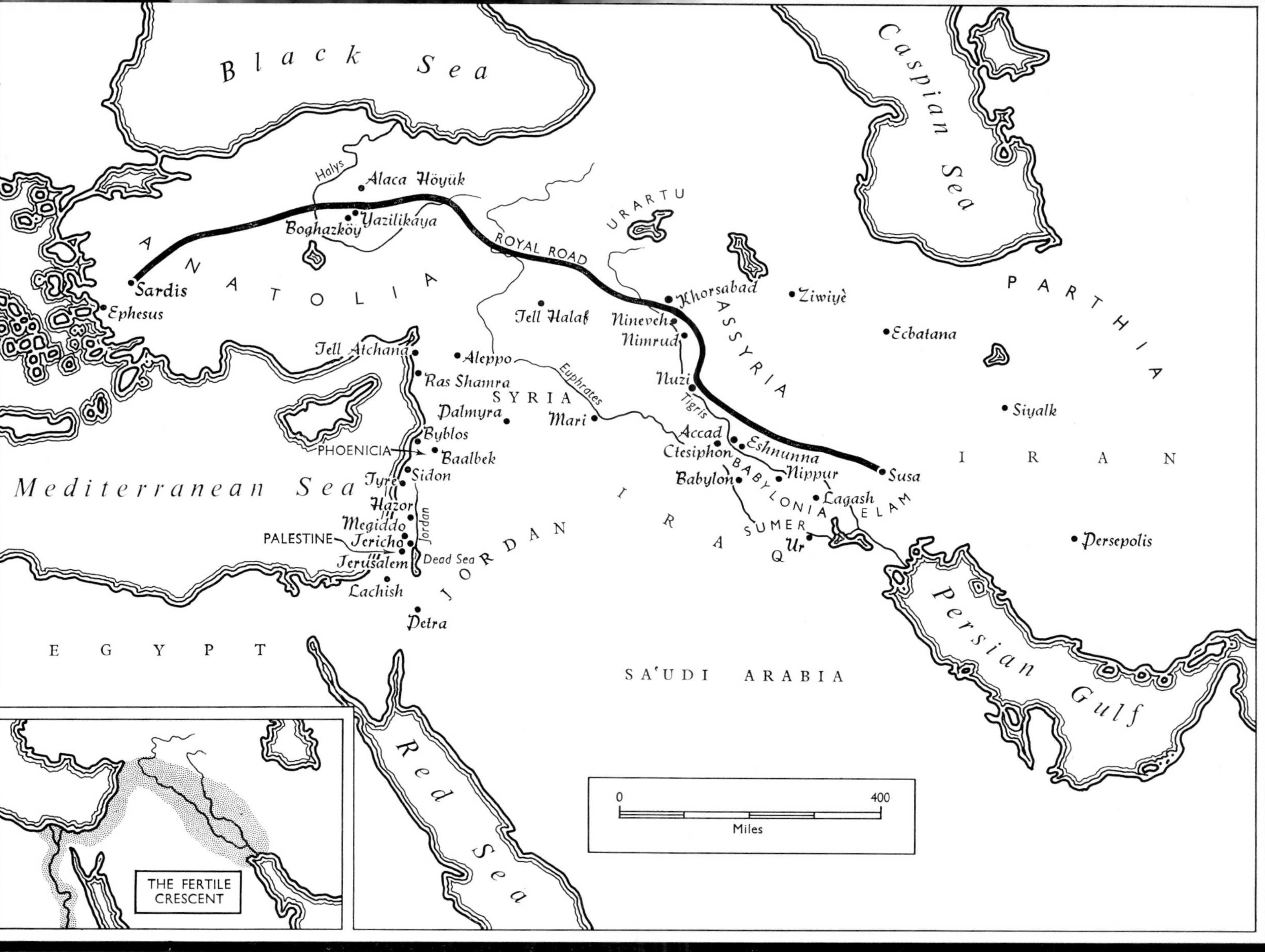

PLATE 159. THE MIDDLE EAST: map showing principal sites.

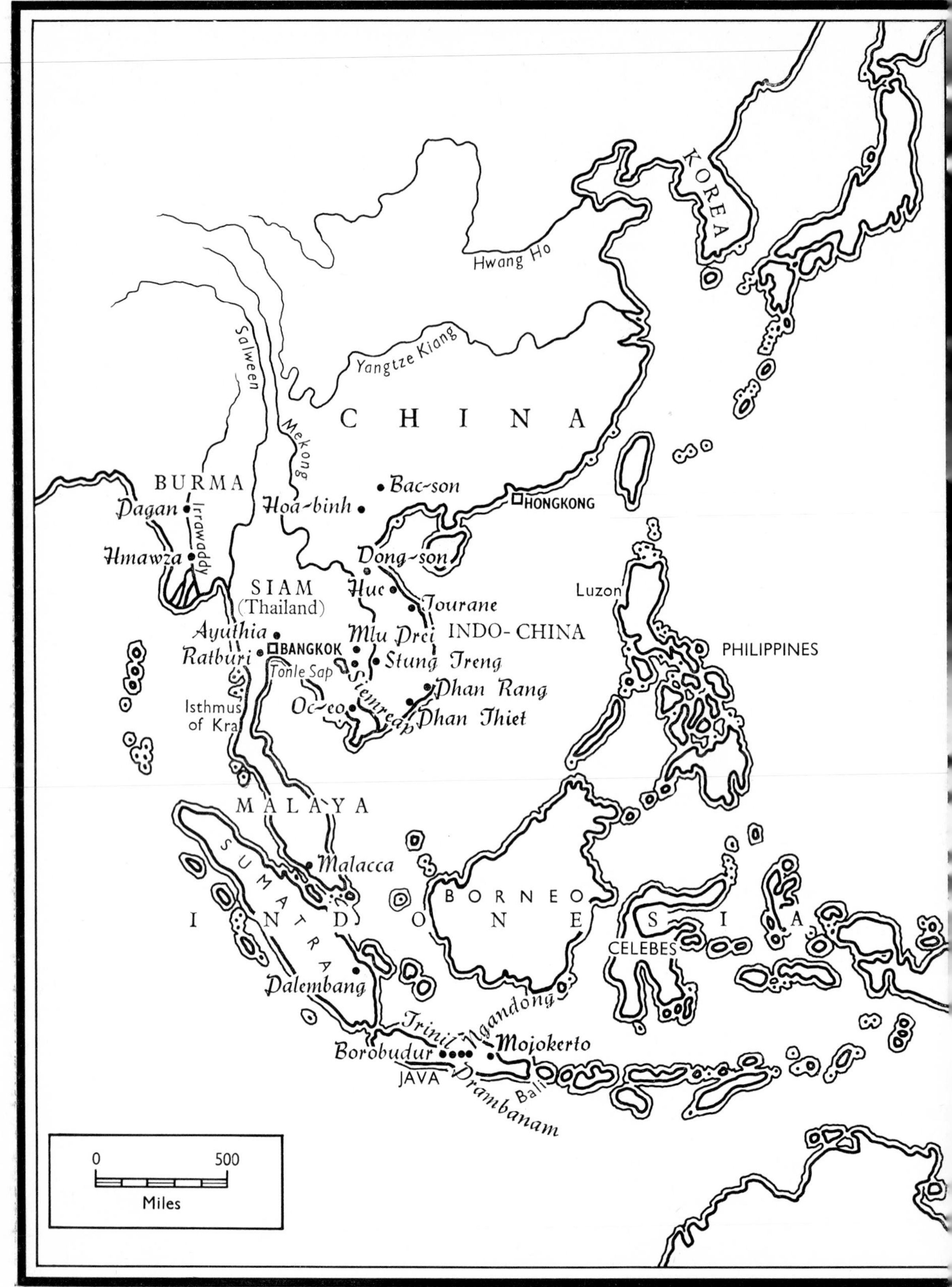

PLATE 160. SOUTH-EAST ASIA: map showing principal sites. See also map of Early Man.

mutilation or "being placed upon the wood", a reference perhaps to impalement or chaining to a stake.

Tools, Stone, *see* Stone tools.

Torc or **Torque.** A necklace of twisted metal.

Totem. A totem may be described as the guardian spirit of a unit of human organization such as the clan or tribe. It can be a plant, an insect, an animal, a bird, or even, though rarely, some mythical entity. The members of the clan regard themselves as being in a particular relationship with their totem; it is not just a name or badge, as the Boy Scouts take an animal for their patrol name, but something very much more. Indeed, they regard the members of the clan as being directly related to the totem, so that it becomes abhorrent even to think of killing it; nor would they dream of eating it, even though it may be an animal or plant that can be used as food.

The possession of a common totem binds the members of the clan together in such a close relationship that a very frequent consequence is that they are forbidden to intermarry, and the young men have to seek their wives from outside the clan, a practice which is known as exogamy.

Such beliefs in the existence and power of totems are to be found among primitive peoples at the present day. It cannot, of course, be proved that they existed in similar form among prehistoric peoples, but it is extremely probable that they did. Certainly, when civilization began in Egypt, the **nomes** seem to have sometimes adopted names which have a totemic origin. It appears probable, for instance, that Elephantiné and **Hierakonpolis** (Falcon-town) refer to the areas acknowledging the elephant and the falcon respectively as their totems.

Totonac Culture, *see* Mexico.

Tower of Babel, *see* Babylon *and* Ziggurat.

Tower-tombs, *see* Palmyra.

Tra-k'ieu: is situated south of Tourane, in central Viet-Nam. No buildings remain at the site which was once the capital of the **Cham** kingdom from A.D. 605 until it was moved further southwards in the tenth or eleventh century under the pressure of attacks by the Vietnamese. It is situated in the heart of what has been called the Cham holy land where **Mison** and Dong-duing are also situated, a region continually enriched by the kings of various dynasties who added new temples there. The importance of Tra-k'ieu lies in the rich collection of statuary and carved stone-work which was found there and which is now largely housed at the Museum of Tourane. The material shows a remarkable unity of style, and probably belongs mostly to the tenth century A.D., which seems to have been a high period in Cham art. In addition to anthropomorphic statuary, there are lions, usually treated in what may be described as a heraldic manner, and superb elephants which combine a high degree of naturalism with a well-conceived idealization. Figures of dancers reveal the sculptors' skill in the presentation of movement, while the treatment of ascetics conveys a real sense of detachment and meditation. The use of a breast motif on horizontal features of altars and pedestals is common, and seems to owe nothing to Indian art tradition. Small scenes are often vivid and valuable for the material culture revealed. One scene shows two men playing polo. The figures of divinities, while their themes are of Indian origin, show a marked ability to treat them in a wholly native tradition. In the whole art of Tra-k'ieu there are signs of an Indonesian strain which may in part be due to Javanese influences, which is very clear in the contemporary architecture of [Mison A1] – but it is also probable that this strain owes something to a wider Indonesian connection, since the Chams belong to the Indonesian group.

Transhumance. Transferring live-stock from one region to another according to the season of the year.

Tree-ring Dating. This technique, which has been practised for a long time, depends on counting the number of "rings" within the trunk of a tree, one "ring" representing a year's growth. Though of limited application, it can be of considerable value on sites where fossilized trees are present.

Trepanning or **Trephining.** An operation for removing part of the bone of the skull; it was done in **Neolithic** times by scraping the bone with a

flint knife to produce a round hole. Astonishingly, the patient did not always die. In at least one case the bone healed during life.

Tres Zapotes, *see* Mexico.

Troy. In *The Iliad* **Homer** describes the war fought by Agamemnon, king of **Mycenae,** and other **Achaean** princes against Troy. The site of Troy on the Aegean coast of Asia Minor was lost to history until the German amateur archaeologist, Heinrich **Schliemann,** discovered it in 1871 near the modern spot known as Hissarlik.

Further excavations since then have revealed the remains of nine settlements stratified one above the other. As a result Troy provides us with the fullest picture of **Bronze Age** development in western Asia Minor in the remains of its successive cities, though earlier remains have recently been found at Kum Tepe nearby, and at Poliochni in Lemnos. An important settlement, contemporary with Troy I, has also been excavated at Thermi in Lesbos. The first city of Troy belongs to the first half of the third millennium B.C. It is strongly fortified, and includes a small "palace" of a chief or king, though its greatest diameter is only fifty-four yards.

Troy II is an important settlement, belonging to the second half of the third millennium B.C. It lasted a long time, and went through several phases, but it still seems to represent the fortress of a local chieftain rather than a full-scale city. Nevertheless, it was rich and prosperous, and before the end it had become a city in the economic sense.

Metal was used already in Troy I for the manufacture of trinkets, tools and weapons, but by Troy II times it was possible to use it more extensively, and to manufacture metal vases also. Bronze, gold, silver and lead were all employed, and demonstrate the wealth and far-flung trade connections of the settlement. The ruler's palace was much larger than before and was built on the plan of the Homeric **megaron,** consisting of a rectangular hall with a central hearth, approached through a deep porch. Troy II was ultimately destroyed by enemies, and much of our knowledge of its wealth comes from the numerous hoards of metal-work and jewellery hidden by the inhabitants before the catastrophe. The most famous of these is the so-called "Treasure of Priam" found by Schliemann. A fine hoard of similar type has recently come to light at Poliochni.

The three succeeding settlements were not so important or powerful as Troy II, but Troy VI which began round about 1900 B.C. saw the central citadel surrounded by a fine wall of **ashlar masonry** with a pronounced **batter.** Indo-European-speaking people were moving westward into the Aegean about this time and seem to have settled in Troy, to judge from the fact that large quantities of the bones of the horse, previously unknown on the site, have been discovered at this level, for the horse is associated with the Indo-European. It is interesting in this connection to note that Homer in *The Iliad* describes Hector as "tamer of horses".

Troy V had been a settlement of small houses. Troy VI was much more important, with a central royal stronghold of concentric terraces. In the middle there presumably stood a palace, but nothing remains to show if this were so, since all the buildings were destroyed to make way for later buildings. The whole city was violently destroyed by an earthquake and fire round about 1800 B.C. It is doubtful whether this was the city of which Homer speaks in *The Iliad* – though many people believe it to be – for the traditional date for the Trojan war is some six hundred years later. It is held, however, that the rebuilt city of Troy VI came to a final end as a result of an earthquake about 1100 B.C. The settlement known as Troy VIIA is in fact probably that spoken of by Homer.

Alexander the Great did his best to revive the city but, though it passed through some fine phases both then and in the later Roman period, the settlement decayed and finally disappeared for centuries until excavated by Schliemann. (*See* **Mediterranean, the Eastern.**)

Tuff. Soft volcanic rock.

Tule Springs, Nevada, *see* America, Early Man in.

Tumbian Culture, *see* Sangoan.

Tumulus (plural-tumuli). A burial mound. The term is now becoming obsolette (*see* **Barrow**).

Tun-huang. This oasis to the west of Su-chow in Kansu, China, served for a number of centuries as a roadhead and entrepôt for two of the main routes of Eurasiatic trade. It was a cosmopolitan centre through which many ideas from the west reached China, and through which Chinese products and culture reached the west. It was in existence and a centre of Buddhism before the fifth century A.D. (some of the translators of Buddhist texts into Chinese were natives of this region) and continued until the tenth century, though its importance diminished in the eighth century under Tibetan threats. Some idea of its size can be gained from the report that in the fifth century "30,000" families were removed from this region by the victorious T'o-pa (Toba) armies of northern Wei. The main feature of the region is the hundreds of caves with Buddhist paintings, made famous in Europe by the work of Paul Pelliot and Sir Aurel **Stein.** These paintings show at the beginning strong western influences, from India and from the Middle East, but the Chinese artists absorbed these foreign strains and incorporated them into a native tradition which dominated the later period, and which was important for the history of Buddhist art in China. The work on silk and wood as well as on paper is remarkable for its highly professional competence, and it is clear that the school of Tunhuang was of the very highest class. In addition to the mural paintings, on plaster on the rock walls, a very small number being true fresco, an enormous quantity of manuscripts of every sort, though predominantly Buddhist, was collected here. Large numbers of documents which throw light upon economic and administrative matters provide a major source of knowledge for the history of China and the central Asian trading and political systems.

Tutankhamun, Tomb of. In his book, *The Tomb of Tutankhamun*, Howard Carter, the excavator, described his discovery: "We were preparing to leave the **Valley** [**of the Kings** at Luxor in Egypt] and try our luck elsewhere; and then – hardly had we set hoe to the ground in one last despairing effort than we made a discovery which far exceeded our wildest dreams". The first indication of the whereabouts of the tomb was a flight of steps cut into the rock. After ten years' searching Carter and his patron, Lord Carnavon, had been rewarded. Carter continued his story: "With trembling hands I made a tiny breach in the upper left hand corner [of the outer door of the tomb]. Darkness and blank space as far as an iron testing-rod could reach showed that whatever lay beyond was empty, and not filled [with rubble] like the passage we had just cleared. At first I could see nothing, the hot air causing the candle flame to flicker, but presently, as my eyes grew accustomed to the light, details of the room within emerged slowly from the mist, strange animals, statues and gold – everywhere the glint of gold".

Carter was looking into the first room only of the tomb in which were piled all the personal effects of the king which he would need in the next world. Robbers had entered the tomb within a short time of the funeral and, in their search for articles which they could easily remove, had turned everything upside down. Officials in charge of the necropolis had attempted to tidy this room and to secure the tomb from further violation. No other hand had touched the seals on the door until Carter removed them in November 1922. Such a hoard of treasure had never been known in the history of Egyptology and great public interest was aroused by the discovery.

For ten months Carter and his helpers, who included skilled draughtsmen and chemists from Egypt and America, worked at drawing, photographing and preserving the multitude of objects in this room which was known as the Antechamber. The king's chariots and armoury, furniture inlaid with gold, ivory and coloured glass, caskets of jewellery and clothing were piled upon each other. A portrait of the king with his queen, Ankhesenamun, decorated the back of a golden throne. Tutankhamun was shown seated nonchalantly upon another throne while the queen anointed his shoulder with oil. Behind them was the sun's disk with rays terminating in human hands, the symbol of the cult of Aton practised by **Akhnaton,** Amenhotep IV, in his capital at **Tell el Amarna.** This throne belonged to the Amarna days, and King Ay, who buried Tutankhamun, did not erase this heretical symbol.

Hunting appears to have been a favourite pastime with the king. His bow, decorated with the heads of nine captives, the traditional enemies of Egypt, was found in the Antechamber. A picture of the king accompanied by his queen shows him fowling, with his lion-cub standing beside him. His prowess in war was another subject frequently used for decoration, but it is unlikely that he ever set foot outside Egypt. However, scenes of massacre were the traditional embellishment for royal possessions and monuments, and Tutankhamun chose imaginary battle scenes for decorating his caskets and weapons.

By February 1923 the Antechamber was cleared

of objects and the long postponed opening of the door into the burial chamber took place. Carter described his first view of it in these words: "Within a yard of the doorway, stretching as far as one could see and blocking the entrance to the chamber, stood what to all appearance was a solid wall of gold".

The "wall of gold" was the outer-post of the shrines containing the sarcophagus and the royal mummy. Engraved on the gold covering of the shrine were the magic texts and symbols which Tutankhamun would need to protect him on his journey through the underworld. In the Antechamber the mourners had placed the everyday things he would need when he arrived at the end of his journey; in the Burial Chamber and between each of the coverings of the sarcophagus were the magic things he would need during his journey. Seven magic oars lay ready to ferry him across the waters of the Underworld. Lamps made of translucent calcite, with delicately carved supports in the form of **lotus** stems, were provided to light his path. The silver trumpet which may have been carried before him when he reviewed his armies lay beside the shrine. Jars of perfume and unguents, made in delicate shapes, were ready for the king to use. Four shrines covered the sarcophagus and when the lid was raised: "A gasp of wonderment escaped our lips ... a golden effigy of the young boy king, of most magnificent workmanship, filled the whole interior of the sarcophagus". On his brow had been placed a small wreath of flowers, perhaps a tribute from his queen.

The tomb was again closed and the task of opening the coffins containing the royal mummy was left until November 1924.

Three coffins covered the body and each was decorated with gold and glass inlay depicting protective deities. Each coffin bore an effigy of the king represented as the god Osiris. The innermost covering was a life-size mask, placed over the head and shoulders, made of beaten gold. On the mummy-bandages were plaques bearing the utterances of the gods who waited for him in the netherworld: "Thy soul liveth: thy veins are firm. Thou smellest the air and goest out as a god ... O Osiris Tutankhamun".

Inside the bandages were many personal belongings of the king each associated with a religious or political role: his diadem, jewelled collars, **amulets** made of semi-precious stones, his gold dagger decorated with hunting scenes, and his iron dagger in its golden case – a treasured possession in an age when copper and bronze were the hardest metals known – rings, bracelets, pectorals (breast-plates) in the form of symbols of eternity or the gods or goddesses of Egypt. The bead "tails" used in certain rituals were fixed to gold girdles and on his feet were sandals made of sheet gold embossed to resemble wicker-work. After detailed examination by anatomists and chemists the royal mummy was returned to the Burial Chamber – there to remain.

Two rooms had not yet been explored: they were a Treasury, which the excavators had seen when they first entered the Burial Chamber but had boarded up while working on the shrine and the coffins, and another room which led off the Antechamber and contained more furniture and personal possessions of the king.

The entrance to the Treasury was guarded by a figure of Anubis seated on a gilded coffer resting on long carrying-poles. The purpose of this room was to house the great golden canopy for the **Canopic** Chest which stood gleaming opposite the doorway. Facing inwards on each side of the chest were life-size figures of four goddesses, their arms outstretched to protect the alabaster chest on which were carved the same four goddesses – Isis, Nephthys, Neith and Selkis.

Gilded statuettes of the king performing ceremonies connected with the myth of Horus and the myths of the hereafter were found, and statuettes of many Egyptian gods all having some magic influence to help the king in his after-life. There were model boats for transport and models of baking and brewing to provide the means of making food after the joints of meat and other offerings in the tomb had been consumed. Robbers had found this room and ransacked the delicate wood and ivory boxes for jewellery, but nearly half had escaped their attention. A large number of **ushabti** figures of the king, housed in boxes, were stored here and in the Annexe.

Among the finds of greatest human interest in the tomb were the mummified remains of two still-born infants, presumably the children of Tutankhamun and Ankhesenamun, and a lock of hair of Queen Ti, wife of Amenhotep III and grandmother of Ankhesenamun. The lock was encased in the innermost of four model coffins together with a gold statuette of Amenhotep III.

In the last room entered by the excavators in their fifth season no attempt had been made by the necropolis officials to restore order – even the footprints of the plunderers remained visible on a bow-case. The room, called by the excavators the Annexe, was a store for unguents and oils, wine and food. Amid the confusion of fallen jars and baskets stood the religious throne and footstool of the king. On the back-panel of the throne was the emblem of the Aton cult, picked out in **faience,** glass and coloured stones on a gold background. The seat was made of ebony inlaid with ivory. On the footstool, made of wood overlaid with violet glazed pottery, were inlaid figures of the nine traditional enemies of Egypt.

Since the tomb was not only much smaller than the tombs of his predecessors but also too small to hold adequately some of its furniture (e.g. the shrines) it has been suggested that Tutankhamun may have intended to build a larger tomb and that he died before doing so. In design the tomb resembles the tomb of Akhnaton at Amarna. Unlike the other royal tombs of its period at **Thebes**, the walls, apart from the sarcophagus chamber, are undecorated. Equally unusual for a royal tomb is the choice of subjects for the decorations. They show the mummy of the king inside a coffin enclosed within two shrines being drawn on a sledge by twelve courtiers, the ritual of opening the mouth of the king in the form of Osiris being performed by his successor Ay, the king in the presence of the goddess, Nut, and the king followed by his **ka** (double) in the presence of Osiris. On another wall are two scenes: the arrival of the sun-god in the underworld and the king in the presence of the deities Hathor and Anubis.

The tomb of Ay had very similar decorations and both tombs share the peculiarity of being the only royal tombs which have scenes, like the transport of the mummy, which are not strictly of a religious character. In this respect they resemble more nearly the private tombs of the period. Their style is much influenced by the artistic conventions of Amarna.

Perhaps Tutankhamun had been preparing for himself the large rock tomb near that of Amenhotep III, but died before it was ready. Ay buried him in the smaller tomb, which may already have been hewn, but not "decorated" for Ay himself. Ay in due course was buried in the tomb begun by Tutankhamun, which suffered the fate of all the other royal tombs.

The importance of Tutankhamun's tomb lies in its being discovered almost intact. Never before had archaeologists been able to see all the funerary equipment of a king massed together, although many royal tombs had been explored. Here it was possible to observe models of the enacting of scenes described in the religious texts. However, no new written material was found and no historical documents to help to elucidate this period of history. *See* colour plate XVI, plate 145, page 465.

Tuxtla Statuette, *see* Mexico.

Tylissos. This **Minoan** site in northern Crete west of **Knossos** has no surviving remains earlier than the Middle Minoan period (about 2000–1550 B.C.), though it is possible that it was already in use in Early Minoan times (about 2500–2000 B.C.). Several finds of interest have been made there: pieces of fresco of the Middle Minoan period on a miniature scale show boxers advancing. An inscribed clay figurine belongs late in the period, as also does a small bronze statue of an elderly male votary. A hoard of gigantic legless cauldrons is of the Late Minoan era (about 1550–1100 B.C.). There are indications of a break in habitation in Late Minoan times, probably as a result of the same catastrophe that overtook many Cretan cities at that time. A Late Minoan cremation burial here constitutes the first of this kind in Crete. The tomb may be that of a foreigner since there are no other examples in Crete until the succeeding period.

Type-site. Objects belonging to a common **culture** are usually named after the site at which they were first found, e.g. **Aurignacian, Magdalenian.**

Typology is the method the archaeologist uses to follow the way in which prehistoric man gradually improves his weapons and tools, slowly making them more efficient and functional (or, sometimes, allowing them to degenerate); his essential conservatism retains features from generation to generation, and so enables the archaeologist to arrange **artifacts** in a scheme of gradual development (*see* **Archaeology**).

Tyre. A famous city of the ancient **Phoenicians,** Tyre was situated on a promontory on what is now the Lebanese coast, twenty-five miles south of Sidon. Its fame rested on its power as a seaport.

Already a flourishing port under Egyptian protection in the eighteenth dynasty, it established close trade relations with Israel in the time of Solomon. The coming of the **Assyrians** to the Phoenician coast and the growth of factions within Tyre reduced its power; Dido, leader of one faction, left to found Carthage, and Tyre finally succumbed to Sennacherib. By retreating to its island, however, and destroying the causeway linking this with the mainland, Tyre successfully resisted Nebuchadnezzar, and on the island a new Tyre grew and prospered. Alexander the Great subdued the city after constructing a huge mole, but it revived and flourished under the Seleucids and Romans. It was an archbishopric in Christian times but fell to the Arabs in A.D. 636. It was finally abandoned by the crusaders in 1291 and was destroyed by the Moslems. The remains of the city were looted or buried under sand and sea. Underwater foundations, possibly of the ancient harbour, have been studied and photographed. The Tyrian purple dye made from the mollusc *Murex grandaris* was an important manufacture in Roman times. Tyrian coinage was widely current from the fifth century B.C.

Tzolkin, *see* Maya and Mexico.

U

Ugarit, *see* Ras Shamra.

Uncials. A form of writing in which the letters are printed separately in a manner resembling modern capital letters, and not run together as in **cursive writing**.

Uniformity, Principle of, *see* Lyell, Charles.

Ur lies nine miles west of Nasiriyeh on the River Euphrates in southern **Iraq** about two hundred miles from the Persian Gulf. It is locally named Tell el-Muqaiyar ("mound of bitumen") from the sixty-foot-high ruins of the **ziggurat** which still dominate the desolate site.

In 1854 J. E. Taylor, British Consul at Basra, dug into the mound to find inscriptions at the base of the ziggurat. Since from these the place was identified with "Ur of the Chaldees", the biblical home of Abraham, great interest was aroused. More work was done there both by the University of Pennsylvania and the British Museum (1918–19) and with such success that full operations by a joint expedition of the two institutions were started. Work was carried on systematically during 1922–34 under the direction of Mr (later Sir) C. L. **Woolley** with outstanding and spectacular results.

Deep soundings to virgin soil showed that Ur's earliest inhabitants lived in a village of huts with reed walls coated with mud, similar to some of the local marsh Arabs today. They used **flints**, made clay figurines and richly decorated pottery called **Al Ubaid** ware after a nearby site first cleared by the same expedition. These peoples traded with distant places until they were cut off by a severe flood which deposited three to eleven feet of silt over most of the lower site. As abruptly as the level of occupation thus ceased so it began again with similar types of **artifacts.** This flood, Woolley believes, covered the whole of low-lying Iraq and was the Great **Flood** mentioned in the **Gilgamesh Epic,** in Sumerian texts and in the Bible. The levels above the flood were named after the characteristic pottery, building techniques and grave-goods known from other sites as **Uruk** and **Jemdet Nasr**. In the later period, about 3000 B.C., there were already traces of a ziggurat, and inscribed tablets, jar sealings and **seals** were found.

While clearing a cemetery area to the south-west of the temenos or ziggurat platform in 1922 Woolley first came upon the royal cemetery which was finally cleared in 1927–30. The upper graves, long lost beneath the rubbish pits of the subsequent city, could be clearly dated by seals and inscriptions to the dynasty of **Agade**. Below them tombs of the early dynasty III (about 2500 B.C.) were found, many unfortunately robbed, for here, as in Egypt, professional tomb robbers had been at work. Some, however, were intact and in the finest of the private graves, that of Mes-kalam-shar, his golden-shafted spear lay by the head with gold-mounted daggers, an axe-head and other jewellery at the side. His engraved helmet of beaten gold, one of the finest examples of Sumerian art, still lay on the rotting skull.

In sixteen royal brick-graves the deceased was generally found to have been accompanied in death by attendants. The number varied from six to eighty. The most spectacular **shaft grave** opened was that of Abargi and Queen Shubad. The bodies of sixty-four ladies of the court and four harpists in ceremonial dress and jewels lay near the remains of the wooden **sledge** used to carry the queen's body into the tomb. The asses that drew it had been slain and then their drivers, with the whole assembly, had taken poison and been laid out before the tomb was sealed. It is interesting to note that the very men who dug the shaft for Shubad had plundered the adjacent tomb of her husband Abargi and resealed its vaulted roof to conceal their entry.

Fortunately the contents of Queen Shubad's grave were found unrobbed though flattened by the weight of overlying debris. Now restored, the queen's head-dress, jewellery, four inlaid lyres, a pair of statues of standing goats made of gold, lapis-lazuli and white shell, and many objects and vessels of gold and silver are among the finest antiquities yet discovered in ancient Mesopotamia.

These royal graves are no example of indiscriminate massacre, of fertility sacrifice, or of sombre pageantry to accompany the burial of some unknown personification of the god Tammuz who is thought by some to have died and been mourned annually. The attendants were part of the grave equipment, as in the first dynasty in Egypt where they were soon to be replaced by the elaborate models used as substitutes for the actual person when activated by magical spells. These men and women at Ur appear to have gone voluntarily into the grave in the hope of continuing service for their ruler in the next world. Among the **Sumerians** these rites were soon dropped and forgotten, but among other non-Semitic peoples in central Asia they were long continued, as is witnessed both by literature and by such discoveries as the tombs at Pasyryk of the fifth to fourth centuries B.C. Among Mongoloid races like the Ahoms of Assam the practice survived into the seventeenth century A.D.

Ur was to experience another period of splendour under the kings of the third dynasty (about 2110–2015 B.C.) founded by **Ur-Nammu**. He rebuilt the walled city, the ziggurat, Ehursag and the royal palace and many of the religious and public buildings within the oval town which was protected on three sides by the River Euphrates and wide canals. More than two thousand inscribed tablets described the active economic life and trade (as far as India) from which came the revenue for all this activity. The texts range from accounts of the offerings and taxes paid to Nannar (the moon god), the chief deity of the city who was also the principal landowner, to school reports and literary works. A victory **stele** shows some of the military activity of Ur-Nammu when he controlled all of southern Iraq. The vaulted mausolea of Ur-Nammu, and his successors Shulgi and Amar-Suen were cleared by Woolley.

The subsequent levels of occupation show how slowly Ur recovered after it had been taken over by the semi-nomadic Semites about 2000 B.C. The role of capital passed first to Isin whose ruler Ishme-Dagan rebuilt a great house for his daughter Enannatum whom he dedicated as high-priestess to Nannar. His reconstruction of the ziggurat and its terraces was continued by Warad-Sin of Larsa. In 1930–31 Woolley excavated about ten thousand square yards of the residential suburb south-east of the **temenos**. Most of the houses were built in this Isin-Larsa period and followed a conventional pattern only varied by the exigencies of the site. From the narrow streets the single gateway led to an inner court from which opened reception, guest-rooms and servants' rooms, kitchen, lavatory and stores. The family proper occupied rooms on the first floor leading off balconies over the open courtyard and reached by a brick or wooden staircase. Some houses had private chapels, and in some the changing fortunes of their merchant owners can be traced by the expansion or contraction of the premises. A street chapel and school house were among the more unusual buildings uncovered. Woolley estimates that the city must have had a population of more than a quarter of a million.

In 1737 B.C. Ur was again destroyed and for about three hundred years only squalid buildings seem to have been built. Then in about 1400, Kurigalzu, a **Kassite** king, devoted great efforts to restoring the Ningal Temple, the great gateway (Egishshirgal) into the sacred area, and the House of Tablets.

Ur saw few innovations in its long subsequent history until the Chaldean kings. Nebuchadnezzar II set out towards the end of his life to rebuild Ur as he had his capital **Babylon**. The main temples were remodelled on an open plan but it was left to his successor Nabonidus (556–539 B.C.) to complete the work. The height of the ziggurat was increased by making it in seven stages instead of three as previously. The Harbour Temple and the huge E-gi-par building, or residence for his daughter Belshalti-Nannar, the sister of Belshazzar, now installed as high-priestess, testify to Nabonidus' religious zeal. This lady used one room to house her antiquities, among which were a carefully preserved Kassite boundary stone, part of a statue of Shulgi, king of Ur about 2058 B.C., as well as objects of the Larsa period and copies of inscriptions from the third dynasty of which the originals also survive. A small drum-shaped clay object was inscribed with an inventory of some of these prizes and is thus probably the earliest known museum catalogue.

The neo-Babylonian buildings continued in use at Ur until the late Persian period. The latest document found in them was dated 316 B.C. About this time the Euphrates changed its course leaving the ancient city buried beneath the rubble and sand. *See* plate 146, page 466.

Urartu. The name Urartu was used by the **Assyrians** to describe a land probably called Biaini by its inhabitants, lying north of Assyria and centred on the lake in eastern Turkey now called Lake Van.

The annals of the Assyrian King Shalmaneser I record that at the beginning of his reign (early in the thirteenth century B.C.) he marched on, and reduced, the whole land of Uruatri, imposing heavy tribute on its people. His successor of two centuries later, Ashur-bel-kala, also claims to have marched on the land, and lists the cities which, no doubt (if the text, found in fragments in the ruins of Ashur on the Tigris, were complete), succumbed to him; and both King Adad-nirari II (912–891 B.C.) and King Ashur-nasir-pal II (884–859 B.C.) mention Uratri or Urartu in describing the extent of their conquests. King Shalmaneser III (859–824 B.C.), however, is the first to refer to a king of Urartu, in a campaign of 856 B.C.; and Seduri, the Urartian leader mentioned by Shalmaneser twenty-five years later, is no doubt the Sarduri who is the author of the first inscription of the Urartians themselves, incised in **cuneiform** writing in the Assyrian language on blocks of stone forming part of a great platform set up below the Urartian capital of Tushpa on the citadel of Van.

The successors of Sarduri extended their kingdom by conquest in many directions, and introduced their own language (expressed in cuneiform borrowed from the Assyrians) to record both their military successes and their civil achievements. His son Ishpuini (probably contemporary with Shamshi-Adad V of Assyria, 824–811 B.C.) carried his arms as far south-east as the pass of Kelishin (on the modern Iraq-Iran frontier north-east of Rowanduz), where, with his son Menua, he set up a bilingual inscription in his own language and in Assyrian; and inscriptions of Menua himself are found as far afield as Palu (on the Euphrates, nearly two hundred miles west of Van), where he records his subjecting to tribute the king of Melitea (now Malatya), and near the Aras River beyond Mount Ararat (which seems to preserve the name Urartu) in the north-east, where he also claims to have reduced a city to tribute.

Menua's son Argishti recorded on the side of the rock of the citadel of Van not less than thirteen years of military campaigns, at least six of them against the land of Mana in the south-east near the Assyrian frontier; and six seasons of the reign of the contemporary King Shalmaneser IV of Assyria (781–773 B.C.) are recorded as occupied with campaigns against Urartu. Argishti's son Sarduri III claims to have received the submission and tribute of Melitea and to have conquered the land of Ashurnirari V of Assyria (755–745 B.C.); but he was heavily defeated in the west in 743 B.C. by the Assyrian's successor Tiglath-Pileser III (745–727 B.C.), and later driven back to his citadel at Van.

Sargon II of Assyria carried out an extensive campaign against Urartu (now under Rusa, son of Sarduri III) in 714 B.C., receiving or imposing submission as he went, and on his return journey ravaging the city of Musasir in the south of the Urartian country and carrying off rich booty, much of it from the Temple of Haldi, the principal god of the Urartians. Rusa's grandson Rusa II of Urartu nevertheless claims to have conquered lands far to the west of Van; and he sent an embassy of greeting to king Ashur-bani-pal of Assyria, who later received a similar embassy from Sarduri IV, one of the successors of Rusa II. Perhaps the last Urartian king, about the end of the seventh century B.C., was Rusa III, son of Erimena, whose name suggests that the Armenians, colonists, according to **Herodotus**, of the **Phrygians**, were beginning to move eastward and to supersede the old dynasty of Urartu. The kingdom of Ararat still appears, however, among those called upon by Jeremiah to help in the destruction of **Babylon**; and the name of Urartu survives on a Babylonian clay tablet dated as late as 418 B.C.

The artistic proficiency of Urartu, notably in metal-working, attested by Sargon's account of the treasures of Musasir, is displayed by material excavated at Toprak Kale, near Van, including bronze shields bearing incised figures of lions and bulls, as well as human and animal figures in ivory;

and much light is being thrown on Urartian life by excavations at Karmir Blur, near Erivan in Soviet Armenia, where more decorated bronze shields, quivers, helmets, arrows, harness, bowls, goblets, and inscribed clay tablets are among the extensive discoveries made in a citadel-building of over a hundred rooms. But although the language of the Urartians is known to be related to the **Hurrian** language, it is still imperfectly understood; and although some Assyrian influence can be recognized in their art, its origins are still largely unknown.

Ur-Nammu, king of **Ur** in southern Babylonia about 2000 B.C., was the inaugurator of a line of five kings (the third dynasty of Ur) who ruled from that city over the whole land of the **Sumerians** and Accadians (i.e. the southern part of modern **Iraq)** and extended their power over the north of the country (**Assyria**) as well, and over a wide though uncertain territory both east and west of this central realm. Under these kings was revived for a time the supremacy of the **Sumerians,** which had been eclipsed both by the Semitic dynasty of **Agade** and by the century-long oppression of the uncivilized Gutians.

At first Ur-Nammu was only governor of Ur under the control of Utu-khegal, king of **Uruk** (the biblical Erech), the national hero who had defeated the Gutians. But soon he appeared not only as independent but as strong enough to subdue, in his turn, the neighbouring cities and to carry his arms abroad. Unfortunately there are no historical records of his reign, only a few formulae giving names to his years (he reigned for eighteen), and most of these refer to civil or religious occasions. One, however, reads "year when Ur-Nammu the king made straight the way from below to above", and this could possibly indicate, according to Babylonian phraseology, a victorious march from the Persian Gulf to the Mediterranean. It is also known, from the prologue to his laws, that early in his reign he defeated the ruler of **Lagash,** an important neighbouring city.

Babylonia has long been famed as the home of the earliest legislation, and a recent discovery has revealed that Ur-Nammu was the promulgator of the earliest collection of laws at present known. Even the little which remains of these is enough to prove that the form and also in part the contents of **Hammurabi's** famous "code" (about 250 years later) were already traditional. Ur-Nammu's laws begin, like Hammurabi's, with a prologue; the gods, by a regular tradition, conferred the kingship of Ur upon Ur-Nammu, who at once set himself to re-establish and reform the institutions of his city. He cleared the canals and revived navigation, regulated weights and measures, suppressed illegal practices of extortion, and championed the poor and defenceless against the rich and the oppressors. Of his laws only a few remain, much damaged; those which can be read concern charges of witchcraft, the recapture of fugitive slaves, and assaults on persons. Most of these provisions reappear with little difference in the Hammurabi code.

Construction-works were undertaken by Ur-Nammu in various parts of his kingdom. He dug out many canals and thereby restored an important overseas trade with the country of Magan. He also restored temples and cults at **Nippur** and Uruk as well as in his own city of Ur. There he has a lasting monument in the great surviving mass of his **ziggurat**, recently excavated: its lowest part, which alone survives, is a rectangular structure tapering upwards; it is finely built with a thick revetment of baked bricks, each bearing the king's name, set in bitumen. Part of a stone relief set up by the king and found at Ur shows incidents in the course of this work (*See* plate 146, page 466.)

Urn People. A culture found in England in the **Bronze Age**, a feature of which was that the dead were cremated and their ashes buried in urns; it was the discovery of such urns which prompted Sir Thomas **Browne** to write his great classic, *Urne Buriall.*

Uruk, *see* Sumerians.

Ushabti figures, made of wood, stone or **faience,** generally measuring about four to nine inches in height are found in large numbers in ancient Egyptian tombs. Their purpose seems to have been to act as substitutes for their deceased owner when the gods called on him to perform menial or tiring tasks in the after-life. At some periods, these figures were inscribed with the following quotation from the sixth chapter of the **Book of the Dead**:

"N. says: O Shabti! If N. is detailed for any tasks to be done there [in the underworld], as a man is bound, mayest thou be chosen instead of me on every occasion, namely to cultivate the fields, to flood the banks [i.e. to water the fields], to carry away sand to the east or to the west, then say thou, 'Here am I'."

During the New Kingdom, when the finest ushabtis were made, they were represented in mummified form and thus resembled their dead owner. They also bore his name. Some of the ushabtis of Tutankhamun are carved in the likeness of the king. Implements for working in the fields are provided with some of the figures; these consist of a basket, hoe, pick, yoke and a water vessel.

The placing of ushabtis in the tomb was a duty performed either by the relatives or by the servants of the deceased person. The number varied from one or two figures to about five hundred.

Ushabti figures were probably first used in the First Intermediate period (about 2280–2052 B.C.). They were very rough and made of wax, and naked but for roughly-made head-dresses. Later the figures were represented as being wrapped in bandages in the same manner as the mummy, and were made of wood, stone or faience.

Whatever the origin of the name, which is uncertain, it is clear that ushabtis formed an important part of the funerary paraphernalia which were intended to provide the dead person with all the comforts he had enjoyed in this world and to preserve his identity in the next.

Usher, James (1581–1656). James Usher, or Ussher, was Archbishop of Armagh, Ireland, from 1625 until his death. He wrote numerous books, one of which – *Annales Veteris et Novi Testamenti* – worked out the age of the world from the information given in the Bible. According to his calculations the earth was created in the week which ended on Saturday, 22 October, 4004 B.C. In 1701 the printers inserted his dates in the Authorized, or King James, Version of the Bible, and thereby gave them such authority that the early geologists met stubborn and bigoted religious opposition to their theories that the world was in reality many millions of years old.

V

Valley of the Kings. The necropolis of **Thebes** lay on the west bank of the River Nile in Egypt. It was here that the kings and queens of the eighteenth and nineteenth dynasties were buried, the kings at the northern end in the Valley of the Kings, and its neighbouring valley the Western Valley, and the queens and some princes at the southern end of the necropolis in the Valley of the Queens. The first of the kings to be buried in the Valley of the Kings was probably Amenhotep I. The tombs are carved out of the rock, and consist of a number of descending corridors and chambers, the final one of which contained the stone sarcophagus. Corridors and chambers were decorated with religious scenes and texts, describing the journey of the sun through the underworld. The tombs mark a radical departure in Egyptian practice. In the Old and Middle Kingdoms the royal burial places had been marked by a **pyramid**; at Thebes it was partly the nature of the terrain which forbade the elaborate monumental construction of an old-style pyramid, and it was undoubtedly the intention of the pharaohs to conceal their actual tombs. The earlier tombs, like that for instance of Tuthmosis III, are remote in the valley and difficult of access. But later the intention of concealing the tombs completely was abandoned and the entrance was constructed with a sculptured façade. The tombs have always been one of the great attractions for the visitor to Egypt; Strabo writing in the first century A.D. mentions forty as worthy to be visited. Only in one case, that of **Tutankhamun** have the tombs escaped the plunderer; the majority were violated within a short time of the interment (*see* **Tomb Robbery Papyri**).

Varves. When at the end of the **Ice Age** the glaciers finally retreated, their melting released sediment into lakes. The larger grains sank quickly, the smaller much more slowly; each year therefore produced one layer grading from coarse at the bottom to fine at the top, the thickness showing whether the summer was warm, so producing thicker layers, or cold. The colour often changes in the layers, so that the band appears striped (from which came the name "varve", from the Swedish for "banded" – *varvig*). Counting the varves and correlating the data with that from elsewhere makes it possible to estimate dates very accurately.

Ventris, Michael George Francis (1922–56). Few men achieve world-wide fame before reaching the age of thirty-five, yet Michael Ventris had done that when he was tragically killed in a road accident. He was by profession an architect, and was highly esteemed by his teachers and colleagues. But his fame rests upon his decipherment of one of the prehistoric **Minoan Scripts** known as Linear B, an achievement which ranks his name among the great pioneers of unknown scripts such as **Grotefend, Champollion** and **Rawlinson.**

Ventris was attracted to this problem while still at school in England by a lecture given by Sir Arthur **Evans.** Evans was convinced that the Minoan scripts contained the unknown language of the **Minoan civilization**; and, despite the subsequent discovery in 1939 of Linear B tablets on the mainland of Greece, Ventris remained of the opinion that the language would prove similar to Etruscan, right down to his successful decipherment in 1952. He put forward this Etruscoid theory for the first time in an article written while he was still at school, and published in an American journal in 1940. After the second world war, during which he served as a navigator in the Royal Air Force, he resumed in his spare time the study of the scripts, and in 1950 persuaded ten scholars of international repute to contribute replies to a questionnaire on this subject. The analysis of their answers, accompanied by Ventris's own views, was presented in a masterly survey called *The Mid-Century Report*, which he had duplicated and circulated privately at his own expense. The next two years saw the publication of the texts of all the tablets found up to that time. Ventris now began a methodical analysis of the richer material which was becoming available, circulating his results and suggestions in a remarkable series of *Work Notes*; by June 1952 these had reached number twenty, comprising 176 typed foolscap pages. This immense industry is the more notable when we remember that throughout this period he had regular professional work.

The methods he employed are described in the account of Linear B. The first hint of the Greek solution came in the last *Work Note* of 1 June, 1952: "Are the Knossos and Pylos tablets written in Greek?" Ventris still did not believe this suggestion when he wrote the note, which he described as a "frivolous digression". He had, however, been led to it by the application of a sound method, and subsequent testing did not confirm his expectation that the first tentative results would prove a "chimera". Instead he rapidly found large numbers of Greek words which yielded acceptable sense. His first public claim was made in a talk broadcast by the B.B.C. in July 1952. He now received encouragement from some foreign scholars, and in England began to collaborate with John Chadwick. The first detailed presentation of the theory was in an article entitled "Evidence for Greek Dialect in the Mycenaean Archives", published by the *Journal of Hellenic Studies* for 1953. This was greeted with acclaim by Greek scholars all over the world; and the early doubts were quickly silenced by the discovery of a new tablet at **Pylos** which, when deciphered, showed a Greek text agreeing closely with the **pictograms** of vessels on it.

This was the starting point of a new and flourishing branch of Greek studies, which has already shed much light on prehistoric Greece, and has added some seven centuries to the history of the Greek language. Ventris's only printed book, *Documents in Mycenaean Greek* (1956), written in collaboration with John Chadwick, was on the point of publication at the time of his death.

He was decorated with the Order of the British Empire in 1955, received an honorary degree from the University of Uppsala, and was made an Honorary Research Associate of University College, London. In 1956 he was awarded the first research fellowship given by the *Architects' Journal.*

Villafranchian, *see* Africa, North *and* Ain Hanech.

Vix, the Treasure of. Vix is a village in northern France, about three miles north-north-west of Châtillon-sur-Seine (Côte-d'Or). Overlooking the village is a hill-fort, known locally as Mont Lassois, where excavations had started as early as 1929. This site was very rich, especially in Early **Iron Age** finds, and yielded an immense quantity (one and a quarter million) of pottery sherds. However, it was not till 1952 that burials were deliberately sought in the vicinity of the hill-fort. In the following year the excavators came upon a most spectacular grave which illustrated the richness and power of the **Hallstatt** aristocracy of northern France. The circular burial mound of large stones which covered the grave had been forty-five and a half yards across, and about six and a half yards high. It seems to have been built by the wayside, following the classical tradition, as it was only 130 yards from a prehistoric road. Although the mound or **barrow** was removed later, the burial chamber was intact. Sunk beneath the old ground surface it was almost ten feet square, and lined with wood. The tomb was intact, the wooden roof having soon collapsed and the water-table having subsequently risen; the grave-goods were therefore magnificently preserved.

The tomb itself was of an amazing richness. In one corner stood an enormous covered krater (mixing-bowl for wine) and placed around it in a profusion of wealth, a silver bowl, Attic cups, a wine jug (*oinochoe*) and three bronze bowls. In the centre, with the head to the north, lay the body on a chariot-carriage, whilst stacked neatly along one side of the grave were the four detached wheels. The deceased, a young woman of about thirty years had been magnificently bedecked with jewellery: bronze anklets, an additional bronze **torc** laid on her body, bracelets of **schist** and amber beads on her wrists; her clothes were fastened by bronze and iron brooches, a necklace of amber and diorite was at her throat, and a golden diadem still on her head; the burial chariot itself had a blue and vermilion coloured drape embroidered with bronze ornaments.

Thus must she have appeared on her last journey to the grave. But who was she? Certainly a Late Hallstatt princess, but her closer identity remains hidden. She died about 500 B.C., for the contents of the grave such as the wine-jug and brooches indicate this. The black figure and plain Attic cups can be dated to between 530 and 520 B.C., and 515 B.C. respectively, and the large bronze bowl to about 520 B.C. These are, however, treasured imports of classical workmanship and are likely to have been kept for a few years before finding their way into the grave. She lived in the period in France known as Hallstatt II b, which may have continued at least locally, for some time after 500 B.C. without any interference from the Later **La Tène** I peoples.

A chariot burial was a rare honour among the Hallstatt peoples. Only sixteen of this period are known in France, concentrated mainly in the north east; of these Vix belongs to an even more select group of five or so royal tombs, so called from the richness of the graves, which included Greek and Etruscan imports and gold finery of Celtic workmanship.

Such burials were normally under barrows with all the grave furniture wrapped in cloth, even the chariot wheels which were in any case usually ritually detached, perhaps to signify that the vehicle was no longer for use in this world. A bronze bowl was the most common grave-good in these graves.

Although rare, other female chariot burials have been found and this may reflect the positions of power which women held, often in their own right, in Celtic society.

The chariot, or more properly four-wheeled wagon, of the luxurious "royal" type is in keeping with the rest of the burial. A very accurate reconstruction was made possible by the minute recording of all the parts of the decayed vehicle during excavation. This showed it to have had wooden wheels of about thirty inches diameter, each with ten spokes and a bronze sheathed hub. The carriage was rectangular, four feet five inches long, surrounded by a decorative brass balustrade, and had a vertical wooden back, lined with fur. Four iron handles enabled the carriage to be easily detached from the chassis. The shortness of the carriage meant that the princess must have been propped up against the back in a half-reclining position. This alone suggests that the chariot had other functions than that of a bier, and the complete absence of harness need not imply that it was only a processional vehicle drawn by men and not by animals. This was the type of burial traditional to a nomadic warrior aristocracy. A vast group of Hallstatt chariot burials are found in Europe, beginning in eastern Bohemia, spreading through Austria, southern Germany and Switzerland and ending in the French group.

The most spectacular of the imports from the classical world is a vast bronze krater with volute handles, richly ornamented and decorated with a metope of applied metal figures on the neck. It is five feet three inches high, and weighs over 457 pounds, the biggest metal vessel known to have survived from antiquity. These large kraters were in any case very rare and frequently offered as presents on diplomatic occasions. One similar in size is mentioned by **Herodotus** as having been offered to Croesus, king of Lydia (560–546 B.C.), by the Lacedaemonians. It seems to have been made in one of the Laconian colonies in southern Italy.

Although an import, the solid gold diadem is less easily identified; consisting of a plain curved gold bar terminating at each end in a lion's paw clasping a poppy-head ball, and ornamented with a pegasus and filigree work, it seems to be of Greco-Scythian manufacture.

From the **Etruscan** metal workers came an *oinochoe* with a trefoil spout, one of the first to have been imported into France, while from Greece itself came a small silver bowl with a golden base and Attic pottery including a painted cup of the "Droop" type.

These imports illustrate the scope of late Hallstatt trade and the fashionable habit of buying a "wine-set" (mixer, pourer and cups) to accompany the equally fashionable Greek wine. How strange the sophisticated design and technique of these classical imports must have appeared to those accustomed to the relative roughness and barbaric splendour of Hallstatt goods!

Rich as this burial was it was not the only one at Vix; there seem to have been at least three others, forming the cemetery of the family or families who controlled the town of Mont Lassois. This power must have been based on a control of the very trade of which the grave-goods are such an eloquent witness.

W

Wallace, Alfred Russel (1823–1913). In 1858, contemporaneously with Charles **Darwin,** Wallace arrived at a theory of natural selection by "the survival of the fittest". He communicated with Darwin and the same year they presented to the Linnaean Society in London a joint paper giving their views on the theory of evolution.

Warka, *see* Sumerians.

Wat Phu, *see* Laos.

Weaving, *see* Clothing.

Weep-hole. A drainage hole in a wall or a roof as a precaution against damp.

Wheel. The invention of the wheel revolutionized transport. It transformed the **sledge** from a vehicle that had to be dragged over the ground by main force into one which ran comparatively smoothly and easily. It was developed thousands of years ago in Asia, yet curiously enough, though the Pre-Columbian Americans produced high forms of civilization, the wheel was not known in America until it was introduced from Europe in the sixteenth century A.D.

The wheel was probably developed originally out of the use of tree-trunks as rollers for transporting heavy loads. If the middle part of the trunk were chopped away to leave an axle with a solid wheel at either end, this could be fixed underneath a sledge and so produce a wheeled vehicle.

It is not known when this – if this is how it did happen – first took place. The earliest carts, being of perishable wood, have disappeared, and it is not until models or drawings appear that the archaeologist can be sure of the existence of wheeled vehicles. It may have come into use in the **Halafian** culture in **Neolithic** times but this is not definitely established. It was certainly known among the **Sumerians** as early as 3500 B.C., and by 3000 B.C. was in general use throughout the eastern half of the **Fertile Crescent.** The **Indus Valley civilization** possessed it by 2500 B.C., and it appears in the **Minoan civilization** in Crete by 2000 B.C. and by about the same date in Asia Minor. The Egyptians, however, who were so advanced in many other ways, did not use the wheel until their **Hyksos** conquerors introduced it in about 1650 B.C. It appears in the **Anyang** civilization of China round about 1400 B.C.

It might be expected that the two main ancient uses of the wheel – vertically for transport, horizontally for pottery making – would have come into use simultaneously in a civilization, but this did not prove to be the case. The Egyptians used the wheel for making pottery a thousand years before they used it for transport. In Crete and northern Europe it was the other way round. Model carts have been excavated in Crete which are some two hundred years older than the first wheel-made pots. In northern Europe wheeled transport appears round about 1500 B.C., but wheel-made pots not until some thousand years later.

The earliest forms of vehicle known to us are two-wheeled carts, with solid wheels in one piece with the axle; the latter was fastened underneath the body by leather straps. Such carts – ox-drawn, as they would have been in prehistoric times – are still to be found in parts of the world today. Two-wheeled carts remained much more popular than four-wheeled wagons because of the failure to evolve a method of making the front wheels pivot while turning a corner; even the Romans do not seem to have achieved this, though scholars are divided on this point, some thinking they did.

Wilton Culture, *see* Africa, East *and* Africa, Stone Age Man in South.

Wonders of the World, *see* Seven Wonders of the World.

Woodhenge is situated in Wiltshire in England, two miles north-east of **Stonehenge.** In 1925 Wing-Commander Insall, V.C., noticed, from the air, concentric rings of white chalk marks in the ploughed soil within the ditch. These were holes which had contained massive posts, up to three feet in diameter.

Excavation by B.G. and M.E. Cunnington in the period 1926–28, revealed a bank and ditch surrounding six concentric rings of posts. The name Woodhenge was coined during this excavation. The bank was twenty-five feet wide and 250 feet in diameter from crest to crest. A berm (ledge) five feet wide separated the bank from an inner ditch which was shallow and flat-bottomed, being only seven feet deep but sixteen feet wide on the floor and thirty feet wide at ground level. To the north-north-east an undug causeway across the ditch formed an entrance thirty feet wide. Short concrete pillars now mark the exact position of each post-hole in the interior.

Here then was a religious monument small in size, but massive in detail. As the prehistoric worshipper came through the entrance and approached the centre he would first of all pass through a ring of sixty posts, then of thirty-two posts, then through the most massive of all, sixteen posts some three feet in diameter, then two rings of eighteen posts and finally one of twelve, only thirty-nine feet in diameter. The most massive ring had had ramps cut to help in the fitting of the large posts into their holes.

The religious function of this monument is, of course, unknown but it belongs to Class I of a group known in Britain as "henge monuments", of which Stonehenge is the most famous.

The uprights may have had lintels (like Stonehenge) but there is no evidence for this, nor were they arranged in pairs. It is suggested that the uprights may have supported the roof of a circular timber building.

The long diameter of the six rings coincides approximately with the direction of the midsummer sunrise. On this line, in the south-west segment of the innermost ring, a grave was uncovered. It had been hollowed out one foot into the chalk and in it lay the crouched skeleton of a three-year-old girl who had been buried facing the midsummer sunrise. The child's skull had been cut open before burial and there were no grave-goods. All circumstances point to a dedicatory or sacrificial rite. A similar burial seems to have taken place on the east side of the monument in the bottom of the ditch, where there was another shallow grave containing the crouched skeleton of a young male adult and a cremated burial had been placed in the ditch. Two chalk models of Breton jadeite axes were also found and they also had a jadeite votive significance.

What was the date of this sanctuary? In the lowest filling of the ditch, in the old turf-line under the bank and in some of the post-holes, were found numerous sherds of Rinyo-Clacton Ware. Beaker pottery came only from the later silting. The site may therefore be assigned to the Secondary **Neolithic** culture, immediately after 2000 B.C.; although it had later been used by **Beaker People** at a later stage.

Woolley, Charles Leonard (1880–1960). Sir Leonard Woolley's distinguished career as an archaeologist and author began with the excavations of Corbridge while he was Assistant Keeper of the Ashmolean Museum in Oxford (1905–07). But experience in the Sudan at Buhen (1907–11) turned his attention to the Middle East where, with T.E. Lawrence, he cleared the **Hittite** city of Carchemish (1912–14, 1919) and explored surface remains in Sinai.

After two seasons' work at **Tell el Amarna** for the Egypt Exploration Society he was chosen to direct the joint British Museum and University of Pennsylvania Expedition working at **Ur** of the Chaldees in Babylonia from 1922 to 1934. The long seasons' work, often in difficult weather conditions, was amply rewarded. The complex of religious buildings which were uncovered near the **ziggurat** revealed many features of **Sumerian** architecture hitherto unknown. Tracing the history of the city back from its abandonment after Persian times to its prehistoric foundations, Woolley came upon the famous Royal Graves resplendent with jewellery and fine objects mainly of the Early Dynastic III period (about 2500 B.C.). These he succeeded in recovering and restoring at a time before the latest scientific techniques and aids were available. He traced a deposit of clay which he attributes to the **Flood** mentioned in the **Gilgamesh Epic** and in the Old Testament and cleared a residential quarter of the city which, with the thousands of **cuneiform** inscriptions found, showed the daily life of the Sumerians and their successors.

The discoveries at Ur, made widely known by Woolley's lucid writings and lectures, did much to further interest in Mesopotamian archaeology and history. He constantly sought for new information to fill in the numerous gaps in the growing knowledge of the ancient Middle East and believed that all his archaeological work should be specially directed to this end. The need to find out the connection between the Aegean, Cyprus, Greece and the known civilizations of Mesopotamia led him to work at the Syrian seaport of al-Mina (1936) and at **Tell Atchana** (ancient Alalakh) during 1937–39 and 1946–49. Although only partially successful in tracing the trade and cultural influences, the site provided new evidence of a small kingdom of mixed Semitic and **Hurrian** populations which flourished near Aleppo in the eighteenth and fifteenth centuries B.C. *See* plate 147, page 476.

Writing, *see* Alphabet.

Y

Yang-shao. The **Neolithic** Yang-shao culture was apparently confined to the mountain regions of Honan Province in north-west China, and was perhaps the product of Turkic and Tibetan tribes living in these regions though it may have spread through the mountain system to parts of mainland south-east Asia and to the Philippines. The pottery is a fine brick-red ware, decorated in three colours, white, red and black, and a number of forms, notably tripods, seem to be related to historical Chinese types which also occur in the bronze repertoire. (This may, however, be due to the fact that the Yang-shao culture persisted until at least 700 B.C. and its potters may therefore have copied Chinese metal vessels in their ceramics.) The Yang-shao people made extensive use of jade in addition to the more usual stone for their tools, the axes being of the rectangular type. Bone implements were also found. Agriculture and cattle-raising were the apparent basis of the Yang-shao economy. The pottery has affinities with that of Kukuteni and Anau, but it is important to note that it is the later phases of Yang-shao which have the closets links with Anau. As the earliest phases seem to belong to central China, the later phases only occurring in the more westerly Yang-shao sites, it seems that in fact this is a local culture with fortuitous resemblances to those of westerly Eurasia. (This view is contrary to that held by Andersson, the discoverer of Yang-shao, who was convinced of the great antiquity of the site, because of the Anau parallels, and not because of its actual archaeological context in China.)

Yayoi, *see* Japan, Prehistoric.

Yueh. The term Yueh subsumes a complex hybrid cultural zone which in the second millennium B.C. appears to have occupied the whole coastal region from Korea to Indo-China in the Far East. It seems to have emerged from a mixture of a collecting and hunting culture, known as Yao, in the mountain areas of central China, which was in the process of turning to slash-and-burn agriculture, and the valley culture, depending upon the cultivation of rice, which was associated with **T'ai**-speaking peoples. The Yueh culture seems to have been responsible for maritime developments along the coasts of the Far East, and it was this development which enabled some of its component peoples to move into the Indonesian islands where their presence is probably typified by the rectangular section **Neolithic** axe. In some areas of China the Yueh long resisted sinization and as late as the eighth century A.D. much of Fukien still retained a distinctive cultural autonomy. Farther south the last considerable migrant group of Yueh which had occupied the Tonkin delta at the beginning of the Christian era, or a century or so earlier, formed the nucleus of the Viet-namese cultural zone, the term Viet being the Annamite form of Yueh. The persistence of common cultural traits which link east Java with the north China coast as late as the sixteenth century A.D. is undoubtedly due to their common culture in the second millennium B.C.

yün-kang is a Buddhist cave site near Ta-t'ung, north Shansi. Work began here in A.D. 460, under the aegis of the Wei dynasty, and continued until A.D. 494. Twenty major shrines and a large number of smaller ones were executed in this period in the sandstone cliffs; a number of smaller shrines and niches containing fine examples of mature Wei style work were added in the period A.D. 500–36. The earliest caves are five in number, dedicated to the king and his four predecessors, and contain enormous Buddha images, one seated figure being forty-five feet high. The prototypes are clearly to be seen in the colossal images of the Buddha near Bamiyan, Afghanistan. From this style a Chinese one rapidly developed, under the influence, it seems, of surviving Han traditions and the last of the caves of the main period, number six, shows the evolved style. A central pillar is carved as a wooden pagoda. The walls, in a series of horizontal registers, are decorated with Buddhas, with attendants and musicians, scenes of the life of Gautama Buddha, and so on. The style is essentially linear (in the later period there is greater depth), and may be said to have evolved as a fully Chinese one, comparable with the contemporary examples from **Lung-men.**

Z

Zapotecs, *see* Mexico.

Ziggurat ("high point") is the designation of the temple-tower built in all the principal **Sumerian, Babylonian** and **Assyrian** cities. It is a characteristic architectural and religious feature of their civilization and as such is represented in art and written texts. The interest of early explorers was drawn to the ruins of these distinctive buildings by their resemblance in form and purpose to the **"Tower of Babel"** of the Bible (Genesis II).

In the late fourth millennium B.C. the early inhabitants of southern **Iraq** built the main temple on a single raised **temenos,** and thus created an artificial citadel. This was done from motives of reverence rather than for protection from floods or attack, since there appears to have been free access to the temple. The earliest "temple on a high terrace" was found at Eridu and this was a prototype reproduced at **Uruk** (Level IV), the so-called Ziggurat of Anu and its associated white temple, and as far north as Brak in the Habur region. Not all such temples were sited on rectangular platforms for, by the Early Dynastic II period (about 2700 B.C.), the temple and its outbuildings are found within an oval-walled sanctuary area raised above the surrounding buildings. Khafaja, by the Diyala River, and **Al Ubaid,** four miles north of Ur, are good examples of this.

In 1940–41 the Iraqis excavating Uqair found a temple set upon two terraces and approached up two short flights of steps. This, together with representations of other three-tiered ziggurats and references to Gudea's construction at **Lagash** shows that by the second half of the second millennium such multi-staired buildings were common practice. Few remains can, however, be traced since these structures often provided the basis for later rebuilding. Thus, at **Ur, Ur-Nammu** (about 2150 B.C.), founder of the third dynasty, used the remains of a first dynasty ziggurat, built at least four centuries earlier, as the core of his new work. He made the lowest platform a rectangle 190 feet by 130 feet orientated to the north-east. For strength, walls thirty-six feet high were built on a curve at a pronounced **batter** and relieved by buttresses at every sixteen feet with the four corners especially reinforced. The outer skin was of kiln-dried bricks, often inscribed with the king's name and titles, with bitumen mortar and layers of matting, the whole being frequently pierced by **weep-holes** for drainage purposes.

Access to the upper stages of the ziggurat was by a main stairway of brick set at right angles to the north-east face. This led direct to the temple on the summit but, at the place on the edge of the first platform where it was joined by two staircases rising diagonally across the face from the north and east corners, it passed beneath an impressive copper-domed arched doorway. The terraces surrounding the upper and smaller stages were covered with bitumen, and there is evidence that trees had been planted here and watered from hoists which worked up the sloping sides of the ziggurat. Some scholars think that a similar decoration of the temple-tower at **Babylon** may have given rise to the description of the "Hanging Gardens" as one of the **Seven Wonders of the World.**

Later ziggurats are known from other excavations. Two dating from the time of **Hammurabi** are known from **Mari** and Kish. The **Kassites** built one at Dur-Kurigalzu (Aqarquf near Baghdad) and the **Elamite** Untash-Huban (1265–1245 B.C.) erected an unusual one at Choga-Zambil, sixteen miles south-east of **Susa,** dedicated to the god Inshushinak with gateway chapels in the middle of three sides at the top of separate stairways. This ziggurat was originally 114 yards square at the base and was forty-five yards high.

The **Assyrians,** heirs of the **Sumerian** civilization, built temple-towers at their capital cities.

Tiglath-Pileser I (about 1105 B.C.) had twin ziggurats dedicated to Anu and Antum, the god and goddess of Ashur. About the same time one was built at **Nimrud** and both were kept in careful repair by Shalmaneser III. Sargon II, the conqueror of Samaria, perhaps influenced by the towers at Nimrud and Babylon, provided the ziggurat at his newly built capital at Khorsabad with ascending ramps which encircled the outer face and thus replaced the stairway.

The best known ziggurats are those repaired by the neo-Babylonian kings, for their remains are still visible today. Nabonidus (556–539 B.C.) refaced the ziggurat at Ur and increased its height, providing seven stages of which the lowest, at sixty feet, can still be seen. Nebuchadnezzar continued work on a similar building at Babylon called Etemenanki – "The Building [House] of the Foundation of Heaven and Earth". An inscribed clay tablet dated 229 B.C. gives details of this and its associated temple called Esagila – "The House whose top is as [high as] the Heavens". The base, as confirmed by excavation, measured 98 yards square and upon this seven platforms topped by the temple of Marduk-Bel rose to a similar height. These must have been the "eight towers in all, one upon another, flanked by a spiral staircase which runs around the outside", seen by the Greek historian **Herodotus** when he visited Babylon about 460 B.C. Thus by the Late Babylonian period the "temple on a high terrace" had become a tower with a crowning sanctuary upon it. The ziggurat was destroyed by Xerxes, cleared by Alexander and later robbed of its bricks by local builders.

Most early explorers saw in the lofty ruins of Babylon (Mujellibeh) the biblical Tower of Babel, though some identified this with Aqarquf. The remarkably vitrified upper brickwork of the ziggurat at Borsippa (Birs Nimrud), seven miles southwest of Babylon, has, however, also been equated with it. The latter was an ancient building only partially restored by Nebuchadnezzar. There is no certain support for the view of **Rawlinson** and others that the seven stages of the ziggurats of Borsippa and Babylon were coloured black, white, orange, blue, scarlet, silver and gold and represented the planets Saturn, Venus, Jupiter, Mercury, Mars, the moon and the sun. The Babylonian order of designating the planets was different and at Ur traces of the colours black, red and blue (uppermost) were found.

The full conception of the ziggurat has as yet been only partially recovered. **Layard** dug into the solid masonry of the Nimrud ziggurat in the belief that it housed a royal tomb as did the pyramids of Egypt. Some think that it was an artificial mountain reproduced by the earliest inhabitants in the plain in keeping with their original hilly homeland; others that it was merely an artificial means of protecting the temple. But it is known that the summit temple was only used on special occasions when the patron deity descended to the top to pass the night there with its solitary occupant, a priestess. There is some ground for the view that the ziggurat was intended to reflect on earth what was in heaven. The upper temple, *Shahuru* or "waiting room", had its counterpart in the town below and terms like *Absu* ("the Deep") are applied both to the ziggurat and to the water pool (an inverted ziggurat) where dwelt Ea, the god of wisdom. The top temple was also called a *Gigunu* ("a dark" or "leafy chamber") a term equally applied to a subterranean cloister. To the Sumerian the ziggurat was unmistakably a pointer or ladder to the skies. It was the gateway to heaven.

Zimbabwe. The ruined stone buildings known by this name lie in well wooded country about fifteen miles south-east of Fort Victoria in southern Rhodesia.

Although much of the walling is broken down and vast quantities of stone clutter the ground, the place is extremely impressive, both because of the great walls which remain and also because of the unexpected appearance of a large stone building in the heart of Africa. All the walling has been built "dry", the building material being the local granite which splits naturally into slabs a few inches thick.

The actual ruins cover about seventy acres and are divided into two distinct areas; the larger lies in a broad valley, and the remainder stands about a quarter of a mile to the north on the top of a rocky hill. The principal building in the valley is an elliptical enclosure, commonly called "The Temple" although its old name *imbahuru* means merely "the great room". On the top of the hill the buildings have naturally been called in recent years "The Acropolis" although such Africans as will talk about the place call it quite simply *zimbabwe*.

The literal meaning of this Shona word, now usually used in its plural form *madzimbabwe*, has been forgotten, but its present meaning is "the chiefs' burial ground and the place of tribal intercession". The earliest account of the Zimbabwe Ruins gives details of the use of Zimbabwe Hill as a place of tribal prayer.

There is nothing in the Portuguese records so far published to show that the Portuguese ever visited this particular building, although one rather obscure passage in de Barros' *De Asia* (published in 1552) may indicate that they knew of the place.

The ruins are said to have been first seen by white men in 1868, but the earliest description available in Europe was that of Carl Mauch, a German geologist, who was held by a neighbouring tribe as a "guest prisoner" during 1871–72. From Mauch's time onwards until early in this century Zimbabwe was the goal of gold hunters, who dug quite indiscriminately and did great damage to the archaeological deposits in the structures.

The first published excavations were those of Theodore Bent (1891) and Sir John Willoughby (1892), but both were in the nature of antiquarian treasure hunts. In 1902–4 R.N. Hall was given the task of clearing the ruins and making them available to tourists but in the process he removed several feet of deposit in the principal buildings. Limited excavations were made by Randall-MacIver (1905) but the only really useful archaeological work was that done by Dr Caton-Thompson in 1929. Further excavations, in areas not examined by Dr Caton-Thompson, were undertaken by the Monuments Commission in 1958.

The absence of any written record, the unusual finds discovered by early investigators, the romantic notions of local commentators, especially R.N. Hall, and the absence of any considerable body of informed archaeological opinion among the Rhodesian public until quite recently has led to a mass of romantic legend being woven around this monument by European settlers. The romantic fog is most difficult to dispel and even today Dr Caton-Thompson's work is adversely criticized by popular writers.

The fullest description is to be found in Hall's *Great Zimbabwe* (1905) which contains a mass of most useful factual material about the surface remains, although the records of digging are too meagre to be of much value and the interpretations are no longer regarded as valid.

The Great Enclosure (or "Temple") is a more or less elliptical building 288 feet long and 220 feet wide with its major axis lying almost exactly north-west to south-east; the circumference of the outer wall is 832 feet. This wall is one of the principal features of the ruin-field, rising in places to a height of thirty feet and sometimes reaching a width of fourteen feet. Some 260 feet of the outer wall bears a chevron pattern, built into the topmost courses of the wall at the south-eastern end of its main axis. No other principal walls are decorated.

This wall was very dilapidated when the ruins were first discovered and it has been much rebuilt. Although no description exists of the wall in its original state, it is known that Mauch saw lintels over one of the entrances. The reconstruction of the entrances as V-shaped slits is therefore regarded as inaccurate, as it is believed that these were originally lintelled doorways. Within this wall is a maze of similar enclosures and passages and at the south-east corner there rises the well known Conical Tower, an apparently solid stone structure about eighteen feet in diameter and now thirty-one feet high.

In the course of Hall's 1902–4 operations he found that the interior of the Great Enclosure had been floored with smooth cement-like material made from ant-heap, on which there had stood at one time a number of mud huts. There were at least three such floors, laid down at various times and between them Hall found a mass of occupation material – potsherds, iron tools and weapons, copper and gold ornaments, carved stone-bowls and other objects, glass beads and other imports from China, India and Persia. This magnificent stratification was nearly all destroyed without its significance being understood or adequate records kept.

These floors, when new, were practically waterproof and, since there is no sign whatever that there was ever a roof over the building, it is clear that the courtyards would require storm water drains; these have been found in the foot of some of the Great Enclosure walls.

The Great Enclosure stands high up on the side of the valley and below it in a north-easterly direction stretches a series of ruined buildings, covering over 500 yards in length and about 150 yards or less in width. These buildings, known collectively as the Valley Ruins, are thickest near the Great Enclosure, where they form a continuous mass of walling and tail off into separate ranges of buildings as one descends to the floor of the valley. It was in one of these separate buildings, known as the Maund Ruins, that Dr Caton-Thompson's principal excavations were made. (The Valley Ruins were divided in arbitrary sections by Hall and named by him after Rhodesian pioneers, many of whom had no connection whatever with Zimbabwe.)

Stretching north-west from the Great Enclosure for about 250 yards is another group of badly ruined structures which have been completely ransacked and partly robbed of their stone.

Looking down on the Great Enclosure and the valley generally is a rocky hill, on the summit of which the so-called Acropolis stands. This is a maze of small enclosures and passages built up between the great rocks which form the top of the hill. Most of the ruins are packed into a narrow space about forty yards wide bounded on the north by immense rocks and on the south by a sheer drop of nearly one hundred feet.

The western end of this space is closed by a thick high wall, comparable in size and style to the outer wall of the Great Enclosure. Like the Great Enclosure wall this too was in a tumbledown condition, but sufficient indication of doors remained for it to be reconstructed according its original design.

The approach to the main buildings of the Acropolis from the valley is up a stairway (reconstructed as far as possible on the old lines), whose topmost part is a passage between rocky walls.

The western slope of Zimbabwe Hill has been built into a series of terraced platforms by the construction of retaining walls and a passage runs from valley level right up to the Great West Wall.

These ruins have challenged the imagination not only of archaeologists and antiquarians but also of architects, and a number of specifically architectural studies have been made.

In all cases the architects have pointed out the lack of plan, the lack of foundations, the ignorance of the arch and of masonry principles generally, all of which is coupled with an empirical approach to building problems and a high degree of competence in workmanship. Altogether, the architectural opinion is that the building is barbaric and has no common ground with established architectural traditions anywhere in the civilized world.

It is now known that there are remains of some two hundred buildings constructed of coursed drystone work in southern Rhodesia and just over its borders. In addition to those examined by Dr MacIver and Dr Caton-Thompson, many others have been examined by the Inspectors of Monuments during the past ten years. None is as large as Zimbabwe but every single architectural feature found at Zimbabwe can be paralleled elsewhere with the one exception of the Conical Tower.

There are therefore good grounds for believing that Zimbabwe architecture belongs to a tradition which has developed locally in the granite areas of the Rhodesian plateau.

The earlier antiquarians had nothing with which to compare their finds, but later and more objective investigators noted that all finds of pottery and other objects were of characteristically African type. As the volume of comparative material has steadily increased, the predominantly African nature of the finds has become even more apparent.

The existence of other buildings of similar tradition has already been mentioned. Test excavations have been made in many of these and all have yielded finds which bear great similarity to, and often complete identity with, those of Zimbabwe.

There are, however, certain finds for which there are no known ethnographical parallels: soapstone birds on tall beams, which were found standing erect in the easternmost part of the Acropolis in 1888, when they were removed; they cannot therefore belong to any very ancient culture and are probably of African origin; soapstone bowls – large shallow dishes of which fragments are found throughout the deposits; soapstone "phalli" – found in considerable quantities throughout the deposits. Similar objects in clay have recently been found, some of which have been proved to be female figurines. These latter are undoubtedly African.

The archaeology of Zimbabwe and of the Rhodesian Iron Age generally is a matter of current research and much work is still unpublished. The completely African nature of Zimbabwe and its culture was made clear by Dr MacIver and by Dr Caton-Thompson more recently, but during the last ten years it has been confirmed time and again.

There are three lines of dating evidence available: (*a*) historical; (*b*) extension dating, from a consideration of imports; (*c*) direct dating, by **radiocarbon** analysis.

(*a*) As already mentioned, there are no definite written references to Zimbabwe before the late nineteenth century; the Portuguese records relate to a number of "Zimbabwes" which were in fact merely royal towns.

(*b*) The earliest datable import is a Persian **faience** bowl, probably of thirteenth century A.D.

in the country of its origin; there are also a number of fragments of Ming celadon of the fourteenth or fifteenth century A.D. All these appear to have come from early occupation levels in the Great Enclosure and suggest that it should not be dated earlier than about the fourteenth century. Dr Caton-Thompson used glass beads from India and elsewhere in the East as the basis for her dating and suggested ninth century A.D. as a possible date. In 1931, when this date was suggested, bead-dating was in its infancy and it is only now that additional evidence from Indonesia and the Far East is being collected, as a result of which it may be that the ninth-century date will require adjustment. Unfortunately, cross-dating is impossible as African exports mentioned by Arab writers – gold, iron and ivory – were raw materials, not manufactures, so we cannot find any African articles in Arab, Indian or Chinese archaeological contexts.

(*c*) The new method of radiocarbon dating has been applied to two pieces of timber which formed the lintel of a drain in the base of one of the inner walls of the Great Enclosure. The average dates obtained, after tests in Chicago and London, were A.D. 591 and A.D. 702, both figures having standard deviations of error of about 100 years.

Unfortunately there are a number of possible sources of error and these dates are regarded as but doubtful to the age of the building.

At present, therefore, Dr Caton-Thompson's date of about the ninth century A.D. still stands as the most probable date for Zimbabwe. *See* plates 149, 150, pages 469, 470.

Zinjanthropus is the name given by Professor Leakey to the skull of a **Fossil Man** which he discovered at **Olduvai Gorge** in July 1959. Because the skull was found in association with pebble-tools it is classified as that of a **hominid**, and is regarded as a contemporary to **Australopithecus.** The great size of the teeth, especially the molars, has led to Zinjanthropus being given the nickname of "Nutcracker Man", and indicates that his diet was mainly vegetarian. He is dated to the Lower **Pleistocene**, about half a million years ago.

Ziwiyè. The site of Ziwiyè, identified with ancient Zibia, a fortified city of the Mannians, is near Sakiz in Azerbaijan, seventy-five miles south-east of Lake Urmia. Archaeologically, Ziwiyè is renowned for a treasure-trove accidentally discovered there by a shepherd boy in 1946. This collection, housed today in several national museums, contains ivory, gold and bronze objects of fine workmanship, but of uncertain origin and date; these mainly fall within the period 675–600 B.C., but certain ivory pieces suggest the last quarter of the eighth century B.C. It is possible that part of this treasure, enclosed in a bronze coffin, formed the royal dowry of Esarhaddon's daughter on her marriage to the Scythian King Partatua.

Stylistically the collection may be divided into four distinct groups: Assyrian, Assyro-Scythian, Scythian and Mannian. Urartian influence, however, is not altogether absent. Motifs which constantly recur in Assyrian and Scythian art are freely incorporated into the designs; these are often found in conjunction on a single object. This reflects the influence of two important cultures which bordered the country of the Mannians. Anthropomorphic symbols are used – the man-bulls and winged genii of Assyrian reliefs. The animal style includes composite creatures, such as winged sphinxes and gryphons, which in many examples wear the typical Phoenician kilt. The gold pectoral, one of the chief objects of the treasure, displays such figures, placed within registers, and moving in opposed files towards a centrally placed tree of life.

An outstanding piece of Ziwiyè jewellery, found intact, is the splendid Lion Armlet in gold. This is a remarkable example of the Assyrian jewellers' skill, and the working of the lions' heads, with heavy "eye-warts" and stylized facial markings, is reminiscent of many examples of Assyrian art.

The Scythian animal style is seen to advantage in a gold scabbard ornamented with ibex heads; its chape (the metal cap at the point) terminates in a highly stylized mask-head. Further examples influenced by Scythian art are gold furniture terminals of gryphon heads, which find marked parallels in objects from Scythian graves in southern Russia.

Local art of the Mannians, which adopts the animal style of Luristan, is represented by gold plaques worked in **repoussé**, used as applied ornamentation to leather or textile surfaces, a fashion well-known to the Scythians.

The significance of the Ziwiyè Treasure, which displays a blending of such varied west Asiatic influences, lies mainly in the light it throws on Median art, for authentic objects of this period of the history of **Iran** have as yet escaped discovery. *See* plate 148, page 468.

For Further Reading

This list of books is far from comprehensive. Generally more difficult books have been excluded unless they have some claim to be classics; books in languages other than English have also been kept to a minimum.

AFRICA

GENERAL

L'Afrique Préhistorique by H. BREUIL, Paris, 1931

AFRICA, EAST

The Prehistory of East Africa by SONIA COLE, Penguin, London and Baltimore, Md, 1954

The Old Stone Age in the Anglo-Egyptian Sudan by A. J. ARKELL, Sudan Antiquities Service, Khartoum, 1949

The Stone Age Cultures of Kenya Colony by L. S. B. LEAKEY, C.U.P., London, and Macmillan, New York, 1931

AFRICA, EASTERN COAST RUINS

Arab City of Gedi, Excavations at the Great Mosque, Architecture and Finds by J. S. KIRKMAN, O.U.P., London and New York, 1954

"Historical Archaeology in Kenya" by J. S. KIRKMAN, in *Antiquaries' Journal*, 37, 1957

Gedi and Fort Jesus, Royal National Parks of Kenya Handbook, London, 1959

AFRICA, NORTH

The Badarian Civilisation by G. BRUNTON and G. CATON-THOMPSON, British School of Archaeology in Egypt, London, 1928

Palaeolithic Man and the Nile Valley by K. S. SANDFORD and W. J. ARKELL, C.U.P., London and Chicago U.P., Chicago, Ill., 1939

The Prehistoric Archaeology of North-west Africa by F. R. WULSIN, Papers of the Peabody Museum of American Archaeology and Ethnology, Cambridge, Mass., 1941

AFRICA, PREHISTORIC ART IN

Rock-Drawings of Southern Upper Egypt, vols 1–2, by H. A. WINKLER, O.U.P., London, 1938–9

"Some Rock-paintings in Central Tanganyika" by A. T. CULWICK, in *Journal of Royal Anthropological Institute*, 61, London, 1931

AFRICA, STONE AGE MAN IN

The Prehistory of Southern Rhodesia by N. JONES, C.U.P., London and New York, 1949

Stone Age Africa, by L. S. B. Leakey, O.U.P., London and New York, 1936

"The Stone Age Cultures of South Africa" by A. J. H. GOODWIN and C. VAN RIET LOWE, in *Annals of the South African Museum*, 27, Cape Town, 1929

AFRICA, STONE AGE MAN IN SOUTH

The Prehistory of Southern Africa by J. DESMOND CLARK, Penguin, London and Baltimore, Md, 1959

Rock Paintings of the Drakensburg by A. R. WILLCOX, Max Parrish, London, 1956

South Africa's Past in Stone and Paint, by M. C. BURKITT, C.U.P., London and Macmillan, New York, 1928

AFRICA, WEST

"Archaeology in the Gold Coast" by C. T. SHAW in *African Studies*, 2, 1943

ETHIOPIA

The Abyssinian at Home by C. H. WALKER, S.P.C.K., London, 1933; Macmillan, New York, 1934

Cinq Années de Recherches Archéologiques en Ethiopie by R. P. AZAIS and R. CHAMBARD, Paris, 1932

Essai sur l'Histoire Antique de l'Abyssinie by A. KAMMERER, Paris, 1926

Historia Aethiopica by LUDOLF, tr. J. P. GENT, Samuel Smith, London, 1652

The Sacred City of the Ethiopians by J. T. BENT, Longmans, London and New York, 1893

Some Records of Ethiopia 1593–1646 by C. F. BECKINGHAM and G. W. B. HUNTINGFORD, Hakluyt Society, London, 1954

HAMITIC PEOPLE

The Galla of Ethiopia by G. W. B. HUNTINGFORD, International African Institute, London, 1955

Peoples of the Horn of Africa by I. M. LEWIS, International African Institute, London, 1955

Peoples of South-west Ethiopia and its Borderland by E. CERULLI, International African Institute, London, 1956

The Non-Bantu Languages of North-east Africa by A. N. TUCKER and M. A. BRYAN, O.U.P., London and New York, 1956

NEGROES, ORIGIN OF THE

The Opening Up of Africa by Sir H. H. JOHNSTON, Williams & Norgate, London, 1911

Races of Africa by C. G. SELIGMAN, O.U.P., London and New York, 1957

The Races of Man and their Distribution by A. C. HADDON, C.U.P., London, and Macmillan, New York, 1925

SUDAN

A History of the Sudan to A.D. 1821 by A. J. ARKELL, Athlone, London and De Graff, New York, 1955

ZIMBABWE

Great Zimbabwe by R. N. Hall, Methuen, London, 1905
The Zimbabwe Culture by G. Caton-Thomson, O.U.P., London and New York, 1931
The Zimbabwe-Monomata Culture in South-east Africa by H. A. Wieschoff, Banta, Menasha, Wis., 1941

AMERICA

AMERICA, EARLY MAN IN

Ancient Man in North America by H. M. Wormington, Denver Museum of Natural History, Denver, Colo., 4th. ed. 1957
Early Man in America by E. H. Sellards, Texas U.P., Austin, Texas, 1952
Early Man in the New World by K. MacGowan, Macmillan, London and New York, 1950
Los Origenes Americanos by P. Martinez Del Rio, Mexico D.F., 3rd ed. 1952

AMER-INDIANS

Handbook of South American Indians, vols 1–6, ed. J. H. Steward, Smithsonian Institution, Washington, 1946
Heritage of Conquest; the Ethnology of Middle America, by S. Tax and others, Free Press, Chicago, Ill., 1952
Indians before Colombus by P. S. Martin, G. I. Quimby and D. Collier, C.U.P., London and Chicago U.P., Chicago, Ill., 1947

AZTECS

The Aztecs of Mexico by G. C. Vaillant, Penguin, London and Baltimore, Md, 1950
Mexican Archaeology by T. A. Joyce, P. Lee Warner, London and Putnam, New York, 1914
The Conquest of New Spain by Bernal Diaz, tr. A. P. Maudslay, Hakluyt Society, London, 1911–16
La Vie Quotidienne des Aztèques by Jacques Soustelle, Paris, 1955
See also Mexico

INCAS

Inca Land by H. Bingham, Constable, London and Houghton, New York, 1922
Lost City of the Incas by H. Bingham, Phoenix House, London, 1951; Duell, New York, 1948

MAYA

An Album of Maya Architecture by T. Proskouriakoff, Carnegie Institution of Washington Publications, 588, Washington, 1946
The Ancient Maya by S. G. Morley, ed. G. W. Brainerd, Stanford U.P., Stanford, Calif., 3rd ed. 1956
A Glimpse at Guatemala by A. P. and A. C. Maudslay, Murray, London, 1899
Landa's Relación de Las Cosas de Yucatán by A. M. Tozzer, Papers of the Peabody Museum of American Archaeology and Ethnology, Cambridge, Mass., 1941
Maya and Mexican Art by T. A. Joyce, Studio, London, 1926
Maya Hieroglyphic Writing: Introduction by J. E. S. Thomson, Carnegie Institution of Washington Publications, 589, Washington, 1950
The Rise and Fall of Maya Civilization by J. E. S. Thomson, University of Oklahoma Press, Norman, Calif., 1954

MEXICO

Arquitectura Prehispanica by Ignacio Marquina, Instituto Nacional de Antropologia e Historia, Mexico, 1951
Excavations at Teotihuacan Mexico by S. Linne, Stockholm, 1934
Mexico before Cortez by J. E. S. Thomson, Scribner, New York, 1933
Zapotecan Antiquities by S. Linne, Stockholm, 1938

PERUVIANS

The Ancient Cities of the New World by Désiré Charnay, tr. J. Gonino and H. S. Conant, New York, 1887
Ancient Civilisations of the Andes by P. A. Means, Scribner, London and New York, 1931
The Conquest of Peru by W. H. Prescott, Bickers, London, 1878; Harper, New York, 1847
Peru, by G. H. S. Bushnell, Thames & Hudson, London, 1956
Relation of the Discovery and Conquest of the Kingdom of Peru by P. Pizarro, tr. P. A. Means, Cortez Society, New York, 1921
Accounts of the Incas and Peru by the Spanish Conquistadores tr. and ed. Sir C. R. Markham, Hakluyt Society, London, 1864, 1907, 1913

EARLY MAN

GENERAL

Fossil Men by M. Boule, ed. H. V. Vallois, tr. M. Bullock, Thames & Hudson, London, 1957
History of the Primates by Sir W. Le Gros Clark, British Museum (Natural History), London, 5th ed., 1958
Mankind So Far by W. W. Howells, Sigma, London, 1947; Doubleday, New York, 1944

MESOLITHIC

The Mesolithic Age in Britain by J. G. D. Clark, C.U.P., London, and Macmillan, New York, 1932
The Mesolithic Settlement of Northern Europe by J. G. D. Clark, C.U.P., London, and Macmillan, New York, 1936

MESOLITHIC, NEOLITHIC AND COPPER AGE

Our Early Ancestors, by M. C. Burkitt, C.U.P., London, and Macmillan, New York, 1929

NEOLITHIC

The Danube in Prehistory by V.G. Childe, Clarendon Press, Oxford and New York, 1929
The Neolithic Cultures of the British Isles by S. Piggott, C.U.P., London and New York, 1954
"The Origin of Neolithic Culture in Northern Europe" by V.G. Childe in *Antiquity*, 23, 1949
The Prehistoric Chamber Tombs of England and Wales by G.E. Daniel, C.U.P., London and New York, 1950

PALAEOLITHIC

Adam's Ancestors by L.S.B. Leakey, Methuen, London, 4th ed., 1953
Dating the Past by F. Zeuner, Methuen, London and Longmans, New York, 4th rev. ed., 1958
Flint Implements by W. Watson, Trustees of the British Museum, London, 1950
Man the Toolmaker by K.P. Oakley, Trustees of the British Museum, London, 4th ed., 1958
The Old Stone Age by M.C. Burkitt, Bowes and Bowes, London, and New York U.P., New York, 3rd ed., 1956
Prehistory of Southern Rhodesia by N. Jones, C.U.P., London and New York, 1949
Stone Age Cultures of Kenya Colony by L.S.B. Leakey, C.U.P., London, and Macmillan, New York, 1931
Stone Age Cultures of North Rhodesia by J.D. Clark, Claremont, Cape Town, 1950

PALAEOLITHIC ART

Four Hundred Centuries of Cave Art by H. Breuil, tr. M.E. Boyle, Montignac, 1952
Painted Caves by Geoffrey Grigson, Phoenix House, London, 1957
Prehistoric Painting by A.H. Brodrick, Avalon Press, London, 1948

PILTDOWN SKULL

Counterfeit by S. Cole, Murray, London, 1955
The Piltdown Forgery by J.S. Weiner, O.U.P., London and New York, 1955

EGYPT

GENERAL

History of Egypt by J.H. Breasted, Hodder & Stoughton, London, 2nd rev. ed., 1905
The Legacy of Egypt by S.R.K. Glanville, O.U.P., London and New York, 1942
Life under the Pharoahs by Leonard Cottrell, Evans, London, 1953
The Lost Pharoahs by Leonard Cottrell, Evans, London, 1950

The Egyptians by Cyril Aldred, London, 1961
Egypt of the Pharaohs by Sir Alan Gardiner, Oxford, 1961

ABYDOS

See Egypt, General

AKHNATON

Tell el-Amarna by J.D.S. Pendlebury, Lovat Dickson, London, 1935
The City of Akhenaten by H. Frankfort and J.D.S. Pendelbury, O.U.P., London and New York, 1934

AMARNA

See Akhnaton

BELZONI

Narrative of the Operations and Recent Discoveries within the Pyramids, Temples, Tombs and Excavations in Egypt and Nubia by G.B. Belzoni, London, 1821

BOOK OF THE DEAD

"The Negative Confession" tr. J.A. Wilson in *Ancient Near Eastern Texts Relating to the Old Testament* pp. 345–6, ed. J. Pritchard, O.U.P., London, and Princeton U.P., N.J., 2nd rev. ed. 1955

BREASTED

Ancient Records of Egypt, vols 1–5, by J.H. Breasted, Chicago U.P., Chicago, Ill., 1920–3
A History of Egypt by J.H. Breasted, Hodder & Stoughton, London, and Scribner, New York, 2nd rev. ed. 1924
Pioneer to the Past, The Story of James Henry Breasted, Archaeologist by C. Breasted, Herbert Jenkins, London, 1947; Scribner, New York, 1943

CARTOUCHE

See Egypt, Hieroglyphs

CHAMPOLLION

See Hieroglyphs

COPTIC LANGUAGE

"The Value of Coptic" by W.C. Till in *Bulletin of John Rylands Library*, 40, Manchester, 1957

GIZA

See Pyramids

HIERATIC

See Hieroglyphs

HIEROGLYPHS

Egyptian Grammar by Sir A.H. Gardiner, O.U.P., London and New York, 3rd rev. ed. 1957

KARNAK

See Thebes

LEPSIUS

Denkmäler aus Aegypten und Äethiopen, vols 1–12, Berlin, 1849–58

LUXOR

See Thebes *and* Tutankhamun, Tomb of

MASPERO

Histoire Ancienne des Peuples de l'Orient Classique, vols 1–3, by G. C. C. MASPERO, Paris, 4th rev. ed. 1886

The Dawn of Civilisation by G. C. C. MASPERO, tr., M. L. MACLURE, ed.: A.H.SAYCE, S.P.C.K. London, and Macmillan, New York, 2nd ed. 1922

MUMMIES

Egyptian Mummies by G. E. SMITH and W. R. DAWSON, Allen & Unwin, London, 1924

NUBIA

See Sudan

OBELISK

Cleopatra's Needles and other Egyptian Obelisks by E. A. W. BUDGE, The Religious Tract Society, London, 1926

OXYRHYNCUS

"The Oxyrhyncus Papyri" by various authors in *Egypt Exploration Fund*, 1–25, 1898–1958

PAPYRUS

Paper and Books in Ancient Egypt by J. ČERÝY, Inaugural Lecture delivered at University College London, 1947

PYRAMIDS

The Development of the Egyptian Tomb down to the Accession of Cheops by G. A. REISNER, O.U.P., London, and Harvard U.P., Cambridge, Mass., 1936

The Mountains of Pharoah by L. COTTRELL, Hale, London, and Rhinehart, New York, 1956

Pyramids and Temples of Gizeh by W. M. F. PETRIE, Field and Tuer, London, rev. ed. 1885

The Pyramids of Egypt by I. E. S. EDWARDS, Penguin, London and Baltimore, Md., 1947

THE ROSETTA STONE

The Rosetta Stone by E. A. W. BUDGE, Trustees of the British Museum, London, 1913

SAQQARA

The Buried Pyramid by M. Z. GONEIM, Longmans, London, and (with title *The Lost Pyramid*) Rhinehart, New York, 1956

Egyptian Antiquities in the Nile Valley by J. BAIKIE, Methuen, London, and Macmillan, New York, 1932

SCARABS

Scarabs and Cylinders with Names by W. M. F. PETRIE, British School of Archaeology in Egypt, London, 1917

SERAPEUM

Le Sérapeum de Memphis by A. MARIGÈRE, Paris, 1857

TANIS

Tanis, vols 1–2, by W. F. PETRIE, Trubner, London, 1885 and 1888

THEBES

A Topographical Catalogue of the Private Tombs of Thebes by Sir A. H. GARDINER and A. E. P. WEIGALL, Quaritch, London, 1913

See also Saqqara *and* Egypt, General

TOMB ROBBERY PAPYRI

The Great Tomb Robberies of the Twentieth Egyptian Dyasty by T. E. PEET, O.U.P., London and New York, 1930

TUTANKHAMUN, TOMB OF

The Tomb of Tut-Ankh-Amen by H. CARTER and C. MACE, Cassell, London, and Doran, New York, 1923

Tutankhamun's Treasure by P. FOX, O.U.P., London and New York, 1951

EUROPE

GENERAL

British Prehistory by STUART PIGGOTT, O.U.P., London and New York, 1949

The Mesolithic Settlement of Northern Europe, by G. CLARK, C.U.P., London and New York, 1936

The Old Stone Age; a Study of Palaeolithic Times, by M. C. BURKITT, Bowes and Bowes, London, and New York U.P., New York, 3rd ed. 1956

Prehistoric Europe, the Economic Basis, by G. CLARK, Methuen, London, and Philosophical Library, New York, 1952

ALTAMIRA

The Cave of Altamira at Santillana del Mar, Spain, by H. BREUIL, translated by M. E. BOYLE, Madrid, 1935

AVEBURY

Articles by H. ST G. GRAY in *Archaeologia*, 1935, and by M. E. CUNNINGTON in the *Wiltshire Archaeological Magazine*, 1931

CARNAC

Menhirs et Dolmens: Monuments Mégalithiques de Bretagne by P. R. GIOT, Editions d'Art Jos le Doaré, Chateaulin, Finistère, 1957

Lascaux and Carnac, by G. E. DANIEL, Butterworth Press, London, 1955

DRUIDS

The Druids, a Study in Keltic Prehistory, by T.D. KENDRICK, Methuen, London, 2nd ed. 1928

HALLSTATT

"From Bronze Age to Iron Age, Middle Europe, Italy, and the North and West" by C.F.C.HAWKES in *Proceedings of the Prehistoric Society*, n.s. 14, 1948

Guide to Early Iron Age Antiquities in the Department of British and Mediaeval Antiquities, Trustees of the British Museum, London, 1925

"A Survey of the Evidence Concerning the Chronology and Origins of the Iron Age in Southern and Midland Britain" in *Reports of the Institute of Archaeology*, 8, University of London, 1952

Catalogue of Treasure of Carniola by A.MAHR and others, American Art Association, New York, 1934

MAIDEN CASTLE

"Maiden Castle" by R.E.M.WHEELER, *Society of Antiquaries Research Committee Report*, 12, 1943

MEDITERRANEAN, THE WESTERN

The Dawn of European Civilisation, ch. 12–15, by V.G. CHILDE, Routledge, London, 6th ed. 1957

The Etruscans by RAYMOND BLOCH, Thames & Hudson, London, 1958

The Etruscans by M.PALLOTTINO, Penguin, London and Baltimore, Md, 1955

The Iberians of Spain and their Relations with the Aegean World by Sir P.DIXON, O.U.P., London and New York, 1940

The Iron Age in Italy by D.RANDALL-MACIVER, O.U.P., London and New York, 1927

Malta by J.D.EVANS, Thames & Hudson, London, 1959

Préhistoire de la Méditeranée by M.R.SAUTER, Paris, 1948

Préhistoric Malta; the Tarxien Temples by Sir T.ZAMMIT, O.U.P., London, 1930

Sicily before the Greeks by L.BERNABÒ BREA, Thames & Hudson, London, 1957

The Stone and Bronze Ages in Italy and Sicily by T.E.PEET, O.U.P., London and New York, 1909

Two Celtic Waves in Spain (Rhys Memorial Lecture) by P.BOSCH-GIMPERA, British Academy, 1939

Villanovans and Early Etruscans by D.RANDALL-MACIVER, O.U.P., London and New York, 1924

PITT-RIVERS

Memoir, Excavations in Cranborne Chase by H.ST G. GRAY, privately published, 1905

SKARA BRAE

Skara Brae by V.G.CHILDE, Kegan Paul, London, 1931

STONEHENGE

Stonehenge by R.J.C.ATKINSON, Hamilton, London, and Macmillan, New York, 1956

SUTTON HOO

"The Excavation of the Sutton Hoo ship-burial", by C.W.PHILIPS and others in *Antiquaries' Journal*, 20, 1940

The Sutton Hoo Ship-burial, A Provisional Guide by R.L.S.BRUCE MITFORD, Trustees of the British Museum, London, 1947

LA TÈNE

Les Celtes depuis de l'Epoque de la Téne et la Civilisation Celtique by H.HUBERT, Paris, 1945

"The Coming of the Celts" by M.DE NAVARRO in *Cambridge Ancient History*, 7, C.U.P., London, and Macmillan, New York, 1928

WOODHENGE

Woodhenge by M.E.CUNNINGTON, Devizes, 1929

FAR EAST

GENERAL

The Art and Architecture of China by L.SICKMAN and A.SOPER, Penguin, London and Baltimore, Md., 1956

The Art and Architecture of Japan R.T.PAINE and A. SOPER, Penguin, London and Baltimore, Md., 1955

The Art of Indian Asia by H.R.ZIMMER, ed. J.CAMPBELL, Pantheon, New York, 1955

The Birth of China by H.G.CREEL, Ungar, New York, 1954

Children of the Yellow Earth by J.G.ANDERSSON, Routledge, London, and Macmillan, New York, 1934

The Chinese, their History and Culture, vols 1–2, by K.S. LATOURETTE, Macmillan, London and New York, 2nd rev. ed., 1934

La Civilisation Chinoise by M.GRANET, Paris, 1929

Epochs of Chinese and Japanese Art by E.F.FENOLLOSA, Stokes, Philadelphia, Pa, 1911

Handbook of Oriental History ed. C.H.PHILLIPS, Royal Historical Society, London, 1951

Histoire de l'Ancien Cambodge by E.AYMONIER, Strasbourg, 1924

Histoire des Arts du Japon, vol. 1, by J.BUHOT, Paris, 1949

A History of Indian and Eastern Architecture by J. FERGUSSON, Murray, London, rev. ed. 1910

Japan, a short Cultural History by Sir B.SANSOM, Cresset Press, London, rev. ed. 1947; Appleton-Century, New York, rev. ed. 1943

"Recent Archaeological Progress in Siam" by G. COEDES in *Indian Art and Letters*, n.s. 1, 1927

Researches into the Prehistory of the Chinese by J.G. ANDERSSON, Stockholm, 1943

Science and Civilisation in China, vol. 1., by J.NEEDHAM, C.U.P., London and New York, 1954

A Short History of Chinese Art by L.BACHHOFER, Batsford, London, 1947; Pantheon, New York, 1946

South-east Asia by B.HARRISON, Macmillan, London, and St Martins, New York, 1954

BUDDHIST ART AND ARCHITECTURE

A Concise History of Buddhist Art in Siam by R.S.LE MAY, C.U.P., London and Macmillan, New York, 1938

INDONESIAN

Indonesia by F. A. WAGNER, Methuen, London, and McGraw-Hill, New York, 1959

JAPAN, PREHISTORIC

Prehistoric Japan by N. G. MUNRO, Yokohama, 1911
The Prehistory of Japan by G. J. GROOT, ed. B. S. KRAUS, O.U.P., London, and Columbia U.P., New York, 1951

KHMER

L'Art Khmer Primitif by H. PARMENTIER, Paris, 1927

PITHECANTHROPUS

Man, Time and Fossils by R. MOORE, Cape, London, 1954
Meet Fossil Man by G. H. R. VON KOENIGSWALD, London, 1958
The Fossil Evidence for Human Evolution by W. E. LE GROS CLARK, Chicago, U.P., Chicago, Ill, 1955

SIEMREAP

L'Art Khmer by G. DE CORAL REMUSAT, Paris, 1940
Pour Mieux Comprendre Angkor by G. COEDES, Paris, 1947

TRA-K'IEU

L'Art du Champa et son Evolution by P. STERN, Paris, 1946
Les Sculptures Chams au Musée de Tourane by H. PARMENTIER, Paris, 1922

GREECE AND THE EASTERN MEDITERRANEAN

GENERAL

The Aegaean Civilisation by G. GLOTZ, Kegan Paul, Trench & Trubner, London, 1925
The Anvil of Civilisation by LEONARD COTTRELL, Faber, London, 1958

ATHENS

The Greek Commonwealth by A. E. ZIMMERN, O.U.P., London, 5th ed. 1931
Hellenistic Athens by W. S. FERGUSON, Macmillan, London and New York, 1911

THE CYCLADES

Excavations at Phylakopi in Melos by T. D. ATKINSON and others, Macmillan, London, 1904

DORIANS

See Greece, general

EVANS, SIR ARTHUR JOHN

Time and Chance by J. EVANS Longmans, London, 1943

GOURNIA

Gournia by H. B. HAWES, American Exploration Society, 1908

HERODOTUS

Standard editions and translations; translation with a commentary by GEORGE RAWLINSON, rev. and ed. A. W. LAWRENCE, Nonesuch, London, and Random House, New York, 1935
Herodotus, Father of History by Sir J. L. MYRES, O.U.P., London and New York, 1953

HOMER

There are numerous editions and translations of *The Iliad* and *The Odyssey;* for the social and archaeological background see especially:
Everyday Things in Ancient Greece by M. and C. H. B. QUENNELL, Batsford, London, 3rd imp. 1957
Homer and the Monuments by H. L. LORIMER, Macmillan, London and New York, 1951
Homer and History by W. LEAF, Macmillan, London and New York, 1915
The World of Homer by A. LANG, Longmans, London and New York, 1910
Life in the Homeric Age by T. D. SEYMOUR, Macmillan, London and New York, 1907

KNOSSOS

See Minoan Civilization

MALLIA

See Minoan Civilization

MEDITERRANEAN, THE EASTERN

The Civilisation of Greece in the Bronze Age (The Rhind Lectures) by H. R. HALL, Methuen, London, 1928
The Dawn of European Civilisation, ch. 3–5, by V. G. CHILDE, Kegan Paul, London, and Knopf, New York, 1925
Early Anatolia by S. H. F. LLOYD, Penguin, London and Baltimore, Md, 1956

MINOAN CIVILIZATION

The Archaeology of Crete by J. D. S. PENDLEBURY, Methuen, London, 1939
The Bull of Minos by L. COTTRELL, Evans, London, 1953
The Palace of Minos, vols 1–5, by Sir A. J. EVANS, Macmillan, London and New York, 1921–36
See also Minoan Scripts

MINOAN SCRIPTS

Achaeans and Indo-Europeans by L. R. PALMER, O.U.P., London and New York, 1955
The Decipherment of Linear B by J. CHADWICK, C.U.P., London and New York, 1958
Documents in Mycenaean Greek by M. VENTRIS and J. CHADWICK, C.U.P., London and New York, 1956

MYCENAE

Mycenae: an Archaeological History and Guide by A. J. B. Wace, O.U.P., London, and Princeton U.P., N.J., 1949

PHAISTOS

Crete, the Forerunner of Greece, by C. H. and H. B. Hawes, Harper's Library of Living Thought, London, 1909
See also Minoan Civilization

PYLOS

Excavation reports by C. W. Blegen in *American Journal of Archaeology*, Princeton, N.J., 1939, 1953, 1954, 1955, 1956, 1957

SCHLIEMANN

Ilios, Mycenae: A Narrative of Researches and Discoveries at Mycenae and Tiryns by E. Ludwig, 1880
See also Troy

THOLOS TOMBS

The Royal Tombs at Dendra near Midea by A. W. Persson, Lund, 1931
See also Mycenae

TROY

Ilios – The City and Country of the Trojans by H. Schliemann, Murray, London, 1880
Troy, vols 1–4, by Carl W. Blegen and others, O.U.P., London and Princeton U.P., N.J., 1950, 1951, 1953, 1958
Troy and its Remains by H. Schliemann, Murray, London, 1875
See also Schliemann

TYLISSOS

See Minoan Civilization

INDIA

GENERAL

Art and Architecture of India by B. Rowland, Penguin, London and Baltimore, Md, 1953
India and Pakistan: A General and Regional Geography by O. H. K. Spate, Methuen, London, 1954; Dutton, New York, 1953
The Wonder that was India by A. L. Basham, Sidgwick and Jackson, London, 1954; Macmillan, New York, 1955

AJANTA

Ajanta Frescoes, parts 1–4, by G. Yazdani, O.U.P., London and New York, 1930–55
India, Paintings from the Ajanta Caves by M. Singh, introduction by J. Nehru, Zwemmer, London, and New York Graphic Society for UNESCO, 1954

AMARAVATI

Sculptures from Amaravati in the British Museum by D. E. Barrett, Trustees of the British Museum, London, 1954
Amaravati Sculptures in the Madras Government Museum by S. Sivaramamurti, Madras, 1942

ARIKAMEDU

The Commerce Between the Roman Empire and India by E. H. Warmington, C.U.P., London, and Macmillan, New York, 1928
Rome Beyond the Imperial Frontiers by Sir R. E. M. Wheeler, Penguin, London and Baltimore, 1955

ASOKA MAURYA

Asoka, the Buddhist Emperor of India by V. A. Smith, O.U.P., London and New York, 1909

CAVE TEMPLES AND ELLORA

The Art of Indian Asia by H. Zimmer, completed and ed. J. Campbell, Pantheon, New York, 1955
Cave Temples of India by J. Fergusson and J. Burgess, Allen, London, 1880
History and Culture of Indian People, vols 2–3, chs. by S. K. Saraswati, Bombay, 1951 and 1954

GANDHARA

"Gandhara Sculptures" by J. Burgess in *Journal of Indian Art*, 8, 1898–1900
"Romano Buddhist Art" by Sir R. E. M. Wheeler in *Antiquity*, 23, 1949
"A Survey of Ancient Gandhara" by M. E. and D. H. Gordon in the *Journal of the Indian Anthropological Institute*, n.s., 1945
The Western Aspects of Gandhara Sculpture by H. Buchthal in *Proceedings of the British Academy*, 31, 1945

HINDU ART AND ARCHITECTURE

Development of Hindu Iconography by J. N. Banerjea, Calcutta, 1952
History of Indian and Indonesian Art by A. K. Coomaraswamy, Goldston, London, 1927

INDIA, PREHISTORIC

The Personality of India by B. Subbarao, Baroda, 1956
Prehistoric India to 1000 B.C. by Stuart Piggott, Penguin, London and Baltimore, Md, 1950

INDUS VALLEY CIVILIZATION

Excavations at Harappa by M. S. Vats, Delhi, 1940
The Indus Civilization by Sir R. E. M. Wheeler, Penguin, London and Baltimore, Md, 1953
Mohenjo-daro and the Indus Civilization by Sir J. H. Marshall and others, Arthur Probsthain, London, 1931

MARSHALL

Revealing India's Past ed. Sir J. Cumming, The India Society, London, 1939

MAURYAN EMPIRE

"Iran and India in pre-Islamic Times" by Sir R.E.M. WHEELER in *Ancient India*, 4, 1947–48

RIGVEDA

The Religion of the Rigveda by H.D.GRISWOLD, O.U.P., London, 1923

SANCHI

A Guide to Sanchi by Sir J.H.MARSHALL, several editions, Delhi

The Monuments of Sanchi by Sir J.H.MARSHALL and A. FOUCHER, Calcutta, 1947

SARNATH

Guide to Sarnath by B.MAJUMDAR, Delhi, 1937

TAXILA

Taxila by Sir JOHN MARSHALL. C.U.P., London, 1951, and New York, 1952

"Taxila (Sirkap), 1944–45" by A.GHOSH in *Ancient India*, 4, 1947–48

THE MIDDLE EAST

GENERAL

Art and Architecture of the Ancient Orient by H.FRANKFORT, Penguin, London and Baltimore, Md., 1954

THE ASSYRIANS

The Assyrian Sculptures by C. J. GADD, The Trustees of the British Museum, London, 1934

Everyday Life in Babylon and Assyria by G.CONTENAU, tr. by K.R. and A.R.MAXWELL-HYSLOP, Edward Arnold, London, and St Martins, New York, 1954

The Rise and Progress of Assyriology by E.A.W.BUDGE, Hopkinson, London, 1925

The Stones of Assyria by C.J.GADD, Chatto & Windus, London, 1936

BABYLON

The Excavations at Babylon by R.KOLDEWEY, tr. A.S. JOHNS, Macmillan, London, 1914, and New York, 1915

Herodotus' Description of Babylon by O.E.RAVN, Copenhagen, 1942

History of Babylon by L.W.KING, Chatto & Windus, London, and Stokes, New York, 1915

CTESIPHON

Ruined Cities of Iraq by S.H.F.LLOYD, O.U.P., London, and New York, 1944

GARSTANG

The Heritage of Solomon by JOHN GARSTANG, Williams & Norgate, London, 1934

GILGAMESH EPIC

The Epic of Gilgamesh definitive text and transliteration by R. C. THOMPSON, Clarendon Press, Oxford and New York, 1930

GROTEFEND, GEORGE F.

The Discovery and Decipherment of the Trilingual Cuneiform Inscriptions by A.J.BOOTH, Longmans, London and New York, 1902

HAMMURABI

The Babylonian Laws, vols 1–2, ed. and tr. G.R.DRIVER and Sir J.C.MILES, O.U.P., London and New York, 1952–55

Letters and Inscriptions of Hammurabi ed. and tr. L.W. KING, Luzac, London, 1898

IRAN

Iran by R.N.FRYE, Allen & Unwin, London, 1954; Holt, New York, 1953

Iran from the Earliest Times to the Persian Conquest by R. GHIRSHMAN, Penguin, London, 1954 and Baltimore, Md, 1955

Survey of Persian Art ed. A.U.POPE and P.ACKERMAN, O.U.P., London, 1938–39, and New York, 1939

IRAQ

Chronicles of Chaldaean Kings (626–556B.C.) by D.J. WISEMAN, Trustees of the British Museum, London, 1956

Foundations in the Dust by S.H.F.LLOYD, Penguin, London and Baltimore, Md, 1955

History Begins at Sumer by S.N.KRAMER, Thames & Hudson, London, 1958; (with title *From the Tablets of Sumer*) Falcons Wing, Indian Hills, Colo., 1956

Twenty-five Years of Mesopotamian Archaeology by M.E.L. MALLOWAN, British School of Archaeology in Iraq publication, London, 1957

MARI

Mari, une Ville Perdue by A.PARROT, Paris, 1936

MESOPOTAMIAN SCULPTURE

Tells by A.PARROT, Paris, 1948

Sculpture of the third millennium B.C. from Tell Asmar and Khafajah by H.FRANKFORT, London and Chicago U.P., Chicago, Ill., 1939

NIMRUD

Nimrud and its Remains by M.E.L.MALLOWAN (in press)

NINEVEH

A Century of Exploration at Nineveh by R.C.THOMSON and R.W.HUTCHINSON, Luzac, London, 1929

Nineveh and Babylon by A.H.LAYARD, Murray, London, 1867

PARTHIANS

A Political History of Parthia by N. C. Debevoise, C.U.P., London, and Chicago U.P., Chicago, Ill., 1938
See also Iran

PALMYRA

Decline and Fall of the Roman Empire, ch. 11, by E. Gibbon, London, 1776–88
Caravan Cities by M.I. Rostovtzeff, tr. D. and T. Talbot Rice, O.U.P., London and New York, 1932

PERSEPOLIS

Persepolis, vol. 1, by E.F. Schmidt, C.U.P., London, 1954; Chicago U.P., Chicago, Ill., 1953

PETRA

Petra, the Rock-City of Edom by M. A. Murray, Blackie, London, 1939

SMITH, GEORGE

Chaldaean Account of Genesis by G. Smith, Low, London, 1875–80

SUMERIANS

New Light on the Most Ancient East by V.G. Childe, Kegan Paul, Trench & Trubner, London, 1952; Praeger, New York, 1953
Sumerians by Sir C.L. Woolley, Clarendon Press, Oxford and New York, 1928
Twin Rivers by S.H.F. Lloyd, O.U.P., London and Baltimore, Md., 1947
Ur of the Chaldees by Sir C.L. Woolley, Penguin, London and Baltimore, Md., 1938
See also Iraq

SUSA

See Iran

TELL ATCHANA

"Alalakh (Tell Atchana)" by Sir C.L. Woolley in *Report of the Research Committee of the Society of Antiquaries*, London, 1955
A Forgotten Kingdom by Sir C.L. Woolley, Penguin, London and Baltimore, Md., 1953

UR

Excavations at Ur by Sir C.L. Woolley, Benn, London and Crowell, New York, 1954

Full reports on the excavations have been published by the British Museum, London and University Museum, Philadelphia, in a series of volumes by Sir C.L. Woolley and others, 1936–59

UR-NAMMU

See also Ur
Cambridge Ancient History vol. 1, ch. 12, C.U.P., London, and Macmillan, New York, 1924

ZIGGURAT

The Tower of Babel by A. Parrot, tr. E. Hudson, S.C.M., London, 1955; Philosophical Library, New York, 1956

WOOLLEY, SIR C.L.

Digging up the Past by Sir C.L. Woolley, Benn, London, 1930; Scribner, New York, 1931
History Unearthed by Sir C.L. Woolley, Benn, London, 1958
See also Sumerians, Tell Atchana *and* Ur

Notes on the Contributors

P. J. Adams, *B.S., Ph.D., F.G.S.*
Senior Geologist with Her Majesty's Geological Survey and Museum. Publications include contributions to *Discovery*, *Fuel Economy Review* and *Meddelelser am Grönland.*

J. Alden Mason, *Ph.D., Curator Emeritus, University Museum, University of Pennsylvania.*
Editor and Archaeological Adviser, New World Archaeological Foundation, Orinda, California. Publications include *The Ancient Civilizations of Peru*, 1957; and contributions to *Annals, New York Academy of Sciences, Journal of American Folklore and Scientific Survey of Porto Rico and the Virgin Islands.*

F. R. Allchin, *B.A., Ph.D., F.S.A.*
Reader in Indian Studies, University of Cambridge. Publications include contributions to *Antiquity*, *Bulletin of the School of Oriental and African Studies* and *Man.*

A. J. Arkell, *M.B.E., M.C., D.Litt., F.S.A.*
Reader in Egyptian Archaeology, University of London; Keeper of the Flinders Petrie Collection at University College, London; formerly Commissioner for Archaeology and Anthropology, Sudan Government. Publications include *Early Khartoum*, 1949; *Shaheinab*, 1953; *Old Stone Age in Anglo-Egyptian Sudan*, 1955; *A History of the Sudan to A.D. 1821*, 1955; and many contributions to *Sudan Notes and Records.*

D. G. Bridson
Senior feature writer and producer for the British Broadcasting Corporation. Has done research on the Dead Sea Scrolls in the Middle East for the British Broadcasting Corporation.

Douglas H. Carpenter, *F.R.A.I.*
Contributor to *Man.*

Anthony Christie, *M.A.*
Lecturer in the Art and Archaeology of South-east Asia at the School of Oriental and African Studies, University of London. Publications include contributions to *Asia Major*, *Bulletin of the Society of Oriental and African Studies*, *Burma* (*H.R.A.F.*) and *Encyclopaedia Britannica.*

J. Desmond Clark, *O.B.E., M.A., Ph.D., F.S.A., F.R.A.I.*
Director of the Rhodes-Livingstone Museum, Livingstone. Publications include *The Stone Age Cultures of Northern Rhodesia*, 1950; *The Prehistoric Cultures of the Horn of Africa*, 1954; *The Prehistory of Southern Africa*, 1959; and numerous articles on the prehistoric archaeology of South Africa and the early history of Northern Rhodesia.

John Chadwick, *M.A.*
University Lecturer in Classics, University of Cambridge. Publications include (with W. N. Mann) *The Medical Works of Hippocrates*, 1950; (with M. Ventris) *Documents in Mycenean Greek*, 1956; *The Decipherment of Linear* B, 1958; and contributions to *Antiquity*, *Greece and Rome* and *Transactions of the Philological Society.*

Sonia Cole, *F.G.I., F.R.A.I.*
Research associate at the British Museum (Natural History). Publications include *An Outline of the Geology of Kenya*, 1950; *The Prehistory of East Africa*, 1954; *Counterfeit*, 1955; and contributions to *Antiquity* and *American Anthropologist.*

J. M. Cook, *F.S.A.*
Reader in Classical Archaeology, University of Bristol; formerly Director of the British School of Archaeology at Athens.

Leonard Cottrell
Member of the Royal Institute of Archaeology, the Egypt Exploration Society and the Hellenic Society; Lecturer on archaeology and producer of numerous radio documentaries on the subject for the British Broadcasting Corporation. Publications include *The Lost Pharaohs*, 1950; *Life Under the Pharaohs*, 1953; *The Bull of Minos*, 1953, and *Enemy of Rome*, 1960.

Ahmad Hasan Dani, *M.A., Ph.D., F.R.A.S.*
Reader in History, University of Dacca; formerly Assistant Superintendent of Archaeology, Government of India, and Superintendent of Archaeology, Government of Pakistan; publications include *Dacca, a Record of its Changing Fortunes*, 1956; *Bibliography of the Muslim Inscription of Bengal*, 1958; and contributions to *Epigraphica Indica*, *Journal of the Asiatic Society of Bengal*, *Journal of the Asiatic Society of Pakistan* and *Journal of the Numismatic Society of India.*

P. E. P. Deraniyagala, *M.A., A.M.*
Director of the National Museums of Ceylon; formerly Acting Archaeological Commissioner, Ceylon. Publications include *The Pleistocene of Ceylon*, 1943–56; and contributions to the *Journal of the Royal Asiatic Society.*

Guy Daniel, *M.A.*
Vicar of Colnbrook, Buckinghamshire. Publications include *The Bible Story*, 1955; and contributions to *The Bible Companion*, 1959.

Adrian Digby, *M.A.*
Keeper of the Department of Ethnography in the British Museum. Publications include (with G. H. S. Bushnell) *Ancient American Pottery*, 1955; and contributions on anthropological subjects to *Chambers's Encyclopaedia.*

JOHN D. EVANS, *M.A., Ph.D.*
Professor of Prehistoric European Archaeology at the University of London. Publications include *Malta*, 1959; and contributions to archaeological journals.

C. J. GADD, *C.B.E., M.A., Hon. D.Litt.*
Professor of Ancient Semitic Languages and Civilizations at the School of Oriental and African Studies, University of London. His publications include *The Early Dynasties of Sumer and Akkad*, 1921; *The Fall of Nineveh*, 1923; *History and Monuments of Ur*, 1929; *The Stones of Assyria*, 1936 and *Ideas of Divine Rule*, 1948.

D. H. GORDON, *D.S.O., O.B.E., F.R.A.I.*
Honorary Correspondent of the Archaeological Survey of India; formerly officer in the Indian Army. Publications include contributions to *Ancient India*, *Antiquity*, *Ipek* and *Iraq*.

GEOFFREY GRIGSON, *M.A.*
Author and broadcaster. Publications include *The Painted Caves*, 1957 and *Art Treasures of the British Museum*, 1958

G. LANKESTER HARDING, *C.B.E., Star of Jordan, F.S.A.*
Formerly Director of Antiquities, Hashemite Kingdom of Jordan; Assistant Director, Wellcome Archaeological Expedition at Tell Duwier (1936). Publications include *Some Thamudic Inscriptions from Jordan*, 1952; *Four Tomb Groups from Jordan*, 1953; and contributions to the *Quarterly of the Department of Antiquities of Palestine*, *Annual of the Jordan Department of Antiquities* and *Palestine Exploration Quarterly*.

THOR HEYERDAHL.
Author and Ethnologist; organized and led Norwegian Archaeological Expedition to Easter Island and the East Pacific, 1955–6. Publications include *The Kon-Tiki Expedition*, 1948; *Archaeological Evidence of Pre-Spanish Visits to the Galápagos Islands*, 1955; *Aku-Aku: The Secrets of Easter Island*, 1957, and contributions to anthropological and geographical journals.

A. HINGSTON QUIGGIN, *M.A.*,
Formerly University Lecturer in Archaeology and Anthropology, University of Cambridge and Director of Studies, Newnham College, Cambridge.
Publications include: *Survey of Primitive Money*, 1949; *The Story of Money*, 1956; and articles in *Encyclopaedia Britannica* and *Chambers's Encyclopaedia*.

P. HULIN, *M.A.*
University Lecturer in Near Eastern Archaeology, University of Oxford. Publications include articles in *Anatolian Studies*, *Iraq* and *The Numismatic Chronicle*.

G. W. B. HUNTINGFORD, *B.Sc.*
Lecturer in East African Languages and Cultures, School of Oriental and African Studies, University of London; Honorary Editor, *Journal of the Royal Anthropological Institute*. Publications include *The Nandi of Kenya*, 1953; *The Northern Nilo-Hamites*, 1953; *The Southern Nilo-Hamites*, 1953; and contributions to *African Studies*, *Antiquity* and *Journal of the Royal Anthropological Institute*.

R. W. HUTCHINSON, *M.A., F.S.A., F.R.A.I.*
At present engaged on archaeological and linguistic research; formerly Lecturer in Classical Archaeology, Universities of Cambridge and Liverpool. Publications include *A Century of Exploration at Nineveh*, 1929; and contributions to numerous archaeological magazines including *Antiquity*, *Archaeologia*, *Journal of Hellenic Studies* and *Iraq*.

VERA S. KATRAK, *B.A., Ph.D.*
Library Assistant at the School of Oriental and African studies. Author of *Analysis of Achaemenian Art and Architecture with reference to Origins, Influence and Development*; and contributor to *Journal of Hellenic Studies*.

J. EDWARD KIDDER, Jr., *A.M., Ph.D.*
Associate Professor of Art and Archaeology at the International Christian University of Tokyo. Publications include *The Jomon Pottery of Japan*, 1957; *Japan Before Buddhism*, 1959; and contributions to *Archaeology* and *Artibus Asiae*.

JAMES KIRKMAN, *M.A., F.S.A.*
Warden of the Coastal Historical Sites of Kenya. Publications include *The Arab City of Gedi: Excavations at the Great Mosque*, 1954; and contributions to *Antiquaries' Journal*, the *Journal of the Royal Asiatic Society* and the *South African Archaeological Bulletin*.

G. E. LAW, *M.A.*
Contributor to *Chambers's Encyclopaedia* and the *Encyclopaedia Brittanica*.

L. S. B. LEAKEY, *M.A., Ph.D., Hon.D.Sc.*
Curator of the Coryndon Memorial Museum, Nairobi; formerly leader of East African Archaeological Research Expeditions. Publications include *The Stone-age Cultures of Kenya*, 1931; *Stone-age Africa*, 1936; *Olduvai Gorge*, 1952; and contributions to scientific journals.

C. B. M. MCBURNEY, *M.A., Ph.D., F.S.A.*
University Lecturer in Archaeology, University of Cambridge. Publications include (with R. W. Hey) *Prehistory and Pleistocene Geology in Cyrenaican Libya*, 1955; *The Stone Age of Northern Africa*, 1958; and contributions to *Antiquity*, *Nature* and *Proceedings of the Prehistorical Society*.

ALEXANDRA MACFARLANE, *B.A.*
Archaeologist.

B. D. MALAN, *B.A., F.R.S.* (*South Africa*)
Director of the Archaeological Survey of the Union of South Africa. Publications include many contributions to *Antiquity*, the *South African Archaeological Bulletin* and *South African Journal of Science*.

Notes on the Contributors

RAYMOND A. MAUNY, *Docteur en Droit, Docteur ès Lettres.*
Head of the Prehistoric Archaeology Department of L'Institut Français d'Afrique Noire, Dakar, Senegal. Publications include a very large number of works on African (chiefly west African) pre-history and history.

J. V. S. MEGAW, *M.A.*
Extra-mural Lecturer in Archaeology, University of London. Publications include contributions to *American Journal of Archaeology*, *Antiquity*, *Folk-Lore* and *Proceedings of the Society of Antiquaries of Scotland*.

T. C. MITCHELL, *M.A.*
Research Assistant, Australian Institute of Archaeology.

MARGARET ALICE MURRAY, *D.Lit.*
Member of the General Committee, British Association for the Advancement of Science; formerly Assistant Professor of Egyptology, University of London. Publications include *Saqqara Mastabas* 1905, 1937; *The Witch Cult in Western Europe*, 1921; *The God of the Witches*, 1931; *The Divine King in England*, 1954; *The Splendour that was Egypt*, 1959; and contributions to *Ancient Egypt*, *Folk-Lore*, *Journal of Egyptian Archaeology*, *Journal of the Royal Anthropological Institute* and *Man*.

K. P. OAKLEY, *D.Sc.*, *F.B.A.*
Senior Principal Scientific Officer in charge of Anthropology Section at the British Museum (Natural History). Publications include *Man the Toolmaker*, 1949; and contributions to *Advancement of Science*, *Bulletin of the British Museum (Natural History)*, *Geology*, *Yearbook of Physical Anthropology*, *A Histor of hnology*, *Proceedings of the Prehistoric Society*, *Antiquity* and *Proceedings of the Geological Association*.

J. J. ORCHARD, *M.A.*
Assistant Keeper, Department of Antiquities, Ashmolean Museum, Oxford.

ROBIN PLACE, *M.A.*
Lecturer at the L. C. C. City Literary Institute; Lecturer at Whitelands College, Putney. Publications include *Britain Before History*, 1951; *Our First Homes*, 1951; *Finding Fossil Man*; 1957; *Prehistoric Britain*, 1958; and contributions to some volumes of the Penguin *Buildings of England* and *The Times Educational Supplement*.

REAY ROBERTSON-MACKAY, *M.A.*, *F.S.A.*, *Scot.*
Assistant Inspector of Ancient Monuments, Ministry of Works; Extra-mural Lecturer in Archaeology. University of London. Publications include contributions to *Proceedings of the Society of Antiquaries of Scotland* and *The Journal of Medieval Archaeology*.

A. F. SHORE, *M.A.*
Assistant Keeper of the Department of Egyptian Antiquities in the British Museum.

H. S. SMITH, *M.A.*
Lady Wallis Budge Fellow in Egyptology, Christ's College, University of Cambridge.

ROGER SUMMERS, *F.S.A.*
Keeper of Antiquities, National Museum of Southern Rhodesia; Chairman of the Historical Monuments Commission of Southern Rhodesia. Publications include: *Inyanga: Prehistoric Settlements in Southern Rhodesia*, 1958; *Prehistoric Rock Art of Rhodesia and Nyasaland* (in press); and contributions to *Antiquity*, *Archaeological News Letter* and *South African Journal of Science*.

LORD WILLIAM TAYLOUR, *M.A.*, *Ph.D.*, *F.S.A.*
Archaeologist. Publications include: *Mycenean Pottery in Italy and Adjacent Areas*, 1958; and contribution to the *Annal of the British School at Athens*.

D. J. WISEMAN, *O.B.E.*, *M.A.*, *F.S.A.*
Assistant Keeper, Department of Western Asiatic Antiquities in the British Museum. Publications include: *The Alalakh Tablets*, 1953; *Illustrations from Biblical Archaeology*, 1958; *Cylinder Seals of Western Asia*, 1959; and contributions to *Iraq* and *Journal of Cuneiform Studies*.

H. M. WORMINGTON, *Ph.D.*
Curator of Archaeology, Denver Museum of Natural History, Colorado. Publications include: *Ancient Man in North America*, 1939; *Prehistoric Indians of the Southwest*, 1947; and contributions to professional journals.